How did the organ become a church instrument? How did it develop from an outdoor, Mediterranean noisemaker to an instrument which has become the embodiment of western music and responsible for many of that music's characteristics? In this fascinating investigation, Peter Williams speculates on these questions and suggests some likely answers. He considers where the organ was placed and why; what the instrument was like in 800, 1000, 1200 and 1400; what music was played, and how. He re-examines the known references before 1300, covering such areas as the history of technology, music-theory, art history, architecture, church and political history. Central to the story he uncovers is the liveliness of European monasticism around 1000 and the ability and imagination of the Benedictine reformers. Professor Williams's approach is new in both tactics and strategy, giving an interdisciplinary idea of musical development relevant to those both in and out of music.

CAMBRIDGE STUDIES IN MEDIEVAL AND RENAISSANCE MUSIC

The organ in western culture, 750–1250

CAMBRIDGE STUDIES IN MEDIEVAL AND RENAISSANCE MUSIC

GENERAL EDITORS:

Iain Fenlon, Peter le Huray,
Thomas Forrest Kelly, John Stevens

This series continues the aims of the Cambridge Studies in Music but now focuses on the medieval and Renaissance periods. As with the earlier series, the central concern is to publish books which make an original contribution to the study of music in its widest sense. Thus the relationship of music both to a broad historical and social context and to the other arts is seen as an important feature.

PUBLISHED TITLES

The organ in western culture, 750–1250
PETER WILLIAMS

Gothic song: Victorine sequences and Augustinian reform in twelfth-century Paris
MARGOT FASSLER

The organ in western culture

750–1250

PETER WILLIAMS

CAMBRIDGE
UNIVERSITY PRESS

Published by the Press Syndicate of the University of Cambridge

The Pitt Building, Trumpington Street, Cambridge CB2 1RP

40 West 20th Street, New York, NY 10011–4211, USA

10 Stamford Road, Oakleigh, Melbourne 3166, Australia

First published 1993

Printed in Great Britain at the University Press, Cambridge

A catalogue record for this book is available from the British Library

Library of Congress cataloguing in publication data

Williams, Peter F.
The organ in western culture, 750–1250 / Peter Williams.
   p.   cm.
Includes bibliographical references and indexes.
ISBN 0 521 41843 7
1. Organ – History – 500-1400.   2. Church music – 500-1400.
I. Title.
ML553.W54   1993
786.5' 19' 09 – dc20   92–19196 CIP

ISBN 0 521 418437 hardback

Contents

Illustrations

Photographs

Drawings

Preface

The first working title for this study was a question: 'How did we come to have the organ in church and what difference did it make?', and although the eventual title became shorter and the text lost many actual question-marks, some such question remains the book's chief impetus. If in the end I do not really know the answer – or cannot find one that explains the facts obviously better than another – nevertheless trying to ask in the right way what I believe are the right questions may give some focus to a field of study that often looks too wide to control. One can feel that nothing known about churches and monasteries in the year 1000 is irrelevant to the question of how some of them came to have an organ. In turn, that question leads to many others, for organs cannot be understood in isolation.

Some points about the book's method and organisation:

(1) In several of the topics touched on here, it has been common to treat the evidence in a positivistic, even uncritical manner. Yet it is clear that both terminology (for example the uses of the word *organum*) and technology (for example the invention of returning finger-keys) need the most wary treatment, the first because it exists on paper with too many different meanings, the second because it barely exists on paper at all. This dual problem totally dominates the subject: evidence as it exists needs to be seen in the context of what it is aiming to say, while evidence that does not exist needs to be deduced or at least its absence accounted for in some way. Consequently, firm answers to many a question cannot now be given, and I have not contrived them except where they are beyond reasonable doubt, which is very rare. An example might be the certainty now that Pope Vitalian did not 'introduce the church organ', as used to be claimed, although this too leads to other questions such as, Why exactly was it that later historians claimed he did? In trying to deal with such questions as this, the book as a whole does frequently imply some kinds of answer. Thus while it cannot be deduced one way or another from the Utrecht Psalter's pictures themselves whether the water-organ was known in northern France in the early ninth century (Chapter 10), nevertheless references to organs in Carolingian annals (Chapter 9), in somewhat later music-theory from this area (Chapter 3) and in other related topics (Chapters 11, 14, 16) make it likely that if it were, it was an exceptional piece of engineering not relevant to any regular monastic organ (if such there was) in the year 900.

(2) Because of a constant attempt to raise questions from several angles, I have not prevented certain items of information from appearing in more than one chapter or in more than one connection. I hope that much might be said for looking at the report of a tenth-century church-dedication from the different viewpoints of various chapters (musical, architectural, liturgical, organological) or for suggesting in various connections that no kind of evidence is always what it seems. Some particular questions – what happened to the organ in the ninth century? did its keyboard always have an ordered sequence of notes? – are particularly difficult and crop up in different forms in the book, with different kinds of answer being implied in different connections. Of course I hope that the result of using the same information on different occasions is neither repetition nor contradiction.

(3) Because of the need to look at evidence within different contexts, I discovered that unfortunately the book could not be arranged in simple chronological order – 'unfortunately' because when one needs to move in and out of the centuries, it becomes more difficult to grasp whether the various kinds of evidence do come together at any single moment in time. On the other hand, this difficulty is true to the subject. It is unlikely that there was a single or straightforward linear evolution in organ-building before the thirteenth century (if then), so that giving the story a chronological shape such as is generally taken for granted today – first came this element, followed by that, under such-and-such an influence – would be contrived.

(4) Latin texts have been translated, in the belief that this can serve to raise useful questions of word-use and thus of meaning. It is more than usually true that for such a book as this, translation is interpretation. There is barely a quotation here that is quite free of ambiguity in the words themselves or that has a context totally clear to any reader but the original author (if to him). Such translations, since they serve to question use and usage, will also tend to lead to questions rather than to definitive conclusions.

(5) As a non-specialist in many areas of this study, I have preferred citing early authors mostly from the classic editions (PL, RBMAS, MGH etc.), moving to more recent editions only if it seemed particularly useful for the context. For present purposes I felt that the simplicity and the convenience of having a few particular locations for so many citations and quotations (which are mostly short) justify my referring to these old editions. Also for convenience, secondary literature is often cited either when its sources are given in full enough detail (for example Wallace-Hadrill, Schuberth, Frend) or, as happens occasionally, when they are not and when a subsequent search has failed to turn up an original. In order for the bibliography to be selective – a guide to basic materials for this particular study – I have put it in the form of a 'List of References', i.e. books and articles that constitute such materials and/or that have been cited in more than one chapter.

(6) One problem with such a book is its order: the background areas before the technical, or vice versa? In practice, however, documentation of any kind concerning organs is so incomplete as to make it hardly feasible to start with the

instrument as a familiar piece of technical equipment. There is so little certain to describe and so much to speculate about that an indirect approach through the various possible background areas – music, liturgy, architecture, iconography, written descriptions – seemed to me to be the most useful.

(7) Another problem is what the book's end-date should be. A date of around 1250 would imply the point at which organs seem to have begun growing in overall size, with an encased wooden structure and all that this would mean – or certainly came to mean eventually – in the way of enlarged sound-spectrum (pipes from the very large to the very small), volume-level, tone, variety of sounds, compass and therefore 'musical potential'. But since even the vaguest idea of the organ in or before *c.* 1250 can be achieved only by guessing what in the organ of *c.* 1450 was new and what might have led to it, so much material in the book actually concerns organs after 1250. However, this does not lead to anything like an account of the high-gothic or Renaissance organ. One of the most pressing needs in musical and instrumental history today is for a comprehensive account of the organ a century or so either side of 1450, with hypotheses on its unparalleled significance to the history of music and the evolution of diatonic harmony, to sound-perception and instrument-technology, to liturgy, musical sociology (public concerts) and the methods of musical archaeology (extant material).

(8) Since all the illustrative material of the book is anachronistic in manner and totally unknown in this form to the people of the period concerned – line-drawings of architectural sections and plans, exactly replicated and colourless illuminations, five-line musical staves, etc. – I have also modernized the note-names while preserving the useful distinctions for B-flat and B-natural:

> B = B-flat
> H = B-natural

When octave-pitches are specific, as in a hypothetical keyboard-compass, the notation is:

> C – c – c' – c" (in which c' = Middle C)

and when they are not, the capitals are used:

> CDEFGABH

The potential ambiguity of this – C could mean both bass C and C-in-any-octave – seldom if ever arises, in part because the complete 'bass octave' as such does not exist in the period.

Acknowledgments

An interdisciplinary study of this kind, particularly one in gestation for a long time, is impossible without the kindness of colleagues across the disciplines who, though of course without responsibility for any errors, do their best to keep one on the straight and narrow. I would like to express thanks to various groups of experts: specialist historians in the USA (Wilson Barry, Edmund A. Bowles, Herbert L. Kessler, †Edwin M. Ripin, Eugene L. Szonntagh and †Lynn White, Jr.) and the keepers of two particular European treasures (Melinda Kaba, Budapest, and Koert van der Horst, Urecht); former colleagues in the University of Edinburgh (Kerr Borthwick and Terry Coppock) and present colleagues in Duke University (Samuel Hammond and Daniel Rettberg, Caroline Bruzelius and Annabel Wharton, Keith Falconer and Ellen Foster, Diskin Clay and Francis Newton, Anne Firor Scott and Ronald Witt); also Frits Knuf, Publisher, and James Flecker, Headmaster of Ardingly. Norman Ryan, Curator of Organs and Harpsichords at Duke, kindly redrew the sections of hypothetical actions (Figures 7 and 8); Isabelle Bélance-Zank neglected her own work to read proofs; and my colleague Larry Todd kindly demonstrated the wonders of word-processing. For research-grants I am indebted to the University of Edinburgh (two) and Duke University (four). The book would probably not have been planned without the encouragement to write an essay for †Maarten Albert Vente's *Festschrift* (Williams 1980) or have been finished without the support of †Peter le Huray.

Peter Williams

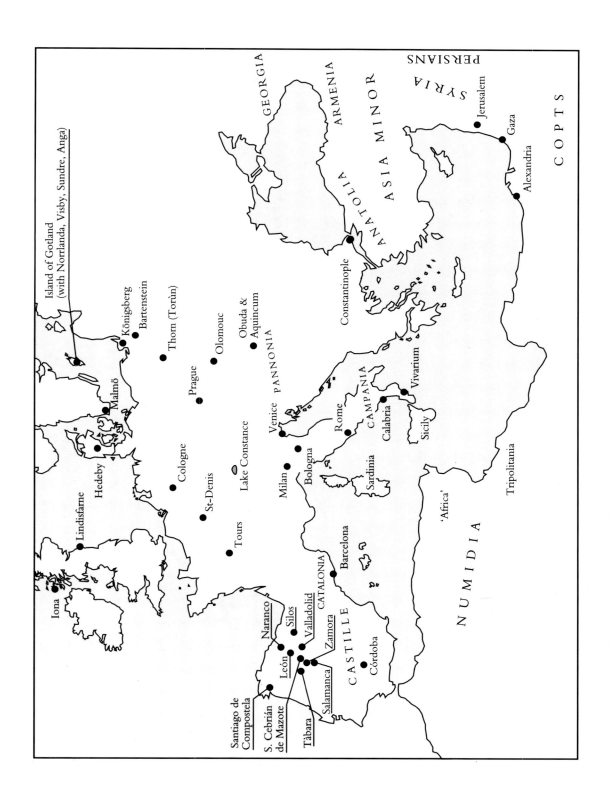

Island of Gotland
(with Norrlanda, Visby, Sundre, Anga)

Königsberg
Bartenstein
Thorn (Toruń)
Olomouc
Obuda &
Aquincum
Prague
Malmö
Hedeby
Lindisfarne
Cologne
St-Denis
Lake Constance
Venice   PANNONIA
Milan
Bologna
Tours
Rome
Sardinia
CAMPANIA
Vivarium
Calabria
Sicily
Barcelona
CATALONIA
'Africa'
Tripolitania
N U M I D I A
Iona
Naranco
Silos
Valladolid
Zamora
León
Salamanca
Santiago de
Compostela
S. Cebrián
de Mazote
Tábara
CASTILLE
Córdoba

GEORGIA
ARMENIA
ANATOLIA
ASIA MINOR
SYRIA
PERSIANS
Jerusalem
Gaza
Alexandria
C O P T S
Constantinople

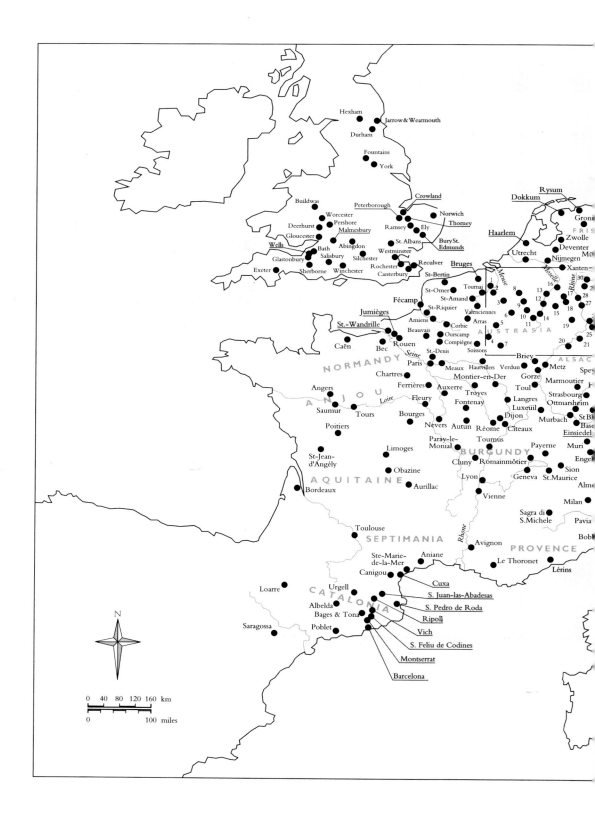

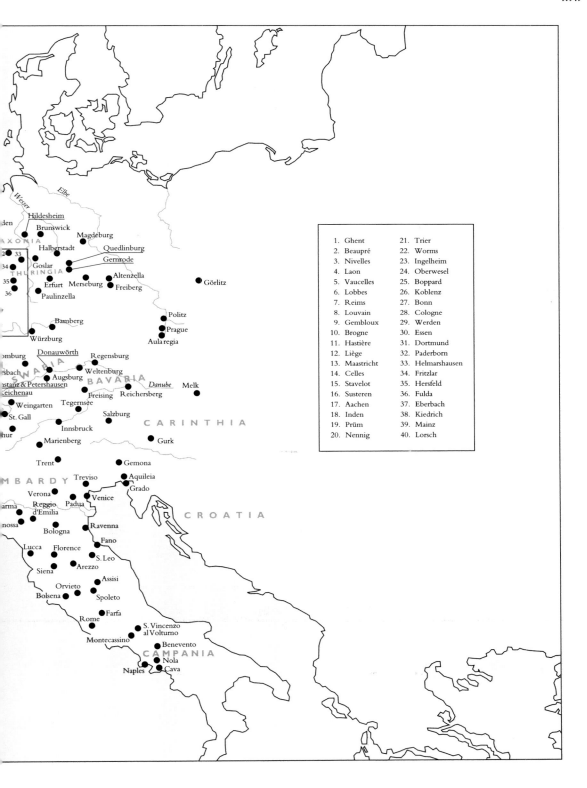

1. Ghent
2. Beaupré
3. Nivelles
4. Laon
5. Vaucelles
6. Lobbes
7. Reims
8. Louvain
9. Gembloux
10. Brogne
11. Hastière
12. Liège
13. Maastricht
14. Celles
15. Stavelot
16. Susteren
17. Aachen
18. Inden
19. Prüm
20. Nennig
21. Trier
22. Worms
23. Ingelheim
24. Oberwesel
25. Boppard
26. Koblenz
27. Bonn
28. Cologne
29. Werden
30. Essen
31. Dortmund
32. Paderborn
33. Helmarshausen
34. Fritzlar
35. Hersfeld
36. Fulda
37. Eberbach
38. Kiedrich
39. Mainz
40. Lorsch

How did the organ come to be accepted by the Church? Some earlier answers

General

Asking such a question as this makes certain assumptions – such as that there may be an answer – and it is not a question that monastic writers of 750–1250 would have asked. Quite why they would not is itself a difficult question. Was it that they were not interested in the origin of man-made objects which, after all, could always be interpreted allegorically? Or that whatever their interest may have been, writing about them would have been too novel for the usual subject-matter of books? Literacy had certain purposes, and describing local practices and how they originated was not one of them. Since complex equipment was often found in major churches – where else could it have been in *c.* 1000? – there may have been felt no need to justify it. Like so many other things that went on in churches, it was outside the liturgy and therefore of no particular concern to monastic writers; thus instruments being 'in church' was not the same thing as being 'accepted by the Church'. In any case, the question of how organs came to be *in* church was not important when so many liturgies and festive events centred on processions partly or even wholly out of doors.

In festive events neither a bellows- nor water-organ played a part that was strictly necessary to the liturgy, and it is by no means certain that either was for 'music' at all. In written records, neither a bellows- nor water-organ (*organum*) would normally be distinguished from the various other 'instruments' (*organa*) taking part (if any were) in the 'organized music' (*organa*) of such events, so there is little use in relying on written documentation to convey much idea of how things actually were. On the other hand, the many meanings themselves of *organum* imply that while organs may not have had a recognizably distinct identity, they 'slipped in' to participate in events when they were available. To do so, they would never need to be officially accepted by the Church.

It seems likely, therefore, that the earliest justifications for the organ would appear when and because it had become a normal musical part of the liturgy, an acknowledged instrument made according to a particular technology, found often enough in the main churches and no longer evoked only for its usefulness in allegory – of the soul (Tertullian), the Church or community of the faithful (Origen), chastity (Arnobius), the praise of God (St Gregory) or whatever it was a poet and Christian moralist found it useful for. But it is difficult to believe that the allegorical significance of organs[1] had much to do with their acceptance by the Church, despite all the written references of this kind. For such allegory – literate creations far removed from the craftsmen – it would be of only marginal relevance whether the instrument was located in church or took part in the liturgy at all, what its functions were, what kind of potential it had, and even what exactly 'church music' was. But as these became standardized, each is described and even prescribed.[2] It may be a reflection of what organs had achieved technologically and liturgically by the thirteenth century that it is no longer the organ but the viella that is most often invoked in the many literary genres – sermon, music-treatise, psalm-commentary, gloss on Aristotle, secular romance (Page 1987: 133). By then, the organ was less novel and its purpose more familiar and accepted.

The late Middle Ages saw different explanations for the instrument. From at least the early thirteenth century, writers began to say such things as the following:

et hoc solo musico	and this is the only musical
instrumento	instrument
utitur ecclesia in diuersis	that the church employs in the various
cantibus et in prosis,	songs [chants?], *prosae,*
in sequentiis et in hymnis,	sequences, and hymns,
propter abusum histrionum	because of abuse by play-actors,
eiectis aliis communiter	the other instruments having all
instrumentis.	been banned together.

(CSM: Gill of Zamora, late thirteenth century)

The phrase *in diversis cantibus* does not appear in an earlier and similar passage attributed to another Franciscan writer, Bartholomeus Anglicus, *De proprietatibus rerum*,[3] where the section follows St Augustine's definition of the organ (see p. 297), as it does too in Gill. Like much that was written, the passage could have been common property and as such is more an indication of what was written than what was known in practice. A century or so earlier, Gerhoch, Augustinian canon of Reichersberg (†1169), had remarked in a commentary on Psalm 80.4 (Psalm 81.3) that instruments participate in praise:

unde et nos in divinis officiis	and whence we in the divine offices	
utimur organis. Tota ecclesia	use organs. The whole church	
est organum Dei, electi sunt	is the organ of God, the elect are	
fistulae dulcisonae.	sweet-sounding pipes.	(PL 194.500)

---

[1] Summarized in Bowles 1966 and in H. Giesel, *Studien zur Symbolik der Musikinstrumente im Schrifttum der alten und mittelalterlichen Kirche*, Kölner Beiträge zur Musikforschung 94 (Regensburg, 1978). Later allegories, such as Athanasius Kircher's drawing of an organ from whose façade-pipes gushes all at once the *harmonia* of the world in birth (*Musurgia universalis* (Rome, 1650), plate xxiii), belong to the same tradition. On comparable symbolisms or allegories for bells, see Chapter 6.

[2] In much later writings that give organ-registrations, prescribing again seems to follow standardization rather than vice versa: stops are specified not where there is huge variety as between instruments (when some advice might be thought necessary) but when there is already uniformity – as in Italy *c.* 1600, France *c.* 1700 and England *c.* 1800.

[3] Oxford, Bodleian Library, Bodley 749, of c. 1250. H. Müller, 'Der Musiktraktat in dem Werke des Bartholomeus Anglicus De proprietatibus rerum', in *Riemann Festschrift*, [ed. C. Menecke] (Leipzig, 1909), 241–55.

From such allegory, traditional with psalm–commentary, one learns only that here *organum* does seem to mean 'organ' and not 'instruments in general', much less 'vocal ensemble music'. As a reformer pressing for strict observance of Canon Law in the new big secular cathedrals and elsewhere, Gerhoch may well have been deliberately rejecting other instruments in the office,[4] distinguishing the sacred from the non-sacred as someone at the period might.

While it is possible that Gerhoch, Gill and Bartholomeus (also in his French translation, Paris, Bibliothèque Nationale, fr. 22532) speak for typical German, Spanish, English and French practice, just as possible is that their remarks aim at an ideal known to none of them directly, merely something read about and freely quoted between one author and another. Nevertheless, any custom would eventually need justification. During the fifteenth century, two quite different kinds of explanation for the Christian acceptance of the organ emerge, speaking on one hand for the pious–irrational side of the period, on the other for its scholarly–rational. Neither will give the same kind of answer as today's approaches, although these presumably derive from the latter.

St Cecilia

Firstly, the organ is an instrument graced by St Cecilia, a virgin martyr not at first associated with the organ except in so far as it may have been part of her wedding music towards which the 'music' of her soul was indifferent:

> And whil the organs maden melodie,
> To God Allone in herte thus sang she.

> (Chaucer, *Canterbury Tales*, Second Nun's Tale 134–5)[5]

There is a faint hint here of the way David is illustrated for the text of Psalms 70/71 in the Utrecht Psalter and perhaps in other psalters now lost: he points to his mouth while he holds one instrument unplayed and while two others (including an organ) lie silent on the ground, thus illustrating the text

exultabunt labia mea cum cantavero	my lips shall rejoice when I sing
tibi et anima mea	to you; and my soul
quam redemisti.	which you have redeemed.

The idea of a saint indifferent to musical instruments in the interests of another kind of ecstasy could well have its origin in David rather than Cecilia. For an Israelite king and a Christian martyr to be seen in a similar light would not be difficult when the king was David; and for a Christian to reject musical instruments would be easily understood in a period when people still remembered, even observed, pagan

---

[4] Cf. K. F. Morrison, 'The Church as play: Gerhoch of Reichersberg's call for reform', in *Popes, Teachers and Canon Law in the Middle Ages*, ed. J. R. Sweeney & S. Chodorow (Ithaca, 1989), 114–44, here 135.

[5] From the *Golden Legend*. On the virgin ideal, see S. L. Reames, 'The Cecilia legend as Chaucer inherited it and retold it', *Speculum* 55 (1980), 38–57; on some interconnections traditionally made between music, virginity and blindness (*caecitas*), see Connolly 1978 and 1980.

practices. The idea is not restricted to David and Cecilia: the virgin martyr St Agnes also disdained marriage, music and *organa* for the sake of her Saviour's gifts, according to a *vita* attributed to St Ambrose (*Acta SS* 2.715) and versified by the tenth-century Saxon nun Hrotsvitha of Gandersheim (MGH rer. ger. ius. 34). Shortly before Cecilia's story was written down, another Church Father St Jerome (†420) had actually directed Christian virgins to remain deaf to *organa (surda sit ad organa* – PL 22.875).

The sources for the story of St Cecilia are the *Passio* of the late fifth century (Connolly 1978: 6f) and the Great Responsory and lesson at mattins on 22 November, of the eighth or ninth. The *Passio* account is as follows, with the words as found in the responsories in *italics*:

venit dies in quo	there came the day on which the
thalamus collocatus est et	wedding was arranged and
cantantibus organis	as *organa* were sounding [? see below]
illa in corde suo soli	she sang to the Lord alone
Domino decantabat dicens:	in her heart, saying:
fiat cor meum et corpus meum	let my heart and body be made
immaculatum ut non confundar.	immaculate that I be not confounded.

The antiphon for vespers and lauds omits *illa in corde suo soli* and *et corpus meum*, in which form – one inadvertently implying that Cecilia sang to the organ – the description became well known particularly, one supposes, amongst the less well-read.[6] One hypothesis on how St Cecilia came to have her connection with music is presented in Connolly 1978, 1980; the present discussion is concerned with the part played by organs in that story.

A crucial point is that although Augustine (†430) and Boethius (†524) sometimes used *organa* to mean the organ, no fifth-century text of a non-technical kind, such as Cecilia's *Passio*, necessarily meant by it any kind of musical 'instrument'. It had other meanings. Perhaps what was *organized* were the sung texts themselves, such as those authorized for matrimony and sung with preconceived melody. Thus not only might Cecilia have been ignoring instruments, had there been any there, but she might have been ignoring all kinds of orderly human *music*. (If this is so, then her abstinence went beyond the mere *cantica mundi* forbidden to Christian virgins by Jerome – PL 22.871.) Music as chant to prescribed texts, as the act of singing in orderly ensemble, perhaps as a form of polyphony – all this was a human activity such as would distract Cecilia from her inner music.[7] All could have been called *organum*, and only with this word does the text make any mention of 'music'. *Musicis* would not have seemed the obvious word to go with *cantantibus*, for although the terms *musica, melodia* and *harmonia* were familiar enough to Boethius and other theorists, they were too technical–theoretical for such a context as this.

6   Better known, according to R. Luckett, 'St. Cecilia and music', *PRMA* 99 (1972), 15–30, but this is questioned by Connolly 1980: 5. The editor of the *Passio* as published many centuries later (Antonio Bosio, *Historia passionis B. Caeciliae virginis* (Rome, 1600)) claimed to base his account of the saint on a Vatican manuscript unnamed.

7   The idea of 'organized music' or consonant ensemble singing is contrasted with the crowd's unorganized, dissonant shouting of '*Holy!*' or '*Alleluia!*' on other occasions and public acclamations: see Chapter 5.

One would not say 'singing *music*' but would use another word: perhaps *modulationi-bus* or (if one wanted to specify ensemble singing?) *organis*. In the fourteenth century, Chaucer still does not say 'singing music'. By the late fifteenth century when so many artists picked up the theme of St Cecilia and the organ, few would know the older significances of the words *musica* and *organum* and would assume that the latter simply meant 'organ'.

Partly as a consequence of all the newly printed liturgical books being more widely distributed in the later fifteenth century, more people must quickly have become familiar with 'St Cecilia and music'. It is not yet possible to pin down the period or country or genre in which she is first shown holding or touching an organ,[8] but it can be supposed that this finished icon resulted from several currents. Firstly, her virginal-healing-musical *persona* became more associated with musical instruments as the word and idea of *musica* became less philosophical (music the audible sign of the proportions that rule the world) and approached the more mundane, modern sense of 'music' as something sung, played, listened to and enjoyed. If Cecilia were 'musical', it must mean that she was involved in music-making, and the layers of subtle and ancient association between virgin, healing and *musica* would melt to produce – a saint who played the organ.

Secondly, popular saint-study must have quickly found organs a very convenient emblem for the saint, as eye-catching in a stained glass window as the wheel for St Catherine. A common purpose for emblems – that they reminded the viewer of the saint's trials – made the organ quite appropriate for Cecilia. Thirdly, she was at first merely associated with the organ as an emblem, not directly involved in actually playing it – if the emblem signified something else, as an allegory would. In time, the representations would move from portraying instruments (*organa*) present at her public wedding to the organ's becoming something she played herself in her religious ecstasy, losing its force as allegory but becoming part of an instantly recognizable portrait. The combination of ecstasy and indifference must be difficult for an artist to represent (numinous ecstasy plus indifference to *organa*), and in paintings Cecilia could easily appear to be merely casting her eyes heavenward as she got carried away by the *musica instrumentalis* of her fingers – precisely what the story meant originally not to say.

Fourthly, *organa* came to mean only 'organs'. In 1500, it was not the invention of the organ so much as its connection to an early Christian martyr that must have been of interest. The martyr in question was a native Roman acquainted with several popes, and she could not have been more central: the church of St Cecilia in Trastevere, associated with the early house-church (*titulus*) of the Caecilian family, served to link the people of 1500 with the city's venerable Christian past and with the saint's ancient cult in Rome, known from a liturgical source of the seventh century.[9] In this way she would be part of Rome's Christian history and its

---

[8] Connolly 1980: 36–8. A. P. Mirimonde's *Sainte-Cécile: métamorphoses d'un thème musical* (Geneva, 1974) does not describe the early historical evolution of the motif.

[9] On the Roman *tituli*: Baldovin 1987: 108. The church of St Cecilia was rebuilt several times, e.g. in 817–24 (Krautheimer 1937–77: 1.94ff). On the Leonine Sacramentary of Verona (*c.* 600): T. H. Connolly, 'The *Graduale* of S. Cecilia in Trastevere and the Old Roman tradition', *JAMS* 28 (1975), 413–58.

incomparable martyrology. Perhaps it reflected the desire of Anglo-Saxon England to remain closely linked with the Holy City, whence Augustine of Canterbury had been sent by Gregory the Great, that St Cecilia joined a select group of Roman saints in the late tenth-century *Benedictional of Æthelwold*.[10] As books of the Roman rite circulated from the late eighth century on, so did knowledge of the martyr, but it is typical of her story in the earlier centuries that the *Benedictional's* Blessing for St Cecilia's day made no reference to music or instruments.[11] Nor, very likely, did the ceremonies concerned with the translation of the saint's relics in the ninth century do so, when the church in Trastevere became one focal point for the early Christian history of Rome as it was already being developed. Perhaps in the Renaissance period the strengthening of the apostolic and by then unrivalled authority of Rome was not the least reason for the popularity of the St Cecilia legend.

Early writers of books on musical instruments, such as Arnold Schlick (1511) and Sebastian Virdung (1511), do not refer to her, nor do much earlier commentators referring to *organa* or early medieval theorists formulating the proportional measurements of organ-pipes (see Chapter 16). For such authors, how the organ had come to be there was not yet a subject for research. A century after Schlick, Adriano Banchieri dedicated his influential treatise *Conclusioni nel suon dell'organo* (Bologna, 1609) to St Cecilia and cited her antiphon *Cantantibus organis* in support. But he also pointed out that several printed authorities on the saints found no evidence for her having been an organist, and noted that there were two problems with the texts as he knew them: *organa* could mean 'organ of the human voice' (*organo della voce humana*), and the early third century is too early for the bellows-organ she is often portrayed as playing.

This scepticism about both terminology and chronology is a refreshing characteristic of the period, but whether Banchieri is quite correct is doubtful. Bellows for small organs are not out of the question for that early period, even if Renaissance painters did not know it and were only guessing. Presumably Banchieri was unaware of the bellows-organ(s)[12] sculpted on the obelisk of Theodosius in Constantinople (late fourth century), although Venetian gazetteers described it; and probably he relied on sixteenth-century editions of Hero of Alexandria to learn about water-organs, which were imaginatively illustrated in these editions.[13] He would not be the last reader of the Latin and Greek authors to assume that their detailed descriptions of water-cisterns meant that such were the only means known by the ancients for raising wind for organs – which, after all, is very unlikely. Also, Banchieri is not

---

[10]   London, British Library Add. 49598: see also p. 96. There had been earlier English references to Cecilian virtues, by St Aldhelm of Malmesbury (late seventh century) and Alcuin of York, Charlemagne's adviser (late eighth: see Connolly 1980: 26–30).

[11]   A sixth-century mosaic in S Apollinare Nuovo, Ravenna, gives St Cecilia no emblem. Also, despite Cologne's putative significance to organ-building in the twelfth century (see Chapter 15) it is striking that the entrance-typanum in St Cecilia's, Cologne (*c*. 1160), shows no musical motif as the saint receives the victor-martyr's laurels.

[12]   I agree with Degering 1905: 76 that what appears to be two such organs on the obelisk is probably a quasi-panoramic view (front and back) of the same organ.

[13]   For Constantinople and its obelisk: P. Gyllius, *De topographia Constantinopoleos*, 2 vols (Leiden, 1561). For Vitruvius: D. Barbaro, *I dieci libri dell'architettura di M. Vitruvio* (Venice, 1556). For Hero: F. Commandini, *Heronis Alexandrini Spiritalium Liber* (Urbino, 1575). By 1609 all three books had had two or more editions.

clear with his phrase 'organ of the human voice': does he mean with it something anatomical (the 'vocal organ') or is he alluding to the old formula *vox organica* or *organa vocis* (the latter already present in the familiar solmization hymn *Ut queant laxis*, text of *c.* 800?). Using 'organ' as an anatomical term was not new[14] in Italian (or English), but he probably meant merely that St Cecilia's *organo* was her own voice – which is a doubtful reading of the *Passio*.

Banchieri's dedication to St Cecilia was a recognition that she was associated with the instrument. Neither he nor others were implying that if a saint had such association with an object then the Church took it into its daily life, for this would mean many an unsuitable object being so accepted. Rather, it was that since the organ was known to everyone, then its being a saint's emblem was one way in which to regard it. Association with a saint was enough to authorize it after the event, all the more necessary in view of the organ's rejection by many a Protestant movement in Banchieri's time.

Pope Vitalian

In an early printed book of *The Lives of the Popes*, the historian Platina attributed the regularization of chant and the admission of the organ to Pope Vitalian (657–72), and many later writers took the idea from him directly or indirectly. The reference in Zarlino 1588: 17 must have been particularly authoritative for musicians. A history book's statement based on earlier documents must have seemed one way to explain how chant was organized or organs admitted, yet its usefulness would hang on at least two factors: whether the words as originally used had changed in meaning by the fifteenth century and whether the aims of original documents, of Platina's version of them and of the uses to which either would be put later, had much in common.

The *Liber de vita Christi ac omnium pontificum* of Bartolomei Sacchi detto il Platina (1474) was republished in various forms, including the *De vitis pontificum* (Venice, 1479), the *De vita & moribus summorum pontificum historia* (1529, printed 'with the Emperor's privilege': Vitalian, pp. 75–7), and *Opus, de vitis ac gestis summorum pontificum* (1564, pp. 178–9). These relate acts of somewhat inconsistent nature in the life of Pope Vitalian and include two passages that are relevant here:[15]

quique Evangelia aureis	[his representatives] had gospels
literis scripta,	copied with golden letters,
ac multis gemmis ornata,	and decorated with many jewels,
beato Petro condonarent . . .	and gave them to St Peter [the basilica?]. . .
Ac Vitalianus cultui	And Vitalian, intent on the
divino intentus,	holy liturgy,

---

[14] Isidore of Seville referred to the lungs of the body, and it is possible that the artist of the Stuttgart Psalter knew this association when he drew his bellows: see Chapter 11 below. Further details on Isidore and the term *organa vocis* in Reckow 1975: 95–6.

[15] In the edition by G. Carducci & V. Fiorini, *Rerum italicarum scriptores: raccolta degli storici italiani del cinquecento al millecinquecento ordinata da L. A. Muratori* (Bologna, 1903), 3.1.109, said to be based on the 1479 edition and the manuscript Rome, Biblioteca Apostolica Vaticana, lat. 2044, *consonantium* is replaced by *ad consonantiam.*

& regulam ecclesiasticam composuit,	composed the ecclesiastical rule [= the office],
& cantum ordinavit,	and set the chant in order,
adhibitis consonantium	employing *organa* (as some would have it)
(ut quidam volunt) organis. . .	for sounding with it [?]

The phrase *consonantium organis* is a crux and sounds archaic. It is difficult to squeeze a reliable interpretation from it because of (a) the different meanings of *organis* (organs/instruments, ensemble music, a book/psalter) and accordingly, (b) the range of meanings that *consonantium*, if not a mistake, can then take. Two possibilities are:

'instruments of consonances [with the chant?] having been employed

or

'employing the instruments of those sounding in harmony'

but since both of these need further paraphrase, they could each have suggested to later writers an 'organ playing with the chant' or one used in some way in its behalf, for example in teaching its notes to neophytes. But a third possibility is that *organis* are the organs not of music but of learning or authority, and what John or his source meant was:

'having employed books of agreeing [texts]'

i.e. having established a liturgical canon. To credit a pope with regularizing the texts of the office seems particularly appropriate. Whichever is the likeliest, the parenthesis *ut quidam volunt* may indicate uncertainty on the transmitter's part: does it apply to *organis* or *consonantium*? Perhaps he is uncertain and assumes *organis* means 'organs'; or on the contrary, he knows it could once have meant a book such as a psalter or antiphoner; or he recognizes something odd about *consonantium* and guesses that in the proximity to *organis* it must have a musical meaning.

While the version *adhibitis ad consonantiam* (see note 15) is clearer and suggests that *organa* were added to produce harmony – thus that *organa* meant the instrument and not music or a psalter – the problem is that this is precisely what is uncertain. Such ambiguity was lost in later translations, including the *Historia delle vite dei sommi pontefici* (Venice, 1594), 70:

ora Vitaliano intento al culto divino, ne compose la regola ecclesiastica, e ne ordinò il canto aggiungendovi (come alcuni vogliano) gli organi

which is literal enough for the same English to serve except that *aggiungendovi gli organi* ('adding the organs' to the chant) is a definite interpretation of *consonantium organis*. By 1594 it would have seemed that *organa* meant organs and that the phrase 'as some call them' was quaint and meaningless.

Platina derived this passage from an earlier account belonging to a group of manuscript histories connecting Vitalian with *organa*, in particular that of Tolomeo Fiadoni of Lucca (1236–1327):[16]

---

[16] Identified in the 1903 edition of Muratori (see note 15) as Ptolomaeus Lucensis, *Historia ecclesiastica*, ed. L. A. Muratori, Rerum italicarum scriptores 10 (Milan, 1727), 741–1244, here 940.

Hic cantum Romanum composuit	He compiled [composed?] the Roman chant,
ut scribit Martinus, & Cusentius,	as Martinus Cusentius [*sic*] writes,
& organo concordavit.	and made it harmonious with the organum
	[= in vocal polyphony?].

Not all histories of the popes did connect Vitalian with *organa*, the most conspicuous and influential of those that did not being the *Liber pontificalis* (see below). In this and other details Tolomeo is careful to cite Martinus (Martinus Polonus or Cusentius, †1278, a Dominican friar), a source that itself goes back directly or indirectly to John the Deacon in the ninth century. But John did not use the word *organum* as later writers did, and the result is that Platina (or at least *his* readers and interpreters) misunderstood the source and then transmitted their misunderstanding.

This is what seems to have happened. In the *Sancti Gregorii magni vita* (*c.* 880) of Johannes Hymmonides or John the Deacon, Vitalian is reported to have sent out a Roman cantor to establish the chant:

occidentales ecclesiae ita	the western churches were so
susceptum modulationis	spoiling the received *modulationis*
organum vitiarunt, ut	*organum* that
Joannes quidam Romanus cantor	John, a certain Roman cantor,
cum Theodoro aeque cive	was sent with Theodore, another
Romano, sed Eburaci	Roman citizen but [also] Archbishop of
archiepiscopo	York,
per Gallias in Britannias	via Gaul to Britain,
a Vitalliano sit praesule	by Vitalian the pope.
destinatus.	(PL 75.91)

This report is one of a complex of texts concerned with the early history of authorized chant (or chant-texts) and may well be based in part on the Venerable Bede's accounts of John the Cantor's mission (*Hist. Eccl.* 4). Quite where John the Deacon acquired the phrase *modulationis organum* and quite what he meant by it are by no means certain, but it is the crucial phrase to connect Vitalian with *organum*: the *Liber pontificalis*, accepted as generally authoritative for the seventh century, does not have the phrase or so connect them.[17] Recognizing that in any case John the Deacon was concerned to support the Bishop of Rome's authority during the tempestuous ninth century, one can suppose *organum* to mean (a) the psalter or office-book (an organ of papal authority?), and perhaps in particular (b) the musical or chant repertory that goes with it, but not (c) *organum* in the sense of formal polyphony, much less (d) *organum* as that particular instrument with pipes and bellows.[18] Whether *modulationis* has a general or musical sense ('in the arranged order', or 'of

---

17 For the text of the *Liber* and a seventeenth-century English translation, see below p. 11. Editions used: Duchesne 1886–92: 2.343, also ed. T. Mommsen, *Gestorum pontificum romanorum: Libri pontificalis pars prior*, MGH (Berlin, 1898), 1.186–9, here 186. On the claim for Gregorian chant's papal authority, see texts in Stäblein 1970: 142★ff, 52★ff. Bede's *Life of the Abbots* speaks of John the Cantor's being sent by Vitalian's eventual successor Agatho (PL 94.711, 715, 717).

18 *Organum* meaning both musical instrument and an organ of learning such as a book closely parallels the use of *psalterium* for both psaltery and psalter.

modulated sound' or 'melodic'), the first two meanings of *organum* would fit. It would be natural for a historian of the popes or of the Church to attribute to particular popes so important a part of church-life as the arrangement of the daily (hourly) liturgies: he would know that the 'Roman component [with] its strong emphasis on the Psalter as a source of stichs' or phrases in liturgical texts (NOHM 1990: 228) did not occur by accident and that however slow to accumulate, someone somewhere must have authorized it. On about a dozen occasions, the *Liber pontificalis* attributes various elements in the Roman stational liturgy to various popes (texts assembled in Baldovin 1987: 120–2).

As various authors between John the Deacon and Platina worked on the material, *organum* came more and more to mean organ. When some copies of the *Chronicon pontificum* by Martinus Polonus (see above) gave the report in these terms:

[Vitalianus] cantum romanorum	Vitalian compiled [composed?] the
composuit	chant of the Romans
et organo concordavit	and made it harmonious with the organ [?]

(MGH SS 22.423)

the juxtaposition of *organo* and *concordavit* would by then easily suggest something as concrete as 'made the chant agree with the organ'. For a thirteenth-century non-expert, it must have been plausible both for the chant to agree with – play in alteration with? – the organ and for someone to deserve the credit for authorizing such common practice.

In repeating or compiling the work of earlier writers such as John the Deacon, later clerical historians glossed the quotations with colourful terms, producing phrases like *dulcisono organo concordavit* or *cum organo et melodia concordavit*, each of which makes it clear that the writer understood his source to mean organs.[19] But it is also possible that authors reproduced these or similar words and phrases not quite knowing what they were supposed to mean. Perhaps this is the case with Platina, who is not necessarily referring to organs in the passage above, whatever his later readers and translators thought.

The attributing of organs in church to a long dead pope recalls the claims for St Gregory and authorized chant,[20] and there were other attributions. One sixth- or seventh-century example was Pope Gelasius (492–6), accredited with writing hymns: *fecit et ymnos in modum beati Ambrosii* ('he wrote hymns in the style of St Ambrose'), according to the *Liber pontificalis* (Duchesne 1886–92: 1.255). Sabinian (604–6) established the custom of ringing a bell for the office hours, and his predecessor St Gregory had the credit for founding the two *scholae. . . de Cantu, & Officio Ecclesiastico*, both according to the same sources still quoted in the *Historia* of Tolomeo (see

---

19   The first by Riccobaldus Gervasius of Ferrara († after 1312), the second by Amalricus Augerius (writing *c.* 1362): quoted in Stäblein 1970: 144*-5*.

20   It seems wide of the mark to attribute the phrase *cantum romanorum . . . organum concordavit* to medieval-Renaissance writers 'because they were irritated by the claim for Vitalian as against Gregory' (H. Hucke, 'Toward a new historical view of Gregorian chant', *JAMS* 33 (1980), 437–7, here 441).

above).[21] Perhaps such achievements are sometimes attributed because a case had to be made for Rome (Gelasius's hymns imply that Rome was not far behind its powerful rival Milan) or because the pope concerned had not been quite beyond criticism (as in the case of both Vitalian and Sabinian). John the Deacon's attributions to Gregory and Vitalian were made during the troubled papacy of – perhaps at the instigation of – John VIII who has another part in the history of organs, probably likewise due to a misunderstanding: see Chapter 13. Some later Protestant historians have been critical of Vitalian as one weakly – his apologists say diplomatically – avoiding condemnation of the Byzantine emperor's heresy: he was 'a courtier to whom it mattered less what he did or said, than that he should keep good friends with the supreme power' in the imperial capital.[22] The emperor, Constans II, is known to have sent Vitalian a book of gospels adorned with gold and precious stones; perhaps that given to St Peter's as reported by John the Deacon above. The description of Vitalian being 'intent on the holy liturgy' may therefore be a response to the monothelite criticism. Despite all this, however, it is also perfectly possible that Vitalian's cantors did form or reform the liturgy and its chant, for at least the pope's own stational services.

Many later versions of the lives of the popes are based on the *Liber pontificalis*, and its text appears verbatim in, for example, the *Anastasii . . . historia di vitis romanorum pontificum* (Paris, 1649), 51–2:

et Evangelia aurea cum	and a golden gospel with
gemmis albis mirae magnitudinis	white stones of wonderful size
in circuitu ornatas. Hic	around its edges. He maintained
regulam ecclesiasticam, atque	the ecclesiastical rule and
vigorem, ut mos erat,	its vigour, as the custom was,
omnimodo conservavit.	in all kinds of ways.

Clearly, the *Liber*, the 'Platina' and the 'Martinus Polonus' texts are related, but how is very obscure. The parallels between the verbs (*conservavit, composuit, ordinavit, concordavit*) and between the nouns (*vigorem, cantum/organis, organo*) – even between the two parentheses (*ut mos erat, ut quidam volunt*) – are such as to suggest a relationship but not what it may have been. Against the *Liber* version is that it does not seem to be saying anything noteworthy, unless it was that a pope 'preserving' or 'conserving' the *regula* was exceptional at the time. But what would 'all kinds of ways' be? If the vigour is that for observing the monastic hours (one wonders if *vigorem* is a misreading of *organum* or vice versa), what was customary, the vigour or the office? On behalf of the *Liber*'s version might be John the Deacon's remarks, for assuming his *organum* to mean something other than 'organ', Vitalian's sending out a cantor and an archbishop could well be an example of his efforts at vigorously preserving the ecclesiastical rule as authorized. Either way, the interpretation implied in the 'Martinus Polonus' text need have no ancient authority.

---

[21] As note 16: pp. 916, 915. Tolomeo also knew of Pippin's organ (glossed as *organa suavissima*, p. 977 – source in A[i]monius/Ammianus, see note 23) and of the performance of *Te Deum, Laudes* and acclamations for Louis the Pious (source in Einhard); see also Chapters 9 and 5.

[22] G. F. Browne, *Theodore and Wilfrith* (London, 1897), 77f.

The 'Platina version' appears in Paul Rycault's translation, *The Lives of the Popes* (London, 1685), 114:

But Vitalianus being intent upon sacred things composed Ecclesiastical Canons, and regulated singing in the Church, introducing Organs to be used with the Vocal Musick.

Although a definite interpretation, the last phrase does at least bring in the idea of ensemble performance. Like other English Catholic sources, Rycault seems to have been little known by later establishment musicians such as Hawkins and Burney, who knew of the claim for Vitalian rather from French and Italian accounts. Martin Gerbert's *De cantu et musica sacra* of 1774 quotes several versions of the Platina report which he finds scattered here and there in books on the popes, and the *De cantu's* account is quite the fullest before the twentieth century. J. U. Sponsel, *Orgelhistorie* (Nuremberg, 1771), 45, and J. Anthony, *Geschichtliche Darstellung der Entstehung und Vervollkommnung der Orgel* (Münster, 1832), 29, give a version virtually identical to that of 1529 above, and this is also found in Perrot 1965: 285. Buhle 1903: 61 quotes another version but cites Forkel, Antony, Sponsel and Calvör's *Ritualis ecclesiastici* (Jena, 1705) as further sources.

In some Protestant treatises of the seventeenth and eighteenth centuries, the authors make use of the histories of Platina and others to show how recent and uncanonical were so many of the Church of Rome's practices. In *William Perkins his Probleme of the forged Catholicisme* (Cambridge, 1604), there is a list of the 'Appurtenances of the Masse, at this day', including organs, for which he cites Platina and 'Amonius'.[23] Also against organs, Joseph Bingham in *Christian Antiquities* (1708–23)[24] not only refers to authorities to show that the organ was brought in to the church only from about 1250 but is aware of its having been used in the palace of the western emperor from the eighth century on. Bingham's account of the references to organs in early writers such as Chrysostom or Theodoret shows a better grasp of the context of their words than does that of many a later music-historian.

Praetorius refers to Platina and several later historians including Perkins and Cranzius,[25] quoting the dates they offer for the organ's introduction. From other archival histories Praetorius too knew of Pippin's organ of 757 and pointed out that Vitalian only 'approved and confirmed' (*approbiret und confirmiret*) the use of organs: for long they had played a part in the understanding of the tetrachord, hexachord and so on, up to the creation of the twenty-note keyboard. Already by Praetorius's time, then, it was assumed that organs had taught practical harmony and that the Church first used them for such purposes. While there may be some truth in this assumption (see Chapter 4), its real significance is rather that Praetorius resisted the idea of the organ's owing its presence and use to particular people at particular times.

---

23 Complete edition: William Perkins, *The Works of that Famous & Worthy Minister of Christ in the Universities of Cambridge M. W. P.* (London, 1631), 2.565. The edition of A[i]monius/Ammianus to which he refers is probably the *Aimoini monachi . . . libri quinque de gestis francorum* (Paris, 1602), based on late ninth-century annals.

24 Quoted here from the complete edition, J. Bingham, *Origines sive Antiquitates ecclesiasticae* (Halle, 1717), 3.275–9.

25 *Syntagma musicum* 2 (Wolfenbüttel, 1619), 90–1. Cranzius = A. Krantz, *Ecclesiastica historia, sive metropolis* (Basle, 1568).

Other answers

There is a further story that bells were invented and/or introduced by St Paulinus of Nola (353–431), a story very likely prompted by *nola* being one term for 'bell'. The tradition for linking Nola with a type of small bell, already reported by Walahfrid Strabo in the middle of the ninth century (MGH Cap. 2.479), may have lead to the Paulinus attribution being made by well-read scribes. Paulinus's period would not be one in which desolated Rome itself was credited with achievements in such difficult technologies as bronze bell-casting. But when the ringing of the office-bell is attributed to Pope Sabinian (see above) credit is brought back to Rome and to the golden Gregorian period:[26] in the *Liber pontificalis* and comparable sources, chant is owed to Gregory, hymns to Gelasius, bells to Sabinian and organs to Vitalian. The story of Paulinus could also reflect another tradition: Nola, a settlement between Naples and Benevento, had been known for its bronze-casting from early Roman times, and the story linked Nola's Christian saint-bishop with its historical, traditional technology.[27] Some concrete or actual element, therefore, played a part in the legend.

So it may have done in the legend of St Cecilia. While polyphony and/or instruments have no particular known association with the Trastevere part of Rome, there are two motifs in the story that are common in early Christian literature around the year 400. Firstly, there were *organa* at wedding celebrations in many Mediterranean societies, as various references make clear, and it is possible that they do play a part in the organ becoming a church instrument, directly or indirectly, sooner or later. Secondly, the chaste in mind and body would have been obliged to shun such celebrations, especially the improper activities – the charivari-like carousing – incited by musical instruments present for that very purpose. Early Christian writers often recommend the faithful to avoid such events. The Anglo-Saxon poet St Aldhelm (†709) interpreted the *organica harmonia* of Cecilia's wedding as representing 'fleshly enticement . . . siren music', while in the ninth century Hincmar of Reims was still regretting the festive licentiousness of wedding celebrations.[28] Against this background, the story of St Cecilia served as one particular example of abstinence from both marriage and *organa*, and only long after the Church of north-west Europe regularly used organs did her association with them become more positive.

Historians quoting Platina's remark about Vitalian and the organ would eventually question what they thought he was claiming with it, using increasingly more sources than he did (not least the Carolingian annals) and successively refining what their

---

[26] Attributions to Paulinus and Sabinian in the manuscript Rome Biblioteca Apostolica lat. 8430 f. 137, according to N. Bossi, *Le campane: trattato storico, liturgico, canonico, legale* (Macerta, 1897), 25. Gerbert (1774: 159–60) also reports the attributions but is sceptical as to Paulinus; so is Bingham (note 24): 3.284.

[27] This would be so even if the interest for Walahfrid Strabo was the play on words (*campana* [a tolling bell] > *campanula* (diminutive) > *campanola* > *nola*), as suggested by J. Smits van Waesberghe, *Cymbala* (Rome, 1951), 15. In that case, *nola*, like *hydra* written on the little organ of Aquincum (see Chapter 14), is an abbreviation.

[28] Selections from St John Chrysostom and others in McKinnon 1987: 72, 83–5, 119, 133–4. For Aldhelm's poem on virginity, see below pp. 78f; quotation here from Connolly 1980: 30. For remarks on Hincmar and festive celebrations, see Chapter 5.

predecessors wrote. This is already the case with Praetorius in the seventeenth century and continues with Gerbert in the eighteenth. For such historians, Platina's *organum* must have meant instruments in general or even vocal music in general, according to Bedos de Celles, *L'art du facteur d'orgues* 1 (Paris, 1776), preface. Or perhaps some particular instrument such as *tuba* was signified by this ambiguous word.[29] But Gerbert (1774: 141) assumed that Vitalian's contribution lay not in organs but in vocal music – a particularly good suggestion (and one picked up by Bedos?) in view of the meanings of the word *organum* that have been more fully traced in recent years. In Hopkins & Rimbault (1877: 17ff), E. F. Rimbault referred to the published claims and evidence from some of these sources, adding one or two of his own and appearing to believe that the answer to the question 'How do we have the organ?' does lie in documents if only one searches far and wide and can assemble enough of them. But he does not question what, for example, Johannes Lorinus could have meant when he said in his *Commentatorium in librum psalmorum* (1611–16, apropos Psalm 33) that organs were known in fifth-century Spain. (So they might have been, but not as liturgical church instruments.) A still later historian asks whether the question of the organ's introduction can be answered at all:

car on ne connaît pas à ce jour de texte officiel, dans les archives pontificales, consacrant l'usage de l'instrument à l'église. (Perrot 1965: 285)

Cet étrange silence can be explained in this way: for a long time the clergy closed their eyes to organs and then, having been seduced by the new instrument thanks to the early ninth-century priest Georgius (who was acting at Louis the Pious's behest), recognized it to be better suited to the liturgy than fiddles or cornets. In any such view of history, therefore, explanations like Platina's can appear to be *sans valeur historique*.

There seem to be three main anachronisms here. Firstly, the idea that there could be or would have been any *texte officiel* authorizing organs in church. Secondly, that a vast movement or gradual development could owe so much to one single person, not now a saint or pope but a craftsman, a well-travelled Carolingian monk mentioned in monastic *annales* (on this Georgius, see Chapter 9). Thirdly, that Platina's words can be taken at present-day face-value. The remarks made by Thomas Tudway in *c.* 1720 are no more anachronistic than Perrot's, despite their brevity and a view of historical progress more typical of the Baroque centuries:

It is certain, that Organs, whatever they were, have not been us'd in ye Western Xtian Church, above 4 or 500 years, & tis as certain, that ye inventors therof, made but a small progress, in comeing to an perfection.[30]

Not only with that 'whatever they were', Tudway put his finger on the crucial point – the appearance of the organ in the one province of the Christian Church –

---

[29] J. U. Sponsel, *Orgelhistorie* (Nuremberg, 1771), 45–59. Is it possible that Sponsel made this suggestion from knowing the tradition transmitted by the *Letter to Dardanus* (ninth century?) according to which some kind of siren-organ as made by the Arabs was called *tuba*? See p. 247.

[30] In C. Hogwood, 'Thomas Tudway's history of music', in *Music in Eighteenth-Century England: Essays in Memory of Charles Cudworth*, ed. C. H. & R. Luckett (Cambridge, 1983), 19–48.

and it is a point that is still obscure today. One recent suggestion is that the organ entered church through imperial ceremony:

Es handelt sich vorerst noch gar nicht um eine Ablehnung oder Duldung von Musikinstrumenten im Gottesdienst, sondern um die Beteilung der Christen und der Kirche an der Kaiserehrung. (Schuberth 1968: 55)

Mostly, it a matter not so much of refusing or tolerating musical instruments in the service but of Christians and the Church participating in ceremonies honouring the emperor.

But if the organ did become a norm of imperial ceremony in the church or churches of the emperor's city, a question would still be: How did it get into the monasteries? Was the ceremony held only in Aachen and Constantinople or was a portable organ moved to any Carolingian *villa*? If so, how did it migrate from palace to abbey? Because of these difficulties, another link in the chain had to be made:

Die karolingische Orgel – ursprünglich Instrument der kaiserlichen Hofmusik – hatte im 9. Jahrhundert ihren Einzug in den fränkischen Kirchenraum gehalten und war im 10. Jahrhundert, offenbar im Zuge der benediktinischen Erneuerung, in englischen Kirchen übernommen worden (Holschneider 1968: 142)

During the ninth century, the Carolingian organ – instrument originally of imperial court-music – found its way inside Frankish churches, and during the tenth, evidently in the train of Benedictine reform, got taken over into English churches.

But this does not explain how it got taken over from 'court-music' into the churches of certain Benedictine abbeys a century and more later in a country beyond the sea, even if it were certain, as it is not, that the *organum* known from documents of the Carolingian and Byzantine courts played music as distinct from noise. Is it really plausible that Ramsey Abbey would have had no organ in the tenth century or that St Oswald would have remained in ignorance of them (see Chapter 12) had it not been for that single gift two centuries earlier from the Emperor of the East to the King of the Franks? Must there not have been instrument-makers dotted about western Christendom independently of both emperors?

Whatever it was that Carolingian annalists were recording when they noted the Byzantine gift of an organ to Pippin in their brief notes on the events of the year 757, and whatever their reasons for doing so (see Chapter 9), neither they nor anyone else ever recorded those day-to-day habits on the basis of which such things as organs became a part of many a monastery's assets, without doubt many more than we know about. Post-Carolingian historians have been too dependent on the notion of the datable event, their approach founded on the very work of the annalists who document Pippin's organ and relay history as a series of dated events. What organs were like and how they were used are questions that lie in very misty regions, glimpsed only now and then as one tries an approach from one or other angle. The value of written documentation cannot be high for a subject like organs when its practice is informal and seldom described and when its technology is something beyond the interests or abilities of contemporary literates to describe.

In the end, the history of the organ cannot rely on documentation such as it has been understood in different ways over the centuries. Not a mattins text for 22 November nor a papal archive, not a royal annal nor today's accumulation of all known references to *organa*, will quite show 'what happened'. This has to be reasoned along the likely stages of development and will depend on such considerations as technology, music, liturgy and architecture, and what they all meant in the periods concerned. Much apparent evidence about organs turns out to be evidence only about the sources themselves – in any case it would be this – and what it was that writers or artists learnt about organs from predecessors working in the same genres (psalm-commentaries, psalm-illustration etc.). Recent thinking might now see the question 'Who invented or introduced organs?' as a subset of the old question 'Who invented music?' and one that can be illustrated with similar material.[31] What organs were like and how they were used are not clear, and the story can be told only as a hypothesis or series of questions.

[31]   As in J. McKinnon, 'Jubal and Pythagoras, quis sit inventor musicae?', *MQ* 64 (1978), 1–28, esp. 11.

Organs, music and architecture

2

Some thoughts on melody and harmony

One needs to imagine somehow what 'melody and harmony' were to the player of an early organ, or any instrument, in a revitalized Benedictine abbey of the ninth or tenth century. This is difficult because so little is certain about the player's background: what contemporary illiterate musics were like, what a monk knew or understood of earlier accounts of music, what effect his overriding contact with chant had on his ideas of music. Since most writing now focuses on the period's literate musical theory (particularly on notes and the relationship between them) and written-down details of its church practice (particularly chant and written polyphony), a more general approach to musical matters may be appropriate to the present study. The following remarks are prompted by, I hope, not too arbitrary a collection of references and aim to put in some sort of context music's impact on the early organ and the early organ's impact on music.

Melody

The difficulty of imagining what could have been to contemporaries so seductive a melody as the Song of the Sirens in the *Odyssey* – a difficulty already there in imperial Rome[1] – is not much less than it is for music composed a millennium and a half later.

In the *Odyssey* 12, the Sirens use words to attract Odysseus to come closer in order to be fully seduced, to hear the 'sweet tone', 'liquid song' and 'beautiful voice',[2] terms that suggested basic elements of melody and timbre both to the ancient Greeks, it seems, and to many a later poet who used the same kinds of phrase. When Achilles sings of famous men in *Iliad* 9, it was presumably more in the narrative style, a style traditionally distinguished from the imitative: the first keeps a simple rhythm and mode (*harmonia*) while the second requires many changes in both and was especially liable to be criticized by those mourning a golden age (Plato *Republic* 3). The ideal of bewitching mellifluence conveyed in the myth of the Sirens is also

---

[1] According to Suetonius (*Twelve Caesars*), who had his own reasons for reporting imperial decadence, the Emperor Tiberius carried literary researches to such a ridiculous point as to ask questions like 'What song did the Sirens sing?'

On Cicero's idea that Odysseus was attracted by something other than the sweetness of melody, see also p. 146.

[2] μελίγηρυν, λιγυρὴν ἀοιδήν, κάλλιμον.

shown in the details of the poetic (and hence musical) style in which they speak or sing, details in the text that can be recognized as 'hinting at the lyric' in its rhythms. This lyricism, added to the 'liquid consonants' and many vowel sounds found in the lines sung by two other women with a 'lovely voice' in the *Odyssey* (Circe and Calypso),[3] may suggest what it was that seductive melody was held to contain. It was neither narrative nor imitative. For one thing, the performance itself clearly has a part in the melodious effect, because the liquid consonants are not theoretical but realized in performance with a lovely voice.

A 'conception of melody [which] entailed qualitative performance aspects'[4] – in other words, how it was sung as well as what the notes were – surfaces also in the Carolingian period, as in the comments on antiphons and modes by Aurelian of Réôme (*c*. 850, in CSM 21), whose descriptions speak of the modes from the practical viewpoint of a monastic singer. Judging by the nature of his treatise as a compilation, Aurelian transmits ideas about varying voice-production in the chant such as were current in northern Francia at the time. Earlier, Isidore of Seville (*Etymologiae* 3.20.4) also spoke for more than the seventh century in claiming that *euphonia* is the 'sweetness of voice' (*suavitas vocis*) and that *melos* is so called 'from sweetness and honey' (*a suavitate et melle*), an association apparently supported by Greek derivatives of *mela* and *melos*. However unscientific such etymology, sweetness is a motif to occur frequently in various kinds of writing about music. And since sweetness and honey are likened, one can assume that the definition of sweetness has not much changed, although this would not explain what precisely the analogy music/honey was meant to convey, or how taste and sound can actually be likened.

The following definitions formulated at the beginning of the *Scolica enchiriadis* (*c*. 850?) for readers in the Carolingian monasteries come, via St Augustine, from at least the first century BC.[5]

musica quid est?	What is music?
bene modulandi scientia.	knowledge of how to regulate sounds well.
bene modulari quid est?	What is regulating well?
melos suavisonum moderari.	managing a pleasant-sounding line.

While the portmanteaus of word-association make any modern translation brusque, at least *sweetness* provides a certain field of meaning. For example, no species of sweetness would characterize either the sound produced at acclamations of kings or bishops or, probably, when the congregation cried *Sanctus!* in the mass (see Chapter 5). On such occasions the communal sound would be more a matter of noise, less ordered than sung ensemble music, no doubt rhythmic but not 'melodic' or in any other way 'organic'.

---

[3] One of Calypso's words is a 'miniature vocalise: by its very nature it calls for a melisma': W. Anderson, 'What song the Sirens sang: problems and conjectures in ancient Greek music', *Royal Musical Association Research Chronicle* 15 (1979), 1–16, here 13.

[4] L. Treitler, 'Reading and singing: on the genesis of occidental music-writing', *EMH* 4 (1984), 135–208, here 158.

[5] Augustine in PL 32.1083. Perhaps the use made in both *Enchiriadis* treatises of classical authority – Plato's *Timaeus* (including its dialogue form) and Boethius's *Institutiones* (including its theory of notes) – was one reason why they circulated so widely.
   Blumröder 1983 traces the phrase *bene modulandi* becoming *recte modulandi*, as in Aurelian of Réôme.

Was it in order to make this kind of distinction that writers of the Carolingian period used the term *organum* for music when they reported on the singing at such occasions as a church dedication – to distinguish the kind of sound which was mellifluously organized from the kind which was not? *Organum* would be music while *acclamatio* was noise, perhaps a rhythmic shouting; and *musica* was theory rather than the experience in sound now called 'music'. Whether the ninth-century phrase *organicum melos* refers to formal counterpoint – diaphony sung only partly in parallels, as in *Musica enchiriadis* (see Chapter 3) – or something like the regulated heterophony as described in late Latin sources,[6] the main element was nevertheless the kind of mellifluity that would come from sound 'organized' in some way, in particular by singing the tetrachordal or diatonic notes (a) in tune and (b) in an ordered fashion. In such a treatise as the *Instituta patrum de modo psallendi sive cantandi*, the phrase *dulci melodia, nectareo iubilo, organica voce* (GS 1.8) preserves the ideas of 'sweet melody' (solo or unison chant?), of 'sweet jubilation' (alleluias or spiritual acclamations, 'honey-like' in sentiment if not in sound?) and of 'orderly music' (music for trained voices, using diatonic notes?).

By nature, *enthousiasmos* is difficult to reconcile with music meaning sweet or organic sound. A culture without conventionalized religious music-making can seem to another to have no sweet cantilena, and it is customary to find other peoples' music harsh or discordant, as Tacitus does of both the British and the Germans (*Agricola* 33, *Germania* 3). Something of this kind is probably the reason for a tenth-century Arab report on the Schleswigers' 'horrible singing . . . like the barking of dogs only still more brutish'[7] in the Viking town of Hedeby, or for the remarks of Venantius Fortunatus (†*c.* 609) on the singing of the early Franks, who were unable to tell a goose's screech from a swan's song (*aut stridor anseris aut canor oloris* – MGH AA 4.1.2). In contrast to this brutishness outside the blessed pale of Christendom, music within it was sweet, a part of the Church's life. In addition, music was not alone in the City of God: 'very sweet singing' (*vocem cantantium dulcissimam*) matches the 'surpassing fragrance' and 'wonderful light' in the heavenly abodes described by a seventh-century Northumbrian man who returned from death, according to a story told by Bede (*Hist. Eccl.* 5 – PL 95.250). *Sound, fragrance* and *light* are often mingled in early references to the Church and its practices, and other examples will be found in the present book. Fragrance and light are to music as evil odours and darkness are to disorganized noise, and the Church naturally desires and provides one rather than the other, both actually and metaphorically.

Given that timbre, in particular voice-quality, can by itself make a music acceptable or not acceptable, what was considered 'melodious' in the Carolingian period need not have been 'expansive cantilena': no long or wide-ranging melody in any later definition of the words. The melodiousness of the brief recitative formulas in readings and psalms relies on only a few different notes, generally lying so close

---

[6] Interpreted as counterpoint in e.g. Perrot 1965: 364 but more plausibly as heterophony in N. C. Phillips, *Musica & Scolica Enchiriadis: the Literary, Theoretical and Musical Sources* (Ph.D. diss., New York University, 1984), 10, 316. Fuller discussion in Reckow 1975: 83ff.

[7] Quoted in J. Brøndsted, *The Vikings*, trans. K. Skov (Harmondsworth, 1965), 43.

together that any leap is a conspicuous and 'beautiful' gesture. Formulas being so repetitive are unlikely to be freely lyrical, but a mere two or three notes sung well and in tune can be melodious, as also they can be in much later music. Consequently, it is a mistake to infer that for

the whole body of Homeric epic, the natural conclusion is that melody has little importance for the oral delivery of the text and still less for the accompaniment[8]

since this implies a later definition of 'melody'. Similarly, if the Arab Call to Prayer became more 'melodic' in the tenth century, as has been claimed,[9] this implies expansive melody as so understood by western listeners a millennium later; earlier Calls would also have been melodic but according to another definition. In contemplating different definitions of 'melody' it can be useful to think of Christian psalmody as a version of the Greeks' 'narrative style', and one that produced very melodious formulas for the tenth-century monk: short repetitive phrases, with recitation notes and few large intervals, little in the way of soaring melisma and yet with a striking sweetness of melody. Since the 'imitative style' cannot have seemed very relevant to that same monk – at least, not in liturgical music – his natural interests in mellifluous melody would turn to the creating of new hymns and sequences whose melodies tended to move beyond the formulas and melismas of narrow compass.

It is possible to think that the lyrical Gregorian hymn, for all its sweetness and regular periods, loses something of the natural, uncontrived *melos* of a psalm formula. It serves to re-define what is melody, so that any early organ relying on a few hexachordal[10] notes and combinations would gradually seem to be not very melodious, and there would be a constant drive to increase its compass. Then there was official uniformity: the attempt to make Benedictine Europe unanimous in its chant must have meant (ideally) fewer and fewer regional differences in how such music was performed and in how 'sweet melody' was defined. When Augustine had compared the singing of Christians at Alexandria and Milan (*Confessions* 9), his words certainly imply that different parts of Christendom had different ideas on singing:

[at Alexandria:]
pronuncianti vicinior   closer to speaking
quam canenti   than singing
[at Milan:]
melos . . . cantilenarum suavium   a melos . . . of sweet melodies

but to what extent these kinds of variety would still have existed in *c.* 1000 can only be guessed. In any case, not the least interesting implication of Augustine's remarks is that musical content and performance were seen to go hand-in-hand, as they do in his other terms such as *suavi, liquida voce* and *convenientissima modulatione*.

Such phrases, both as they occur in Augustine and as they are repeated afterwards, do tend to be formulas traditionally deferring to what has been written before, but that need be no reason to regard them as empty. When a certain ninth-century

---

8   Anderson (see note 3): 12.
9   By H. G. Farmer in NOHM 1957: 439–40.
10 In general remarks of this kind, I am using 'hexachord' to signify 'the six basic diatonic notes' up from C or D.

commentator at Luxeuil likens the work of biblical exegesis (i.e. the drawing out of a spiritual meaning) to the organ (sweetly drawing out a pleasing melody from its bronze pipes – *dulci cantilena melos . . . suaviter . . . fistulae aeris*),[11] he was no doubt alluding to what he had read in such authors as Cassiodorus (see p. 299); but he could also have been showing that this is indeed what the player of organs was supposed to do. If the writer had never seen an organ, if the vocabulary being used is entirely conventional and if 'organ' itself is a traditional metaphor, the remark still invokes the idea of a player being able – and expected – to draw a *cantilena* and a *sweetness* of some kind from his pipes, presumably via a keyboard. A bigger problem is knowing what was such sweet melody: chant of course, but chant includes simple formulas and need imply no long, lyrical cantilena.

Melody would come from organ-pipes if they merely played over a simple psalm-tone, for the notes would be those of a sustained and in-tune wind-instrument.[12] By definition, that must have been 'sweet' as it was also 'organic'. Distinctions now made between cantillation of lessons, chanting of psalms and singing of hymns[13] are useful in leading one to suppose that although all three are a form of melody, it was the third kind – pure singing – that would be open to most 'melodious' development. It would do so if not in metrical hymns themselves then in other musical additions to the liturgy, in which probably the organ too began to take part from time to time (for the Winchester *prosae*, see p. 39). Once admitted to this area of music-making, organs, their compass and their playing-mechanism would stimulate and grow with melody as it too changed and developed. Eventually the organ would lose the high screeching tone and signalling siren-function it must have had in much of its earlier life.

Harmony or polyphony

Presumably Plato's *organon* meant heterophony (Vogel 1965: 58f), which after all is a form of polyphony and one that was very fertile. Deep, tuned sounds of long strings or pipes remained too rare or exceptional to turn the ear in the direction of 'bass lines' until the fourteenth or fifteenth century, with the appearance all over Europe of organs with fuller compass and (in major, influential churches) suboctave ranks. But aside from this peculiarly western development, and in the centuries before it could develop, music can have been open only to a limited number of possibilities for combining notes:[14]

---

[11] J. J. Contreni, 'Carolingian biblical studies', in *Carolingian Essays = Andrew W. Mellon Lectures in Early Christian Studies*, ed. U.–R. Blumenthal (Washington DC, 1983), 71–98, here 89.

[12] *Organum* and *organicus* as used specifically in connection with wind-produced sound, are described in Reckow 1975.

[13] In E. Wellesz, 'Early Christian music', NOHM 1954: 1ff, speaking of early Christian practices some of which (psalm-singing) may be a later development than once thought (J. H. Smith, 'The ancient Synagogue, the early Church and singing', *ML* 65 (1984), 1–16).

[14] Good pointers in E. Wellesz, *Ancient and Oriental Music* = NOHM 1957; A. Hughes in NOHM 1954: 270–86; E. Gerson-Kiwi, 'Vocal folk-polyphonies of the Western Orient in Jewish tradition', in *Yuval: Studies of the Jewish Music Research Council*, ed. I. Adler (Jerusalem, 1968), 169–93 (examples, pp. 16–25); and Wiora 1955.

heterophony;

imitation of one voice by another;

canon (partial or temporary);

drone or bourdon (including more than one note at once);

ostinato;

hocket;

parallels at the octave;

parallels at the fourth, fifth or other interval (varying in interval);

chance.

Later versions of these techniques would include such treatments as:

contrary motion

and presumably, counterpoint is most readily sustained at length by:

combining or alternating two or more of these.

On any given occasion most of the techniques would operate only for a time. Whatever the settled technique of some later repertories of music suggests, singing entirely in parallels is less likely to have occurred than alternating one polyphonic technique with another. Among the points made in one of the best surveys so far of widespread polyphonic techniques are the following:[15]

pure parallel organum is nowhere found as a primitive form;

parallel fifths are not older than parallel seconds or thirds;

bourdons are held throughout a piece relatively seldom, in various kinds of music and in many cultures;

early notated western organum (Enchiriadis, Hucbald, Winchester, Guido) has few interval-parallels and is full of 'dissonances';

imitation is generally more common than canon as such.

One consequence of such observations is that a traditional 'sweetness of concordant sound' has to be understood as implying something much broader than consonance of constant fourths, fifths and octaves. Some short two-part Winchester organa of *c.* 1000 refer in their titles to the 'very sweet, mellifluous' or the 'very charming, delightful, lovely sweet-sounding, very beautiful' (*dulcissima, melliflua, amoenissima, jocunda, pulchra, dulcisono, pulcherrima*), and while this may be traditional and conventional – such texts keep the diction of late classical poetry – it is certainly the case that the organa are not particularly marked by these consonant intervals.[16] Such polyphony and the way it was sung must have agreed with old ideas of 'sweetness' unless the words were indeed merely empty formulas.

Chance may not seem a genuine option for combining notes, and yet it would play a part in any improvised counterpoint – say the harmony produced by two voices of which the upper was more melismatic than the lower, or the effect of sustained chords when many a simple canon (like children's rounds of today) is sung. When the notes are primarily those of the diatonic heptachord – C D E F G A H – 'chance' combinations do not produce marked discordance, any more than

[15] M. Schneider, 'Origins of Western polyphony' in *International Musicological Society: Report of the Eighth Congress, New York 1961*, ed. J. LaRue (Kassel, 1961), 161–78.

[16] Transcriptions in Holschneider 1968: 110ff (see Chapter 3), texts 156ff.

the intervals made by the combination of similar tones in, say, the Winchester organa do. (See Ex. 3.2.) Like melody, harmony needs to be defined in such a way that it does not necessarily and always imply sweetness of effect, even if 'sweet concordance' is a word-formula that does appear from time to time. If melody does not necessarily mean 'expansive cantilena', harmony does not necessarily mean 'constant consonance'. It could be an anachronism, therefore, to describe the combined tones made by heterophonic octave canon as 'entirely haphazard and filled with tone-clashes of harsh dissonance'.[17] 'Clashes' and dissonance' do not seem quite appropriate terms when the notes are sung sweetly, when they are those of the diatonic series and when the nature of such lines ensures an independent counterpoint such as most organum (and the invertible counterpoint of a much later period) will not.

Yet many results of combining notes are by nature full of non-concords, in particular heterophony (where the discordance may be slight, resolved in the aura of the unison) and canon. Canon has its own logic and clear purpose, irrespective of the dissonances it may produce;[18] in it discordances occur that are unlikely to be encountered otherwise, and they might be as often as not left 'unresolved'. But in the seven notes of music as fixed by the organ keyboard, the most severe dissonance will be the tritone (F–H) or major seventh (C–H), and both of these will be easily resolved in one way or another. The situation is quite different once the lyric semitone B is admitted on an instrument of fixed notes. The resulting stretch of three semitones (A B H C) increases the number of major sevenths and minor seconds available, requires the organist to work out what pairs of notes go together, and makes temperament a potentially burning issue. Perhaps the larger number of notes and a need to define tempered intervals also encouraged organists to add a third part in order to create 'harmony'.

Early written polyphony: *Musica enchiriadis*

The first notated example of musical notes being combined is the passage found in the handbook *Musica* (usually called *Musica enchiriadis*), a treatise once attributed to Hucbald, extant in over fifty copies[19] and probably originating in (the area of) Laon or St-Amand in the middle of the ninth century and circulating at first in the diocese of Tournai.[20] Some account of it is necessary here because it demonstrates certain ways in which a culture that may have had organs was able to combine notes, and because it also implies a general principle relevant to any instrument. This is, that music is to be made by embellishing a melody – extending, doubling or 'reinforcing'

---

[17] E. Gerson-Kiwi (see note 14): 183, who speaks of such polyphony as not being 'a musical form in the narrow sense'.

[18] It is possible to think that just as certain twentieth-century composers have returned to basics and reminded listeners how three notes can be melodious (perhaps even one, in the first movement of Stravinsky's *Concerto in D*), so others have returned to the idea of the logic of the canon irrespective of dissonance (e.g. Bartók).

[19] Eight before *c.* 1000. Listed in H. Schmid, *Musica et scolica enchiriadis una cum aliquibus tractatulis adiunctis* (Munich, 1981), viif.

[20] Laon or St-Amand: Phillips (see note 6): 499f, 516f. Particularly the Tournai diocese: M. Huglo in Corsi 1989: 361 (where the treatise is said to have been 'probably composed by an Irish master'). The only extant ninth-century copy of Aurelian of Réôme (see p. 87) is also from St-Amand.

it – by adding further notes above or below each of its original notes adding a short drone, weaving notes heterophonically around it, running in parallels with it and so on, always provided that both parts belong to the same scale of C D E F G A (B) H.

The treatise uses melodies in Lotharingian–East Frankish forms and may well transmit very traditional practices from this part of the continent:[21]

(chant + fifth below)

al – le – lu – ia_____   al – le – lu – ia_____

(chant + octave below or above)

al – le – lu – ia_____   al – le – lu – ia_____

Ex. 2.1. From the *Musica enchiriadis*: based on H. Schmid, *Musica et scolica enchiriadis una cum aliquibus tractatulis adiunctis* (Munich, 1981), 26, 27

To Example 2.1, boys may add a second octave above. Counterpoint at the fourth below provides a 'pleasant harmony' if sung with tact and care (*organum . . . suavem concentum . . . modesta dumtaxat et concordi morositate*).[22] While it is possible that the last five words only mean singing in tune, nevertheless the description does bring in a practical observation: the pleasantness of harmony again depends in part on the performance itself. The vocal lines of Example 2.2 can also be doubled at each octave above.

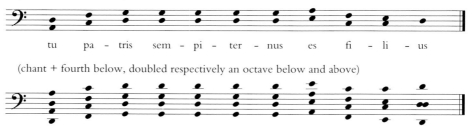

(chant + fourth below)

tu   pa – tris   sem – pi – ter – nus   es   fi – li – us

(chant + fourth below, doubled respectively an octave below and above)

Ex. 2.2. From the *Musica enchiriadis*: based on H. Schmid, *op. cit.*, 38, 39

Clearly, such music is not a matter of independent part-writing but of troping or duplicating the melody. Whether this treatment was close to that of non-literate, non-ecclesiastical music-making outside the monastery or to music very commonly sung within it, is obviously unknown, but both are likely despite the difficulty of producing evidence to show it.[23] The treatise has been called less an exposé of organum

---

[21] Lotharingia in *c.* 850 is defined as the eastern stretch of the Carolingian empire, roughly from Liège down to Reggio d'Emilia.

[22] Waeltner 1975: 2–3 and the translation of the *Musica* in L. Rosenstiel, *Anonymous: Music Handbook* (Colorado Springs, 1976), 20–1.

[23] There is 'no scientific evidence extant to prove beyond question that there was a rudimentary polyphonic practice before the organum of the ninth century', according to L. B. Spiess, 'An introduction to the pre-history of polyphony', in *Essays on Music in Honor of Archibald Thompson Davison by his Associates* (Cambridge, MA, 1957), 11–15, here 14; but points made in e.g. Huglo and Göllner (see below, note 45) imply a more modern definition of 'scientific evidence'.

than a presentation, for local or wider use, of 'all the facets of the theory of liturgical chant',[24] including how to perform it in an *organal* way. (On regular chant being treated like the non-liturgical verses used for illustration here, see below, final remarks.)

In general terms, the treatise must also relate to two other Benedictine interests of the ninth and tenth centuries: musical notation and organs (either pipe-calculation or organ-building). At one point it refers to notation as a means of learning notes and intervals (§6), and at another to instruments as a means of recognizing the 'equal-sounding octave' (§10). It is clearly concerned with the notes of music. Since there will be tritones when the organum to some chants is sung only or consistently in fourths or fifths one must vary the intervals; and one should not go below c (if the final is d) or f (if it is g).[25] To demonstrate the notes by which the organal voice would avoid tritones, *Musica enchiriadis* constructs a scale that would also tend to encourage organum in the form of parallel fifths:

G A B c d e f g a h c' d' e' f♯' g' a' h' c♯"

This series of notes is produced by 'transposing' (in the mind's ear or eye) any tetrachord such as d e f g (but also any other) down one fifth and up successive fifths. Both the author and any organ-builder knew that other notes were required and arose naturally if the chant and its counterpoint were sung in octaves; these additional notes were

b f' b' c" d"

The *Musica enchiriadis* scale was also one way to understand notes such as the low B and the high f♯' that were heard in some chants. One wonders if its 'proto-tonal' nature – the sharpened notes look like 'leading notes' rising to the 'key' above, with a 'sub-dominant' movement as the line descends – had any effect on organum of the period and whether the seeds were already here for the leading notes that emerge in later medieval music. If no organ up till then had had an f♯, it is easy to believe that such theory would encourage a builder to make one. Conversely, if there were local organs with an f♯ specially provided by the builder because the tetrachord e f g a was needed a tone higher in pitch (so f♯ g a h), then it is easy to believe that a theorist would explain the f♯ in terms of such tetrachords. But builders were surely not constrained by a paper-theory of tetrachords or anything else.

There are various practical implications of the *Musica enchiriadis's* organum and scale. On the rule that the organal voice does not go below tenor C: this coincides with Hucbald's instrument compass (see Chapter 3), including his organ keyboard, and although neither author refers to the other's reasoning, a C-compass organ of the later ninth century in the St-Amand area would have been able to play the organal counterpoint of the *Musica*, though at what pitch is unknown. On the theoretical scale[26] with f♯' and c♯": if these notes were getting known – i.e. were found on

[24] M. Huglo, 'Bibliographie des éditions et études relatives à la théorie musicale du Moyen Age (1972–1987)', *AM* 60 (1988), 229–72, here 261.

[25] Some have described the organum rule demonstrated in Example 2.3 as being merely that the added voice does not go below tenor C (e.g. T. G. Georgiades, *Music and Language* (Cambridge, 1982), 17), but that is not so for such an example as 2.2.

[26] The word 'absurdity' for a scale of augmented octaves, used by e.g. C. Dahlhaus, 'Zur Theorie des frühen Organum', *KmJb* 42 (1958), 47–52 and still sometimes found today (e.g. M. S. Gushee, 'The polyphonic music of the medieval monastery, cathedral and university', in McKinnon 1990: 143–69) does not seem quite appropriate. Is it a vestige of the very interpretation the authors are discounting, i.e. that the *Enchiriadis* describes a simple scale in the later sense?

some organ keyboards – and produced sharp Pythagorean thirds with D and A, as they probably would, one might then understand more easily why the Cologne Treatise of *c.* 900 objected to thirds in vocal organum (Waeltner 1975: 54–5), though the stricture could also apply to hexachordal thirds, major or minor. Even the seconds, also criticized in this later treatise, might be absolutely unpleasant on a fixed-note instrument. It needs to be considered in future examination of the organum treatises whether any tenth-century doctrine of organum based on unisons, octaves, fifths and fourths (for example in the Paris Treatise) was formulated not because sacred music needed to be distinguished from non-sacred (which was used to all kinds of intervals?) but because the fixed notes of organ keyboards had shown how unpleasant other intervals could be.

Whatever the broader implications, the organum in Example 2.3 already offers a useful general model. It can be seen as a sophisticated amalgam, in miniature but unambiguous, of various basic means of making polyphony: repeated notes (brief quasi-drone), parallels and the kind of unison that occurs in heterophony at the various closes or half-closes in the text.

(chant above)

Ex. 2.3. From the *Musica enchiriadis*: based on H. Schmid, *op. cit.*, 49, 51

Unisons are required at colon and comma, according to such different sources as the Cologne Treatise and the Winchester organa.[27] Or an octave will serve a similiar purpose to a unison, according to later formulations (John 'of Afflighem', CSM 1. 1 57). No doubt such recommendations reflect the tendency of 'natural polyphony' to reach unisons or octaves at the ends of phrases,[28] and in turn they suggest that the examples of purely parallel fifths in Part 2 of the *Scolica enchiriadis* – a consistent line of fifths below the chant, either of which could be then duplicated at the octave below or above – were textbook demonstrations.

Although it may be so that the *Enchiriadis* examples illustrate organum 'not for its own sake' but to show 'the properties of the *symphoniae*' (intervals of fourth, fifth and octave),[29] they must surely at times reflect one or more kinds of music as actually

[27]   Waeltner 1975: 54–5 and Holschneider 1968: 123–8. Parallels between musical and grammatical punctuation are usefully made by L. Treitler, 'The early history of music writing in the West', *JAMS* 35 (1982), 237–79.
[28]   'Popular' examples from Georgia, Croatia, Sicily and Sardinia in P. Collaer, 'Polyphonies de tradition populaire en Europe méditerranéenne', *AM* 32 (1960), 51–66, here 52–3.
[29]   On the *symphoniae*: Fuller 1981: 53. But is it certain (p. 82) that in distinguishing consonance (with its *suaviter* or 'smooth effect') from dissonance (with its *aspera* or 'rough effect'), Boethius is marking the difference between two intervals (e.g. octaves and sevenths) rather than between organized and non-organized music?
        On the *Rex caeli* in particular: N. Phillips & M. Huglo, 'The versus Rex caeli – another look at the so-called archaic sequence', *Journal of the Plainsong & Mediaeval Music Society* 5 (1982), 36–43.

practised, whether for spiritual songs or liturgical texts, for secular or sacred contexts. In addition, Example 2.3 already establishes the six notes of Hucbald's instrumental scale (see Chapter 3) and Guido's hexachord (C D E F G A, thus with no tritone). Made from the four modal finales, the basic tetrachord described by Hucbald (D E F G) may have theoretical justification but it also has a practical property: adding a note to either end produces the C D E F G A hexachord, which is 'perfect' in itself. (Adding the H and B above this hexachord only produces transpositions of tetrachords already present: thus H C D E = E F G A.) It is possible to imagine theorists coming to music from the active experience of singing an established chant-repertory, looking at the notes of music and recognizing the limited number of patterns of tones and semitones that can be made with them, and accordingly seeing tetrachords as the building-bricks of music. While the music of the *Musica enchiriadis* examples is certainly something basic, it bequeathed two sophisticated things, both developed in the following centuries, for example in Guido d'Arezzo's *Micrologus* (*c*.1025/33): it recognizes that the categories of parallel and drone are not distinct, and it demonstrates that music is demonstrable by succinct example.[30] It shows that parallels do not simply begin or remain consistent but would emerge, run for a time, alternate with a drone now and then, merge in unisons or octaves, and so on; it also shows that a phrase of chant could be treated in more than one way.

After such treatment it is hard to believe that other musical ideas such as true contrary motion had to wait until they were written about by theorists in the eleventh century, or that melismatic organum – with a freer new line – was unknown before the twelfth-century Codex Calixtinus (see note 43) notated it. All of these techniques were possible on an organ keyboard of seven or eight notes and multiples thereof, undocumented though any such practice remained and rare though the occasions for it may have been in any one church year.

Drones and other harmony

Chance and *heterophony* are already evoked in the classical period by the remark of Pseudo-Aristotle (*Problems* 19.9) that there is 'more enjoyment' when a soloist sings with one aulos or lyre than with several, because the singer can then sign to the instrumentalist more easily when he 'hits his target'. (This seems to mean when they meet at cadences in their heterophony – the greater the number of performers, the smaller the freedom?) A lively picture suggests itself here, in which the soloist and instrumentalist perform freely enough not always to 'hit the target' together but to give 'more enjoyment' than by merely duplicating each other. In the same source and in others such as Plato (*Laws* 812) and the Plutarchian treatise (*On Music* 1141), a heterophony called 'accompaniment under the melody [*oden*]' as distinct

[30] Examples of held or repeated notes, as in the *Enchiriadis*, given in E. Jammers, *Anfänge der abendländischen Musik*, Sammlung musikwissenschaftlicher Abhandlungen 31 (Strasbourg, 1955), 73f. On the notion of giving examples in a treatise, a new idea in which 'man has his eye on music itself . . . comprehending it as *doing* . . . the beginning of western music as historical phenomenon', see T. G. Georgiades, *Nennen und Erklingen* (Göttingen, 1985), 116.

from 'accompaniment in unison with the voice' is referred to amongst the various treatments of narrative or imitative song. 'Under' the melody presumably means 'subordinate to' and could involve one or several of the techniques briefly referred to in the present chapter. Elsewhere in the *Problems* (19.17),[31] a distinction is made between two parts singing at an octave and singing at a fifth or fourth: the latter 'consonances' are 'not the same'. Although here this distinction is a theoretical one – notes at a fourth or fifth do not have the same function in the scale as the eighth – it may also express something heard by the ear: singing at the fifth creates a totally new line while singing at the octave does not? The octave must always have been of interest to theorists, leading, for example, certain Arabic sources of the ninth and tenth centuries to deal from time to time with singing in parallel octaves, or singing in octaves with the lute (see Shiloah 1979: 348).

Drones are particularly difficult to establish as historical phenomena, being neither notated nor remarked upon in those repertories for which they could well have been characteristic. A sustained bass note can be held through the *Rex caeli* of the *Musica enchiriadis* (Ex. 2.3), but it is only a guess to suppose that the technique is not described there because bourdon elements were 'not of value for the theorists'.[32] Georgiades's sugestion that in one kind of troped Kyrie of the Carolingian period, the singer(s) with the main text might hold the tonic as a bourdon while the singer(s) with the interpolated text sing their notes – similar in principle to held notes in alleluia tropes – is colourful and plausible but also necessarily a conjecture.[33] So is any suggestion that Pippin's organ of 757 contributed held notes to vocal lines, producing a *diaphonia basilica* or 'imperial two-part music' (?) such as might have befitted the Carolingian court by imitating the supposed drone-singing in orthodox chant (Schuberth 1968: 117–18).[34] The rules for improvisation in the so-called Vatican Organum Treatise (thirteenth century) suggest that chant-notes are held against improvised decorations, a kind of interpolation since the chant-notes are longer, sometimes very much longer, than they would otherwise be.[35] Following the custom already there in the *Enchiriadis*, the author calls the new melismatic line *organum*. For some typical examples, see Example 2.4.

Both the *Enchiriadis* and the Vatican Treatise show that note-against-note counterpoint (discant) and melismatic organum can involve a quasi-drone element, not dissimilar to the recently documented but traditional techniques found in certain

---

[31] Translations and notes on these texts in A. Barker, *Greek Musical Writings* 1 (Cambridge, 1984), 191, 235 and 194 respectively.

[32] W. Krüger, *Die authentische Klangform des primitiven Organum*, Musikwissenschaftliche Arbeiten 13 (Kassel, 1958).

[33] In the translation *Music and Language* (Cambridge, 1982), 15. It is not clear quite how this conjecture fits in with the idea that Kyries were by nature a troped form. (On ways of performing Kyries: NOHM 1990: 271–7.) For a similar idea about performance of tropes in general, see O. Marcussen, 'Comment a-t-on chanté les prosules? Observations sur la technique des tropes de l'alleluia', *RM* 65 (1979), 119–59, esp. 126, and further on held notes in alleluia tropes in R. Jacobsson, 'Le style des prosules d'alleluia, genre mélogène', in Corsi 1989: 367–75.

[34] In the phrase of c. 1200 *diaphonia basilica*, the second word may derive from 'basis' and have nothing to do with the *basileos* or emperor (Stäblein 1970: 59). See also p. 44.

[35] Georgiades (see note 33): 25 and F. Zaminer, *Der Vatikanische Organum-Traktat (Ottob. lat. 3025)* (Tutzing, 1959), e.g. 44.

Ex. 2.4. From the *Vatican Organum Treatise*: based on F. Zaminer, *Der Vatikanische Organum-Traktat (Ottob. lat. 3025)* (Tutzing, 1959)

Jewish music.[36] Although the Vatican Treatise does not say so, with a short-compass organ of short pipes it is conceivable that an alto counterpoint could indeed be improvised or prepared in the manner of Example 2.4. With a large-compass organ and its ability (one assumes) to provide a slow-moving foundational tone, it is equally conceivable that the two could be exchanged: organ takes *cantus firmus* while voices take the counterpoint. Such would be a conception of polyphony to reap an endless harvest over the following centuries.

But drones are elusive. It may be that they 'can be found in many variants over an inter-continental area, among both early and high music civilizations',[37] but it is hardly possible to verify this beyond noting the number of drone-playing instruments traditional in India, Persia and Arabic countries, or the impression given by representations of the High Middle Ages that by then drone-music was one of the norms in both sacred and secular music. It may be so that it is only 'a small step' (Vogel 1965: 63) from the antique or traditional bagpipes to the organ, but it is a crucial step: one could reason that the keyboard of Hero or of the Aquincum organ was there precisely to make it possible to move away from the single or constant or one-time tonic. More stimulating is the idea that some Arabic music without drone nevertheless implies one, having a pivotal or tonal centre running through the music.[38] There seems little reason to think such a 'centre' specific to Arabic music. Another thought-inspiring remark of the same author is that 'the acoustical presence of a

---

[36] As in E. Gerson-Kiwi (see note 14). For western examples, see Walter 1981.
[37] E. Gerson-Kiwi, 'Drone and dyaphonia basilica', *Yearbook of the International Folk Music Council* 4 (1972), 9–23.
[38] E. Gerson-Kiwi, 'Archetypes of the prelude in East and West', in *Essays on the Music of J. S. Bach and other Diverse Subjects: a Tribute to Gerhard Herz*, ed. R. L. Weaver (Louisville, KY, 1981), 60–8. For points made about 'tonal centres' ('hovering about a note') in Aquitanian sequences, see N. van Deusen, 'Syle, nationality and the sequence in the Middle Ages', *Journal of the Plainsong and Mediaeval Music Society* 5 (1982), 44–55.

tonal center [of this kind] is part and parcel of non-European music cultures which rely on oral tradition' (*ibid.*), for if this is true for non-European oral music over the last seven or eight hundred years it would be true for European oral music before it. Such 'tonal centres' can also be the product of jumbled background sound, such as the sound given by clanging bells.[39] It can not be unlikely that some early organs contributed a similar jangling hexachordal 'chord' to certain chant, playing a kind of tone-cluster behind the jubilant chant of feastdays. (On the Sanctus and *Te Deum* in particular, see Chapter 5.)

Because the Byzantine chant's instrumental *ison* (bourdon) is not documented before the sixteenth century is no proof that it did not exist previously. Nor is it evidence that when it did, it was introduced to confirm tonality and 'to mark the underlying tonal course of the melody' to which by then 'Ottoman and other Eastern musical traditions' had given 'complex and ambiguous chromatic alterations' to Byzantine chant.[40] 'Chromatic alterations' can certainly be ironed out by fixed or fairly fixed notes (particularly those of an organ), but it would not contradict what is known of many western and eastern musics if the idea of holding or restriking an instrumental note goes back to early, pre-Ottoman idioms in the Orthodox Church.[41] In the West, whatever tendency there was amongst singers to sing drones in ordinary music-making, a part must have been played, perhaps as early as the tenth century in a few main centres, by gradual awareness of those mid-eastern stringed instruments that were bowed in such a way that strings on a flat bridge were liable to sound all the time (Bachmann 1969: 92ff. For further remarks on these various points see Chapter 3). But it is not easy to imagine precisely how stringed instruments related to such musical elements as drones. On one hand, the *organistrum* or hurdy-gurdy might have been a western invention reflecting increased interest in such sounds during the twelfth century (see Bachmann 1969: 92ff),[42] originating as an 'improved monochord' in monasteries known for technical expertise and resounding to fabulous effect in gothic cathedrals. On the other hand, for eastern chant an instrumental ison *in the lowest part* of the compass – thus a 'held bass note' – is certain to be a later medieval development. It was a function of neither hurdy-gurdy nor the Byzantine *ison* to provide a held note necessarily 'in the bass', and in any case neither of them became more than optional.

What references there are to drones, as to heterophony, may expose the tip of the iceberg. For example, Guido d'Arezzo gives an alternative to the usual organum-by-fourths for those melodies that have a low tessitura: the organal voice remains on the final throughout (Babb 1978: 81), or, having remained on a C rises to join the principal voice on a D at the close. It is not out of the question that the mid-twelfth-century

---

[39] Wiora 1955: 323 and 331, is surely correct also to emphasize the harmonic character of bell-clanging, as of certain kinds of ostinato or canonic music-making. All these forms work towards a 'tonal centre'.

[40] D. Conomos, 'Experimental polyphony "according to the . . . Latins" in late Byzantine psalmody', *EMH* 2 (1982), 1–16.

[41] Perhaps to the period of the Arab conquest: E. Wellesz, 'Byzantine music and its place in the liturgy', *PRMA* 81(1954–5), 13–28. On the *ison* neume, an eleventh-century sign for the repeat of a note, see NOHM 1990: 51–3.

[42] C. Page, 'The medieval *Organistrum* and *Symphonia* I: a legacy from the East?', *GSJ* 35 (1982), 37–44, here 41.

Codex Calixtinus includes in its organum some instrumental lines of drone-like purpose.[43] Aribo's *De Musica* (1069/78), a somewhat isolated treatise, has directions for a measurement-scale (in addition to that for strings, bells and pipes) that may relate to the *organistrum* or hurdy-gurdy with drone,[44] and the treatise *Summa musice* of *c.* 1200 describes a counterpoint (diaphony) created by one voice singing a cantus above a note held by another (Page 1991: 124, 200). But whatever the evidence, such means of 'creating harmony' as drones or heterophony must have remained opportunistic and irregular, improvised not notated, offering a view of counterpoint different from that given by later historians relying on a few carefully notated books of fulldress organum.

Although the examples in *Musica enchiriadis* may at first imply that metrical texts are particularly appropriate for polyphonic treatment, that may have been unintentional. Two-part organum of a sort is thought to have been sung even for the ordinary of the mass by at least the eleventh century, and it is quite believable that some Frankish singers treated Charlemagne's *Gregorian chant* heterophonically or with some notes held from time to time – on occasion, or who knows how regularly – right from the moment it was distributed.[45] Perhaps they had previously treated the chant it was replacing in the same way, centuries before such practices became 'regular polyphony'.

---

[43] W. Krüger, 'Zum Organum des Codex Calixtinus', *MF* 17 (1964), 225–34, and 'Ad superni regis decus', *MF* 20 (1967), 30–44. On the Codex reflecting northern French music and its compiler being a Parisian, see C. Hohler, 'A note on Jacobus', *JWCI* 35 (1972), 31–80, here 38f.

[44] Thus a century before known representations of the hurdy-gurdy: Aribo in CSM 2.44–5 (and Sachs 1980: 218ff).

[45] On these points, see T. Göllner, 'Tradition and innovation in early polyphony', and M. Huglo, 'Les origines de l'organum vocal en France et Italie . . .', in Corsi 1989: 181–8, 355–65 respectively.

3

Organs and polyphony

The idea that the organ supported chant in some way or that polyphonic organum is so called because the organ somehow offered models for vocal polyphony[1] was plausible only so long as the words used by the documents were not critically questioned. Neither the role of the organ nor the route by which a type of instrument and a type of music shared the same name is straightforward. It is always possible that by *c.* 1000 in a few special churches, organs did indeed play melodies and drones with certain chant, or imitate or participate in or even inspire certain techniques of vocal *organum*; and some of these possibilities are more likely than others. But what evidence there is suggests a more complicated picture, and as is clear from the exhaustive survey of the term *organum* by Fritz Reckow (1975), its meanings have to be fathomed on each occasion. The purpose of the present chapter is not to add to the interpretations presented by Reckow so much as to outline persistent questions about organs *vis-à-vis* vocal polyphony, and to do so by reference to a few particularly important written sources.

One important task is to understand 'polyphony' in a broader sense than the carefully conceived parallel or melismatic organum familiar from certain late, largely non-monastic repertories. To distinguish 'polyphony' (*Mehrstimmigkeit*) from the kind of 'singing together' (*Zusammensingen*) supposedly demonstrated by the examples in *Musica enchiriadis c.* 850,[2] may be an anachronism, a distinction reasonable in the light of later music but not one that would have been understood in the ninth century. Polyphony *is* singing or sounding together. As it affects the early medieval organ and vice versa, polyphony arises when any second sound different from unison melody is added to it, and it therefore includes heterophony and parallel octaves. Some attempt is made here and in Chapter 2 to suggest ways in which organs – themselves in large measure imitating vocal techniques of one kind or another – could have contributed such 'polyphonic' elements.

---

[1] An idea most thoroughly reasoned in W. Krüger, *Die authentische Klangform des primitiven Organum*, Musikwissenschaftliche Arbeiten 13 (Kassel, 1958), 26 *et passim*, where the evidence, all of which appears in the present book, is used in a positivistic manner. Other writers of that period (e.g. Vogel 1965) also assumed that the added voice in the *Musica enchiriadis* – the first systematically notated *vox organalis* – is so called because 'obviously' the organ played it.

[2] The date is still open: a recent view is *c.* 850, as in L. Treitler, 'Reading and singing: on the genesis of occidental music-writing', *EMH* 4 (1984), 135–208, here 142. On the division between *Mehrstimmigkeit* and *Zusammensingen*: T. Göllner, 'Tradition and innovation in early polyphony', in Corsi 1989: 181–8, where the distinction is between 'pseudo and genuine polyphony' (184).

Organum

It is tempting to see the term *organum* in §13 of the *Musica enchiriadis* as an allusion – one likely to be so understood as the treatise circulated widely – to instrumental practice known to (known about by?) its author. For readers in obscure monasteries, knowing of no instruments (*organa*) themselves, did the term *organum* stir their imaginations to wonder about mixed ensemble music such as the *Enchiriadis* writer implies in this and his following chapter? The intervals produced by two notes are discussed,

Haec namque est, quam diaphoniam cantilenam vel assuete organum nuncupamus.	For this is what we call diaphonic song [= polyphony] or, usually, *organum*.

Although voices can mix with instruments, such vocal counterpoint itself resembled music played by or with an instrument. The more that the *Enchiriadis* examples resembled improvised polyphony as known in popular or secular music – not merely a formal church practice – the more likely that instruments ideally had some part in it. However, this is far from saying organum is so called because it has anything to do with church organs. While *Enchiriadis's* author would have known St Augustine's definition of *organum* (see p. 297) and would therefore see it as ancient usage, in his own century he would also come across the word to mean ensemble or 'organized' music as distinct from disorganized crowd noises (see Chapters 1 and 13). Perhaps such music ranged from popular songs to psalms, performed by many voices.

Something similar may be intended when Regino of Prüm takes up Isidore's distinction between *succentor* and *concentor* (in PL 82.292f):

Concentus est similium vocum adunata societas. Succentus est, quando varii soni conveniunt sicut videmus in organo.	*Concentus* is the alliance-as-one of similar voices [= unison]. *Succentus* is when diverse sounds [= notes] come together, as we see in *organum*.	(GS 1.234)

In organo means music combining the correctly calculated notes of a diatonic scale, including those of instruments if any were available, which in church must have been seldom. How this early 'organized music' was organized must have varied, but most basic, universal techniques of polyphony would have needed little planning or directing: The *Musica enchiriadis*'s phrase 'diaphony or organum' could be understood as an attempt to pin down one type of such *organum*: this 'music in two dissimilar parts' (as distinct from unisons and octaves?) was a means of making ensemble music 'or what we usually call *organum*'. The same definitions would apply to instruments as voices (§14):

possunt enim et humane voces, et in aliquibus instrumentis musicis non modo binae et binae, sed et ternae ac ternae hac sibi collatione misceri, dum utique uno impulsu.	for human voices can mix together and with any musical instruments in this collective, not only in two parts but in three, in any case with one beat.

The last might mean sung and played homophonically. But the passage is not a description of 'the technique of instrumental accompaniment' (Huglo 1981: 109) in the sense of organ *accompanying* sung liturgical music in church, rather a general explanation of how a rational ensemble of music is made up.

In his *De ecclesiasticis officiis* (*c.* 821/35), Amalar of Metz uses a passage from St Augustine's commentary on Psalm 150 to describe the idea of ensemble sounds joining in praise:

non ut singulae sonent, sed ut diversitate concordissima consonent sicut ordinatur in organo. Habebunt [!] enim etiam sancti differentiam ad suos consonantes, non dissonantes.	so that they sound not singly but together in the most harmonious diversity, as is ordered in *organum*. For the saints too will keep a difference in harmony, not disharmony, with their fellow saints.

(Augustine: PL 37.1964, Amalar: PL 105.1107)

'Praise him on the strings and pipe' (*in chordis et organo*) therefore indicates something more than single (unison? solo?) sounds of praise. Whether *sicut ordinatur in organo* meant 'as is organized in vocal polyphony' (so in the ninth century it might be for Amalar) or 'as is arranged in the organ' (which the original context suggests it did for Augustine), it conveys a sense of musical ensemble or unity-from-diversity. To what extent an instrument (*organum*) is actually involved in the organized, non-unison music (*organum*) seems to be a secondary consideration; and whether the instrument (*organum*) might be an organ (*organum*) would be secondary to that. Also, neither *organum* as polyphony nor *organum* as organ need involve parallel fifths and fourths: ensemble music for voices can be organized with octaves and unisons only, and so can the multi-rank chorus of organs (see pp. 351f). Amalar is therefore not implying that in the cathedral at Metz the choir sang complex parallel polyphony and was joined in it by the sound of a full Blockwerk organ playing accompaniments or solo interludes. Only some four hundred years later might it have done so.

It is important to see that while the word *organum* does not necessarily mean organs or imply some organ-like quality, it does not exclude them: they could be included within what it does broadly signify. Even if so many references to *organa* in pre-thirteenth-century sources do not indicate organs, they are not lost to the organ-historian for they offer one explanation of how the organ came to contribute: it slipped in to the broad definition of the monastic community's ensemble music (*organum*) just as here and there one was constructed in the community's church itself. Therefore, although it could well be that no author of the period suggests polyphony is called organum because it is analogous in sound or performance-technique to any instrument,[3] there is nevertheless a logical development of ideas behind the terminology. A writer wishing to be specific had to find other terms, and

---

[3]   Reckow 1975: 161. Explaining one word as 'coming from' another was and has been such a tradition that this observation of Reckow's is striking. For Hucbald's terms, see also p. 49.

already by *c.* 900, when he wished to refer unambiguously to both organs and other instruments, Hucbald calls neither merely *organum* but creates a phrase 'hydraulis or any other kind of instrument [*instrumentum*]',[4] something as unambigious as he could make it. If by the early eleventh century a theorist may think *organum* correct only as a term for vocal counterpoint (Sachs 1980: 234), it could be because after all he is more likely to have heard such counterpoint than the sounds of an actual organ. For many centuries and for most purposes connected with the life of monasteries and cathedrals, it must have been more important for books to define vocal polyphony than to describe organs made with pipes and bellows.

Vocal organum before the *organa* of Winchester or Limoges must have been simpler in several respects, although in the nature of things the simpler techniques would not get either described or notated. In the newly established genre of music theory in the ninth and tenth centuries, the 'term organum was considered to apply properly only to *symphoniae*' (Fuller – see p. 28), i.e. the music produced by partially parallel movement in fourths, fifths and octaves; and texts of the tenth and eleventh centuries concerned with organ-pipe measurement make a point of noting those same intervals (Sachs 1980: 307–8). Theory cannot have very much to say about unisons and octaves. And yet a pipe-measurement text would also point out that seconds and thirds are produced from the same basic intervals – for a second, come down a fourth from the fifth above, etc. – and it could be arbitrary and theoretical for writers then or now to use the term *organum* to mean polyphony based on the primary intervals but not on the secondary. 'Early' or 'simple' organum could have been very varied (see Chapter 2).

By the time of John 'of Afflighem' (early twelfth century) both polyphony and organ were established on certain clearcut lines. In a brief but nevertheless 'first attempt at an etymology' of the word,[5] John supposed that polyphonic vocal organum is so called

eo quod vox humana	because the human voice,
apte dissonans	[with notes] different but matching,
similitudinem exprimat	expresses a likeness
instrumenti quod organum	to the instrument that is
vocatur.	called organ.

(CSM 1.157)

Only if one reads the last four words to mean 'the instrument specifically called organ' does John suggest that the organ creates some kind of complex sound, perhaps in its tone (it can sound more than unison pipes per key) or in its ability to make counterpoint with itself ('the polyphonic instrument' – Schuberth 1968: 118). But if it means merely 'instrument or, to use another word for instrument, *organum*' (cf. Reckow 1975: 47), then the latter does not necessarily denote or connote 'organ' but is a Latin synonym for 'instrument' in general. In that case, John is not implying either that organs play polyphony or that polyphonic organum is so called because organs do play polyphony.

[4]   Babb 1978: 24 and R. Weakland, 'Hucbald as musician and theorist', *MQ* 42 (1956), 67–84, esp. fig. II.
[5]   Reckow 1975: 146, who also points out that John was not followed in this explanation by later theorists.

The very array of ways in which the word *organum* was used, however, leaves it open as to whether organs played, or played in, the ensemble effort called polyphony. If orderly or organized or composed music (*organum*) can take some form of polyphony (*organum*) which on occasion can be produced by or with or somehow like the music of an instrument (*organum*) such as organ (*organum*), then one needs to speculate on what the 'somehow' could be. One could imagine four main functions for the organ embraced within the vocal term *organum*, each becoming prominent at different periods:

> organs played in unison or (more likely?) heterophonically with voices singing a melody;
> organs contributed to *diaphonia* (non-unison music)[6] like any other voice or instrument, when and where present;
> organs could and did play *diaphonia* themselves, alone;
> organs have a tonal make-up that itself resembles one form of *diaphonia* i.e. with octaves or even an octave-and-quint chorus of pipes.

By the thirteenth century all four were or had long ago become familiar in practice, except perhaps for the quint ranks. A difficulty lies in speculating which of them was true at which point in the history of music, i.e. as universal polyphonic elements became conventionalized in the church music of the West, notated and embroidered. As for the quint ranks: even if it were so that 'organum in parallel fourths is of Syrian origin and with antiphony found its way to Western Christianity', it would not follow that

the European organ with its fifth-and-octave registers . . . may be a last instrumental reminder of the old Syrian vocal practice[7]

unless 'reminder' is taken figuratively, without musicological significance.

All one can assume with some certainty is that if an eleventh-century treatise speaks of *organum* as a music for *voces sive humanas seu alias* ('voices either human or other', i.e. instrumental – GS 2.74), it does not imply that organs played polyphony themselves or with others as part of the definition of *organum*,[8] only that an organ could participate in 'organized ensemble music' if one happened to be there and was constructed to provide more than a signalling noise. In the writings of successive theorists, 'organized ensemble music' might come to be synonymous with carefully conceived polyphony of one kind or another; but it is not so by definition.

---

[6] 'Diaphony' is a useful alternative to 'polyphony' for the non-unison music referred to by *Musica enchiriadis* above, and implies 'sounds discrepant or dissonant' (Isidore's phrase: *voces discrepantes vel dissonae*, in *Etymologiae* 3.20.3f) only in so far as its intervals are not solely those of the perfect octave, fifth and fourth.
[7] H. Husmann, 'The practice of organum in the liturgical singing of the Syrian churches of the Near and Middle East', in LaRue 1966: 435–9.
[8] As is still often suggested, e.g. in Barassi 1983: 15.

Organs playing polyphony?

For theorists, knowledge from their many sources that the term *organum* was common to both a kind of music and a kind of instrument must have encouraged the idea of linking them. But the interlarding of a treatise on organ pipe-scales with sentences on organum-singing, as in the late tenth-century Sélestat manuscript, is an example in which there is not a true mingling but a surface juxtaposition made by a compiler, perhaps in this case the scribe (Waeltner 1975: 53, 58f). Both topics were of little use to the crafts of organ-building and organ-playing, nor is there anything much in common between them. Organum-singing does not elucidate organ pipe-scales, while on the other hand no one needed organs to discover diaphony or polyphony in the first place.[9]

Considering how difficult it is to relate instrument to music, it would be immensely useful if Andreas Holschneider were correct in thinking that the letter-notation added at the time to neumes of monophonic *prosae* (new melodies and texts) in a copy of the Winchester Troper was for organ and even that one of its scribes was the same Wulfstan who wrote the poem on the Winchester organ.[10] The letters A–G are those of a diatonic scale with semitones between C/D and G/A – thus an alphabet with the 'difference of a third' (*Terzdifferent*), in which letters A–G correspond to the modern C–B. It is certainly possible that the Winchester organ keys were so labelled. The alleluia-sequence melody in Example 3.1 is a most melodious development of melodic cells, with recurrent cadences, varied formulas, welcome changes of tessitura and variable lines, each line syllabic and repeated. Perhaps the repetitions even suggest antiphonal performance. The cadence notes are missing, but any musical player could have added them without needing to be told what they were.

What appears here to be a picking out of certain notes may – though this is frankly conjectural – give a picture of the kind of heterophony in which a few notes on the organ could be held over to produce 'harmony'. The idea of holding a note for a short time below or through others is known in other connections and would be a kind of 'reinforcement' of the chant, therefore in principle much like other musical devices of the period. The letters appear only in the first half of each double versicle and in the single verses, either (if for the moment one can treat this as an 'organ part') because the user could assume that they were repeated or because the second half was *tasto tacet*.

The problems with accepting the idea that we have here an organ part, a notated organ heterophony of the kind sometimes improvised, come under various headings: diplomatic, palaeographic and practical. Diplomatic: the manuscript, surely not an organist's performance copy, was a record of what and for which purpose? Palaeographic: letters could be confirming pitch-identification for the neumes and

---

[9] It is hard to agree that the diaphony with long held bass-notes in Bulgarian or Russian popular music is the result of the organ's influence, as suggested in M. Raghib, 'Descriptions d'orgues par les auteurs turcs et persans, IV', *RM* 14 (1933), 86–91, here 89.

[10] The copy is Cambridge, Corpus Christi College, MS 473 (dated between 996 and 1006 in Planchart 1977: 26ff). Holschneider 1978: 155–66. The direct connection with Wulfstan is accepted in M. Lapidge, 'Æthelwold as scholar and teacher', in Yorke 1988: 89–117, here 111.

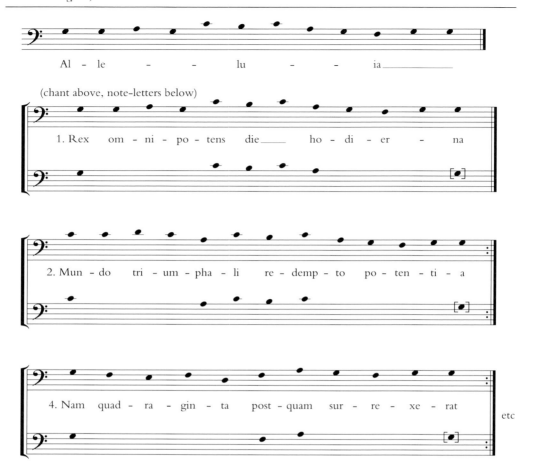

Ex. 3.1. From the *Winchester Troper*, based on A. Holschneider, 'Die instrumentalen Tonbuchstaben im Winchester Troper', in *Festschrift Georg von Dadelsen*, ed. T. Kohlhase & V. Scherließ, (Neuhausen-Stuttgart, 1978), 155–66

would thus be only a notational device. Practical: was the organ located near any liturgy, and could the slider-keys be manipulated fast enough for the unison sections? If the copy was a cantor's hand-copy,[11] are we to imagine him standing near the slider-keys ready to operate them while he held the manuscript, or showing some other player(s) what organal notes were to be played while he himself sang the original chant?

Answers to these various questions can be conjectured, and although the matter cannot be settled one way or the other, the very possibility that we are dealing here with 'early organ music' leads to various useful conjectures. The manuscript, for whatever archival purpose, could represent or even record the kind of heterophony sometimes practised and known to the scribe. The letters could have more than one

---

[11] It was a copy 'for the precentor', according to H. Besseler & P. Gülke, *Schriftbild der mehrstimmigen Musik*, Musikgeschichte in Bildern III/5 (Leipzig, 1973), 30; to be held by the cantor, according to M. Berry, 'What the Saxon monks sang: music in Winchester in the late tenth century', in Yorke 1988: 149–60, here 157.

purpose, and *prosae* might be particularly appropriate for instrumental participation, i.e. moments at which the cantor might move to the instrument and play it. The two organists in Wulfstan's poem could produce a genuine organum of their own, one with the melody, the other sustaining the salient notes as they occur – C F G of the hexachord, the mode finals and the top and bottom notes, etc. But further counterarguments could be assembled in turn, particularly against the idea of two organists (see Chapter 12). Also, even if the 'alphabet notation . . . was in fact geared to the alphabet on the Winchester organ keyboard' (a plausible guess but no more) and the copy was later 'used by several other cantors' (Planchart 1977: 53–4), the question of what function the manuscript itself had can not be regarded as quite settled.

Holschneider makes no claim for organ participation in the regular organa of the Winchester Troper, only in those *prosae* with additional letter-notation. This could be an important musical distinction since the organa contain repeated notes and liquescent neumes more suitable, one supposes, for voices; also, the crossed parts as they appear in Holschneider's interpretations do not suggest keyboard music. Nevertheless, any such hexachordal organa would produce the kind of counterpoint or *diaphonia* that two-part organ-playing could also have produced, with whatever agility its keys allowed (see Ex. 3.2).[12]

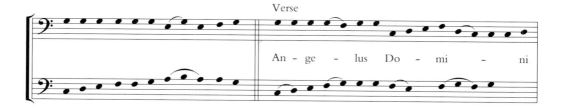

Ex. 3.2. From the *Winchester Troper*, based on a reconstruction in Holschneider 1968: 110f

[12] Holschneider 1968: 110–11. The author's reasonings – interpretation of the neumes, hypothesis on the intended chant-form or *cantus firmus* – are accepted fully for the purposes of illustration here. For further reconstruction of this organum based on fourths and excluding fifths, see S. Fuller in NOHM 1990: 505–8.

For both parts to be played on the organ, like a 'transcription', several conditions have to be right: the player would have had to know from memory or write out the lower of the two parts; his reading of neumes would have to identify fixed organ-pitches (particular keys for particular neumes); one of the lines (the organal?) would have to be read at a higher octave; and there would presumably have had to be an occasion outside the regular office on which the organ would play such music. Of these, the 'crossed parts' need be no problem, since they are those of a modern transcriber, and a cantor could read neumes at various pitches and octave-levels. But constructing two-part music when the notation gives only one part is less plausible, so much so as to 'prove' that this cannot be organ music, at least in this particular copy.

However, whether the layout of Example 3.2 in Holschneider's reconstruction is a 'keyboard score' is a different question from whether it represents more generally the kind of music that could have been played by the organ on various occasions. The answer to the second question is much more likely to be 'Yes' than to the first. Such vocal music transcribed for organ – or imitated by it – must have formed one of the staples of early repertories. In other words, the Winchester organa illustrate a possible organ music, one more developed than basic polyphonic techniques such as drones but still centred on the facility a keyboard would have for providing hexachordal melodies either to sung chant or as a second part in its own solo music. Even the 'repeated notes' shown by the neumes in some pieces might merely imply the length of a note that would be held by the organ in any note-against-note polyphony.

In general, if one is to make a case for some organa being organ-music, it is not impossible to solve the various problems (diplomatic, palaeographical and practical) offered by the musical sources of the Winchester organa. The *prosae* of *c.* 1000 (Ex. 3.1) would represent perfectly a conjectural model of the crucial step in the history of the organ: the step from heterophony as a universal means of making music to the kinds of festive liturgical music of the thirteenth-century Church in which the organ contributed both 'melody' (chant in alternation with the choir) and 'polyphony' (in the accompaniment to its own chant), some of it notated. In turn, this supports the idea that heterophony is a crucial element in the evolution of music. Was it the sound of a late romanesque and early gothic church that encouraged singers also to expand the cantilena lyrically by singing in contrary motion (recommended by John 'of Afflighem') or in florid lines above slower chant-notes (certain Aquitanian polyphony)? In such buildings traditional heterophony and close-interval organum would be blurred and chaotic, whether sung by voices or played by organs.

In its illustrations of *symphoniae* – the intervals sung by two voices – *Musica enchiriadis* does support the idea that

> early medieval *organum*, as a consciously applied device, was viewed essentially as the departing from and returning to a unison rather than as a mere bald progression of fifths and fourths: such a type of polyphony [bears] obvious sign of a heterophonic origin.[13]

Singing consistently in parallels was not the first step.

---

[13]   G. Reese, *Music in the Middle Ages* (New York, 1940), 258. However, in a pure hexachordal system, untempered fifths are powerful, natural sounds, creating no 'mere bald progression'.

Species of polyphony

The very formula-like nature of so many chant repertories – Syrian, Jewish, Byzantine, Arabian, Coptic, as well as Ambrosian, Beneventan and Old Roman – make it likely that in favourable circumstances performance might be heterophonic. Both an idiom that made much of repeated formulas and of centonization techniques ('patchwork' composition)[14] would also speak for heterophony as a technique stimulating invention, since any formulas must tempt singers and players to vary them, in different ways at different times,[15] including heterophonically.

Western modal theory as it was emerging in the northern monastic scriptoria also confirms the prevailing importance of melodic formulas when Aurelian of Réôme described in 'somewhat metaphorical language . . . some features of the eight *toni* and their formulae'.[16] Such 'classification was based at least in part upon the similarity of motifs or formulas found in one group of chants as compared to another',[17] and it could well be that certain melodic formulas had gradually emerged in response to certain sequences of diatonic notes. F A H C, for example, would prompt one group of recurrent melodic phrases, D F G A another. Although Aurelian's references to what he has learnt of Byzantine theory or practice, as well as his early date (ninth century), make it likely that his observations have nothing much to do with organs, one can conjecture that were any organ to have been available – as it was for Hucbald (see below)? – it would have had little difficulty in contributing to special ceremonies by playing various formulas, perhaps heterophonically, perhaps even as a kind of ostinato. It could also have made some kind of counterpoint.

In principle the keyboard of the organ allows it to make counterpoint to the voices according to various techniques such as were listed in Chapter 2. If the keyboard were long enough (more than one octave), it could play by itself most of those techniques:

with seven or eight notes	*with eight to fifteen notes*
heterophony	heterophony at the octave
canon	canon at the octave
parallels (various – seconds, fourths, fifths)	parallels (now including octaves, some twelfths)
antiphony or hocket	antiphony at the octave
drone	drone (doubled, tripled, etc.)
ostinato	ostinato
combination of these	more combinations of these

The ostinato need not be consistent, the canon could alternate with the drone, and so on. Clearly, the larger the compass the more techniques are feasible, and interesting

---

[14] Useful observations on formulas in Strunk 1977: 191–201; L. Treitler, 'Homer and Gregory: the transmission of epic poetry and plainchant', *MQ* 60 (1974), 333–72 (here 352–3, 369) and '"Centonate" chant: *übles Flickwerk* or *e pluribus unus?*', *JAMS* 28 (1975), 1–23. Examples of Beneventan repetition in Kelly 1989: 109–37.
[15] Characteristic examples of Coptic chant in NOHM 1990: 19, 20.
[16] Gushee 1973: 389. Aurelian giving no guidance on the actual relationships in the scale rather resembles pipe-measurement authors not giving concrete measurements.
[17] D. Pesce, *The Affinities and Medieval Transposition* (Bloomington, 1987), 1.

speculation can be made on whether players who anticipated musical possibilities prompted builders to increase compass or whether builders who gained experience with larger compass – i.e. a wider range of pipe-lengths – prompted players to expand their musical techniques. (My own guess would be the latter rather than the former, since the builders, whoever they were, were working in more isolation than performers, were less bound to tradition and ruling convention, and were therefore more inventive than either monastic chant-singers on one hand or the old Roman hydraulis-makers on the other.) In any case, the organ must gradually have found its own basic forms of polyphony: heterophonic elaboration, for example, may well be more suitable for an organ or any instrument to add to the precentor's alleluia than for voices.

And yet not a single one of these techniques is described in the references to organs. Even the drone, which is the simplest of them, is barely documented for organs before the thirteenth century and then only in reference to or in drawings of *bourdons* (Sachs 1980: 348), for which word there hangs a complicated etymology that is not very informative about what organs actually played (see pp. 301ff). It is only guess-work that in normal church usage the organ was meant as a *Borduninstrument* playing the C and F of so-called instrumental tuning.[18] But perhaps it is not difficult to believe that any form of organ-keyboard, however early, would have led to various experiments in sound on at least the rowdier feastdays. Even a simple keyboard would make possible not only unison, octave and heterophonic melody but certain basic methods of polyphony as known from various sources:[19]

> note-against-note 'counterpoint', perhaps favouring now parallels, now contrary motion;
> additions to single-line melody, i.e. drones – short or long, fixed or moving, from one stretch to another;
> an independent contribution such as ostinato;
> a background sound-mass, the equivalent of the clangour of bells.

That the first of these four methods, implied in *Musica enchiriadis* and Example 3.2, remained a widespread means of making music is clear from the later medieval tradition of *cantus planus binatim* documented in Italy and elsewhere, in which certain chant-melody (now more tonal) is accompanied by a second voice note for note, keeping its free rhythm and very likely following formulas that allowed it to be 'more a matter of performance practice than of real composition' (See Ex. 3.3).[20]

Such counterpoint is a reminder of a music that could be made in more places on more occasions than the fulldress polyphony usually the subject of historical study.

---

[18] Jammers 1962: 196, 190. Equally conjectural is the idea that the *diaphonia basilica* described in the *Summa musice* of *c.* 1200 (see Page 1991:201) was (a) old imperial counterpoint from Byzantium, (b) brought to Francia by Roman singers, (c) intended to bolster Charlemagne's imperial pretensions, and (d) a musical term indicating organum with a drone (Jammers 1962: 185, 199). See also p. 30.

[19] For examples of some of these, see Wiora 1955: 32.

[20] On *binatim*: see L. Treitler, '*Cantus planus binatim* in Italy and the question of oral and written traditions in general', in Corsi 1989: 145–61. On *ostinato*: note that the verse structure of two-part organum as interpreted by Holschneider 1968: 110ff for Winchester will sometimes produce a repetitiveness not totally unlike ostinato.

(chant below, organal voice above)

Ex. 3.3. *Binatim* polyphony (fifteenth century), from the Benedicamus trope *Verbum patris hodie*; based on Treitler (see note 20)

It is also a kind of music that could be imitated or transcribed by generations of organists in need of preludes or interludes, players who saw themselves as providing a kind of transferred vocal music. However much attention modern historians have paid 'the first genuine keyboard music' (Robertsbridge, Faenza manuscripts), most organists before the seventeenth century cannot have had much idea that there was such a thing as a specially composed solo repertory for organ. Their organ music came from improvising and transcribing.

Not the least important of the four methods listed above is the last (the background sound-mass), though it too is virtually impossible to document. Sixteenth-century triadic sirens – the single sustained chords given out by the townhall *lion* of Görlitz and by the *steer-organ* on the townside wall of Salzburg castle – are likely to be only late examples of an organ-chorus designed to make sustained penetrating sounds, in these instances without a keyboard but conceivably related to a type of early monastic organ or to one of the uses to which early monastic organs were put.

Hucbald and organ compass

Towards the end of the ninth century the theorist Hucbald already had spoken of an organ – actual or theoretical – with a compass that would make possible various musical contributions involving octave counterpoint, although how agile a polyphony the mechanism allowed is quite unknown. References to actual organs at that period virtually do not exist, so these remarks and their *en passant* nature (implying that organs were nothing extraordinary to his readers?) are exceptionally important.

Hucbald, who seems to have operated within the area Reims–Laon–St-Amand–St-Bertin, describes in *De harmonica institutione* the series of notes to which instruments are tuned (Babb 1978: 21–5),[21] the equivalent of:

c d e f g a h c' d' e' f' g' a' h' c" d" (and e" f" g" a" h" or higher)

This is the organ scale. By no means does it imply that these or any instruments were being used in church either in organum or (as suggested by Huglo, note 21: 192) to *accompany* the eight psalm-tones. As for the archetypal stringed instrument – the cithara – it is likely that Hucbald includes a reference to it in his discussion of scales because Boethius and Isidore do.

There could be as many as twenty-one or even more notes in Hucbald's scheme, to allow 'sufficient scope' for all the modes, that is, to produce up to two octaves above any final between c and h. In practice, Hucbald says, the *synemmenon* or 'added note' between the other tetrachords (B♭ or 'B') is 'unlikely to be found on the hydraulis or other instruments' (*quo tamen ydraulia vel organalia minime admisso* – GS 1.112b). Most will therefore be unable to play the liturgical melodies (*cantus*) that have both H and B. Of course, with the monochord as used later for demonstration purposes (in the *Dialogus* of *c.* 1000, once attributed to Odo of Cluny), a note of any pitch could be made by shifting the bridge a few millimetres, but this tool had no musical potential comparable to the fixed notes of a keyboard instrument.[22]

Hucbald's compass is of greater significance for what it suggests about instrument-makers, including organ-builders: although theorists might theorize about vocal scales from particular chants already in existence, and give an arithmetical explanation for them, instrument-makers must long have known and produced scales for their instruments. How they made these scales and what they consisted of can only be guessed, but it is not certain that, for example, the seven strings of the cithara mentioned by Isidore were tuned to the notes produced by the Pythagorean proportions, any more than the pipes of the Aquincum organ were (see pp. 249ff). Yet Hucbald makes the point that instruments do not contradict understanding: intelligent men have long made their scales (which start at c) to the same intervals as vocal music

---

[21] For a discussion of what letters Hucbald himself used (A–P? F–F–F?) see Sachs 1980: 159–61, 274. The letters A B(=H) C D E F G a . . . come from the *Dialogus* of *c.* 1000 (see below). Further brief remarks on the cithara- and organ-scales in M. Huglo, 'Les instruments de musique de Hucbald', in *Hommages à André Boutemy*, ed. G. Cambier (Brussels, 1976), 178–96, here 183ff.

[22] This is so even if in the context of music-teaching it may be true that 'with its exclusive reliance on the monochord, the *Dialogus* seems the most pragmatic of early treatises': R. L. Crocker, 'Hermann's major sixth', *JAMS* 25 (1972), 19–37, here 25.

(which start at A).[23] For him, therefore, practice conformed to theory, but one wonders how long or generally this had been so. Was it still quite new, a characteristic of the ninth-century monasteries and their flourishing music?

Few remarks in medieval music-theory are as stimulating as Hucbald's that instrument-compass is 'so planned as to ascend' (Babb 1978: 25) with two whole tones followed by a semitone, for this is the start of the major hexachord C D E F G A as later formulated by Guido and by Hermannus Contractus. Since no discussion of notes necessarily implies absolute pitch – a choir's flexible A is not necessarily a 'minor third' below the organ's fixed c – the starting notes of the scale are indeed significant, more so than can be easily understood on a later and longer keyboard. It is also surely not a coincidence that the first written examples of organum in another treatise of northern France (the *Musica enchiriadis* – see above, pp. 25ff) use the same scale based on c. This arrangement of notes would strike players of a keyboard, however primitive, more than would any scale theoretically expressed for they could now *see* it, especially if the keys were labelled and compass was small. Although naturally Hucbald illustrates this 'major scale' with some chant that happens to show it, the implication is that pipe or stringed instruments – and the music they are used to playing – start from, play in, revert to, or tend towards something that looks rather like 'C major' or G-mixolydian.

While, then, Hucbald may be writing with an eye to what he had read in Boethius or Isidore, he may also be speaking from practical experience when he says that readers can find instruments starting at c. Even if it is rather simplistic to read this as describing a six-stringed cithara typical of the ninth-century diocese of Tournai (Huglo 1981: 99), personal observation was not incompatible with using ancient, written authority. In any case, all such remarks as these on the 'major hexachord' scale could go on to alert and influence cantors elsewhere when they too read earlier authors on music. If Augustine's remarks on Psalm 150 inspired them to see organs as a fit vessel of worship, Hucbald's gave them ideas on what notes it would contain.

Thus by the early or mid-tenth century, those engaged in musical affairs (chant, theory, liturgy) from St Gall right across to Glastonbury could feel justified in using whatever organological craft-knowledge was available to create – an organ. Such dating agrees with known documentation, as does the idea that Hucbald was describing actual instruments.

It is also possible that Hucbald, or his copyist in the Brussels manuscript (see Plate 1),[24] further deferred to organology in a less sophisticated way, when making the diagram to show Boethian note-names and the tone-semitone scale. The diagram, ostensibly a frame around the list of note-names, is of a vertical rectangular strip (length : width about 8 : 1), rounded at the lower end, pointed at the top. This could represent the round end of a slider-key played by the hand and the pointed or tapered end that

---

[23] Is Hucbald implying that this was not always the case? Since it is known that 'Hucbald of St-Amand' owned a translation of Plato's *Timaeus* (e.g. R. McKitterick, *The Carolingians and the Written Word* (Cambridge, 1989), 135), is it possible that he was also familiar with the philosopher's criticisms of those over-interested in the minutiae of tuning (see p. 291)?

[24] Line-drawing in Babb 1978: 24; also in Weakland (see note 4): plate III.

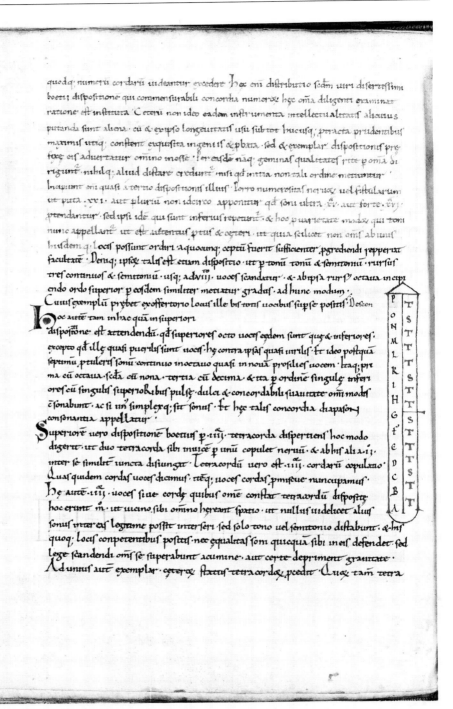

Plate 1 Diagram of note-names (copy of Hucbald): Brussels, Bibliothèque Royale Albert 1er, Codex 10078–95, f. 87'

travelled in the chest. Or perhaps it is not a key but an organ-pipe, in the form of an open pipe-metal sheet pointed at one end (the foot) and rounded at the other (to suggest a circular section); the 8 : 1 ratio would be that of conventional pipe measurements (see Chapter 16). All this is uncertain, but then, so is Hucbald's very term *ydraulia vel organalia*. This has been taken to mean that he was distinguishing between hydraulic- and bellows-organs,[25] but the phrase is almost certainly a synonym, meaning simply 'organ'. By *c.* 900, this would automatically mean bellows-organ, as it seems to have done already for St Augustine and after him Isidore of Seville, to either or both of whom Hucbald was surely alluding when he used a Greek term mentioned but not actually given by Augustine (see p. 297).

A century or so before the Winchester poem speaks unambiguously of its keyboard having both B and H, Hucbald says that the B (*synemmenon*) is unlikely to be available on organs and (diatonically strung) instruments, and that this means a 'great many melodies' (*cantibus* – Babb 1978: 29) cannot be played by them. Quite apart from the glimpse this may give of what instruments played – melodies in church? in the liturgy? in the *schola*? – it raises some important questions about scales. If the diatonic scale without B was archaic to a theorist of Hucbald's time, then perhaps organs had been previously built for hexachordal music of one kind or another (melodic or harmonic) and were limited in their choice of tonic. But equally likely is that only in the ninth century was the organ-makers' scale becoming a single, standardized sequence of diatonic notes. If this were so, it would suggest that less familiar scales, associated earlier with music quite different from the Frankish chant of the Carolingian period, had once been known to organs and, so to speak, surrendered as they entered monasteries. (On possible scales for the third-century organ of Aquincum, see Chapter 14.) Music-theorists, compilers of pipe-scales and manuscript-illuminators all aimed to confirm what perhaps did not seem obvious or inevitable: that notes on a keyboard should be ordered in a single, reliable, regularized sequence.

Presumably, the sample complete octave in the organ of the Harding Bible (1109 – see Plate 10) aims to show a set of levers that includes both B and H, but it need not be a literally drawn compass such as one would find on an actual organ. Simpler diagrams of keyboards drawn by scribes with scant personal knowledge[26] would not necessarily have both B/H since their source could have been very much older. Otherwise, there is no knowing whether the organ in a drawing had the usual distribution of tones and semitones or not even whether the artist knew of such things – and therefore whether the 'b-natural key' was indeed H or B. This would be so whatever the purpose of the drawing and however far it was meant to be 'real'.

Equally uncertain is the significance of note-names if or when there is no pitch-standard. A player or builder would know that a missing B – the 'minor sixth' in the mode based on D – could be obtained by 'transposing' the whole thing down to the mode on A, assuming he had some such terminology for his notes. (If they had no names, he could find the points at which semitones occurred and choose the one that

[25] E.g. Huglo (see note 21): 194. Babb (1978 *passim*) translates always as 'water organ'.
[26] E.g. an English Boethius copy of *c.* 1130. See Plate 13.

was followed above by three whole tones.) A line G A B C that was unplayable because there was no B could be 'transposed' down to D on the organ, and there would be no 'drop of a fourth' unless – as it is not easy to believe – the choir had the idea of a fixed A. If Hucbald does not give the option to transpose, it would be because he is not concerned here with simple, so to speak, everyday practice. If he refers only to the problem of melodies unavailable when there is not both H and B (Babb 1978: 29–30), it would be because the latter is a burning issue for the teacher and player.

The theorists' notion of 'transposing by the affinities' – one tonic can be exchanged (in thought or in sound) for another if the two have the same tone-semitone sequence – was a reasonable way of viewing the scale. From practice a player knew that the notes a cantor called A H C D had the same sequence as keys labelled D E F G, and he soon learnt whether the sixth note in the second scale was missing, i.e. whether he had the B-flat above D that corresponded to F above A. As players desired more such 'transferences', extra notes became necessary: not only B♭ but F♯ and G♯ (in the treatise *Summa musice* of *c.* 1200?) and eventually F♯, C♯, D♯ and G♯. Some such *falsae* were also necessary for the few chants with both E and E♭ or F and F♯. While theorists might explain E♭ and F♯ as something produced by polyphony,[27] players – who also sang polyphony – would know that instruments of fixed pitch needed them when sung music had variable pitch. Transposition was a practical need. In any case, it seems unlikely that all organ-keyboards began with the same C, or that if keyboards began at the top with two full tones (as Gerbert of Reims implies is the case for his *organa* of *c.* 985),[28] all such top A's had the same pitch. Variable pitch-standards and other conditions must have meant that musicians transposed without knowing they did so.

In fact, one wonders how a player would even know what the builder had made for a particular keyboard until he tested the first three keys from top and bottom, or unless the alphabet was written on them. Using letters to show where the semitones lay was particularly important when – was this the case? – anyone in the monastery could have been the organist and when 'playing' was an occasional hebdomarian duty rather than the regular practice of a professional organist. Knowing which notes were the semitones was also important when, as a dozen or more diagrams in the *Scolica enchiriadis* (*c.* 850) are intended to show, differences of mode result from – i.e. the concept of mode is based on – the semitone being in different positions relative to the other notes.

In one respect, keyboard-compass as observed by Hucbald did show a clear musical concept: that the gamut consists of successive octaves, as many as art or technology could furnish. The alphabet notation introduced in the *Dialogus* of *c.* 1000 expresses

27 E.g. W. G. Waite, 'Two musical poems of the Middle Ages', in *Musik und Geschichte: Leo Schrade zum sechzigen Geburtstag*, ed. W. Arlt (Cologne, 1963), 13–34. One of the two poems (in Rome Biblioteca Apostolica Vaticana lat. Palat. 1346 f. 3 = RISM BIII2, p. 108), dated to the early thirteenth century by Waite, has the line *setque de lignis sunt organa siue metallis* in connection with the placement of E♭ and F♯ (*falsae*): this presumably means 'but there are instruments of wood or metal', not 'organ-pipes are of wood or metal'.

28 Texts in Sachs 1970: 62, 65; discussion in Sachs 1980: 274.

once and for all this concept of successive octaves, of course much more clearly than would the individual note-names of the Greek systems:

A B c d e f g a b h c d e f g $\frac{a}{a}$

but one can imagine organ-builders already thinking in these terms. Can organ-builders ever have used the Greek names, must they not always have leaned towards a simple letter-code? For the teaching of chant or as aids for understanding its notes, a few – eight at the most – would have served, and indeed these could be seen to produce various possible sequences of tones and semitones according to a particular octave species. But Hucbald's organ keyboard gave physical identity to the octave interval such as produced by men and boys singing the 'same' note – which is how Hucbald refers to octaves (GS 1.107). It also implied that enlarging the compass meant multiplying the number of octaves. Since any builder knew that an octave rank for the note c required exactly the same pipe as a unison rank at c', this would have been no new revelation to him. But to the theorist it would have given perspective to, for example, the remark in the *Musica enchiriadis* concerning notes at the fingertips of Virgil's Orpheus:

septem discrimina vocum	seven different voices [= notes]
quod scilicet sonorum ordo	because of course the series of sounds
disparibus septem continuetur	is to be continued in the seven different
vocibus	voices [= lyre-strings],
et in octavis in novum mutetur.	and in the eighths is to begin anew.

Recognizing the acoustical nature of octaves – that they meant the halving or doubling of string-length, etc. – would not necessarily mean recognizing their musical function, but anyone could see and hear on a keyboard that 'every sound is reborn at the octave'.

Music-theory's metaphysical explanations of the octave also suggest that a new understanding was evolving. For while the Greek parallel was between the seven notes of music and the seven planets – which would not easily explain why the eighth is reborn as the first, and would have been pointless to an instrument-maker – Guido's parallel is to the seven days of the week, which does indeed begin anew on every eighth day:

ita primas et octavas	so the first and eighth notes	
semper voces easdem figuramus.	always we fashion the same.	(CSM 4. 108)

The idea of being 'born anew' on the eighth note suited any keyboard that had more than a few notes, for it would hardly be feasible for every note to have a different name. When the author of the *Musica enchiriadis* (§10) mentions instruments as a means for the listener to recognize the 'equal-sounding' octave, perhaps one or two of his readers could have taken his advice to an organ.

Further on keyboards

There is also the question of how keyboards worked and thus what they could play. One can assume that the more agility the keyboard allowed, such as would come with press-keys instead of sliders, the more busy or melodic the organ's line could be. Conversely, sliders gripped by the hand and then left in position would be better for the drones or sustained chords of the signal- or siren-organ, since press-keys or spring-loaded slider-keys can play them only by having the hand kept on the key. Thus automatically returning slider-keys would lose one facility without, one imagines, replacing it with another (i.e. agility), at least at first. Each kind of key-mechanism, therefore, has its conveniences, and agility as such cannot be assumed to have been universally desired.

Perhaps agility was needed more for heterophony than for some other forms of polyphony, as it was for the lively lines of soprano melody evolving in the repertories of the fourteenth century. The keyboard must have become more agile just at the time when there was a 'sudden multiplicity of styles in [vocal] counterpoint between *c.* 1050 and 1250',[29] but it is not possible to document a link between this music and the organ. It still need not have been obvious that keyboard agility was desirable. Even in the fourteenth century there may have been little call for major organs to have had light, slender, closely packed keys, so balanced that they required minimal pressure to open their pallet. Small portatives of soprano compass were another matter, however, and only uncertainty over crucial steps in the development of organ-mechanism means that one does not yet know how far a more agile keyboard depended on the makers of little portable organs. Perhaps entirely.

It seems reasonable to think that the eight 'keys' of the Harding Bible organ (see Plate 10) show a monk pulling sliders one by one in order to provide the sustained organal notes or *tenores* such as were beginning to appear in written organum (St-Martial) – and for which the small compass of eight notes would probably suffice. Such would be a conventional interpretation of this drawing (for example Chailley 1937), but as so often the drawing is marked by uncertainties. Can the eight notes be taken literally? Is the drawing more than a pictorial interpretation of what the artist may have read? If it was reliably modelled on an 'actual' organ, can we be sure that the sliders had no return-spring, that there was no technical information cut off by the right-hand margin, that in any case the organ was anything like up-to-date? In such respects as these, pictorial evidence is always problematic, and connecting the Harding Bible drawing with musical practices in the liturgy is at least premature (see further in Chapter 11).

But arguing from what the miniatures do appear to show of organists having or not having to return their slider-keys to the rest position, one recent writer (Körte 1973: 13ff) suggests that Winchester had sliders operated by keys which returned to

---

[29]   J. Smits van Waesberghe, 'Einleitung zu einer Kausalitätserklärung der Evolution der Kirchenmusik im Mittelalter (um etwa 800 bis 1400)', *AfMw* 26 (1969), 249–75, who also asks why it was that there is such little (known) development in free organum over the period 850–1050.

position through a spring. This is entirely possible, but the poem does not supply clear evidence.[30] If the Winchester organ were so loud that no other sound could be heard at the same time (line 164), then it is hard to imagine it playing agile melodies. Similarly, however conventional the poem's reference to 'thundering' images might be, thunderousness would be increased the more notes were played at once, as perhaps they were meant to be. (On the possibility of a quadrillon-like clash of tetrachord notes played by an organ keyboard, see remarks on the Utrecht Psalter, p. 158.) In addition, since with non-returning sliders a drone could play while the hands were left free to push-and-pull melodic notes at a tempo that would serve at least some purposes, the organ may have been able to produce both melodies and a lot of sound. Altogether, therefore, the questions of how the keys worked and what the organ was there to play are so inter-involved that one cannot use either to reason very far about the origin of the other.

On later developments of the keyboard, see Chapters 17 and 19.

Remarks on the organ's impact

The tuning of fixed notes, the timbre of bronze pipes, the sustained nature of organ sound, the novelty of instrumentally combined notes: potentially, these produce a sound-world of startling character. Such sound is one that must have anchored the chant-singers to its reliable notes – when singers heard them – and given them an even stronger sense of what it was that 'tonic' meant for the psalm-tones. This would happen not only if the organ were used for teaching melodies but particularly if it played drones when a chant such as a Sanctus was being sung or its text acclaimed. Since nothing is known of organ-scales in *c.* 800 – one can only guess that they were already like Hucbald's – it is impossible to trace how the modal tonics of Gregorian music, the instrumental scales of organ-builders and the systems of the theorists bear on each other, i.e. which influenced which and how. But it is at least possible that organ-scales not only encouraged theorists' interests in naming names but governed the chant as it spread and developed in the North. In Beneventan chant, where a 'pair of finals [G and A] accounts for the whole repertory' (Kelly 1989: 154–6), few if any modal distinctions can be heard between the two, although finals respectively on G and A do hint at the fundamental major/minor distinction implied by Hucbald's C and A scales. It is tempting to draw wide-ranging conclusions from the fact that non-Gregorian repertories with the characteristics of an earlier chant dialect seem to have led no more to organs than they did to modal theory.

Thirteenth-century theorists, surely reflecting decades if not centuries of familiarity with the keyboard, refer to the keys of the organ in order to illustrate for their readers particular musical concepts such as dissonance (can be produced by *duas claves in organis* – Guido of Cherlieu), vocal trills (Jerome of Moravia) and, most of all, the sharps and the inequality of semitones (an earlier topic, now discussed by, for

---

[30] Similarly, a question is begged in the claim that 'it is sensible to reconstruct an organ only if one knows what music was played on it' (Körte 1973: 19), since the reverse is equally true.

example, Jacques de Liège).[31] One can only guess whether at this late period the theorists or their readers were familiar with the keyboard through church organs, portatives in ensemble music or instruments in the *schola*, but the references are practical, not theoretical – without doubt, Jacques de Liège's remark on unequal semitones reflects what organ-builders actually did. Nevertheless, one needs to visualize the effect of keyboards on singers and composers without too much help from theorists. If the treatise *Summa musice* (south German, *c.* 1200?) refers to the need to change octave when instruments have only seven or eight notes and the chant goes beyond compass (Page 1991: 84 and 167) it may be merely drawing on earlier tradition – the 'seven or eight' notes of music – and gives no indication of organ-compass in a major cathedral of the early thirteenth century.

Unlike other instruments, the organ has fixed sounds immediately graspable by the ear, offering to a fourth-century poet (Prudentius), a ninth-century theorist (John Scottus Eriugena) or a thirteenth-century encyclopedist (Albertus Magnus) a useful reference when they need to speak of consonance being produced by *difference and diversity*, i.e. harmony produced by separate, different pipes.[32] St Augustine expresses a related idea (see p. 36). Meanwhile, for voices still working very much with pure fifths – to sing which requires a good and practised ear – an untempered organ offered a constant reference. Conversely, ever since it had included eight notes to the octave, the octave's easy ability to combine them must have given to those that heard it either the experience of fixed sharp thirds (C–E, F–A, G–H, B–D) or the desire to temper them and to flatten the fifths. The dissonance of Pythagorean thirds, already remedied in some Greek theory, must have been modified in tenth-century Arabic theory, judging by its recognition of major and minor thirds in organum (Al-Fārābi *c.* 870–950),[33] and there too the question would have been a burning one if organs were used to play chords. On the other hand, one consequence of the fixed sound could be that its Pythagorean tuning – A H C D E F G B tuned by pure fifths – produced a taste for even large major thirds and sixths 'striving' towards the octave-and-fifth finals of vocal music,[34] as the more mannered harmonies of the high-gothic followed that earlier organum in which thirds had been avoided.

Another consequence of the fixed sound could be that any less purely diatonic notes in music as customarily sung here and there across Europe – any chromatic or quarter-tone notes sung around recitation tones and finals, for example – would be ironed out if or as the brothers became familiar with organ sounds.[35] The fractional tones or slides in Syrian or Ethiopian chant (examples in NOHM 1990: 8, 24) could

---

[31] References and further remarks in Reckow 1975: 150–1. On the semitones, see below pp. 347ff.

[32] References and further remarks in Reckow 1975: 151–2.

[33] As interpreted by F. V. Hunt, *Origins in Acoustics: the Science of Sound from Antiquity to the Age of Newton* (New Haven, 1978), 50–1.

[34] By the fourteenth century, this awareness of interval-character is clear in both music and theory: cf. J. W. Herlinger, 'Marchetto's division of the whole tone', *JAMS* 34 (1981), 193–216. It could well have been a characteristic of fourteenth-century mannerism that the sharpness of the tonic and dominant leading notes was exaggerated in performance by singers, and the reason in physics why the ear can tolerate a greater sharpness in thirds than a flatness in fifths was equally valid from the tenth to the twentieth century.

[35] An observation already made in E. Jammers, 'Einige Anmerkungen zur Tonalität des gregorianischen Gesanges', in *Festschrift Karl Gustav Fellerer*, ed. H. Hüschen (Regensburg, 1962), 235–44, here 240. For further remarks on organs discouraging microtones and modal inflection, see Chapter 4.

not have been imitated by any organ of the western kind, although the question remains open whether that was also true of instruments of (late) classical antiquity, such as early eastern Christians may have known. The 'Hucbaldian organ' would have driven home the nature of diatonic notes as nothing else would, and the acclimatizing of singers' ears to fixed notes in this scale is a contribution to the history of music quite as important as any counterpoint the organ may have produced.

Speculations about the effect of fixed organ-scales are necessarily difficult to develop. It is possible that they encouraged the tendency of northern European melodies to make more leaps than those of Mediterranean countries, where a 'stepwise motion predominating' in 'most Italian dialects' of chant (NOHM 1990: 73) was typical. Equally, they may have encouraged newly composed sequence-melodies to centre on those tonics above which the next note is a whole tone.[36] In both cases, any truth to such speculation would come from the fact that the keyboard was in effect encouraging 'major and minor' scales. Rather less speculative and easier to imagine is the disappearance of microtones as ears became trained to such scales as that of the *Dialogus* (see above). Can there have been any pronounced microtonal inflection in the octave organum illustrated by John 'of Afflighem' or Guido d'Arezzo when they quote a phrase at three octave levels, sung 'with a minimal difference of sound . . . as if a single thing' (Babb 1978: 62, 113)? One might just (barely) imagine the top voice embellishing its melody with divided semitones in the manner of certain expert female singers likened to the Sirens – i.e. singers in the treble range – by Arnulf of St-Ghislain in about 1400 (GS 3.318). Either way, before later builders learnt to split treble sharps any such music imitated by an organ would be 'purified' of its inflection, both deliberate microtones and the pitch-variance of actual singing. Organs offered an ideal of 'pure notes' to the world of elevated sacred music.

Recent work on later medieval instruments, particularly viella (fiddle) and hurdy-gurdy, recognizes what the following string-tuning would imply:

> d Gg d'd'

With this tuning, the player 'produces both melody and heterophony: auxiliary noises clustering around any tune he played' (Page 1987: 127–8). Although they were not obliged to do so, the strings could easily sound simultaneously, tending to make drone effects or open fifths and fourths, and producing a melody embroidered around with an 'auxiliary noise' that was a kind of fiddle's equivalent to the keyboard's polyphonic techniques outlined in this chapter. Of course such melody, if it was written down at all, appeared as single notes, and no notation will show quite what happened in performance. While to some extent the organ's chorus corresponded to this 'auxiliary noise' – every key played more than its unison pipes – the keyboard itself made further 'auxiliary noises' possible and was able to emphasize open fifths and fourths as well as any fiddle. It seems entirely likely that for centuries the organ contributed in many cases not a reasoned counterpoint but various kinds of 'auxiliary noise', thus something more like the music made by stringed instruments of the thirteenth century than that made by liturgical organs of the sixteenth.

---

[36] I.e. D F G A c rather than E or H: sample percentages of sequences in H. Avenary, 'The northern and southern idioms of early European music – a new approach to an old problem', *AM* 49 (1977), 27–49.

Postscript

It would not be difficult to find theoretical–theological reasons for the organ's presence in church, and scholarship's eager reliance on a period's writings could lead today to some such thesis as that the organ as a diatonic instrument of fixed tones was a symbol, metonym or paradigm for the perfect proportions of divine *harmonia*.[37] But any such explanation must be at best retrospective: organs were known and their sound used for many different purposes irrespective of symbolic exegeses worked out at the time or afterwards by those not necessarily themselves involved in making them. It is striking that the classic symbolist-interpreter of the High Middle Ages, Gullielmus Durandus (*c.* 1295) has no symbolic interpretation for the organ[38] as he does for other attributes of a church. Any such explanation would also require that both pipe-scale theorists and manuscript-illuminators be taken much more 'literally' or positivistically than would otherwise be suggested from a circumspect reading of them (see Chapters 16 and 10). More likely is that if a theoretical or theological justification for having organs were ever sought by Frankish cantors and abbots – and it may be an anachronism to expect that it was – it came from their being so intimately familiar with two kinds of texts: the Old Testament descriptions of liturgy or praise (Psalms, 2 Chronicles 29.26ff, etc.) and, perhaps more importantly, the great psalm-commentaries which describe organs and explain their older and quite conventional symbolisms (see Chapters 1 and 17).

It is also possible that such practical consequences of the organ's presence as may now be conjectured – its fixed tones confirming for ever the octave diatonic and eventually chromatic scale, compelling makers and players to raise practical questions of tuning and compass, and offering counterpoint alone or as 'auxiliary noise' to sung music – were not expected or originally planned. Did the organ first appear in a monastery church only to create occasional public noise not so different from that familiar on the streets of Constantinople or even classical Rome? Did it already have a fixed diatonic scale and was therefore useful – either in its sound or in the living proof it offered of Pythagorean proportions – to early Frankish cantors when they were making a practical theory of music and classifying their chant accordingly? Hucbald's phrase concerning the diatonic scales of formal vocal music – that they had been known 'for a long time now' on instruments – may suggest that he was aware of there being times or places when other scales were used. For the organ certainly had the effect of establishing that scale which, as a Renaissance theorist six or seven centuries later pointed out, could not accommodate the intervals of French, German, Spanish, Hungarian, Turkish and Hebrew songs.[39] Even he, in dealing with keyboard instruments, could not offer an organ with all the required microtones, only a harpsichord.

---

[37] I had written this sentence before reading in the Abstracts of Papers for the American Musicological Society Fifty-sixth Annual Meeting (November, 1990) one entitled '*Organica instrumenta*: the medieval symbolism of precisely-tuned instruments', which not only calls organs 'aural icons of the divine plan' on account of the 'proportions among pitches in the Pythagorean scale' such as would render music 'inherently divine', but finds here an explanation 'why the organ was installed in churches'.

[38] Pointed out by Sauer 1964: 140. On Durandus, see also p. 82.

[39] N. Vicentino, *L'antica musica ridotta alla moderna prattica* (Rome, 1555), f. 85'.

4

Organs, politics and chant

Hypotheses on what in an early period is technologically significant and what must have been its impact are difficult to make, for written sources give so incomplete a picture of crafts and techniques that any hypothesis has a short life-expectancy. It will be sure to need replacement as further technical details emerge, which they tend to do only outside written sources. The concrete and practical are not easy for conventional scholarship, and for every five studies on 'Developing Concepts of Carolingian Kingship' or 'Papal–imperial Relations', there will be scarcely one on what it was people were developing with their hands, although in addition to its own importance, this too will affect concepts of kingship. What people actually believed as Christians may not be easily discerned in a major book entitled *The Frankish Church*, although it was surely relevant.

Because the practical is so elusive one is likelier to reach a wrong conclusion on a material question such as the location of Charlemagne's main hall at Aachen than on an immaterial question such as Charlemagne's perception of his rôle as defender of the faith. And imaginative attempts to understand the concrete and practical are all too easily challenged by traditional historians whose knowledge of documents can appear to bring them nearer the truth than one who makes those imaginative attempts. A good example is the reaction to Lynn White's stimulating ideas on the introduction and significance of the stirrup (White 1962), more or less contradicted in a recent survey of Carolingian scholarship.[1] But not the least interesting of White's observations is the practical one that stirrups appear in the work of certain important ninth-century monastic artists (White 1962: 26), which suggests that some people, for some reason, were newly alerted to them or wished to show that they were. If this too turned out to have been an over-simplification, the value of White's original stimulus becomes all the clearer since it focused questions on riding equipment and what might have been its impact on the lords of a developing feudal system or on the artists of an expanding monastery library.

One development in traditional scholarship, however, does have implications for the practical question of how organs came to develop. The known appearances of the organ fit the recent thesis that it is not the period of Pippin and Charlemagne

---

[1] D. A. Bullough, '*Europeae pater*: Charlemagne and his achievement in the light of recent scholarship', *EHR* 85 (1970), 59–105, here 84–9. Criticisms of White's theory already in R. H. Hilton & P. H. Sawyer, 'Technical determinism: the stirrup and the plough', *Past & Present* 24 (1963), 90–100.

but the years around 1000 that are those of major development in so many directions – a period of European 'rebirth' barely foreseen even fifty years previously.[2] The old idea that the organ was introduced into the western Christian church by one or more particular events in the lives of the Carolingian kings – the gift to Pippin in 757, or Louis the Pious's welcome for a Venetian organ-builder in 826 (see Chapter 9) – has seemed inadequate for some time now, an idea that came originally from depending too much on the many written sources of the Carolingian period. An organ-historian too can now usefully ask whether the 'generally accepted version of the Carolingian world [is] an "imagined" world, existing only in the minds of modern historians'.[3] But as attention moves to the late ninth and tenth centuries, when documentation is so sparse, the organ-historian might ponder how the previous Carolingians came to leave such voluminous records and what they meant by it.

In general, both in so far as they exist and in so far as they do not, the sources leave it very unclear how organs came to be known at all. Because of the changing nature of documentation, every half century between the years 750 and 1250 leaves behind a somewhat different impression about organs and how they were used. Various kinds of evidence suggest that there were developments in late eighth-century Europe conducive to the crafts of organ-making, and since both the threefold increase in church lands between 751 and 825 and the 'intensified craft production'[4] that went with it could have prompted bell-founding and other bronze work, the absence of clear written reference to organs is difficult to understand. Do the two ambiguous references to *organa hymnorum* in the *Regula magistri* of the early ninth century (Anon – PL 88.958, 970) mean even as much as 'the music of the hymns', or is the old phrase used because the author was uncertain what his texts (in the first instance, Psalm 136/137) meant? Is the later ninth century's silence on organs, in those very areas of Europe likely to have had them, a result of something so very concrete as the Viking raids of *c.* 880–90? If so, did this affect both England and Normandy, right across the Carolingian homelands from Tours and Fleury, Jumièges and St-Wandrille, to Corbie, St-Amand, Luxeuil, Prüm and on to Aachen? Perhaps, since those raids may not always have been as totally devastating as Christian chroniclers suggest,[5] it is less a question of the lack of ninth-century references to organs than the existence of clusters of references at certain moments in the eighth and tenth centuries. If only because the Viking raids were hardly worse than some of the inter-Christian barbarities chronicled centuries earlier by Gregory of Tours, one might think that it was not because they had all been destroyed that organs were so seldom mentioned.

There are also interesting silences in the next century or so, with no mention of organs in the Winchester *Regularis concordia*, the Cluniac customary (see p. 72) or

---

2   R. Fossier, *Enfance de l'Europe, Xe–XIIe siècle: aspects économiques et sociaux*, 2 vols (Paris, 1982).

3   R. E. Sullivan, 'The Carolingian age: reflections on its place in the history of the Middle Ages', *Speculum* 64 (1989), 267–300, here 279.

4   E.g. in the case of pottery, glass and stone querns: R. Hodges & D. Whitehouse, *Mohammed, Charlemagne and the Origins of Europe* (Ithaca, NY, 1983), 103–4, 171.

5   E.g. St-Amand's library was saved despite the spoliation: A. d'Haenens, 'Les invasions normandes dans l'empire france au XIe siècle', *Settimane* 16 (1969), 233–98. Also, 'the activities of English *scriptoria* were never seriously interrupted during the years of the trouble': F. M. Stenton, *Anglo-Saxon England* (Oxford, 1971), 396.

St Bernard's quite detailed indictment of Cluny (see pp. 217f). Although such silences are a disappointment to the organ-historian, it is clear that documents were aiming to be specific about very little but the matter in hand, and consequently one learns at least that any organs which did exist were not central to that matter. For example, they might have been a sign of wealth known to only a few main houses, not mentioned unless that wealth happened to be itemized. Not only does silence prove nothing about organs but any reference to them is likely to be less 'real' than it seems, based on some literary tradition that may have nothing to do with the work of craftsmen, monastic or lay.

Events in the eighth century

The Byzantine Emperor Leo's attack on so-called worship of images that began in 726 (the dispute over iconoclasm) had as one of its consequences the removal of Greek-speaking provinces, including those in Sicily and southern Italy, from the pope of Rome to the patriarch of Constantinople in *c.* 732/3. Rome's authority was curtailed, and relations with the North became more crucial. But neither Pope Stephen's well-documented agreement with Pippin in 754 nor Pope Leo's crowning of Charlemagne in 800 would have anything to do with organs were it not that the collaboration of Roman popes with Carolingian kings had at least two relevant effects, one general and one specific: such collaboration must have encouraged the Carolingian belief in the written record, and it may have occasioned the diplomatic exchanges between East and West that brought a special organ to Compiègne and other exotica to Aachen (see Chapter 9). If Rome's authority for the early Carolingians can be seen in the sending of its liturgical books, so Byzantium's can be in the sending of its technical apparatus such as organs.

As Charlemagne's later biographer The Monk of St Gall (Notker Balbulus †912) put it:

semper omnes Graeci et	as usual, all the Greeks and	
Romani invidia	Romans were consumed with envy	
Francorum gloriae carpebantur.	at the fame of the Franks.	(MGH SS 2.735)

This *invidia* is something of a leitmotif for the author, who seems to have picked up the idea in Einhard's *Vita caroli magni* (MGH SS 2.458): it became an important element in Carolingian claims of legitimacy, surviving to be taken at face value by later historians. While the Merovingians before Pippin, like the English saints chronicled by Bede (†735?), had not omitted to seek authorized material from Rome, it was 'Pippin and his successors [who more] systematically insinuated themselves as protectors' of the Church in Neustria.[6] Music – chant, perhaps even

---

[6] P. J. Geary, *Before France and Germany: the Creation and Transformation of the Merovingian World* (Oxford, 1988), 179. On English imitations of Rome: something comparable to Notker's *invidia* is suggested by William of Malmesbury's remarks in the twelfth century that there was 'Roman ambition' in the old church of Hexham, the like of which could not be seen this side of the Alps (*ambitionem Romanam* – RBMAS 52.255).

organs – was not the only beneficiary of the drive to establish an authority blessed by Rome: constant reference to Rome's apostolic claim, to Carolingian legitimacy, and to the benefits of Benedictine evangelization (either against pagans or against other kinds of Christians) must have helped to produce in the ninth-century Church a fertile ground for the flowering of various arts. The connection between organs and Rome is indirect: if organs were known in churches during Charlemagne's son's reign, it was not because they came from Rome. On the contrary, the influence is the reverse: whenever it was that a church in Rome first had a fixed organ, the idea for it probably came from the north. The most fertile ground was there in the North. The region may not have had much of an architectural technology in *c.* 800 to compare with the Byzantines' but at least metallurgical and other crafts were developed, and this over a large area.

On the immediate level, as groups of missionaries traversed Frisia or Saxonia or Carinthia or Catalonia, a base-of-operations would have been physically conspicuous. In many areas it meant a clearing of the forest and the creating of a thriving community;[7] sometimes monasteries were built on fortified hilltop sites, often where there had been a previous if less conspicuous religious settlement.[8] When Boniface (†754) destroyed a pagan tree he may have delivered the pagans from the captivity of the devil, but he would certainly have found the task easier when he had something special to offer in return: perhaps a Christian tree (a cross, eventually a crucifix), ideally a stone building, with special light (a large and brilliant bronze candelabrum), wafting fragrance, a set of bells (in a tower), and so on. One is bound to wonder whether so many of the major centres of Saxon conversion – Paderborn, Münster, Hildesheim, Halberstadt – were later associated with technological advance as a direct consequence of arts and crafts developed there during this early missionary period.

East of the line of monasteries that eventually documented some of this technological advance – from Theophilus's Paderborn area down via Hirsau and Murbach to Notker Labeo's St Gall (Chapters 15 and 16) – was the wide stretch of converted peoples whose allegiance one can imagine being won partly by means of miracles technological as well as religious. (In this way, there is a deep connection between organ-building and the transposing of relics, beyond *organa* merely playing on such festive occasions: they were both wonders of a kind.) The activity of the 'freelance Irish missionaries of early centuries'[9] across more western and southern lands never stimulated such interest. Nor so far as is known were their converts threatened with capital punishment for lax observance, as the Saxons were by Charlemagne in his *Capitulatio de partibus saxoniae* (MGH Cap. 1.68–70), perhaps in imitation of the Lord's command to Moses in Exodus 31.14–15. No doubt converts needed fewer threats the more wonderful or awe-inspiring the new Christian liturgies

---

[7]   A vivid idea of the process is given in R. E. Sullivan, 'The Carolingian missionary and the pagan', *Speculum* 28 (1953), 705–40, with bibliography.

[8]   Central German examples in D. Parsons, 'Sites and monuments of the Anglo-Saxon mission in Central Germany', *AJ* 140 (1983), 280–321.

[9]   As it is called in Sullivan (see note 7): 710. Is it owing only to later events that two particular Irish foundations – St Gall and Bobbio – did become associated with organs and comparable crafts (see Chapter 13) or was there already some interest in musical instruments there?

turned out to be, and the Saxons at least saw, as Bishop Daniel of Winchester advised Boniface to point out to them, that Christians were better off than the pagans. When Charlemagne destroyed their temples, it would surely have been effective to substitute a fine church and other wonderful novelties.[10] Stone structures were built where there had been forests before, according to early documents (MGH SS 15.115);[11] at Fritzlar a vineyard was planted (MGH SS 15.41); there was metalworking at Fulda (MGH SS 2.375) and, as at Freising, organized chant everywhere.

Tenth-century reform

To the extent that Byzantine monasticism could be described as having no Orders, no reforms, encouraged no individual initiative, was less of a community in each case than in the West, was less specialized, business-like, international or involved in state affairs than western monasticism,[12] so to that extent the church organ of the tenth-century Anglo-Saxon Benedictines typified the West. For it expressed the opposite of every single one of these Byzantine traits, at least as they had developed by 950 or so. Benedict himself, 'wisely unlearned' according to Gregory (*sapienter indoctus* − PL 66.126), may not have advocated liberal arts learning, much less the *artes mechanicae* studied by a few later monks for church equipment and decoration, but in so describing Benedict, Gregory doubtless had his own purposes (Stäblein 1970: *60). In actively re-establishing Christian learning he would lead some later western bishops to make use of technology in their pastoral efforts towards the laity, and they would see here nothing to contradict their founder's spiritual aims. Already in the twelfth century, William of Malmesbury saw the reform of English monasteries under St Dunstan (†988) as involving 'great wonders' such as bells and organs (PL 179.1660), and these would have been quite as much for the benefit of the people as for the monasteries.

In tenth-century sources from Benedictine monasteries in England the organ served to demonstrate the qualities of the reforming bishops, who were generous, or made things 'with their own hands', or were knowledgeable, or encouraged the offering of expensive embellishments and technological wonders to the church *ad majorem gloriam Dei* (see Chapter 12). Each of these acts as reported in their vitae and elsewhere could serve as models for others or, as in the case of making things 'with their own hands' (see p. 201), helped to establish something that was politically desirable, i.e. that abbots and bishops were no longer aloof aristocrats and their monasteries not merely royal enclaves. Such records also have something of a legal status, in so far as the reference to an organ would help prevent its future removal: the gift was recorded on parchment.

---

[10] On Boniface, Sullivan, *ibid.*, 717. On the destroyed pagan site the *Irminsul*, see *ibid.*, 720, and on its removed treasures, Fichtenau 1982: 79. This site was up-river from Theophilus's Helmarshausen (see p. 255).

[11] But Celtic missionaries further south and west in the seventh and eighth centuries had also developed the idea of communal work, e.g. in clearing arable land: F. Prinz, *Frühes Mönchtum im Frankenreich* (Munich/ Vienna, 1965), 537–9.

[12] Points listed in D. Savramis, *Zur Soziologie des byzantinischen Mönchtums* (Leiden/Cologne, 1962), 87–9.

Equally effective, though for different political purposes, was the documentation concerning Pippin's assembly of 757 and the organ sent there from Constantinople (see Chapter 9). In both cases – the eighth-century Frankish kingdom of Pippin, the tenth-century English kingdom of Edgar – reporting on organs had a political dimension, therefore. If for the Carolingian chroniclers the gift was a sign of recognition by the chief foreign and Christian power in a period of political pact-making, so for the Saxon chroniclers it typified the bishop–saint's practical work in re-establishing the minsters of Edgar's kingdom, this in a period of relative peace from the Vikings. One version of the *Anglo-Saxon Chronicle* described Winchester's Æthelwold – the bishop making organs at Abingdon and Winchester – as being determined to restore all of those minsters. If the tenth-century reform as a whole, as has been recently claimed,[13] had as its central objective the restoring of monastic observance rather than any political programme as such, nevertheless the two were inter-involved, so much so that it would be hard to say whether the organ was there for well ordered liturgy – part of the 'summoning' necessary for major services, especially where the people (*plebes*) were concerned – or for the new, splendid occasions when the powers of Church and state met together, as they frequently did.

Despite the Cluniac's regard for splendour of liturgy and buildings, particularly in the bigger houses, it is possible that in the provinces Cluniac development did not encourage the making of organs, since the *plebes* and what was needed to attract them were not by then its prime concern. The Order was not evangelical in this way. A large part of the Cluniac agenda was to get exemption from the authority of bishops, such as it had been wielded in Benedictine houses,[14] and if bishops were no longer allowed to celebrate public masses as a matter of course in the larger abbeys,[15] then there was less occasion and less need for a large organ. Thus it is likely that the royal/Benedictine impetus in England produced results rather different from the aristocratic/Cluniac in Burgundy and Aquitania, and if organs were indeed as rare in Cluniac abbeys as documentation is silent about them, then one implication is that in the Benedictine abbeys they were there for *plebeian* occasions. From such origins, the organ would be a natural piece of equipment in the great secular cathedrals and eventually parish churches of the gothic period.

Tenth-century reforms then, had different effects on the introduction of organs, depending on the kind of reform. In any event, the increased reference to organs in the late twelfth and, especially, thirteenth centuries is mostly in connection not with Benedictine or Cluniac monasteries but with bishops' churches, the secular cathedrals.

---

[13] On the part played by Æthelwold, including the donation of books to one of those minsters (Peterborough), see M. Lapidge, 'Surviving booklists from Anglo-Saxon England', in *Learning & Literature in Anglo-Saxon England: Studies presented to Peter Clemoes*, ed. M. L. & G. Greuss (Cambridge, 1985), 33–89, here 52–5. For emphasis on liturgy in tenth-century reform, M. McC. Gatch, 'The office in late Anglo-Saxon monasticism', *ibid.*, 341–62.

[14] H. E. J. Cowdrey, *The Cluniacs and the Gregorian Reform* (Oxford, 1970), 24–7 *et passim*.

[15] The question still exercised Benedictine monasteries in the twelfth century: see remarks on Peterborough Cathedral, p. 85.

'Gregorian chant' and organs

In no chant repertory, from Syria to Ireland, from Iona to Benevento, can it be shown that organs were introduced to play chant or that when they were first known, they contributed to it. For the possibility that in the later thirteenth century, quire organs became an accepted part of the furnishings – literally the woodwork – in the stalls of larger monastic or cathedral churches, see remarks on woodworking in Chapter 18. For the earlier period, the most that can be said is that the connection between organs and chant is indirect. In so far as organs first become documented in annals, vitae, chronicles or other distinct literary genres, they do so in the region that is associated with Gregorian ('Frankish–Roman') chant rather than with Mozarabic, Beneventan, Ambrosian, Old Roman or any other – with the chant, therefore, that tended 'towards fixation' in its various systematic arrangements (of psalm-tones, antiphons, chant-types), in its notations and in its taught theory.[16] The connection between chant and organs is one of cultural context rather than liturgical collaboration and is therefore difficult to define.

The origin and nature of Frankish–Roman chant being still far from clear in all respects,[17] many questions remain about the local situation both at the Carolingian centre and on the peripheries. In England, 'Gregorian chant' must date only from Charlemagne's period despite an old tradition of deference to the pope who had sent missionaries to Kent two centuries earlier.[18] In the Lombardic south of Italy already at the same period, Frankish–Roman chant was superseding the so-called Ambrosian, but precisely why Carolingian claims to the region took this form is not immediately obvious: if Pippin (714–68) asked Pope Stephen III (752–7) for clerics to teach the chant in Carolingian lands, and Paul I (757–67) sent Roman chant-books (presumably without notation) to the same area, was it only 'to increase unity throughout [Pippin's] domain by imposing the Roman rite'?[19] Rather than unity as such, a more likely motive was the search for authority, an exclusive apostolic authority not least in Italy itself where competing traditions meant that rites and usages were not uniform. Any wish to impose uniformity of chant would be a consequence of such authority: if it were *correct*, it needed to be the same everywhere.

How 'Gregorian chant' originated – how Frankish a version of contemporary Roman chant it was, and what of 'Old Roman' chant it ironed out – is less important for present purposes than the authority it assumed as something claiming to come from Rome, whose own apostolic succession was also assumed (and by now

[16] Summary of tendencies for such chant by R. Crocker in NOHM 1990: 221.

[17] Some useful remarks on Gregory I and Gregory II (715–31) and the claims for chant-origin, in McKinnon 1990: 88–119. Also NOHM 1990: 111ff.

[18] More than once Bede (c. 673–735), familiar with *vitae* of the popes, mentions Gregory I or his disciples in connection with church practice (e.g. PL 94.715), while in Einhard's and Notker Balbulus's *vitae* of Charlemagne, the focus of authority appears to be Rome rather than St Gregory himself. In England, Sts Benedict and Gregory represented the desired canonic authority; perhaps by chance, the oldest extant copy of Benedict's Rule is Anglo-Saxon (see Gatch (note 13): 347).

[19] Levy 1984: 49. Carolingian texts in e.g. G. Ellard, *Master Alcuin, Liturgist* (Chicago, 1956), 48–67; various earlier and later texts in Stäblein 1970: ★140ff. On 'Ambrosian' (here, Beneventan) chant being superseded, see Kelly 1989: 21f.

constantly claimed) for this purpose. The desire of the Carolingians for unification by means of chant-books or authorized cantors from Rome is frequently stressed today[20] and is indeed already made clear by Notker Labeo in his phrase *unitas et consonantia* ('unity and agreement' – MGH SS 2.735) when he is discussing what it was Charlemagne had in mind with his canonical books. But Charlemagne's own word in the *Admonitio generalis* of 789 was *unanimitatem*, the 'one spirit-ness' desired by a Christian king who looked to the seat of apostolic authority in Rome (MGH Cap. 1.61).[21] This is no ordinary unification but something subtler, leading amongst other things to an otherwise surprising degree of uniformity ('unanimity') in chants as transmitted into the eleventh century, especially those associated with the oldest fixtures in the liturgical year. Accuracy of copy was crucial, for 'to error was in some sense to sin'[22] or rather – to lose authority. No merely secular, imperialistic unification could produce this, but a desired spiritual unanimity might.

That unanimity means something more than unity is suggested by contemporary church-design, where spiritual unanimity does not mean loss of variety in design from one region to another. Except in the most general terms of layout there was no question of unanimity meaning identical form even in the special cases of direct architectural copy, such as the petrine basilica in Fulda or the Aachen octagon in Bruges, Nijmegen, Ottmarsheim and elsewhere. But while obviously churches and furnishings could vary, the texts and evidently the way they were sung ought to be the same across the Carolingian world. Naturally, total liturgical or musical uniformity was also hardly feasible, and already by *c.* 825, presumably as neumatic notation was circulating, Amalar of Metz gave various reasons why there would be discrepancies between one usage and another (PL 105.1152, 1243–5, 1314).

Having Roman authority for how the liturgical texts were to be sung was second only to knowing the authorized texts themselves. Any such Roman texts were the latest instance of the age-old respect given to books (especially Gospels) as instruments of authority. Sacred books were objects over which Celtic saints and kings had once quarrelled (Columba) or which a Benedictine missionary of more recent times was said to be holding in his hands as he was martyred (Boniface). The authority of the book was important to the biographers of saints, who then expressed it by – writing a further authoritative book. An antiphoner of Pippin's or Charlemagne's period was a liturgical equivalent to relics, giving the same sense of direct contact with the founts of truth, and it is no accident that relics from Rome were also being sought for all the new Carolingian foundations of the later eighth century. In Mozarabic and northern Ambrosian provinces, where the claims of Rome were less in evidence before the Benedictine–Cluniac thrust of the early eleventh century, older regional chant-repertories remained, as no doubt they did in other

---

[20]   E.g. L. Treitler, 'Homer and Gregory: the transmission of epic poetry and plainchant', *MQ* 60 (1974), 333–72, here 338; H. Hucke, 'Toward a new historical view of Gregorian chant', *JAMS* 33 (1980), 437–67, here 445.

[21]   *Unitatem* in Levy 1984: 49, note 3, but correct in Levy, 'Charlemagne's archetype of Gregorian chant', *JAMS* 40 (1987), 1–30, note 14.

[22]   D. G. Hughes, 'Evidence for the traditional view of the transmission of Gregorian chant', *JAMS* 40 (1987), 377–404, here 400.

centres with important traditions,[23] and it was naturally in the central Carolingian lands that the original local repertory (Gallican) 'was the one most thoroughly suppressed' (Levy 1984: 49). Already in 789 Pippin was credited by his son with the *unanimitatem* this suppression had the effect of bringing about, although no actual decrees from Pippin to this end are known.[24]

The hoped-for *unanimitas* of the church's books in north-west Europe over the late eighth century and the advent then or soon after of musical notation – whether of the early 'graphic' or the more advanced 'gestural' neumes[25] – do not obviously impinge on organs. Yet chant that was (a) ordered or regulated and (b) notated, belonged to the culture that saw organs as highly desirable objects a century and a half after Charlemagne's death and quite likely much earlier. As one tries to sense a connection between organs and chant it is useful to think in terms of what was authorized in each instance, not by papal decree – neither was authorized in so many words – but by use and usage. A particularly interesting case is that of psalters. The Stuttgart Psalter of *c.* 820/30 which contains three early organ-pictures (see pp. 165ff), transmits the psalm-texts with the same two kinds of authority as those of a chant-book. In both the texts are 'regulated' and 'notated' in an appropriate way: the Psalter transmits an accepted interpretation (i.e. the paintings illustrate with imagery drawn from the authoritative commentaries) and notates the canonic text (i.e the words are written down) and even an accepted performance practice (there are some ecphonetic signs for cantillation). A chant-book too gave both a text and an 'interpretation'.

Not long after the Stuttgart Psalter, Hucbald implies an indirect but powerful link between organs and psalms when he mentions organs not in connection with psalms themselves but with the notes of music as used for singing them or other authorized texts. The connection between psalm-teaching and organ-making is that for both of them one had to understand the nature of *notes*. In this way, while the kinds of authority transmitted by an antiphoner, a psalter and a theory-book in one and the same Carolingian monastery are of different orders, they can be seen as working to a common end. There may be no direct connection between an abbey's concrete interest in organs and any copy of Aurelian's *Musica disciplina* (see p. 20) its library may have had – as at St-Amand, Arras St-Vaast or Erfurt St Peter[26] – but a book describing modes was not irrelevant to a ninth-century organ-maker's 'interest in notes'. (Later, when two pier-capitals in the ambulatory at Cluny were elegantly carved with allusions to the eight tones of music, there can have been little if any such relevance: they represent pure Boethian theory, a platonic learning distinct from – inimical to – instrumental practice.)

---

[23]   E.g., in 1058 the Chronicle of Montecassino records Pope Stephen IX's forbidding of *ambrosianum cantum* (MGH SS 7.693). Further in J. Boe, 'Old Beneventan chant at Montecassino: gloriosus confessor Domini Benedictus', *AM* 55 (1983), 69–73.

[24]   C. Vogel, 'Les échanges liturgiques entre Rome et les pays francs jusqu'à l'époque de Charlemagne', *Settimane* 7 (1960), 185–295, here 237.

[25]   Terms from K. Levy, 'On the origin of neumes', *EMH* 7 (1987), 59–90.

[26]   See L. Gushee, preface to CSM 21, respectively pp. 49 (copy *c.* 900), 17 (twelfth century), and 47 (tenth–eleventh century). For organs in Arras and Erfurt, see pp. 211 and 222.

If there is any possibility that organs contributed to sequences in the early period (see Chapter 5), then it may be significant that such new music is also associated with the earliest known neumes (Levy 1984: 81): for some, there may have been a natural link between 'newly composed' music, the notation for it and an interest in instruments. Similarly, if notation aided the teaching of boys, as later the *Dialogus de musica* (*c.* 1000) said was the case with notated antiphons,[27] so would instruments, particularly an instrument with a keyboard. Arguing in the same way – that in particular ways ninth-century musical activities encouraged interest in organs – one can see that written documentation, indeed writing in general, also played a part. First, if revising the liturgy was 'set in motion by the Frankish monarch Pippin during Stephen III's visit to the Frankish realm in 753–4' (Levy 1984: 79), then contacts with Rome and Constantinople would be key items for an annalist of the period to record in his chronicle. While the Byzantine organ of 757 may have had nothing to do with this liturgy, it would have aroused in at least some of the annalists an interest in musical technology. Second, as an interest in writing about the practice and theory of music grew during the ninth century (*Musica* and *Scolica enchiriadis*, Aurelian, Hucbald), so pipe-measurement texts created an area of learning. While these treatises may have had nothing to do with organ-building as such – though they too surely aroused copyists' interest in instrumental sound – practical details did creep into them (see Chapter 16). Any emphasis on written records that can be seen to be typical of Charlemagne's administration[28] indirectly helped to make organs more familiar, in name and eventually in sound. Re-copying chronicles was surely not so thought-numbing a drudgery that copyists' curiosity was never kindled by the entry for 757, 'Francia received its first organ'. Similarly, while in principle studying the theoretical scale of organ-pipes need not lead to an interest in organs, it obviously had a far greater potential for practical music-making than studying the theory of monochords or bells.

Whether much of such curiosity was roused during Pippin's, Charlemagne's or Louis's lifetime, however, is not known, for documents were not so very complete and do barely mention musical matters. But it is possible after all that just as authoritative books sometimes circulated before Pippin or Charlemagne marshalled effort on behalf of *unanimitas*, so organs were previously known here and there without there being any reason to report them. The clear agendas behind the various kinds of written record that do exist make it out of the question that *no mention* means *nothing was happening* – a conclusion that one can reach also by surveying written technologies, which describe neither every technique that was known nor, of those they do describe, necessarily practised far and wide. Just as one might be tempted to seek a common ancestry for all musical notations, so one might for organs. But in both cases, more likely than a common ancestry as such is a common function: if organs (or notations) resembled each other closely in what they were there to do, they could well turn out to resemble each other physically, in principle if not in detail.

---

[27] GS 1.252–3 = 'Odo of Cluny' in O. Strunk, *Source Readings in Music History* (New York, 1950), 103–4. See also above, pp. 50f.

[28] Documented in F. L. Ganshof, *The Carolingians and the Frankish Monarchy* (London, 1971).

For both, the wide scatter of known accomplishment in the tenth century – both notation and organs are documented in far-apart regions of western Christendom – argues against too much weight being given to Charlemagne's drive for unification. The most direct connection between Winchester's chant-notation or its church organ and Charlemagne's *unanimitas* two centuries earlier is likely to have come via the activity of the monasteries, reformed after an intervening low period. It is they who forge the link between 800 and 1000, regularly producing notations and (probably) organs by 900 but having learnt to do so by steps that are now very uncertain.

The 'imposition by fiat' of Frankish–Roman chant was among other things a means towards encouraging ninth-century musical composition, the creation of music whose 'forms are the sequence, Kyrie, Gloria in excelsis, hymn and trope, with the sequence as the most important', a product of the 'infinitely expressive art of the Gregorian melisma'.[29] Notating the music of these sequences prompted this art to expand[30] and its influence to spread. If organs of any kind were heard in the bigger abbeys about the year 800, particularly for special liturgical or extra-liturgical events, it would not be difficult to suppose that they were associated from time to time with the new musical forms, especially the hymn and sequence (see Chapter 5). The more plausible this is, the more probable that organs developed for such purposes in the abbeys noted for sequence composition, particularly St Gall, and so the more likely it is that they remained simpler signal-sounding instruments where chant-forms were less developed. There is no reason to assume that all major abbeys across Europe in *c.* 1000 put to *exactly* the same use any organs they might have possessed, and it would be logical that where they were used more for purposes of music than of noise, there the technology for such parts as the key-action and chest-size would be the most intensely developed.

But since it is not proved that organs were 'more for purposes of music than noise' in connection with new chant-forms, a question is whether there would be other links between organ and chant. Perhaps the Numerical Office – a liturgical programme in which 'the components (antiphons or responsories) are arranged in modal order' for the sake of Frankish cantors who 'wanted a more varied repertory of melodies for their new antiphon sets' than Roman singers did[31] – provided one such link. The organ's fixed scale would demonstrate very clearly the nature of the different psalm-tones formulated first, or only, in the monasteries of the 'Carolingian Renaissance'. It could also make immediately clear – visibly and audibly – the concept of four authentic modes (melodies largely within the octave above the finals D, E, F or G) and four plagal (melodies equally below and above the final). Sources of *c.* 900 do not make this link between organs and chant or chant-learning, and yet the same period saw music-theory dealing both with the keyboard-scale and with attempts to describe eight modes; see Chapter 3. Is it only coincidence that contemporary Rome had neither the organ, as far as is known, nor a modal classification

29 Quotations from R. L. Crocker, 'The early Frankish sequence: a new musical form', *Viator* 6 (1975), 341–51, here 341–3.

30 Perhaps the same is true of the basic chant-repertory, now thought by some to have been notated already by or before 800: Levy (1987; see note 21).

31 Quotations from R. L. Crocker, 'Matins antiphons at St-Denis', *JAMS* 39 (1986), 441–90, here 445, 488.

for its chant?[32] And this despite establishing the vast corpus of liturgical texts for the whole year (the *circulum anni*), along with music that would have benefited from classification. On the other hand, organs would not show the finer points of vocal performance, such as the inflections or changes of voice-tone identified by Aurelian for certain chants in certain modes, or any microtones that sometimes, in some regions, may have been sung.[33] The vast musical world opened up when the organ produced normality from diatonic notes and established once and for all that the scale made up of multiple octaves was not to be one with much microtonal inflection.

If the organ did not participate in the chant during office or mass, and even if it never had anything to do with instruction in singing or learning the notes – though this is difficult to believe – it would still have had some connection with new liturgical chant. As mass and office 'became the exclusive expression of the clergy, and the congregation were spectators', so the laity's 'comprehension and participation' would increase 'as the beauty and ornament of the liturgy increased'.[34] (Similar points were made above concerning Saxon converts.) The excitement of mass on feastdays or special occasions such as a church-dedication was precisely what the clamour of bells and organs was for, judging by such references as there are from the tenth century on (see Chapters 5 and 13). If 'Gregorian chant' was essentially the clergy's, and its troped and polyphonic forms were even more exclusive (for trained singers), then there was all the more reason why on grand public occasions the organ would play a role, producing for the *plebes* a stirring sound – melodies or chords or drones as the case may be. In major abbeys, the organ would be part of the Gregorian style. Perhaps the consecration at Cava in 1092 (see p. 212) was well documented in order to remind churches in the Italian south that, just as Montecassino under Desiderius was finding at that period, Rome with its Gregorian chant and its reforming Cluniac energies meant to be the dominating presence in the region.

And perhaps all the time there was an undercurrent of lay interest in organs. Since the production of useful texts in the vernacular languages (as at Fulda from *c.* 820) led to German versions of organ-treatises by the end of the tenth century or so (as at St Gall), one might wonder whether in some areas instrument-making was and had remained a layman's craft, actively practised in many a settlement. Was instrument-making important to members of the active new church in certain German provinces because it was something well developed outside the monastery and needed to be brought within it? Nothing yet known makes it impossible for the Winchester organ to have been made by lay craftsmen, perhaps in monastery workshops under a cantor's supervision, but in any case so made as a special object for special occasions when the *plebes* were passive observers of an intricate liturgy.

---

[32] H. Hucke (see note 20): 442, may rely too much on extant sources in claiming this. But arguments summarized in his 'Die Herkunft der Kirchentonarten und die fränkische Überlieferung des gregorianischen Gesangs', in *Kongreßbericht Berlin 1974* (Kassel, 1980), 257–60 seem compelling.

[33] Telling example from Aurelian discussed in L. Treitler, 'Reading and singing: on the genesis of occidental music-writing', *EMH* 4 (1984), 135–208, here 157–8. On possible microtones between the semitones E/F and B/C in Burgundian practice, see Hughes (note 22): 395f.

[34] Quotations from R. McKitterick, *The Frankish Church and the Carolingian Reforms 789–895* (London, 1977), 181, 203.

There is a further analogy between notating chant and making organs in so far as they both 'fix' the notes and the relation between them. One does it symbolically on parchment, the other materially on a keyboard. Neither need have originated for the purpose of fixing notes but both became more specific as musical practice depended more and more on them, which it would in a relatively *unanimous* Europe. Hucbald pointed out that the note-names of instruments identify pitches more reliably than did neumatic notation, for which one needs one's memory or a teacher (Babb 1978: 36). But 'there was a great deal of chant to be sung: and if the Roman *schola cantorum* was content with rote memorization, the Frankish monasteries clearly were not'[35]. Both notation and instruments would be useful. In early instruction books such as the *Musica enchiriadis*, notation of one or other West Frankish sort could be used both to demonstrate vocal polyphony and to illustrate those sections chanted by the non-expert priest as distinct from the expert cantor; and it is not difficult to imagine the keyboard being used for comparable aural and visual purposes.

As the musical staff gradually emerged, the early keyboard had something very basic in common with it: in themselves, neither the lines-and-spaces of any form of staff nor the notes of a keyboard without raised flats or sharps gave any indication whether the space between two adjacent notes was a tone or a semitone. On both the staff and the keyboard, D–E and E–F look the same. But like the keyboard's note-names, the most common clefs of the eleventh century – f and c' – had the effect of indicating where the semitone lay. This was so whatever form they took (letters or coloured lines) and whatever their theoretical purpose.[36] It was unimportant that the organ had a fixed C while the voice did not, for any such connections between chant and organs as conjectured here do not imply that organs actually accompanied regular chant in any way.

---

[35]   R. L. Crocker, 'Hermann's major sixth', *JAMS* 25 (1972), 19–37, here 25.

[36]   E.g. to indicate the natural and soft hexachord (those based on C and F). For the *litterae vel colores* given by Guido, see the *Prologus in antiphonarium*, ed. J. Smits van Waesberghe, Divitiae musicae artis A.III (Buren, 1975). That the third or hard hexachord in the 'Guidonian system' is based on the note that eventually supplied the third main clef (G) must be a coincidence, since early *litterae* had also included f, c, D, a and others as well as g, and in any case not g' itself (Smits van Waesberghe, *De musico-paedagogico et theoretico Guidone Aretino eiusque vita et moribus* (Florence, 1953), 65–6).

5

When might organs have been heard?

To ask the question in this form, rather than 'What did early organs play?', is to recognize that the sound of organs need not at first have been for the sake of music any more than the sound of bells was. Organs were heard on exceptional occasions and, as far as can be seen, always for positive effect (jubilation and clamorous noise), not for negative (funeral dirges or commemorations of the Passion) or even for neutral (regular music alternating with psalm-tones). Since the stages by which the organ developed as a provider of music are no clearer than the stages by which it developed as a mechanical contrivance, the questions about both are comparable: what functions did it usually have, what did it first play, how did that gradually change to its later forms of music, and what is the nature of the sources on which any hypothesis can be based – why do they not say more, and why do they say anything at all?

While there are no certain answers to any of these questions, it is at least clear that any imagined scene in an important church in the late Middle Ages, in which organ alternated more or less discreetly with priest or choir at certain moments in mass or office, says nothing about what organs first played. But there is a theme common to most of the opportunities for organ-sound listed in the present chapter: the lay people (*plebes*) are involved. Organs contributed to various public occasions and even, in the case of the Anglo-Saxon instruments of the late tenth century, are likely to have been introduced for the purpose, part of the reformers' thrust to involve the people. For whatever reason their smaller organs were used, many a non-monastic cathedral, collegiate church and major parish church of later centuries had a large organ for similar purposes, and there need have been no great change of policy or use when by the later fifteenth century Utrecht Cathedral or Haarlem St Bavo was providing the people with regular concerts on the organ.

Before and into the Carolingian period

The Mediterranean climate must have given the organ in both pagan and Christian communities a natural usefulness out of doors. The occasion might be night-time street serenades in January as described in a fifth-century Syriac poem from Antioch (an early form of carnival? – Farmer 1931: 48–50): it seems the hydraulis (*hedhrula*) was louder than other instruments, and it must have been movable, set up in different positions, as it was later in out-of-doors events in Byzantium (see Chapter 9). Two other valuable references to organs come from this period. First, a sarcophagus from Provence shows an organ at the raising of Tabitha as if to show that pagan and/or Jewish funerals had such sounds, as indeed they did (Perrot 1965: plate X). Second, Sidonius Apollinaris reported of the Visigothic king Theodoric something he seems to have considered unusual for a ruler: Theodoric had no sound of *organa hydraulica* during meals (MGH AA 8.31).

In a similar way, Notker Balbulus still thought it reprehensible in his *Life of Charlemagne* for a certain bishop to have all kinds of instruments at his equally reprehensible banquets (*cum omnibus organis musicorum*: MGH SS 2.739). Weddings are frequently the occasion for late classical reference to *organa* (examples in Perrot 1965: 95f), and it could be that Christians' associating instruments with licentious festivity at weddings[1] prompted the story of St Cecilia. In Visigothic Spain, the eighth-century *Carmen de nubentibus* referred to instruments evidently celebrating weddings in the classical manner, but later hymns invoked the *sonora organa* for a more symbolic wedding: the marriage-to-faith of holy martyrs.[2] Such symbolizing could well have reflected actual practice at more mundane weddings. In the ninth century Hincmar of Reims was still warning of regrettable behaviour at weddings (PL 125.776), but it is always possible that these clerical authors admonished from the moral heights only of book knowledge.

Occasions on which *organa* might have been heard include processions for the Roman emperor, the music in the arenas, noises (rhythms?) at the acclamations of rulers and, at least in the imperial apogee of Constantinople, as splendid artefacts for show in the reception rooms of the palace.[3] Splendour of sight and sound was by no means the least important of the organ's attributes and was surely one of the reasons for its appearance in reformed monasteries in the Christian West in the years around 1000. Scenes in the Byzantine hippodrome could include the sound of organs as part of proclamations. The *trisagion* ('Holy God, Holy Mighty, Holy Immortal!') was acclaimed in some way to such sound, saluting both God and his regent: the organ must have played (screeched?) either during or in alternation with the people's *Holy!* Also, it would not be out of character for *organa* to accompany the acclamatory *Holy!* on other occasions in Constantinople, such as when the emperor was first acclaimed at his coronation (for example Constantine VII, 912–57 – in Schuberth 1968: 56ff). Another possible occasion was when the *Holy!* was used, from the fifth century onwards, as a popular addition (*troparion*) before psalms or eucharist chant (Baldovin 1987: 226). These moments in Byzantine ceremonies were allusions, however witting, to the salutations of Solomon and David; see below. Perhaps by

---

[1] Was it the banqueting and drinking (thus Rites of Bacchus) or the charivari-like processions for the bride (thus Rites of Venus) that recalled too vividly Roman and other pagan practice?

[2] H. Anglès, *Historia de la musica medieval en Navarra* (Pamplona, 1970), 40–1. In 1144, for one Spanish royal wedding, the chronicle still uses the phrase *canentium in organis* in describing the music (text in Llovera 1987: 297).

[3] Various texts in Schuberth 1968: 45ff. *Organa* in such sources indicates instruments, not yet (it seems) 'ensemble vocal and instrumental music'.

coincidence, an 'authoritative Byzantine tradition for the Trisagion melody' uses precisely the seven basic notes of the (organ) scale C D E F G A H[4] in a clear, straightforward manner.

By the tenth and eleventh centuries at Cluny, the *Sanctus, sanctus, sanctus* was there neither to serve the emperor nor was it a congregational acclamation as it had been for six or seven centuries earlier.[5] But clamour of some kind, perhaps with instruments, was just as appropriate for this moment of the mass on at least certain special occasions in the Cluny calendar, even if there is no documentation to say so. The Sanctus was a chant that 'shows at its most striking the liturgical and musical relationship between East and West.[6] Similarly, the Roman *adventus* or ceremonial arrival of emperor or consul in a city (for example Caracalla at Alexandria in 215 – Schuberth 1968: 18) took a form that became familiar to the rulers of both the Byzantine and Carolingian empires, not only for emperors and kings but for at least the more powerful bishops. As for arena scenes: the third-century mosaics at Zliten in Tripolitania show wind instruments including two organs sounding (or poised to sound) during combat between the gladiators (see Perrot 1965: plate II). Such arenas were presumably included in the phrase 'large theatres' (*magnis theatris*) about whose water-impelled sounds an earlier poem speaks.[7]

For all such occasions a question is: What did the organ play? Assuming that the graded pipe-lengths shown in early representations corresponded to a pitch-sequence sounded by the key-levers – whatever the scale and however the levers worked – then some kind of chords could have been produced as well as some kinds of melody. Any set of key-levers (a 'keyboard') could also produce discords, arbitrary sounds, mechanized screeches, and do so with any amount of rhythmic patterning. For at least Byzantine practice of the ninth and tenth centuries – where it cannot have been a question of organ-polyphony as such (Hammerstein 1986: 57) – there may be a clue about its general effect in the report that the singing of prayers during processional liturgies began as the organs stopped sounding, i.e. ceased their high, loud, sustained cry? Such a break in the sound was also the signal for the *trisagion* after the emperor had processed back to the palace from the Church of the Holy Apostles on Easter Monday (sources in Schuberth 1968: 68–71, 82). Stopping the organ-sound served as a signal, as did stopping the bell-sound at the end of the procession at Cluny or for the beginning of the office in the Winchester *Regularis concordia*. A similar point can be made about the procession described in twelfth-century Bury St Edmunds (see below). What needs to be envisaged here is not today's quiet organ-prelude receding before service begins in a church but a noisy outdoor sound, continuous, sustained at a volume-level or pitch-complex closer to that of bells, the silence after which then becomes solemn and expectant. Ironically,

---

[4] I.e. with this series of notes, as transcribed in NOHM 1990: 94–5.
[5] The Sanctus, perhaps coming from Constantinople, seems to have been known at Cluny before it formed part of the mass ordinary in Rome: E. Werner, *Die gesellschaftlichen Grundlagen der Klosterreform im 11 Jahrhundert* (Berlin, 1953), 49f.
[6] K. Levy, 'The Byzantine Sanctus and its modal tradition in East and West', *Annales musicologiques* 6 (1956–63), 7–67, here 7; on the Sanctus being originally congregational (as still in the East), see 14, 18f.
[7] The Aetna poem, attributed to Virgil: Perrot 1965: 379.

a key element in the way organs have always been used is the special nature of the silence when they stop playing.

Although the late classical or Byzantine references to organs do not concern churches, it is unlikely that crowd acclamations would have the noise of instruments accompanying them *only* if they were in the palace-grounds, not if they were in church, as they frequently were – for example when in 1040 the empress adopted the future Michael V in the crowded church of Blachernae, when Michael was crowned in church in 1041, or when Theodora was proclaimed empress in Hagia Sophia in 1042.[8] Furthermore, for a caesaro-papist ruler there was no absolute separation between secular and sacred location, even if one of his own palace churches had special liturgies with organ-sounds[9] in the way that the big city churches probably did not. Or perhaps written records of the emperor's movements are simply fuller than for those of the patriarch or bishops of the time, who may not have been far behind in using special ceremonial equipment but left no accounts of it. An organ as used in the palace liturgy would be something very desirable, one imagines, for a wealthy monastery to have. Some bishops were able to imitate imperial processions and *adventus*, as at Alexandria in 346 when the bishop made a Palm Sunday entrance (PG 35.1113–17), but how far instruments became regular equipment is unknown.[10] So it is too for public events in the churches of Constantinople, as when the emperor participated in Easter processions to H. Sergios-&-Bakchos (remaining in the gallery as the people pressed below) or was crowned before the people in a city church after the private ceremony in a palace church.[11] Perhaps a small organ was moved about.

So far, no historian has shown in detail why or how the Orthodox Church in general, and the Byzantine in particular, came to be without organs in the Middle Ages and, except where westernized, in all later periods.[12] Perhaps it was merely that imperial organ-sound in Constantinople never became ecclesiastical? If so this could imply in turn that when it did become so in the West, one reason was that similar bishops on feastdays were as emperors, *in statu regis*, attracting similar if less grand musical noises of one kind or another.

As a general rule, however, one can see that extravagant objects like organs must have been both acceptable and inacceptable to the Church. On one hand, Hagia Sophia in the sixth century had a fanciful clock and automatic fountains like an

---

[8] According to trans. E. R. A. Sewter, *Fourteen Byzantine Rulers: the Chronographia of Michael Psellus* (London, 1966), 102, 123, 144.

[9] During the Easter vigil, it seems (Schuberth 1968: 86–7). On caesaro-papist rulers, see a similar point concerning Charlemagne, p. 128.

[10] For example, no organs are recorded in the massive church-construction projects of the sixth century undertaken by evangelizing Byzantines then settling in North Africa (see Frend 1984: 834). Sources of the use of the church spaces in Constantinople itself are examined in T. F. Mathews, *The Early Churches of Constantinople: Architecture and Liturgy* (London, 1971).

[11] T. F. Mathews, 'Architecture et liturgie dans les premières églises de Constantinople', *Revue de l'Art* 24 (1974), 22–9. For Hagia Sophia, R. J. Mainstone, *Hagia Sophia: Architecture, Structure and Liturgy of Justinian's Great Church* (London, 1988).

[12] A common explanation is that 'the canons of that church have never permitted the use of musical instruments in its services' (NOHM 1990: 29), but nor in a formal sense did those of the Church in the West.

imperial palace: the clock in the south-west corner of the church, the fountains in one or other atrium (Mango 1986: 97, 101). On the other, a contemporary account of a Byzantine church in Gaza notes, with evident approval, that its splendid decoration was kept within bounds – the mosaic artist did not make his birds actually sing (as he could have done, perhaps, with one of the organ-automata known in that part of the world) since this would then have prevented one from 'hearing divine things' (Mango 1986: 62). As to written reports of organs, circulating widely and maybe arousing curiosity: they could also have remained largely non-actual, merely literary. An eighth-century wedding in Spain or a bishop's procession in eighth-century England might conceivably have involved *organa* of some kind, but it is over-simple to see references to them as meaning an actual organ was heard even though the occasions are appropriate for jubilant sound. In at least one Spanish reference the list of instruments appears to have been taken straight out of Isidore's *Etymologia* (III 1119–20): *tuba, fistula, lyra, tibia, vasa organica* (= 'wind-instrument implement'?), *cithara, cymbalum, nablum*. This suggests what the term *organa* brought with it when it was conventionally referred to,[13] and there is no reliable evidence here for organs. Nor need there be in the report of a Merovingian king (Clovis) being acclaimed with all the clamour of a traditional *adventus* and the authority of a psalm:

sub tegmine ecclesiae	under the roof of the church
taliter psallebatur:	the psalm was sung as follows:
'adprehende arma et scutum	'take hold of shield and buckler,
et exsurge in adiutorium mihi'.	and stand up for mine help' [Psalm 34.2].
Dicunt enim proceres regis:	For the king's nobles spoke:
'magna nobis organa hodie	'today the organa will sing to us
religiosaque canent auspicia'.	mighty and sacred omens'. (MGH rer. mer. 7.316)

Nevertheless, whether *organa* meant instruments, a kind of music or a psalter, this report is useful since the event was taking place in a church.

Processions

It cannot have been only in funeral processions, such as reported by Eusebius (*Eccl. Hist.* 9.8), that flute-playing was heard in Christian lands of the fourth or fifth century, although the aulos itself was traditional in this context.[14] Processions were a normal manifestation of communal religion, and the local *instrumentarium* must have played a familiar part in them, even perhaps in the airy basilicas themselves in which 'the whole congregation is like a huge procession, being led by the priest and moving east towards the sun'.[15] In Constantinople,

---

[13] See also Anglès (see note 2) and H. Anglès, *El còdex musical de Las Huelgas* 1 (Barcelona, 1931), 28. Such Spanish references are taken as evidence of actual organs in Schuberth 1968: 98, 101 and Llovera 1987 *passim*.

[14] G. A. Williamson, *Eusebius: The History of the Church from Christ to Constantine* (London, 1965), 367.

[15] J. A. Jungmann, *The Early Liturgy to the Time of Gregory the Great* (Notre Dame, IN, 1959), 138.

the average worshipper did not so much 'go to mass' as participate in the worship-life of the city as it unfolded . . . on the basis of the fifth-century evidence, as well as that of the tenth century, liturgical processions were part and parcel of this urban worship-life.   (Baldovin 1987: 211)

In at least the processions or events in which the Byzantine emperor was present, *organa* participated (see Chapter 9), and if nothing is known about organs or instruments participating in festive processions at Rome during the same period – as large pontifical groups walked from the church where they assembled (*collecta*) to another where they held a service (*statio*) – it may be only because there are no descriptive details comparable to those that were written down in documentation for the Byzantine court. In general, various kinds of exuberant music were sung for joyful processions, as the later commentator Johannes Bethel notes (*responsoria, antiphonae*: PL 202.19). Accordingly, it must be possible that *organa* sometimes contributed to the antiphons sung by the *schola* before the Kyrie in a Roman station-church of the day (see Baldovin 1987: 133ff) or even to the hymns sung *en route*: instruments if not necessarily organs. Although neither the instruments nor other musical details are prescribed in the processional *ordines* of St-Riquier purporting to have been made in about 800, the movement of monks and laity through the complex antechurch, nave, galleries and crypts, even on solemn occasions during Holy Week (Heitz 1963: 60f), could well have involved more sound than that which could ever have been produced by the regular singing of psalms and antiphons. Using *organa* for processions in or around the church, or for the arrival of a procession before mass, is more likely than for the mass or office itself. Similar things could be said of the 'hymns' sung on many such occasions.[16]

Though exceptional, like the imperial palace at Aachen, the Abbey of St-Riquier served as one model for large-scale ceremony.[17] The nature of its documentation (church annals, liturgical *ordines*, customaries, property records) is such that it does not – and was not likely to – refer to *organa* or any optional musical equipment; but the using of three carefully spaced choirs for the Good Friday vigil at St-Riquier suggests that its community knew about siting music interestingly (Heitz 1963: 79). So do similar choir-placements in the Winchester *Regularis concordia* (Symons 1953: 36), and if St-Riquier did not have an organ, which is hard to believe, Winchester certainly did. (The *Concordia's* silence about organs – a silence standard for such documents – is a reminder of what good luck it was that Wulfstan of Winchester should write his poem.) It is difficult to imagine the Easter Day procession in and around the huge cloister at St-Riquier without some form of continuous or clamorous sound for its great train of people, a thousand or more: bearers of holy water and censers, seven crosses, seven reliquaries, seven deacons, seven under-deacons, seven acolytes, seven

---

[16] But it is not clear how the 'church songs' (*ecclesiastica carmina*), referred to in the closing sentence of the *Musica enchiriadis* as something open to organum embellishment, prove that instrumental music was heard in the Carolingian liturgy, as is sometimes claimed (Schuberth 1968: 127–8).

[17] This would be so even if (as suggested in D. Parsons, 'The pre-romanesque church of St Riquier: the documentary evidence', *Journal of the British Archaeological Association* 133 (1977), 21–51) the layout of church and cloister in the well-known engraving on which recent writings have depended, were those not of the late eighth century but of the early eleventh. For the liturgical directions of *c.* 800 (?), see E. Bishop, *Liturgica historica* (Oxford, 1918), 314–32.

exorcists, seven porters, the rest of the monks seven by seven, the *schola* and finally seven further crosses, presumably all followed by the *plebes* who may or may not have appreciated that the sevens alluded to the seven stational crosses of Rome (cf. Baldovin 1987: 162). In a larger city such as Metz similar processions moved from church to church in imitation of the Roman stations: a Palm Sunday procession began outside the city walls as it did in Jerusalem itself, and moved to locations (shrines, altars) within the main churches. Psalms and antiphons were sung on the way. The sheer number of people gathered together in a major abbey-church on Sundays and feastdays is vividly described by Abbot Suger in remarks on his building projects at St-Denis (1146/7).[18]

For the Roman stations at which people collected and stood for a ceremony, special equipment such as altar vessels circulated among the station-churches, as is recorded already in the fifth century and as would be suitable when the stational service was 'the local church's main liturgical celebration' of the feastday.[19] For practices further north, the *ordines* of St-Amand (ninth century) speak of a procession formed at the starting-church, with candles and antiphons, an antiphon as more candles are given out, a procession to the next church whereupon the *schola cantorum* begins the litany and eventually the introit-antiphon for mass.[20] This was on such feastdays as the Purification. At St-Riquier, a complex church and vast cloister laid out for ambulatory liturgy,[21] two types of procession are discernible: regular morning and evening procession from the main church to the other cloister-churches and back (thus within the *monasterium*), and the bigger Sunday and feastday processions that moved further away but gradually turned towards the main church for mass with festal introit. The first corresponds to the daily office, the second to festival mass when the music was presumably more expansive.

Comparable ambulatory liturgy was suited to those cathedral complexes with several churches (see pp. 117ff), to imperial palaces with various buildings (Aachen, Ingelheim, Compiègne)[22] and to those complexes that included both abbey and royal palace (Westminster in the eleventh century).[23] *Statio* services were a 'normal way for Roman–Frankish liturgy to show itself' and are recorded for the (archi-)episcopal centres of Cologne, Trier, Mainz, Strasbourg, Chur, Augsburg, Paris, Chartres, Autun, Angers, Verona and Pavia.[24] By the time of the vast gothic cathedrals, processions were the occasion on which 'the ecclesiastical establishment would come forth from

---

[18] Panofsky 1977: 87 translates *in solemnibus diebus* as 'feastdays', but the phrase presumably included Sundays as well.

[19] On the vessels, attributed to e.g. Pope Hilary (461–8) in the *Liber Pontificalis*, see C. Mohrmann, 'Statio', *Vigiliae christianae* 7 (1963), 221–45. For a definition of stational liturgy: Baldovin 1987: 36–7.

[20] R. Hierzegger, 'Collecta und Statio: die römischen Stationsprozession im frühen Mittelalter', *Zeitschrift für katholische Theologie* 60 (1936), 511–45, here 523. A. A. Häussling, *Mönchskonvent und Eucharistenfeier*, Liturgiewissenschaftliche Quellen und Forschungen 58 (Münster, 1973), 191, estimates that a quarter of the days in the year saw *stationes* in Rome.

[21] Heitz 1963: *passim*; Häussling (see note 20): 57ff.

[22] The Carolingian palaces had personnel connections with major abbeys: ex-chaplains of the court moved on to St-Denis, St-Martin-de-Tours, St-Wandrille, St-Bertin (St-Omer), St-Riquier, Jumièges, Ferrières, Reichenau and St Gall: see J. Fleckenstein, *Die Hofkapelle der deutschen Könige* I (Stuttgart, 1959), 108.

[23] Reconstruction in R. Gem, 'L'Architecture préromane et romane en Angleterre: Problème d'origine et de chronologie', *BM* 142 (1984), 235–72.

[24] Listed in Häussling (see note 20): 199.

its walled enclave [*monasterium*] to celebrate in other parts of the church or of the town',[25] and as such could not easily have used any fixed organ for *alternatim* chant.

One can suppose that while outdoor processions used hand-held instruments, those indoors used any organ that might have been there as they did bells, i.e., for clamour. If *organa* were first used by the Church for processions, it is quite possible that by 1000 or so a major monastery would have both such a processional 'aid' as a movable organ and, fixed in a gallery or aisle, a larger instrument for crowd-scenes in the church itself. In such a way might have begun the tradition for two organs, one large and one small. In any case, in all such ambulatory liturgies the musical elements could easily develop, and the introit of the mass that followed the processing might especially encourage tropes.[26] Only in the late fourteenth century or so is the organ, as a fixed artefact like the clock, referred to in rubrics concerned with processional liturgy.[27] If in Rome itself stational processions were still prominent in the thirteenth century (Stäblein 1970: ★47), it is difficult to believe that organs had come to play no part in them.

Indirectly, reference to processions or to any moving around in the course of services gives some idea of how music or sound contributed. In the *Regularis concordia* antiphons are specified for some processions, as too sometimes is absolute silence (Symons 1953: 15, 19, 31). A visitor of 1200 to Hagia Sophia, Constantinople, speaks of lauds beginning in the narthex, moving to the centre of the church, then to the quire where, on Sundays and feastdays, the singers proclaim the patriarch and continue to sing until mass (Strunk 1977: 112). At St Gall in *c.* 911, the three days of Christmas were marked by jubilant processions and a troped introit to the mass.[28] Palm Sunday remained particularly appropriate for processions, and the sumptuous processing for it at Cluny was prepared for at the Saturday vespers by the clamour of all the bells ringing. Then bells rang while the main procession was out and until it returned to the antechurch, to the west of which was an atrium for the waiting people;[29] keeping back the *plebes* in the atrium at Cluny (see p. 112) suggests that there may usually have been a chaotic throng of people on such occasions. Did they follow the *fratres* into church or was it in the Cluniac style to exclude them? For vespers and other processions at Beauvais, as recorded three hundred or more years later, sections of the *responsorium* have the rubric *cum organo*,[30] presumably meaning organum or an ornate vocal setting such as would long have been normal on these occasions, improvised or composed, with instruments or not.

---

[25] M. Fassler, 'The Feast of Fools and *Danielis ludus*: popular tradition in a medieval cathedral play, in *Plainsong in the Age of Polyphony*, ed. T. F. Kelly, Cambridge Studies in Performance Practice 2 (Cambridge, 1992), 65–99.

[26] This would conform with one thirteenth-century definition of trope, as understood in practice: a kind of versicle sung on important feasts immediately before the introit, as if a prelude (R. L. Crocker, 'The troping hypothesis', *MQ* 52 (1966), 183–203, here 184). Introit tropes were still common practice on the major feasts in Notre-Dame, Paris, during the twelfth century (Wright 1989: 91).

[27] 'Near the organ' or 'near the clock' at St Matthias, Trier: ed. P. Becker, *Corpus Consuetudines Monasticarum* 5 (Siegburg, 1968), 60–1. See also reference below to St Albans in 1235.

[28] W. Arlt, *Ein Festoffizium des Mittelalters aus Beauvais in seiner liturgischen und musikalischen Bedeutung* (Cologne, 1970), 43–4.

[29] Ed. P. B. Albers, *Consuetudines monasticae* 5 vols (Stuttgart/Vienna, 1900–12), 1.43–4, 137.

[30] In Arlt (see note 28): 230–3.

The only fully rubricated processional of the Middle Ages,[31] originating in Salisbury but usable in other secular English cathedrals, may be very exact as to topography, personnel and the sequence of events, but details of the music seem to have been left to the cantor and his control of local conditions. In the case of thirteenth-century processions in Notre-Dame, Paris, it is known that processional responses were sung in organum at the station 'before the cross' or rood above the pulpitum (screen at west end of quire) 'on at least a dozen major feasts of the year' (Wright 1989: 267). If either at this point or when organum was ordinarily sung at the lectern in the centre of the choir,[32] an organ had participated, it must have been placed near the choir and designed for such use. Alternatively, if Notre-Dame had an organ but none participated in organum (see Chapter 20), it would imply that – large, inflexible and very public? – it was placed elsewhere in the church. The same would go for organs in any major non-monastic cathedral of the twelfth and thirteenth centuries.

Special music and special use of instruments are alike in this, that only latterly are they ever mentioned, if at all, and then with too little detail for one to be sure quite what is being spoken of. But in the graphic report of the abbot-elect's reception at Bury St Edmund's in 1182 (RBMAS 96.1.230–1), there is a particularly evocative detail. At one point, the abbot's procession halts at the high altar (*ad magnum altare*) and the organ and bells are silenced as the prior begins prayers: perhaps they are again located close together, either near the crossing and the door from the cloister (south) or on the contrary in the massive west complex. But either way, these *organa et campanae* had not been mentioned previously, nor are they later when the *Te Deum* is sung, suggesting again how much by chance it is that one knows anything about organs before the fourteenth century. Particularly evocative here is the idea of silence, which must have been as dramatic as the clamour was otherwise continuous. Presumably the clamour stopped when the choir sang the responsories on the abbot's entry into the church and re-started at, before and even during – the *Te Deum*.

Church dedications

In cathedrals bishops were consecrated, no doubt much more often with '*organa*, bells and who knows what token of gladness' than is documented on one occasion (the *Life of St Bruno* – see pp. 206f). In the sources, dedications of buildings or altars or altar-vessels appear as occasions on which there was a special appreciation of church arts,[33] and it is not surprising that this sense of 'appreciation' and occasion would lead to reports of music of various kinds. Hence the *organa* in ninth- and tenth-century Catalonia (see Chapter 13) or the musical terms in a poem attributed to St Aldhelm (†709) concerning the dedication of an Anglo-Saxon church and its altar to the Virgin: *modulemur carmina, dulcibus accentibus, antiphonae, psalmorum*

[31] So described in T. Bailey, *The Processions of Sarum and the Western Church* (Toronto, 1971).
[32] R. A. Baltzer, 'The geography of the liturgy of Notre-Dame, Paris', in Kelly (see note 25): 45–64.
[33] I. Wood, 'The audience of architecture in post-Roman Gaul', in Butler & Morris 1988: 74–9, concerning sixth-century Lyons, Vienne, St-Maurice and elsewhere.

concrepat, hymnistae, clamoso carmine, voce tonantem, cantibus, psalterium, lyra (PL 89.289f). Virtually all of these words appear in other quotations elsewhere in the present book, reminding one of the kind of texts used for sequence and of their pedigree in the poetry of late antiquity (see Chapter 3). Although lyres and psalteries are most unlikely to have been played at this particular dedication, the words bring with them a justification for using any instruments the abbey may have possessed. The dedication of one tenth-century rebuild at Winchester certainly included the sound of instruments, perhaps organ amongst them, and in both the Winchester and Limoges repertories of tropes, there are pieces for the dedication of churches. These events also included mass,[34] which by nature would be jubilant on such occasions. Presumably even during the shorter processions in such services as baptism, or while the *trisagion* is sung before the lessons in the East, some music could have filled the gap while the priests moved, as it did and does for the gradual of the mass.[35]

In full-dress dedication rites, the processions and a great deal of movement mark the sequence of events: a threefold circuit of the building outside, tracing of a cross upon the entire length and breadth of the pavement of the church inside (marked with Greek and Latin alphabets), a threefold circuit within the building, blessing of the altar (after the bishop has walked round it seven times), the whole followed by mass. At various moments antiphons, responsories, hymns and liturgy were sung, complete with several alleluias.[36] At the grand papal dedication at Cava in 1092 the *organa ac tibia* are mentioned immediately after the pope is reported as 'delineating the walls' (*delinivit parietes*) and completing the dedication, as if they were played in church as part of the rite (see p. 212). The report makes it clear that the ceremony is distinct from both eucharist and mattins, i.e. both mass and office (*Acta SS* 7.333-4). No doubt local usage varied in detail, but the processions and jubilation gave opportunity for instruments, especially (one imagines) when the company processed outside. This must have been the case at major dedicatory events like that for the rebuilt St-Denis in 775 when Charlemagne was present, or later when the annual Feast of the Dedication marked another consecration. But indoors too, it is difficult to imagine that the 1,250 lamps used at St-Denis on feastdays, according to a description of 799,[38] were not matched by equally brilliant and artificial music .

One of the most evocative of all church-dedications is that described for Ramsey Abbey on 8 November 991 by the author of the *Vita S Oswaldi* (written *c.* 995/1005):

---

[34] E.g. Gallican rites in G. G. Willis, *Further Essays in Early Roman Liturgy* (London, 1968), 159ff; Spanish rites in M. S. Gros, 'El Ordo romano-hispánico de Narbona para la consegración de iglesias', *Hispania sacra* 19 (1966), 321–401, e.g. 394; for St-Denis, see Suger's *De consecratione* in Panofsky 1977: 118f.

[35] Baptism in e.g. T. C. Akeley, *Christian Initiation in Spain c. 300–1100* (London, 1967), 150; *trisagion* in e.g. D. Conomos, 'Communion chants in Magna Graeca and Byzantium', *JAMS* 33 (1980), 241–63.

[36] L. Bowen, 'The topology of medieval dedication rites', *Speculum* 16 (1941), 469–79. The most useful source for the early period (summarized above) is from the tenth century: *The Pontifical of Egbert, Archbishop of York*, ed. W. Greenwell, Surtees Society 27 (1853), 26–51.

[37] A. Walters, 'The reconstruction of the abbey church at St-Denis (1231–81): the interplay of music and ceremony with architecture and politics', *EMH* 5 (1985), 187–238, here 190, 193.

[38] B. Bischoff, 'Eine Beschreibung der Basilika von Saint-Denis aus dem Jahre 799', *KC* 34 (1981), 97–103.

introoeuntibus praesulibus et	the bishops, nobles, abbots and
ducibus, abbatibus et militibus,	knights having entered,
populus est aggregatus immensus	a large crowd of people congregated
. . .	. . .
Explicito sollemni jubilo	When the solemn, jubilant responsory
responsorio,	was completed.
laus laudibus hymnisque	praise upon praise and hymn upon
hymnus allectus est.	hymn were sung in sequence [?].
Namque magister organorum	Whereupon the master of the *organa*
cum agmine ascendit populorum in	ascended with the crowd of people to
altis sedibus, quo	the upper floor where with
tonitruali sonitu excitavit	thundering sound he stirred up
mentes fidelium laudare	the souls of the faithful to praise
nomen Domini.	the name of the Lord.
Haec audiens gratulans chorus	The joyful choir, hearing this
auribus benignis, Christo,	with kindly ears, for Christ,
sanctorum qui est decus Angelorum	who is the glory of the holy angels,
studuerunt melos psallere,	applied themselves to psalmody,
dulces alternatim concrepando	singing lustily the sweet praises
laudes. Cum dextera	in alternation. When the right-hand
pars sonum melodum personaret	part [of the choir] sang out the
inclytis vocibus,	melody with glorious voices,
tum sinister jubilando	then the left jubilantly
organicis desudabat	exerted themselves in *organic*
laudibus.	praises. (RBMAS 71 1.464–5)

(For the organ at Ramsey, see Chapter 12, and for an interpretation of the upper floor location, see Chapter 8.) If the description means that there was antiphonal music of the later familiar kind between organ and chorus, or that a precentor with three 'fellow cantors' and the organ made the 'five voices' (*quinis vocibus*) referred to a little later,[39] then any organ at Ramsey would have had to be thoroughly modern and able to play agile melody. Perhaps it was and could, but both *organorum* and *organicis* would then have to denote 'the organ', which would be unusual in such reports despite Ramsey's being known to have had such an instrument (see p. 199). If on the other hand *organorum* and *organicis* refer to vocal organum or ensemble music that contrasted with the psalms, then the description concerns the variety of vocal 'scoring' implied by the term *organum* in non-technical sources and is not a description of early *alternatim* music. Even if there were an organ there, if it were located in an upper gallery (see p. 126) and if it was this that produced the thunderous sound (see the Winchester poem line 163 for a similar verbal formula), what followed the organ's noise could have been vocal ensemble music only.

The account is nevertheless of great interest for the impression it gives of a special occasion. It is not clear why the people should climb up to the gallery with the organist, why they should want to be as near the organ as possible, and whether

---

[39] Antiphonal music claimed in Holschneider 1968: 136–7; interpretation of the 'five voices' in M. Berry, 'What the Saxon monks sang: music in Winchester in the late tenth century', in Yorke 1988: 149–60, here 159.

they processed separately from the dignitaries who were presumably traversing the whole building below for the rites of dedication. And yet there is an evocative picture here: as the monks and nobles enter a new church for an exceptional event of thanksgiving, a large crowd gathers, the monks begin to sing the office of vespers, a procession takes the crowds to a gallery where they are then incited by the organ, and various *organal* music follows. Incense is not mentioned, but a sense of clamour, music, fragrance and light would be typical of such occasions, even in the late autumn fens of Saxon England.[40]

Acclamations

Formal acclamation of praise sung in the presence of the Frankish king, the so-called *laudes regiae*, is chronicled before Charlemagne's time, and marked days on which the king wore the crown.[41] Its roots in early Christian litanies such as the fourth-century Sanctus gave it special significance at the period when Pippin and his son (who was received with *laudes* at Rome in 774) were establishing liturgical practice as authorized in Rome, or claiming to.[42] The melody of certain Frankish *laudes* centres on the same E G A as the *Te Deum* and the (congregational) Sanctus; being repetitive, it would be suitable for the organ to play too (see Ex. 5.2). By the eleventh century, a major feastday in a major cathedral might well have two such moments, the *laudes regiae* before the epistle (though neither king nor duke need be there)[43] and acclamations for the bishop before the dismissal 'Ite missa est'.

Organum either as 'ensemble music' or as 'a musical instrument' does not appear in sources of the *laudes*, which however do sometimes refer to them being heard in church, as at Aachen in 812 (*in ecclesia* according to Einhard – MGH SS 1.199), probably in imitation of Charlemagne's reception at St Peter's in 800. In St Peter's, *laudes* were sung or shouted at the east end of the basilica. It is striking that the Byzantine emperor should have sent Pippin an organ so soon after the king was anointed by the pope in St-Denis in 754 (see Chapter 9), for coronations of all kinds traditionally included *laudes*. When the people acclaimed the newly crowned *basileos* himself in Hagia Sophia, they repeated the singers' various chants such as Gloria[44] three times, and one imagines these moments to have been rather rowdy, the kind of clamour in which a siren-organ could join. It is difficult to believe that when nearly two centuries

40 Was *decus angelorum* a reminder, on the occasion of a new dedication, of St Gregory's famous pun as reported by Bede (*anglorum/angelorum*)?
41 So called in E. H. Kantorowicz, *Laudes regiae*, University of California Publications in History 33 (Berkeley, 2/1958). Texts in B. Opfermann, *Die liturgischen Herrscherakklamationen im sacrum Imperium des Mittelalters* (Weimar, 1953).
42 Frankish formulation in G. Knopp, 'Sanctorum nomina seriatim: die Anfänge der Allerheiligenlitanei und ihre Verbindung mit den "Laudes regiae"', *Römische Quartalschrift für christliche Altertumskunde und Kirchengeschichte* 65 (1970), 185–231, esp. 223–6.
43 Kantorowicz (see note 41): 80, 87f. Probably from the time of its gothic quire, Notre-Dame, Paris, had royal lauds for its bishop at Easter Day mass, sung before the epistle (Wright 1989: 199).
44 St Peter's in Opfermann (see note 41): 21. Hagia Sophia in E. Wellesz, *A History of Byzantine Music and Hymnography* (Oxford, 2/1961), 109. On the Sanctus: G. Nickl, *Der Anteil des Volkes an der Messliturgie im Frankenreiche von Chlodwig bis auf Karl den Großen* (Innsbruck, 1930), 19–27.

later Otto the Great was elected, enthroned and acclaimed in the basilica at Aachen, the ceremonies were without the sounds of *organa*, though none is mentioned in Widukind's report of *c.* 936 (MGH SS 3.437).[45]

Normally in the monastery, *laudes* would have had broader meanings. Thus in the early twelfth century, Honorius of Autun remarks, apropos the Sanctus, on practice in the Temple:

Hoc sacrificium concentus	at the *sacrifice* David and Solomon's
angelorum David et Salomon	songs of angels [Holy, holy, holy!]
sunt imitati, qui instituerunt	were imitated, and they
hymnos in sacrificio Domini,	established hymns in the Lord's sacrifice,
organis, et aliis musicis	to be sounded aloud by organs [?] and other
instrumentis concrepari, et	musical instruments, and
a populo laudes conclamari.	praises to be shouted out by the people.
Unde solemus adhuc	Whence we are still accustomed
in officio sacrificii organis	to sound aloud from organs in the office
concrepare, clerus cantare,	of the mass, the clergy to sing,
populus conclamare.	the people to call out together. (PL 172.556)

Although the reference is not specific enough to show the organ as having won a regular place in the liturgy – the trio of instruments, voices and people follows a traditional formula – it surely does not argue against it. From such readings of Old Testament reports (especially Chronicles) the liturgical writer would understand the organ to be there to 'add its harmony' at the congregation's acclamation in the mass, i.e. the Sanctus. Such an interpretation is found in one particularly influential treatise on church practice and symbolism, Durandus's *Rationale* of *c.* 1286–9, where amongst church ornaments or furnishings, organs are mentioned in the chapter dealing with the Sanctus.[46] It is unclear whether Durandus meant that the Sanctus in major churches customarily included organ-sound or only that Solomon's and David's rites did – perhaps both, but he depends a great deal on earlier writers.

One can assume that in certain major churches of *c.* 1000 organs were heard at some point in the mass and that writers, drawing on older writings rather than contemporary practice, would find authority for them in scripture. Occasions of praise are clearly occasions for special effects, and both Gloria and Sanctus are forms of acclamation. Probably the Sanctus was more purely congregational before the tenth century, thus a form of jubilation kept for the congregation to contribute during a monastic mass on feastdays. (Evidence that seems to show the Sanctus being sung by congregations in the eighth century but by choirs in the ninth[47] may not distinguish between regular monastic mass and the more public feastdays: perhaps both ways of performing it were heard on different occasions or at two points in the mass.) When various twelfth-century reports mention organ at mass, there is a likelihood that it was sometimes heard at the Sanctus closing the first part of the

---

[45] The priest's *lituus* as reported by Widukind was presumably not a trumpet but a bishop's crook.

[46] *Rationale divinorum officiorum* 4.34: cf. G. D., *The Symbolism of Churches and Church Ornaments* (Leeds, 1843; repr. New York, 1973), 97 and G. H. Buijssen, *Durandus' Rationale in spätmittelhochdeutscher Übersetzung: das vierte Buch* (Assen, 1966).

[47] As suggested in Levy (see note 6): 198.

Eucharistic prayer chanted by the celebrant. Is the reference in an ordinal of 1337 to organ-playing after the Sanctus at mass in Exeter Cathedral merely a late expression of an old custom known widely in the larger monasteries? The directive apparently concerns any occasion, probably by implication a feastday:[48]

Ex licencia, si placet	By special leave, if the senior
senioribus, loco	brethren please, in the place of
Benedicamus ad Vesperas	*Benedicamus* at vespers
et ad Matutinas, et ad Missam	and mattins, and at the mass
post Sanctus, poterunt	after the *Sanctus*, they [the choir?] will be
organizare cum	able to perform ensemble music [?] with
vocibus vel organis	voices or organa

The last five words serve to link a fourteenth-century ordinal with much older usage, and one can only guess whether *organa* is used in an old or new sense, thus meaning either 'vocal organum' or 'organs'. Either way, whenever it was that organs in the West began to sound at the Sanctus the authority for it was ultimately the Old Testament, either directly (one could read there that Solomon and David had something of the kind) or indirectly (bishops preserved the timeless tradition for acclamations).

The likelihood that *laudes* were known in Carolingian buildings with westworks of various types (see Heitz 1963: 154f) suggests a connection between the two: such moments could be celebrated indoors in those parts of Europe where the open Mediterranean atrium would have been less usable throughout the year. Equally, however, the acclamation for Queen Matilda at Winchester in 1068 could have imitated Roman custom, with the 'performers' near the eastern apse, and the organ (fairly) close by. In any case, noise rather than sweet music gave character to such occasions. The noise of bells in such phrases as *clangore signorum* or *signorum cum strepitu* is spoken of by one tenth-century writer in connection with the priests' *laudes* (Ratherius in 951 – PL 136.360, 378): perhaps bells and organs were understood as sounding together at such moments, centuries before documents couple them.[49] It is certainly the case that references to *organa* frequently evoke the great noise they make – or were reputed to make – even in situations far removed from acclamations or the Sanctus. *The Voyage of St Brendan*,[50] which probably dates from the tenth century and was translated into ten early vernacular languages, tells at one point of a great bird

strepitum faciens sicut	making a great noise like
sonitum organi magni	the sound of a large *organum*

and two versions of the *Life of St Wilfrid*[51] from much the same period refer to the saint's gospel-preaching:

[48] Ed. J. N. Dalton, *Ordinale Exon*, Henry Bradshaw Society 37 (London, 1909) 1.1920.
[49] For Winchester, see Opfermann, (note 41): 157. For a German reference of 1377 see G. Rietschel, *Die Aufgabe der Orgel im Gottesdienst bis in das 18. Jahrhundert* (Leipzig, 1893), 7.
[50] C. Selmer, *Navigatio Sancti Brendani from Early Latin Manuscripts* (Notre Dame, IN, 1959), 43.
[51] Campbell 1950: 13. A further tenth-century version reads *gimnasia* for *ydraulia*. However, the prose version of Wilfrid's *Life* also refers to organ (vocal organ? wind-organ?) at this point: Wilfrid preaches with 'the organ of the spirit singing through him' (*organo spiritali de se canente*: B. Colgrave, *The Life of Bishop Wilfrid by Eddius Stephanus* (Cambridge, 1927), 16).

latae penetrans ydraulia   sounding like hydraules across
Romae.   broad Rome.

Brendan's bird might have been any kind of screeching instrument, but *ydraulia* must mean organ. Even if such references come only from book-knowledge, clearly for some purposes some authors associated *organa* with loud sounds rather than with 'sweet song'.

Mass and office

The comprehensive treatise of Walahfrid Strabo, *De ecclesiasticarum rerum exordiis et incrementis* (†849 – MGH Cap. 2.474–576), presumably originated in an East Frankish house that may well have known organ-making: Reichenau or Fulda. And yet despite his references to bells, to the singing of monastic hours, to hymns and even to wooden *tabulae* beaten in Holy Week (the last copied from a report by Amalar of Metz? – see below, p. 98, and despite his knowledge of practices in imperial Aachen, Walahfrid says nothing here about organs. Nor is there anything in Charlemagne's *Admonitio generalis* of 789 (MGH Cap. 1.53–62) which directs the people to collect on Sundays and feastdays for sermon at mass. Nor in Amalar who, in the *De ecclesiasticis officiis* of *c.* 821/35, notes that 'our singers' hold no instruments but are themselves instruments (PL 105.1106), a standard reference to Old Testament practices compared to Christian. Amalar is marking the separation between those performing the liturgy (*cantores*) and those standing for its instruction (the *plebes*), being aware perhaps that it was in the Sanctus that Charlemagne's capitulary directed priest and people to join together (MGH Cap. 1.59). In pointing out what lesson it is that musical instruments can teach about faith – that certain kinds of diversity can produce concordance, as between different saints of like mind (see p. 36) – Amalar is neither rejecting them nor referring to totally unknown objects. On the contrary, using objects as symbols implies that they are familiar enough for the reader to see the point.

Similar remarks could be made about many a psalm-commentary. When Gerhoch of Reichersberg calls the whole church the *organum Dei*, he is expressing the twelfth-century view of the Augustinians, who of all people knew their patron saint's description of the organ (see p. 297). When Gerhoch distinguishes between types of instrument, as in the remark

instrumentis hujus artis   with instruments of this kind
ut organis, cymbalis et   such as organs, small bells and
campanis deo servimus   large bells [?], we serve God   (PL 194.500)

he may be using old formulas but his words could still relate to actual organs. For organs to play music as distinct from noise, changes must have come about since Roman times, and some psalm-commentaries, however derivative in general or based on St Augustine in particular, were made over the period in which such change came about. Although 'virtually all medieval references to instruments can be classified within well-defined literary and iconographical categories',[52] they may still reflect a literate monk's idea of real description. How else is he likely to allude to actual practice? He does not write books on the origin and use of instruments, and treatises that are organological (see Chapters 15 and 16) say nothing, even obliquely, about their use.

Although there is no evidence of an organ participating in the late twelfth-century organum sung in Notre-Dame, Paris, on some forty or more days a year, it is suggestive that such music was concentrated 'at the procession before Mass, at the solemn Mass itself, and at Vespers' (Wright 1989: 267, 75), since such occasions were very likely those on which organs were played, when they were. It would also be because it was becoming used in the regular mass that the organ needed to be gradually more 'flexible' (with tone-changes, adequate compass etc.) as time passed. For regular mass, though not for public entertainments on the feastdays of old, the organ could be quite small: the 'organ for the mass' as described by Henri Arnaut de Zwolle in the mid-fifteenth century is the smaller of two particular instruments (*organum misse Domini* – Le Cerf 1932: 30). Before 1450 organs cannot have participated in services so very often, nor were quire-screen organs 'relatively large',[53] except in relation to portatives. In general, however, the steps by which the organ came to be an instrument for the regular mass as distinct from the big public masses are very unclear. Up to the twelfth century in some cases, monasteries were being protected against such 'public masses' (*missas publicas*) said by the bishop, for it was not fit for laymen to penetrate the convent.[54] Any such tendency to divide responsibility for the church's services would mean that large organs (if there were such) remained near points of public access, while the conventual office would be left without organs and only gradually would the conventual choir have as a matter of course its own quire organ.

Tropes

Ekkehard of St Gall reported of the monk Tuotilo (see p. 317) that he not only dedicated tropes to Charles the Fat (883–7) but

per psalterium seu per rothtam,	by means of psaltery or rote,
qua potentior ipse erat,	in which he was particularly gifted,
neumata inventa dulciora sunt . . .	yet sweeter melodies were found . . .
in omnium genere fidium et	[he was] in all kinds of stringed and
fistularum prae omnibus.	wind-instruments pre-eminent.

(MGH SS 2.101, 94)

---

[52] J. W. McKinnon, 'Musical instruments in medieval psalm commentaries and psalters', *JAMS* 21 (1968), 3–20, here 3, 18.

[53] As suggested by F. L. Harrison, 'Tradition and innovation in instrumental usage 1100–1450', in LaRue 1966: 319–35, here 321.

[54] Papal Bull of 1146 for Peterborough: ed. W. T. Mellows, *The Chronicle of Hugh Candidus, a Monk of Peterborough* (Oxford, 1949), 114.

This makes some kind of connection between composed melodies and the playing of instruments: not that instruments played these melodies in any liturgy but that in general terms instruments aid composition – or that in this instance, a musician very skilled in one was very skilled in the other. The importance of tropes for the history of the organ is not that either was necessarily made for the other but that they both represent creative music-making, and do so particularly for the feastdays of the year.[55]

An introductory trope before the full choir's introit on a feastday in a major late ninth-century monastic church in northern Francia or Germania could appropriately have been prefaced itself with some organ-sound, either of a clamorous kind not so different from simultaneously jangled bells, or of a more melodic kind anticipating the trope melody in some way. That introit tropes make particular use of the notes or note-patterns associated with the modes – classic melodies, as it were – would make such anticipation likely. If this is at all a plausible picture, one could speculate further on the chronology. Thus at first, an organ contributed some clamour, especially if it were in a public part of the church where the people milled; or it could repeat a phrase of melody in one of the tropes or *prosulae*, like an intermittent ostinato; then it began to anticipate the trope-melody more fully; then, especially if placed near the quire, it contributed to the introit (or Sanctus or eventually other movements including canticles in the office) in the form of 'replacing' a section of it. In this way a full *alternatim* practice would emerge, though not simultaneously in the same way all across Europe. This sequence of events is conjectural and telescopes different practices over several centuries, but it is one way to explain later medieval conventions that are otherwise puzzling. (See also below on *alternatim* in the *Te Deum*.)

While the many references to instruments in trope verses and sequences from Winchester or Limoges are not evidence that instruments were used in their performance[56] – one could reason that they are referred to in the texts because they are not used – a certain widening of musical expectation could result from them. Although the terms in Limoges texts belong to a traditional poesy – *cantica, ypodorica, paraphonista, jubila, carmina, organa, agmina, enarmonica, yperlidica, mela symphonia, tuba sonora, diatesseron, organicis, instrumentis, hydraulica mela* – and no more imply practices in the mass than do their references to dancing, nevertheless these are musical terms beyond the norms of everyday mass or office. Had organs and organ-music never developed, one would not imagine such terms to have played any particularly practical part; but since they did, the terms can be seen to represent various musical effects of great interest to composers and those who played instruments.

Whatever the purposes of the note-letters in the Winchester *prosae*, of the manuscript itself (not a performance copy?) and of the cathedral's organ (located near enough to the specialist singers at the central altar?), it is so that the letters could be read as cues for instruments in heterophonic performance: see Chapter 3. Perhaps the Winchester *prosae* were transmitting certain details from lost sources originating

---

[55] Ekkehard's words have been interpreted as referring to a particular moment before or during mass, perhaps an offertory trope (Schuberth 1968: 114), but this is not made explicit.
[56] Holschneider 1975; J. Chailley, *L'Ecole musicale de Saint Martial de Limoges* (Paris, 1960), 308ff.

in Corbie or Fleury,[57] abbeys which may or may not have had an organ in the 980s. In general, close and practical connections between music and instruments are not easily proved, and it is difficult to sustain any such idea as that the (apparent) bottom notes C and F of the (very much later) short-octave compass show the organ to have originated as a drone-instrument in such music as the alleluia. On the other hand, since it is certainly plausible that organa including organs participated in teaching and that certain sequence-texts probably refer to this, then some sequences could be 'accompanied' by instruments, creating a vocal-instrumental organum. This argument could be pressed further and a case made for the well-known Engelberg sequence-melody *Audi chorum organicum* (see p. 221), for example, being played 'not only on the medieval organ but even being doubled at the octave in accordance with the rules of vocal organum'.[58] The compass given by Hucbald, if taken literally as evidence for actual organs (see pp. 46f) would make this possible, but it is a conjecture difficult to justify except by generalities – such as that references in Aurelian of Réôme (c. 840/9) and elsewhere possibly assume that organs are one of the instruments associated somehow with organum. Then the question arises whether an author was doing more than compiling snippets of information and interspersing them with his understanding of word-derivation (organum must imply *organa*) in order specifically to describe some non-liturgical practices. Yet the conjecture is reasonable if it is understood that organs might so participate only occasionally, in full-dress performance or for special effect.

No musical sources, written references or organological details as known, quite enable one to connect organs with alleluias or Gloria-tropes in such a direct way. Despite this, Alleluias in public mass on feastdays – even the ornate chants of the *Benedicamus domino* in the monastic office, performed at certain places in the quire[59] – do provide a context for organ-sound. If the early repertory of sequences owed 'its genesis largely to artistic impulse' and marked a 'creative leap' in western church practice over the years 830–50,[60] there could well have been new interest in jubilant sound (organs, bells). If scribes and cantors did feel free to 'change, recast, expand or entirely recompose the musical and literary texts' of the standard chant,[61] it is unlikely that such musical invention stopped with vocal music.

For clear reference to organs playing 'at the sequence' (*ad prosam* – before, during?) in the thirteenth century, see p. 225.

---

[57] Fleury in E. Jammers, *Das Alleluia in der gregorianischen Messe*, Liturgiewissenschaftliche Quellen und Forschungen 55 (Münster, 1973), 148f. Corbie in D. Hiley, 'Observations on the Derivation of two early repertories of polyphony', in Corsi 1989: 377–91, here 385.

[58] The idea on C/F compass proposed by Jammers 1962 (see p. 44), that on the Engelberg conductus in Huglo 1990.

[59] A. W. Robertson, 'Benedicamus domino: the written tradition', *JAMS* 41 (1988), 1–62.

[60] R. L. Crocker, *The Early Medieval Sequence* (Berkeley, 1977), 408, 401; also, 'Some ninth-century sequences', *JAMS* 22 (1963), 367–402.

[61] A. E. Planchart, 'The transmission of medieval chant', in *Music in Medieval and Early Modern Europe*, ed. I. Fenlon (Cambridge, 1981), 347–63, here 348.

'Liturgical plays'

In so far as the Easter text *Quem quaeritis* and other brief dialogue-tropes[62] were preceded by liturgical processions and closed with *Te Deum* or joyful clamour of some kind (bells, instruments), such plays provided opportunity for organs. Whether the sepulchre dialogue was enacted as a celebration text belonging to mattins or sung as a trope to the mass introit, as in the Prüm Troper of *c.* 995,[63] there could well have been some sort of clamour. The more that organs and bells participated, the stronger the case for seeing the dialogue as not a trope but an independent ceremony separate from the Easter mass.[64] Whichever is the case, directions associated with Farfa, Fleury and Cluny show what happens as the little dialogue closes:[65]

demum, pulsantibus pariter	and then, as all the bells
omnibus signis de turri,	are rung at the same time from the tower,
in choro inchoetur	in the quire the mass
missa sollempniter.	is to begin in solemn manner.

Only much later are the (more developed) plays recorded as having made use of instruments, when they often served programmatic purposes.[66]

Regular Palm Sunday processions typify the ninth and tenth centuries' tendency towards a liturgy more expressive and more understandable by lay people,[67] who then become passive. Perhaps the papal procession for the Vigil of the Feast of the Assumption, at which the *Te Deum* was sung, allowed the Roman congregation to participate more intimately. The *Visitatio sepulchri* (*Quem quaeritis*) of *c.* 930, performed as an annex to Easter mattins at Winchester and Reichenau, resembled the introit-trope for Christmas Day in the St Gall troper,[68] something to mark and make more expansive a special moment in the church year. Such an enactment of the scene at the sepulchre on Easter morning was something 'to instruct the ignorance of this people', as a copy of the *Pontificale romano-germanicum* puts it (*ad instruendam huius plebis ignorantiam*).[69] It did so with very little in the way of stage directions, which would have limited the usefulness of a general description, as would the reference to an organ in other kinds of service-directive. The kind of book in which the dialogue appears, a troper, is seldom rich in rubrics: the most that would be said is that the dialogue is played near the (or an) altar. When these plays were first

---

[62] An 'introductory polystich [whose] melody is in the idealized antiphon style used for Introit tropes': R. Crocker, NOHM 1990: 269.

[63] R. Jonsson, 'The liturgical function of the tropes', in *Research on Tropes*, ed. G. Iversen *et al.*, (Stockholm, 1983), 99–123.

[64] See T. J. Mcgee, 'The liturgical placement of the *Quem quaeritis* dialogue', *JAMS* 29 (1976), 1–29.

[65] See J. Drumbl, 'Ursprung des liturgischen Spiels', *Italia medioevale e umanistica* 22 (1979), 45–96, here 77.

[66] Late examples given in E. A. Bowles, 'The role of musical instruments in medieval sacred drama', *MQ* 45 (1953), 67–84.

[67] B.-D. Berger, *Le drame liturgique de Pâques*, Théologique historique 37 (Paris, 1976), 60.

[68] Texts in K. Young, *The Drama of the Medieval Church*, 2 vols (Oxford, 1933), 1.1781–97. The dating of *c.* 930 at Fleury is in J. Drumbl, *Quem quaeritis: teatro sacro dell'alto medioevo* (Rome, 1981). See also D. A. Bjork, 'On the dissemination of *Quem quaeritis* and the *Visitatio sepulchri* and the chronology of their early sources', *Comparative Drama* 14 (1980), 46–69.

[69] Quoted in Drumbl (see note 65): 48.

performed a public westwork may have been particularly appropriate, as were more easterly sites later, particularly if or when the high altar migrated further east.

From the late eleventh century, as the number of dramatic compositions increases, *Quem quaeritis* becomes a sepulchral play and both music and movement become more expansive not least in cathedral schools removed from monasteries.[70] The fourteenth-century *Liber ordinarius* of Essen may record much earlier practice when it describes Easter processions entering the elaborate west-end complex (built *c.* 1000) before the *Te Deum* is sung at mattins.[71] The Essen play closes with one of the disciples moving up to the Michael-altar in the open westwork near the organ, and while no reference is made to the organ actually being played, it clearly could have participated in the *Te Deum*. It is not known precisely where the organ was, but the altar to St Michael was on the upper floor, like other Michael shrines and chapels, and the organ-chest could have been there in the gallery.

No doubt a strong influence on the early development of para-liturgies of this kind were the ceremonial interests of Cluny and of other reformed centres, as late as eleventh-century Halberstadt.[72] As the number of observed feastdays rose in the tenth and eleventh centuries across the continent so did the production of monastic crafts, many of which must have been geared to ceremony. Which churches had organs and how they were used on festive occasions is not well documented, but it is possible that the distinction implied between bell-noise and organ-sound in a fourteenth-century Annunciation play at Padua – a bell tolled at the beginning but organ and choir alternated for the *Gloria Patri* at the end[73] – had been normal for some time.

Te Deum

Since the *Te Deum* incorporates the text of the Sanctus, it could be that if *organa* and bells were appropriate for the one on certain occasions, so they would be for the other. The melodic similarity between the two – the separate and the incorporated Sanctus – confirms this.

Quite what the organ played and when it played it is never described in sufficient detail, but it is tempting to see it sounding forth the hymn's 'melodic cell' E G A C H A as the *plebes* and/or full choir were singing (see Ex. 5.1).

Although the melody in this form (*Liber usualis*, pp. 1832ff) is not known from sources before the twelfth century, one may assume for present purposes that it gives some idea of what was traditionally performed. Probably one is not to imagine the organ at first playing its own systematic counterpoint – two-part polyphony, a free voice above longer notes etc. – but rather that it played a drone (E) or a cluster, or

---

[70] E.g. the twelfth-century *Play of Daniel*, from Beauvais: NOHM 1990: 349ff.
[71] On westworks for the plays, see Heitz 1963: 181, 188; on the layout of Essen, 189–97. For a note on the gallery spaces in Aachen, Bruges and Essen, see Chapter 8.
     One cannot always assume that fourteenth-century ordinals speak for earlier periods, as is clear from those at Hamburg and elsewhere, where it is unlikely there was a much earlier organ.
[72] D. Dolan, *Le drame liturgique de Pâques en Normandie et en Angleterre au moyen âge* (Paris, 1975), 36ff.
[73] W. L. Smoldon, *The Music of the Medieval Church Dramas* (Oxford, 1980), 382.

sounded the repeated phrase almost like an ostinato, playing it between verses or
during them or instead of some of them? The last possibility would be an early form
of *alternatim* organ music, and a more systematic counterpoint for the organ alone
would develop as the organ came to play a complete verse, or vice versa. Since the
Te Deum had only one melody – one that is repetitive – and was sung at the close of

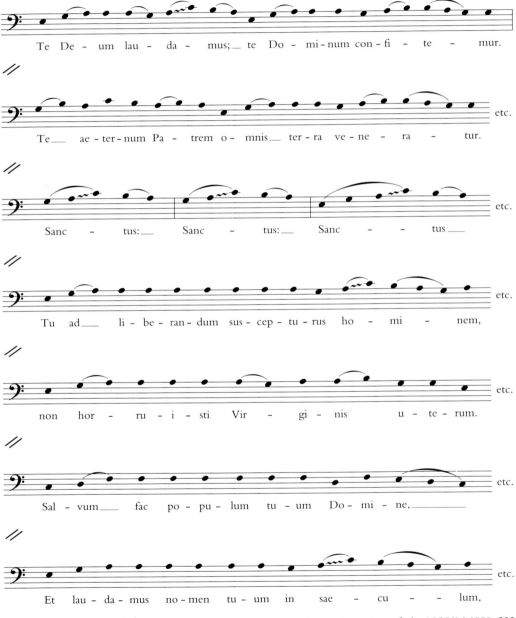

Ex. 5.1. From the *Te Deum* (sample verses); based on *Liber usualis* 1832–4, cf. also NOHM 1990: 232

every festal mattins and special thanksgivings such as consecrations, it must have been particularly familiar to the *plebes*. One can imagine its E G A C H A motif jubilant on a hexachordal organ, not least during the words *Sanctus, sanctus, sanctus,* which also use it. Also repetitive was the *laudes* chant, as in the melody in Example 5.2 from a late twelfth-century southern French source.

1   Rex____ re - gum, Chri - stus____ vin - cit, Chri - stus____ reg - nat, Chri - stus im - pe - rat
2, 3, 4, (each + one repeat by *scola*)

5   mi - se - ri - cor - di - a   no - stra   Chri - stus   vin - cit
6, 7, 8, 9, 10, 11.

Ex. 5.2. From a *Laudes regiae* melody (sample verses): based on H. Hucke, 'Eine unbekannte Melodie zu den laudes Regiae', *KmJb* 42 (1958), 32–8

And again, though there is no documentary evidence for it, the organ can be imagined joining in with its diatonic notes before, during or in place of some of the verses.

Dante's reference to *organi* in connection with the *Te Deum*, as the Pilgrim is admitted through the grating gates of Purgatory (*Purgatorio* 9.139–45), has generally been taken as a literal description of *alternatim* practice of the kind that became familiar in later periods:

Io mi rivolsi attento al primo tuono,

e *Te Deum laudamus* mi parea
udire in voce mista al dolce suono.

Tale imagine a punto mi rendea
ciò ch'io udiva, qual prender si suole
quando a cantar con organi si stea;
ch'or sì, or no s'intendon le parole.

I turned attentive at the first sound [of the
    following hymn? –],
and the *Te Deum laudamus* I seemed
to hear in voices mixing with the gentle
    sound.[74]
What I heard gave me exactly such an
impression as one is used to getting
when one stands to sing with the organ;
that now one hears the words, now one
    does not.

(*Purgatorio* 9.139–5)

But it is not certain how these words should be taken. In the first place, it would be nothing unusual for a poet to be following literary tradition: earlier Latin verse too

---

[74] Is this the sound of the chant in which priests and *plebes* mix, or of the gates (so understood in Hammerstein 1986: 213) which are now sweet-sounding because they are more open?
    The *dolce armonia da organo* is also referred to in *Paradiso* 17.44 in a complex simile: as the sweet harmony of the organ strikes the ear (i.e. music unfolding over time and anticipated with pleasure?) so visions of the pilgrim's future unfold to his guide. Dante's references in *Purgatorio* 9 and 31 are given and discussed in Zarlino 1588: 291–2.

had described jubilant occasions with *organa*, by which an early fourteenth-century poet would understand the organ. The theme of the creaking gate is rich in association (for example, the gates of Tartarus in *Aeneid* 6) and would give a certain familiarity to any scene in which gates opened on to hidden rites or, as in Dante's source (Lucan's *Pharsalia* 3.154–5), great treasures. Since the *Te Deum* is not in the first mode, *primo tuono* is unlikely to be relaying any technical information, and the alliteration (of *tuono, Te* and the other t's in the hymn) suggests merely that the 'first sound' is that of the hymn, not the creaking gate. And yet *primo tuono* is a striking phrase for a reader versed in music-theory, and it is unlikely that a poet would use it without some allusion.

In the second place, even if the words do refer to current practice and are more than simple allusions to earlier poetic tradition, they need not mean regular *alternatim* music. The hymn being sung in Purgatory was audible only now and then through the sound of the mighty creaking gate, not because alternate verses were missing. The effect was therefore like that in church when organists used their instruments not for fully fledged organ-counterpoint alternating discreetly with clerics' voices *alternatim* but when they spontaneously joined in the repetitious chant, repeating the motif at regular points, playing partial ostinati or drones, and otherwise making a loud sound during some of the verses. Not the least interesting and realistic touch here is the reference to the standing *plebes* (cf. Ailred's remarks in Chapter 13).

By the later fourteenth century, organs and *Te Deum* are reliably documented together, and presumably Dante's reference, whatever it conveys of the musical detail, agreed with what he knew of practice in the larger and richer churches of the day.[75] In Notre-Dame, Paris, there was a distinction between the *Te Deum* sung as a regular mattins hymn (when the organ did not play) and sung as a special offering at one or other kind of celebration, as at the end of a sepulchre play (Wright 1989: 114). One may reasonably assume that singing *Te Deum* in *organis* at coronations in fourteenth-century Aachen, or using the organ in thirteenth-century Bohemia when a king's succession was announced or when a church was dedicated, was a well-established tradition.[76] Much earlier still, the association seems rather to have been *Te Deum* and bells, as at the close of the sepulchre play in the tenth-century *Regularis concordia* when the prior begins the *Te Deum*:

quo incepto una pulsantur	this begun, all the [large] bells
omnia signa.	are rung together. (Symons 1953: 50)

So tied to bells is the *Te Deum* that the *Concordia* specifies that in the days after Christmas, 'although the *Te Deum* is not sung . . . nevertheless the bells are rung' (*licet Te Deum laudamus non canatur . . . tamen . . . signa pulsantur*: Symons 1953: 30).

---

[75] E.g. in Rietschel (see note 49). Fifteenth-century examples in E. A. Bowles, 'The organ in the medieval liturgical service', *RBM* 16 (1962), 13–29. In 'The organ in the medieval Latin liturgy', *PRMA* 93 (1966–67), 11–24, J. Caldwell sees Dante as simply referring to the *alternatim* practice (p. 18).

[76] Aachen cited without source in Ronig 1980: 24. For conventional references to instruments when Wenceslas II was acclaimed in 1283, see *FRB* 4.20; for the Bohemian Benedictine church of Politz dedicated in 1294, see ed. K. J. Erben & J. Emler, *Regesta diplomatica, nec non epistolaria Bohemiae et Moraviae*, 4 parts (Prague, 1855–92), 1202.

Te Deum was also sung before certain liturgical dramas, such as that after Christmas mattins or before the gospel of the third Christmas mass.[77] But there are no references to suggest when it was that organs joined or replaced bells for the *Te Deum* on such occasions, nor quite how they would join in if they did – perhaps by letting the motif resonate against the bells? (Did tuned bells play the same motif?) The clearest directive is given in the fourteenth-century Exeter ordinal: bells begin to play while the *Te Deum* is being sung, beginning at the verse *per singulos dies* ('day by day' – last six verses) and ending for the start of lauds that follows.[78] Presumably this means that there was a constant jangling, something that would create a kind of multiple drone to the chant if the bells were tuned diatonically.

The report of another event at St Albans, this time in 1235, evokes the character of one such special celebration. The report itself is special, having a political purpose[79] without which it is quite likely that it would never have been written and never have given its glimpse of monastery practice. On this occasion, as the new abbot-elect was led to the church and then in procession to the high altar, the *Te Deum* was begun, and the bells, the organ (*burdones* – for text see pp. 302f) and the clock all sounded as candles were lit around the altar. Thus a special occasion, a procession, a liturgy, the *Te Deum*, bells, choir and noise (organ, clock), were all involved in the jubilation. Exactly what happened is not clear: did the clock (*cum horologio*) signal the start of the ceremony and produce a continuous sound for 'the third hour'? Did its bells and the larger tower-bells sound only before or during the *Te Deum*, while the organ added some drones or ostinato motifs?

In general, organs can be imagined to have gradually moved from a less to a more 'musical' rôle, eventually playing regular, carefully conceived *alternatim* verses particularly in the more intimate context of conventual office or chantry-chapel mass. (The latter probably played a crucial part in the development of fifteenth-century organ music.) Perhaps *alternatim* as a musical practice originated in the way the organ participated in the communal *Te Deum*: not very systematic at first, and heard on special occasions only.

---

[77] S. Rankin, *The Music of the Medieval Liturgical Drama in France and England* (New York, 1989), 195–6, 188, 193 (cf. 195).

[78] Given in Dalton (see note 48): 2.535.

[79] There had been a power struggle at St Albans, involving both king and pope, over the election of this wealthy house's abbot; see RBMAS 28 and 57. The careful record of the ceremony was clearly meant to establish the election's legitimacy.

6

When were bells heard?

In two particular respects bells offer a useful parallel to the early medieval organ: they relay a technology from pre-Christian times which was then applied and developed by craftsmen in or for monasteries; and they are there to make a noise for various monastic activities, not necessarily the liturgy. One of them having a measurable mass of metal for striking and the other a measurable tube of metal for blowing through meant a third element in common: both were used as exempla for the arithmetical proportions expressed by the different pitch of musical notes. This third element, explored by theorists still categorizing instruments as *strings*, *percussion* or *winds*, is not basic to the present chapter, nor in any case can any text concerned with measuring a sequence of bells be certainly dated before the eleventh century (Sachs 1980: 114).

Winchester and other Anglo-Saxon bells

Tenth-century England left both a monastic custom in which the use of bells is described and various documents that refer in one way or another to bells as they do to organ.[1] Such documentation gives some idea of the importance of bells in the revitalized monasteries of England, where, however, readers would have been aware that smaller bells had been used in convents for several centuries. Bede's *Life* of St Cuthbert (†687) has a more informative reference to bells than is usually found:

at ubi consuetum	and when the usual bell rang,	
in monasterio nocturnae	in the monastery	
orationis signum insonuit.	for the night office.	(PL 94.787)

This remark may reflect knowledge of the passage in St Benedict's *Rule* in which the abbot is made responsible for the *signum* to wake the community;[2] like the information that Cuthbert took the tonsure, it has the effect of demonstrating that the saint observed the canon, that the bell of the wandering saint has become the fixed bell of Roman custom. Although church organs may not have been able to claim papal approval, the office bell could: its use as a signal for the office was attributed by authorized sources to Gregory I's successor, Sabinian (see p. 10).

---

[1] Winchester in RBMAS 71.1.426 (concerning the Winchester sacristan ringing the *clocca* as the bishops met the king); Abingdon on RBMAS 2.1.345; Ramsey in RBMAS 71.1.464; and St Albans in RBMAS 28.4.1.
[2] *Rule* 45.1, 11.12–13: in *Regula Benedicti,* ed. T. Fry, (Collegeville, MN, 1981), 206f, 246f.

At the time that its organ was being made, Winchester was equipped with, and evidently had the technology for, not only small liturgical bells (perhaps for use near an altar inside the church) but large summoning-bells in a tower. 'Evidently' because a large bell (perhaps some 4' rim-diameter) appears to have been cast in the floor of the nave of the Old Minster during the rebuilding of 971–80.[3] Malmesbury too had bells of wonderful size according to William of Malmesbury (RBMAS 83.301), and a bell-casting pit of the Anglo-Saxon period has also been found in the foundations of the Saxon minster of St Oswald, Gloucester, for a bell of about 1' diameter.[4] The Winchester pit is the largest known, and such archaeology rather contradicts any claim that the city's emergence as a cultural centre in the tenth century is 'hardly observable in metalwork',[5] although it is true that any extant fine-scale or ornamental metalwork it may have produced is now scarce.

The 'Winchester monastic custom' or *Regularis concordia*, now attributed to Æthelwold,[6] Bishop of Winchester and late Abbot of Abingdon, describes three distinct sound effects with signalling purposes in the monastery:

unum tintinnabulum pulsetur, 'let one small bell be struck': this was probably a small bell in the church, struck continuously, for example, until the boys had entered church for nocturns (Symons 1953: 13);[7]

omnibus signis motis, 'all the bells having been rung': probably the large bells in a tower, rung before such services as the first mass on the Vigil of Christmas (Symons 1953: 28–9);

tabula pulsetur, 'let a wooden board be struck' after the Chapter meeting, to signal the time for the daily manual labour (Symons 1953: 20).

The significance of the *signorum motus* or 'ringing of bells' for mass on feastdays is that it summons the lay people or *plebes* (Symons 1953: 19), presumably from outside the new monastery walls, at Winchester or anywhere else. But it is not always certain that the compiler or clerk of the *Regularis* wrote *signa* to indicate the large bells and *tintinnabula* the small, since in the same paragraph (Symons 1953: 13) there are three signals for nocturns described rather differently:

pulsetur tintinnabulum, 'let the little bell be struck'; *sonetur secundum signum*, 'let the second bell [signal?] be sounded'; *pulsatis reliquis signis*, 'the other bells having been struck'.

Elsewhere, the 'signal is made' (*facto signo*, 15), there is the 'signal of the little bell' (*tintinnabuli signo*, 15) within the church (?) after a first bell is sounded for prayers (*sonet signum*, 16); and for terce, other bells are sounded (*campana pulsata*). It looks as if the clerk varied his vocabulary with less purpose than might first appear, or perhaps

---

[3] Details in ed. M. Biddle, *Object and Economy in Medieval Winchester*, 2 vols (Oxford, 1990), 1.102–8. See also Chapter 8, note 22.

[4] References in H. M. Taylor, *Anglo-Saxon Architecture*, 3 vols (Cambridge, 1978), 3.1063.

[5] D. A. Hinton, 'Late Anglo-Saxon metal-work: an assessment', *ASE* 4 (1975), 171–80, here 175. See also Biddle (note 3): *passim*, for evidence of metalworking in Winchester.

[6] On Æthelwold's writing the *Regularis concordia*, see M. Lapidge, 'Æhelwold as scholar and teacher', in Yorke 1988: 89–117, esp. 98–9.

[7] Symons 1953 cited here for its translation. Text in T. Symons & S. Spath, *Consuetudinum saeculi X/XI/XII monumenta non-Cluniacensia*, Corpus consuetudinum monasticarum 7.3 (Siegburg, 1984), 61–147.

this variety is some indication that the Regulation was compiled from different originals. In general, however, *motus* does seem to mean pealing as distinct from tolling and suggests a clash of many or all of the bells. The distinction between a pair of bells rung (*pulsentur*) on ferial days and all of them rung on feastdays is still clear in John of Avranches's book on liturgy of the eleventh century (*Liber de officiis* – PL 146: 32). *Omnes campanae* must mean increased clamour.

The sketch of several (five?) bells placed in the central tower drawn in the *Benedictional of Æthelwold*[8] is probably more 'real' than those drawn in manuscripts classifying instruments for didactic purposes, though it too represents objects that have symbolic significance. The scene of the *Benedictional*'s drawing is liturgical and evokes practices in the reformed Anglo-Saxon abbeys, including a 'real' detail concerning the altar (in front of the chancel arch?): it appears to be free-standing, thus making it possible for the bishop to walk around it seven times at the church's dedication. Perhaps the bells are being rung – their presence suggests that they were doing something in the scene – and paten, chalice and altar-cloth imply imminent communion. That realistically drawn objects also have symbolic importance is clear from the picture's two weathercocks: one of them was probably gilded, as reported in Wulfstan's poem and both must have carried the usual significance.[9]

No organ is drawn in the *Benedictional*, any more than the directives of the *Regularis concordia*[10] ask for one, and without doubt clanging bells were a far more regular contributor to the liturgy, one way or another. Perhaps some early organs imitated clanging bells and played chord-clusters. As special equipment they corresponded to the bell-wheel used on feastdays in Æthelwold's abbey at Abingdon – no ordinary bell for daily services but some special turning apparatus, gold-plated, fitted with little bells and twelve lamps shining forth like the Apostles. The good bishop set up

rotam tintinnabulis plenam . . .	a wheel full of little bells . . .
quam in festivis diebus	which on feastdays [including Sundays?]
ad majoris excitationem	for the inspiring of greater
devotionis reducendo volvi.	devotion, turns round and round [?].

(RBMAS 2.1.345)

Æthelwold's connection with both *rota* and *organum* at Abingdon (see also pp. 200f) may underline their common purpose. Whether Fleury, on whose customary it is supposed the *Regularis concordia* drew, had such special equipment has not been recorded.

The Saxon bell-pit at Winchester, and a later pit nearby made presumably for bells in the new Norman cathedral, raises a question also of importance to organs:

---

8 London, British Library, Add. 49595 f. 118'; discussion and reproduction in ed. J. J. G. Alexander *et al.*, *F. Wormald: Collected Writings* (Oxford, 1984), 85–100 and plate 106. On the *Benedictional* being prepared for Æthelwold's own use, see A. Prescott, 'The text of the Benedictional of St Æthelwold', in Yorke 1988: 119–47, here 147. Remarks on the 'Benedictine' theme in such manuscripts in R. Deshman, 'Benedictus monarcha et monachus: early medieval ruler theology and the Anglo-Saxon Reform', *FMSt* 22 (1988), 204–20 and plates xviii–xxvi.

9 The signifier of Peter's denial, the awakener of the dead, the preacher of the word, the messenger of the morning and therefore its first monastic hour: sources in Sauer 1964: 143–6.

10 Although the scene does not necessarily represent Winchester, there were enough monastic foundations with an organ for it to have been included had it played in the liturgy of Benediction.

who were the craftsmen? Technical historians have assumed itinerant artisans,[11] and in view of what one supposes the demand for bronze bells to be, this is not unlikely for large-scale work of this kind. But so far, clear evidence is missing for this early period. In the case of organs, such as were made for the same group of English monasteries, only the pipe-making and perhaps the casting of bronze sheets were unusual jobs for a given workshop, and even these were not remote from other monastic crafts: small 'pipes' (*fistulae*) were rolled in connection with the necessary liturgical vessels, as Theophilus explains (Chapter 15). Bellows and gold leaf too must have been made in-house, as could have been the small bells on Æthelwold's gold-leafed wheel. This was presumably made of wood, and in so far as it was a wooden artefact with modestly sized sounding-parts of metal made to sound by man-made power, it offers definite parallels to the Winchester organ.[12] It may also suggest that while itinerant craftsmen for organ-making cannot be ruled out, tenth-century organs were being made in a monastery's workshop.

Bells elsewhere

The freestanding tower with three bells in a pair of Italian manuscripts dealing with instrument-classification (Seebass 1973: plate 41, tenth to twelfth century) seems more purely diagrammatic than that in the *Benedictional of Æthelwold*. The claim that one of these manuscripts gives sufficient detail to imply that the bells had pitches of unison, fifth and octave certainly seems excessive,[13] although no doubt bells did differ in pitch and the artist was certainly intending to convey some such difference. Like organs, church-bells and their towers received allegorical or symbolical interpretation, particularly in the High Middle Ages when they had long been familiar: one such idea is that as a trumpet marshalls forces for a military battle, so a bell does for a spiritual.[14] Presumably, illustrations of towers and/or bells can reflect such interpretation as much as they do 'reality', and it cannot always be certain which of the two is dominant in a given picture or whether the symbolism reduces the realism. An example of 'realistic' bells and tower, whatever the spiritual symbolism they convey, can be seen in a tenth-century Spanish manuscript from Távara, Zamora (*c.* 970).[15] Here, a balcony runs around the top of the tower which is located next to the scriptorium, a sure sign that the two were not in simultaneous use: when the bells sounded, the scribes were elsewhere.

[11] Brief notices in the *Foundry Trade Journal* 117 (1964), 460–2 concerning the Saxon pit, and 119 (1965), 537–41 concerning the Norman.

[12] Of the many possible methods for turning the wheel, two are known from later examples. For the later *flamboyant gothic* bell-wheel at Fulda drawn by Athanasius Kircher (*Musurgia universalis*, (Rome, 1650), 339), the axle was rotated at each end by ropes which were wound around a second rotating axle in the roof. If the Abingdon wheel was simple and light enough it could have been turned like a windmill, i.e. wind raised by bellows was directed against vanes at the hidden end of a rotating axle, as in the later smaller Zimbelsterne of organs.

[13] J. Smits van Waesberghe, *Musikerziehung*, Musikgeschichte in Bildern, ed. H. Besseler & W. Bachmann, III.3 (Leipzig, 1969), 156.

[14] Symbolism of bells and bell-towers summarized in Sauer 1964: 140ff.

[15] Seebass 1973: plate 52. Part of this tower still exists in the present romanesque structure at Távara.

If in certain influential churches of the tenth or eleventh century the organ began to participate at such moments as the sequence on certain feastdays, and if a bell or bells sounded before, during or after the singing, it does not follow that either bell or organ had a musical rôle as such or participated in the chants with pitched melodic notes. If 'organ and cymbala frequently go together' in texts of various kinds and 'cymbala are shown hanging in a row by the side of or above the organ' in psalter illustrations, this is no indication that they somehow played notes together. Nor do bell-measurement texts (*mensura cimbalorum*) suggest in themselves that actual bells were used 'to distinguish the intervals in teaching music';[16] one has only to think of the complex frequencies mingling in any bell-sound to see that intervals could not have been easily taught by these means. Whether it was to make it possible for bells and pipes to play at the same pitch in church that measurements for both appear together in several brief treatises,[17] is also quite uncertain. The practical questions of pitch-standard are not raised, and there is no description of their 'use together'. Little can be made of the fact that sources do not actually forbid such collaboration, since documents follow the conventions of their genre – whether treatise or drawing – and are not concerned with practice one way or the other.

The term *signum* for bells, used in the *Rule* of St Benedict and ever after, must indicate a signalling function: a signal to alert the community both literally and meta-phorically. Cicero, Ovid and Caesar (*Histories*) use *signum* in connection with military standard-bearing, and this is an association by no means irrelevant to monasteries and missionaries from one end of Christendom to the other. In the ninth century a bell at Lobbes was inscribed

nocte dieque vigi	awake night and day,
depromam carmina Christo	I will bring forth songs to Christ

– a reference to its signalling function[18] and to the literal and metaphorical significance of wakening. Percussive sounds were important, as when Hraban Maur in ninth-century Fulda referred to the *signum ecclesiae* (the bell alerting people to a funeral procession) or when Amalar of Metz, after a visit to Rome in *c.* 820 reported on the wooden board (*tabula*) used in St Peter's instead of metal bell during the last three days of Holy Week (PL 105.1201). This *tabula* is interesting as yet another Roman convention adopted by reform Benedictines of the tenth century, as is clear in the phrase from the Winchester *Regularis concordia* above. The Trier custom of *c.* 1000 speaks of the *signum* arousing monks for the night offices at Trier and Gorze, while a century or so earlier at St Alban, Mainz the bell for vespers is reported in the same terms as in the *Regularis concordia* (*signo ad vesperas pulsato* – MGH SS 2.97).

At Farfa, a major house near Rome reflecting eleventh-century Cluniac customs, the two bell-towers flanking the quire may have been so placed as to enable the

16   Quotations from J. Smits van Waesberghe, *Cymbala* (Rome, 1950), 18–19.
17   Suggested by C. Vivell, *Frutolfi breviarium de musica et tonarius*, Sitzungsberichte der Philosophisch-historischen Klasse der Akademie der Wissenschaften in Wien 188.2 (Vienna, 1919), 24.
18   Fulda and others in P. Price, *Bells and Man* (London, 1983), 112; Lobbes in Blumröder 1983: 3. On the Lobbes bells, see below, p. 211. For other references *c.* 796–826, see Bullough (p. 247, note 37).

ringers to see and respond to liturgical action.[19] (Although evidence is not clear, organs too may well have begun to be located with the same purpose in mind; they certainly were by the fourteenth century.) At Einsiedeln by the tenth century, bells were contributing more than summoning noises and must have suggested sooner or later various ways in which loud organs too could serve the community:

in summis festivitatibus	on the highest feastdays
ad *Te Deum laudamus* omnia	at the *Te Deum laudamus* all
signa, similiter ad	bells, similarly at the
Sequenciam in die . . .	sequence on the day. . .
vel quando rex novus vel	or when a new king,
episcopus vel abbas	bishop or abbot
constituitur, dum *Te Deum*	is installed, until they have finished
laudamus excelse cecinerint,	singing the *Te Deum laudamus* jubilantly,
cuncta percuciantur, vel	all are to be rung, or
quando vadant ad cruces.	when they process to [with?] the crosses.

(Schuberth 1968: 107)

Even if *excelse* implied merely the physical location ('on high'), it looks as if the bells were playing continuously during the singing of the *Te Deum*. For the chant's prominent hexachord of diatonic notes, such as could be clanging forth from tuned bells, see Chapter 5. It is striking that at the point when organs were able to add their clamour to the *Te Deum* they must by then have lost their older, pre-Christian purpose of participating in outdoor processions.

Although such tenth-century phrases as *clangore signorum cum melodia hymnorum* ('the sound of bells with the melody of hymns' – PL 136.360, 378) appear to say that pitched bells were giving out hymn-melodies, they are unlikely to have done so. Assuming that 'hymns' is to be understood literally, the reference may mean at the most that one was able to hear both clanging bells and melodious hymn-singing on certain festive occasions. Bells were normal, and there can be no comparison between how often bells and organs were each heard: in most cases and to most people, bells must have been the only familiar 'instrument'. Even iconography may suggest that they alone had an actual, sacral use, for only they are 'realistically' portrayed in the ninth and tenth centuries (Seebass 1973: 55 and plate 112). St Benedict's stipulation that the abbot is responsible for *signa* is not matched by any reference to organs in any later document, nor is Charlemagne's directive that the bellringer be a priest.[20] Walahfrid Strabo remarked that bells signify times of the office (*significantur horae* – MGH Cap. 2.478), but in this they are anticipating clocks, not organs. Some six hundred years after Walahfrid, Jean Charlier le Gerson expressed epigrammatically the use of bells in a way no one ever spoke of organs (Gerbert 1774: 2.163):

---

[19] C. B. McClendon, *The Imperial Abbey of Farfa: Architectural Currents of the Early Middle Ages* (New Haven, CT, 1987), *passim*.

[20] W. Reindell, 'Die Glocke der Kirche', in *Leiturgia* 4, ed. K. F. Müller & W. Blankenburg (Kassel, 1961), 876.

laudo Deum verum	I praise the true God
plebem voco	I call the people
congrego clerum	I collect the clergy
defunctis ploro	I lament the dead
pestem fugo	I drive away the plague
festa[m] decoro.	I embellish the festival.

Yet it is possible that the organ of Winchester did all of these things (including the penultimate?) by the year 1000.

Such are the typical references to the only musical instrument blessed by Benedict's *Rule*. For most of such purposes the bell could hang in the dorter[21] away from the church itself, and for more public purposes – inviting the public, as Walahfrid Strabo implies (MGH Cap. 2.478) – large clapper-bells were hung in free-standing towers within the *monasterium* or enclosure, towers which themselves became a hallmark of the Church in the West. While all such bells were more familiar to most scribes than other musical instruments, they did resemble organs in requiring special technologies to be mastered for the sake of Christian observances.

St Paulinus of Nola

On the legend of St Paulinus inventing the church bell in the fourth century see also Chapter 1. As there was some foundation to the idea of Gregory I or Gregory II composing or compiling chant, or St Benedict personally composing or compiling a rule, so there was to St Paulinus inventing such church equipment, since he was known to be an active church-builder.[22] He also had family estates in Campania and in localities where there was long tradition for bronze-casting. But his known papers, including poems about paintings or mosaics, a letter to Sulpicius Severus and an admonitory letter from St Jerome,[23] make no mention of church bells or bell-towers. Perhaps bells, like organs after 1000 or so, could be naturally assumed to be part of building-projects if these were on a sufficiently grand or public scale. Or perhaps the association of Paulinus with bells came about partly because like organs they required justification, not because they had pagan associations but because they were not so obviously necessary to liturgy as to justify the expense or labour. But bells had useful functions when, as at Nola, the church complex was accustomed to crowds of pilgrims processing or acclaiming in the manner summarized in Chapter 5. Other fourth-century complexes, in particular Rome and Jerusalem, would have found bells useful for the same purposes, as would the later 'cathedral groups' in the West.[24]

---

[21] As was the case at Gorze, Fleury and other abbeys of the late tenth century: see L. Donat, 'Recherches sur l'influence de Fleury au Xe siècle', in *Etudes ligériennes d'histoire médiévale*, ed. R. Loins (Auxerre, 1975), 165–74.

[22] Summary of sources in Frend 1984: 713–5; also R. Goldschmidt, *Paulinus's Churches at Nola* (Amsterdam, 1940).

[23] Which circulated and was quoted by Louis the Pious to the new Abbot of Fulda in 818 (MGH SS 15.1.227–8). Bells of various kinds (and perhaps their towers?) must have had a part in the building-work undertaken at Fulda over the period 817–22.

[24] E.g. E. D. Hunt, *Holy Land Pilgrimages in the Later Roman Empire 312–460* (Oxford, 1984). Bede's report on the Constantinian basilicas at Jerusalem (*Hist. Eccl.* = PL 95.256–7) ensured widespread knowledge of them in the eighth century. For the layout at Nola, see R. Krautheimer, *Early Christian and Byzantine Architecture*, Pelican History of Art 24 (London, 4/1986), 196.

In the first half of the ninth century, Walahfrid Strabo reports on the connection of bells with Campania and Nola: for him, the local monastic world had established practices which needed describing and which may or may not have had long-standing tradition behind them. Up to the period of Theophilus, German abbeys with known bell-casting traditions include Tegernsee, Weingarten, Fulda, Erfurt, St Gall and Reichenau. In his treatise, Theophilus was surely speaking for interests and traditions that had led this northern monastic world to develop techniques beyond those of an earlier Christianity. There must have been foundries in other provinces – Neustria, Aquitania, Catalonia, Lombardy, Campania – but they had no commentator to compare with Walahfrid, who speaks of bells as customary (*ut modo est*). The German customaries too are very rich in references to bells used to announce office or mass, as well as other daily events. If a fraction of what the *Corpus consuetudinum monasticarum*[25] has to say about bells and their use were devoted to organs and their use[26] the history of organs would be very much clearer than it is.

Elsewhere Walahfrid refers to the 'bronze trumpets' (*tubas aereas*) authorized in the Old Testament but does not take the opportunity to extend the idea to organs, either for signalling or for more musical rôles in the church's music – the *cantilena, psalmodia, ymni metrici at rithmici* (MGH Cap. 2.478–9, 506–8). Nor does Amalar. It looks as if neither knew organs – or organs in church – and yet it is possible to imagine that the kind of church appurtenances or furniture that Walahfrid or Amalar does mention would easily admit organs (like pictures and statues) when the stimulus for craftsmen to make them was there. If that came at the end of the tenth century, a path of a kind had already been laid. The same can be said for clocks, which took the function of the bell for marking the office-hours and at the same time aroused wonder in anyone gazing on them. A bell to ring automatically, as reported by Bishop Liudprand of Cremona of the clepsydra in the church of St Michael, Constantinople, in the early tenth century,[27] did so in a wonder-inspiring manner, like the sounding pipes of Winchester half a century later, or the fully mechanical clocks of much later centuries. The precursor of such organs and clocks, however miraculously new to the *plebes* they may have appeared, had been the large bell.

A note on organ-builders/bell-founders

During the thirteenth century as more and more types of document record details of trades and crafts – see excerpts in Chapter 13 and remarks on contracts in Chapter 17 – one and the same person is often mentioned as a maker of bells and organs, as

[25] E.g. K. Hallinger *et al.*, *Initia Consuetudinis Benedictinae: Consuetudines saeculi octavi et noni*, Corpus consuetudinum monasticarum 1 (Siegburg, 1963). The *index terminorum* of these volumes also records the frequency with which the Roman military term for the trumpet-signal (*classicum*) appears for bells.

[26] E.g. for detailed reference to each bell (by name) and the combinations in which by then various bells sounded during the several services on the major feastdays, see the thirteenth-century Canterbury Customary (Thompson 1902–4).

[27] PL 136.895. See ed. J. Becker, *Liudprandi episcopi cremonensis opera*, Scriptores rerum germanicarum i.u.s (Hanover/Leipzig, 1915, Hahn), 90. Was the 'Church of St Michael' the chapel attached to St Peter's church in the palace?

later of clocks and organs. The information may appear in connection with property or the use of premises, as in the fabric accounts at Exeter in 1284 (see p. 355) or as in the case of the first documented name of an organ-builder in Cologne,[28] one Johan, variously mentioned between 1250 and 1310 as *campanarius, magister Johannes organicus, organarius* and *factor organorum*. Although Cologne's known secular sources before the fifteenth century are not otherwise known to refer to any organ-builder, Johan's workshop may not have been unique, for organ- and bell-making seem to have been associated together in the city since at least the twelfth century, though on monastic premises (see Chapter 15 on Theophilus). Very likely bells of bronze and pipes of bronze or copper (or perhaps 'fine pewter', i.e. copper and tin) were made in the same workshop in many a large monastery of the eleventh century and on secular premises in many a growing city of the thirteenth and later. If as centuries passed organs became more the product of workshops away from monastic premises – assuming that they were ever regularly made on the premises, which is barely established by the documents – one would naturally assume that organs were becoming larger. But so far it is not possible to say whether this would be a result or a cause of workshops re-locating.

Although tin was also used by bell-founders, the general turn towards pewter pipes, in as far as it can be chronicled, could have meant a separation between the crafts of making bells and organs. The many late medieval references to bells-and-organs would then have been marking only the tail end of earlier practice: the references exist not because there was a new practice but because documentation in general happened to be growing more voluminous. But it is by no means clear what the references do imply about old and current practice. Since the same Cologne sources list two early fourteenth-century bell-founders (*Glockengießer*) but mention no further *organarius*, does this mean that organs required no special mention – making pipe-sheet was an easy and minor part of the founder's craft? Or that the crafts were entirely separate by then, and records happen not to be complete enough to transmit names of organ-builders?

If the crafts had become separate, it could be because organ-making was seen as a woodwork craft quite as much as a metalwork. In that case one can assume that the building of (large) organ-cases, chests and playing actions had made organ-building more like instrument-making in general: organs may have been larger than other instruments but were like them in developing specializations, in this case three particular crafts – to work wood, to make and voice soft metal pipes, and to draw and use hard wire. At this stage, various technologies became common to organ- and clock-making.

7

Architectural plans and the placement of organs

It is clear from the masterpieces of church design in those non-western lands that never had church organs – for example, Syria, Georgia or Numidia – that however large or spectacular the site, however spacious or inventively designed the interior of church or courtyard, organs were not a basic part of any building's design or purpose in the way that the bishop's throne or the ambo/lectern would have been. Although processions around the spectacular monastic sites of eleventh-century western Christendom – Loarre, S Pedro de Roda, St-Martin-du-Canigou, Durham, Komburg, Melk, La Sagra di San Michele, Canossa, Montecassino – seem such ideal occasions for organs and bells that one wonders quite what else would have served (see Chapter 5), organs still need have been no more than optional extras for special events. Even when present, they need not necessarily have entered the church building itself or formed part of its furnishings or equipment. But in western Europe there is at least a chance that organs were known from time to time, whereas for comparable sites of the same period in Christian Armenia or Georgia (such as the monastery David Gareja) there was never any question of organs, as far as is known.

Organs and church-design

Church-design in western and north-western Europe from 750 to 1250, though too vast a topic for any simple overview, bears on the organ's gradually becoming a familiar part of church-furnishings, and suggestions need to be made on where an organ was or could have been placed. Something is known of the plan of several churches in which early organs are recorded: Winchester, Abingdon and Ramsey (see Chapter 12), Fécamp, Lobbes, Bruges St Donaat, Canterbury, Petershausen, Constance, Freising and later organs (see Chapter 13). Also well documented are three churches not known for certain to have had an organ but very closely connected in one way or another with the instrument: Charlemagne's chapel at Aachen (see below) and the monastery churches at Helmarshausen and Cologne St Pantaleon, probably homes to Theophilus, author of an organ treatise (see Chapter 15). There is good architectural documentation for monasteries associated with the few pipe-scale texts whose details suggest that the copyist/author knew something about actual organ-building – monasteries such as Reichenau or Murbach, with which Reichenau was connected (for the 'Bern Anon' treatise – see Chapter 16); or associated with monks who, extant writings suggest, were engaged in some aspect of organ theory or practice (Reims, Bobbio, Fleury, Hirsau, Komburg, St Gall), perhaps copying out Vitruvius or Theophilus. Like any period, the years in which such monasteries are particularly relevant to organ theory or practice also saw the rebuilding, even the massive reconstruction, of their church, part of which may have been for the sake of an organ, though accounts do not say so. At Hirsau just before and during the abbacy of William of Hirsau (1067–91), who was certainly interested in *organa* (see Chapter 16), the church was rebuilt to a three-aisle basilica plan with two-tower westwork, and gave several possible sites for an organ even though extant documentation of that time and later says nothing about it.

In all of these cases, from Wessex to Lake Constance, the building had some form of complex western structure by *c.* 1000: facing east down nave and aisles (if there were such) was an upper-floor liturgical space of some kind with a shrine or altar, or a two-storeyed (perhaps multi-storeyed) westwork, or an axial western chapel in a tribune with a narrow view of the nave, or even a whole west-church which itself had two floors. Some churches had a tribune or gallery elsewhere in the building and nearer the main altar or crypt, perhaps a two-storeyed bay or porch (*porticus*) whose upper floor was a good location for an organ. But since over the whole period concerned, *c.* 800–*c.* 1100, it cannot be shown that the organ directly served office or mass, a likelier location than quire or crossing was one of the more public, less conventual areas of the building, such as a westwork open at least in part to the nave (see following chapter) or a pavement-level space removed from the quire.

The uniqueness of each of the major churches of Europe would have meant in each case an individual solution to the question of where the organ was placed, and the silence of documents makes the early solutions very elusive. At Cluny in 981, the west end of the church probably gave on to the atrium: was there a west gallery or tribune (perhaps open to the atrium, as at S Ambrogio, Milan, eleventh century) where an organ could contribute to a procession? In the later, vast Cluny III of 1088–1130, there was now an antechurch or Galilee divided from the main church by a wall thick enough to hold within it a tribune above the entrance to the inner nave: was the space more than a secluded 'chapel of St Michael',[1] perhaps a gallery for singers? No known document at Cluny mentions an organ, and if it did one would not know whether it was large enough to be fixed and where it was placed if it were, in the sight of the *plebes* or, on the contrary, hidden and mysterious. But it may be relevant that the extant Galilee in the Cluniac church of Paulinzella (1124–) has an upper floor with an open arcade across the nave-width, looking down on the main nave below. If there was an organ here, as is quite possible, it could have been reflecting local German interests in organs (Paulinzella was a day's

---

[1] Cluny tribune according to Conant 1959: 83ff, still accepted in Klukas 1978: 538 and Heitz 1987: 228ff. Klukas's careful distinctions between galleries, tribunes, tribune-chapels, westwork altars and 'axial western chapels' (*passim*) may not bear much on the place of organs when they were taken off the pavement: any kind of upper floor would have been suitable.

ride from Fulda) rather than any Cluniac custom. But if either Cluny III or Paulinzella did have an organ and if the antechurch was where the *plebes* stood, such a gallery could have become the conventional location for an organ.

Conditional tenses and subjunctive clauses are inevitable in any history of the early organ. Nevertheless, certain generalizations can be deduced from the later history as known, often expressed in terms of either/or. Thus, all the increasingly frequent references to organs in the twelfth and thirteenth centuries mean either that they were merely part of the sudden flowering of timberwork (choirstalls, wooden screens) in the equally sudden flowering of gothic construction; or a few had been there before the gothic expansion around 1200 and had been located in the various public places of earlier romanesque and yet earlier Carolingian churches. If either were so, then it would mean that the late twelfth century did see a major change with respect to organs: occasional, individual, even idiosyncratic structures gave way to a more common, more conventionalized instrument. Perhaps in this newly 'conventionalized' period they were much more alike from one part of Europe to another than has ever been the case from *c.* 1500 onwards.

Plans and Sections

The ground plan of Winchester as shown in Chapter 8 suggests a complex western structure, single-bay 'transepts', and a kind of crossing: see the plan and reconstruction on p. 133. The massive west end may have borne some resemblance to those a century earlier at Corvey or Auxerre. In more southern provinces, an atrium open to the sky is even likelier, perhaps with a further chapel or circulating space as at Cuxa (955–74 and later) (see Fig. 1). It is tempting to see some such plan and elevation as a version of the layout at Bages in 972 when *organum* was heard at its dedications (see Chapter 13). Atria such as can still be seen in Essen (now much shortened) were known in many larger, early northern churches (Cologne Cathedral

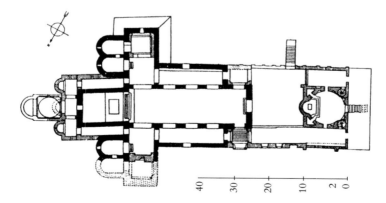

Fig. 1. Plan of Cuxa: based on X. Barral i Altet *L'Art pre-ròmanic a Catalunya Segles IX–X* (Barcelona, 1981). Atrium to right.

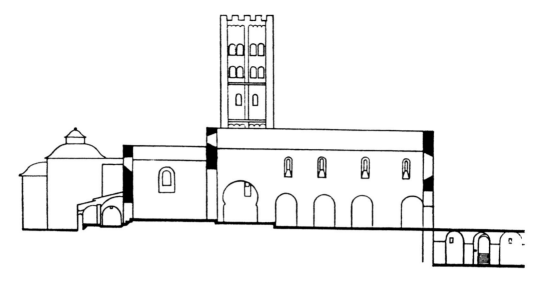

Fig. 1. Section of Cuxa: based on X. Barral i Altet *L'Art pre-ròmanic a Catalunya Segles IX–X* (Barcelona, 1981). Atrium to right.

and Fulda Abbey by *c.* 800) only to disappear under a later extension of the church. Complex western structures within the building as a whole could then have served for housing the *plebes* inside and separating them from the *fratres*, though how far this was their purpose is not yet well understood.

A characteristic example for the eleventh century in the central Meuse region (Nivelles to Trier) is Lobbes, of *c.* 1070–90 (see Fig. 2). Although there was no nave gallery there were complex east and west ends, rebuilt and added to from time to time, with various suitable sites for an organ away from the pavement. Lobbes was a widespread church-type, and the documentary reference to an organ here (see p. 211) might suggest that similar churches, not so documented, had one as well. In the houses reformed under the local Brogne–Gorze influence, there were three main altars – at the westwork, in the middle of the nave and in the quire above the crypt – and an organ was appropriate near either of the first two, as it would have been at Winchester. At Lobbes, bells are also mentioned in the text: perhaps organs and tower-bell were located near each other, viewed liturgically in somewhat similar light, i.e. as signals or backgrounds. This church-type too must often have had an atrium, like nearby Brogne.[2] The very long naves of English Norman churches of a similar period (complete with massive west complexes as at Winchester and Ely) must reflect a similar need for lengthy processional spaces indoors, as if the porch, enclosed atrium, narthex and processing aisle were all replaced by one long nave divided by altars or screens and planned for the processional *stationes.*

---

[2] A. Dierkens, *Abbayes et Chapitres entre Sambre et Meuse (VIIe–XIe siècles): Contribution à l'histoire religieuse des campagnes du Haut Moyen Age* (Sigmaringen, 1985), 133ff (Lobbes), 220ff and 258 (Brogne). Also, L.-F. Genicot, *Les Eglises mosanes du XIe siècle* (Louvain, 1972). For comprehensive catalogue and analysis of Rhine–Meuse churches of the period, see Kubach & Verbeek 1976–89.

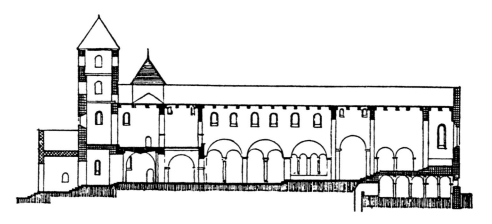

Fig. 2. Section of Lobbes: based on L. Grodecki, *L'Architecture ottonienne* (Paris, 1958), 206

Unique in many respects though the Aachen chapel was, it does raise some general questions for the organ-historian (see Fig. 3). (The small basilicas to the north and south are now accepted as later additions: Krautheimer 1969: 255.) Whenever the emperor received acclamations standing in the outside tribune and looking down into the atrium, or seated on his throne and facing down into the octagon, a suitable place for a movable Byzantine organ of the type that may have been used in Louis the Pious's time (*c.* 825 – see Chapter 9) would have been the first-floor gallery of the building, on the west side. This was a space secreted from the *plebes* but one from which the sound could be heard, both in the atrium and the octagon.

There is a hint of such a secreted organ at Aachen in the report of St Donaat, Bruges, in 1127, when the Count of Flanders hid from his murderers in the organ-chamber, if this is the correct interpretation of the words (see p. 266). St Donaat was an octagon, perhaps of the ninth century, very closely imitating Aachen[3] and probably with the same gallery-spaces in which an organ could be secluded. (The semi-octagon or semi-hexagon at Essen offers similar locations: see p. 89.) If Bruges had an organ located there by the early twelfth century, did Aachen in the ninth? And if the Aachen galleries gave a safe 'secret place' (*monasterium*) for an organ, does this suggest similar possibilities in other round/octagonal churches such as Ottmarsheim or Almenno S Bartolomeo and in churches with spacious west galleries such as Corvey and Lorsch? (By coincidence, the lowering organ now filling the western bay of the octagon gallery at Ottmarsheim occupies a traditional location, according to this kind of reasoning, except that it is a much bigger instrument than the builders of the original church could have imagined.) A further question is: since the gap of a century between two great periods of round-church design – up to the end of the ninth, and then again from the late tenth century[4] – is also that in

[3] On the imitation see J. Mertens, 'The Church of Saint Donatian at Bruges', in J. B. Ross, *The Murder of Charles the Good, Count of Flanders by Galbert of Bruges* (New York, 1960), 318–20.

[4] Dates and analysis in A. Verbeek, 'Zentralbau in der Nachfolge der Aachener Pfalzkapelle', in *Das erste Jahrtausend: Kultur und Kunst im werdenden Abendland an Rhein und Ruhr*, ed. V. H. Elbern (Düsseldorf, 1964), 989–47.

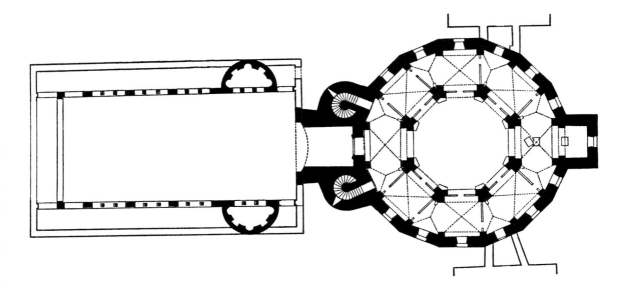

Fig. 3. Plan and section of Chapel at Aachen: based on W. Braunfels, *Die Welt der Karolinger und ihre Kunst* (Munich, 1968), 129, 131. Atrium to left.

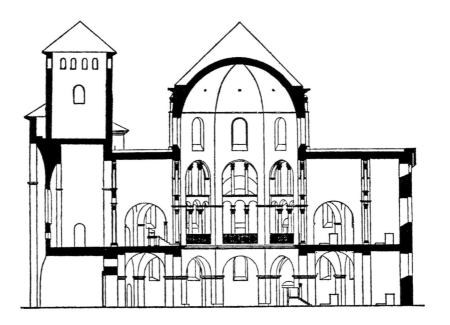

which the organ rather disappears from view, is there any significance in the coincidence? Either way, perhaps there was a sudden interest in organs around 1000 partly in connection with the re-development of westworks and galleries.

In one of the first influential churches of the late tenth-century revival in central Germany, Gernrode St Cyriacus, one can see several places suitable for an organ such as would excite the converted Thuringians (see Fig. 4). Particularly appropriate might have been that bay (with lower floor for bellows?) between nave and rebuilt westwork, a feature kept when the west end itself was later modernized and re-modernized. The nave galleries, assumed to have been built for the canonesses' community of St Cyriacus, are very early (982)[5] and passed directly to the westwork upper floor. They are already placed higher above the aisles – thus rather more remote from the nave-floor, as suited such women – than the slightly later and very spacious galleries at Montier-en-Der, where the *plebes* standing there (men, women or both) must have felt very much part of the monastic proceedings below if and when they moved along from the upper west chapel to the transepts. They must still have felt so in galleries early in the next century, such as S Eufemia, Spoleto, where one could walk through to the eastern apse. Despite its early galleries Gernrode

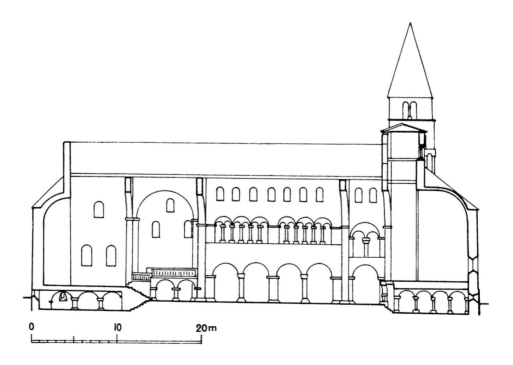

Fig. 4.1. Section of Gernrode (see 4.2)

[5] Analysis in F. Oswald, 'Beobachtungen zu den Gründungsbauten Markgraf Geros in Gernrode und Frose', *KC* 18 (1965), 29–37. Gernrode seen as particularly significant in Heitz 1987: 260.

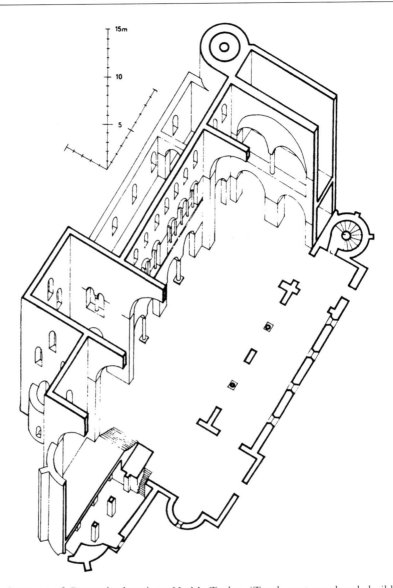

Fig. 4.2. Cutaway of Gernrode: based on H. M. Taylor, 'Tenth-century church building in England and on the Continent' in Parsons 1975: 141–68

belongs to a familiar type in central Germany, where a certain uniformity must indicate that the churches had similar liturgies; although being a nunnery, Gernrode may have had galleries for purposes other than those in a men's monastic church.

Elsewhere, there seems to have been more variety in design and layout, as in Catalonia and other Spanish provinces, where the principle of 'interestingly planned space' is applied with great inventiveness, both in the Benedictine–Cluniac areas of the re-christianized north-east and in the Mozarabic regions further west, which saw some double-ended designs for church (S Cebrián de Mazote, Valladolid) and palace (Naranco, 848). On the other hand, the northern churches of Europe were more frequently rebuilt and suggest a more restlessly developing culture, one that would by nature make use of newer technologies. An average-sized church like the Abdinghof, Paderborn, had five very different plans before the end of the twelfth century.[6] By *c.* 800 it had already been rebuilt as a double-ended church with a large west transept, turrets and small galleries; by 1031, there was no such transept but an atrium and porch; by *c.* 1078, a new west quire; by *c.* 1163 the whole now vaulted in stone, with a quire screen. Any organ it had could have belonged to either the   *c.* 1031 or *c.* 1163 stage.

Basilicas and atria

The new type of large public church signalled by Constantine's basilica of St John Lateran resembled the classical Roman assembly-hall not only in its architecture but in so far as the Roman basilica had already carried 'religious overtones, ever inherent in public building through the obligatory presence of a divinity's or the emperor's effigy'.[7] No single church-basilica in Rome, or centrally designed church in Milan is known from documentation to have had an organ for nearly another thousand years, but since the long naves of basilicas were partly for public processional purposes (particularly solemn at the Lateran) small processional instruments would not have been out of place. (On the smaller basilica at Grado, see p. 112.) The same would be true for any atrium prefacing the basilica's western entrance, and again in early churches for any propylaeum or colonnaded cross-arm prefacing the atrium (S Lorenzo, Milan). Perhaps from time to time even the early Christian house-churches gradually replaced by the basilicas had themselves known *organa* whether in the sense of 'instruments' or 'ensemble music that might include instruments' (cf. the legend of St Cecilia). That all known references to actual early instruments concern buildings quite different from Christian basilicas (see Chapters 9, 10, 13) suggests several things: basilicas never had organs; or what instruments they had never grew beyond the portable or movable size; or the whole subject is simply not one that was documented. While the second and third of these must be more likely than the first, the third does not help and the second leads only to other imponderables – in particular, why would Mediterranean (and especially Roman) church technologies not develop? If Rome was a place of wretchedness for much of the key period (ninth to twelfth centuries), would this really account for stagnant instrument-technologies? In view of such questions, it may be more useful to scan the uses to which basilican spaces like the atrium was put.

[6] B. Ortmann, *Die karolingischen Bauten unter der Abdinghof-Kirche zu Paderborn und das Kloster Bischof Meinwerks (1016–1031)* (Ratingen, 1967).
[7] R. Krautheimer, *Three Christian Capitals* (Berkeley, CA 1983), 18. On the remains of Roman house-churches beneath various basilicas, see Krautheimer 1937–77.

For centuries the atrium had various religious uses while the church itself remained as a temple-like sanctuary. From at least the third century AD, penitents and cate-chumens remained in the atria or porticoes of church-complexes. The atrium built in the fifth century around the site of St Stephen's martyrdom in Jerusalem was large enough for ten thousand monks, while a little earlier that at Nola in southern Italy (see p. 13) was serving as courtyard for three churches, the upper floor of its arcaded sides (cloisters) being used as a pilgrims' dormitory.[8] The whole was a model for the 'cathedral group' discussed below.[9]

The crowds (*plebes*) using the atrium on Sundays, feastdays and similar occasions in northern European monasteries also did so for particular events, for example the gathering for the Council of Clichy in 626 held in the modest atrium of St-Denis (Wallace-Hadrill 1983: 127) or the mattins at Aachen when, the Monk of St Gall implies, the clergy assembled before the octagon (MGH SS 2.745). Both Gregory of Tours and Pope Gregory I imply that feasts were held in atria, either monastic (Gregory of Tours, PL 71.453) or in the less formal surroundings of an old Romano-British temple (Gregory I, according to Bede in PL 95.71). But neither Gregory can have known much about the climate at Lindisfarne or Iona where it is hard to believe anything often happened out of doors.

From such varied congregational use it seems a long way to the atrium of tenth-century Cluny, where the *plebes* remained so as not to interfere with the monks' processions into the antechurch, according to early documentation (see Davis-Weyer 1986: 129 and above, p. 77). Perhaps in monasteries of the grander sort atria were naturally plebeian. When attached to Roman basilicas of both pre-Carolingian (St Peter, St Paul) and Carolingian periods (S Prassede), atria gave straight on to the nave and aisles behind the basilica's west wall, with no western complex or galleries.[10] (Is it an accident that no famous basilica, however large, is known for certain to have had an organ, or does the 'organ of Grado' as reported by Zarlino – see p. 261 – give a glimpse of Italian basilicas that had both small early atria and, perhaps, an organ?) A modest version of the northern European atrium-and-basilica such as ninth-century Inden is likely to have had a two-storeyed western porch to the nave, while in buildings on a grander scale, such as eighth-century Lorsch, there may have been a whole series of structures as one entered. At Lorsch, there was first an entrance, then a courtyard to the still-extant *Torhalle*, then a large atrium, followed by towers-and-gate, a small atrium, a westwork and only then the modest nave. Such layouts preserved the feeling of – and were there presumably to make possible – Mediterranean processional liturgy.[11]

---

8   Early atria described in e.g. Frend 1948: 410–11. In the fourth century, Eusebius said that atrium fountains were for foot-washing before one entered the holy places (*Eccl. Hist.*, 4.42), as at e.g. Hagia Sophia in sixth-century Constantinople (Mango 1986: 101).

9   References to pilgrims at Nola etc. in E. D. Hunt, *Holy Land Pilgrimages in the Later Roman Empire AD 312–460* (Oxford, 1984), 25, 242. On Greek temples lying axially to the entrance into the colonnaded courtyard, see e.g. J. J. Coulton, *Ancient Greek Architects at Work: Problems of Structure and Design* (Ithaca, NY, 1977), 122–3.

10   Of course, this also became the case in the later gothic church as earlier west-end structures were replaced by new gothic bays to the nave (e.g. at St-Rémi, Reims or Worcester Cathedral).

11   Inden in L. Hugot, *Rheinische Ausgrabungen*, 2: *Kornelimünser* (Cologne/Graz, 1968), figs 7, 8. Lorsch in Horn & Born (see note 25 below): 1.254.

It is not difficult to imagine that one or other of Charlemagne's and Louis's atria at Aachen (one of which could take five thousand people, according to Conant 1959: 14–15) was the place where the *plebes* greeted the king. The outside tribune at the west end of the chapel must have been there for the purpose. If nothing else, the study of Vitruvius's *Ten Books of Architecture* made at Aachen by those associated with the chapel octagon[12] would have introduced them to organs; no doubt they were more attentive to Vitruvius's theories of architectural proportion, but are we to imagine no interest in the musical (or military) equipment described in the treatise? After all, the Vitruvian proportions of the Aachen chapel are no more explicitly documented than an organ was, and are merely deduced by today's readers of the *Ten Books* from the extant fabric and measurements of the chapel. Any organ-fabric at Aachen has long since disappeared, so one is not now in a position to make similar kinds of deduction about the Vitruvian organ. But the possibility remains that when the expert Georgius was referred to Aachen in the 820s for materials for his instrument (see pp. 114ff), it was because there was already an interest there in Vitruvian water-organs.

At Aachen there must have been at least bells. In the ninth century, several northern atria, perhaps based on Roman precedent,[13] had bell-towers associated with public atria to provide both jubilant sound and a summons to the liturgy (Cologne, Fulda, Plan of St Gall).[14] While more southern monasteries such as St-Martin-de-Tours or Nola may have offered models, Rome was surely the inspiration for the large atrium of some northern churches as it was for several elements at Fulda in *c.* 800,[15] a centre of active evangelization in a major region. Roman elements there included the basilican plan with full open transept (a plan giving the cross's T-shape), the martyr's altar in the west apse, the atrium-cloister to the west, and the scale of the whole (Krautheimer 1969). Such *Romanism* was not unlike that of contemporary scribes of Gregorian chant, for while neither architecture nor chant was by any means really Roman, or able to suppress regional variety, the authority of both came from official association with Rome.

Galleries

The uncertainty still surrounding so many parts of a church – what were they there for? – is particularly severe in the case of tribunes or galleries, no doubt partly because there is no single answer. It seems unlikely that a women's convent church made the same use of them as a men's, a monastic church the same as a secular, a Saxon church the same as an Aquitanian; or that their use did not change between the tenth century and the twelfth. Also, the different uses to which they were put

---

[12] Vitruvian elements at Aachen analysed and literary allusions collected in Boeckelmann 1957.
[13] W. Meyer-Barkhausen, 'Die frühmittelalterlichen Vorbauten am Atrium von Alt St Peter in Rom, zweitürmige Atrien, Westwerke und karolingisch-ottonische Königskapellen', *WRJb* 20 J(1958), 7–40.
[14] Where, however, bells are not mentioned – perhaps they could be taken for granted on a ground plan, i.e. one that showed only the objects located at ground level. See below.
[15] According to Conant 1959: 8, the atrium of Mainz Cathedral (987–1036) could hold some 15,000 people.

did not necessarily lead directly to the way they were designed, such as what depth they had or how wide their sightlines to the nave and quire were. It is not always even clear now whether a church had galleries or not: from Vignory in central France to Hereford on the frontier of Wales upper-level arcades now have no galleries behind them (i.e. there are no floors) but could well have had them once.

Nevertheless, in so far as all galleries took people away from the main pavements below, and for whatever reason this was necessary, they would have provided several locations suitable for an organ. This would be true even if, as Theophilus implies (Chapter 15), the organ then had to be protected from people passing by. It would also be true whether the complete transept and quire galleries of Norman churches (example still at Gloucester) were to keep the *fratres* above away from the *plebes* below – or, as is more likely, vice versa, with men on one side and women on the other.

Both the *gemino solo* of the organ in Winchester (see p. 187, Wulfstan's poem line 142) and the option given by Theophilus for placing the bellows on the floor below (see p. 264), suggest that a two-floor layout had technical advantages when an organ was set up in church: the bellows and their noise were removed from the vicinity of the pipes. The various two-storeyed spaces in a building were not only those of side-chapels (*porticus*) facing into the nave but those of westworks wherein a king sat from time to time, as was the case in many a major monastery that kept at most only the briefest record of such visits. One may think that at Winchester in 980, 'such a connection with the ruler is particularly appropriate, for the westwork stood immediately opposite the royal palace',[16] as no doubt it did elsewhere.

However, that there is no inevitable connection between galleries and organs is clear from earlier history. Sixth-century reports of Constantinople and Gaza speak of the galleries carrying the congregation's women, including the empress in the case of Hagia Sophia (Mango 1986: 70–85), while the men thronged the nave in such non-monastic churches. No doubt circular churches from S Vitale, Ravenna (sixth century), to S Stefano, Bologna (eleventh), had gallery spaces around their octagons for similar purposes, and if men and women were segregated in basilica naves, so they presumably were in the galleries of more complex structures. In general, it seems that Italian galleries remained merely 'additional accommodation for worshippers' (Klukas 1978: 107), without liturgical significance.

In design and presumably function, northern Europe's nave galleries, such as they were, look like a dark, primitive and more enclosed version of the great open upper spaces at H. Irene, Constantinople. Some early transept tribunes in Fulda and elsewhere (perhaps imitating St Peter's Rome), must have been more open, something perhaps for singers. For ceremonies held inside at Aachen in Charlemagne's time, judging by the present location of the throne (Fichtenau 1978: 54), the king sat in the gallery, where there was an altar to the Saviour, while presumably the *plebes* were below, where there was the altar to St Mary. The nobles stood on either level. In the Saxon cathedral of Canterbury the people stood below on the floor of the nave while the priest celebrated at the altar in the raised west quire,

16 M. Biddle, '*Felix Urbs Winthonia*: Winchester in the age of monastic reform', in Parsons 1975: 123–40, here 138.

facing east over their heads; in the Norman cathedral of Canterbury, the organ was on the upper floor of the south transept (see p. 129), a grand two-storeyed *porticus*. Upper westwork altars, as at St-Riquier in the ninth century,[17] remained in use for centuries, and upper spaces with good sight-lines must have been particularly suitable for pilgrimage churches in which the *plebes* circulated in galleries as well as aisles and crypts.[18] Altars in the very spacious galleries of Santiago de Compostela – galleries such as were rare, unique even, in Spain – are described in the twelfth century,[19] and despite an absence of evidence, comparable galleries in major churches on the Santiago route (for example Toulouse St-Sernin, larger than Santiago), in much of contemporary Normandy and in all of Norman–Benedictine England, may well have been liturgical spaces.

Although so little is certain about the purpose of nave galleries, that they were associated at least in part with lay spectators is suggested by their frequent absence from churches that had the kind of westwork or west chapel from which the *plebes* could overlook the nave, as at St-Philibert, Tournus (1007–19), or churches in the Meuse region (Maastricht St Servaas, etc). For the same reason – particularly in order to house the *plebes* women perhaps – one finds them in the new town cathedrals, such as Tournai in the early twelfth century. From the point of view of the *plebes* it would not be important whether galleries were cubical bays (as at S Ambrogio, Milan, early twelfth century) or more continuous upper aisles (as at Modena Cathedral, same period) except that the latter might be less spacious. In basilicas without nave galleries, special eastern galleries or raised quires might take monks or canons away from the *plebes* in the nave and give potential sites for an organ, as at S Lorenzo fuori le Mura, Rome, *c.* 1200.

Three particular types of short galleries in important German churches of the eleventh century may suggest where organs could have been placed. These are churches without nave-galleries above the aisles. At the *Quedlinburg Stiftskirche*, a double pair of large, round-headed gallery openings at the west end looked out on to the nave not far below, and did so on a more open scale than in less developed versions of the same thing (for example St Georg, Reichenau). Some such opening on to the nave was originally known in many another church since altered, as in the Upper Meuse romanesque. Secondly, at *St Michael, Hildesheim*, the west transepts have various galleries and spaces: that on the north side has two upper storeys, both very spacious, serving in part as chapels with altars. The main quire was that at the west end, although processions after vespers also moved to the eastern quire (Klukas

---

[17] At St-Riquier, the prominent altar to St Peter was not in the westwork but on the east side of the main crossing: had there been an organ dedicated to St Peter, as at Winchester, it could have been placed in a gallery at the crossing, with access from the spiral staircases in the eastern angles of quire and transepts. These eastern galleries are not referred to in the accounts of ceremonies: were they private? (On *monasterium* meaning a secluded space, see also Chapter 15.)

[18] On these aspects of the St-Riquier plan see E. Lehmann, 'Zu Querschiff, Vierung und Doppeltransept in der karolingischen-ottonischen Architektur', *Acta historiae artium academiae scientiarum hungaricae* 28 (1982), 219–28, here 226. See also p. 75 (note 17).

[19] Early galleries in the larger churches of Spain, as at La Seu d'Urgell, had rather small openings too high up for anyone behind them to participate in a liturgy. For Santiago's gallery altars, see Davis-Weyer 1986: 148, 154.

1978: 36). Thirdly, at *Alpirsbach*, the north-east corner of the crossing has a small gallery open to the crossing but in other respects secreted from the circulating people, while in other churches – Werden St Lucius, Werden St Ludgerus, *c*. 1000 and Essen Minster (*c*. 1050, since changed) – comparable arcaded galleries were found at other points near the crossing, facing into the nave or south transept. Also, in churches with one or more of these three gallery-types – west end, west transept, east transept – there was one other prime location for organs: the blank wall of the nave above the arcade and below clerestory windows. This would have served for Theophilus's organ-arch made in the stonework, where the organ was so placed that the pipes could face the nave while the bellows and player were housed behind.

In these German churches, then, a general sequence of events might have been:

during the ninth or tenth century, an organ in one or other west gallery, perhaps a gallery frequented by processing *fratres* and *plebes*;

later, an organ in a more private gallery further east in the church; by the early twelfth century, an organ in a specially made opening in the nave wall, with the player behind, and with little or no wooden casework framing the pipes;

in the following centuries, an organ in much the same position but now with a complete wooden casework developed into a full ' swallownest' organ, with player sitting in the organ's own little gallery, and the woodwork including large decorative pendentives etc.[20] Such would be the pattern adopted by the larger of the new non-monastic town churches or cathedrals.

The massive timberwork necessary for the last suggests the fourteenth century, by which time the gothic design of newer churches had given the stone walls above tall nave-arcades shallow arcaded 'galleries' within and in front of which some later swallownest organs still lie (for example at Metz and Strasbourg Cathedrals).

A sign that tribunes or upper gallery-spaces were part of the 'unquiet' side of Benedictine ceremony, being used in festive events or public processions, is the Cistercians' disregard for them. Cluniac churches, where there are occasionally galleries (Nevers St-Etienne, Modena Cathedral) although customs do not require them (Klukas 1978: 93), would not have been on principle inimical to organs even if they were not geared to lay congregations, and although some Cluniac churches had no view into the nave from the westwork (for example Payerne and Romainmôtier). But classical twelfth-century Cistercian design – from Fontenay to Poblet, Eberbach to Fountains – had no galleries or gallery-like upper spaces at all, just a modest west porch. While it is so that galleries do not necessarily imply organs,[21] it is also true

---

[20] At St Michael, Hildesheim, a pair of early eleventh-century pillars at the east end of the northern arcade of the nave has plain capitals (unlike the other pillars, which date from 1175) that might suggest an organ having been placed against and above them, like a gothic swallownest organ but before 1175. At some point an access door was made in the wall above these pillars, to a roodscreen but also perhaps to an organ on the wall. (In the nineteenth century, the organ was on this screen.) For details of these pillars, see H. Beseler & H. Roggenkamp, *Die Michaeliskirche in Hildesheim* (Berlin, 1954), 72.

[21] E.g. galleries comparable to those of Benedictine churches in north-western Europe but found in contemporary Georgia (Kumurdo, 964; Alawerdi, early eleventh century) may have served the *plebes* but undoubtedly had no organs. Examples in E. Neubauer, *Altgeorgische Baukunst: Felsenstädte, Kirchen, Höhlenklöster* (Leipzig, 1976), 92, 122. Examples of twelfth-century German naves with galleries of various kinds in Kubach & Verbeek 1976–89.

that the Cistercian churches of the early or 'Bernardine' kind were by nature inhospitable to organs and to any of the public festivities that used them.

That striking Italian church-type without galleries but with a raised eastern quire that stretches across the building above a largely open crypt, often with processional stairs to the side – Verona S Zeno, Florence S Miniato, the Cathedral of S Leo (Urbino) – would have offered several very suitable locations for an organ. Faintly similar examples can be found in the North (for example Poitiers St-Hilaire, eleventh century, Jerichow Praemonstratensian, twelfth). The raised quire would make an organ effective to eye and ear without compromising its privacy, both removing it from the *plebes* and at the same time making a two-storeyed structure for it (the *gemino solo*) possible. So far, however, no details of any such organ have come to light.

Cathedral groups

Another architectural arrangement in late Roman and post-Roman Europe – the cathedral group containing several churches in one enclosure (cathedral, basilica, baptistery, shrine, chapels) – would have made processions very practical, and with processions, the organ. From a physical point of view, there can have been little real change between the Roman city-spaces of a city like Trier and the kind of space made by its 'cathedral group' in the fourth century onwards, after the legions had left.[22] The Trier group was a large, northern version of Mediterranean layouts with a pair of churches and other processional spaces, as in fourth-century Aquileia. Reconstructions of such episcopal or monastic enclaves at Geneva, Lyons, Tours, Metz and – more typical of high-medieval layouts – Arras,[23] suggest ideal processional–musical spaces in which a bell or quite modest organ would be so effective as to have no need of great size or carrying power. Similar points could be made about enclosures such as those of tenth-century Winchester or of those sites in which several churches or chapels were arranged either in a west–east line (Glastonbury, Canterbury St Augustine) or within one domain (Nivelles, St-Wandrille, St-Riquier, Corbie, St-Bertin), sometimes within a closely confined space (eight churches at S Vincenzo al Volturno by *c.* 850; various spaces at SS Quattro Coronati, Rome). On a typical Rogation Day in the High Middle Ages in an episcopal town such as Arras, the whole city was full of processions for which the three central churches around the cathedral served as focus, and the kind of clamour being made by the city's 'hundred belfries' was a flamboyant version of what had long been traditional for feastdays in the old cathedral groups.

In some tenth- and eleventh-century instances, the church itself was large enough to incorporate various large spaces: entirely indoor (at Dijon St-Bénigne, a long

[22] For Trier, see Heitz 1987: 11ff. Other comparable Roman sites and subsequent adaptations illustrated in e.g. T. Berchert, *De Romeinen tussen Rijn en Maas* (Dieren, 1982).

[23] N. Gaulthier *et al.*, *Topographie chrétienne des cités de la Gaule des origines au milieu du VIIIe siècle* (Paris, 1986–7): Trier = 1.21ff, Geneva = 3.43ff, Lyons = 4.22ff, Tours = 5.28ff. Processions at Arras are described in *The Monastic Ordinale of St. Vedaast's Abbey, Arras*, ed. Dom L. Brou, Henry Bradshaw Society 86 (London, 1957), esp. 67, 71. For Metz, cf. *BM* 142 (1984), 100–1.

nave, several levels, large eastern rotunda and further east-end chapel) or partly outdoor (church, atrium, chapels or baptistery, perhaps western processional steps, at St-Michael-de-Cuxa, Montecassino and Magdeburg). The thirteenth-century lay-out at Assisi gives some idea of the tradition for inventively created spaces suitable for the many regular processions of pilgrims: double churches, terraced outdoor levels, atria, steps, porches, all sufficiently enclosed for musical sound to express the communal spirit and to summon attention to one or other focal point.

The Plan of St Gall

The celebrated and puzzling Plan appears to be a partly traced, partly re-drafted copy made at Reichenau in *c.* 826/30[24] and is thus about contemporary with the Utrecht Psalter. It is unlikely that, as is still sometimes claimed, it owes its origin to the monastic reform councils at Aachen (Inden) in 816 and 817 under Louis the Pious and St Benedict of Aniane, since the length of the church and the prominence of its many altars suggest rather the 'Romanism of Charlemagne's day'. Furthermore, the present plan may be a version of an original made about 800, inspiring the builders of Reichenau at that time and forwarded later to St Gall, where the church was built in reference to it not as an exact plan to scale but as a 'schematic guideline'. Many monasteries can be shown to share characteristics with the Plan's church and general layout, leading to the idea that it served as a model or paradigm.[25] The best candidate for such a church seems to be Cologne Cathedral but it is not impossible that a Mediterranean model lies behind the Plan of church and monastery as it now exists.[26] Further parallels between the plan and the cathedral monastery at Metz have also been drawn and connections made between the Aachen councils and the *Regula canonicorum* of Metz sixty years earlier (Heitz 1987: 108). On the other hand, very close similarities between the Plan and known monasteries are elusive and the direction of influence (which influenced which?) uncertain.

Whatever purpose the plan was meant to have and whomever it directly influenced, its patterned layout is clearly expressing some desire for regularity and

---

24 Recent examinations include W. Sanderson, 'The Plan of St. Gall reconsidered', *Speculum* 60 (1985), 615–32 and, connecting the Plan with the church of Reichenau as it was *c.* 800, A. Zettler, *Die frühen Klosterbauten der Reichenau: Ausgrabungen – Schriftquellen – St. Galler Klosterplan*, Freiburger Forschungen zum ersten Jahrtausend in Südwestdeutschland 3 (Sigmaringen, 1988), esp. 14–15, 235–47. G. Noll's connecting of the Plan with Canterbury Cathedral in the seventh century (e.g. 'The origin of the so-called Plan of St. Gall', *Journal of Medieval History* 8 (1982), 191–240) seems to have gained little support.

25 Advocated in W. Horn & E. Born, *The Plan of St. Gall: a Study of the Architecture and Economy of, and Life in a Paradigmatic Carolingian Monastery*, 3 vols (Berkeley, CA, 1971): and W. Horn, 'On the selective use of sacred numbers and the creation in Carolingian architecure of a new aesthetic based on modular concepts', *Viator* 6 (1975), 351–90 and 50 plates.

26 Aachen councils: Wallace-Hadrill 1983: 343 and K. Hecht, *Der St. Galler Klosterplan* (Sigmaringen, 1983). Romanism: E. Lehmann, 'Die Architektur zur Zeit Karls des Grossen', in *Karl der Grosse: Lebenswerk und Nachleben, 3: karolingische Kunst*, ed. W. Braunfels & H. Schnitzler (Düsseldorf, 1965), 301–19. Reichenau *c.* 800: T. Puttfarken, 'Ein neuer Vorschlag zum St. Galler Klosterplan: die originalen Maßinschriften', *FMSt* 2 (1968), 78–95. Cologne: D. Parsons, 'Consistency and the St. Gallen Plan: a review article', *AJ* 138 (1981), 259–65. The possibility of a Mediterranean origin for the Plan (cf. the oil-press and catalogue of plants for the monastery garden) is pointed out by D. Hägermann in a review of Hecht, in *Technikgeschichte* 54 (1987), 1.34–5.

system, a desire unknown to the familiar, less planned, more open spaces of large monasteries across Europe, spaces that followed more individually the contours of their site. Compared to St-Riquier, Hirsau or Bury St Edmunds, the Plan of St Gall brings everything of the monastic community into neat, symmetrical order, physically and therefore spiritually. In the process of doing this it has the effect of emphasizing all the ancillary sectors of a monastery – the regularly spaced workshops and so forth. At a stroke, all 'loose' processional spaces are removed, the liturgy becomes monopolized by the central church, types of ceremony can be reduced (few outdoor *stationes*?) and accordingly the range of music can be curtailed.

In four particular points, the Plan may bear on the history of the organ though only obliquely and even negatively. Firstly, there is no organ indicated in the church or the chapels. Several explanations for this are possible: it was still too early for a plan to show them, they were too small to be fixed, they were too exceptional to be shown as necessary furniture, or they were regarded as variable equipment like altar vessels, which also are not shown. At first glance one could hardly have expected a fixed organ to appear on a plan of *c.* 800, for it is by no means certain that such a thing yet existed. But since the Plan does not mention bells either, although they were surely familiar enough (see note 14), the last explanation is not out of the question: the large or fairly large fixtures such as altars or font are shown but not the smaller or more variable equipment such as might have included the organ.

Secondly, the main space of nave and aisles is cut up for chantry and processional liturgies that move from altar to altar; barely 'one sixth of its area was accessible to serfs, pilgrims or guests'.[27] Despite this, there is a clear entrance for the *populus* at the west end, between the towers (where the bells would be) and into a circulating space (perhaps where an organ might be). Thirdly, the western layout – a public area – has a concentric porticoed enclosure, atrium and apse like at least one influential cathedral of the time (Cologne, 787–800) and not totally unlike some other monastic churches over a wide stretch of Europe (St-Maurice-d'Agaune, Fulda, Anglo-Saxon Canterbury), thus giving a *locus classicus* for any festival music, traditional or new, as might still have been performed in major churches.[28]

Lastly, as was also in effect recommended at the Synod of Aachen in 816 (MGH Con. 2.1.312–464), workshops were indicated in the Plan. They included space for those craftsmen who would have contributed in one way or another to the making of organs, had a monastery desired this. The Plan's turners (*tornatores*), leatherworkers (*fellarii*), blacksmiths (*fabri*) and goldsmiths (*aurifices* – meaning also coppersmiths and tinsmiths?) are a kind of concrete manifestation of interest in the *artes diversae* as occasionally evoked in literary sources of the time, for example at Fulda and St-Riquier in *c.* 800. Writers were beginning to acknowledge workers: Wala of Bobbio (*c.* 835) referred to carpenters and metalworkers, Adalhard of Corbie (*c.* 822) to workers in base metals and gold (*fabri*), bronze-casters (*fusarii*), carpenters and masons (Schwind 1984: 1067 112–13). It was through such craftsmen that the major

---

[27] As calculated in L. Price, *The Plan of St. Gall in Brief* (Berkeley, CA, 1982).
[28] However, at St Gall itself, such western parts (including towers) seem not to have been built: see Sanderson, (see note 24): 622.

houses were able to develop organ-technology when it was needed, whether or not the workshops were neatly laid out as in this Plan.

Furnishings

Compiled for a variety of reasons, lists of church furnishings mention bells from time to time, as in the report of Angilbert of St-Riquier who listed among the things aiding prayers for the soul of Charlemagne, thirty altars, the relics of fifty-six martyrs, and fifteen bells (MGH Con. 2.2.785ff). Usually, however, lists of furnishings throughout the period make no mention of instruments of any kind. Einhard listed Charlemagne's gifts to the Aachen chapel as gold, silver, the bronze lattices and doors, imported marble columns, lamps, altar vessels and robes (MGH SS 2.457). One can see similar lists for Byzantine churches, such as Justinian's gifts to Hagia Sophia (Mango 1986: 100f), and more modestly in the documents recording monastery dedications in Catalonia. These last, by way of recording how things were at the time the church was dedicated, sometimes list the *vasis sacris*: silver calix, paten and thurible at Canigou in 1009, gold calix and paten, missal, lectionary and vestments at Ripoll in 888.[29]

In general, wooden objects are not mentioned unless sheathed in gold or encrusted with precious stones. When in 1144/5 Abbot Suger of St-Denis listed the ornaments in his church (altars, crucifix, altar-panel and altar-vessels of gold, lectern, pulpit, throne, windows and seven candlesticks) and included what seems to have been wooden choirstalls (*chorum fratrum* – see Chapter 18), it could be that in so doing he is showing that wooden furnishings were beginning to receive new attention and probably newly improved techniques.[30] The references to stalls in the eleventh-century *Constitutiones Hirsaugiensis*, where they are called *formae* or *scammae*[31] imply similar developments. No doubt it was the expensive metalwork that occasioned the references to organs in tenth-century records of gifts to English monasteries (see Chapter 12). Here too, however, there was an element of novelty. To whatever extent earlier exegetists like Amalar of Metz (*c.* 821/35) were still being read in later tenth-century England, it would have been known that his list of furnishings refers to the Old Testament's musical instruments as objects replaced by the hearts of the Christian faithful: the singing faithful are 'themselves the trumpet, psaltery and cithara' (*ipsi cantores sunt tuba, ipsi psalterium, ipsi cithara* – PL 105.1106). If the writings of Amalar and the technology of Winchester were both characteristic of their time and place, and if such remarks as Amalar's actually mean that instruments were never used – admittedly two very big ifs – then a change had come about between their two periods (*c.* 825 and *c.* 975).

---

[29] Documents in Marca 1688: 971–2, 817. The record of an organ given by a late monk in the Weltenburg *Necrologium* (see p. 220) is matched by other entries in which lay donors gave e.g. a calix (MGH Nec. 3.370, 382).

[30] Suger's *De ornamentis ecclesiae* in Panofsky 1977: 52ff.

[31] W. Loose, *Die Chorgestühle des Mittelalters*, Heidelberger Kunstgeschichtliche Abhandlungen 1 (Heidelberg, 1931), 5f.

But perhaps it had, and furnishings conform to the time-plan suggested earlier in some remarks on the theorist Hucbald (†931 – see p. 47): however realistic were his descriptions of the psalm's strings and pipe (cithara and organ), however true it is that in his writings 'we glimpse a Dark Age instrument' (NOHM 1990: 458) beyond merely regurgitated Boethian theory, Hucbald's words were surely influential in their time. They must have interested and even inspired early readers in a period when attention was already being paid to equipment and furnishings in church, particularly to attract the laity. In imagining what an Anglo-Saxon church of *c.* 975 was like – a building

composed of small spaces, many altars, brightly painted carvings of animals, birds, patterns and foliage, dimly seen by candlelight, everything enhanced by the gleam of gold and silver[32] –

one can also imagine the burnished copper pipes of an organ, its gold-leafed chest like (and at much the same height as) the panelled altar near which it was sometimes placed. The scene at Malmesbury, for example, may well have been something like this.

Furnishing-lists reflect important changes in outlook or conditions. Perhaps Charlemagne's gifts were made by lay craftsmen and separately purchased, whereas Suger's objects were all produced by the monastery's craftsmen?[33] If so, Suger's list gives a good idea of what a major monastery could produce for itself, as in a different way does the Plan of St Gall. It seems likely from reports of Leo Marsicanus at Montecassino (*Chronica monasterii casinensis*, before 1099) that during the eleventh century at least, the more energetic abbots of the greater houses were encouraging the brothers to develop practices in the arts and crafts. One can assume that there had gradually developed a greater and greater tendency in this direction. At Montecassino under Desiderius (1058-87)[34] the community included artists in mosaic, silver, bronze, iron, glass, ivory, wood, alabaster and stone, each of which substances supposes an individual, discrete craft. Several such items, along with images of light, fragrance and sound, are listed in a poem written on the dedication of the new church in 1071 when a pope and cardinals celebrated, presumably on a grander scale than at Cava a century before. But unlike Cava, there is no reference here to *organa* (PL 147.1237f – for Cava, see p. 212). By *c.* 1023 an illustrated copy of Hraban Maur's writings was probably to be found at Montecassino (see p. 247), in which readers could have learnt a little about organs, if only enough to whet their appetite or increase the mystery about them. When a century later Peter the Deacon, writing in the *Chronica monasterii casinensis*, refers to St Augustine himself as 'the organ [tool? voice?] of the church' (*organum ecclesiae* – MGH SS 34.460) one is bound to wonder whether this was the only kind of church organ he knew about.

[32]   C. Heighway, *Deerhust St. Mary and Gloucester St. Oswald: Two Saxon Ministers*, The Sixth Deerhurst Lecture ([Deerhurst, *c.* 1988]). On the location of the Malmesbury organ, see Chapter 12.

[33]   Suger had four groups of goldsmiths working for him, including the *Lotharingi* (Meuse Valley men, East Frankish descendants?) who worked on the copper parts of the Great Cross at St-Denis. See D. Gaborit-Chopin, 'Suger's liturgical vessels', in *Abbot Suger and St-Denis*, ed. P. L. Gerson (New York, 1986), 283–93. At Winchester in the late eleventh century, there was a monk Blacheman Aurifaber, presumably not one of the immigrant Normans (A. W. Goodman, *Chartulary of Winchester Cathedral* (London, 1927), 18).

[34]   Translations of Leo and Desiderius in Davis-Weyer 1986: 135ff.

He must have known of the hydraulis from the copy he made of Vitruvius at Montecassino (Reynolds 1986: 444).

Perhaps no instruments of any kind are included in any known eleventh-century document at Montecassino not because there were none but because they were not dedicated solely to sacred things, as were the objects or the skills that did find themselves listed. Reference to an organ at Montecassino in the late eleventh century would be invaluable, since one could relate it to Desiderius's suppression of Beneventan chant for the sake of Gregorian, that is to say, for the official music of Christian Rome. In its absence, the most one can do is note that several of the skills under Desiderius do relate to the arts described in Theophilus's treatise where, in the version of it that includes instruments, organ appears before bells. Whether or not Theophilus's arts were those actually practised by craftsmen at Montecassino, it should not be forgotten that one of his justifications for writing about such things was that knowledge of them would enable its possessors (in Lower Germany) to avoid the trouble of importing such objects – from such centres as Montecassino?

8

Organs in the westwork and elsewhere

Chapter 7 referred to westworks of one kind or another, and some emphasis on these structures is useful here not because there is good and widespread evidence that organs were found there – of course there is not – but because organs may have started to become familiar in the same area and period to which so many westworks belonged: the territory of Louis the Pious during the ninth century. The various new energies given to monastic life in the earlier ninth century (Benedict of Aniane's reforms, the Aachen Councils, Louis the Pious's personal interests) seem to have resulted in amongst other things strikingly uniform church-plans in the territory. From Corbie and Reims during Archbishop Ebbo's time (see Chapter 10) to Corvey and across to Halberstadt, most churches had no nave galleries but did have complete upper churches or chapels in their west-end complexes. Later reforms in the conduct of monastic life and rites, such as those spreading from Gorze in about 1000, seem to have led to similar developments in architecture in the affected churches, particularly the upper west chapels as at Lobbes in 1020 and similar locations in, for example, Gembloux, Stavelot, Toul and as far afield as Merseburg.

There is nothing to show that any upper church-spaces required for liturgies in the wake of reforms by St Benedict of Aniane then in turn required the organ. The Gorze reforms may have had use for upper chapels (Klukas 1978: 139ff) but do not ask for an organ to be placed there or anywhere else, any more than does the Winchester *Regularis concordia*. But in so far as there was a sense of ceremony in the church and a spirit of enquiry in the scriptorium – late ninth-century music-theory in this same region certainly suggests the latter – it is possible to imagine that organs were getting known in this same monastic culture. If Hucbald is referring to actual organs he knows (see Chapter 3), they must have belonged to that stretch of monasteries for which Reims or Corvey was an ideal, wherever they were placed in the monastery and for whatever purpose they were used.

The example of Anglo-Saxon Winchester

While it is certainly possible that the reference to 'thunderous' organ-tone audible around the town of Winchester alludes to both a passage in Virgil and to the

'Talmudic report about the Temple organ in Jerusalem sounding as far as Jericho',[1] it is also likely that early organs were located so as to be audible far and wide. They always had been audible in this way, and there seems no reason why they should be different in a Christian setting. In the atrium of a Mediterranean church-complex, and in the open porch of a northern abbey (such as can still be seen at Fleury) or a southern (at the north-west corner of S Apollinare in Classe, Ravenna), the sound of an organ standing there would certainly travel, and was meant to do so. Like large tower-bells, it linked the monastery with the people. The same could well be true were it placed on the upper floor of a westwork, where it is not certain that the window-spaces were always or necessarily filled in.

At Winchester, the westwork was called *atrium* in Wulfstan's poem (line 41 – see plan below). Its ground floor probably centred on St Swithun's shrine, and one con-jecture is that 'the central space containing the tomb probably rose the full height of the [westwork] building like a lantern tower, surrounded on three if not four sides by aisles and galleries'.[2] An organ placed on its upper floor, in a chapel open to the *plebes*, would have had potential as a summoning or signalling device second in carrying power only to bells – whether in a tower at the eastern crossing of the church, at the west end (St Martin's Tower) or elsewhere in the *monasterium* enclosure. The westwork was clearly important, being the main object of the first stage of the rebuilding project, dedicated in 980 and no doubt imitating to some extent what the builders knew of Carolingian west-complexes on the continent.[3] Other possibilities for where the organ was placed are discussed in the present chapter, but since it is likely that the earliest organs were associated with a saint's altar, an open westwork is one possible location since such an altar or shrine might be placed there. In any case, at Winchester the organ's signalling must have been kept for those feastdays on which the town's inhabitants congregated, summoned from outside the conventual walls. (Such newly built walls were themselves sign of a newly reformed monasticism, secluding and excluding.)

References to organ-location such as they are before the large, open churches of the twelfth and thirteenth centuries resulted in conventional solutions to the problem, are usually quite unclear. Probably what organs had in common was not their actual location from church to church but their associations – having no common purpose in the liturgy as yet, they would not need to be in the same place. Wherever they were, they were associated with a particular saint, whether the donor of the organ, the patron of the church or a martyr for whose relics pilgrims came to the church, and in each of these cases the organ would be something seen and admired by the people. None of the spaces in a tenth-century monastic church was normally any-where near as large as those in the Mediterranean basilicas or the occasional northern

---

[1] For *tonitrus*, 'thunder', see p. 196. For the suggestion about Taldmudic reports, see Holschneider 1968: 142–3; but the extent to which Talmudic accounts, written several centuries AD, influenced the Benedictine scribes or poets of north-west Europe is doubtful. On the *Letter to Dardanus* that refers to the Jerusalem siren, see p. 247.

[2] E. Fernie, *The Architecture of the Anglo-Saxons* (London, 1983), 99. On the shrine, M. Biddle & R. N. Quirk, 'Excavations near Winchester Cathedral, 1961', *AJ* 119 (1962), 150–94, here 174–5.

[3] M. Biddle, 'Excavations at Winchester, 1966', *The Antiquaries Journal* 47 (1967), 251–79, here 270.

abbey that imitated them. In England, only gradually did the west–east sequence of small, separate cell-churches within the *monasterium* enclosure become 'united' in one compartmentalized building: Winchester in the second half of the tenth century was a conspicuous early example of such a unified building, and it seems hardly a coincidence that its organ belonged to the same period of restructuring.

Upper-storey chapels in west-complexes can still be seen across Europe from Deerhurst to Gurk, Corvey to Tournus, built in the course of several centuries to different sizes, shapes and liturgical potential. For all of them it is possible to imagine an organ located somewhere nearby – in the chapel itself or at the west end of nave or aisle – so as to sound for the *plebes* both in the upper chapel and below in the various spaces. The same goes for those churches whose original westworks or west gallery-chapels were much more enclosed than is now suggested by the large, wide arches built later to open them out to the nave (Celles, Jumièges both churches, Werden, etc.). Although Wulfstan does not describe the organ in connection with the westwork at Winchester, its spaces were large and public enough for special music and ceremonial events. So they were in the pair of galleried transverse structures at St-Riquier two centuries earlier: the westwork itself and a somewhat similar transept at the 'crossing'.

Locations implied in the sources

In describing the second consecration at Winchester in *c.* 994, Wulfstan appears to refer again to the organ (Campbell 1950: 72):[4]

11. 239–42

cimbalicae voces calamis miscentur acutis	bell-like voices are mingled with high pipes [= organ?]
disparibusque tropis dulce camena sonat,	and melody sweetly sounds in very varied kinds of trope,
insuper et cleri iubilat plebs omnis, et infans,	and above, all the common people rejoice, clergy and also the boys,
et deitatis opem machina trina tonat.	and the triple machine thunders forth [in praise of] God's help.

Machina trina sounds Virgilian, and were it not for the musical context of *tonat*, one might think that it could refer to the three estates just mentioned: clergy, choir and people. But it could also refer to the three main structures of the cathedral: nave, westwork (structure called *machina* in line 58), and crypt (also called *machina* in line 137).[5] Other possibilities are that the phrase is a subtle allusion to the *trina oratio* ('thrice-daily prayer') listed in the *Regularis concordia* of Winchester (before 975), or

---

[4] For source, see Chapter 12. Less critical interpretations of the musical aspects of the Winchester and Ramsey dedications in Holschneider 1968: 140 and 136–7.

[5] On later word-use in this tradition: William of Malmesbury (*c.* 1120) refers to a certain fallen tower as a *machina* (RBMAS 90.2.379).

even to the threefold *instrumentarium* of musical theory.[6] That the last is not out of
the question is suggested by the musical context and the fact that Wulfstan's phrase
cimbalicae voces calamis already alludes to three categories of music-making from
Cassiodorus's list of wind, strings, percussion and voice. The most likely, however,
is that as so often Wulfstan is alluding to word-use in St Aldhelm, where the *nomino
trino*, like the *substantia triplex*, appears in connection with the Trinity (PL 89.239).
Whatever is the case, *machina trina* is not obviously a reference to an organ, as is
sometimes suggested (for example Sachs 1980: 309).

Westworks or west-end galleries were locations in which the people were
assembled, particularly for processional liturgies, and lay people (or their aristocratic
representatives) are clearly visible in the celebrated picture of a church interior in the
Benedictional of Æthelwold (971/84), standing in the gallery west of the 'crossing' while
monks and the bishop (who is giving the benediction) are below.[7] On this picture,
see also Chapter 6. The illustration appears to be the most 'realistic' in the manuscript,
whether it is Winchester that is depicted (as has often been assumed)[8] or, since the
manuscript may have been made at Ely, some kind of generic Saxon monastery-
church with a tower and a short quire. From any such upper floor the more public
altars in the nave like that in front of the crossing wall could be viewed, and from
there steps might lead down to side aisles for processional liturgies at altar-stations.
The brief report of a church-dedication at the Abbey of Bages, Catalonia, in 972 (see
pp. 207f) is of a family with that at Winchester described in Wulfstan's poem, in so
far as both give a sense of crowd and space.

At Ramsey in 991, the newly reformed and endowed Benedictine foundation
was dedicated in a *vespera* service: see pp. 79f for the report in the *Life of St Oswald*.
Bishops and other eminent people were gathered with the *plebes*, as the monks
began to sing the service:

namque magister organorum	whereupon the master of the *organa*
cum agmine ascendit populorum	ascended with the crowd of people
in altis sedibus, quo	to the upper floor (?) where with
tonitruali sonitu excitavit	thundering sound he stirred up
mentes fidelium	the souls of the faithful
laudare nomen Domini.	to praise the name of the Lord.

(RBMAS 17.1.464f – see also p. 199)

Since the Ramsey documentation also speaks of an organ, and since 991 seems rather
early for *magister organorum* to mean 'composer of organum' these lines do make it
appear that as the liturgical singing began (or was about to begin) the organist led the
people in a procession to the upper floor,[9] where he played loud sounds apparently

---

[6] On the *Concordia*: Symons 1953: xxxii, xliii. On the *instrumentarium*: cf. Amalar of Metz's statement in his
discussion of the monastic office of terce, that there are three varieties of music: *triformis est natura musicae
artis* (strings, winds and voice – PL 105.1174). Such phrases certainly influenced psalter-illustrators (cf.
Seebass 1973: 108).

[7] Quirk (see note 2): 163, sees the people as richly dressed, therefore eminent persons.

[8] E.g. J. Gage, 'a dissertation on St. Æthelwold's Benedictional', *Archaeologia* 24 (1832), 1–117, where there
is a coloured facsimile of the picture in question.

[9] Holschneider 1968: 138 translates *altis sedibus* as 'high seats', as if they were some kind of stalls in the
gallery, but that seems unlikely.

in the festive vespers itself. (On the question of organ performing antiphonally with the choir, see p. 80.) The *Life of St Oswald*, Archbishop of York 972–92, describes the church at Ramsey as cruciform:[10] three *porticus* (chapels, bays or apses) to east, south and north of a central tower, to the west of which Oswald had added a 'church' or nave ending in a smaller west tower (a modest westwork?). There are various possibilities for an organ on an upper level here: in the tower itself, perhaps a lantern tower opened out towards the nave like a kind of eastern westwork; in the (two-storeyed?) *porticus* either to the north or south of the central space; or above the nave-aisles, as at Hexham in the seventh century, which had 'stone stairs and passageways and turning corridors . . . devised so cunningly that it was possible for a large crowd of people to be there and to walk around the nave of the church without disturbing anyone within it'.[11] The *Life* is ambiguous about there being a further tower to the west, but either way, there is no doubt that Ramsey had some kind of gallery to which the *plebes* ascended before the liturgy and where there was an organ, presumably too large to be portable. One could imagine something similar at St Pantaleon, Cologne, in *c.* 1000: spiral staircases next to the westwork led to upper spaces in which *plebes* and organ could have been accommodated.

English abbey churches with 'westworks or axial western chapels'[12] included Abingdon, Ramsey, Worcester and Winchester (Old Minster, New Minster), three of which are reported to have had organs. These western chapels, along with the two-storeyed transepts also found in the major churches, served as oratory chapels or provided altars or *stationes* for processions, as did those churches in Europe associated with the Gorze reforms, such as St-Riquier, Cologne Cathedral, Cologne St Pantaleon, Corvey, Hildesheim St Michael, Hildesheim Cathedral, Lobbes, Essen, St Gall, Stavelot, Trier Cathedral and Reims St-Rémi. Quite by chance, one of these (Lobbes) is known to have had an organ (see Chapters 7 and 13), and it is inconceivable that some or most of the others did not too. Two of them – Cologne St Pantaleon and Stavelot – are now associated with Theophilus, the author of the technical treatise (see Chapter 15).

Dedication ceremonies at such churches provided a particular opportunity for reporting either the sound of organs or of ensemble music (*organum*) that could well have included instruments. If it is not clear at Bages in 972 or Cava in 1092 whether *organum* means music or instrument (see pp. 207–9), at least the occasion that suits both also suggests one way in which organs entered church: as optional participants in the timeless Mediterranean custom for public liturgical ceremonies. On such occasions instruments were heard mostly out of doors, mostly in processions and mostly, no doubt, very noisy when it was a question of an exuberant monastic dedi-cation. At Bages, if there were a fixed organ, the west-complex was the most

[10] RBMAS 71.1.433–4 (translated in Davis-Weyer 1986: 111–12). Discussed further in R. Gem, 'Towards an iconography of Anglo-Saxon Architecture', *JWCI* 46 (1983), 1–18.

[11] Twelfth-century account translated in Davis-Weyer 1986: 76–8. Irrespective of its relevance to Ramsey, this description of the *plebes'* access to galleries and what they did there away from the monks below, is uniquely valuable. See also p. 199 (note 29).

[12] Phrase from Klukas 1985: 81–106, to allow for the term *westwork* not being always appropriate for complex western structures.

appropriate location for it; if it had not been fixed, the atrium (mentioned in the report) was; and it is possible to imagine that if the small *organa* traditionally heard in Mediterranean atria on festive occasions ever included organs, these naturally migrated indoors near the west end if or when they became bigger.

The festive character is usually clear. At Cava, a pope was taking part, while at Bages, the foundation in 950, the translation there of St Valentine's relics from Rome in 951, and the consecration of the church in the presence of the donor's children, were only the most recent of reform-Benedictine achievements in a Catalonia still then on the very threshold of the Infidel.[13] At Winchester, perhaps the evocative description of the organ in action as given in Wulfstan's poem was evoking the dedication ceremony itself: he was describing what the organ did at one or other of the reconstructed church's dedications, some of which must have involved the westwork and what it contained. At Ramsey, the occasion was certainly one such dedication, and at Winchester there is the possibility that so many blowers were needed because the event took so long and the noise had to travel outside as the clergy and congregation beat the bounds (see Chapter 12).

In the Aachen chapel during the century before these Anglo-Saxon dedications, the two storeys of the octagonal central space had different significance: rulers on the upper floor, people below (see Chapter 7). On the western facet of the octagon was a further structure having some of the characteristics of a westwork: from it dignitaries of church and state could address crowds in the atrium to the west and perhaps did so with the benefit of a siren-organ – certainly a *signum* of some kind. In *c.* 825/30, Ermold spoke of the *organa* 'kept now in the hall of Aachen' (*nunc Aquis aula tenet* – see Chapter 9), and although the position of the Carolingian palace's aula is not certain, any organ kept there would have corresponded to one or other in the palace of the Byzantine emperor during the same period. But *aula* could mean any kind of large space such as a nave,[14] and questions that one might ask about the Aachen organ in the early ninth century – what was it for, where was it, what was it like? – will have to remain without answer.

When Einhard speaks of Georgius making an organ 'in the palace of Aachen' (*composuit . . . in Aquensi palatio* – see Chapter 9), he too could be referring to the chapel and its 'westwork' as part of the palace. Similarly, if Louis the Pious was acclaimed and saluted in the tribune of the chapel's westwork facing the outside atrium, or inside on its upper floor, this would still be 'in the palace', for the chapel was no monastery church. Furthermore, since acclamations of a caesaro-papist emperor were sacred, the division between 'secular palace' and 'holy chapel' was likewise not at all clearcut. It is certainly possible that much later two-storeyed west porches, often (as at Soest) on a very big scale but still pre-gothic in conception, witnessed imperial or other acclamations and sent forth the sound of various *organa*.

---

[13]   The province around Bages lies just north of the Arab line as it was in *c.* 878. Examples of such monastic activities in E. Junyent, *Catalogne Romane: La Nuit des Temps 13*, Numéro spécial de Zodiaque, 2 vols (1961). For the musical aspects, H. Anglès, 'La Musique en Catalogne à l'époque romane. L'Ecole de Ripoll', in *Scripta musicologica*, ed. T. López-Calo (Rome, 1975), 279–96.

[14]   E.g. for Gervase of Canterbury in the late twelfth century: see note 15.

Another puzzle concerns Canterbury Cathedral. The Saxon cathedral is not known to have had an organ, but the raised part of the church at its west end would not have been inappropriate for one.[15] From an altar on the east side the priest could look down to the *plebes* below in the nave, as in churches with westworks (for example St-Riquier, Cologne St Pantaleon) or west quires of double-ended naves (for example Trier, Hildesheim St Michael, Essen). The main entrances at Canterbury were through south side-towers (about halfway along the nave), and the choir near the eastern apse was separated by screens from the people (*turba*).[16] The Norman cathedral of *c.* 1080– did eventually have an organ, built now in the south transept[17] (a public part of the church, next to the town) where there were again two floor-levels, on the upper of which the organ was located. It seems unlikely that it had a part in the regular conventual services, at least those in the quire. (See p. 223, also p. 224 for a hint that the twelfth-century organ in nearby Rochester was also on the south side.) In the large church of Canterbury, the south transept was successor to the Saxon cathedral's southern entrance and may have been 'public' in the way that the north transept, leading to the cloister, was not. An organ in the upper floor of this transept – a 'platform-transept' in which the whole limb was two-storeyed – was therefore audible and visible to the *plebes* and also safe from it. So it could have been in other large abbey churches from the late eleventh century, which had vaulted galleries on three sides of the transepts, as at Winchester (Norman church – Plate 2), Caën St-Etienne, Fécamp and elsewhere in Normandy (see p. 214). At Norman Winchester, the gallery or 'tribune platform' at the end walls of both transepts was open, with stair-towers at both pairs of outer transept corners; an organ would have been suitable in either tribune, particularly if one or other of the towers was meant to carry a bell.[18]

Another possibility for the open (south) transepts in the larger English monastic cathedrals is that they sometimes had clocks well before famous or spectacular examples were documented in the later Middle Ages. One might wonder – alas, without evidence to call upon – whether the now functionless engaged column in the spandrel between the arches at Winchester (see Plate 2), as at Caën St-Etienne, was meant to support, or to appear to support, some wooden structure placed above: a clock, an organ, some other wooden apparatus. Such an engaged column would serve rather like the plinth for the Beauvais clock (see Plate 19). Either way, the fourteenth-

---

[15] Interpretations of the Saxon cathedral as destroyed in 1067, in N. Brooks, *The Early History of the Church of Canterbury: Christ Church from 597 to 1066* (Leicester, 1984) and H. M. Taylor, 'Tenth-century church building in England and on the continent', in Parsons 1975: 141–69. Translations of the descriptions by the precentor Eadmer (eleventh century) and by the chronicler Gervase (twelfth century) in Davis-Weyer 1986: 112–14 and 141–2 respectively.
 Perot 1965: 296 contains errors about both date and location of the Canterbury organ.

[16] Interpretations in D. Parsons, 'The pre-Conquest cathedral at Canterbury', *Archaeologia Cantiana* 84 (1969), 175–84.

[17] Conjectural plan of the cathedral as it was in 1174, with remarks on the vaulted galleries in the transepts, in R. Willis, *The Architectural History of Canterbury Cathedral* (London, 1845), 37–9. (Eadmer's text and a translation, 9–12.)

[18] On the 'tribune platforms' in the transepts of Winchester Cathedral, probably complete by 1093 when the monks moved across from the Old Minster, see J. Crook & Y. Kusaba, 'The transepts of Winchester Cathedral: archaeological evidence, problems of design, and sequence of construction', *JSAH* 50 (1991), 292–310. The south transept probably had no door for either monks or *plebes*; that in the north transept was on its west side, first bay from nave.

Plate 2 Winchester Norman Cathedral, the north transept: from J. Britton, *The History and Antiquities of the See and Cathedral of Winchester* (London, 1817)

century clock at St Alban's was evidently placed near the organ,[19] almost certainly somewhere in the open south transept. Since (as here) monastic buildings were usually connected to the south transept – though not at Canterbury Cathedral – it could be that by then both organs and clocks had become more monastic, less public, near the entrance used by the monks rather than by the *plebes*.

Taken at face value, Ailred of Rievaulx's complaint about organs (see p. 217) implies that in the twelfth century the people were close enough to the organ to wonder at its bellows; it also implies that a reader of his words would easily grasp the picture. Getting the people to admire a technological masterpiece must have been one of the reasons for organs entering the church, and they often remained near one or other entrance:

organa solemnia in introitu	festive instruments at the entrance
ecclesiae superius situata	of the church, placed above

as a fifteenth-century English source[20] said of the organ at Crowland, a fenland hermitage-monastery imitating nearby Ramsey. An occasional but further use for westworks that was of particular relevance to music or to any organ they contained was found in liturgical drama and in the processions associated with them: see Chapter 5. The possibility that organs somehow contributed to such events exists in the cases of Winchester, Fleury, St-Riquier, Gorze, Metz, Laon, Soissons, Toul, Verdun, Limoges St-Martial, St Gall, the Reichenau, Augsburg, Minden and (above all) Cluny, all in the eleventh century.

There is necessarily a good deal of speculation in a discussion of organs and westworks, not only because sources rarely describe location in such a way as to be understood by the modern reader but because references to organs are rare and fall into certain groups of sources – Carolingian annals, Anglo-Saxon records, dedication reports, *en passant* reference in chronicles. However, the more clearly distinct these groups of sources can now appear, the more likely it is that the few references to organs that do exist stand for many others, unrecorded because to record was exceptional. Up to a point, late medieval practice may help to confirm something already suspected in the earlier centuries, such as that the placing of organs in or near side-chapels dedicated to specific chantry use – as in the Brotherhood chapels at Zwolle (1447) or 's-Hertogenbosch (1454) – developed from the old practice of placing organs near altars in the name of certain saints, as at Saxon Winchester and Norman Canterbury. That an organ may typically be very close to an altar is suggested by the report of a fire in Erfurt St Peter in 1291, when the same lightning-stroke destroyed both. As at Canterbury, the altar in question was dedicated to All Saints:

organa eciam ex opposito magna	also the great organ facing [it]	
ex eodem ictu fulminis vel	was thus shattered by the same	
tonitrui sic sunt contusa.	stroke of lightning or thunder.	(MGH 30. 1.425)

[19] On the clock, J. D. North, 'Monasticism and the first mechanical clocks', in *The Study of Time* 2, ed J. T. Fraser & N. Lawrence (New York, 1975), 381–9. For the organ sounding with this clock (or a predecessor) the source is RBMAS 28.

[20] Quoted in Hopkins & Rimbault 1877: 46, probably from ed. W. Fulman, *Rerum anglicarum scriptores* 1 (Oxford, 1684), 1.536.

Any major church had many altars for an organ to be overlooking. When in the fifteenth century a larger organ was fixed to the wall of a big church in its nave, aisle, transept or quire – what its position may have been partly reflecting was the fact that the *plebes* no longer congregated at the west end or in a western gallery but wandered over a spacious pavement from which the choir was secluded by screens. It was the seventeenth century before west-end organs became common again, and then mostly in Protestant churches where fixed pews and a sedentary liturgy prevented the *plebes* from ambulating. It is a strange irony that musical technology developed to such a degree that several early churches have their once-active and ceremonial western structures now hidden and cut off from the nave by large, in some instances celebrated, organs (Corvey, St-Denis, Marmoutier, Tournus, Werden and Fleury).

Further on the example of Winchester

Winchester remains one of the most useful of all pieces in the puzzle of early organs, for despite the many uncertainties in the poem, its text is the most suggestive now known, belongs to the crucial tenth century and is part of a church important in itself, in its connections and in its position within the Benedictine revival. Although known references to organs in *c.* 1000 are so few, it would not be out of character with all the reforms emanating from Gorze or Cluny[21] to suppose that many of the reforms' larger churches had a comparable organ.

At Winchester, Wulfstan's poem appears to include its account of the organ in that section dealing with the recently completed building-work in the eastern, not western, part of the cathedral; see Chapter 12. The following plans and reconstruction by Martin Biddle, though necessarily speculative in detail, make clear the possi-bilities as to where the organ could have been played. Despite being a unique church, Winchester serves to identify these possibilities in many another building, such as Werden St Liudger (dedicated in 943) or other late Carolingian buildings from which Winchester has been said to derive directly (see Fig. 5).[22]

By *c.* 994, the church was 159' long, with an aisleless nave, a western structure some 79' square (larger than Corvey or Werden), a shrine-crypt below the high altar at the eastern 'crossing' (a space with north and south apses), an eastern apse and a crypt further east (above ground, as still at Werden). Possible locations for the organ are:

> *Towers and porch.* Either might have been more open to the outside than appears in this conjectural reconstruction, and in any case could have contained an upper storey or gallery-space of one kind or another (as in the separate towers-and-porch structure still at, for example, Paray-le-Monial, 999–1004). Perhaps this new work dedicated in 980 then housed an instrument built over the next few years.

---

[21] Doctrine, governance and rites for the network of reformed monasteries, though not often practical matters connected with them, are described in K. Hallinger, *Gorze-Kluny: Studien zu den monastischen Lebensformen und Gegensätzen im Hochmittelalter*, 2 vols (Rome, 1950–51).

[22] Gem (see note 10): 7. Perhaps the north and south bays given triple roofs in the Reconstruction above were large single-space chapels (*porticus*), their foundations those of narrow burial chambers or shrines, like the Merovingian crypts still at St-Médard, Soissons?

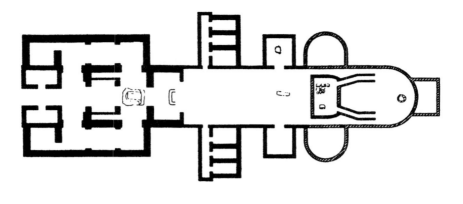

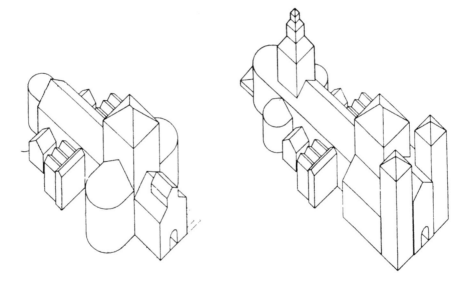

Fig. 5. Plan and reconstruction of Winchester Old Minster: from M. Biddle, 'Archaeology, architecture and the cult of saints in Anglo-Saxon England', in Butler & Morris 1986: 1–31. Reconstruction: *Left,* as in *c.* 974 before *Right,* new westwork of *c.* 980 and the east end rebuilt between *c.* 980 and 993/4.

Westwork. A structure east of the western towers, the wide tower-space that prefaced the nave presumably had an upper floor looking out and down on to the nave (as still at Gernrode).

North/south porticus. The three successive limbs at the sides of the nave could each have housed an organ, with the bellows at ground level and the chest and keys on the floor above. For any such purpose, the first-floor opening need not have been large (perhaps not much larger than that still at Deerhurst), or it could have been enlarged for the pipe-front (cf. Theophilus's suggestions on p. 264). The nave itself probably corresponded to, or even contained some of the fabric of, the seventh-century church of SS Peter and Paul, and it is assumed that the minster's high altar was dedicated to SS Peter and Paul (Klukas 1978: 253). As elsewhere, however, the old double name may by then have been reduced to one, so that the reference to S Peter in line 172 of the poem would imply that the organ was close to this high altar, perhaps in the southern side-bay.

Apses at the 'crossing'. If the organ had a public function not necessarily liturgical, a plausible location was also the central space near the shrine and the steps below it, where processions no doubt congregated and emerged from the eastern crypt-spaces. The curved easternmost bays to north and south were quasi-transepts which appear to have belonged to the same building-phase as the organ, thus *c.* 980–94. An organ in this south bay would be equivalent in its way to the later organ on the upper (and lower?) floor of the south transept at Canterbury. In fact, one might wonder if Canterbury was following a convention established earlier at Winchester.

Showing with such remarks that virtually any place in the church could have served for the organ is more useful than it may seem, for indeed all of them reflect one or other function the organ might have had and each covered an area large enough to provide room for the bellows, its framework and the large chest. Indirectly, the poem suggests that the organ was (a) somewhere in the eastern part, and/or (b) near the unlocated altar to St Peter. A further detail might help to identify the spot: archaeological evidence for the bell-casting pit, some feet west of the central space of the crossing,[23] suggests the main bell to have hung in the crossing-tower. Since organs and bells were often associated in sound and probably in location, there may be further support here for placing the Winchester organ in the northern or southern *porticus* of the 'crossing'. Curiously, the very choices for interpreting the situation at Winchester anticipate a key question in the history of the organ in Christian Europe: does it belong to the western or eastern parts of the church?

---

[23] Although a large bell would presumably be cast as directly as possible below where it was to hang, the pavement below the tower at Winchester was the top of some steps, and for various reasons the pit would have had to be dug further west. The *Benedictional of Æthelwold* (see note 8) may well be further evidence for the main bell's being hung in the central tower, and therefore for the organ to be nearby.
On this bell, see also p. 96.

Organs and documentation

Organs in the Carolingian and Byzantine courts

Annals and comparable sources have left reports of three organs in the Carolingian court during the successive reigns of Pippin, Charlemagne and Louis the Pious. It is the first of these that has been credited in the past with being 'the first organ re-introduced to the West' and hence the first in the western Christian Church.

Pippin's organ of 757

Over twenty annals refer to this instrument, sometimes giving supplementary details of unknown authority or authenticity. The following list reflects the number of times a detail is mentioned, from the most to the least:[1]

> the date is 757 (or 756);
> the organ (*organum* or *organa*, once *organo musico*) was given to Pippin;
> it was sent by Constantinus, Byzantine emperor (*rege grecie*);
> it arrived in the country of the Franks (*venit in franciam*);
> along with other gifts (*munera* or *dona*);
> Pippin was at the time in his *villa* of Compiègne, where the people were then
>   gathered (*generalem conventum*);
> it was brought over from Constantinople (*de graecia*);
> it was otherwise unknown in the country (*antea non visum fuerat in francia*);
> it was the year the eastern emperor 'made his peace with the Franks' (*pacem cum*
>   *francis statuit*).

While the large number of references to the organ need not mean the report was true or (more to the point) worded reliably, Byzantine gifts of this kind were certainly known. The following version appears in the royal Frankish annals, formerly attributed to Einhard:

Constantinus imperator misit	The Emperor Constantinus [V] sent
Pippino regi multa munera,	King Pippin many gifts,
inter quae et organum [*or* organa];	amongst them an *organum*;
quae ad eum in Conpendio villa	which reached him in the *villa*

---

[1] Extracts from MGH SS 1 and 5, assembled in Perrot 1965: 394–5 and Schuberth 1968: 114–16.

pervenerunt, ubi tunc	of Compiègne where at that time
populi sui generalem	he was holding a general
conventum habuit.	convocation of his people. (MGH SS 1.141)

This version, like other early references, omits the point about its being otherwise unknown; perhaps this was a gloss that gradually appeared. (On another celebrated organ not having been seen before, compare the opening remark in the Winchester poem, p. 187.) The plural form *organa* has been taken by some recent commentators to mean 'instruments in general'.[2]

That the annals were related or dependent on common sources is clear enough in general terms but not enough for one to know how reliable are the extra details: were they creative glosses? While it is plausible that Pippin should receive eastern delegates at Compiègne where regular assemblies were called by the king, the chroniclers probably had another aim in recording the event: it was important to establish the emperor's recognition for Pippin, ouster (some would say usurper) of the Merovingian kings but recently acknowledged and anointed by, so it was claimed, the pope.[3] Such a story about an organ sustained the idea, current in Francia since at least the sixth century, that Byzantium acknowledged Frankish sovereignty in the West, and the emperor did so on this occasion by presenting a piece of clever mechanism (*organum* = 'device, mechanism'?) which, as anyone ought to have seen, also proved Byzantine's cultural–technological superiority. It is not certain that diplomatic 'gifts' were more than long-term loans or, if they were more in the nature of gift-exchanges, what it was Pippin sent the emperor in return, either on this occasion or after another mission had arrived in 765.[4] These dates are significant, for 757 and 765 lay within the first period of the Byzantine Destruction of Images (726–842)[5] when an emperor might well have found it inappropriate to send to a fellow Christian an ornate piece of church furniture or an object for the liturgy.

The questions of what kind of special organ the Byzantine gift to Pippin was and what it was used for are secondary to questions about the sources themselves. Does their political character leave technical terms such as *organum* reliable – was this an organ or some other kind of complex machinery? If an organ, was it an instrument of music or a military siren splendid to look at, like the richly decorated organs in Constantinople (already suggested in Riemann 1879: 194), or a piece of engineering apparatus quite miraculous in the volume-level it produced? How did annals know anything about it except by hearsay or through a court annalist whose technical vocabulary was generic and unsure? Perhaps the annalist had heard a legate refer to the gift as an *organon* ('engine'). Aimonius's ninth-century version of the report as transmitted by Tolomeo of Lucca (*c.* 1300) refers to the organ of 757 as *organa suavissima*, but this

---

[2] E.g. Riemann 1879: 192, who recognizes that *organa* was sometimes used as a feminine singular noun.

[3] See Chapter 4. The same Pope Stephen II (752–7) had also been responsible for establishing further stational processions in Rome, according to the *Liber pontificalis* (Duchesne 1886–92: 1.443). From its report in MGH Cap. 1.37–9, it seems that the Compiègne convention of 757 also included delegates of the pope and was concerned chiefly with marriage and questions of consanguinity.

[4] Report of the missions in F. W. Buckler, *Harunu'l-Rashid and Charles the Great* (Cambridge, MA, 1931), 7ff.

[5] The iconoclastic troubles led to the Frankish response contained in the *Liber carolini* written in the early 790s by Theodulf of Orleans: MGH Con. 2, supplement.

is a formula that could have been added by any scribe:[6] it is certainly no evidence against the original device being a high-pressure siren. Nor is another late report quoted by Praetorius (1619: 91): in speaking of 'a first-rate large instrument' (*ein trefflich groß Instrument*) with lead pipes and bellows, its author was surely guessing, interpreting the information in the light of more recent word-use. The only hint about the instrument itself in the early annals is that it was otherwise unknown, but it can only be guessed whether this reflects the nature of the organ (its size and volume something quite new), the aims of political annals (a Byzantine salute to the new dynasty had to be unusual) or the convention whereby special objects had to be described as unique. In any case, was 'not seen in Francia' meant to be specifically the area between the Loire and the Rhine? Or is the whole phrase a gloss?

The annals, though made, copied, circulated and preserved by monks or in monasteries, do not concern monastic life except in so far as some affairs of state involved churches and some churches witnessed events of interest to state chroniclers. But if it is so that annals' entries do not bear on monastic or church life as such, nor would their words then be proving that organs were unknown in monasteries of the time. It would be possible for an annalist of *c.* 775 to use an antique, non-vernacular term like *organum* in several senses on different occasions; he could write that 'the organ was not previously known' when his own monastery had instruments (*organa*) of various kinds, because he could take his source's word *organum* to mean some other complex mechanical device, or because the organ he knew was called *hydraulia* (as in Hucbald), or because he did not question a source. The scribe who wrote *cum organo musico* could well have been trying to bring a little less ambiguity into the reference, like another scribe's added word *suavissima*. It is true that there are many crippling uncertainties in such discussions, but what is certain is that if any monasteries in the later eighth century had had an organ, Frankish annals would not have been the place in which to look for a record of it.

Since no unambiguous references to church organs in the later eighth century have ever been found, the Byzantine gift of 757 has played a major part in later history books. And yet, if there had been no reports in such annals, the history of organs would be exactly the same, and one would still have to conjecture what happened in the century and a half between the time of Charlemagne's son Louis, who had an organ, and certain Benedictine reformers of the later tenth century, who also had organs. It is the presence of annals that is exceptional in the story. Since at least the *Liber historiae francorum* of 727,[7] court-associated historiography played a major part in establishing the authority of the Carolingians, drawing attention to various kinds of individual, dated events. The annals concerning Pippin's organ fall exactly into the period when there was a 'deliberate impetus'[8] towards more written documentation in Carolingian government: a crucial development in western culture.

---

[6] For Aimonius and Tolomeo, see pp. 11, 12 notes 21, 23 (Tolomeo = 1727 edn, p. 977). Further additions in Riemann 1879: 192–3, from eleventh- and sixteenth-century versions.

[7] MGH S rer. merov. 2. Probably written at St-Denis, the *Liber* was one of the documents in which 'the Franks had been learning to see themselves as a regenerate people' and was 'a record of Carolingian doings as seen from their point of view' (Wallace-Hadrill 1983: 300, 199).

[8] R. McKitterick, *The Carolingians and the Written Word* (Cambridge, 1989), 25.

Whether it was this impetus that encouraged writers in other, non-political areas such as music-theory and notation is beyond the present book to examine, but a connection between them is not difficult to imagine. Even then, it was another two hundred years before monasteries documented much in the way of special objects, and did so then as a means of recording the work of charismatic reformers. Before the tenth-century monastic revival, church records such as they are remained uniformly unenlightening with respect to organs, and even then became only fitfully otherwise.

If vocal organum was already known at much the same period as Pippin's organ[9] and if there is any possibility that in some sources organum was understood to be connected with the organ,[10] then there is even less reason to suppose that music and instrument developed as a consequence of the Byzantine *organum* of 757. It surely cannot be that the *Musica* and *Scolica enchiriadis*, though originating at no great distance from Compiègne, gave attention to vocal organum and pipe-scales only because a century or so earlier the King of the Franks had received Greek envoys bearing gifts? Nor can it be that Hucbald is referring to an actual copy of Pippin's organ when a little later he mentions the *hydraules*[11] – a copy made in or for one or other monastery in the region of St-Amand? To suggest that organs became church instruments through a kind of 'model' offered to monasteries by the Carolingian court is to over-emphasize the significance of this extraordinary instrument reported in the annals: whatever it was, it was meant to be unusual.

If the Byzantine gift was a particular kind of device not known or even seen before by Franks or Saxons or Lombards, what was it? A twelfth-century copy of the Arabic treatise by the engineer 'Muristos' (see below, this chapter) speaks of a hydraulic siren-organ made by him for the 'King of the Inner Franks', and the question will always remain whether this was indeed one and the same instrument as the gift to Pippin in 757.[12] No doubt a high-pressure siren of one or more pipes (up to five, according to the Arabic descriptions) would have been unknown in Francia and previously 'unseen' by Frankish chroniclers. In any case, if Muristos's siren-organ for the Franks had an otherwise totally unknown high wind pressure it would surely have got reported in documents one way or another. The possibility that Pippin's *organum* was a siren is strengthened by the specious report of a Byzantine organ for Charlemagne, for this suggests there to have been some nebulous knowledge, some folk-memory of an exceptional device still invoked a couple of generations later.

---

9   S. J. P. van Dijk, 'Papal Schola versus Charlemagne', in *Organicae voces: Festschrift J. Smits van Waesberghe*, ed. P. Fischer (Amsterdam, 1963), 21–30, here 23.
10 The arguments for this in e.g. Schuberth 1968: 119 cannot easily survive the evidence of complex word-use surveyed in Reckow 1975, even if vocal organum is understood to include many kinds of polyphonic technique.
11 Suggested in M. Huglo, 'Le développement du vocabulaire de l'Ars musica à l'époque carolingienne', *Latomus* 34 (1975), 130–51, here 139–41.
12 Farmer 1931: 150ff. Hardouin 1966 bases part of the argument on the word 'king' being strictly appropriate only to the years between 754 (when Pippin was anointed, unlike the Merovingians he succeeded) and 812 (when Byzantium acknowledged Charlemagne's title of *emperor*). But 'king of the inner [= distant] Franks' is unlikely to be so specific in an Arabic source?
    Schuberth 1968: 81 claims the Muristos organ to have had a wind-pressure of 6 m (!) but this may be a misreading of Farmer's measurements: see p. 248.

However, this could also have been the case if Pippin's *organum* had not been a siren but the alternative: a regular Byzantine ceremonial organ with a timber framework and precious decorations (see below, this chapter), something that could have been similarly sacred or ceremonial in function, i.e. in so far as it accompanied a sacred ruler who entered a church or chapel for whatever purpose. Had the emperor known of Pippin's efforts to establish and reform both the royal *cappella* and the realm's liturgy, sending him an organ might have seemed particularly appropriate. But appropriate for what? Even in these circumstances, it would not have been a 'church organ', either for the Byzantine emperor or the Frankish king, in the way that became familiar later: it was not a piece of furniture for church or a regular piece of equipment in its services, for which presumably other special objects then being imported – the sacred books and relics from Rome – were intended. Whether he sent a siren or a (more tuneful?) ceremonial organ, the emperor did not know 'church organs', nor did any monasteries in his empire.

Objects also dispatched by Pope Paul I to Pippin about this time – perhaps the same year – do not relate directly to the Byzantine organ but do give a glimpse of the period's crafts, for he sent not only an *antiphonale et responsale* for Pippin's liturgical reform (and some Aristotle and other Greeks) but 'last but not least, a nocturnal clock' (*nec non et horologium nocturnum* – PL 89.1157). A 'nocturnal' clock meant something other than a sundial, probably some kind of clepsydra useful for marking the time for mattins. But useful for whom? If Pippin's *cappella* rose in the night like monks in a convent, or if the pope's gift was meant to encourage them to do so, a clock had in effect as sacred a purpose as the liturgical books, and soon no doubt major monasteries made their own copies of both. Assuming that the pope's gifts originated in Rome, there were clockmakers at work there, and although nothing whatever is known about organs in eighth-century Rome one might conjecture that modest musical instruments would have given skilled clockmakers little trouble. Again the question arises: were modest organs being made all the time but did not reach the pages of annals and chronicles unless they were exceptional, like Pippin's? Whatever Pope Paul's clock had been, it too did not get recorded in the Carolingian annals.

Somewhere in central Italy there had been a tradition for water-clocks, water-organs and automata, judging by the request of 507 by Theodoric, King of the Ostrogoths, to his chancellor Boethius for such gifts to be sent to the King of the Burgundians (according to Cassiodorus – MGH AA 12.39f). These gifts commissioned from Boethius were diplomatic too, for Theodoric, having become King of the Romans and Ostrogoths in Italy, was developing a confederation with the Burgundians, Franks and others. Making such gifts was a recognized way of proceeding. Theodoric's request to Boethius also makes it unlikely to be true, as is still sometimes claimed, that it was only through the Arabs that water-clocks can have been known in such ex-Roman provinces as Spain.

Not least in view of this shadowy activity, a fundamental uncertainty still surrounds the annals' record of the year 757 and how such phrases as 'never seen or heard before' are to be understood. This was a phrase used elsewhere by chroniclers, for example in an account in the Fredegar Chronicle of another gift: the relics of St Peter sent to Charles Martel by Pope Gregory III in 739.[13] Yet relics of the apostle – like gifts from Byzantium, signalling a conferred authority – had circulated earlier, not least in England.

'Charlemagne's organ of 812'

The sole report of this organ, as given below, is by Notker Balbulus[14] who, in his *Life of Charlemagne*, written after 883, reports on 'all kinds of instruments' (*omne genus organorum*) being brought to Aachen by a Byzantine legation of 812. Since the organ was said to have been copied by Charlemagne's workmen, the story may be reflecting those occasions on which gifts were taken back when the legation left for home (Schuberth 1968: 121). However, recent historians, from Degering onwards (1905: 61), have cast doubt on the whole report, suggesting that Notker was confusing it with Pippin's organ or with an Islamic legation of 806, which also brought diverse exotica such as great tents and many silk robes. Organs are too sophisticated to have been included in the baggage of other legations sent to Charlemagne and his son, for example those by the warring Avars.[15] It is also possible that Notker had in mind Einhard's earlier reports of the official homage paid Charlemagne by both the caliph and by successive emperors of Byzantium (*Vita caroli magni, c.* 830 – MGH SS 2.451–2), which no doubt included the dispatching of gifts. Einhard's influence on Notker has already been mentioned in Chapter 4.

Notker does not say that any of the *organa* were gifts, rather models that were then copied. Even if the story as a whole is unreliable – a confusion of other stories made several reigns later – this is a plausible detail for complicated equipment being imported to a nerve-centre such as Aachen. Clearly, copying was necessary if any import had anything to do with the spread of the organ across Carolingian Europe. The account also transmits certain technical details:

adduxerunt etiam idem missi	the same envoys also brought
omne genus organorum, sed	all kind of instruments (indeed
et variarum rerum secum.	of various things) with them.
Quae cuncta	All of which
	were very carefully inspected
ab opificibus sagacissimi	by the craftsmen of the all-wise
Karoli quasi dissimulanter	Charles with simulated indifference,
aspecta acuratissime sunt	
in opus conversa,	[and] copied in their work,
et praecipue illud musicorum	and especially that outstanding
organum praestantissimum,	*organum* of the musicians

[13]   J. M. Wallace-Hadrill, *Fredegarii Chronicorum Liber Quartus cum continuationibus* (London, 1960), 96.
[14]   Preface to the edition in MGH rer. germ. n.s. 12, ed. H. H. Haefele (Berlin, 1959).
[15]   Islamic embassies described in Buckler, (see note 4): 31ff (esp. 36–7). For scepticism about any close relationship between Charlemagne's court and the caliphs, see E. A. Belyaev, *Arabs, Islam and the Arab Caliphate in the Early Middle Ages* (London, 1969), 221. For no less than eight Avar legations to the Franks (in 782, 790, 795, 796, 797, 805, 811 and 822), see MGH S rer. ger. in usum schol. (1895).

quod doliis ex aere	which with vessels★ cast in bronze
conflatis follibusque taurinis	and bellows of bullhide
	blowing magnificently
per fistulas aereas	through the bronze pipes,
mire perflantibus	
rugitum quidem	matched the very roar
tonitrui boatu,	of the crash of thunder,
garrulitatem vero lyrae, vel	the chattering of the lyre, or the
cymbali dulcedine[m] coaequabat.	sweetness of bells.
Quod ubi positum fuerit	Where it was set up
quamdiuque duraverit et	and how long it lasted
quomodo inter alia (rei publicae)	and how, with other public things
	[among other losses to the state?]
post dampna perierit,	it later perished,
non est huius loci vel	this is not the place or
temporis enarrare.	time to report. (MGH rer. germ. n. s. 12.58)

★ *dolium*: large jar for wine, etc.
perhaps a barrel (see below)

The reference to thunder, lyre and bells is formulaic: cf. the Bishop of Dol's letter of *c.* 1125 – pp. 213f. If it can refer to anything as concrete as the low, middle and high sounds on a bronze chest,[16] then this could be an organ of Notker's own period, nearly a century later. 'Vessels of bronze' is puzzling: are they the words of an eye-witness (not Notker)? Or are they the words of someone knowing something about the old *hydraulis*, guessing that this is what his original source meant and finding *dolium* or *doelium* a good term for the cistern? (Theophilus's term for a cooper was *doliarius* – 1.17.) In that case, the bullhide bellows would have replaced cylinders as feeders for the cistern which, though possible, is not otherwise recorded; but see the organ of Aquincum: Chapter 14. Either way, *taurinis follibus* is also formulaic, and a well-read scribe would know Virgil *Georgics* 4.171. If *dolium* meant the bronze chest, then perhaps the Byzantines worked with shapes different from the rectangular box implied by the usual terms for chest (*capsa, cista*). Another possible reading of the lines – that *doliis ex aere conflatis* means 'vessels blown up with air' (*aĕre*) – could apply to either chest or cistern.

Two other points in this account may be significant. The reference first to 'all kinds of instruments' and only later to that 'instrument of the musicians' (*organum musicorum*) sounds as if the Byzantines brought various complex devices with them, not necessarily musical instruments. In that case, perhaps there had indeed been a Byzantine or Arabic siren-organ known by Charlemagne or his father or both, and that knowledge of it percolated down to Notker. None of this has anything to do with the Church or its liturgy, nor with the polyphonic vocal organum that seems to have been known at Charlemagne's court, judging by a phrase or two of Walahfrid Strabo (*c.* 809–49), poet and editor of Einhard's *Vita caroli magni*.[17]

[16]   Taken by Hardouin 1966: 42 to mean an organ of 'without doubt, three octaves'.
[17]   So understood by M. Schuler, 'Die Musik an den Höfen der Karolinger', *AfMw* 27 (1970), 23–40, here 29–30. But perhaps *organum* for Walahfrid means 'organized ensemble music' rather than regular polyphony.

The second point concerns the last sentence. Despite its coyness, it does suggest that an author of *c.* 900 asked certain questions – where was the instrument placed, over what period was it used, and what happened to it[18] – probably none of which any source would have told him. There are various possible answers to the questions raised. An organ in the palace of Aachen would have suffered from the Viking raids in the late ninth century; these were raids whose success did not flatter Carolingian claims of unique and divine authority and might best be glossed over by any monk of St Gall.[19] Or since a signal/siren-organ had military uses, as the Arabic sources made clear (Farmer 1931: 121ff), it was no doubt vulnerable on campaigns under latterday Rolands fighting the pagans or each other. In either event, the instrument would not have survived.

Louis the Pious's organ of 826

Charlemagne's biographer Einhard and other contemporary sources, such as Walahfrid Strabo and the author of the *Life* of Louis the Pious, report in similar terms on a further instrument, now with other concrete details:[20]

the date is 826;
Venetian *presbyter* Georgius was brought to court [at Ingelheim?] with one
 Count Baldric and said he could make an organ;
in the Greek or Byzantine style (*in more graecorum*);
Louis sent him to Aachen and authorized the treasurer to supply what he
 needed;
because it was something that had not been in use previously (*ante se inusitata
 erant*);
Georgius built the organ with great skill;
at or in the palace of Aachen (*in aquensi palatio*);
an organ called in Greek *hydraulica*.

Another poet, Ermold, also remarked of the *organa* that Francia had never seen one before (*organa . . . quae nunquam francia crevit* – MGH SS 2.513) and that the Greeks were 'proud' of it (*superba*). This latter remark resembles the point made a generation later by Aurelian of Réôme that the Greeks boasted of their eight modes (CSM 21: 82), prompting Charlemagne to have four others developed. The words of Ermold that follow the remark are also boastful:[21]

Et quis te solis,	And the only thing,
Caesar, superasse putabat	Caesar, in which Constantinople

---

[18] Cf. the similar questions asked about Pippin's organ in Hardouin 1966: 43.
[19] Since accounts of the inhuman atrocities committed by the Northmen are given mostly by Christian monks (as deeds of the Saracens were also reported in Bede's *Hist. Eccl.*), was the pagans' real affront their success against the Lord's anointed?
[20] MGH SS 1.214, 359; MGH SS 15.1.260; MGH SS 2.629-30 (Thegan, *Life*). In Schuberth 1968: 122–3 and Perrot 1965: 395–7.
[21] Part of his campaign to clear himself of accusations of disloyalty? – cf. Wallace-Hadrill 1983: 238.

Constantinopolis,	used to think itself superior to you,
nunc Aquis aula tenet.	now the Palace of Aachen possesses.
Fors erit indicium, quod	Perhaps it will be a warning for them
Francis colla remittant.	to cede to the Frankish yoke. (MGH Poet 2.76, 92)

The hyperbolical diction of Louis's poets – Walahfrid and Ermold in particular[22] – may not make what they say totally unreliable but nor does it convey much technical information. At most one can see that Ermold's words do suit a high-pressure military siren (something requiring sophisticated metallurgy) better than they do an organ used indoors. It is hard to see how even a flattering poet could imagine that a few ranks of copper pipes placed in the gallery of the Aachen octagon would cause hearts in Constantinople to quake with fear.

Salient points in the different reports of Louis's instrument are that a monk from Venice was the expert in this Byzantine technology, that Louis (then at Ingelheim) sent him to the empire's administrative centre for materials, that Georgius built the organ in the *palatio* or *aula* ('palace, hall') of Aachen, and that it may have been a water-organ. Whether in *more graecorum* was intended to convey the idea of a military siren such as the Byzantines must have used on campaigns, and as Ermold's words above suggest was the case here, is not known. It is not unlikely that a Venetian priest–craftsman would use Byzantine terms: *hydraulis* appears in two sources (Einhard and the Annals of Fulda), and perhaps it was for the complex metalworking of bronze cylinders that Georgius needed to go to Aachen and its workshops. If the legates visiting Pippin had used the word *organon* for their instrument (see above) but Georgius had used *hydraules* for his, one might expect two different kinds of 'device' to be intended. But Hucbald's use of *hydraulica* suggests that ninth–century authors used it simply to mean the organ as distinct from other *organa* (see Chapter 3).

Hydraules is not the only ambiguity: *inusitata* may say less than appears (cf. Pippin's organ 'not seen' before), and *aula* can mean many things: perhaps the nave of the chapel, perhaps the main hall.[23] On the Aachen chapel and sites for an organ, see Chapters 7 and 8. Another uncertainty is whether the Georgius of this episode is the Georgius who became Abbot of St-Saulve, Valenciennes, and took with him from Aachen relics of saints recently brought there from Rome, according to Einhard (MGH SS 15.1.260f). Organs from Venice or Constantinople and relics from Jerusalem or Rome share the same kind of Mediterranean authority sought by the Carolingians, or at least by their chroniclers.[24]

The possibility that Pippin's and Louis's organ – either or both – were high-pressure hydraules is not lessened by a passage in an obscure poem of Walahfrid Strabo which speaks of a woman losing her senses and dying from the sweetness of the sound of, it seems, this organ (*decedens sensibus . . . perdiderit vocum dulcedine*

---

[22] Recent examination of such poetic idioms in P. Godman, 'Louis "the Pious" and his poets', *FMSt* 19 (1985), 239–89.

[23] On the uncertain location of the *aula* and *lateran* at Aachen, see L. Falkenstein, *Der 'Lateran' der karolingischen Pfalz zu Aachen* (Cologne/Graz, 1966), 55f.

[24] Greek theological writings were also sent to Louis by the emperor Michael over this same period: in 827, works of Pseudo-Dionysius (see Wallace-Hadrill 1983: 226–7). St-Saulve was in the centre of the Lobbes–Loan–St-Amand area: see Hucbald above, p. 46.

vitam: MGH Poet. 2.374). Elsewhere, Walahfrid uses *organa* probably to mean a string instrument, as in the case of the instrument played by Louis's wife Judith (*ibid.*, 2.376). The 'sweet melody' (*dulce melos*) accompanying outdoor events at Aachen, according to this poem, implies something very different from a siren, but the phrase is too glibly allusive to mean anything specific here. The four or five pipes, such as Muristos describes for his siren (see Chapter 14), are enough to create sweet melody, it is true, but not if they all sounded at once. The whole tenor of Walahfrid's account resembles that of ninth- and tenth-century Arabic reports of hearers losing their senses on hearing Muristos's organ, or dying from frenzy at the sound of the siren (Farmer 1931: 58, 64, 137). One needs also to remember that Cicero's translation of some lines from the Sirens' scene in the *Odyssey* could mean that learned poets of Walahfrid's kind were familiar with the legends and certain interpretations of them.[25]

A further speculation has been that Louis's organ of 826 was like those drawn in the contemporary Utrecht Psalter and that the Psalter's artist saw Louis as an *imitatio David* (Schuberth 1968: 125f). Both are possible, but in that case other organ-references of the period are no less likely to relate to some particular instrument or setting. One example is the remarks on organs drawn from St Augustine by Amalar of Metz for his liturgical treatise *De ecclesiasticis officiis*, first dedicated to Louis (PL 105.1107); but rather than relate to a particular instrument, it could be all such references are doing no more than passing on knowledge traditional to their medium, whether in words or pictures. Nevertheless, Louis is known to have had contacts with Byzantine Italy (see Chapter 10) and in 831 received a diplomatic mission from the Caliph of Baghdad. For the Emperor of the West, as for the Emperor of the East, various locations in his chief palace – chapel, main hall, 'Lateran' hall – could have served for royal ceremony of the kind that in Constantinople was the occasion for the sound of organs.

Organs in the Byzantine court

The various references in ceremonial and other books of ninth- and tenth-century Constantinople relate to occasions or situations that consciously kept alive practices of late imperial Rome and were based on sources two or more centuries old. Organs played at state arrivals (*adventus*), at the hippodrome, weddings, palace ceremony, diplomatic receptions and banquets; and they also served as proud technological feats impressing both the Franks and the Arabs.[26] Seldom, however, is any technical detail clear, and from the descriptions one can make only such surmises as the following:

---

[25] Cicero, *De Finibus* 5.49, where it is not the sweetness of the voices (*suavitate vocum*) that attracted Odysseus but his thirst for knowledge, something Cicero found more worthy than mere idle song (*canticulis tantus iretitus*). However, the oldest copy now known is eleventh century (Reynolds 1986: 112–13).
     Walahfrid's verse is no clearer when it deals with such concrete objects as the statue of Theodoric in the Palace of Aachen: discussed in Falkenstein (see note 23): 55f.
[26] A convenient selection and arrangement of sources is in Schuberth 1968: 56–93. On the late date of the sources for the *De ceremoniis* (book of imperial ceremonies), see also Baldovin 1987: 197–8.

on a platform (πούλπιτον) in the entrance or reception hall of the palace (χαλκῆ) stood a golden organ (χρυσοῦν ὄργανον) on one side, a throne on the other, a standing cross between the two (a Ceremonial of 838: Schuberth 1968: 56);

in the Hall of Justinian was another tribune on which stood the high throne: on either side, below (κάτωδεν) and on the inside of two curtains (ἔσωδεν τών δύο βήλων), were two silver organs (ἀργυρᾶ ὄργανα). Those blowing the organs (τὰ αὐλοῦντα) stood outside (= behind?) the curtains (Ceremonial of 957: *ibid.*, 57).ῆ̃

Such reports seem to indicate an organ with a lot of gold leaf (chest and frame? also the pipes?), imposing enough in size to be called the 'chief wonder' (πρωτόδαυμα); and two organs either silver-plated (including the copper pipes?) or with a chest and frame embellished with silver panels (a kind of revetment, as on many relics-caskets and altars of the period). Whether either organ was an automaton is not clear, although Hammerstein 1986: 50ff assumes both were: 'those blowing' could mean the apparatus itself, such as bellows or pistons, as well as bellows-blowers or pump-operators in person. The first location makes the golden organ a kind of equivalent to the throne, the second gives the silver organs a subservient rôle as instruments of the Blue and Green factions. One can imagine that these organs stood before the curtains, the men blowing them standing behind. But the report does not quite say this, and it is possible that there were curtains on the extreme left and right, then the organs inner left and right (seen only when the curtains were pulled back), and the throne in the middle.[27] The curtains, traditional protectors of the divine, surely cut down any reverberation of sound there might have been.

Since the ceremonies of the New Rome do not make a distinction between sacred and secular, the *organon* that sounded as a signal in the hippodrome of Constantinople was no mere circus noise in any modern sense. The hippodrome may not have been a church but its ceremony used organs like any imperial ritual. The ceremonial books mention only the 'imperial organ' (βασιλιςὸν ὄργανον) at the hippodrome, and other instruments appear for other occasions, such as banquets or bridal processions. For all such occasions, hydraules would be appropriate; but bellows-organs with many ranks or speaking at higher pressure than later western organs built for enclosed spaces, would also serve. The fourth-century obelisk of Theodosius shows in relief an organ (or two organs – see p. 6) with bellows trodden by two boys (or slaves represented by a smaller scale) and with windtrunks curving somewhat like those of the Stuttgart Psalter, whose row of pipes similarly looks Roman (see p. 169). The whole scene is as symmetrical in its way as the Utrecht Psalter illustration for Psalm 150 and observes a similar hierarchy of levels, with musical performance on the lowest. If the obelisk does mean to show two organs, then they could have been those of the Byzantine factions or their predecessors in the fourth century.[28] The deep organ-chest(s) indicate(s) more than one rank of

[27] The significance of curtains – drawn back to signal an approachable Presence – is clear from many representations of the period, East and West. In the Utrecht Psalter there is a veil for most temples.

[28] Reproductions (e.g. Degering 1905: plate IV.2) do make it look as if the two organs have different numbers of pipes, eight (?) on the left (with the pipe-mouths towards the spectator), eleven (?) on the right.

pipes; the longest appears to be about 3', in relation to the blower on the far right, but since the scale is symbolic rather than literal, this may be misleading. One interpreter of this carving sees two organs, both hydraules with their base behind a balustrade, the boys as singers not slave wind-raisers, the pipes long enough for the player to have to look round them, not over as in the Nennig mosaic (Hardouin 1966: 46). As at Aachen, the music was behind a latticework screen.

That organs were carried about is clear from the ceremonial book concerning weddings and the acclamations for the bride, and presumably they participated in processions in much the same manner as those accompanying certain church events elsewhere in Christendom (text in Schuberth 1968: 64). Whether those carried by the Factions were the same silver organs from the palace or another pair kept for such purposes is not known: it could be either. A golden organ appeared also in the Golden Hall, and whether there were one or two such gold-leafed or plated organs, the need was probably for portable or movable instruments.

A report of the diplomatic reception in 946 of Saracen representatives in the Great Hall (*magnaura*) speaks of the golden organ between pillars on the right side of the hall and outside the draped curtains. Beyond it was the Blues' silver organ, opposite which was the Greens' (text in Schuberth 1968: 72–3). A little later in the description there are two golden organs in the Clock Room (the emperor's organs) and two silver (the Factions' organs). An eleventh-century report also speaks of two large organs of pure gold decorated with different stones and glass or crystals (Mango 1986: 160–1); this was a later document praising the emperor Theophilos (829–42) and may be running together more than one account. In the main hall or *magnaura* itself was also the throne with the celebrated automata: a growling lion either side, whistling birds in a tree (two trees?) and perhaps other moving beasts.[29] Evidently organ(s), lions and birds all sounded together at certain moments, in imitation of the throne of Solomon. (Like David, Solomon is a name to occur often in connection with ceremonial splendour and musical elements in the liturgy; he is also invoked in the mechanical treatise of Theophilus Presbyter – see p. 270.) If the lions' roar had to be carefully timed, perhaps bellows not cylinders were used for the wind-raising.

A further Arabic source of the later ninth century describes the ceremonials at Constantinople (Schuberth 1968: 74–5) with details that offer other, different light on the organs' structure. Three 'crosses' are brought in to the public hall and fitted before the organ is played; then the organ is brought in and set up; it has a central square wooden structure like an oilpress; it is covered in leather, with sixty copper pipes plated in gold or standing behind a gold panel; bellows 'like smiths' bellows' are fitted into one side; two men blow, a third plays.[30] Useful details here are the

---

[29] Described by Liudprand, Bishop of Cremona (*c.* 920–72) in MGH SS 3.338 and Mango 1986: 209; discussed in Hammerstein 1986: 43–58. Brett 1954 emphasizes the Arab interest in Hero and his designs for automatic mechanisms (see Chapter 14), an interest amply documented from the ninth century onwards (p. 480).

[30] According to the translation used by Hammerstein 1986: 53, the organist 'counts' (*zählt*); but this suggests nothing certain about how the keys worked (sliders? like an abacus? like the later checkers?). Similarly, although the account mentions the blowers and their function before it mentions the organist and his, it does not have to imply (as suggested in Hardouin 1966: 46) that (a) they began their task first, nor that (b) the pressure had to be built up because (c) it must have been a *hydraulis*.

likening of the chest to an oilpress – a waist-high or shoulder-high rectangular
wooden box with sides? – and the number of pipes, 'sixty' no doubt meaning 'a
large collection'. The initial setting up is also important, for 'crosses' sound like the
steadying framework mentioned by Muristos (see p. 249). A firm, rigid construction
would be necessary for bellows-levers if the organ and bellows were large. So it
would be for hydraules, and even the small water-organ as described by Vitruvius
needed a sure fixture for its side-cylinders (the so-called 'ladders', one of the first things
he describes: see Chapter 14). One interesting possibility about this report of 'crosses'
is that some such text (not this one) was known to the artist of the Utrecht Psalter for
Psalms 150 and '151', leading him to make his decorative, crossed upper framework.
Another is that wooden framework of this or another kind – eventually a complete
structure with a decorative side facing the player – gradually became the rigid timber
casework for the western church organ. In the first half of the twelfth century
Theophilus Presbyter was still recommending that the chest be fixed to the wall
with iron rods (p. 265), thus securing the windtrunk without structural casework.

Accounts of these Byzantine organs suggest that not only were there several in
and around the palace but that they were built or replaced from time to time. The
Emperor Theophilos had two organs of solid gold made (ὁλόχρυσα) as well as the
golden or gilded tree: mention of 'smelting' seems to confirm that something more
than just gold leaf is involved here, as do the reports of Michael III (842–67) later
melting down the solid gold lions and organ. One imagines gold panels or a complete gold revetment, as for many an altar. Assuming the scribes were not misled,
such detail as the square wooden structure must therefore relate to other organs – the
original organs' replacements, perhaps. On the whole, however, these various sources
allow for definitive statements about neither the number of organs nor their materials,
and it is arguing too much from an absence of clear evidence – in this case, proof in
the sources that the organs needed players – to conclude with Hammerstein 1986:
56 anything as definite as that all the Byzantine palace organs were automata.

10

The organs of the Utrecht Psalter

The significance of the three representations of hydraules in the Utrecht Psalter (*c.* 816–30)[1] is unquestioned: they are the only certain early Christian drawings of a water-organ and, with the bellows-organs of the Stuttgart Psalter (see p. 165), the oldest extant 'realistic' representations of any organ after late antiquity. More than in any other known psalter, music and its instruments form a major theme in the illustrations of the Utrecht Psalter.[2]

In view of the Psalter's vast literature, which can by no means claim to have answered all the questions to be asked about it, this chapter will summarize relevant issues before remarking on the organ-drawings.

Origin, influence and 'reliability'

Perhaps like one of the Winchester tropers (see p. 39), the Psalter was a precentor's book, large enough and its layout clear enough to be read by a small choir. Carolingian features of the Psalter include its liturgical additions (including canticles) and the psalm-text itself (St Jerome's 'Gallican' psalter). This was the text favoured by the dynasty – the Psalter was known at the court of Charles the Bald (†877) – as too by reformers in tenth-century Winchester. One of the reasons why the Utrecht and Stuttgart Psalters were so strikingly fashioned may be because they represent official policy. However, for the drawings in both psalters the artists could have had more than one version of the psalms in mind, as well as one or more psalm-commentaries.[3] In any case, many seemingly antique details in the drawings are

---

[1] Utrecht, Universiteitsbibliotheek, MS 32. Although *c.* 850 is still sometimes suggested, *c.* 830 is sustained in F. Mütherich, 'Die verschiedenen Bedeutungsschichten in der frühmittelalterlichen Psalterillustration', *FMSt* 6 (1972), 235 and Dufrenne 1978: *passim.* H. L. Kessler, in a review of Dufrenne in *AB* 63 (1981), 142–5, suggests a date between 816 and 823, i.e., the earlier half of the archiepiscopate of Ebbo of Reims (see below).

[2] The most recent comprehensive coverage is K. van der Horst & J. H. A. Engelbregt *Utrecht Psalter,* Codices selecti phototypice impressi Facsimile LXXV (Graz, 1982) and Kommentar LXXV (Graz, 1984). Here, the Psalter's ink is said to follow the recipe of Theophilus (1984: 14).

[3] For a summary of the psalm-texts and their history, written with musical considerations (chants) in mind, see J. Dyer, 'Latin psalters, Old Roman and Gregorian chants', *KmJb* 68 (1984), 11–30. On the Utrecht Psalter's text: D. Panofsky, 'The textual basis of the Utrecht Psalter illustrations', *AB* 25 (1943), 50–8 and Wormald 1953. Comprehensive summary in Kessler (see note 1). On this aspect of the Stuttgart Psalter: McKinnon 1968: 15.

found nowhere else in extant Carolingian art, and conversely, other elements in that art are not found here.

It has long been recognized[4] that stylistic similarities between the Utrecht Psalter and a Gospel made for Ebo or Ebbo, Bishop of Reims 816–34, probably in the scriptorium at Hautvillers (south of Reims), could indicate a similar time and place for the two manuscripts, although the Psalter may be a little earlier than the Gospel.[5] Probably there were once other manuscripts in the same 'series'. At least the text of the Psalter was the work of several scribes and was written in a script ('Rustic capitals') similar to such earlier manuscripts as the fourth-century Vatican copy of Virgil.[6] The drawings were not completed in one operation but went (or were meant to go) through two or three phases. While some are conjectured to have been copied from a Greek (Byzantine) psalter, consensus is now that the Psalter is a typical Carolingian creation in its drawing on various sources. Since including the canticles and 'Psalm 151' is known only from this period, it seems unlikely that the illustrations for them could have antique 'originals'.[7]

Yet it is also agreed that however Carolingian the finished product, for some of the details the artist could have been using a Christian psalter of the fourth or fifth century[8] along with other books known in Hautvillers, where antique sources such as Terence were also copied at the period. Some elements in the drawings surely come from such secular sources. Ebbo's milk-brother was Louis the Pious (emperor 814–40), who had close contacts with Brescia, Ravenna and Italy south of Rome, bringing southern artists to Aachen after 814 and no doubt new illustration-types (Wallace-Hadrill 1983: 227), possibly including the representation of a water-organ. So Greek a motif as a water-organ was probably meant to be Mediterranean or 'oriental', though hardly anything as specific as a salute to St Helena, whose cult became known in Hautvillers. If the Psalter is based on any such 'early models', and if these included 'originals' for the organ-drawings, the questions still remain: do the organs transmit details of late antiquity accurately or inaccurately, did the artist know of more up-to-date organs but preferred the antique for various reasons, or was this an organ-type also still known in the West in *c.* 800? If in the end the Psalter is indeed a *pasticcio all'antica* (Kessler, see note 1), what can it tell us about organs? Some attempt to deal with these questions, which are still not answerable as they stand, will be made in this and the following chapter.

4   A. Goldschmidt, 'Der Utrecht Psalter', *Repertorium für Kunstwissenschaft* 15 (1892), 156–69. Other hypotheses on origin: H. Graeven, 'Die Vorlage des Utrecht Psalters', *ibid.* 21 (1898), 28–35.

5   Summary of previous literature in J. H. A. Engelbregt, *Het Utrechts Psalterium: een eeuw wetenschappelijke Bestudering (1860–1960)* (Utrecht, 1965). On Psalter and Gospel, D. Tselos, 'Defensive addenda to the problem of the Utrecht Psalter', *AB* 49 (1967), 334–49 and Dufrenne 1978: 21. F. M. Carey, 'The scriptoria of Reims during the archbishopric of Hincmar (845–882 AD)', in *Classical and Mediaeval Studies in Honor of Edward Kennard Rand*, ed. L. W. Jones (New York, 1938), 57, provisionally dates the Gospel to 800–25, the Psalter to 825–45.

6   On the handwriting, see P. Durrieu, 'L'origine du manuscrit dit le Psautier d'Utrecht', in *Mélanges Julien Hovet* (Paris, 1895), 639–57. On related manuscripts: Horst 1984 (see note 2): 29ff.

7   For Greek models, arguments are already summarized in A. Hulshof, 'Het Utrechtsche Psalterium', *Het Boek* 3 Spec. Nr. (1914), 116–40; for Carolingian origin, Engelbregt 1964: 142ff and Horst 1984 (see note 2): 41; on the question of the canticles, Wormald 1953.

8   Dufrenne 1978: 175, 218–19; also Kessler (see note 1).

The Psalter seems to have been at Christ Church, Canterbury, by *c.* 1000 or earlier, remained in England[9] for some seven centuries, and is related to three other psalters: London, British Library, Harley 603 (from Canterbury, *c.* 1000 but some drawings later twelfth century), a direct copy of it; Cambridge, Trinity College, R. 17. 1 (the 'Eadwine Psalter', *c.* 1147), based on an intermediate copy, as too Paris, Bibliothèque Nationale, lat. 8846.[10] The Gallican text evidently suited the aims of the English Benedictine reform of the tenth century. Unlike the Utrecht Psalter but like the Stuttgart, the Harley Psalter shows an organ in connection with Psalm 136/137, 'By the waters of Babylon', in this case a row of seven pipes without chest or bellows (panpipes?), perhaps alluding to the *septem discrimina vocum* of music-theory and paired with a harp, also probably of seven strings. (Harps in the Harley manuscript appear 'realistic', even 'actual'.) At this point the Utrecht Psalter pictures some stringed instruments of the cithara kind, perhaps either because the artist assumed the words *organa nostra* meant an instrument resembling 'David's harp' or because he also bore in mind a further translation of the psalms: one version of the St Jerome's psalter, probably not known to the Harley Psalter artist, reads *citharas nostras* instead of *organa nostra.*[11]

The main organological question about all of these psalter illustrations is how 'reliable' is their technical information for an organ of any period: what are they showing wittingly and unwittingly, and how far does either kind of information fit the actuality of a craft like organ-building? Original 'sources' for the Utrecht Psalter could be visualizations of written documents the author had read (for example Vitruvius or other late antique scientific books available in ninth-century Reims); reproductions of ancient painting, stuccoes or carvings (some known in Reims?); earlier manuscripts (not necessarily Byzantine – perhaps Syrian?); actual objects, new or old; or – most likely of all – a combination of these, along with what the artist imagined or intended to convey of antique, scriptural practice.

One or other of these factors could 'explain' the two organists for Psalm 150: this could be a scene created by an artist's other intentions (for example to make symmetry), by his visualizing polyphony (i.e. music produced by more than one person), by visualizing certain phraseology known from books (on the 'concordant brothers', see Chapter 12), and by sheer imagination (for example, what would convey the energy and exaltation of mood in Psalm 150). Whether any 'actual practice' is behind the

---

9   Perhaps first at Reculver Abbey before being removed to its mother church at Canterbury (Engelbregt 1964: 9; Wormald 1953: 1) or brought to Winchester from Fleury by Bishop Æthelwold before 984 (G. R. Benson & D. T. Tselos, 'New light on the origin of the Utrecht Psalter', *AB* 13 (1931), 13–79).

10 Comparison between Utrecht, Harley and Eadwine Psalters is already illustrated in W. de G. Birch, *The History, Art and Palaeography of the Manuscript Styled the Utrecht Psalter* (London, 1876). On these and other manuscripts influenced by the Utrecht Psalter, see Horst (see note 2): 55f. For an Anglo-Saxon psalter of *c.* 1050 (Paris, Bibliothèque Nationale, lat. 8824), whose few tiny drawings may be based directly or indirectly on the Utrecht Psalter, see B. Colgrave, *The Paris Psalter*, Early English Manuscripts in Facsimile 8 (Copenhagen, 1958), preface.

11 St Jerome: PL 28.1297. The Harley Psalter organ/panpipes is illustrated in Page 1979. It is possible that in this Psalter the instruments were added by another hand; the artist also drew three quite different kinds of tree for Psalm 136/137, as if he had reasons for showing variety.

Harp and organ are both *organa* in the sense implied by the Vulgate, viz. an equivalent to the Septuagint's *organon*, 'instruments or tools'; see also note 19 below. The Hebrew versions speak of *kinoro*, however, a stringed instrument generally thought to resemble the Greek *kithara*. (Remarks on the texts and terminology of the various Latin psalters in Richenhagen 1984: 187–8).

conception of two organists will probably never be certain, nor – a question seldom asked about medieval sources – whether this representation might have led to any such practice.

Naturally, the questions about organs in the Psalter are not isolated: a typical puzzle is the drawing of a church for Psalm 26/27 on f. 15. In its domed tower at the crossing, its eastern apse, two transepts (east and west, latter with an entrance), aisles with entrance, and pedimented western entrance (with drapes and cross), users of the Psalter in Reims or Canterbury would have had a 'realistic' model before them. There are even certain parallels with the then recent, exceptional and renowned church of St-Riquier. Yet the building on f. 15 is very similar to that on a somewhat later ivory carving,[12] suggesting – since in this instance it is clear which was copying which – that this was a type of building found useful for ninth-century representations irrespective of what either illustrator knew personally. In other words, an actual church could well have served for a model which then became conventionally re-interpreted by a succession of artists. Organs, being generally less familiar and relevant to artists, have a much less certain pedigree. But it seems common sense to assume that the illustrator of Psalm 150 in the Utrecht Psalter did not wilfully change what he knew of the instrument – from a previous drawing, from a treatise or 'from life' – as much as his drawings were later changed by the artist of the Eadwine Psalter (see below).

On some sources of knowledge for the Stuttgart Psalter's artist, see Chapter 11.

Psalm 70/71, f. 40 (Plate 3)

Assuming that the Psalter's psalms were illustrated in order, this (or Psalm 136/137 in the Stuttgart Psalter) is the oldest manuscript illustration of an organ, and was identified as such earlier this century.[13] Compared with the two other drawings, it looks unfinished and could give the impression of being the work of a different artist. There seems to have been either a new quill at this point in the manuscript or the artist used his ink in such a way as to give the darkest hue, apparently without a preparatory sketch. Most likely is that the apparent carelessness of the drawing is a means of conveying the topos, the subject's indifference to certain objects: for like St Cecilia, David is indifferent to instruments (see p. 3). Although he is capable of singing to the cithara and so making use of instruments, it is his lips (*labia*), tongue (*lingua*) and soul (*anima*), that rejoice in praise, not his fingers as they sound pipes or strings. Such an interpretation of these particular words goes beyond St Augustine's commentary on Psalm 70/71 (PL 36.900) but is not incompatible with it.

The organ has pipes deftly suggested by single vertical lines making an oblique row at the top (increasing in length from the viewer's left to right), either nine or seven pipes, depending on the purpose of the two outer lines. Either these represent pipes in sequence or are outer frame-limbs following the sloping contour, probably

---

[12] Comparison in Dufrenne 1978: 190 figs. 88, 89.
[13] A. Brom, 'Afbeeldingen van Orgels in het Utrechtsche Psalterium', *Het Boek* 3 Spec. Nr. (1914), 141–4.

Plate 3 Illustration of Psalm 70/71 in the Utrecht Psalter: Utrecht Bibliotheek der Rijksuniversiteit, MS 32/484, f. 40

the former. Judging by the two other drawings in the Psalter, we face the front of the organ so that David, were he to move across to play the instrument, would pick up the lyre or stand behind the organ to face us. The shallow chest and two water-cisterns can be seen, but no *pnigeus* (the cone-shaped vessel inside the cistern, the top of which is visible in the other drawings) nor cylinder-and-piston at the sides. The base seems to be hidden by a fold in the terrain: a sign that the organ was of relegated importance? However, the hoops binding the round cisterns are clear enough. Hoops are not mentioned by Vitruvius or Hero, nor known from mosaics and most other representations, and their effect is to suggest a detail observed from real-life cylinders by the artist or his source. They may also have been known in Arabic manuscripts (see p. 247) and do appear for the organ-cylinders in the terra-cotta oil-lamp from Carthage[14] – a species of useful ornament not unlikely to have been known in late Roman or Merovingian Reims. A butter-churn on f. 86 of the Utrecht Psalter is hooped, and it is not at all impossible that for the organ the detail could be both antique and modern, both allusive and realistic.

That the pipes are in one sequence, unlike the double sets in both other drawings (see below), also raises questions. Assuming that some symmetry was desirable in the drawing for Psalm 150 and by extension for 'Psalm 151', are we to think that the single long-to-short sequence was normal and the double sets less so, shown for special effect? True symmetry in Psalm 150 would have produced the mitre-shape for a row of pipes, i.e. an inverted V with the longest pipe in the middle. But this may have been far too speculative for the Psalter's artist, who was probably going far enough in changing from the standard long-to-short sequence of pipes as they are in Psalm 70/71 to the double set of pipes for Psalm 150 and '151'.

Psalm 150, f. 83 (Plate 4)

In few respects is the information in this famous picture clear, and, as with the Winchester poem, there have long been conflicting interpretations of it.

On a firm (wooden?) base, four piston-and-cylinders – the hinged levers worked reciprocally by four energetic blowers using both arms – feed two round water-cisterns bound with hoops (barrel-hoops of iron?). One of each pair of cylinders has a decorative (?) vertical band, making it look at first as if there were three cylinders per set: an error in the draft, confusion on the artist's part, or the carefully drawn mark of a soldered seam? From these cisterns two *pnigeus*-necks pass into a shallow chest on which are placed two identical rows of four graded pipes, treble to player's right. The structure below the chest is shaded as if there is a back panel preventing one from looking through this part of the organ.[15] Two organists are standing behind (?), one with the fingers of both hands doing something on the chest, the other with the fingers of one hand similarly placed while the other directs two blowers. Blowers and players are producing sound, as are the other instruments in the drawing;[16] this association of horns with the organ recalls various representations

---

[14] Reproduced in Degering 1905: plate I (1–3) and Perrot 1965: plates XI–XII.
[15] In this detail, the structure does rather resemble an altar, and one could imagine decorated panels of beaten copper etc. on the other side, as for the front of an altar-table.
[16] Air (= breath, sound) is drawn coming out of the ends of the wind instruments, though not from the organ pipes.

Plate 4 Illustration for Psalm 150 in the Utrecht Psalter: Utrecht, Bibliotheek der Rijksuniversiteit, MS 32/484, f. 83

of Roman ceremonies. The decorative framework of the organ (two double uprights and a cross piece) could most plausibly be understood as turned woodwork, the material therefore a hardwood; but the conscious contrast between the frameworks of the two organs (Psalms 150 and '151') could be more the musings of an artist than a strictly observed detail.

Uncertainty about the detail arises in several respects, some from the nature of the drawing (it was done in more than one stage), some from the content (there is little to compare it with from elsewhere). Several interpreters have seen two rows of five pipes each (Perrot 1965: 346; Dufrenne 1978: 175), although it is not quite the case that the ambiguity arises from the perspective (Hardouin 1966: 36) since the ghostly 'fifth pipe' at the treble end of each row has what would be the correct length. More likely is that the drawing is ambiguous because the artist was uncertain and wished merely to give an impression of multitude. Also possible is that the drawing results from revision(s) of a first sketch. In the normal way, the pressure and volume of wind produced by such pistons would feed far more than four pipes, and one can imagine various possibilities: that they speak at very high pressure, that four stands for a bigger row or more than one row, that they express the artist's understanding of the tetrachord and are therefore a visual synecdoche (like the heptachord of later medieval illustrations) and so forth. Whatever is the case, close inspection of the manuscript does suggest there to have been at some point a fifth pipe for each set, not perhaps very precisely allowed for in the first sketching.

Some interpreters have also assumed the players to be Christian monks, robed and tonsured, but comparison with other figures in the Psalter makes this unlikely. Nor can we know the length of the robes in question. In general the Psalter appears to avoid a presentation that is liturgical or even spiritual (Engelbregt 1973: 26ff), which may or may not give a true impression of how organs were seen at the time: they would not have been Christian, liturgical nor indeed objects of piety other than in their role as representatives of the Temple practices of Solomon and David (see p. 82). But this role was all-important and, together with St Augustine's commentary on the psalms, must have helped to win acceptance for the instrument sooner or later. Although, therefore, it is virtually out of the question that either monks or quasi-liturgical performances are being portrayed, the picture does give a clear indication of one way in which organs were perceived.

Both the cylinders with their windtrunks and the decorative frame at the 'front' (?) of the chest suggest that we are looking at the back of the organ.[17] Either the personnel were placed 'incorrectly' in order to show as much detail as possible, or altar-like organs were played from the front – presumably the latter. A different uncertainty arises from what the players appear to be doing. If the black marks lying on the chest represent press-keys, as the curved position of the fingers suggests, then there is here the total picture of an organ in action: keys and fingers, pipes, chest, wind-raising apparatus and two organists standing at the front of the organ, which has some kind of casework or decorative framework.

What does seem an obvious impossibility is for the organists to be threading their fingers through the pipes: something due to error or ignorance on the part of the artist? Since it is not at all unlikely that his knowledge of how the organ was played came from books, one might guess that for this detail his source was Cassiodorus, whose mention of fingers and mechanism is so brief that it leaves the reader to imagine what a player actually did (see quotation on p. 299). The drawing surely cannot mean that the vertical pipes themselves were somehow slid into and out of position above their wind-holes, as has been confidently proposed recently (Hammerstein 1986: 91)? There is a further and distinct possibility: the players' gesture is metaphorical, conveying an impression of the puzzling and labyrinthine skill (such as a non-organist might see it) behind musicians' being able to produce the right sounds in the right order. A literal reading of the picture, therefore – which would lead to the idea that the player's hand-position has 'nothing to do with organ playing at any period of its history' (McKinnon 1974: 11) – may not be what it is asking for.

That the players appear to be sustaining several (but not all?) of their notes is neither more nor less certain, like the left organist's gesture to his blowers. Is this exhorting them to great and sustained effort such as would be necessary for a high-pressure cylinder, or a signal for the beat and musical phraseology such as would need regularly

---

[17] Clear evidence that cylinders are towards the rear of the organ-plinth (not in the front plane) is given in the Carthage lamp terracotta (as in Perrot 1965: plate XI.6). Horst, see note 2 (1984: 92), mistakenly calls the cistern and cylinders 'bellows'.

alternating wind-supply? The Winchester poem line 145 may imply a similar question (see p. 192), although the idea of pumping on or for the beat is not one that is familiar in recent centuries for wind-instruments with reservoirs, such as the bagpipes. A further question concerns the pipes: unlike Psalm 70/71, Psalms 150 and '151' show two sets of pipes cut (less exactly in the latter) to a proportional length in which pipe 3 is half pipe 1, and pipe 4 half pipe 2. Is this a vague interpretation of the Pythagorean tetrachord or something more realistic – the representation of four sounds[18] used in various combinations, for variable noises like a signal or acclamation, something 'unmelodic'? The four bells being struck by David in some later medieval psalters may represent the same idea of clamour, when organs themselves had longer compass and therefore could play wide-ranging melodies. Earlier, perhaps they did play four diatonic notes at once, in tetrachordal clusters.

Apocryphal Psalm or 'Psalm 151', f. 91' (Plate 5)

The psalm speaks of David as shepherd and musician, 'making' an *organum* and playing a *psalterium* (v2):

manus meae fecerunt organum	my hands have made the *organum*
et digiti mei aptaverunt	and my fingers have fitted the
psalterium.	*psalterium.*

The Greek or Septuagint terms are *organon* and *psalterion*:[19] neither term in Greek or Latin necessarily implies a musical instrument (see also 'Psalm 151' in the Stuttgart Psalter, Chapter 11).

The drawing, not certainly by the same artist as Psalm 150, shows the hydraulis with some of the same features: two cisterns, three pumps (the fourth hidden in the perspective?), eight or nine pipes in two sets, decorative framework (now a flat frame, looking like joined wood), a shallow but deeper chest, and a player 'behind' the organ but again perhaps meant to be at the front (with the decorative framework on his side of the organ). It looks like a less careful drawing: the left-hand pistons are joined by a redundant third lever (? see below), and the right has no lever unless it is hidden by the sheep. There are no windtrunks, and there appears to be a ghostly ninth pipe at the player's right-hand or treble end, as if the drawing for Psalm 150 was being loosely copied. The pipes have a less geometric pipe-top line, and the organist (in shepherd's clothing?) looks as if he were added: in fact, in both drawings the organists could have been added after the organs were already drawn. In 'Psalm 151', the organist's fingers are given less detail and are not positioned over the 'keys'.

---

[18]   Hardouin 1966: 38–9 points out that the clanging of four bells together leads to the terms *quadrillon* and hence *carillon*.

[19]   On the inclusion of 'Psalm 151' in English–Roman psalters from at least the eight century, see D. H. Wright, *The Vespasian Psalter*, Early English Manuscripts in Facsimile 14 (Copenhagen, 1967). Old English glosses in this psalter, thought to have been added in the ninth century, give *organan* as an equivalent for *organum* in Psalms 150 and '151', *hearpan* for *psalterium* in 'Psalm 151'.

Plate 5 Illustration for 'Psalm 151' in the Utrecht Psalter: Utrecht, Bibliotheek der Rijksuniversiteit, MS 32/484, f. 91'

It looks as if he is playing with no wind in the chest, although the piston-levers could be at rest, not simply abandoned. The cylinders are bound with hoops and the player is looking towards the king,[20] not unlike the watchful hydraulis-player in gladiatorial mosaics – an antique, allusive detail, as if in the right circumstances a barbaric practice could be converted to a sacred? Perhaps the organist, David as shepherd and maker of musical instruments, is still engaged in constructing an unfinished organ,[21] or perhaps he is not playing because the psalm speaks only of his building it (Vellekoop 1984: 194).

Close examination of the manuscript suggests that the little half-lever to the left does not belong to the finished drawing (an unerased error, an incomplete element in darker ink or a later mark?), that the sheep to the right were drawn in first (the organ re-inked?) and that at one point there were meant to be nine pipes (with the round top of the ninth not shaded in like the others). But since the drawing was not the work of a single act, it is even more difficult to be certain of the intention behind it.

[20] Or 'awaiting pensively the arrival of the blowers' – Hardouin 1966: 35.
[21] E. T. De Wald, *The Illustrations of the Utrecht Psalter* (Princeton, [1932]), 72.

Arguing that the probable date and place of the Utrecht Psalter could make its scenes particularly deferential to Louis the Pious,[22] Schuberth thinks the organ of 'Psalm 151' specific, even possibly a portrayal of the organ at Aachen (Schuberth 1968: 91, 125–6). David as the anointed one, as king in majesty, as conqueror of Goliath and as artist (performer, psalmist, instrument-maker) is pictured in the Psalter and serves as a model for Louis himself; Aachen, with its temple and throne, already suggested associations with Solomon. While such speculation as this cannot be rejected out of hand, it cannot be easily developed further.

General questions

Uncertainty about the nature of the pictures in the Utrecht Psalter centres on a question even difficult to frame without anachronism. To ask 'are these drawings fact or fancy?' begs other questions, and it might be more pertinent to ask the following:

Did the artist know an organ of this kind? While it is pure conjecture that the drawing for Psalm 150 is of the very organ given to Pippin in 757 and/or of Muristos's siren-organ described during that period (Hardouin 1966: 35–6), there is a possibility that Reims or its neighbourhood, with several Carolingian palaces and great abbeys within a day or two's ride, did still know the water-organ. The organ built for Louis the Pious in the 820s by the Venetian or Greek Georgius may have been some kind of hydraulis (see pp. 128 and 144 for the possibility). A century and a half later, owing to Archbishop Gerbert's interests, Reims had both a hydraulis and a mechanical clock, according to William of Malmesbury (see p. 216). Although there is no known connection between these items, it seems unlikely that personal knowledge would be ignored by an artist clearly interested in giving his instruments variety and who shows himself to be a keen observer of other practical details, such as the tuning pins of stringed instruments on f. 63'.

In that case, however, since bellows-organs were certainly known (or had once been known) here and there for centuries before *c*. 825, one has to ask why the Utrecht Psalter illustrator (and/or his source) used only water-organs. At least part of the answer must be: for the authority of the antique. Hydraules were harder to make and were the only organs described – so to speak authorized – by the *ars mechanica* treatise most influencing the Carolingians (see below). Because of this 'authority' they would be assumed to be older than bellows-organs, which, had they been known in the Marne valley in the ninth century, might have been no more than little instruments of itinerant juggler-musicians. So might some of the plucked stringed instruments idealized by the artist, however, and it would be difficult to argue that water-organs alone were associated with the sacred. A related puzzle is that nowhere in the Psalter does the illustrator draw bellows, and yet the forge he depicts for Psalm 117 on f. 6'

---

[22] According to the Notker Balbulus (MGH SS 2.753) a monarch still claiming dominion over the Holy Land, i.e. the home of the psalms.

must have had them; one can see there a standing figure who would be the bellows-blower. Perhaps the artist knew only whole-skin bellows (see Chapter 15) and for some reason found them unsuitable for Old Testament illustration.

Is the drawing based on an understanding of verbal sources? During the ninth century Vitruvius was copied and known across the area in which Hautvillers is situated, with known copies from Aachen, Corbie and Soissons as well as Corvey, the Reichenau and Murbach (see p. 241 for copies). From what written sources ninth-century writers such as Walahfrid Strabo and Hucbald knew of *hydraules* (*hydraulia, hydraulicis*) is unknown; perhaps they knew of Vitruvius directly or indirectly, although one would then expect Hucbald (like the author of the treatise *Cuprum purissimum* – see Chapter 16) to use the word *hydraules* for water-organs only, which seems not to be the case. Whatever the truth of the matter, Vitruvius was well known in the libraries of monasteries associated with the artists of the Utrecht and Stuttgart Psalters and with the authors of important music-theory books (Hucbald, *Enchiriadis*).

Somehow the Utrecht Psalter artist knew about such practical details as cisterns with hoops. Vitruvius describes paired cisterns (see Chapter 14) but unless any Byzantine or Syrian sources known to the Psalter artist[23] also portrayed them, the hoops must have come either from actual observation or from the practical under-standing that a cylinder under stress from piston and compression needs structural reinforcement. The cisterns do not correspond to Hero's *bomiskos* (a geometric solid, for example as left when the upper part of a prism is sliced off parallel to the base), but two other descriptions may be relevant. While Vitruvius presumably meant by *ara* a stone 'altar' of familiar Roman form, taller than wide – as drawn elsewhere in the Psalter (for example, Psalm 149 immediately above the present drawing) – a ninth-century Christian may have had a different mass-altar in mind, like those of Anglo-Saxon England. For the cisterns, is it possible that the Syriac/Arabic *tanur* ('oven', as translated in Farmer 1931: 52, 129) was somehow known to the Psalter artist? Muristos's description of a siren-organ says:

and let its base be broad, and as it rises to the top, it gets narrower . . . like the form of an oven. And it is roofed, that is to say covered [i.e. hermetically sealed?].

There is also a faint resemblance between the Utrecht Psalter's cisterns and a pump described by the antique author Philo of Byzantium: this was a cylindrical bellows of leather, 'kept distended by wooden hoops', on the top of which 'is a wooden lid, tight fitting, with the discharge pipe fitted to it'.[24]

On the other hand, the decorative framework for the Psalter's organs might well be an 'artist's impression' of frames described in written sources such as the eastern reports quoted in Chapters 9 and 14, assuming such reports – not necessarily those now known – circulated. This framework does not appear to have had any structural function, and may therefore have been imaginary.

---

[23] Byzantine in G. R. Benson & D. T. Tselos (see note 9), and Dufrenne 1978; Syrian in Farmer 1931: 53 ('probably influenced by Syrian art').

[24] Text and interpretation in Drachmann 1948: 6. Compare p. 247 below.

Did the artist have other considerations in mind? While the drawings of the Psalter undeniably 'radiate an otherwise unknown concrete liveliness'[25] that must have resulted from some personal perception, it is not possible to know how original were his instruments. Was he able to ignore his period's secular and sacred music and/or those connected with Orpheus in late antiquity as he attempted to imagine the instruments of the Temple? Unlike the Stuttgart Psalter, the Utrecht makes no link between psalter-scenes and contemporary liturgy, although the scene in Psalm 150 could be representing a generalized outdoor acclamation as briefly discussed in Chapter 5. (Farmer thinks it 'a military scene' – 1931: 137.) On the other hand, the timelessness of the psalms and their linking the faiths of the Old and New Testament could well mean that the artist collected images of instruments known both in antiquity (from written sources) and in more recent times, then amalgamated the two. The many buildings in the drawings include those with Christian symbols such as the cross (Psalm 107/108) as well as those with outside sacrificial altars.

The most striking feature of the drawing for Psalm 150 is its symmetry. The orderliness symbolizing eternity is very thorough for this final psalm, as is surely appropriate. The landscape features are totally symmetrical, as are the six angels, four winds, eight priestly musicians, ten lay musicians, four organ-blowers, two organists, each group halved left and right. The left/right antitheses, recognized elsewhere in the Psalter (for example for Psalm 43/44 or the 'butterchurn' scene on f. 86), are most pronounced here. Symmetry not only symbolizes the sounds being made by all the participants 'singing a new song' in the fixed 'firmament of His might' but parallels the symmetry of the doxology-psalm itself: Psalm 150 is a text that begins and ends with alleluia, and its binary verses pair the alternate statements of antiphonal psalm-structure even more markedly than usual. It is this persistent symmetry that explains the two organists, for had there been only one (as for 'Psalm 151'), either he would have taken the same axis as God above or he would have broken the symmetry. Even the organists' leaning outwards contributes to the oblique lines leading to God to whom all are directing praise through wind-produced sound ('all that has breath'). Yet while the two organists lean symmetrically, they do not do so totally – only one gestures to the blowers and nor are the pipes arranged in the symmetrical mitre-shape. Both of these details surely result from a desire for some 'reality' in the picture. In one practical respect, the next drawing in the Psalter for the Canticle of Isaiah (f. 83'), is even more symmetrical: it is placed in the middle of the page itself, rather as if f. 83 (where the drawing for Psalm 150 has to be at the bottom of the page) had prompted the artist to plan the layout of f. 83'.

Is it possible to say what most governed the artist? So complex are the questions surrounding the Utrecht Psalter that an undue focus on the three organs can lead to dubious hypotheses about them, as often in the past. But in view of the technical–architectural interests of the manuscript's time and place, it does seem more than likely that the biggest single factor in these three drawings was the artist's understanding of Vitruvius: see also p. 240 and previous excerpts. Not only the altar-like shape (a

---

[25]   T. Seebass, 'Die Bedeutung des Utrechter Psalters für die Musikgeschichte', in Engelbregt 1973: 35–48, here 37. On a few aspects of the drawing's symmetry, 44–7.

Christian altar) and the pair of hydraulic cylinders but, most of all, the *tetrachordos* of four pipes (two sets of which make an *octochordos*) suggest this.

If there had been some misunderstanding about tetrachords on Vitruvius's part, or a corrupt reading in the single original copy (see p. 241), then all the more reason for thinking that the Psalter artist had him in mind. Symbolisms and other agendas apart, not only do the Psalter drawings not make much musical sense as they stand but they are ambiguous in number of pipes and what the players are doing – precisely the uncertainties with which reading Vitruvius would have left either the Psalter artist or, if he were copying an earlier drawing, some predecessor.

Eadwine Psalter

Like the Utrecht Psalter, this twelfth-century 'copy'[26] shows plucked stringed instruments for Psalm 136/137 (f. 243'). For Psalm 70/71 (f. 121'), the organ discarded by David has no chest, and twelve pipes (counting the outside lines as pipes) come straight from the top of the now prettified cisterns. For Psalm 150 (f. 261') there are also some changes: there are now three hooped cisterns not two, three pumps to the left (two on the right), indistinct windtrunks, eleven 'keys' (small blocks further from the fingers) and ten pipes (six to left, four to right). There is the same personnel with the same gestures, but the pipes join the top edge of the table and are not placed on it. For 'Psalm 151' the pipes are unambiguous (two sets of four) but the player's fingers appear to be placed on or around the pipes.

All these changes suggest the artist to have been interpreting the drawing of an object quite unknown to him at least in this form, unlike the drawing of a harp on the same folio. Clearly he did not convey the Utrecht Psalter's systematic symmetry, although it can hardly have escaped his notice. Since during the period of his work Canterbury Cathedral may have had an organ (see p. 223), two questions would be whether the artist was copying any of its features, and if not (or not very much), why not. As to the first question: the organ is so obviously a glossed version of that in the Utrecht Psalter that any instrument in the artist's cathedral could have informed his drawing only in the variant details – the eleven keys, the ten pipes etc. It is not out of the question that an actual instrument taught him how recent organs generally had more keys than the Utrecht Psalter's. As to the second question: perhaps the artist's duty was to reproduce an already archaic drawing and one therefore carrying psalmic authority. For his own monastery's organ to influence the drawing of a scene in the Book of Psalms could have seemed absurd, however worldly or up-to-date later illuminators became in this respect.

On the other hand, the placement of pipes at the top edge need not be the result of ignorance: this is how a row of organ-pipes might be seen by non-experts on the church pavement below. A similar point may be made about the 'keys': some kind

---

[26] Cambridge, Trinity College, R. 17. 1 (MS M987). Black and white facsimile in M. R. James, *The Canterbury Psalter* (London, 1935). The drawing described in Perrot 1965: 347 (plate XXIII.2), labelled 'Eadwine Psalter' and called 'a very mediocre copy' (of Psalm 150?), is that of the apocryphal Psalm 151 in the Utrecht Psalter.

of little darkened blocks, located somehow on or at the level of the table, and manipulated somehow by the fingers. In both this picture and that for Psalm 150 of the Utrecht Psalter, the non-expert observer may not have been portraying mechanism in any detail and yet – familiar or not with Cassiodorus's remarks – he could still be conveying the shape and approximate location of the playing parts of a ninth-century instrument.

11

Other early illustrations

Stuttgart Psalter

Stuttgart, Württembergische Landesbibliothek, Biblia fol. 23, ff. 152, 163' and 164': *c.* 820/30, probably from the northern French scriptorium of St-Germain-des-Prés.[1]

Large bellows-organs of the kind painted with some convincingly real detail on ff. 163' and 164' of the Stuttgart Psalter are not likely to have come from any early 'italo-byzantine' or seventh-century Milanese models that have been proposed for this psalter.[2] But there is always the possibility that they did, and that these organs are Byzantine, redrawn by a northern Frankish scribe. Another possibility, one less purely conjectural than this, is that the two large bellows-organs are a direct interpretation by the artist of the words of St Augustine and Cassiodorus, describing or defining the organ (see Chapter 17). Technical details in the paintings that could be the result of an experienced artist interpreting the words of a psalm-commentator include the (unclear) wooden key-action for Psalm 150 and '151', which were perhaps suggested by the (unclear) words of Cassiodorus at this point. In the case of Psalm 136/137, the idea for the Stuttgart Psalter's little willow-organs did not come from Augustine, who speaks more symbolically of the trees and *organa* mentioned there (PL 37.1764f), but nor is it contradicted by what he says.

Either possibility – that these organs are 'real' (Byzantine) or 'literary' (St Augustine) – makes the Stuttgart Psalter of great interest, fully complementing and no less important than the Utrecht Psalter, which therefore cannot quite be regarded as 'the only early medieval representation of an organ drawn with some professional knowledge'.[3] Its relative neglect in organ-studies is puzzling, reflecting perhaps a once commonly held view that the illustrations are of an amateurish or primitive quality. But like the Utrecht Psalter, the Stuttgart is no 'simple compilation of various sources' and instead involves a 'many-sided development of them',[4] including

[1] Facsimile and commentary, *Der Stuttgarter Bilderpsalter*. I *Faksimile in Farben*. II *Untersuchungen* (Stuttgart, 1968); date and place of origin according to B. Bishoff, 'Die Handschrift', *ibid.*, II.15–30 and B. M. M. Davezac, *The Stuttgart Psalter: its pre-Carolingian Sources and its Place in Carolingian Art* (Ph.D. diss., Columbia University, NY, 1972), 30ff. Corbie suggested as place of origin by Engelbregt 1973: 27f.

[2] Dufrenne 1978: 33, 176 and Davezac (note 1): 32f.

[3] Seebass, in Engelbregt 1973: 45. There is good coverage in e.g. Seebass 1973: 106–11.

[4] F. Mütherich, 'Die Stellung der Bilder in der frühmittelalterlichen Psalterillustration', in the facsimile edition, as in note 1: 2.151–222, here 201.

well-observed or well-conjectured detail of an organ. The manuscript is like no other: it 'stands alone in a vacuum with no pedigree, no credentials, no civic status to allow it to join the already vast amount of Carolingian documented data', although resemblances have been found between it and the Sacramentary of Drogo, Louis the Pious's half brother.[5] Whether or not the Stuttgart Psalter depended on a sixth- or seventh-century 'picture-world' familiar to artists in Louis's circle and influenced by the imported art of Ravenna, its artist either was merely copying such details as skin-bellows and circulating this knowledge to the Psalter's users, or he knew of them already and needed no tenuous trading routes to teach him. Knowing of bellows presumably from forges, he could easily adapt such knowledge to a drawing inspired by St Augustine's definition of what an organ was.

The Stuttgart Psalter has a Gallican text belonging to a northern French text-group of *c.* 770/90, similar to that of the Utrecht Psalter,[6] and like it has illustrations of organs on three of its pages. However, rather than for the David of Psalm 70/71, its first organ is for Babylon.

Psalm 136/137, f. 152

The pair of small organs hanging on the willows[7] has seven (?) pipes each and seven little key-tabs below the pipes (six for the left-hand organ?); these latter are little rounded tabs at the bottom of the lowest panel of the rather deep chest, appearing in the perspective to protrude below it. The pipes are surrounded by a frame, and an oblique bar runs across them. Such *organetti* could be a miniaturization conjectured by the artist from the larger organs: the bars are similar, and the 'tabs' could be small versions of key-sliders. (For a later example of an organ drawn in three different sizes, see Chapter 17; for later 'tabs' see Hickman 1936: fig. 10, an Italian manuscript.) Although the third-century Aquincum *organetto* already had support-bars front and back, one might question whether the Stuttgart Psalter artist was drawing actual portatives so many centuries before they are regularly depicted.

Rather, if he needed to invent a miniaturized organ he could have drawn on several traditions for his details. For example, a relief on the front panel of a fourth-century Cybelline altar (Vatican Grottos) shows a seven-pipe syrinx with horizontal bar, attached to a pinetree from which it hangs. Or the idea of square frames around an organ could have come from old traditions for illustrating Psalm 136 in Greek psalters with lyres or harps hanging in trees (for example, Rome, Biblioteca Apostolica Vaticana, graec. 1927,[8] and graec. 752[9]), or other kinds of instruments (for example, in the Chludov Psalter, Moscow, Historical Museum, MS 129) or even small objects holding what look like pipes (London, British Library, Add. 19352 of the eleventh century,

---

[5]   Parallels drawn in Davezac (see note 1): 9 and 93.

[6]   D. De Bruyne, 'Le Psautier de Stuttgart', *Speculum* 7 (1932), 361–6. On the artist sometimes following the Old Latin psalter for the content of certain drawings, see Davezac (note 1): 27.

[7]   See p. 152, note 11, for a remark on hanging *organa* (musical instruments or worktools?).

[8]   E. T. De Wald, *The Illustrations in the Manuscripts of the Septuagint* 3.1 (Princeton/London, 1941), plate lvii.

[9]   *Ibid.*, 3.2 [1942], for Psalm 136; here they look more like baskets, perhaps for tools (*organa*)?

and the earlier London, British Library, Add. 40731).[10] While angels of the gothic period do carry portatives, any earlier small organs are probably to be seen as 'reductions' of larger, as when the eleventh-century sculptor of the portal of Jaca Cathedral gave *David and his Musicians* a miniature version of the conventional organ of seven pipes.

All five psalters, Stuttgart, Vatican graec. 752 and graec. 1927, BL Add. 19352 and 40731, have basket-like objects hanging in trees, with thick frames and (in the first two) oblique lines or bars. A Greek copy of the Book of Job (eleventh century, from Constantinople?) portrays a feast-scene for Job 1.13 in which a female figure appears to be holding on her left arm a small portative. Neither keys nor bellows are visible, but it is possible that it represents a portative with pipes arranged in mitre form.[11] This would be such an advance in chest-construction as to imply that the artist was using either his imagination or some exotic source: were there really eleventh-century Byzantine portatives with a bored chest that allowed a symmetrical arrangement of the pipes? Similarly, were little portatives of the Stuttgart Psalter type known in Corbie or Paris in the ninth century, framed in wood, held by straps and blown by a pair of bellows plugged in at the back? If neither is impossible, nor does any known reference make it likely.

The impasse reached by such questions is only too characteristic of the iconographical problem. On one hand, not enough is known of what was technically feasible for the answer to such questions to be 'Yes', so the temptation is to assume that artists either invented instruments according to their conventions, now ill understood, or copied them creatively from somebody else. On the other hand, since what was technically feasible cannot be established when neither literates nor artists were admitted to the crafts, a 'No' answer would imply that craftsmen were not imaginative according to their conventions, which are also now ill understood.

Psalm 150, f. 163' (Plate 6)

The big organ participating in the *instrumentarium* for Psalm 150 (one of the largest pictures in the Psalter as a whole) is instructive. A dancer, a horn, cymbal and stringed-instruments – therefore wind, percussion and strings in the established categories – are joined by three (?) bellows-blowers, two of whom tread a bull or goatskin bellows. This is of the whole-skin type described by Theophilus (*arietum* or ramskin – see p. 267) and is not at all merely a wedge-bellows 'very primitive in form and drawing', as Buhle 1903: 74 describes it. On the contrary, this bellows speaks for a type known far and wide for many centuries, and used for many purposes. From the bellows two trunks, evidently flexible but too thin for them to be realistic, lie below the pipes and take the wind to the chest. (One of the trunks is difficult to

---

[10] For Chludov, see Strunk 1977: 145. Surely the artist did not understand what he was copying. For the BL manuscripts, see S. Dufrenne, *L'illustration des psautiers grecs du Moyen Age*, 2 vols (Paris, 1966), 2 plate 98 and 1 plate 59 respectively.

   Since for Psalm 151 in London, British Library, Add. 19352, David is clearly playing a square harp, it looks as if the instruments for Psalm 136 were meant to be organs. Also possible is that the basket-like appearance of these psalter-organs (see below) reflects a further meaning of the word *cithara*: a 'rib-cage'.

[11] In J. Braun, 'Musical instruments in Byzantine illuminated manuscripts', *EM* 8 (1980), 312–27, here 323.

ad faciendam uindictam innationibus
increpationes inpopulis

ad alligandos reges eorum incompedibus
& nobiles eorum in manicis ferreis

Ut faciant ineis iudicium conscriptum
gloria hec est omnibus scis eius

LELALLELUIA ALLOIA

Laudate dnm insctis eius
Laudate eum infir mamcto uirtutisei
laudate eum inuir tutibus eius Laudate
eum secdm multitudine magnitudiniseii

Plate 6 Illustration for Psalm 150 in the Stuttgart Psalter (original in colour): Stuttgart,
Württembergische Landesbibliothek, Biblia fol. 23, f. 163'

see in reproductions.) The third male figure may be treading a second skin-bellows from which a third trunk curves up to another part of the chest, but only two pairs of legs are visible. Or perhaps this figure represents the organist who would otherwise be hidden behind the pipes and thus not visible, as he should be, in the scene of praise. Another distinct possibility is that he is there at all – and not joined by a partner for another bellows – in order to complete to a conventional eight the number of persons about King David, representing the eight musical forms of praise.

Pipe-mouths are visible at the front, as are ten dark marks which represent either the endblocks of the sliders' morticed channels or the ends of the sliders themselves, brought to the front for a panoramic picture. The wooden (?) elements remind the Psalter's reader of the interior wooden action of an organ briefly remarked on by Cassiodorus in his commentary on Psalm 150 (see p. 299): both commentator and illustrator are vague, but both do refer to the working mechanism. The bellows seem to have their skins reinforced at the folds and edges, and could have been drawn from Byzantine originals,[12] from written descriptions or from personal knowledge of either forge- or organ-bellows. 'Realistic' too are the decoration at the top and the open structure below; and the closely packed pipe-row would seem 'realistic' to a non-expert artist. Is the open structure meant to imply that the chest is on a storey above the blowers, who could not be placed below on the page if the organ-pipes were to be so large? Perhaps also reliable is the shallowness of the chest and the fact that like that for 'Psalm 151' it seems to be made up of joined timber members – a most important detail (see below). In the case of the support-bar for the pipes, the feature is undoubtedly antique (Buhle 1903: 74), but who it was that alluded to the antique models – the organ-builder in the first place or the artist later – is not clear. Two of the blowers have their hand on a bar attached (?) to a rod connected with the end of the bellows, and they are either pulling up the deflated bellows or using the bar for leverage, with their feet attached to the bellows as in the Mariamîn mosaic (see p. 192). The pipe-row is so closely packed as to appear a block of pipes: these have a patently equal diameter, which, with the support-bar and the generous length of the shortest pipe, adds to the antique look and gives an impression not very different from, for example, Roman organ in the Nennig mosaic. It is difficult to believe the Stuttgart illustrator did not know some such mosaic. Certainly if Roman remains in Francia gave the Utrecht Psalter artist some kind of knowledge of the water-organ, they could also have given the Stuttgart Psalter artist the image of a sloping block of tight-packed pipes. But the same image might have come from Cassiodorus's description of the organ as 'a kind of tower' (see Chapter 17).

'Psalm 151', f. 164' (Plate 7)

A second organ, similar to that on f. 163', is pointed at by David whose hands 'made the organ' (*fecerunt organum*) and whose fingers prepared the psalter (*aptaverunt psalterium*), a copy of which lies on the altar. Here *psalterium* is understood as a book not an instrument, therefore, and serves to suggest that the illustrator knew written

---

[12] Such as the fourth-century obelisk of Theodosius (Perrot 1965: 348); see p. 147 above.

sources such as Isidore (see p. 209). On this apocryphal psalm, see Chapters 1 and 10.

Again the mass of pipes for the organ, apparently eighteen in front, go up to the right-hand margin, rising in length while now the support-bar falls to the right. No pipe-mouths are indicated this time. From one laurel- or heart-shaped skin bellows, two flexible windtrunks (coloured red, like arteries) pass to the chest where fifteen thin, short vertical lines correspond to the ten 'end blocks' in the organ of f. 163'. Below the 'end blocks' are nine or ten longer and more widely spaced vertical battens (?) which fill that level of the structure and correspond to the four panels of f. 163'. Below this is a similar frame support (?) through which the trunks remain visible. Whether or not the little vertical marks represent press-keys or sliders, it looks as if the horizontal sections of the structure are built up and joined, not carved from a block. At least the colouring makes this appear to be so, for in both organs two of the sections are coloured red, the others light brown or (for Psalm 150) darkened red. While this could be purely decorative, the size of the organ does make the coloured strips look like separate elements in a wooden structure; furthermore, the 'decoration' could be the organ-builder's as much as the illustrator's. The very possibility that this is a jointed and joined structure of wood opens up questions about what craftsmen knew beyond the techniques described as many as three hundred years later by Theophilus. Were certain symbolisms working in the picture, such as that the heart-and-arteries (lungs-and-windpipe) are the 'organs' of praise, the coloured strips still lead to these questions: how advanced were the skilled woodworkers of ninth-century Francia?

The 'reality' of organological details in these three drawings is not necessarily lessened by the eminences grises behind the psalter's organs, i.e. the psalm-commentaries (especially Augustine) long recognized as important to the Stuttgart Psalter. Apropos 'realism': in the case of the battle-scene for Psalm 59, there seems to have been an array of sources made use of by the illustrator. He must have seen Franks dressed for battle; he must have been aware of how eastern foes were represented during his period; and he would have known of the attempts in contemporary literature to identify the Franks with the chosen Israelites.[13] Whatever the picture is signifying politically, the result suggests an actual battle of the day. Now in the case of the two large organs, the details of their bellows (type, number, dimensions), pipe-row (size, appearance) and structure (frame, wooden elements, stand), as also the connection between them, can be attributed to conventional iconography or literature, to observation or imagination. Of the four, *imagination* is probably the least important here. The other three may be of roughly equal significance: the artist knew some mosaics, some psalm-commentaries and some actual bellows. What realistic *observation* there might be is probably not that of an expert: pipes would not be so tight-packed in an actual organ and the trunks are unrealistically thin. (While a good illustrator could recognize flexibility in a windtrunk and convey it in his drawing, he may not realize that the trunk had to have a minimum diameter.)

---

[13]   On St Augustine: E. T. De Wald, *The Stuttgart Psalter* (Princeton, 1930), *passim*. On the battle-scene: B. S. Bachrach, 'A picture of Avar-Frankish warfare from a Carolingian psalter of the early ninth century in light of the *Strategicon*', *Archivum Eurasiae medii aevi* 4 (1986), 5–27.

psē misit angelum suum·&tulit me de
ouibus patris mei·

&unxit me inmisericozdia unctionissime
rares mei boni &magni·
& non fuit bene placitum ineis dno
xiuit obuiam alienigine·
& maledixit me insimula cris sui·
go autē eucto abeo ipsius gladia· am
putaui caput ei·&abstuli obpbriū afiliis
israhel

Plate 7 Illustration for 'Psalm 151' in the Stuttgart Psalter (original in colour): Stuttgart,
Württembergische Landesbibliothek, Biblia fol. 23, f. 164'

One thing to bear in mind when sources of an artist's knowledge are as nebulous as they are here is that the situation cannot have been so different for the organ-builders themselves. Particularly if they were monastic craftsmen making instruments, they may well have been forced by isolation to work things out for themselves and were equally subject to a whole range of written and other sources.

Pommersfelden Bible (Plate 8)

Pommersfelden, Gräfl. Schönborn'sche Schloßbibliothek, MS 334, fol. II, f. 148ʳ: second half of the eleventh century, Bible from St Kastor, Koblenz.

David and his four musicians represent the instrumental categories, for David plays his harp amongst the percussion, strings and winds. The organ is there for various reasons: to stand for instruments (*organa*) in general and wind-instruments in particular ('those that have breath'); because *organum* was a word familiar from the Vulgate Bible and required illustration; because an organ completed the ideal *instrumentarium* for an eleventh-century artist representing David as the biblical Pythagoras; and because its ceremonial music was associated with David in the Old Testament (see p. 82). The organ appears to have thirteen or fourteen closely packed cylindrical pipes, with mouths visible and with sliders protruding straight from the chest-front. For them the whole hand is used, whether they are being pulled and pushed or pressed and raised.[14] (Any apparent pressing-down action of the hands may be due to 'faulty' perspective, as too in the Harding Bible below?) The pipes look as if they begin in two unison ranks, and while their equal width may not be literal, the small-ness of the top pipes, evidently reached too soon by the artist in his drawing, has some 'reality' about it. Whether at this period of organ-building cylindrical pipes do imply a pipe-metal 'of tin, lead or an alloy of these metals'[15] is not certain. Nor is it clear how the wind is raised, since bellows and blower(s) are not shown; but the plinth-stand could be a stylized windtrunk,[16] again suggesting that the wind is raised from below.

The keys of this organ and those of the Harding Bible faintly resemble those of a unique if not very reliable drawing[17] of a hurdy-gurdy or *organistrum*, a drawing now lost but engraved in Gerbert 1774: 2, plate xxxii (twelfth or thirteenth century). The hurdy-gurdy's 'key' appears to be a tapered rod with bulbous end towards the player, who turns (twists) it to bring the protruding edge of the distal end of the rod into contact with the string, stopping it like the tangent of a clavichord.[18] Although the bulbous keys of the Pommersfelden Bible may simply be roughly drawn – flat key-sliders in poor perspective – it is always possible that some early organ-keys were not pulled out or pressed down but operated by being turned, an action that the left hand of the player in the Pommersfelden drawing could be interpreted as

[14] First in Perrot 1965: 348, second in Körte 1973: 14.
[15] W. Barry, 'A 12th-century English organ', *The Diapason* 74/10 (1983), 10–11.
[16] Buhle 1903: 77. If so, the bellows could be out of sight on a floor below (cf. Winchester, pp. 190f).
[17] 'Undoubtedly been tampered with and cannot be trusted': NOHM 1990: 481.
[18] Each note would presumably need separating from the next unless, as on a *gebunden* clavichord, special effects were intended.

suggesting. While both the poor standard of drawing for the pipe-row and the six keys do not inspire confidence – why six keys when there are seven bells? – yet the hands of all five well-drawn people are carefully done, as they could well be by an artist who did not understand the technical apparatus itself or followed what had been drawn or written before him.

Plate 8 'David and his Musicians' from the Pommersfelden Bible: Pommersfelden, Gräfl. Schönborn'sche Schloßbibliothek, MS 334, fol. II, f. 148'

Harding Bible (Plates 9 and 10)

Dijon Bibliothèque Municipale, MS 14 vol. 3, f. 13': four-volume bible (1109)[19] for Stephen Harding, third Abbot of Cîteaux, an Englishman brought up at Sherborne, according to William of Malmesbury (RBMAS 90.2.380).

[19] Chailley 1937 mentions, but does not give, good reasons for a dating of 1098/1109.

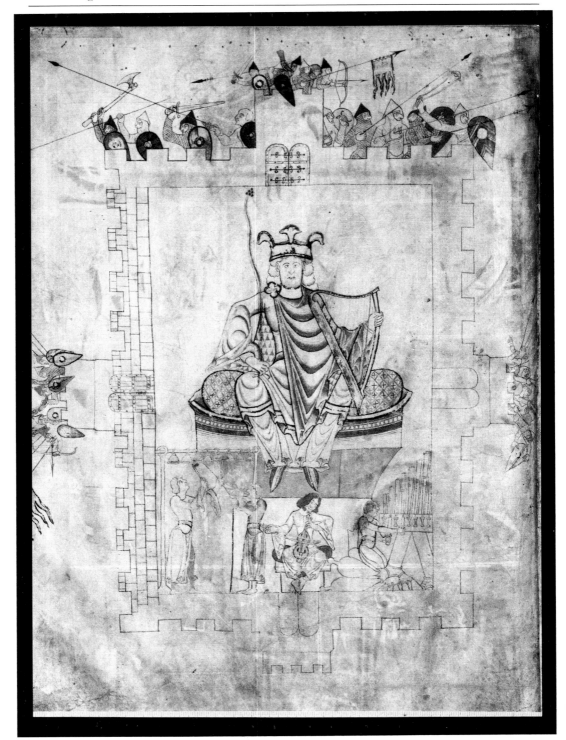

Plate 9 'David and his Musicians' from the Harding Bible: Dijon, Bibliothèque Municipale, MS 14 vol. 3, f. 13'(opposite).

Plate 10 'David and his Musicians' from the Harding Bible: detail (above).

On David and his four musicians, see the Pommersfelden Bible above. In the Harding Bible there are a set of eight bells (in left–right order) and a separate eight-keyed organ, with eight pairs of conical (flue) pipes from treble left to bass right, placed on a deep chest from the upper part of which the eight large sliders protrude. It is possible that the citadel wall cuts off the organ on the right side,[20] but to argue compass on such grounds supposes the drawing to be that of a 'real' organ, which is not proved. In any case, the instruments of David's other musicians are not less than complete. From how much appears of the windtrunks the reader is led to understand there to be twelve hand-worked bellows: two sets of three pairs, each pair of which meets in a socket which joins two others in a *conflatorium*, here more elegant than that described by Theophilus. Twelve bellows for twelve pipes are also shown schematically in a manuscript associated with St Emmeram, Regensburg, dated *c*. 800 and reported on by Gerbert in *De cantu* (Gerbert 1774: 139 and plate 23): twelve is also the conventional number for the pipes of the organ described in the *Letter to Dardanus* (see Chapter 14). All these twelves are easily imagined to represent the Apostles and the text 'their sound is gone out'.

The Dijon representation is celebrated because of the eight alphabet letters above the push-pull sliders, corresponding to the letters as recommended by the eleventh-century text *Cuprum purissimum*, 'for the player to know more quickly what slider he should be working' (*ut citius modulator possit scire, quam linguam debeat tangere* – Sachs 1970: 58) that is to say, where the semitones are situated. In a more careful picture or one more closely tied to a text of music-theory, it would not be out of the question for the 'reverse order' of pipes in the Harding Bible to be illustrating pre-Boethian theory in which the succession of notes descends; but that seems unlikely to be the intention here. It is also difficult to see the pipe-rows as consisting of a principal and a reed or regal, as sometimes interpreted,[21] since both appear to be conical: whatever they are, they look the same.

The artist drew the mouths in a line equidistant from the pipe-ends instead of the pipe-feet, but the conical shape itself may be a reliable detail. The sliders are unlikely to be pulled down and pushed up:[22] the vertical movement represents the perspective of movement towards the viewer, and the organist has to sit at a level (on a chair with a back) to make this possible. Perhaps the left slider protruding much further than is realistic is meant to give an impression of activity and a quick changing of the notes, but the drawing is not expert enough for this to be certain. Similarly, although David's musician is pictured with an organ plausible for the eleventh century, the iconographical genre was too conventionalized for this scene to be certainly representing church ceremony[23] or indeed a 'real' church organ at all. Rather, the eight sliders correspond to the eight bells and other numbers-of-eight in David iconography, and demonstrate here the seven notes of music plus the lyric semitone B.

[20] Suggested by P. Hardouin, 'Encore Winchester', *CO* 39/40 (1981), 20–3. On the right-hand margin in the Stuttgart Psalter, see above.

[21] Suggested by N. Dufourcq, *Esquisse d'une histoire de l'orgue en France* (Paris, 1935), 33–4.

[22] Suggested by Chailley 1937: 5, already questioned by Perrot 1965: 349.

[23] Suggested by Chailley 1937: 7. But the vestment alone of the four players surely suggests no liturgy appropriate even to David in the Temple.

In two particular respects the Harding Bible picture holds an important position. First, certain parallels between it and the first two chapters of Theophilus can be observed: both deal with conical pipes of more than one rank, both have letters above the keys (Theophilus's phrase *in caudis* 'at the end' could suggest to a reader the far as well as near end of the key), and both keep to eight keys (as a model octave?). For the drawing and treatise to have these things in common the drawing could be interpreted either literally or not,[24] but it would be necessary for the treatise to have existed first. It is not impossible that 'Theophilus' as known is a compilation of older material, some of which would then be older than the Harding Bible (on its archaic elements, see Chapter 15); but in the absence of further documentation this is an open question.

Second, the Abbot of Cîteaux was not a black monk, and the drawing represents the earliest known organ in a Cistercian manuscript (or a manuscript prepared for a Cistercian). On one early Cistercian view of organs, see remarks on Ailred of Rievaulx in Chapter 13. Stephen Harding, responsible for the *carta caritatis* or rule for the Order's governance and annual gathering of abbots, seems in this Bible to have liked a style of illumination as flowery as that of contemporary Cluny.[25] Although Cistercian abbeys are unlikely to have had such organs, drawings may have circulated in the less strict pre-Bernardine monasteries, particularly those with an interest in developing technologies. In general the Bible drawing serves a somewhat similar purpose to that of the Munich and Belvoir illuminations of the next century: *nolae* (bells), *organistrum* (hurdy-gurdy) and *organum* (bellows-organ) refer to or salute the David of the Book of Psalms, the sacred Pythagoras who rules sound-proportions.

Cambridge Psalter (Plate 11)

Cambridge, St John's College, B 18(40), f. 1a: beginning of the twelfth century, perhaps from St-Rémi, Reims.

This is the upper half of the first page: sitting on the throne, David plays the cithara of six strings (but eight tuning pins), in the presence of a singer, a wind-instrument, a seven-note panpipe, a seven-key two-rank organ, two bellows-blowers holding on to a bar with both hands, and a figure – perhaps Pythagoras[26] – holding or playing a monochord and striking one of seven bells. (See the Belvoir Castle Psalter in Chapter 17 for a later version of the scene.) Although an old idea that the picture represents 'a reality in church music' is now rejected (Seebass 1973: 139), there remain several quasi-technical details of interest.

The organ appears to have two ranks of cylindrical pipes in order (*bis septem discrimina vocum*) and seven key-sliders in the upper part – or actually on top – of a

---

[24] E.g. the note-letters may not be actually in the picture (located on the chest-front above the keys), merely written without realism on top of the image (so outside it).

[25] See A. H. Bredero, *Cluny et Cîteaux au douzième siècle* (Amsterdam, 1985), 40, 138.

[26] Seebass 1973: 94ff discusses the David–Pythagoras connection. J. Smits van Waesberghe, *Musikerziehung, Musikgeschichte in Bildern*, III.3 (Leipzig, 1969), 52, thinks the figure that of a nobleman, but this would not contradict the idea of a David–Pythagoras.

quite deep rectangular chest standing on four (?) short legs. A curving windtrunk of large capacity is fed via a *conflatorium* by two bellows fixed into it and trodden by blowers, apparently on a lower storey. The blowers are at rest[27] and there is no indication that their feet are strapped on to the upper board. The details of the bellows may be meant to suggest leather and wood: there is a band across the narrow end and the rounded wide part ends with a protruding grip, rather as if the artist knew only hand-held bellows. A major question concerns the keyboard: the 'keys' look not unlike some drawn many centuries later by Praetorius[28] as flat, protruding levers with rounded ends comfortable to press. It is possible that they are placed on the top board of the chest, sticking out over the edge. In that case, they might be press-keys not slider-keys. But a comparison with the Pommersfelden and Harding organs must leave it doubtful whether a drawing can be relied on to show how keys looked or worked, particularly as press-keys must often have kept the older slider-shape.

A second question concerns the pipes: the ends look too complicated for simply open principals. Are they stopped, with caps? Any argument that the pipes cannot be open since the horn in the same picture is drawn with a blackened resonator-end missing on the organ-pipes (Buhle 1903: 91) cannot be conclusive, since the organ-pipes are too small to admit the horn's detail. Perhaps they are ambiguous because the artist was uncertain, whereas he knew that horns were open-ended. Another possibility for the picture is that the throne-animals were also emitting sounds, as in I Kings 10.19 and 2 Chronicles 9.18. If they did, like those in the Byzantine throne-room (see p. 148), they would need some kind of wind-raising equipment, no doubt secreted away below.

Some, perhaps most, of the technical details here can be found in other drawings: the two ranks of equal-length pipes (thus an organ of more than one unison rank), the number of pipes, the shape of the 'keys' and the space between them (rather less than their width, unlike, for example, Harding and Pommersfelden), the shallow chest made up of two planks (? with separate topboard?), the shape of the bellows and trunk, the blowers' support bar and the impression of two storeys (bellows, chest). Although all such details could come from written sources and would easily become conventionalized, someone at some point in the chain of knowledge may have observed an instrument and 'reduced' it in size and scope in order to produce an illustration suitable for the beginning of a psalter. The Book of Psalms was not a recent creation and there is no reason why an instrument pictured in it would have to be up-to-date.

[27]   Not in the view of Perrot 1965: 350, who sees them *en pleine action*, probably in alternation. Körte 1973: 8 sees the windtrunk as *elastisch* and supposes the manuscript to be English.
[28]   So interpreted also by Buhle 1903: 86–7: Praetorius 1619: 97.

Plate 11 'David and his Musicians' from the Cambridge Psalter: Cambridge, St John's College, B 18(40), f. 1a (opposite).

The iconographic genres and 'realism'

All told, extant illustrations of organs from the ninth century to the sixteenth are astonishingly few, and like written documentation they transmit only a few out-of-focus details about the instrument as made by the craftsmen. But since they are so few in the total mass of early medieval illustration, even that concerned with instruments, it must be significant when they are admitted to an established genre, such as *David and his Musicians*. Quite what is being signified is not easy to define, however. David himself, resplendent in his antique authority, may be less 'realistic' than many another figure.[29] At the same time, old significances for the numbers seven and eight make their appearance in drawings and illuminations, as in seven or eight pipes or keys, less than 'reliable' as a sign of what organs actually contained.

That the genre *Illuminated Psalters* followed strong conventions is clear in the twelfth-century copy of the Utrecht Psalter (Cambridge, Trinity College – see Chapter 10) where the copyist re-interpreted the ninth-century drawings but did not modernize them, and even glossed the antique hydraulis by giving it another cistern. Did he understand this early copy of Psalm 150 to have carried a particularly authoritative interpretation? It can have had nothing whatever to do with twelfth-century church organs. But this psalter did at least have the drawing of an organ whereas Byzantine psalters take *organa* to mean 'musical instruments' in general and never at this point, as far as is known, picture a bellows- or water-organ.

Similarly, in the case of certain later medieval genres such as *The Coronation of the Virgin*, portative organs regularly occur, and though this may be merely following convention at least they do appear there and convey a few 'reliable' details. Perhaps the significance of western psalters occasionally showing organs but eastern psalters not is that by *c*. 850 the organ was more likely to be accepted in the West as suitable for the sacred scene, either because a few were known in church or because having been far less familiar in Corbie than Constantinople, organs had fewer secular associations for the artists. The more this is likely, the more it could be that the organ became known in western churches because artists and others were associating it with things sacred, not having known it in other connections.

If pictures of organs are likely to appear only in certain clearly defined contexts, it follows that no one context is necessarily more 'reliable' than another: an illustration for Psalm 150 is not less or more reliable than an illustrated treatise dealing with other genres such as *Classification of Instruments* or *Letter to Dardanus*. Here and there the conventions allow a detail to emerge, as in a later copy of the *Letter to Dardanus* (English manuscript, fourteenth century)[30] in which, though without much instructive detail, there are pictured the organ's three main elements: pipes (two sets of six, thus suggesting multiple ranks?), chest (large and framed, thus suggesting decoration?) and bellows (four and round, illustrating both number and shape?). One has to extract such detail and then extrapolate the information to imagine what a builder of the period – or, rather, the previous period – was capable of.

[29] A psaltery held by David might well be less 'real' than one held by an accompanying musician of lower status (Seebass 1973: 131).
[30] Cambridge, Peterhouse, MS 198 f. 133: in Hammerstein 1959: 122.

Extracting and extrapolating are possible, however, even in tightly controlled genres. Thus in the *Classification of Instruments* accompanying two related eleventh or twelfth-century copies of Cassiodorus and Boethius, both of them Italian, the organ is pictured amongst other wind-instruments (*inflatilia*)[31] and the drawings are little more than schematic. But the *schema* is instructive. In both, the organist and bellows-blower are standing, and the organist reaches up to head-height to play; while this height can hardly be 'realistic', standing might be. So might the equal status of player and blower, suggested by their clothes: two servants in ancient Rome, two *servi Dei* in Christian Lombardy. In the Milan manuscript the 'unrealistically drawn' pipes have the same length, while the Piacenza manuscript has two long-to-short rows arranged not unlike those for Psalm 150 in the Utrecht Psalter: a tight frame around the picture may have forced the pipes to double back.

While the Milan manuscript is organologically inexpert (pipes seem to have replaced keys), the Piacenza manuscript shows two bellows-folds, a clear bellows-shape (not unlike that in the Harding Bible), firmly lodged bellows-mouth in the plinth (= the windtrunk) of the organ, and a frame on which the bellows rest. Doubtless the two manuscripts belong equally to a conventionalized genre, but one of them has better observed detail than the other,[32] particularly of the bellows. Generally, bellows are better observed in medieval organ-drawings than the playing or sounding parts, presumably because they were far more familiar. That bellows are so often realistically drawn does rather suggest that it was because organs were complex and relatively rare that drawings of them were always sketchy and 'unreal', whatever the genre in which the artist was working.

Assessing how well something has been observed, however, is not straightforward. In the Piacenza manuscript, seven *cymbala* have regulated sizes such as to suggest pitches[33] of c' d' e' f' g' a' h', i.e. a diatonic scale. But this 'realism' may be accidental or the result of common sense, it being easier to understand a row of graded bells than a row of organ-keys. Also accidental may be the 'realism' of the first known representations of pipes arranged in mitre form: in the Ivrea Psalter (998–1001)[34] a *David and his Musicians* includes a seven-pipe organ with the longest pipe in the middle. (See Plate 12.) But although the number seven encourages such symmetry, the point here is rather that the stringed-instrument being played by one of the other musicians also has a pointed shape. Both instruments have a peaked frame, and the organ's mitre-shape is therefore unreliable. Yet another detail in the picture, though not exactly 'realistic', may well be representational: the semicircular line at the bottom of the (too deep) chest may be there to give the impression of an organ sitting on a vault, i.e. on an upper floor. It surely cannot be the *pnigeus* of a water-organ.[35] A further example of an 'accidental realism' can be seen in a tenth-century copy of

[31] See Seebass 1973: 184 (Piacenza, Biblioteca Capitolare, MS 65), 179 (Milan, Biblioteca Ambrosiana, MS C 128 inf) and plates 42, 43. Not in Perrot 1965.
[32] The Piacenza manuscript perhaps originating in Bobbio, where Gerbert of Aurillac and Reims may have left a legacy of pipe-measurement texts (see p. 284).
[33] Smits van Waesberghe (see note 26): 156–7.
[34] Seebass 1973: 177, 187 and plate 107. Not in Perrot 1965.
[35] The oldest manuscript now known of Hero is thirteenth century: see Perrot 1965: plate xxiv for the cistern diagram with 'semicircle' or hemisphere.

Isidore's *Etymologiae*[36] where the bellows have what appear to be realistic studs around the edges but which are probably little circles such as decorate other edges in the manuscript's drawings.

A second mitre-shape arrangement of pipes is found in this same copy of Isidore's *Etymologiae*, raising the question whether the mitre was specific to the genre *Classification of Instruments*, and if so why. As before, the pipes might be arranged in this order because otherwise the pipeline would run into the text, or because the figure is symmetrical like others in the manuscript. Perhaps the symmetrical arrangement had to happen only once in an influential manuscript to become a convention belonging to the genre. So clearly aiming at symmetry are twelve strips drawn below (?) the chest (?) of the organ illustrating one copy of the genre *Letter to Dardanus* (French, tenth or eleventh century) that it is not clear whether they represent pipes or bellows,[37] and there may well have been other examples. One may suspect that the less familiar an artist is with an artefact, the more he inclines towards abstractions like symmetry.

The genre *Music-theory* may occasionally yield the hint of a practical detail about organs: see a conjecture on Hucbald's 'slider-key' in Chapter 3. A copy of Boethius's *De musica* made at Christ Church, Canterbury, in *c.* 1130, illustrates the A–P alphabet with a 'comb-like diagram' that may represent a keyboard drawn to scale[38] (see Plate 13). If it does, we are looking down on the front of the organ-plan, with protruding sliders or press-keys, suggesting both playing-length and how big the space was between them – invaluable information. Fifteen pipes labelled A–P are also drawn in stylized form, rectangular, with thin pointed feet (meant to be of uniform length?) and divided into two sets, perhaps B C D E♭ F G A♭ and H C D E F G A B, with a pitch of C = 208Hz and Pythagorean tuning.[39] The first six notes of all eight modes would be possible, some of them transposed, hence the need to label organ-keys, an otherwise puzzling practice? But of course, nothing in other sources – manuscript illuminations, pipe-measurement texts, music-theory – supports the idea of interpreting these drawings so literally or specifically, nor need the artist have been incorporating anything familiar to him as he endeavoured to illustrate Boethius's scale and compass. Nevertheless, the evolution of the keyboard and its compass was doubtless convoluted, both varying enough for one to reject no evidence, apparent or real.

[36] Turin, Biblioteca dell'Università, D III 19, in Seebass 1973: plate 119. Not in Perrot 1965.
[37] Paris, Bibliothèque Nationale, lat. 7211 f. 150, in Hammerstein 1959: 121. The shortest are in the middle, but separated by a wide gap; Hammerstein 1959: 122 assumes that they are pipes.
[38] See also Page 1979. On other materials from the Canterbury scriptorium, see Chapter 10.
[39] Private communication from Mr Wilson Barry, who suggests other interpretations, such as that the two sets of pipes could represent CDEFGAB at two pitches, the second plus an initial H as in later compasses.

Plate 12 'David and his Musicians' from the Ivrea Psalter: Ivrea, Biblioteca capitolare, MS 85, f. 23' (opposite)

Plate 13 Diagram of pipes and keyboard (Boethius copy): Cambridge, University Library, Ii. 3.12, f. 125' (page 184)

Plate 14 'David and his Musicians' from the Rutland or Belvoir Psalter: London, British Library, Add. 62925, f. 97' (page 185). For remarks, see pp. 309f below.

Jdq; pbat̄ hm̄. Nāque÷ mese. w. ihȳpodorio: eade. w. idorio hȳpat̄
meson-abeaque÷ iquouism̄ l̄gue diateſſaron ēsonantia differens.
Jtē mese dorij que÷ η: abea que÷ mese phrigij. id̄. oj. distat tono.
Nā que÷ mese idorio. η. eade iphrigio licanos meson. Rurſ mese phri
gij modi que÷ oj. abea mese que÷ lidij. id̄. f̄ distat tono. Nāque et̄ mphrigio
. oj. mese: ilidio é. licanos meson. Rurſ mese lij modi. abea mese que÷
mixolidij. id̄. η. semitonio distat. Et̄ eñ iſ ordo grec̄ lidij ēt̄iuer
mesen: et ordiu grec̄ mixolidij mese bt̄ cōparat̄. īpagiuila ſ; īſu
distingui̊. Ea q̄q; que÷ mixolidij. id̄. η. ad eū mesen que̊ hipmixolidij.
id̄. f̄. tou differentia hē. iccirco qm̄. η. que mixolidio mese: éade÷
mhipmixolidio licanos meson. Undefit. ut̄ mese dorij abea mese que÷
mixolidij. diateſſaron ēsonantia distet. Jd̄ pbat̄ hm̄. Nā mese que÷ do
rij. id̄. η. eade÷ mixolidij. id̄. η. hipate meson. que ad cui libet modi
mesen diateſſaron ēsonantiā seruat. Jtē mese dorij. id̄. η. ad eā mesen
que÷ hipmixolidij que÷ f̄. diapente ēsonantia seruat. Ea eñ mese
que÷ dorij. id̄. η. iordine hipmixolidij licanos hypaton÷ Lichanos
aūt hypaton admesen idiatonico que iq̄ libet modo ficōpare÷ dia
pente ēsonantia distat. Cur aūt octauus mod̄ q̄ē hipmixolidius adi
icet̄ hm̄c patet. Sic biſ diapason ēsonantia hēe.

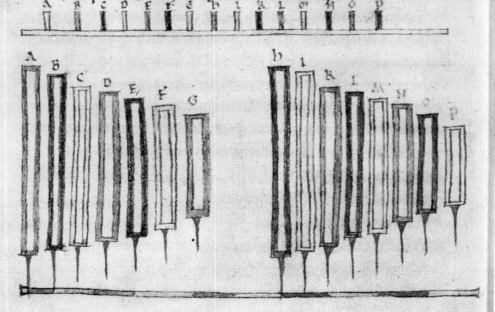

nū tu dn̄s altissimꝰ sup omnē ꞇram: nimis exal
tatꝰ es sup om̄s deos. tionis eiꝰ.
ꝙ diligitis dn̄m odite malū: ꞇ cuſtodit dn̄s aı̄as ſc̄o
rum ſuoꝶ de manu peccatoris liberauit eos.
lux orta est iuſto: & rectis corde leticia.
et ꝛamini in dn̄o: & coꞏfitemini memoꝛie ſc̄ificā

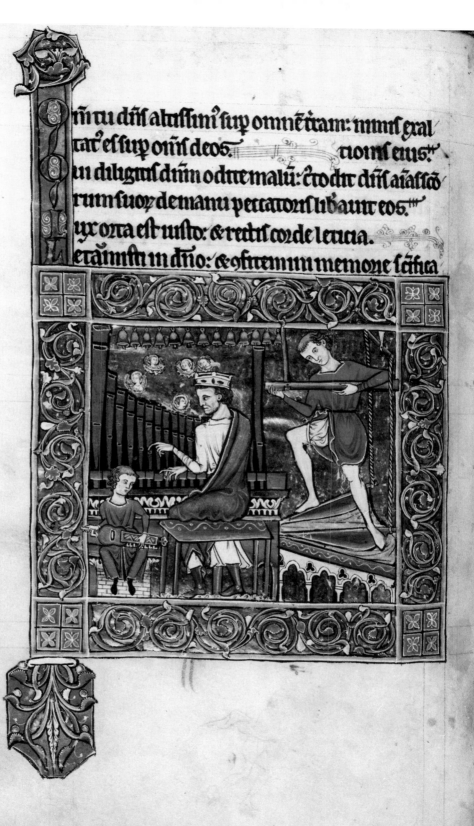

Finally, one technical detail has often been claimed to be 'proved' by drawings: the conical or outward-tapering pipes as drawn in the Harding Bible, in Gerbert (1774: plate 27), a thirteenth-century *Glossary of Solomon*, the Belvoir Castle Psalter (see Plate 14) and others.[40] While Theophilus and a few less clear references in some pipe-measurement texts[41] appear to refer to conical pipes, they may not be corroborating evidence. They, rather than actual instruments, may be the source of information for artists; perhaps the reverse is not out of the question. Nevertheless, for builders the option of giving pipes a conical shape must have existed, irrespective of what the drawings or treatises appear to say; and builders must have experimented with the degrees of taper, some of which may have been scarcely clear to the eye, especially from a distance (see Chapter 17). The question again, therefore, is how literal a reading of the visual information is justified.

The *Glossary of Solomon* of 1241 (see note 40) shows six pipes, three apparently conical, three cylindrical; but in comparison with the 'reliable' details for the bellows – cuneiform shape, a clear hand-grip and tuyère, some studded edges – the pipes are sketchy. To interpret them as standing for a six-rank chest of 8.8.4.3.3.2 of which one was a stopped quint,[42] is not only over-sanguine[43] but distracts the eye from more certain details – such as that the player is sitting down, that the bellows are thrust into the bottom of the chest which stands on four legs (of wood?), and that the keys are long enough for pulling. All these details conform to other drawings in the David-genre. One of the most suggestive of these is found in the Mouzy manuscript[44] (probably eleventh century, from Mouzon, a monastery connected to Reims) where an organ is drawn with three sets of seven pipes (?) in one row on the top line of a chest, which is itself on top of the trunk; there are two rounded cuneiform bellows and a seated organist gesturing as if pulling sliders. Had the artist learnt from a theorist about either three ranks or three octaves of pipes, he may well not have appreciated that it made no sense to have the three sets, each long-to-short, in one row. For his purposes, familiarity with the David-genre, some acquaintance with writings such as Hucbald's, and experience with everyday equipment such as bellows, would have given him all he needed for such a drawing.

---

[40] E.g. in Perrot 1965: plate XXVIII.2 (the *Salomonis glossarium* of Conrad von Scheyern, 1241), plate XXVIII.4, and Hickmann 1936: fig. 7.

[41] From the tenth to the fifteenth centuries: Sachs 1970: 93, 141.

[42] R. Quoika, *Vom Blockwerk zur Register-Orgel* (Kassel, 1966), 10–11.

[43] 'A model for those interpretations that over-estimate by far how real the content in a representation is' (Sachs 1980: 102–3).

[44] Paris, Bibliothèque Nationale, lat. 5371, f. 272'. In Huglo 1981: plate I.2.

12

Winchester and other Anglo-Saxon organs

The poem[1]

Lines 141–72 of a 588-line narrative in verse, consisting of a prologue and *Life* of St Swithun by the late tenth-century cantor, Wulfstan of Winchester, provide the most detailed account of any individual organ before contracts began in the later four-teenth century. Dedicated to Bishop Aelfheah or Alphege, this is a unique document[2] concerning what was probably a unique organ, and the lines occur in the part of the poem that deals with the eastern part of the church: the east end, eastern crypt and eastern (crossing) tower. See also Chapter 8 concerning the westwork at Winchester.

In its references to music and to technicalities of the organ, the poem leaves many uncertainties:[3]

141	talia et auxistis hic organa, qualia nusquam	and you enlarged [endowed?] the organs here, such as are nowhere else
	cernuntur, gemino constabilita solo.	seen, fixed on a double floor [= on two levels].
	bisseni supra sociantur in ordine folles,	Twice six bellows are joined above in a row,
	inferiusque iacent quattuor atque decem.	and below lie four and ten.
145	flatibus alternis spiracula maxima reddunt.	With alternating breaths [vents?] they render a great amount of air.
	quos agitant ualidi septuaginta uiri	Which [bellows] seventy strong men work
	brachia uersantes, multo et sudore madentes,	moving their arms and dripping with much sweat,
	certatimque suos quique monent socios,	each eagerly encouraging his companions,
	uiribus ut totis impellant flamina sursum,	to drive the air upward with all strength

---

1   Text from Campbell 1950: 69–70. A fascimile of the older of two earlier sources (London, British Library, Roy 15 c. VII f. 54–54', written *c.* 1000) is given in Holschneider 1968: plates 14 and 15. The copy insets even-numbered lines, begins each line with a capital, gives verse punctuation and incorporates what appear to be revisions: 151 *s* added to *quadringenta*, 157 *s* added to *quaterdeni*, 164 *preter ut* partly obliterated.

2   Unique in its technicalities but related in genre to e.g. the verse preface by the scribe Godeman to the *Benedictional of Æthelwold* (see also p. 126), prepared in or for Winchester (?) in 971/84. Wulfstan's *Narratio metrica de Sancto Swithuno* has been called 'the longest and most metrically accomplished surviving Anglo-Saxon poem': Lapidge, in Yorke 1988: 110.

3   For the present translation, cf. McKinnon 1974: 5–6.

150	et rugiat pleno kapsa referta sinu,	and make roar the full chest with its ample curve [or: from the full reservoir],
	sola quadringentas, quae sustinet ordine musas,	which by itself supports the four hundred muses in order,
	quas manus organici temperat ingenii:	which the hand of organic skill controls:
	has aperit clausas, iterumque has claudit apertas,	it opens the closed and in turn closes the opened,
	exigit ut uarii certa Camena soni,	as the prescribed song [or: chant] of diverse notes requires,
155	considuntque duo concordi pectore fratres,	and two brothers of harmonious spirit sit together,
	et regit alphabetum rector uterque suum,	and each, like a ruler, rules his alphabet,
	suntque quaterdenis occulta foramina linguis,	and there are hidden openings in four times ten tongues,
	inque suo retinet ordine quaeque decem.	and each holds ten in its own rank [= in due order?].
	huc aliae currunt, illuc aliaeque recurrunt,	Hither some tongues run, thither some return,
160	seruantes modulis singula puncta suis,	serving the individual holes in their own places [= the separate holes in the chest according to their pitches?]
	et feriunt iubilum septem discrimina uocum,	and the 'seven separate voices' strike up the jubilant song,
	permixto lyrici carmine semitoni,	mixed additionally with the song of the lyric semitone.
	inque modum tonitrus uox ferrea uerberat aures,	And in the manner of thunder the iron voice beats upon the ears
	preter ut hunc solum nil capiant sanitum,	that they receive no sound beyond only this,
165	concrepat in tantum sonus hinc illincque resultans,	the sound so clamours, echoing here and there,
	quisque manu patulas claudat ut auriculas,	that everyone closes the opening of his ears with his hand,
	haudquaquam sufferre ualens propiando rugitum,	totally unable to bear the noise when drawing near,
	quem reddunt uarii concrepitando soni,	which the various sounds producing in their clamouring.
	musarumque melos auditur ubique per urbem,	And the melody of the pipes is heard everywhere in the city,
170	et peragrat totam fama uolans patriam.	and flying fame goes through the whole country.
	hoc decus ecclesiae uouit tua cura tonanti,	It was your care that consecrated this glory of the church to the Thunderer,
	clauigeri inque sacri struxit honore PETRI.	and set it up in honour of the holy keybearer Peter.

The poem and the dedication of the enlarged Old Minster to which it is connected are dated 993/4,[4] and since Bishop Alphege succeeded the reformer Æthelwold in 984, the organ would be included in the various works undertaken between 984 and 994. A guess would be that the organ was built or rebuilt on a larger scale, perhaps in part for the dedication ceremonies themselves; see remarks on the Winchester organ in Chapter 5. On a possible (but unlikely) reference to the organ later in the poem, see Chapter 8. It is also possible that Wulfstan refers to the organ again in his hymn for St Birin (†*c.* 650, relics transferred to Winchester in 673), one of four poems that frequently refer to singing and to chant:[5]

Nostra camena tibi canit haec, pia carmina patri	This our muse sings to you; our muse causes pious songs
Intonat et iubilat nostra camena tibi.	to resound to the father [= St Birin] and rejoices to you.
Organa clarisonis reboant tibi dulcia bombis,	In brilliant sounds sweet *organa* resound to you,
Et crepitant modulis organa clarisonis.	and *organa* peal out their brilliant sounds.

Had it not been for Wulfstan's other poem one would assume that *organa* here means either 'organized articulate ensemble singing' or simply 'music'. The vocabulary looks like a *tour-de-force* collection of poetical-musical terms rather than a realistic account of singing and organ-playing: *camena, carmina, canit, intonat, iubilat, organa, clarisoni, reboant, dulcia, bombis, crepitant* and *modulis* are all conventional in earlier poetry. In the circumstances, however, while *organa* may not mean 'the organ', it could encompass it in the general sense of 'organized ensemble sounds'.

The various interpretations of Wulfstan's larger poem make a story of interest in themselves. Evidently from the excerpt in Du Cange 1678 (under 'organum'), Dom Bedos knew of it in the 1760s, questioning whether even so crude an organ really needed twenty-six bellows for four hundred pipes.[6] A century later, Rimbault went to another seventeenth-century edition, the *Acta sanctorum* of 1685, probably aware that Gerbert had also done so in 1774, and now questioned whether there really could be seventy blowers: perhaps it was a 'corruption of the text for seven'.[7] A further hundred years later, other questions have been asked, such as whether 'four hundred' (*quadringenti*) should read 'forty each' (*quadrageni*).[8] Three more recent fundamental studies summarize contrary views of the 'reliability' of the poem,[9] none quite sufficiently stressing Wulfstan's skill in metrical composition and therefore his control of the words. The following section focuses on the technical material in the poem.

---

[4] See e.g. M. Biddle, 'Archaeology, architecture and the cult of saints in Anglo-Saxon England', in Butler & Morris 1986: 1–31.

[5] Lines 25–9, in ed. G. M. Dreves, *Analecta hymnica medii aevi* 48 (Leipzig, 1905), 12, cf. 14. On the 'father' being the 'holy father our bishop Birin', see inscription *ibid.*, 13.

[6] Bedos de Celles, *L'Art du facteur d'orgues* 1 (Paris, 1766), preface.

[7] Hopkins & Rimbault 1877: 20–2; Gerbert 1774: 143. Here *Acta sanctorum* = *Acta sanctorum ordinis S. Benedicti*, ed. Luc d'Achéry & J. Mabillon, saec V [= vol 5] (Paris, 1685), 630–1.

[8] P. Hardouin. 'Qu'il est difficile d'être sûr des descriptions d'orgues anciennes', in Dunning 1980: 271–85 and 'Encore Winchester', *CO* 39/40 (1981), 20–3.

[9] Körte 1973, McKinnon 1974 and Vellekoop 1984. In particular, the first two authors give contrary views on the way in which the poem is instructive, the first positivistic, the second critical.

Technical details

Line 141.

The organ was put up, perhaps 'enlarged'. The following lines make it clear that here *organa* does not mean 'ensemble singing' or 'various instruments' but indeed 'an organ with pipes and bellows'. Whether *auxistis* refers to enlarging a previous organ as usually understood (for example Holschneider 1968: 141), or means rather 'caused to be put up', perhaps 'endowed' or even 'consecrated' (cf. line 171), is an open question. But the possibility that Winchester did have an earlier organ is clearly important, raising questions about how long the instrument had been known to the Anglo-Saxons and what it was like. A guess would be that there had been a smaller instrument made a few years previously under Æthelwold, the bishop also accredited with an earlier organ at Abingdon (see below). These organs were therefore artefacts built within the same period of monastic reform: as Alphege enlarged Æthelwold's recently built crypt, so he did his organ, and the scope of the new one was so extraordinary as to deserve Wulfstan's enthusiastic description. A rebuilt crypt and a rebuilt organ might suggest that they were both aimed at the visiting pilgrims.

On Æthelwold's organ at Abingdon, another recently reformed house, see below.

Lines 141–2.

Such organs were not otherwise known: this remark is much like that made about Pippin's Greek organ (see Chapter 9). Courteous exaggeration can be expected in most lines of such a poem but the next phrase may imply what was new about the Winchester organ and beyond any previous instrument: it was fixed on two levels. *Constabilita* suggests something non-portable and the two floors imply something about the organ's size. *Gemino solo* appears to conform with suggestions made later by Theophilus for locating an organ, i.e. bellows on one level and the sounding parts above on another. (Perhaps there is a punning oxymoron in the words: *gemino*, 'twin or double', *solo*, 'base' but also 'solo or single' in another metre.) Another interpretation of *gemino solo* might be the 'musical foundation or sound source [*Tonquelle*] of two units',[10] implying that there were two chests or sets of pipes, but this would be a more abstract way of referring to something technical than is usual in the poem. By itself, *gemino* occurs in other technical organ-sources;[11] for *solo*, see also line 170 below.

If the organ were on two levels and there was also a double tier of bellows (see following lines), does this mean that one set was placed above, close to the pipe-chest and therefore to the organist, or were both tiers of bellows fixed in one large wooden frame ('twin rows'), with the wind taken off to the floor above? The second is likelier in view of the next lines.

---

[10]   Riemann 1879: 207f for a translation of the passage.
[11]   E.g. in the treatise *Cuprum purissimum* (see Chapter 16), probably (but not certainly) later than Wulfstan's poem, *geminos* is used for the pair of bellows.

Lines 143–4.

Sociantur in ordine gives the impression of a row of bellows linked together to a windtrunk, which could have been lying across their mouths in a straight line, as in Praetorius's drawing of the Halberstadt bellows-chamber (Praetorius 1619: plate 26). This may be an anachronism, however, and the phrase means merely 'grouped and arranged in an orderly fashion', perhaps so as to lead into a single wind-collector (Theophilus's *conflatorium*), which may just possibly be implied in line 150. Whether the bellows were made from whole skins or cuneiform boards, they would very likely have been arranged in two tiers, with the player and pipes on a floor above. This would represent a developed stage of organ-building beyond what is known of Roman organs though not necessarily of Byzantine (see Chapters 9 and 14); it may also suggest that the builder had previous experience.

Although all the terms in Wulfstan's poem that involve numbers are problematic, being useful for the metre or for the clouds of allusion enjoyed by such poets,[12] *bis seni* ('twice six') does sound as if it refers to pairs of alternating bellows. Or since the set of 'four and ten' bellows could also indicate pairs, one might wonder if one or the other group – the set of twelve or the set of fourteen – was a reservoir. Perhaps seven pairs of (wholeskin) bellows fed a reservoir above made from twelve skins? However, twenty-six bellows are not out of the question. Presumably they would have needed thirteen blowers, which would suit Riemann's ingenious suggestion that *septuaginta* should read *sex septemque* ('six plus seven', or perhaps *septem sexque?*) were it not that the suggestion would contradict the metre.[13]

Arguing from well-known medieval miniatures, and relying on what they show of bellows-types and their proportion to the numbers of pipes depicted, Körte 1973 suggests that Winchester had twenty-six hand-held wedge-bellows, pumped energetically in alternation by teams of blowers in shifts, hence seventy (?) being needed. This is all possible but one is at a loss for evidence: surely not miniatures? Wulfstan's figures cannot be relied upon simply because he was the cantor and must know what he was talking about.[14] In the present context, cantor (as Wulfstan refers to himself) also means 'poet', one who may have been using numbers to 'convey a general poetic connotation' or to 'fit neatly into the poetic meter' (McKinnon 1974: 13), a poet-composer[15] no more expert in organs than in bells. Even if it is true, as William of Malmesbury said, that Wulfstan wrote a book on music (*fecit . . . opus de tonorum harmonia* – RBMAS 90.1.167), it would not follow from any interest he had in the theory of the 'lyric semitone' (line 162) that his description of organ-mechanism need be taken literally.

---

[12] Lapidge (see note 2): 112 points out Wulfstan's skill in handling metre, a skill suggesting that he was not being constrained in his choice of words.

[13] Riemann's alternative (1879: 207) gives an inadmissible spondee, but he did think *septuaginta* an exaggeration chosen for the sake of the metre (*übertrieben und des Metrums wegen*).

[14] On *cantor* meaning a practical musician as distinct from *musicus* (a scholar of the *ars musica*), see E. Reimer, 'Musicus-Cantor, *HmT* (1978). On the cantor's duties of supervising all music-making, the scriptorium and the liturgy, see M. E. Fassler, 'The office of cantor in early Western monastic rules and customaries: a preliminary investigation', *EMH* 5 (1985), 29–51.

[15] Some remarks on Wulfstan's interests as a poet in M. Lapidge, 'Three Latin poems from Æthelwold's school at Winchester', *ASE* 1 (1972), 85–113, here 106. On Wulfstan's notating tropes, Planchart 1977: 27–33.

The question of the seventy blowers is a test-case: if, as well a Benedictine poet might, Wulfstan means simply 'a large group of men working together for common benefit' like the seventy translators of the Old Testament or Moses's seventy elders in Exodus 24.1, then the unequal numbers of bellows[16] and blowers is not disturbing. But if the cantor was responsible for hiring servants to work the bellows (cf. the *famuli* at Notre-Dame some centuries later: see p. 331)? he would know how many to hire. Now one occasion on which he may have needed five shifts of thirteen men each (plus a leader to 'spell' the alternating rhythm) was the minster's dedication – this part of the poem may be describing that time when the organ sounded for much of the day as various parts of the structure were consecrated, the bounds beaten, the new monastic enclave consecrated, the people summoned, and so on. For either reason, therefore, 'seventy' is explicable. But it is hard to believe that more than thirteen bellows-blowers were regularly gathered, and there may be another reason for the figure twenty-six: see below.

Line 145.

A great mound of wind is raised by many blowers who alternate and use their arms vigorously. This need not necessarily indicate hand-held bellows since blowers hung on to horizontal bars while treading bellows, pulling up the spent bellows while stepping on to the full.[17] *Spiracula* are vents rather than breaths (*spiramina*), and it could be that Wulfstan is saying that the vents from the bellows are operating alternately, as they would be. *Bracchia versantes* seems to allude to *Aeneid* 8.619, and *sudore madentes* to line 1362 of Frithegodus's *Life of Wilfrid* or its source (Campbell 1950: 60). Eager encouragement of the kind the men are described as exchanging would hardly be appropriate either if they were in sight of the people or if the organ sounded during the regular liturgy. Neither, therefore, was the case?

Lines 149–50.

The wind is driven upward to the chest: this must be another reference to the two-tiered layout. Since *kapsa referta* and *pleno sinu* could be construed as meaning much the same, it is not certain that Wulfstan was referring to the kind of upward-curving windtrunk described by Theophilus, although if an artist was seeking information for a drawing and knew Wulfstan's poem, he could see it as meaning a curving trunk. Other possibilities are that the *sinu* is a curved wind-collector like Theophilus's *conflatorium* or – most likely? – that it is neither trunk nor collector but a metaphor for the 'full bosom' of a singing instrument. *Kapsa* was a familiar term for both 'reliquary' and 'organ-chest'.[18] Three hundred years earlier, St Aldhelm's

---

[16] The late fourteenth-century organs of Halberstadt and Magdeburg were reported by Praetorius to have twenty and twenty-five bellows respectively (the latter 'very small' – *gar kleine*), requiring ten and twelve blowers: Praetorius 1619: 103. Since these bellows must have been remade before Praetorius's time, it is not unlikely that originally there were even more pairs.

[17] Ropes are already clearly visible in a third-century Roman mosaic: see J. Perrot, 'L'orgue de la mosaïque syrienne de Mariamîn', *RM* 59 (1973), 99–105. Perhaps these in turn reflected older practice: a pair of Ancient Egyptian blowers each stepping on a pair of bellows and pulling them up with ropes is shown in Frémont 1917: 28.

[18] Reliquary, cf. the *capsa major* at St-Riquier: C. Heitz, 'Architecture et liturgie processionelle à l'époque pré-romane', *Revue de l'Art* 24 (1974), 30–47. Organ-chest: in the text *Cuprum purissimum* (see Chapter 16).

phrase *auratis capsis* ('gilded chests' – MGH AA 15.2.356) suggested a polished or gilded bronze reliquary-sized chest, and now Wulfstan's *referta* leaves the impression of a chest crammed with wind or mechanism or pipes much as a reliquary would be crammed with relics, both of them breathing forth a spirit of one kind or another.

Line 151.

The idea of twenty-six bellows for only four hundred pipes is not easily convincing, although in itself the ten-rank chorus (with much duplication of pitches per key) is reasonable. Possibilities are that there were fewer bellows raising the wind or that they were very small; alternatively, that 'four hundred' stands for 'several hundred'. (In number alphabets as described in later centuries, 400 represented the last Hebrew letter *taw* or, in some systems, Greek and Latin *y*.) Otherwise it must have been as commentators have said in the past: the apparatus lost so much wind that over-capacity compensated and helped to stabilize the supply.

Any emendation to the text to make it read something like 'two chest-sections each of forty pipes' (*quadragenas* for *quadringentas, kapsa/sola* meaning two chests) raises other questions: forty is too few unless Wulfstan is counting only the front pipe of each slider (see below). The very neatness of the equation (400 pipes = 40 slider-keys × 10 holes each), though often seen as proof that the numbers were real, could suggest that they were given in order to add up. For concrete numbers, Wulfstan would find precedent in the Old Testament, especially the Pentateuch: two, seven (days), ten, forty (years of wandering, or the chapters in Exodus), seventy (the Septuagint or Moses' elders), perhaps four hundred. If a poet knew a count of twenty-six for the Hebrew Old Testament books (or New Testament without Jude?), one could imagine a natural association between seventy blowers or scribes and twenty-six bellows or books. It seems possible that in giving musical-technical details unusual in poetry, Wulfstan used these concrete numbers because the Old Testament had, even that he was implying a parallel: Winchester bishops brought reformed monks to the Old Minster as Moses led the chosen people to the promised land. This would still be so even if the numbers were 'reliable'.

As to the *musas* in line 151: this is not a word used for pipes by Isidore, Cassiodorus, or the *mensura* texts (Chapter 16), although it might appear in lists such as Regino of Prüm's *tibiis, musis, fistulis, organis et his similibus* (*c.* 900 – GS 1.236). The *musas* of line 151, the *melos musarum* of line 169 and the title *Musa* for a sequence in the Winchester Troper, Corpus Christi College manuscript, could denote either pipes or 'the Muses' as intermediaries in terms of Isidore's *Etymologiae* (just as *organa* meant 'instruments').[19]

---

[19] Winchester Troper, see Holschneider 1975. Isidore = Book 3.5.1. On uses of *musa*, N. Swerdlow, 'Musica dicitur a Moys, quod est Aqua', *JAMS* 20 (1967), 3–9, here 5.
  On seventy and twenty six: the numbers may both be approximate, since in fact there were said to be seventy-two translators of the Septuagint, and the Hebrew books are generally counted as twenty-four.

Lines 152–4.

Skill is 'organic' when it makes use of the notes of music as proportionally calculated (Reckow 1975: 67–8). Opening/closing may refer to sliders pulled out/pushed in; or to keys that, when pressed, transfer motion via a square to the horizontal sliders. and need to be pulled up again; or to spring-loaded keys that will return themselves when no longer being pressed. (Riemann 1879: 207 and later writers assume that there is no spring and that the sliders have to be 'closed' by hand.) *Currens/ recurrens* (line 159) suggests sliders but does not make any other part of the action clear, i.e. whether there were keys operating them.

Lines 152–3 could also be allusive (Vellekoop 1984, 193): the organ is the Church, he who rules is Jesus or David, the one 'that openeth and no man shutteth' (*qui aperit et nemo cludit* – Revelations 3.7). This would conform to the idea of the Church as 'the organ of God' (see p. 2).

Line 154.

Camena is the word of a poet and is not found in the *mensura fistularum* treatises. *Certa* suggests something 'prescribed', not the haphazardly produced jumble of sound from bells or the screech of an organ used for signalling. *Varii soni* is unlikely to mean anything as specific as the several church tones,[20] and *sonus* means either sound in general (as in Isidore) or musical notes, an equivalent to the *phthongi* of contemporary theory.[21] The sliders produce the basic sounds of music, and these can be articulated melodically; therefore the phrase 'prescribed song of diverse tones' can be paraphrased as 'regular melodic lines made from the various notes'. Even if line 154 signifies something biblical – David ordering the various sounds of the skies (Vellekoop 1984: 194) – it could still describe what a tenth-century organist did in church.

Lines 155–60.

Two brothers (thus not lay musicians?) together play their own keys with forty slider-keys of ten holes each: *quaeque*, 'each', refers to the tongues. *Concordi pectore* has the ring of poetic diction, and *fratres concordi* has both classical and more recent predecessors, particularly in St Aldhelm.[22] Aldhelm's lines concern the clamour attending the dedication of an altar to the Virgin, and *fratres concordi laudemus voce tonantem* ('brothers of like mind, let us praise the Thunderer [God] with our voice') refers to singers. Particularly in the context of a dedication ceremony, Wulfstan may have had this in mind and thus did not intend 'of like mind' to mean unison in the musical sense. On the other hand, *fratres* and *alphabetum* may well be technical terms: it is monks who play the slider-keys, and the keys are labelled, actually or metaphorically, with the letters of music. For further on the two organists, see below.

---

[20] *Toni* for the eight modes and their formulas in the later ninth century (Aurelian of Réôme – GS 1.39ff).
[21] Examples in *Musica enchiriadis* (opening sentence refers to *phthongi*, 'called *soni* in Latin') and the early pipe-measurement text *Symphonias* (Sachs 1970: 45f), thus both before and after Wulfstan.
[22] For *fratres concordi*, see Cicero *Pro Ligario* 5 and Aldhelm in PL 89.290. For the whole line, Alcuin's *Carmina* 9.144 (= MGH Poet. 1).

There are several possibilities for line 158. The first is that the slider had ten holes: but this is difficult to imagine because even if it had to move only a couple of inches or so to open or close the holes, it would be long; and if it were tightly fitted, as it would have to be, the inertia would not be easily (or at any rate smoothly) overcome. The problem would increase if there were forty keys in a single row from top to bottom, since this could mean pipe-sizes that needed yet longer sliders in the bass. (But see below on the nature of this pipe-chorus.) More likely is that the slider had a single hole: 'ten' refers to holes not in the slider but above on the topboard, thus holes for the pipe-feet. A slider-hole for each pipe would be necessary only if the ranks were separable or it was a question of a copper chest *à la* Theophilus. Otherwise the slider need have only one hole, but Wulfstan, seeing ten pipes per key and not knowing how sliders were made, could think there were ten holes.

There is another major problem, however: several phrases in the poem imply some kind of double organ, particularly those concerning the two organists and the two alphabets. One could suppose the organ to have had two half-chests, with twenty sliders each; their half keyboard could duplicate each other, or the compass could be continuous, or there could be merely a partial overlap. Riemann's suggestion of two keyboards (placed side by side?) each with a twenty-note compass of

> A H c d e f g a b h c' d' e' f' g' a' b' h' c" d"

or

> G A H c d e f g a b h c' d' e' f' g' a' b' h' c"

and each note with ten pipes of octaves and unisons only, is well reasoned if one assumes that the poet's numbers are literal and that the keyboard was continuous (Riemann 1879: 208). But neither is certain. How the keys were labelled is another question: perhaps with the 'third-difference' alphabet used in the Winchester Troper, whereby A–G corresponds to modern C–B (see Chapter 3). The reading 'each of forty pipes' – *quadrageni*, see above – would mean that each organist had ten keys of four pipes per key, and lines 157–8 could then read 'and there are four sets of holes within the sliders' (Hardouin 1966), for unison and octaves pipes only. But this is no more than a guess, as would be the idea that two organists were needed for playing two-part organum.

More needs to be said on the 'double organ' (see p. 198), but in any case it is by no means certain either that forty keys would have been in a single sequence or that if they were this would be 'from bass to treble' as today. A large-size, multi-rank mixture-organ is conceivable in which there were no pipes larger than 4' or even 2': ranks broke back as they descended, like the much later Repeating Cymbel or (perhaps) the much earlier Roman arena organ. Or the compass could repeat every ten or twenty notes, so that each player's keyboard started at some kind of middle C. In either case there was no 'bass' and therefore no 'treble' in the later sense. Unfortunately, this is all very uncertain and yet is a crucial part of the picture: a whole new approach to the development of the organ and its music is opened out by an awareness that the Winchester keyboard need not have had a single sequence of notes 'from bass to treble' in the later sense.

Lines 161–2.

There are eight different tones. Taken literally, this agrees with the alphabet C D E F G A B H of the Harding Bible (see Plate 10), thus a complete octave of notes, the schema for a longer keyboard. Like any other, the Winchester notes are based on the *septem discrimina vocum*[23] of *Aeneid* 6.646, a phrase unlikely to have come to Wulfstan merely through secondary literature familiar to any cantor (for example Isidore *Etymologiae* 3.22), in view of other faint allusions to Virgil in the poem (see lines 163–70). *Permixto* sounds Ciceronian, and lines 159–62 look like a poetic expansion of lines 153–4, with 'lyric semitone' being an allusion to the lyre's extra note beyond its seventh string – in any case a fanciful reference to the B-flat that was about to be discussed extensively in music-theory[24] but evidently familiar already to organ-makers.

Lines 163–70.

The sound is thunderous. The language of passages to do with the organ's impression on the ear is particularly traditional and/or allusive: *vox ferrea* (*Aeneid* 6.626 and *Georgics* 2.44), *fama volans* (cf. *Aeneid* 3.121 and 7.392), *peragrat fama* (cf. Cicero *Pro Milone* 98), *vox verberat aures* (cf. Lucan's *tuba verberat aures* 7.25, and Plautus *Miles* 799 and *Amphitryo* 333), *patulas auriculas* (cf. Horace *Ep*.1.18.70), *resultans* (cf. *Aeneid* 5.150), *pleno sinu* (cf. Ovid *Fasti* 4.432) and *sudore madentes* (cf. Lucretius 6.1187). While some of these may be too commonplace to suggest anything but a well-read cantor, the reference to thunder is formulaic: *tonitrus*, like the *tonanti* of line 171, recalls the *Jupiter tonans* in Ovid, which in turn alludes to *Iliad* 2.478 and 2.781.

Although *hinc illincque* is a set phrase, it may refer to reverberation in the spaces outside the enclosed or monastic part of the church; see Chapter 8 on westworks. The reference to the 'melody of the pipes' heard around the city is part of the verse-form in so far as in the binary structure of the verse, the two lines 169 and 170 say much the same thing. That ears could 'receive no other sound' may be a further reference to St Aldhelm of Malmesbury, whose thirteenth riddle implies that strings grow silent when the organ sounds (MGH AA 15.2.103), and it is likely that he too was alluding to earlier references to organs.

Lines 171–2.

The organ is in honour of St Peter. Like the early Vatican church the original Winchester oratory was dedicated to SS Peter and Paul according to Bede. While St Peter remained the patron saint of many churches, especially in England, Wulfstan's reference here may be more informative: the organ was placed near the saint's altar. It seems unlikely that there is a pun here, since *clavis* for organ-key is unlikely before the later thirteenth century,[25] although one has to allow for unwritten and now unknown usage.

[23] A phrase with Greek antecedents: see D. Wulstan, *Septem discrimina vocum* (Cork, 1983). On the question of seven or eight pipes, see also remarks on Hero of Alexandria, p. 245.

[24] *b quam rotundam* in the *Dialogus c.* 1000 (GS 1.253b), Guido's *Micrologus c.* 1025 (CSM 4.94), and the text *Cuprum purissimum* (an inserted sentence: see Sachs 1970: 174).

[25] *HmT*, under 'clavis'; for pipe-treatises of (or in copies of) the fourteenth and fifteenth century, see Sachs 1970: 140, 141.

Perhaps indicating the upper side-chapels in the Winchester nave, or in a generic church-layout similar to it, the *Regularis concordia* specifies that choirs of boys be located away from the main choir for special effects on Maundy Thursday (Symons 1953: 36f), as the later Essen customary also specifies the west galleries of the eleventh-century minster (Heitz 1963: 190f). Bearing in mind the two-tiered structure of the Winchester organ, there must have been several upper-floor spaces in the Old Minster (Klukas 1985: 86, 91), each of which could have housed an organ. On these various questions, see Chapter 8.

General interpretation

Was there an organ at all at Winchester? Or is Wulfstan's salute to the bishop an elaborate panegyric in which the *organa* – the pipes, bellows and players – serve as symbol for the Christian host? Since the numbers ten, forty, seventy and (probably) four hundred had significance for students of the Old Testament, was the description of an organ no more than a mass of pious allusions?

While such a possibility cannot be dismissed out of hand, there are several reasons for believing there to have been an organ. Since secular descriptions of organs did not exist in *c.* 1000, Wulfstan's diction was not a quaint exception but a perfectly plausible medium. If some numbers in the poem might be allusive (seventy), others seem unlikely to be so (fourteen or twenty six). It is true that not 'a single visitor to so important a city as Winchester ever wrote a word on the instrument' (Vellekoop 1984: 196), but nor did they on any other special objects at Winchester or on organs in influential churches elsewhere (Valenciennes, Lobbes). All early instruments are known about by chance or through exceptional sources. Also, it can only be guessed how long the organ was there to be heard; since the Saxon cathedral was destroyed by the Norman bishop by *c.* 1094, at most there could have been only a century of silence about it, and a century is nothing exceptional. Furthermore, elsewhere in the poem Wulfstan described other material structures known from other kinds of evidence, such as the tower and crypt, and the organ appears to be described no differently from these.

Yet it is not easy to agree with some recent authors[26] that references to organs in earlier poems written in England prove that they existed, much less that they were placed in actual churches. The most that can be said is that poems are neutral: they say neither that the poet knew organs nor that he did not. Similar points may be made about other late tenth-century references to *organa* in Reims and Fleury: see pp. 283ff. Although these may be evidence for the 'great role' played in organ-making by unspecified English–French contacts of the time (as suggested in Vellekoop 1984: 187), it is likely that at the craftsman's level, organ-making was totally removed from considerations of *musica* or *mensura* such as interested the Archbishop of Reims or the Abbot of Fleury.

---

[26] E.g. Apel 1948, Holschneider 1968: 142, Caldwell 1971: 4, Page 1979.

In the case of the Winchester organ, any conclusions have to be based on Wulfstan's poem. Assuming that he did not think merely that there had to be two players to produce two-part polyphony such as could have been heard at the period – a cantor would surely know better – perhaps two players did work two sets of sliders. Holschneider 1968: 141, arguing from the poem's factual accuracy in other connections,[27] interprets the details simply and describes a double organ of four hundred pipes and two players. And yet, if in referring to actual numbers the poem does so at least 'partly according to traditional, speculatively acquired number-relationships' (McKinnon 1974), then no quantity is reliable, being Wulfstan's version of the kind of verse-style in which Ermold described Louis's palace at Ingelheim in *c*. 825/6 (with its hundreds of columns, multitude of apartments, thousands of gates and rooms without number – MGH Poet. 2.63.66).

Similarly, Wulfstan's poem may not give a more 'reliable' picture of an organ than drawings give of their instruments: the Utrecht Psalter does not confirm the idea of two organists, for even if its symmetrical picture for Psalm 150 were taken literally, 'it is entirely possible that Wulfstan [knew this manuscript and] had the two monks of the Psalter in mind when he penned the phrase *duo concordi pectore fratres*. Thus we have a literary allusion to an iconographic inaccuracy'.[28] Yet 'inaccuracy' is not quite the right word either, for if the Utrecht Psalter and the Winchester poem both explore a metaphor or figurative idea – 'two concordant brothers' personifying concord, making a visible 'harmony' – then accuracy or otherwise does not arise.

Nevertheless, some interpretation of the poem's information has to be made. It would have to start with the idea that it was a large instrument for the period, probably unique when made, locally and independently conceived. It contained several hundred pipes, and not necessarily in one keyboard-sequence from 'bass' to 'treble' or made up of five (!) eight-note octaves. Perhaps there really were two sections (or sets) of keys, each with the same compass and pitches; both would not always need to be used, and the cantor would not always require the two players and the crowd of bellows-blowers employed on a special feastday. Assuming that *gemino solo* does mean it was on two floors, the organ could well have had something more complex than a single chest and single row of keys. It need not have had pipes larger than 4' at the most (one would expect Wulfstan to have said if it had) or done more than give out 'certain melodies' in public areas of the church or across the monastic enclosure, like a sustained, tuned, versatile bell-substitute. Speculating beyond the poem, one can imagine a large mixture made up of unisons and octaves, a real compass of two octaves or so repeating over forty keys played sometimes by two organists, and a mechanism such as would allow several if not all of the types of polyphony listed in Chapter 3.

---

[27] Demonstrated in R. N. Quirk, 'Winchester Cathedral in the tenth century', *AJ* 114 (1957), 28–68.
[28] McKinnon 1974: 11. The argument is based on the likely presence of the Utrecht Psalter in England (Christ Church, Canterbury) by 1000 and its possible presence in Winchester before that (see p. 152).

Other Anglo-Saxon organs

Wulfstan's poem is contemporary with a report concerning the life of St Oswald and events in the year 991 at Ramsey Abbey. The phrases at Ramsey

ad honorem Dei et S Benedicti	to the honour of God and St Benedict
et ad decus ecclesiae	and to the glory of the Church (RBMAS 83.90)

recall or anticipate Wulfstan's poem, and other remarks concerning the bellows, melody, location and occasion are instructive if not very clear:

Triginta praeterea	Furthermore [Count Ailwin] granted thirty
libras ad fabricandos cupreos	pounds for making copper
organorum calamos erogavit	pipes for the organ,
qui in alveo suo	which in their cabin [= on their chest?]
super unam cochlearum denso	up on one of the spirals [?] in close-packed
ordine foraminibus insidentes,	rows, sitting on their [topboard?] holes
et diebus festis follium	and on feastdays, set in motion
spiramento fortiore pulsati,	by the strong breathing of bellows,
praedulcem melodiam et	emitted very sweet melody and
clangorem longius	strong sound
resonantem ediderunt.	resonant over some distance. (*ibid.*)

From the sum for 'making the pipes' it seems that neither their materials nor their working would be a standard job for the monastery or for the labourers it hired for building work (RBMAS 83.39, 88), whereas any woodwork involved would be. Lines 4–5 are not clear: do they mean 'each in its socket on the chest', 'on a chest at the top of a pendentive-shaped structure', 'on their chest high in one of the apses';[29] 'in the alcove above a spiral staircase' or something else? The alcove approached from a spiral staircase seems the most likely.[30]

Some time earlier – thus the earliest known English organ? – St Dunstan (†988) had given an *organa* to Malmesbury Abbey, according to William of Malmesbury whose report written a century and a half later still has some bearing on Winchester:

Ideo in multis loco munificus,	Generous with many things in that place,
quae tunc in Anglia magni	things that at that time in England
miraculi essent,	were thought to be great wonders
decusque et ingenium	and to display the honour and intelligence
conferentis ostenderent,	of the donor,
offerre crebro.	he [was] to donate frequently.
Inter quae signa sono	Among them bells oustanding in tone
et mole praestantia, et organa	and size, and an organ
ubi per aereas fistulas	in which, through bronze pipes

[29] *Cochlea* compares with *concha*, the latter of which was frequently used for the apse (e.g. sixth-century Byzantine sources in Mango 1986: 80–1).

[30] *Cocleae* were the spiral staircases for access to the galleries at St-Riquier in contemporary sources (cf. Heitz, see note 18), as also at Aachen in Widukind's account of the Emperor Otto's coronation in 936 (MGH SS 3.437). According to William of Malmesbury, the seventh-century church at Hexham was surrounded by such *cochleae* (*per cocleas circumducta*: RBMAS 52.255), which probably meant spiral stairs in William's putative source, the Eddius *Life of Wilfrid* (in Davis-Weyer 1986: 76).

musicis mensuris elaboratas	prepared according to musical proportions,
'Dudum conceptas follis	'The agitated bellows discharges
vomit anxius auras'	channelled breaths[?]'
Ibi hoc distichon	Then he engraved this distich
laminis aereis impressit:	on the bronze plates:
Organa do sancto praesul	I, Bishop Dunstan, give this organ
Dunstanus Aldhelmo,	to St Aldhelm,
Perdat hic aeternum qui	let him lose the kingdom of heaven,
vult hinc tollere regnum.	who wishes to remove it hence. (RBMAS 52.407)

Since in the previous passage William had also been praising Dunstan's activities at Glastonbury and Abingdon, some readers have taken him to be saying that these abbeys too had an organ (for example Caldwell 1971: 4), but this is not explicit. It seems that like the Winchester organ, that at Malmesbury was dedicated to a saint, whose altar was probably in the south-east corner of the church, open to pilgrims' processions entering on the town side of the church;[31] like Winchester, it was used in festivals (RBMAS 83.301–2). Although *aereas fistulas* sounds formulaic, the Malmesbury organ no doubt had bronze pipes, like Ramsey, and it is possible that *laminis* indicates bronze plates rivetted to a wooden chest, as to some altars and doors of the period. The church was new at the time of Dunstan's gift, reformed by Abbot Elfric as Winchester was by Æthelwold, and it looks as if the organ was given as part of the new furnishings and holy vessels. (On furnishings at the period, see also Chapter 7.) Not the least interesting detail, and one to occur elsewhere at the time, is the permanence of the gift: it is not to be moved. This suggests not so much that the organ was small and too easily removed but that on the contrary, it was a major part of the abbey's endowed property.[32]

At Ramsey, Count Ailwin's gift of thirty pounds for the copper pipes anticipates the 'candelabrum worth thirty pounds' lost in the fire at Freising in 1158 (*candelabrum triginta libris comparatum* – MGH SS 24.322): it was perhaps a formula signifying a general level of value for metal objects. Another formula of uncertain reliability is the phrase 'made by his own hands' in the later report of Æthelwold's activities at Abingdon before he moved to Winchester:

fecit etiam duas campanas	two [large] bells he made	
propriis manibus	with his own hands	(RBMAS 2.1.345)
organa propriis manibus	the organ with his own hands	
ipse fecit. Rotam etiam,	he made. Also the bell-wheel,	
quae aurea dicitur	which was said to be of gold,	
. . . ipse fecit.	he made.	(RBMAS 2.2.278)

[31]   Dunstan also gave a stoup to Malmesbury (RBMAS 52.407), a holy water receptacle likewise greeting the people at the southern or south-eastern entrance?

[32]   The best-laid plans for the inalienability of endowments frequently went wrong, as is clear from the history of a church in the same reformist circuit: see S. Raban, *The Estates of Thorney and Crowland: a Study in Medieval Monastic Land Tenure* (Cambridge, 1977), for the history of Æthelwold's gifts to Crowland in *c.* 996. On the treasures of Abingdon not surviving the twelfth century – some having been previously purloined by the Normans – see A. Thacker, 'Æthelwold and Abingdon', in Yorke 1988: 43–64, here 58. The problems experienced by Æthelwold and the Bishop of Ely in proving ownership are clear in ed. E. O. Blake, *Liber Eliensis*, Camden 3rd Series 92 (London, 1962), 100–1.

WinchesterandotherAnglo-Saxonorgans

(On the bell-wheel, see Chapter 6.) No doubt Æthelwold supervised work on both organs and bells, but *propriis manibus* is unlikely to mean more than that the reformer, with a vigour and ideals praised by the panegyrists, was known to use his hands in physical work,[33] unlike the new aristocratic Cluniacs who were so busy on their knees. It would be important to show an abbot of aristocratic origins engaged in physical work such as ploughing or hammering iron, as Bede had already reported of the aristocratic Abbot Eosterwine of Wearmouth in 682–6 (PL 94.719–20). The activities of such abbots and bishops became even more a matter of record when, during the later tenth century, monasteries became conventually controlled (no longer with lay abbots), their buildings reconstructed and conventualized,[34] new abbeys founded and all of them blessed with holy relics, gospels, customaries and other links with apostolic authority. The *Vita S Æthelwoldi* (*c.* 1000) itself reported of King Eadred that he had measured out the plan of his church at Abingdon 'with his own hands' (PL 137.89).

For the galleries and overall shape of Ramsey (969/91) and Abingdon (955/63), see also Chapter 8. Neither church has been reconstructed in plan, but it is possible that Æthelwold's Abingdon had apses in such a way as to offer a centralized effect not totally unlike Aachen and other buildings which Aachen had influenced;[35] Ramsey may have been cruciform. Both were probably larger buildings than most monasteries had known previously, Abingdon some 200' × 57' excluding *porticus*.

Conclusion

Neither the location of any organ in the Saxon cathedral of Winchester nor its function, neither its sound nor its music, is at all certain. It has long been recognized that the new building-work, codifying the monastic customs, re-establishing the brethren as regular coenobites and notating chant-tropes and other music were all part of the late tenth-century reform at Winchester, even if it might now be claimed that 'the standards of the reform and the reformers were not particularly high' or that 'the knowledge of Latin among the clergy was almost universally low' (Parsons 1975: 1, 74). Neither bells nor organ was private, known only to the cloistered brothers,[36] and on the contrary, both were intended for making a public noise. There is also the possibility that copies of Vitruvius – perhaps 'brought over the Channel in the tenth century' (Reynolds 1986: 443) – aroused some interest in organ-mechanisms in the main English Benedictine libraries.

---

[33] C. R. Dodwell, *Anglo-Saxon Art: a New Perspective* (Ithaca, NY, 1982), 49. For Æthelwold's probably noble birth and evident wealth, see B. Yorke, 'Æthelwold and the politics of the tenth century', in Yorke 1988: 65–88.

[34] The Charter of King Edgar (959–75) created a single enclosure or *monasterium* for the three Winchester foundations, demolishing secular buildings to do so and separating off the new enclosure by a wall. See Quirk (see note 27), and W. de G. Birch, *Liber Vitae of New Minster* (London, 1892), xii.

[35] Various interpretations in M. Biddle *et al.*, 'The early history of Abingdon, Berkshire, and its abbey', *Medieval Archaeology* 12 (1968), 26–69; E. Fernie, *The Architecture of the Anglo Saxons* (London, 1983), 108ff; see also p. 127.

[36] Who in any case were not very numerous; perhaps no more than six monasteries in England had more than forty monks (Parsons 1975: 16).

What is less certain, however, is whether bells and organs were a sign of a new, renewing spirit or whether merely reporting on their presence was. Attributing them to the great tenth-century bishops who organized charters and endowments, and including them in the records of reform, could be taken as evidence either way. Whether St Aldhelm knew organs at Malmesbury (see p. 78), it is difficult to think that the Winchester organ had no predecessors – that the makers knew no earlier organ at Abingdon or in Winchester itself (cf. line 1). Apparatus that made use of the technologies of bellows or bronze tubing or solid-block woodworking were surely known, if only by a handful of specialist craftsmen. From the point of view of those documenting the Benedictine revival of the later tenth century, earlier achievements may simply not have been worth recording. What the monastery and church of Abingdon possessed before Æthelwold's efforts is very uncertain: 'Æthelwold's biographers were not interested in unreformed minsters'[37] before him.

A key figure in the monastic revival, St Dunstan of Glastonbury not only knew continental reforms at first hand (RBMAS 63.25, 83.301) but was accredited by William of Malmesbury some two centuries later with introducing the organ far and wide in England (see p. 229). Even if this was the result of misunderstanding on William's part, one might speculate that Dunstan's interest in liturgy and its music came from his experiences at Ghent and his involvement in the lively group of abbeys, from Ghent to Gorze, that seem to have been agreeing on liturgical practice (very little is known about Ghent). On the strength of this movement Abbo of Fleury came to Ramsey in 986 for two years, and Corbie's music (both mono-phony and polyphony) may have been close to Winchester's.[38] Æthelwold had comparable knowledge of Fleury and of resolutions passed by the Synod of Aachen (816–17) and St Benedict of Aniane. It would be strange indeed if great and active monasteries – Corbie, Ghent, St-Omer, Brogne, Gorze and above all Cluny – knew nothing about organs before Dunstan's return to England in 958. Even his writing an inscription on the bronze *laminae* at Malmesbury suggests acquaintance with the old and widespread custom of inscribing metal objects. On the other hand, if Dunstan and his fellow reformers were the chief or only instigators of such special furnishings as organs, it would help to explain the apparent inactivity after their deaths (Æthelwold 984, Dunstan 988, Oswald 992). While the fashion for recording such things may simply have passed, it is likely that the new, disruptive Danish domination of southern England in the early eleventh century meant a loss of impetus in architecture and furnishings. Or – since 'disruption' is easily exaggerated when written sources are relied upon – the period did not inspire enthusiastic reporting in *vitae* and poems of such concrete things as church equipment once the achieve-ments of the past reformers had been chronicled.

Written evidence leaves many outstanding questions. Did the four or five Anglo-Saxon organs owe something (precedent, technical detail, the very craftsmen?) to

---

[37] Thacker (see note 32): 58. The situation thirty or forty years after Æthelwold is also undocumented.

[38] Among the literature on St Dunstan, cf. the chapter 'Dunstan's shadow over France (950–1000)', in G. Ellard, *Ordination Anointings in the Western Church before 1000* (Cambridge, MA, 1933). Points concerning music at Corbie and Winchester in D. Hiley, 'Observations on the derivation of two early repertories of polyphony', in Corsi 1989: 377–91.

one or more of the northern French abbeys? So far, only the most indirect and obscure hints – the work of monastic theorists (Chapter 16), the indications of organs from Valenciennes to Lobbes (Chapters 3, 9 and 13), the background to Theophilus's treatise (Chapter 15) – support this idea, and then only weakly. But it is plausible. For one thing, if there were so few instruments in the generations that followed the reforming bishops, and yet so many in the twelfth and thirteenth centuries, where did the latter come from? Were they re-introduced or re-invented or did they exist all along, here and there? If organs were at all familiar through the period in which the tenth-century reformers were being praised, there *must* have been an organ at Corbie and Cluny, to name but two. The cluster of references to organs in late tenth-century England reminds one of the cluster of references to Pippin's Byzantine organ of 757 (Chapter 9), and the isolated nature of both could give many misleading impressions.

It must be that the absence of references does not mean the absence of organs. Even in the case of the English reformers' abbeys, the known documents concerning them[39] are unlikely to mention all the instruments they contained. (See also Chapter 13, 'Absence of References'.) The technology to make organs was there: Anglo-Saxon metalwork includes examples of techniques later described by Theophilus (niello, encrustation, filigree); bell-founding was developed (see Chapter 6); there is good evidence of both lead and copper-alloy working at Winchester; carpentry was no problem, nor bellows-making; and the various East Frisian or 'German' contacts[40] in the mid-tenth century could have ensured technological expertise at least on the supervisory level.

No new organ in England is known after Ramsey or Winchester until those of the twelfth century, but the organ's location at Canterbury (in a public place?) and the special nature of the report that refers to it (in a very *en passant* way – see p. 223) suggest a family likeness with Winchester and thus the likelihood that other organs had served as a link between them, stretching over two centuries.[41]

---

[39]   Glastonbury, Malmesbury, Bath, Westminster (Dunstan); Worcester, Ramsey, Pershore, probably Deerhurst (Oswald); Winchester, Ely, Peterborough, Thorney, Crowland (Æthelwold).

[40]   For Winchester metalwork, see ed. M. Biddle, *Object and Economy in Medieval Winchester*, 2 vols (Oxford, 1990), 1.89ff, 2.947ff. For foreign contacts, see Parsons 1975: 33–4.

[41]   The organ at Abingdon, for the maintenance of which certain revenues were specified in the later twelfth century (see Chapter 13), was presumably not then new.

13

Other references to 'actual organs' before *c*. 1300

Ninth and tenth centuries

Although there is a number of references to organs towards the end of the tenth century, it is not at all clear whether this means that there were more of them than there used to be or that for some reason writers were becoming more interested in documenting them. Perhaps there had been organs in the great monastic houses destroyed by the Norsemen in the second half of the ninth century; but there are no known references to them. Perhaps the monks of Montecassino or Hildesheim were able to turn their traditional skills in metallurgy towards organs – bronze organ-pipes can have been no great advance on crown-candelabra – but there is no evidence that they did. Furthermore, of the various references to *organa* in ninth- and tenth-century sources – a letter of Pope John VIII, *Lives* of the English bishops, accounts of Catalonian dedications, the written theory of, for example, Gerbert of Reims – only the second concerns without doubt a church organ. Perhaps this is not the frustrating circumstance it may appear, for the casualness of references when they do occur might suggest that organs were less exceptional than they now seem.

While it may be so that references to *organa* in early Mozarabic hymn-texts suggest actual instruments – something concrete and not merely symbolic[1] – there is no reason that it should mean 'organs' rather than other 'instruments of various kinds'. In the case of early Anglo-Saxon references evidently to pipe-organs (see St Aldhelm, p. 300), the question is rather how free of poetic formulas the words are; failing other evidence, one must assume they do not refer to 'actual' instruments. In the case of the famous letter of Pope John VIII (872–82) written at Rome to Anno, Bishop of Freising, the puzzle is again the word *organum*:

precamur autem ut	furthermore we pray
	that you either bring or send
	(with the said payments)
optimum organum cum	a very good *organum* with a
artifice qui hoc et moderari	craftsman who can both play it

[1] H. Anglès, 'Die Instrumentalmusik bis zum 16. Jahrhundert in Spanien', in *Natalicia musicologica: Knud Jeppesen Septuagenario*, ed B. Hjelmborg & S. Sørensen (Copenhagen, 1962), 143–64, here 145. The phrase *organa resonant* and comparable terms in tenth- and eleventh-century hymns are understood by Llovera 1987: 162–3 as evidence for the existence of organs.

et facere ad omnem	and achieve all
modulationis efficaciam	success in modulation [?]
possit	
ad instructionem musice	to instruct us in the [quadrivial]
discipline nobis	discipline of music.
aut deferas cum eisdem	
redditibus aut transmittas.	(MGH Epist. 7.1.287 and PL 126.651)

This has been generally taken to mean that John VIII is asking for an organ to be sent to Rome from a technologically advanced Bavaria,[2] sent moreover with an organist to teach the members of the *schola cantorum* how to play it. Why a pope should do so in the middle of his other problems – John's requests to Bavaria and Swabia were usually for military help against the Saracens and Italy's seditious dukes – is not known, for Rome remained a desolate city despite a similar call on the West Franks.[3] It seems hardly a moment to be asking for organ-music.

Yet the amanuensis clearly knew contemporary word-use. *Organum, artifex* ('an expert'), *moderari* ('regulate', 'play'?) and *modulationis* seem to be the words of a professional, as does the phrase *musica disciplina*, whether it comes from up-to-date music-theory (Aurelian of Réôme) or earlier classics (Cassiodorus, or Isidore *Etymologiae* 3.2). On the other hand, the early date makes *organum* unlikely to mean simply 'an organ'. Inconclusive though any such argument remains, one might expect two non-experts (a pope and a bishop) to make use of something a little more specific, such as *organum fistularum* or *organum musicorum*. From all such arguments as these there seem to be two possible interpretations of the letter. Firstly, since there was a lively *schola* working for the pope – probably during whose papacy John the Deacon credited Gregory the Great with regularizing chant and Vitalian with furthering the work – it is not unlikely that *organum* was used in the letter to Anno in much the same sense as in the lines dealing with Vitalian (see Chapter 1; perhaps Pope John's amanuensis was the same John the Deacon?). A paraphrased translation might then read:

optimum organum cum	a very reliable [notated?] chant-book with
artifice qui hoc et moderari	an expert able both to perform from it
et facere ad omnem	and achieve the most
modulationis efficaciam	effective music [ordered melody?
possit.	word-setting?].

Secondly, since *organum* can mean an 'apparatus of learning' such as the monochord – perhaps already a speciality of south German monastic craftsmen?[4] – the pope's request is for an aid to teach musical proportions. Then a paraphrase might read:

---

[2] E.g., the letter reflects 'solid experience in organ-building and playing at this time in Bavaria': Barassi 1983: 42.

[3] F. E. Engreen, 'Pope John the Eighth and the Arabs', *Speculum* 20 (1945), 318–30. For John's crowning of Charles the Bald as emperor and his expectations of Carolingian support, see Wallace-Hadrill 1983: 254.

[4] Not documented so early. But knowledge of Boethius's monochord measurements, such as contributed to the *De mensurando monochordo* of Berno, Abbot of Reichenau (1008–48 – GS 1.330ff), may have led to the making of monochords here and there.

optimum organum cum	a very good 'instrument' with
artifice qui hoc et moderari	an expert able both to operate it
et facere ad omnem	and with it effectively
modulationis efficaciam	demonstrate the relationship between
possit.	notes.

One might think the second of these interpretations is likelier if only because the various musical terms relate to the teaching of music-theory.[5] But there is a good reason why *organum* should mean a book, an organ of learning such as a notated antiphoner: John VIII had been given authority over much of southern Lombardy (South Italy) by Charles the Bald (MGH SS 3.722) and was at that moment pressing for papal–Roman observance in his new territories. Such observance no doubt included Gregorian chant for the Roman office and mass, notated examples of which the Bishop of Freising – better than any other of the pope's contacts within a radius of 450 miles? – may well have been able to supply.

Despite all this, even if *organum* does not mean organ and *musica disciplina* not organ-playing, the reference can still be useful for the organ-historian. Pope John may not have been asking for an organ but organs too could be an 'instrument of learning' elsewhere, in other circumstances and on some other occasion. Perhaps a later southern Italian organ like that at Cava (see below) was there to aid the task of romanizing the chant and musical instruction.

A somewhat similar problem concerns the annals' reference to Count Atto donating several ornaments in 915 to a new monastery in the northern Apennines, *in arce Canusina* ('on the rock of Canossa'). He gave gold and silver vessels for divine office, acquired relics of St Appollonius, and

fieri fecit organa	had an organ made	
in dicto monasterio	in the said monastery [church?]	
ad honorem predicti	in honour of the aforementioned	
confessoris.	confessor [= St Appollonius].	(MGH SS 31.431)

This sounds like an organ set up near the saint's altar, like those of the later English Benedictine bishops. Only the earliness of the date might cause surprise. Had gifts from noblemen begun to take the form of organs of music as they had once organs of scripture (gospels, psalters)? Or, since the account itself belongs to the thirteenth century (MGH SS 31.339), the scribe misunderstood his source and Atto's gift had indeed been a book? Canossa had a *scriptorium* associated with the castle, in addition to the monastery of St Appollonius; as a new monastery and seat of princes developing a route to Rome[6] it could have had both famous books and an endowed instrument. In any case, however, it is likely that the date should be later: 950 would fit in better with the construction work of Atto Adalbert, Count of Canossa (†988).

Probably neither books nor organs are intended in a phrase used in the eleventh-century life of Bruno, Archbishop of Cologne (*Ruotgeri vita Brunonis*) concerning the celebrations at his consecration in 953:

5   E.g. the phrase *modulationis efficaciam* recalls *modulamen efficiens* in the definition of *symphonia* in Cassiodorus's *Institutiones* (*c.* 550–60): see Blumröder 1983: 2.

et laudem Deo	and the praise of God
simul universi clamore,	together the assembled company
	had sounded,
quo quisque poterat,	each in his own way,
in organis nihilominus et	no less with *organa* and
cymbalis et quocumque	*cymbala* [= bells?] and all manner of
signo laeticiae	tokens [= large bells?] of joy.
personuerant.	

(MGH SS 4.259)

This might mean 'with instruments and bells' or is an annalist's formula (*cymbalis personaret* is Ciceronian) or both; *signum* may even be meant to have two meanings here, bringing with it older word-use. What is clear is the festive nature of an archbishop's consecration, an event comparable to church dedications in which instruments of different kinds took part and/or were more symbolically invoked by writers (see Chapter 5). One interesting coincidence – if that is what it is – is that Bruno refounded St Pantaleon in Cologne, perhaps the later home of Theophilus (see Chapter 15). In any case, an eleventh-century author would assume that Bruno, brother and supporter of the German emperor Otto I, was consecrated with all available pomp.

Catalonia

One of the most tantalizing of all references to *organum* – tantalizing because the term is ambiguous, the occasion typical and the setting evocative – concerns a dedication, at the Catalonian abbey of S Benet-de-Bages in 972 as reported by Petrus de Marca in the seventeenth century:[7]

vociferabant enim sacerdotes	the priests and Levites [= choir]
et Levitae laudem Dei in	exclaimed praise of God in
jubilo, organumque procul	jubilation, and at a distance the
diffundebat	*organum* poured forth
sonus ab atrio	sounds from the courtyard,
laudentes et benedicentes	[everyone] praising and blessing
Dominum qui regnat in secula,	the Lord who reigns for ever,
reddentes itaque Deo cum omni	rendering thus to God praise and
devotione laudes & gratias.	thanks with all devotion.

Whether *organum* means 'organ' or 'ensemble music',[8] it seems that it was sounding forth in the open air, perhaps as part of a procession – not, it seems, for the liturgy inside. The whole scene is of great interest, for it suggests the kind of music (jubilant),

---

[6]   Cf. the celebrated confrontation between Henry IV and the pope (Gregory VII), with Matilda of Canossa, January 1077.

[7]   Quoted several times by H. Anglès, including *La Música a Catalunya fins al Segle XIII* (Barcelona, 1935), 80, for which the source is Marca 1688: 898, drawing on a document said to be from the archives of the monastery and written *c.* 1290.

[8]   *Vociferabant organumque* carries echoes of *organicae voces* in e.g. John Scottus Eriugena, *c.* 850 (PL 122.883), implying a singing in octaves; but the Bages source is unlikely to be so technical.

occasion (dedication), context (a crowd scene) and location (out of doors) that must have been familiar across Europe in the period when monasteries were consecrated in great public events. The source is one of many reports or *acta* of Catalonian consecrations, but none of the others includes comparable detail. Even the major monasteries of Urgell, Ripoll, Cuxa or Montserrat have left no such descriptions, but nor did Bages itself in another report of the same event (Marca 1688: 404–5). The reference, therefore, is a fortuitous survival.

The present church and monastery of S Benet-de-Bages are twelfth-century rebuilds,[9] the modest church without aisles or galleries, as was common in Catalonia; but there are various spaces for outdoor processions, and there was no doubt a bell-tower (extant early example in S Mateu-de-Bages). Musical and liturgical developments in such centres as Ripoll (Cluniac by 1008) influenced these new monasteries, and it is significant that Gerbert of Reims's studies in Catalonia must belong to much the same period as the Bages dedication.[10] Also contemporary is a Navarrese source for the Life of Abbot Salvus of Albelda which speaks of his skills in *ymnis orationibus versibus ac missis* ('in hymn-writing, sermons, verse and liturgy') in much the same way as an Anglo-Saxon or Alemannic *vita* of the same period might.

Evidently the late tenth century is one in which reformed monasteries across Europe shared activities and vocabularies. In Catalonia, this was before the strong Cluniac drive to re-settle monasteries (and to develop the Santiago pilgrimage route) got underway in the eleventh century. In such respects Catalonia contrasts with the centres of early Mozarabic re-christianization in more westerly provinces where there is no known reference to *organa* in any sense, as 'instruments' or 'books', 'organs' or 'ensemble singing'. Either Mozarabic monasteries did not know the organ at all and it had to be developed by the Catalonian abbeys – which is quite possible, given the significance of the Barcelona area in the later history of the Spanish organ – or they knew it here and there but, following the practices of their southern founders from Córdoba, did not produce the kind of documentation known to the mainstream Benedictines of the north.[11]

Organum remains the most difficult term in the Catalonian reports, although it is possible that since the language concerning Abbot Salvus is rather specific, so is the Bages phrase *in jubilo organumque*. This could mean 'in the jubilus' of the alleluia, implying that vocal polyphony was heard chiefly then; or it could allude to Augustine's definition of the sung jubilation as a kind of wordless work-song sung out of doors.[12] Therefore, either an instrument (*organum*) is contributing to the joyful clamour at the Bages dedication or, on the contrary, organized ensemble music (*organum*) is being

---

[9] Plan etc. in E. Junyent, *Catalunya romànica: L'arquitectura del Segle XII* (Montserrat, 1976), 190–207. The Bages context in X. Barral i Altet, *L'art pre-romànic a Catalunya Segles IX–X* (Barcelona, 1981), esp. 227–32.

[10] See H. Anglès, *Historia de la Musica medieval en Navarra* (Pamplona, 1970), 58–60. But Llovera 1987: 103, who makes use neither of Reckow 1975 nor Sachs 1980, gives no evidence for claiming that Gerbert took an outstanding position on the early Spanish organ. See also note 18 below.

[11] On Albelda: C. J. Bishko, 'Salvus of Albelda and frontier monasticism in tenth-century Navarra', *Speculum* 23 (1948), 559–90, here 582. The last two terms as translated above are uncertain. On the re-settling of west-central Mozarabic monasteries: J. D. Dodds, *Architecture and Ideology in Early Medieval Spain* (Pennsylvania State UP, 1990), e.g. p. 55 (S Cebrián de Mazote).

[12] Or at least in some 'arduous occupation' – McKinnon 1987: 156.

sung at various times in the ceremony. The salient point here is that although the Bages report does not necessarily concern organs, any more than does, say, the phrase *organali . . .in musica* in an eleventh-century poem concerning Sigo of Saumur (in Perrot 1965: 289), ensemble music could well include instruments of some kind on some such occasions. From the rest of the Bages dedication-report (see note 7), it is certain that the monastery was well endowed with sacred vessels, liturgical books and vestments.

At an earlier Catalonian dedication, Tona in 888, sacred or sacral objects listed in the account are *calicem et patenam, missalem, lectionarium et organum* ('chalice, paten, missal, lectionary and organum') in which *organum* sounds very much like an antiphoner or chant-book of some kind.[13] *Organum* meaning psalter – an organ of authority, a canonic text – is already established by Isidore of Seville (*Etymologiae* 6.2.15):

psalmorum liber	book of psalms, called
Graece psalterium	psalter in Greek,
Hebraice nabla	nabla in Hebrew,
Latine organum dicitur.	organum in Latin.

Isidore's influence on word-usage,[14] whatever modern historians of science may think of the compilation-technique and etymologizing of such lexicographers,[15] was especially strong in Frankish Gaul (see Reynolds 1986, 1955) where so many references to *organa* originate. Although he also defines *organum* in the Augustinian sense of instruments and bellows-organ (*Etymologiae* 2.2), non-musical scribes or chroniclers could well have preserved his non-musical uses of the term; see below for the word meaning liturgy or mass at York and elsewhere.

In the reports of dedication ceremonies, such formulas as *in himnis organisque* ('in hymns and spiritual songs' or 'in the music for voices') abound,[16] sometimes coupled with other formulas such as a phrase about the wafting of incense (as at Cava in 1092 – see below). In such phrases, *organisque* will not indicate organs. At Cuxa in 855 there was another meaning of the word: records of endowments and gifts include what seems to be agricultural equipment amongst which are 'eight ploughshares' (*soccas VIII*) and 'three similar tools' (*organas parilias III* – Marca 1688: 788). If this is a correct translation, here is an uncommon example of *organa* in the old sense of 'work-tool'.

As with Pope John's letter, if the word *organum* in Catalonia does not mean organ but denotes ensemble music that can include organ should circumstances permit, then these references are still useful for giving the background against which organs became known. Furthermore if San Benito de Bages had *organum* at its dedication, it is difficult to believe that the churches of Ripoll, S Juan de las Abadesas, Vich,

---

[13] Quoted by Anglès (note 7: 82); Perrot 1965: 287 regards the term as 'equivocal'; Schuberth 1968: 104 takes it as meaning 'instrument' (*organon*); Llovera 1987: 156ff again concludes that it is evidence for an organ.

[14] Discussed widely (e.g. for England) in J. M. Wallace-Hadrill, 'Rome and the early English church: some questions of transmission', *Settimane* 7 (Spoleto, 1960), esp. 537, 543–4.

[15] 'Without access to the hard core of Greek science, the Western world could not rise above the level of the Latin encyclopedists': E. Grant, *Physical Sciences in the Middle Ages* (Cambridge, 1977), 13.

[16] Various phrases and uses listed in Reckow 1975: 105–7.

Silos, Montserrat, Cuxa and Canigou did not,[17] even if reports in such sources as Petrus de Marca are silent about it. Jubilant occasions, processions, noisy liturgy or para-liturgy, ensemble musical performance of various kinds: Catalonia must have been much like Anglia or Neustria or many another monastic province. The more this is so, the less reason there can be to think that the western Christian organ got introduced through Arabic Spain, or even that the Spanish organ did.[18]

Eleventh and twelfth centuries

Although many of the terms used are still within the literary traditions known widely to scribes, a practical detail in references may show the organs to have been 'actual'. In a twelfth-century document at Petershausen, near Lake Constance, *modulatio* implies one of the areas of meaning in Pope John's letter, but now it is part of a factual report of a more up-to-date kind, concerning an organ of *c.* 1130:

Counradus abbas conduxit	Abbot Conrad employed
monachum quendam nomine Aaron	a certain monk called Aaron,
presbyterum de Châmberch	priest of Komburg [?],
musicae artis peritissimum	very skilled in the *ars musica*,
qui fecit ei organa	who made for him an organ
elegantissimae modulationis	of most elegant modulation,
et constituit ea ad meridianam	and set it up in the south
plagam eiusdem	aisle [= pavement?] of the same
basilicae.	church.
Ipse etiam iam antea	Previously he had also made
eiusdem generis instrumentum	an instrument of the same kind
Constantiensi æcclesiae fecerat.	for the church at Constance. (MGH SS 20.669)

This is a rich reference, giving the name of a commissioner employing an organ-builder, who was a full monk. The builder's name, where he came from and where else he built, are given; and the location, even perhaps the organ's tone, is specified. Not many contracts written three centuries later would give better information, merely itemize what is implied here by the word *conduxit*, i.e. materials for the organ bought at the abbot's charge. That a certain monk belonging to the south German Benedictine circuit[19] made two organs suggests that it was his craft-speciality, as

---

17   In *c.* 1000 the churches of S Benet and S Mateu de Bages, Ripoll, Vich, S Pedro de Roda, and S Feliu de Codines had something in common: a type of Corinthian capital, made by itinerant masons. M. Durliat, 'La Catalogne et le "Premier Art Roman"', *BM* 147 (1989), 209–38, here 217–18.

18   So far there seems little evidence for the idea that Gerbert knew any organ in Bages (Llovera 1987: 97) much less that it was through contacts with the Arabs that he became 'initiated . . . in the difficult art' of organ-building (Perrot 1965: 291). William of Malmesbury's claim that he studied the quadrivium with the Saracens (RBMAS 90.2.194), has to be seen against William's interest in and respect for Islam: cf. R. M. Thomson, 'William of Malmesbury and some other western writers on Islam', *Medievalia et humanistica* 6 (1975), 179–87.

19   Petershausen is near Constance and the Reichenau, and its abbots were connected with Hirsau and its reforms; this glimpse of organ-activity, therefore, relates to two or three very important centres. There is an area Chamberich north-east of Regensburg, but probably Aaron came from Komburg (south of Schwäbisch Hall), as so understood in F. Quarthal *et al.*, *Die Benediktinerklöster in Baden-Württemberg*, Germania Benedictina 5 (Ottobeuren/Augsburg, 1975), 352.

further north it probably was for Theophilus at exactly this period. Perhaps Aaron made a third organ: the same period, under Abbot Hartwig (1103–38), saw Komburg developing fine metalwork, including a large-scale and still extant crown-candelabrum shaped like the walls of the *civitas Dei*, with twelve towers.

Abbot Conrad also had a modest bell-tower built at Petershausen, probably over the crossing as at Constance.[20] But there was no gallery to the nave, and in both churches placing the organ on the floor in the south bay of the crossing or in the aisle itself would have served the simple plan of the building. The southern location suggests the organ to have been useful near to the conventual entrance (i.e. from the cloister on the south), therefore away from the more public spaces of the west end. The text itself seems to be moving towards a more concrete description, and it is otiose to seek a more complex translation of *elegantissimae modulationis* than simply 'very refined tone'. If this is correct, the words must carry a hint of how the organ was used (melodies? chant? diaphony?) and perhaps how older organs had sounded (less refined? used less for melodies?).

A concrete reference to organs also appears in the Chronicle of Lobbes for 1134, concerning the organ and bells – both of the previous century? – in that distinguished abbey:

organum quod sanctae memoriae	the organ that Abbot Fulcuin of
abbas Fulcuinus	holy memory had given
in usum divinae laudis	for use in the divine worship
ecclesiae contulerat,	of the church [at Lobbes]
ab ecclesia abstulit,	he took from the church,
quod episcopus Atrebatensis,	because the Bishop of Arras,
qui huiusmodi maxime	who was excellently skilled
incentor erat,	in things of this sort,
in suam fecit transportari	had it transported to his own
ecclesiam;	church [= St Vaast, Arras?].
sic et de cymbalis factum est,	This too was done with the bells
quae . . . divine laudi	which . . . served for divine
subserviebant.	worship. (MGH SS 21.326)

'For use in the divine worship' may mean only that both organ and bells signalled the start or close of particular services or parts thereof, although *in usum* could suggest a more liturgical role for the organ. What exactly the bishop was skilled in, and why valuable assets were so purloined is not known, but the incident is probably one item in the ongoing warfare between bishops and abbots and gives some idea of why it was that a donor might say an organ is not to be moved. (The eleventh-century cathedral of Arras was rebuilt from 1160 in the then new gothic, beginning with the eastern chevet; perhaps the organ remained somewhere at the massive west end or in one of the transept galleries. See also p. 117 for practices at Arras.)

The Lobbes organ is, or would be, of particular interest because the church was so similar to others in the Upper Meuse region, buildings usually smaller (Hastière-

[20] J. Hecht, *Der romanische Kirchenbau des Bodenseegebietes* 1 (Basle, 1928), 240ff; Oswald 1966: 155f.

par-delà, Celles, Susteren and perhaps Brogne) and occasionally bigger (Maastricht St Servaas) but with a similar design of nave, without gallery except in the westwork. Perhaps at Lobbes the organ was made when major work was undertaken between 1070 and 1095 for the large west tower, porch and built-over eastern crypt; for cross-section and comments, see p. 105. As at Winchester, all of these parts of the church contributed to an ambulatory liturgy in which an organ, whether near the west gallery or some other public spot, could have played a summoning rôle.

Ceremonies of dedication often refer to instruments in traditional or formulaic terms, making it difficult to be certain either that *organa* means organ or that if it does, it played music as distinct from noise. The Chronicles of Cava, near Salerno, for the year 1092 show the uncertainties:

tam vero magnifica	indeed the pomp
consecrationis pompa fuit	of the consecration was so magnificent,
ut perpetuo	that without pause
suavissimi odores cremarentur,	the sweetest incenses were burnt,
dulcissimi concentus exaudirentur,	the loveliest sounds were heard,
organorum, ac	the modulations of *organa* and
tibiarum ad iucundissimum	flutes producing a most agreeable
numerum modulationes.	harmony. (*Acta SS Martii* 1.334)

Organorum ac tibiarum is not a reliable reference to the church organ, but the occasion is typical: a new pilgrimage church, its abbey under the Cluny observance (thus independent of the bishop), is now consecrated by a pope (Urban II) in the company of many cardinals and the local duke (who gave an organ perhaps?), all of whom would be personifying the power of the Church of Rome in the Italian south (see p. 63). Since other sources reporting this occasion mention only the psalm-singing – not *organa* – the event at Cava becomes useful as a reminder that there were occasions when *organa* would have been heard but did not get recorded in any extant source.[21]

Uncertainties of documentation concern both minor and major details. At the Abbey of St Ulrich, Augsburg, in 1060, it was reported that Abbot Adalbert

primum organum musicum	placed a first-rate organ of music
	[or first, he placed an organ]
in templum posuit.	in the church. (Buhle 1903: 66)

This has been taken to mean the church's 'first organ', but the word-use *optimum organum* in Pope John's letter (see above) makes this unlikely. 'Placing in the temple' may indicate a particular location, such as a shrine to St Ulrich. At Freising a century later, the term *domus* is similarly ambiguous: during a cathedral fire

ruit domus organorum	the house of the organ was destroyed,
et turris regalis cum	and the royal tower with its
dulcissimo sono campanarum.	very sweet ring of bells. (MGH SS 24.322)

---

21   Other accounts of the consecration in P. Guillaume, *Essai historique sur l'Abbaye de Cava d'après des documents inédits* (Cava dei Tirreni, 1877), 25, 59–66.

Is *domus* the organ-case as a whole, the chest of pipes (see Theophilus's term on p. 262), or its complete gallery with bellows chamber ('housing')? Or is *ruit domus* a poetic reminiscence by the scribe (*domus ruinosa*, in Ovid *Heroides* line 56)? If it were the first, this would be a very useful indication that 'organ-cases', presumably of inflammable wood, were being made by 1158. One might guess that they were, but the evidence virtually does not exist. Probably there is a touch of Ovid about the reference, or at least, the scribe was not averse to rhetoric and wanted to give a dramatic account of the fire:

ruit sedes cathedralis . . .	the bishop's throne was destroyed . . .
ruit ciborium . . .	the communion plate . . .
ruit candelabrum . . .	the [crown?] candelabrum . . .
ruunt laquearia . . .	the panelled ceiling . . .
ruit domus organorum et turris . . .	the organ and tower . . .
ruit palatium	the palace . . .

Here is a topography: having started at the east, the fire moved west, through the crossing (where the candelabrum hung?), down the nave ceiling towards the west tower and adjacent building. The organ was therefore at the west end?[22] At Marienberg (South Tyrol), a much later reference to the 'chapel of St Michael near the organ' (*capella sancti michaelis apud organum*) seems to mean a chapel on an upper floor not at the west end[23] (as at Essen − see p. 89) but at the east, on the south side. This may have been where the organs at Petershausen and Malmesbury were placed.

The report of events after the fire of 1199 in Magdeburg Cathedral (the Augustinian *Petersburg*) gives a glimpse of certain current practice.[24] In 1207,

Tidericus cellerarius	Dietrich the steward
novum organi instrumentum fecit,	made the new instrument of organ,
vetus enim incendio ecclesie	for the old one perished
periit.	in the church fire. (MGH SS 23.174)

So it seems to be the duty of the steward in a non-monastic cathedral to make or commission organs, which by now were found so useful that the church was without one for only a few years. Both these details could be typical of cathedrals *c.* 1200 in north-west Europe.

Although the twelfth century must have been the period of greatest activity in organ-building so far, the evidence is still not very plentiful. In the course of a letter, however, Balderich (1046–1131), Archbishop of Dol, implies various things about the state of affairs and remarks that many churches do not have such things (*multi*

---

[22] A report of the fire of 1356 in Basle Minster implies something similar: the fire reached 'the tower in which the large bell hung . . . destroying the bell and precious organ of the same monastery', i.e. in the same enclosed space? (*Turrim in qua maior campana pendebat . . . et campanam et organa preciosa eiusdem monasterii destruxit*: I. Rücker, *Die deutsche Orgel am Oberrhein um 1500* (Freiburg, 1940), 112).

[23] The quotation (given without source) is understood in Ronig 1980: 22 to refer to the year 1185. But it belongs to the period of the fourteenth-century chronicler who reported it (ed. P. B. Schwitzer, *Chronik des Stiftes Marienberg verfaßt von P. Goswin*, Tirolische Geschichtsquellen 2 (Innsbruck, 1867), as made clear in J. Joos, 'Kirchenmusik in Marienberg', *Singende Kirche* 14 (1967), 175–7.

[24] This was probably the organ of 1173, the date given (without source) in T. Schneider, 'Die Orgelbauer-familie Compenius', *AfMf* 2 (1937), 8–76.

qui tale quid in suis non habentes ecclesiis) – which in fact may imply that many others do. Apparently evangelizing on behalf of organs, he remarks on the instrument in the abbey of Fécamp, a major Norman abbey reformed in 1001 by William of Dijon:[25]

illa in ecclesia unum quid erat	in this church was something
quod mihi non mediocriter	that pleased me more than
complacuit . . .	moderately . . .
ibi siquidem instrumentum	in as much as there I have seen the
vidi musicum,	musical instrument
fistulis aeneis compactum,	composed of bronze pipes [and]
quod follibus excitum fabrilibus	which, excited by smiths' bellows,
suavem reddebat melodiam, et per	produced sweet melody, and through
continuam diapason	a continuous compass [?] and
per symphoniae sonoritatem,	the sound of correct intervals [?],
graves, et medias, et acutas	united low, medium and high
voces uniebat, ut	sounds, so that
quidam concinnentium chorus	it could be thought a kind of
putaretur clericorum, in quo	massed chorus of clerics consisting
pueri, senes, juvenes jubilantes	of boys, old men and youths
convenirent et continerentur;	coming together rejoicing.
organa illud vocabant,	They called this an organ
certisque temporibus excitabant.	and played it at stipulated times
	[= seasons?]. (PL 166.1177)

Not least in this exceptionally interesting source is Balderich's idea that an organ was like a vocal ensemble, making use of notes in several octaves and having the same effect of *jubilation*. One hopes that this is not merely a literary reminiscence. There is also a faint possibility that *continerentur* implies notes 'being sustained' by the organ, an advantage organs had over choirs.

From Balderich's letter and other information about the great church of Fécamp dedicated in part in 1099, it has been suggested that the organ was completed in 1107 and that like its successor (built after a great fire of 1168) it had copper pipes and was placed somewhere in the north transept where there was a vaulted gallery, as in the Norman cathedral of Winchester.[26] While this is possible, the shallow but intricate west-end structure, rebuilt in the new church after a fire of 1168, had originally been a westwork of the kind not unlikely to have housed an organ. That a replacement organ of the late twelfth century was said to have had copper pipes, however, is a more concrete detail: if this was old-fashioned, as it may well have been, was it also a sign of especially high quality?

Balderich's letter is unique in its blend of practical detail and, in other sections, symbol exegesis. He justifies the organ as amongst other things a traditional metaphor

25   On the work of the reformer William of Dijon (or Volpiano) linking the liturgical life at Fécamp, Jumièges, Réôme and elsewhere, see N. Bulst, *Untersuchungen zu den Klosterreformen Wilhelms von Dijon (962–1031)* (Bonn, 1973), 147ff, 174ff.

26   J. Lemaître, 'Dix siècles d'orgue et de la musique à l'abbaye de Fécamp', in *L'abbaye bénédictine de Fécamp*, ed. Anon., 3 vols (Fécamp, 1959–63), 2.193–216.

of man inspired by the Holy Ghost. Like 'gold, silver or decorated silks' in a church (*aurea, vel argentea, vel serica ornamenta*), an organ is something for the praise of God – an interesting remark in view of church valuables frequently listed in this way (see details of furnishings in Chapter 7). He is aware that some people, having no such thing in their churches, criticize those who have, and while acknowledging that it is 'no sacrilege to be without them' (*sine sacrilegio eis carere*), he points out that if there is an organ present, then it is to be used 'according to the church's customary rites' (*uti ecclesiastica consuetudine* – PL 166.1178). In this letter there could be many allusions to contemporary practice in church-music. Since there was no need to say that organs were not known everywhere, it is possible that he makes his points as a bishop reacting to the latest Cistercian criticisms of gratuitous objects in church, especially those in the grander Cluniac–Benedictine monastic churches. *Consuetudo* may also say less or more than it appears to: does it mean 'customs' (the organ has long been used and can now follow precedent) or 'customary' (its use specified in rules for the conduct of monastic life and services)? The last would be more likely if it were not that the organ does not occur in extant customaries of the time.

On splendid Cluniac–Benedictine churches: Balderich was well travelled in the Norman monasteries of Jumièges, Bec, St-Wandrille and Worcester,[27] and it is likely that here and there he had found lay people resisting Cluniac splendours.[28] (Considering the obvious importance of *musica* within the Cluniac scheme of things,[29] it is very striking that there is no early documentation of organs in any of the churches of Cluny itself, more particularly if Fécamp and others had one.) Details in Balderich's letter suggest an organ of some size, with the low/medium/high sounds as described in various literary genres[30] and with bronze pipes, forge-bellows and a bright sound (*jubilantes*). Although it looks as if both organ and choir produced *melodiam*, it could be merely that the organ was 'melodious' in a broad sense, not necessarily playing chant. Despite Balderich's awareness of musical terms, *diapason* and *symphonia* do not appear to be used in the old technical senses of 'octave' and 'basic intervals' respectively; on the contrary, a *continuous* diapason or *sonorous* symphonia makes most sense figuratively, i.e. in referring to the notes of a keyboard instrument which are (a) fixed and (b) tuned. (On such unique and striking characteristics of organs, see Chapter 3.) Since the talk of *diapason* and *sonoritatem* suits Balderich's image of the spiritual harmony that an organ expresses, one can not reason much further from these words about the 'organ chorus' as such.

[27] R. Herval, 'En marge de la légende du précieux sang: Lucques, Fécamp, Glastonbury', in *L'abbaye bénédictine de Fécamp* (as note 26), 1.105–126. Smits van Waesberghe compares Balderich's activities with those of William of Dijon in 'Die Geschichte von Glastonbury' in *Dia-pason: de omnibus. Ausgewählte Aufsätze von JSvW*, ed. C. J. Mass & M. U. Schouten-Glass (Buren, 1976), 159–64.

[28] Probably there was a class element: the quasi-Byzantine pomp and splendour of Cluny were reflections of an aristocratic prestige. Cf. B. H. Rosenwein, 'Fuedal wars and monastic peace: Cluniac liturgy as ritual aggression', *Viator* 2 (1971), 129–58.

[29] E.g. the well-known carved capitals of Cluny III; or the proliferation of David-sculpture, with its musical motifs, in the new Cluniac houses of Spain (Foster 1977: 38). But such musical references concern *musica* and *auctoritas*: theoretical and theological considerations, rather than the practical music performed for the people on feastdays?

[30] Cf. the *graves/acutae/superacutae* in Theophilus and in Guido d'Arezzo (Sachs 1980: 232), or the *graves/medias* in the Engelberg poem quoted below. How does a bishop know of such musical vocabulary?

The early twelfth century saw a further and quite new type of reference to organs in William of Malmesbury's report of Gerbert of Aurillac (†1003) and the cathedral of Reims. Now it is a question of a historian remarking on an actual earlier instrument and its actual maker:

extant apud illam ecclesiam	still existing in [?] that church are
doctrinae ipsius documenta:	proofs of his learning:
horologium arte mechanica	a clock made according to the *ars*
compositum; organa hydraulica,	*mechanica*; an hydraulis
ubi mirum in modum,	in which in an extraordinary manner,
per aquae calefactae violentiam,	by hydrostatic force,
ventus emergens implet	the emerging wind fills
concavitatem barbiti,	the cavity of the instrument,
et per multiforatiles tractus	and by means of channels pierced
	with numerous apertures [?]
aereae fistulae	the bronze pipes
modulatos clamores emittunt.	emit loud, ordered sounds. (RBMAS 90.2.196)

While in some later interpretations this gave rise to ideas of a steam organ (*calefactae* was taken to mean 'warm' rather than 'disturbed'), William's description conforms to reports of fabulous astronomical equipment in early medieval cathedrals,[31] vague if the reader does not know the object. It also shows how William, doubtless from his reading only, understood the hydraulis to work; in its way it is a good, clear summary, perhaps picked up from Vitruvius, which William knew (Reynolds 1986: 443). One also learns how special equipment belonged in or near a church, for the clock was surely to mark office *horae*. On the other hand, William's phrase 'bronze pipes' is formulaic, as are *barbiton* and *ars mechanica*, and the latter may have indicated only that the *horologium* was a sundial, with nothing mechanical about it (see p. 284).

Since the 'extraordinary manner' may also be formulaic, however, it cannot be taken as meaning that something called 'hydraulis' was totally unfamiliar at Gerbert's or William's period, although the water-organ itself surely was. Rather, in view of earlier use of the term *hydraulia* (see Hucbald, p. 49), it is doubtful from the start that William's source – whatever it was – had used it to mean a water-organ. If Gerbert was involved in actual organ-making, it is likely to have been as a quadrivial theorist calculating scales, at most supervising instructional *instrumenta* which, it is true, may have been placed in monastic or cathedral churches. But there seems nothing to connect Gerbert's writings on musical matters (see p. 283) with an actual organ built in the cathedral at Reims for playing music, nor does the late tenth-century *Historia* of Richer of St Rémi mention such things, although it does call Gerbert incomparable and likens his skills to Cicero's (PL 138.155). Unless William had access to other, now lost material concerning Reims, the whole passage may result from assuming that Gerbert's well-known musical studies had taken practical shape.

---

[31] As already pointed out by W. Stubbs in the preface to RBMAS 90.2 (p. lxxi). For another translation, cf. Farmer 1931: 156. Also, the chronicle of Berthold (†1088) had described Hermannus Contractus (†1064) as unequalled 'in making clocks, musical and mechanical instruments' (*in horologicis et musicis instrumentis et mechanicis . . . componendis* – MGH SS 5.268).

The Cistercians and the organ

It is not certain that the *Speculum caritatis* (1141–2) of Ailred, Cistercian Abbot of Rievaulx (1110–67), in which the famous tirade against *organa* appears, was written at the behest of St Bernard for Ailred to use in his work as novice-master at Rievaulx.[32] But its rhetoric was surely framed in such a way as to suggest to the reader that (like Balderich at Fécamp) Ailred had personal experience of the organ:

unde, quaeso, cessantibus jam	why, I ask, since images and
typis et figuris,	statues are now being rejected,
unde in Ecclesia	why [are there] in the church
tot organa, tot cymbala?	so many *organa*, so many bells?
Ad quid, rogo, terribilis ille	For what, I ask, [is] this fearful
follium flatus,	bellows-blast,
tonitrui potius fragorem,	more able to express the crash of
quam	thunder than
vocis exprimens suavitatem? . . .	the sweetness of the voice? . . .
Stans interea vulgus	Meanwhile the people standing,
	trembling and thunderstruck,
	wonder at
sonitum follium,	the noise of the bellows,
crepitum cymbalorum,	the clashing of bells and
harmoniam fistularum	the harmony of pipes.
tremens attonitusque miratur.	

(PL 195.571)

The final chapters of Book 2 of the *Speculum caritatis* concern many instances of *vanitas*, including the *voluptas* of hearing and the *concupiscentia* of sight (PL 195.752–4). Following the lines above on the bellows, Ailred complains about various kinds of singing, so that although *tot organa* obviously means organs here,[33] *organum* meaning vocal music is not far from his mind. In particular, it is the improper nature of certain singing (*lascivas cantantium gesticulationes*) as much as the organ that would make one think that the people were assembled 'in the theatre, not in a place of prayer' (*non ad oratorium, sed ad theatrum*).

But it is uncertain from this whether Ailred had actually experienced either organs or theatres. In the same chapter he refers to the Church Fathers and their attitude to the *theatrum* (PL 195.572), and it is possible that the image is invoked purely on the basis of such tradition,[34] not least in the words of St Bernard for whom monastic life 'had nothing of the theatre' (*non est de theatro*). Much of what St Bernard wrote served as a model for Ailred, such as his criticisms of splendid craft-objects like the

---

[32] M. Powicke, *The Life of Ailred of Rievaulx by Walter Daniel* (Oxford, 2/1978), lvi, xci, xcviii.

[33] Assumed without question in later references, such as the translation in W. Prynne, *Histriomastix* (London, 1632), 280.

[34] Examples in McKinnon 1987: 43–5 (Tertullian), 47–8 (Novatian), 145 (Gregory of Nazianzus), 81 and 84 (Chrysostom). Ailred's remarks are taken as evidence for actual theatres, in G. Cohen & R. S. Loomis, 'Were there theatres in the twelfth and thirteenth centuries?', *Speculum* 20 (1945), 92–5, where Bernard's following remark is also quoted.

crown-candelabra at Cluny and many a Benedictine abbey by 1100 (PL 182.915).[35] That such skilful artefacts might have a decorative detail suggesting Augustine's City of God (for example turrets on the candelabrum at Hildesheim Cathedral, like castellations on many a later organ-case) did not enter into the moral question. Ailred's phraseology recalls St Bernard's rhetorical questions concerning church-decorations (painting mosaics) in the *Apologia ad Guillelmum*:

dicite, inquam, pauperes	tell me, poor men (I say),
si tamen pauperes,	if poor you really are,
in sancto quid facit aurum? . . .	what is gold doing in your sanctuary? . . .
quid ibi immundae simiae?	for what are the dirty monkeys?
quid feri leones?	for what the fierce lions?
quid monstruosi centauri?	for what the monstrous centaurs?
quid semihomines? . . .	for what the half men [caryatids?] . . .
quid venatores tubicinantes?	for what the horn-playing hunters? (PL 182. 914–15)

Such criticisms may deliberately invoke the archaic or the exotic: how common in the northern Europe of the twelfth century were mosaics with monkeys and lions?[36]

Despite the evocative nature of Ailred's attack, therefore, one cannot be sure that it was either spontaneous or actual. Even the reference to people standing recalls earlier remarks he may well have known, such as that of Hraban Maur of Fulda in *c.* 844 explaining that theatres were so called from *apo tes theorias*, 'because in them people stand, watching the games' (*stans . . . spectans ludos* – PL 111.553). Ailred could know of noisy bellows from various sources, and there is nothing concrete enough here to see him as suggesting that 'from the nave [the bellows] can be heard almost as clearly as the music from the pipes' (Perrot 1965: 222). The mingling of organ and bells in the tract also suggests something less than literal: as if he thought them directly related, the bellows causing the clashing, both organs and bells irrelevant to the unsullied Church. It is possible that he knew that they performed on the same occasions, and it would be useful if his words could be taken to mean that they played at the same time, across each other. But Cistercians cared for neither organs nor bell-towers. The fact that in this passage he is criticizing the three categories of sound laid down by Isidore of Seville and others since – voice, wind, percussion (*Etymologiae* 3.20) – makes what he is saying more formulaic than, in the first instance at least, actual.

Yet just as earlier biblical exegesis could well be conveying 'real' detail of instruments in its conventional language, so might Ailred. Perhaps there were some Cistercian abbeys, presumably not of the pure Bernardine kind, that were inclined to have churches with towers, porches and complex west ends, thus elements to which organs were not foreign. The twelfth-century French Cistercians were no enemies

---

[35] Perhaps in response to such criticism Peter the Venerable, Abbot of Cluny, decreed in *c.* 1146 that the Cluny crown should be lit only on a few principal feasts: D. Knowles, 'The reforming decrees of Peter the Venerable', in *Petrus Venerabilis 1156–1956: Studies and Texts*, ed. C. Constable & J. Kritzek, Studia Anselmiana 40 (Rome, 1956), 17.

[36] Roman mosaicists worked here and there into the fourteenth century, e.g. the pavement and other objects in Westminster Abbey in the late thirteenth (e.g. L. Homo, *Rome médiévale 476–1420* (Paris, 1934), 286). By this time, such figures were moving to service-books and other manuscripts.

of advanced heavy technology or certain 'impure' elements of church-design.[37] As far as liturgical books were concerned there might be official objections to gold leaf and stipulations to use only one colour, and yet handsomely illuminated books were produced at Cîteaux in the early twelfth century while Stephen Harding was abbot, including a well-informed organ-drawing (see Chapter 11).[38] While no doubt Cistercians themselves encompassed various degrees of strictness, uncertainty about what was the early Christian attitude to instruments – did the early Church have *organa* or didn't it? – could leave members of this technically minded Order ambivalent about them. Although Cistercian organs were certainly known in the later fourteenth century, supposed references to earlier examples should be treated with caution.[39]

As with Cistercians, so with the new orders of friars. Some of Ailred's words were used by at least one of the poor friars of the next century, and in a sermon attributed to the Franciscan Guibert de Tournai, the title makes it clear that it is aimed at the Benedictines (*ad monachos nigros*):[40]

unde, queso, in ecclesia	why, I ask, [are there] in the church
tot organa, tot cymbala,	so many organs, so many bells,
tot monstruosa? . . .	so many monstrous things? . . .

Perhaps *monstruosa* already includes moving statuary, though this would be early. The tirade is otherwise concerned with the abuses of singers:

stans interea populus	standing meanwhile, the people
miratur attonitus . . .	wonder, thunderstruck . . .
ut non videantur ad	looking as if they had come not to
oratorium, sed ad theatrum	a place of prayer but a theatre.
convenisse.	

Organs, complex polyphony and extravagant singing would be equal targets for purist reformers, particularly if they had been long associated together.

---

[37] For a complex west end in an early Cistercian church, see C. A. Bruzelius, 'The twelfth-century church at Ourscamp', *Speculum* 56 (1981), 28–40. For the iron foundries, summary in Gimpel 1976: 67–9.

[38] Gold leaf castigated in the *Dialogus inter Cluniacensum et Cisterciensem* of the mid-twelfth century: F. Alessio, 'La filosofia e le *artes mechanicae* nel secolo XII', *Studi medievale* ser. 3, 6.1 (1965), 71–161, here 87f. On Harding's book, W. Cahn, 'The *Rule* and the book: Cistercian book illumination in Burgundy and Champagne', in *Monasticism and the Arts*, ed. T. G. Verdon (Syracuse, 1984), 139–72, here 140f.

[39] E.g. the *instrumentis* of 1292 at the new Bohemian Cistercian house of Aula Regia (Zbraslaus) were not instruments of music, despite claims made in some secondary sources; organs are absent both from a list of precious objects and from the founder's obsequies (FRB 4.53, 55, 78). But Meaux in England had two organs by 1396: *organa majora in occidentali fine ecclesiae . . . organa minora in choro* ('the larger organ at the west end of the church, the smaller in the quire' – RBMAS 43.3.lxxxii). Altenzella in Saxony, where there was an incomplete copy of Theophilus probably by then (see p. 271), received permission from the Cistercian mother church in 1368 to make use of organ: J. B. Mencke, *Scriptores rerum germanicarum praec. Saxonicarum*, 2 vols (Leipzig, 1929), 2.445.

[40] Quoted from the manuscript Bibliothèque Nationale, Paris, lat. 9606 in P. Aubry, 'Les abus de la musique d'église au XIIe et au XIIIe siècle', *La Tribune de Saint-Gervais* 9 (1903), 57–62, here 59.

Other twelfth- and thirteenth-century references

For centuries the references, especially when short, are bedevilled by the ambiguities of the word *organum*. The 'organal music' in tenth-century Saumur (see above, p. 209), the *organis* 'suspended' at York in 1147 when a new Cistercian archbishop was resisted (*suspensis ecclesiae organis*), the *organa* given by a monk at Weltenburg (*Dietricus pbr . . . dedit nobis organam* – MGH Nec. 3.376) – these are difficult to translate when the text is so short, although in the case of the much longer Engelberg conductus text (see below),[41] the context is not so very much more certain. At least one of these short references is unlikely to mean an organ: judging from several thirteenth-century excerpts in Du Cange 1678 (under 'organum'), it is probable that what was suspended at York was not the playing of organs but the saying of mass. A pope or bishop could well use *organum* to denote the canonic text of the liturgy, as in the Bishop of Meaux's directive of 1221 to his Chapter:

Vos rogamus ut injuriam et   we request that the injury and
dedecus de hominibus nostris   disgrace concerning our men
incarceratis . . .   in prison
vindicare nobiscum curetis,   you take care to put right with us.
organa vestra in majori Ecclesia   [We are] suspending your services in
nostra, quod in aliis Ecclesiis   our larger church, as we instruct to
fieri praecepimus, suspendentes.   be done [also] in the other churches.

(Du Cange 1678, under 'organum')

This kind of disciplinary action evidently led to the formula 'suspending the *organum*', and it was one used well into the fifteenth century (Bull of Pius II, 1462: Du Cange *ibid.*).

The Engelberg conductus is a twelfth-century verse-text complete with simple sangallian neumes, probably originating in St Blasien but associated with Engelberg Abbey. The opening lines are:

Audi chorum organicum   listen to the organic *chorus*,
instrumentum musicum   the musical instrument
modernorum artificum . . .   of up-to-date artists [craftsmen?]
cantum perfice doctis digitis   play the *cantus* with trained fingers,
sonum musicae neumis   a musical sound with pleasing
placitis.   tones.
Gravis chorus succinat   Let the deep *chorus* play
cui sonorus buccinat   let it loudly trumpet forth,
choro chorus accinat   let chorus sing with chorus
diaphonico modo et organico.   in the style of diaphony and organum [?].

Although generally taken to be a description of organ-playing, in church and on an organ with finger-keys, the poem's diction must make one wary of seeing any

---

[41]   York: without source in A. Freeman, 'The organs of York Minster', *The Organ* 5 (1926), 193–204, here 193. Engelberg Codex 102 f. 12: review of four sources in H. Norbert, 'Der Conductus "Audi chorum organicum"', *Schweizerische Musikzeitung* 119 (1979), 257–62 and of six in Huglo, 1990.
The melody of the conductus became familiar from Kodaly's *Laudes organi*.

technical information in it. The care with which traditional music terms such as *graves*, *acutas* and *medias* for the three pitch-levels have been introduced recalls practice in much earlier tropes and sequences, where texts often made use of a whole array of conventional musical-poetic terms (for example p. 86). Perhaps that is all that is happening here.

Nevertheless, just as the poet Notker Labeo and his monastery of St Gall undoubtedly knew something of organs and other instruments while his poetry is only conventionally allusive, so this conductus poem may still be giving some actual or practical hints. But hints of what? It looks at first as if the organ is playing a melody (*cantum perfice*)[42] as well as ensemble music (*diaphonico, organico*), but *chorus* could mean a group of musician-tumblers rather than a monastic choir, and *cantum* has too many general meanings to be helpful here. Also tempting is to assume that the note-by-note letters added above the words of the first seven short lines in the Engelberg copy:

F E D C F G A F F E D C D F F

are an instrumental notation to enable an instrument to play the short-compass melody; on this basis, the Engelberg manuscript has sometimes been said to carry 'the oldest piece of organ music' (Bormann 1966A: 130). But quite apart from the much older note-letters in a copy of the Winchester *prosae* discussed in Chapter 3, there is no necessity to see a poem about organs as something performed on or with an organ. If these note-letters transmitted some organ music so would the fifteenth-century Thuringian copy of the poem that notates the piece on a four-line staff (see note 43). Similarly, while it is possible that the term *gravis chorus* implies tenor or bass notes – even that they were held like a bourdon – it is also formulaic and poetic. One could therefore argue either way. The lines following those above speak of the 'moving hand' (*manu mobili*) and the 'delighted, admiring people' (*placens populo qui miratur*) who 'rejoice and sing' (*laetatur tunc cantatur* – playing as well as singing?), each of which could be as actual as allusive. The scene is a familiar one of celebration, with the *plebes* (here *populus*) stirred by the jubilation and perhaps by music with fast passagework, as suggested by the words

transvolando salias	flying through dances [?],
saltu nobili	with a noble leap,
manu mobili.	with a swift hand.

For this a player would indeed need to 'practise' (*usum exercites*) unless the poem were merely recalling earlier poetry that spoke of agile fingers.[43] Either way, the secular rhythms of a conductus text suit a small organ or instrumental ensemble but say nothing about organs in church, where it is difficult to imagine any liturgical opportunity for such a poem in praise of organs.

Descriptions of everyday liturgies are equally missing from the twelfth-century *chansons de geste*, where it is the special occasion that is recorded. In the *Roman de Horn* (*c.* 1170) and *Brut* (*c.* 1155), the verbs *chanter* and *organer* appear to relate to singing,

---

[42] *Melodia* is not referred to in the passage, although 'honey' appears twice (*mellis, mellicum*).
[43] E.g. verse of Julian (†363) and Claudian (*c.* 400) in Perrot 1965: 383.

perhaps 'monophonic melody' and 'some kind of heterophonic accompaniment' respectively (Page 1987: 121–2).[44] Brut also refers to organs:

quant la messe fu comenciee	when the mass was begun,
ke le jur fu mult exalciee	which was very exultant on that day,
mult oïssiez orgues suner	you could hear the organs playing loudly
e clers chanter e organer	and clerics singing and making music.

The prose source for the passage, in Geoffrey of Monmouth's *Historia regum Britannie* (concerning King Arthur), had mentioned only *tot organa tot cantu*,[45] which probably means two kinds of vocal music. Was this interpreted as involving organs by chanson-poets in the light of contemporary Norman practice known to them? In a similar way, the Breton cycle *Lancelot* (*c.* 1170) specifies the occasion, gives a context and makes clear that the *plebes* are present (Perrot 1965: 299):

qu'aussi con por oïr les ogres [!]	just as to hear the organs
vont au mostier a	there goes to the monastery on the
feste annuel	annual feast
a Pentecoste ou a Noel	at Whit or Christmas,
les janz acostumeement.	the people customarily.

Orgues is unlikely to mean 'instruments in general', and although such texts have their own conventions and diction, it was in their interest to picture the ideal scene in a major Norman monastery. Whether one could go on to reason that Easter and Ascension are omitted from *Lancelot* because Norman practice was more solemn on those feasts is doubtful; maybe the words did not suit the metre. Generally, however, Easter did become a time suitable for organ-sound, one of the regular feasts for which organs were specified in later *ordines* and contracts. An early recorded example is at the abbey of St Peter, Erfurt, in 1226, when the new organ, a wonderful artifice (*mirificum opus*), was first heard on Holy Saturday (? *in sabatho sancto pasche* – MGH SS 30.1.390), perhaps at the long public mass of the day.

Other concrete details in poetry's references to organs include a clear description of a hand-held portative in the *Roman de la rose* (1270s) and the visionary organs in verses 391 and 398 of Albrecht von Scharfenberg's poem *Jüngerer Titurel* (*c.* 1280). These lines speak of a strange and wonderful *orgelsanc* in the Temple of the Holy Grail, high up at the west end above the door (*vil hoch ob einer porte gen occidente schone*) and contributing to festive mass (*ze hochgeziten daz ambet*). They also describe a further extravagance on the walls of chapels near the quire:[46] a tree-automaton with birds. Knowledge of such automata may have originated in Byzantine or Arabic sources but could also have come from Vitruvius (see Chapter 14). Whatever the many

---

[44] An Old Occitan poem of the same period seems to criticize a musician unable to 'make organum in church or palace' (*ni organar en glieiza ni dedinz maison*): E. Aubrey, 'References to music in Old Occitan literature', *AM* 61 (1989), 110–49, here 145–6. The text is uncertain and suggests the scribe did not know the term *organar;* either way, it hardly refers specifically to the church organ.

[45] Page 1987: 121. Note the contemporary use of Ailred's rhetorical *tot . . . tot* phrase.

[46] Examples of Norman feasts in Heitz 1963. *Roman de la rose*: S. Huot, 'Voices and instruments in medieval French secular music', *MD* 43 (1989), 63–113, here 97. *Titurel*: ed. W. Wolf, *Albrecht von Scharfenberg: Jüngerer Titurel*, 2 vols (Berlin, 1968). On attempts to relate the descriptions in *Titurel* to actual churches and organs, see Hammerstein 1986: 189ff, 199ff.

purposes served by such real–unreal instruments in imaginative poetry, the picture of a west-end organ and various quire or side-chapel organs is real enough, even – since it became usual only in the following centuries – something novel and therefore an ideal.

After the poetry of some sources, Gervase of Canterbury's report of Canterbury Cathedral a few years after the fire of 1174 is more prosaic but if anything even less instructive.[47] In the new Norman cathedral, both nave (*aula*) and quire had a special gilt crown-candelabrum, and the south transept had two floors on the upper of which was the organ, near the altar to All Saints in the eastern apse of that transept. How old the organ was is not clear from Gervase's account, nor whether it survived the fire, which was chiefly in the quire; he probably means it was pre-1174. The upper floor at Canterbury may have occupied more space than peripheral transept galleries at Winchester and elsewhere, for Gervase speaks of the pillar which holds it up as being in the middle of the transept (see p. 129 for further remarks on the Canterbury location).[48]

organa quae supra	the organ which [is? was?] above the
fornicem in australi cruce.	vault in the south transept.

Perhaps the bellows were below, on the ground floor? – if so, the organ would then probably have been in the upper transept-space itself, not in its eastern apse-chapel, since directly below this was another chapel (to St Michael)[49] with the tomb of an archbishop on *its* south side. More public than the north transept, the south may also have served as the lawcourt, like the south-central tower of the Anglo-Saxon cathedral and many a later gothic city-monastery (for example Chester). Positioned some way from the enclosed quire east of the crossing tower, the organ at Canterbury cannot have formed an intimate part of the quire liturgy but was close to pilgrim-processions moving down to the crypt on the south side (altars included St Augustine's) and across to the place of martyrdom of St Thomas Beckett (†1170) in the north transept. Perhaps the organ was built for inspiring such pilgrim-processions.

Other details about organs emerge from brief English references at this period. At Winchester in 1172, a deed of gift by the bishop made over the revenue of a certain parish church for 'the making of books and the repairing of organs' (according to its published translation).[50] One is bound to wonder, however, whether the coupling of *books* and *organs* means that the latter were also books of some kind, such as psalters: no doubt *organa* could still mean this in the twelfth century, especially in archaic legal Latin.[51] (On psalters being made in English cathedrals, see note 58.) Books and

[47] In R. Willis, *The Architectural History of Canterbury Cathedral* (London, 1845), 34–47 and Davis-Weyer 1986: 141–6.

[48] Willis (note 47: 39) likens the two-floor transept to that at St-Etienne, Caën, a church 'the same as the present in its plan and dimensions'. See also p. 129 above, concerning galleries. Whether the Canterbury organ was upholding the Benedictine traditions of England or of Normandy cannot be known.

[49] Chapels (like whole churches) to St Michael were usually located on high; see note above on Marienberg and further examples in Klukas 1978: 452ff.

[50] A. W. Goodman, *Chartulary of Winchester Cathedral* (London, 1927), 3.

[51] See Goodman (note 50): 5, 18 and 20 where the gift of the same church's revenue is confirmed but only for the cost of making books (p. 5 = the gift of 1107, p. 18 = papal confirmation, p. 20 = thirteenth-century re-confirmation).

organa are similarly juxtaposed at Ely in 1133: the bishop gave tithes from one source 'for the maintenance of *organa*' (*ad emendationem organorum*) and those from elsewhere 'for making and repairing the books of the church' (*ad libros ecclesiae faciendos et emendandos*).[52] If *organa* does mean the organ, then Ely could well have been typical of the new (and not always yet complete) Norman cathedrals two generations after the Conquest, which in turn could suggest that the major abbeys had an unbroken tradition from pre-Norman days, from *c.* 1000 onwards. But alas, the meaning of *organa* is uncertain, and it is unlikely ever to be more than a guess that Winchester, Canterbury, Ely and others had this unbroken tradition.

During the twelfth century, Abingdon's *organa* – a more recent instrument than that made by Æthelwold and referred to in Chapter 12, which had been carted off by the Vikings (RBMAS 2.2.278) – was endowed by the donor so that 'it can be repaired and maintained in the future' (*in posterum reparari aut manu teneri possent* – RBMAS 2.2.208). It could well be that such abbeys had a succession of organs, replaced as they became unusable or outmoded. They were still associated with special festive events like the reception and presumably acclamation of new abbots, as at Bury St Edmunds in 1182 (see p. 78). At Rochester in 1192 there is information on both the giving and placing of the organ: a stone cloister (complete with south quire aisle) and an organ were given by the Norman bishop, making good the damage of several devastating fires. It is likely that all three – aisle, cloister, organ – were situated closely together:[53]

G. Rofen episcopus . . .	Gibert, Bishop of Rochester . . .
fecit claustrum nostrum	had our stone cloister
perfici lapideum, &	completed,
organa nobis fieri fecit,	had *organa* made for us
& multa alia nobis contulit	and conferred many other
beneficia.	endowments on us.

(*Fecit perfici* and *fecit fieri* suggest outside workmen?) Here too is a case in which a later source records a gift not mentioned in other documents, including a list made in 1327 that refers to Gibert's gifts and work done to the fabric of the church.

During the thirteenth century, references become more specific in several ways, and information about non-monastic churches gradually emerges. Provision in contracts for maintenance or repair become commoner all over Europe, for example as at Barcelona Cathedral in 1259 when the donor required the organist to be responsible for maintaining the organ (*fer aparellar* – Llovera 1987: 174). A customary of St Augustine's Abbey, Canterbury (the manuscript itself of the second quarter of the thirteenth century), specifies the use of organ on some eleven festivals:[54]

---

[52]   Cited with source in C. W. Stubbs, *Historical Memorials of Ely Cathedral* (London, 1897), xxvi.

[53]   See C. Johnson, *Registrum Hamonis Hethe Diocesis Roffensis AD 1319–1352*, Canterbury & York Series 48 (Oxford, 1948), 2. Quotation here from J. Thorpe, *Registrum Roffense* (London, 1769), 633; for the list of 1327 (see below), 122.

[54]   Thompson 1902–4: 2.293–4 (feastday list) and 2.261/268 (concerning vespers and mass). On 2.259, *organa trahere* in conjunction with *folles* shows *trahere* to mean treading bellows.

Christmas Day, *St John the Evangelist*, St Thomas Beckett, *Epiphany*, St Hadrian, *Octave of St Hadrian*, *Purification*, Annunciation, Easter Day, St Michael, Translation of St Augustine (after the procession – i.e. the organ in church after the procession outside?)

While the customary does not necessarily imply that St Augustine's itself had an organ at this period, comparable major churches no doubt did, whether or not they were monastic and whatever particular festivals local usage required instead of the Octave of St Hadrian or the Translation of St Augustine. Bells are used on many more occasions than organs, and their schedule – which bells ring at what points in the office – is much fuller and more detailed. The organ is used three times on bigger feastdays (*ter in una festivitate*), at both vespers and 'at the sequence before the gospel' of the mass (*ad prosam ante ewangelium*). The references to organs concern payments for treading bellows (*de organis tractandis*), which must mean that it was no ordinary monastic duty to do so; but for the feastdays italicized above, there is no payment for the organ (*nulla sunt stipendia*). This suggests that it was less used on these occasions – for the sequence only? – and blown by monks (novices?) rather than paid servants.

At Exeter in 1286/7, the Fabric Rolls specify 'costs concerning the enclosing of the organ' (*in expensis circa organa claudenda . . . 4s*),[55] and while this has been taken to refer to some newly made wooden casework surrounding the organ in the quire – which would be important evidence for a new style of organ-building – more likely is that it refers only to the work for locking it away (*circa* is used in these records to mean 'concerning', not 'around'). This is the first known reference to organs at Exeter Cathedral, written while extensive work was underway (the building of nave, quire, aisles 1280–1300), and suggests a major piece of fixed equipment – which in turn may mean that the organ had wooden casework. Such reasoning is an uncertain and roundabout way of inferring what an instrument was like, and then only in general terms, but unfortunately there is seldom any other way. The dates certainly suggest that an organ was in use before the church was complete, wherever it was placed: in the extant gallery above the north nave arcade, in the north transept (near a clock?), on a screen, or in the quire.

From annals of the same period at Strasbourg one might draw similar inferences: of the four sentences afforded to the year 1292 in a contemporary chronicle, three relate to the organ:

Item eodem anno comparavimus organas, que constabant quingente libre Argentinensis monete.	in the same year we provided an organ which cost five hundred Strasbourg pounds.
Eodem tempore fuerunt procuratores fabrice Lucas miles et Ellenhardus maior prope monasterium.	At the same time Lucas *miles* and Ellenhardus *mayor* were overseers of the fabric [the workshop?] near the monastery [?].
Et magister Guncelinus de Frankenfort paravit predictas organas.	And Master Gunzelinus of Frankfurt supplied the said organ. (MGH SS 17.103)

[55] A. M. Erskine, *The Accounts of the Fabric of Exeter Cathedral, 1279–1353* (Torquay, 1981), 7. In 1312/13, timber for new bellows (*ad nov' flat'*) cost 8d. and work on making them 3s: this suggests that costs in 1286/7 were either for major construction or involved much ironwork.

Assuming that the two *procuratores* were joint Clerks of Work (evidently men of secular authority) in control of the organ-project, which the placing of the sentences suggests, this would have been a large structure involving the fabric – perhaps a precursor of the fourteenth- and fifteenth-century swallownest organs in the same nave. If the builder 'supplied' the organ rather than merely 'made' it (*fecit* or *fecit fieri*), one may be justified in supposing a large team-project, in the hands of an expert from another city.

One would expect it to be clear from the references whether the Strasbourg instrument was a swallownest organ, and whether that at Exeter was integral with the new stalls (*c.* 1260–80); but it is not. At Exeter the reference suggests that it was either placed on the screen that preceded the stone pulpitum of 1320 or, if locking it away was necessary, built as a separate structure on the quire floor. After a fire at Strasbourg in 1299, the replacement organ was in the hands of a lay joiner of great repute; perhaps a swallownest was involved. A clue about one organ-location at this period is found in yet another list of items burnt in a church fire, at St Maria zu den Staffeln, Mainz, in 1285:[56]

cum quibusdam ornamentis,	with certain ornaments,
organis, libris, ymagibus	organs, books, images of the
sanctorum, altaribus et aliis	saints, altars and other
bonis ipsius ecclesiae.	good things of the church itself.

Once again, the reference to an organ – the first known document to refer to an organ in Mainz – is made *en passant*, as if it were a part of the altar equipment. Since the images, books and altars were surely located near each other, so by implication was the organ. It is not possible to infer even this much from the contemporary report of the Strasbourg fire:

ignis . . . campanas, organa et	the fire devoured the bells, organ and	
ornatus ecclesie devoravit.	ornaments of the church.	(MGH SS 17.139)

While so little is certain about the structure and the location of thirteenth-century organs (on wooden casework, see also Chapter 18), references to any newly built organ in the chronicles – rather than in the detailed fabric rolls or accounts – might well suggest that it was a large, fixed instrument. The chronicles of Erfurt were very selective and certainly not so voluminous as to be recording mere everyday equipment when they report of St Mary's in 1225:

Hoc anno facta sunt organa nova	in this year was made a new organ	
Erphordie in ecclesia beate	at Erfurt, in the church of the	
virginis.	Blessed Virgin.	(MGH SS 30.1.390)

---

[56] F. Bösken, 'Beiträe zur Orgelgeschichte des Mittelrheins bis zum Beginn des 16. Jahrhunderts', *KmJb* 45 (1961), 82–101, here 90. On the likelihood that the Exeter organ was somewhere in the quire, see N. Orme, 'The early musicians of Exeter Cathedral', *ML* 59 (1978), 395–410, here 397. On the Strasbourg organ of 1292 being the successor to an already large organ of 1260, see M. Vogeleis, *Quellen und Bausteine zu einer Geschichte der Musik und des Theaters im Elsaß 500–1800* (Strasbourg, 1911), 3, 17; on the organ of 1327, 61–2.

A question is whether *organa nova* means that there was a previous organ. The phrase is not uncommon in the thirteenth century, and particularly in more important churches one might conjecture that at one or other stages of their construction or reconstruction, they had organs well before the year 1250. The new organs of large secular cathedrals, perhaps already in safer and more spectacular locations such as swallownest galleries in the nave, could well have been up-to-date replacements making use of the period's wood and tin technologies. In the thirteenth-century chronicle recording the organ of Prague Cathedral (Sv Víta), there are only a handful of items for that year but both the cost and schedule for the organ are given:

Eodem anno organa nova	in the same year [1255] a new organ
facta sunt in ecclesia Pragensi,	was made in the church of Prague,
quae constiterunt XXVI	which cost twenty-six
marcas argenti, sed perfecta sunt	silver marks, but was finished
futuro anno tempore quadragesimae.	by Lent of the following year. (FRB 2.293)

These references at Erfurt and Prague, presumably to special instruments, match others of the time in the large area east of the Rhine and south-west of the Elbe, and especially in the non-monastic churches of the Rhineland itself (Strasbourg, Worms, Mainz, Koblenz, Bonn). Taken as a group, they support the idea that the mid-thirteenth century did see new directions in organ-bulding especially in east-central Europe, with large all-encased instruments aiming for a bigger, i.e. less localized, sound in very large churches, sometimes replacing earlier organs and taking some time to build and set up. Documentation was becoming specific about builders as well as the contractual items they were to supply (see Chapter 17), making it look as if organ-building at the beginning of the fourteenth century was a speciality of certain cities like Frankfurt.[57] Whether such centres of activity are as new as the documents suggest, which is unlikely, there is certainly nothing *en passant* about the new kinds of reference to organs: attention is being drawn to them.

Finally, two other word-uses of the thirteenth century need attention: the continued use of the old term *organista* and the new appearance in documents of so-called 'larger organs'.[58]

On the first: how far archaic meanings persisted into the fourteenth century is a major question. If in documents of many a late twelfth-century cathedral *organista* meant, as it did at Tarragona in 1164, a director or creator of vocal organum, does it gradually come more and more to mean an organist – is it any evidence that the church had an organ – at Barcelona, Lérida, Burgos, Toledo and Santiago between

---

[57] E.g. T. Peine, *Der Orgelbau in Frankfurt am Main und Umgebung von den Anfängen bis zur Gegenwart* (Frankfurt, 1956), 13ff, based on e.g. the Strasbourg document above.

[58] Spanish cathedrals: H. Anglès, *Scripta musicologica*, ed. T. López-Calo, 3 vols (Rome, 1975–6), 564, 848 and H. A., as FN 10: 114–15. Olomouc in J. Senhal, 'Die Orgeln der Olmützer Kathedrale', *AO* 15 (1981), 27–75, here 37. Budapest in L. Zolnay, 'Ungarische Orgelbauer und Organisten im 14.–16. Jahrhundert', *Studia musicologica* 14 (1972), 385–400, here 399. (These three authors assume that *organista* implies the presence of an organ.) Paisley in J. Inglis, 'The builders of Scotland's organs – a survey', *J. of the British Institute of Organ Studies* 15 (1991), 50–8, here 51. Durham in ed. J. Raine, *Historiae Dunelmensis Scriptores Tres*, Publications of the Surtees Society 9 (London/Edinburgh, 1839), 46. Although *organum* was losing or had lost its meaning of psalter, see also Raine, *ibid.*, xlviii and 44 for the attention paid at this time in Durham to the making of such books.

1223 and 1279 when *organistae* are mentioned? If for centuries vocal organum might have included some sort of instrumental *organum* in special circumstances (such as major ceremonies in a major church), it is likely that as time passed *organista* did mean someone in charge of the organ, especially in the greater churches and especially as it grew in size and value. 'Someone in charge', however, need not mean its player who, also for centuries, probably needed no great musicianship or special appointment. Whether the *organista seu cantor* at Olomouc Cathedral in 1257 or the *organista* at Paisley Abbey, Scotland, in *c.* 1250 or the *magister organorum* at Budapest in 1303 (Margaret's Isle, Dominican sisters) were as likely to be organists is less certain, since loose terminology probably persisted longer in such peripheral places. One could argue two ways. Since in none of these churches is there independent record of an organ (except at Barcelona in 1259), mention of an *organista* need not imply that there was one; on the other hand, since vocal organum might on occasion include some participating instrument, an *organista* would have been the controller of any *organa* there happened to be there.

On the second: annals at Durham in 1264 report an *organa grandiora* but no smaller organ. If *organa* does not mean a *more ingenious machine* for the bells, or a *larger instrument* distinct from something else used in the priory, it implies two organs, a larger for feastday clamour and a smaller for the office. This was certainly so at Durham in the sixteenth century, but like any other custom, it had to be established. Even a major cathedral is unlikely to have both a large and a small fixed organ before *c.* 1350, and any apparent references to such a pair could well be misleading.[59] But it cannot be out of the question here and there in the mid-thirteenth century, when either one of the organs – the smaller for the new *alternatim* music, the larger incorporating recent technology – could have been the more recent.

Absence of references

The most puzzling question to arise from references to actual organs in this chapter is why there are not more. Many of them that do exist appear *en passant*, and in more than one case there exists a second reference to the church or personnel that makes no mention of the *organa* reported in the first: nothing about organs at Winchester and Abingdon in Wulfstan's prose *Life of Æthelwold* (PL 137.79ff) or in a further account of the Cava dedication in 1092 (MGH SS 3.190). If by 1000 four English abbeys had organs, did not their continental models? Is it feasible that Abingdon and Ramsey had organs but Fleury not, when Fleury was connected with both English abbeys?[60] More generally but importantly: did non-monastic churches have organs only from the thirteenth century onwards?

[59]   A claim that by 1188 the Benedictine Abbey of Donauwörth, Swabia, had two organs, an old and a large new organ (quoted in e.g. H. Fischer & T. Wohnhaas, 'Organa benedictina bavarico-suevica', *Studien und Mitteilungen zur Geschichte des Benediktiner-Ordens* 90 (1979), 315–55, here 326), is probably due to a misunderstanding of (lost) sources.

[60]   The abbot of Fleury had lived in Ramsey for a time (see p. 202), and Æthelwold had sent an envoy to learn the observances at Fleury (PL 137.89).

That there is a chance element in the references to organs – a source may or may not have a reason to mention such things – is clear from material dealing with the English reform-bishops Æthelwold, Dunstan and Oswald (see Chapter 12). At Abingdon, records of donations in both the tenth and the twelfth centuries do include bells and *organa* (see above), but was Abingdon so exceptional or only its chronicles better detailed? Then if Æthelwold's reform at Abingdon and Winchester resulted in special objects including organs, it would be strange if it did not at Thorney as well, particularly since nearby Ramsey had an organ. But none is known about. It also seems scarcely possible that Ramsey had an organ while the major foundations of Peterborough and Ely did not, or that if Crowland did have as many as seven bells in 975,[61] it had no organ. Since Bishops Æthelwold, Dunstan and Oswald were all signatories to the charters of Crowland (966), Peterborough (970) and Malmesbury (974), is it really so that only Malmesbury had an organ or is it rather that only this abbey was fortunate enough to have a later historian to report it?[62] Since lists of furnishings and valuable gifts so rarely include organs, one might think that for some reason the clerks or scribes were not alerted to them. Because organs were not primarily for liturgical use (see remark on Montecassino, p. 122)? Because they were soon out of date and each one of little permanent value?

It has been assumed that when in his *Vita sancti Dunstanti* (*c.* 1120) William of Malmesbury attributes St Dunstan with spreading the organ in England he had good reason to do so:

illud instrumentum quod	that instrument which
antiqui barbiton,	the ancients call barbiton
nos organa dicimus,	and we *organa*,
tota diffudit Anglia;	he dispersed throughout England;
ubi ut fistula	[an instrument] where for the pipe
sonum componat	to produce sound
per multiforatiles tractus	through many-holed channels [?],
'pulsibus exceptas, follis	'the agitated bellows discharges
vomit anxius auras'.	breaths upwards when pumped'. (RBMAS 63.257)

In his *Life of St Dunstan*, William follows the tradition in which *vitae* expound on their subject's artistic and scientific achievements: perhaps Dunstan 'did scatter organs around Anglia' or southern England but the possibility is known only through William's *vita*. If it were true, one would have expected Dunstan to have brought an organ to Canterbury Cathedral, where his works included a chapel used as his later shrine;[63] but if he did, there is no record of it. Furthermore, although William is speaking here of an organ with pipes and bellows, his previous sentence referred to the cithara, and it would not be a surprise if he were confusing what his sources said. The *Life of Dunstan* by 'Britferdus' (*c.* 1000) refers a great deal to the

---

[61] One very large bell before 975, six more (two large, two medium, two small) in that year, rung together according to a report supposedly of *c.* 1090 (H. T. Riley, *Ingulph's Chronicle of the Abbey of Croyland* (London, 1854), 107), but now recognized to have been compiled as late as 1450.

[62] Charters in Riley (note 61): 84f, 91f, 95f; later Malmesbury account in RBMAS 72.1.317–21.

[63] See R. D. H. Gem, 'The Anglo-Saxon cathedral church at Canterbury: a further contribution', *AJ* 127 (1970), 196–201.

music of the liturgy and tells of Dunstan playing the cithara or *hearpe/harpa* (PL 139.1423ff). In other similar sources, both music and instrument might well have been called *organum* as might the liturgical texts themselves: Dunstan's close contact with Frankish monasteries pursuing liturgical reform could have led to an account in which *organum* meant 'chant-repertory' or 'canonic/liturgical texts'. Presumably William of Malmesbury also read the story of Dunstan's miraculous cithara which, hanging on a wall and untouched by human hand, played a certain antiphon melody (PL 139.1435 and *Acta SS Mai* 4.349). From St Aldhelm he would know that the barbiton was also an *organum* and that praise could be sung with the strings of the cithara (MGH AA 15.2.103, 355), and in turn readers would know that the barbiton appears in patristic literature (examples in McKinnon 1987: 73) and in William's reference to Gerbert of Reims. But since it was usually the cithara that was 'called barbiton by the ancients', was it such a stringed instrument, not the organ, on which Dunstan excelled? Unravelling the truth about Dunstan from this complex of allusion and source-transmission is not easy, and it seems a pity to doubt a positive remark about organs when there are so few references to them and their introduction. But eventually the most plausible words are those of 'Britferdus' (PL 139.1454): he does not say that Dunstan filled England with organs but with holy doctrine.

The cult of Dunstan was strong, and it is striking that William says nothing about Æthelwold's organ-building when he reports on his activities (RBMAS 63.303). A typical example of such silence about organs rather than of misleading remarks about them concerns the eleventh-century abbey of Peterborough. It is recorded that the abbot saw to it that the church had special objects of fine metalwork (a great cross of gold and silver, candelabra, altar-frontal, many shrines, vestments, etc.), so much so that it was known as the Golden City (Gildineburch).[64] Did it have neither bells nor organ? Writing in *c.* 1160, Hugh Candidus refers to Æthelwold's having given 'all good things' to Thorney (*bonorum omnium*), richly endowing Ely, building the church and monastery at Abingdon, and reforming the three monasteries at Winchester, all nearly two centuries earlier. But just as William of Malmesbury does not attribute organs to Æthelwold, so Hugh makes no mention of organ or bells at any of the four foundations, although other sources say Abingdon and Winchester had both. Similarly, Hugh reports on the reception or *adventus* of the new Abbot of Peterborough in 1154/5 without mentioning any music with or without *organa*, although it was a ceremony traditionally appropriate for both:[65]

cum magna processione . . .	with a great procession
a conventu	he was welcomed by the convent
in propria sede	in his own seat
Burgi susceptus est.	of Peterborough.

Another occasion on which one might expect a reference to *organa* in one or other sense is at the *Te Deum* sung in *c.* 1131 when the Aquitanian monks of

[64] Ed. W. T. Mellows, *The Chronicle of Hugh Candidus, a Monk of Peterborough* (Oxford, 1949), 66.
[65] Mellows (note 64): 43–6 (Æthelwold) and 127 (new abbot). On Æthelwold's gift of books to Peterborough, see also p. 62. If there had been an organ there in 1154/5, it would probably have been newly built after the massive fire of 1116.

St-Jean-d'Angély elected a new abbot at Peterborough (with which they were connected); but again there is no mention even of bells. Hugh simply seems to have had no interest in music. In particular, Æthelwold's rebuilding of Peterborough and equipping it with 'various ornaments' (*variis ornamentis*), in which state it was visited by Dunstan and Oswald,[66] is not further itemized, and there is no further chronicle, no *vita* or poem to give any detail of Peterborough's expensive equipment, as there was elsewhere. It is possible that a note was made of the organ at nearby Ramsey only because Oswald was a churchman who evidently believed in written documentation.[67]

Such a chronicle as that of Hugh Candidus relates tenth-century events by means of sources either from the tenth century, which might be glossed over or even misunderstood when they mention bells and *organa*, or from intervening periods, when such details may already have been glossed over. Either way, an incomplete record results. The cluster of monastic houses in the Fenlands – Peterborough, Ely, Crowland, Thorney, Ramsey – was much like clusters elsewhere, around Brogne or Arras or Reichenau and many other places in Francia, Aquitania, Catalonia, Saxonia and Germania. An organ in any one of these places must surely bespeak an organ in others, not mentioned because to mention it is the exception.

---

[66] Mellows (note 64): 31. A variant in the manuscript copies – *possessionibus* for *ornamentis* – suggests that sources were less or more specific, without it now being obvious why.

[67] E.g. seventy-six land-leases survive from Oswald's period as Bishop of Worcester, more than seems to have been usual (S. Kelly, 'Anglo-Saxon society and the written word', in *The Uses of Literacy in Early Mediaeval Europe*, ed. R. McKitterick (Cambridge, 1990), 36–62).

Organs and written technology

14

Vitruvius, Hero, Muristos and the organ of Aquincum

Vitruvius's material

The *De architectura*, written probably between *c.* 84 and *c.* 14 BC by the Roman architect Vitruvius, includes various references to music in Books 1, 5, 9 and 10 (Morgan 1914). Before the broader implications are examined, these can be briefly summarized as follows:

Book 1, Chapter 1, §8–9.
Architects should understand the nature of sound in order to make sure that (a) catapult strings are stretched in unison, (b) bronze resonators fixed below theatre seats are tuned correctly, (c) water-organs etc. are made according to the principles of music.
    If in the last Vitruvius is referring to pipe-lengths made in proportional lengths, does it suggest that sometimes they were not and that builders had other means of discovering pipe-measurements?[1]

5.4.1–9.
After an introductory chapter on theatres (5.3) and before their further architecture is discussed (5.6, 5.7, 5.8), an account is given of Aristoxenos's scale and tetrachords, with directions for bronze resonators in theatres (5.5). The number of pitches to which the resonators are tuned depends on the size of the theatre.[2]

9.8.2–4.
Ctesibius discovers that a ball descending in a close-fitting pipe compresses the air and produces a tone; observing this he goes on to make a *hydraulica machina* and water-clocks (working by gravity feed).
    Vitruvius makes no mention of any reed or fipple that would produce the vortices: Ctesibius merely observed that tones were produced by the 'contact between air-under-pressure and free air' and used this principle in water-organs, whose pipes

---

[1] There is no Roman *mensura fistularum* (pipe-measurement text) comparable to those summarized below in Chapter 16.
[2] According to the interpretation in Morgan 1914: 144, for the largest theatres the notes were A H c♯ d e f♯ g a h c' c♯' d' e' f♯' g' a'.
    For references to resonators ('acoustic jars') in churches in England and the Balkans, see NOHM 1990: 33.

must have been either reeds or flues. Neither here nor in Book 10 does Vitruvius describe an organ-pipe or how it speaks.

10.1–16.

The final book concerns machines: in general (10.1), hoists (10.2), levers (10.3), water-lifting (10.4-6), Ctesibius's pump (10.7), the water-organ (10.8), odometer (10.9), catapults, *ballistae* and siege machines etc. (10.10-16).

10.7.1–3.

Ctesibius's water-pump for fountains: the spout or 'pipe at the top is called a trumpet' (*insuper fistula, quae tuba dicitur*). On *tuba* as a pipe of some kind used in pressurized apparatus, see p. 14 and the *Letter to Dardanus* below. In 10.7.4: reference to other devices using water for air-compression and thus motion and sound, such as 'singing blackbirds' (which were presumably automata birds in a tree).

  The first main feature of the instrument described in 10.8, *De hydraulicis*,[3] is the water-stabilizer (cistern) fed by a pair of cylinders. The cistern is contained in a bronze altar-like object (*ara*) placed on a wooden base: the cylinders feed into the central stabilizer much as they do into the central wind-chamber of Ctesibius's water-pump, where there is also a pair of feeders. Whether the two cylinders are operated in alternation (or even necessarily both at all) is not discussed, but two little bronze indicators (shaped like dolphins)[4] indicate the position of the inlet valve attached to their 'snout', and therefore whether the blower is pumping. From the cistern the wind is driven into the three-level chest: a shallow low chamber for the wind to collect (*arcula*); then the section with four, six or eight longitudinal channels (each with 'its own stopcock', *singula epitonia*); then between topboards are placed the perforated, oiled sliders (*regulae*, 'rulers')[5] running latitudinally and operated by *pinnae* ('feathers' = flat or leaf springs?).

  More needs to be said below on the longitudinal channels. The passage concerning the springs (?) reads:

haec regulae habent ferrea choragia	these sliders have iron pins [?]
fixa et iuncta cum pinnis	fixed and connected to feathers [?],
quarum pinnarum tactus motiones	the touching of which brings about
efficit regularum continenter.	motion of the rulers without a break.

The usual interpretation of this is that the 'sliders are fitted with strong iron springs attached to the keys' (Perrot 1971: 38, based on Schmidt 1899: 501?). But this interpretation must be influenced by the knowledge of Hero's key-squares (see below) and is not very precise; also, springs are more likely to have been made of bronze than iron (Callebat 1986: 182). If *pinnae* are springs operating the sliders

---

[3] Further translations and interpretations in C. Fensterbusch, *Vitruv, Zehn Bücher über Architektur, übersetzt und mit Anmerkungen versehen* (Darmstadt, 1964), and in Callebat 1986: 170–86.

[4] Water creatures said to be lovers of music (Callebat 1986: 179).

[5] *Regulae* is the name in 10.8.1 for the bars or rods attached to the left and right sides of the organ-plinth into which, somehow, the cylinder-pumps are fixed. Vitruvius's remark that these bars look like ladders (*scalari forma*) suggests a personal observation.

without keys as such, then *choragia* means no more than 'pins' (pegs, rivets). Drachmann 1948: 8f follows the Schmidt interpretation, but in Drachmann 1963: 195 and Callebat 1986: 26 there is an alternative: the keys (*pinnae*) were thin enough to serve as springs themselves, perhaps placed obliquely, connected (hooked) with an iron rod (*coracia*, 'little raven') to the end of the slider, and flipping back to position when the finger is taken off. Of course, *pinnae* may be the 'key-plates', not themselves bending but attached to a flat spring that was bent down and then sprang back. It could be, however, that all such interpretations proceed from later knowledge of the various forms of spring-loaded key: were there to be no other information from various sources it would be difficult to project this or any other specific key-action from Vitruvius's words.

Nothing is said about the pipes other than that on the top of the chest, above the holes through which the wind passes, there are

anuli adglutinati quibus	rings soldered on, into which
lingulae omnium	the little tongues of all the
includuntur organorum.	pipes are inserted.

The little rings must have been useful to hold flue pipes firm when the instrument was moved about and also perhaps if the pressure was high, but there is always an outside chance that they were the visible parts of reed-boots. As for the terms: *organa* or 'instruments of sound' must mean pipes, while *fistulae* is used for the tubes or little windtrunks from the cylinders into the cistern. Whether *lingulae* mean reeds (i.e. 'reed tongues') or flue-mouths (the languid as 'tongue')[6] is not known: perhaps as elsewhere in Vitruvius, the word denotes merely the 'narrow end' of the pipes, whether flue or reed (Callebat 1986: 184). Like the sounding parts, the key-mechanism of the organ is treated succinctly, even cursorily (see similar remarks on Theophilus's treatise in Chapter 15).

But one of the final remarks of Chapter 8 refers to the organ's music: when the sliders are handled as intended,

e musicis artibus,	by means of musical arts,
multiplicibus modulorum varietatibus	in very many varieties of melody
sonantes excitant voces.	they make resonant sounds [?]

Although the terms, particularly *artibus, modulorum* and *voces*, invite paraphrase and concordance with other texts, it is going rather far to see here a reference to 'extreme diversity of timbres' (Callebat 1986: 27) or even to 'sounds . . . conforming to the laws of music' (Morgan 1914: 300). Although the second is likelier, a 'great variety of melodies' may be too specific for *modulorum*. The phrase *e musicis artibus* must imply controlled or 'organized' sounds, but it is difficult to wring from these words a reliable picture of the organist creating beautiful melodies with colourful stop-changes. Nevertheless, it remains possible that Vitruvius's organ did have stops.

In the description of the chest, the references to 'in whose length are channels' and 'the holes arranged across its width' (*in cuius longitudine canales, ordinata in*

---

6   For usage in earlier medieval treatises (*lingua* or *plectrum* for languid, *zúngûn* in Notker Labeo's German), see Sachs 1980: 318, 321, 353.

transverso foramina) seem to indicate, if ambiguously, (a) channels running under separate ranks, and therefore (b) a chorus of pipes per key.[7] Some reading of Vitruvius may directly or indirectly have led certain thirteenth-century artists to show some slider-like mechanism on two sides of the chest,[8] and in any case various arrangements are conceivable: Schmidt 1899: 50 draws the chest in such a way that the 'stop-sliders' are located at the front below the keys, like many an organ of his own day. But Vitruvius's description is altogether unclear. Since he may have been relying on a Greek account not only for several technical terms but for a description of those parts of an organ he could not see,[9] perhaps he did not correctly understand the design. While it is true that a pair of pumps could easily supply wind for eight channels in a short-compass organ of small pipes, it is puzzling that Vitruvius leaves rather crucial terms unlatinized:

in cuius longitudine canales,	in the length of which [are] channels:
si tetrachordos est,	if it is a tetrachord [type of chest?]
fiunt quattuor,	four are made
si hexachordos, sex,	if hexachordal, six
si octochordos, octo.	if octochordal, eight.

Tetrachord seems an illogical term for 'four chorus ranks', and in Book 5 Vitruvius uses it in the usual sense of note-sequence, i.e. four different and adjacent notes. Perhaps *tetrachordos* could mean much the same as *tetrachoros* ('four-rank'?) or even be a misreading for it, by Vitruvius or the compilers/authors writing under his name or even the later copyists (i.e. of the extant copies)? Textual variants (Callebat 1986: 25) suggest that scribes were unsure of the passage, although other readings such as *longitudine si canales* and *longitudine si canalis* would not remove the questions.

However in further support for the idea of four or six or eight ranks per key is the information on a kind of stop-knob:

singulis autem canalibus	furthermore, for each of the channels
singula epitonia sunt inclusa	there are fitted individual stop-valves [?],
manubriis ferreis conlocatis.	iron handles being attached to them.

It is true, as Callebat 1986: 182 suggests, that through linkwork the stop-handle could be in the front face of the organ, for the convenience of the player. But this is to assume that like the post-Renaissance player the ancient Roman organist 'manipulated organ-stops' or 'changed registrations', whereas if Vitruvius is reliably describing an organ of four or six or eight ranks, its layout could have resembled more that proposed for the Aquincum organ. Here various sets of pitches were probably available, even various tunings, and one changed pitches/tunings rather than 'stops' in the later sense. And yet: are eight different pitches/tunings really feasible,

---

[7] Morgan 1914: 299 translates *in transverso foramina* as 'vertical openings', which would not substantially alter the description of the chest, although it might imply that there were individual vertical windways (i.e. bored holes) up to the pipes.

[8] I.e. both 'key-sliders' in front and 'stop-sliders' to the side: Friuli and Munich manuscripts in Perrot 1965: plates XXVII/1 and XXVI.

[9] Hence the detail on the parts he could? – the *dolphins* fixed to the cylinders' intake-valves, or the side *ladders* for securing the pumps, both visually evocative.

or did makers duplicate ranks – thus one pitch/tuning for four ranks, another for two (ranks five and six), and a third for the final two (ranks seven and eight)?

There is a further difficulty with the following interpretations:

> there were up to eight stops, each rank with a different tone-colour, in the Renaissance organ;
>
> there were up to eight tunings, each rank corresponding to a different modal ethos;
>
> there were up to eight different pitches for one and the same diatonic scale, such as may be implied by a late Greek source, the so-called Bellermann Anon. (Perrot 1971: 136–9)

The difficulty is that musical subtleties of this kind would be useless in a theatre-organ, such as it seems Vitruvius was intending to describe at this point in his treatise[10] – for finesse in salons, perhaps, but not in theatres.

Almost the only thing certain here is that by referring to something having more than one, two or three ranks, Vitruvius is wishing to describe a major piece of apparatus. A conceivable possibility is that Vitruvius confused his information. There were three stop-valves, for four, six or eight ranks respectively, presumably with unison and octave duplications to make three different levels of screeching chorus. But various further conjectures are also possible. For example, the valves were a kind of *Sperrventil* (the 'blocking valve' known to later organ-builders)[11] cutting off wind from a faulty rank. Or the longitudinal channels were not for separate ranks at all but for even dispersal of wind inside the chest. Or – to interpret 'tetrachord' as elsewhere in the *De architectura* – there was a compass of four, six or eight notes; four notes would have been too small for much melody but were enough for a siren (see below, Muristos). Or the range of notes was based on a theory of *tetrachords* and some-how the information became garbled – why, after all, the reference to *four, six* or *eight* but not three, five or seven? 'Tetrachords, hexachords and octaves' (DEFG, CDEFGA, CDEFGABc) would mean merely that the keyboard was arranged in a diatonic sequence, something not obvious in the first century. Practical musicians surely did not have to wait for a 'theory of hexachords' to appear in the eleventh century to know that the diatonic scale could be explained in terms of four, six or eight notes.

Attempts to interpret Vitruvius's words are hampered by their isolation: neither archaeology nor other writing is able to put them into context. But some of the suggestions made above are not incompatible with the organs represented in the Roman terracotta lamps of Carthage and Copenhagen (Perrot 1965: plates xii, xiii). They seem to have had a compass of eighteen or nineteen notes in a regular sequence of some kind, with short but graded pipe-lengths in some four (?) ranks, and with a row of keys attached to the ends of small sliders (?). The technological

---

[10] Callebat 1986: 181 notes the author's penchant for theoretical classification. But he may be over-optimistic in seeing good evidence for organs with different numbers of 'stops' (*jeux*) in the various iconographical sources.

[11] Without any such stopcock, was silence achieved on a (high pressure) water-organ purely from the hermetic seal on the slider-channel? Or was it that so long as there was wind in the cistern the slides preferably had to be operated, with little if any gap between notes?

challenge of any such organ was by no means negligible. Vitruvius's eight ranks, if such there were, would mean a long slider unless the pipes were very small or – as is more likely – the slider opened a single large hole below all the channels. And even a short compass of seven or eight notes, if Hero's model is taken literally, would mean up to sixty-four pipes.

Finally, not the least interesting detail in Vitruvius is his use of the term *organum/organicus* for three different things:[12] various kinds of apparatus or equipment, including a pipe; a particular musical or medical organ (*in organo non medicus sed musicus modulabitur* – Book 1); and musical instruments in general.

Vitruvius and the *artes mechanicae*

A brief remark in one ninth-century Frankish treatise on music – that Vitruvius had spoken of eight winds (four *principales* and four *subjecti*), thus suggesting a parallel to the eight modes of music – serves as a reminder of the range of classical authors familiar to a Carolingian theorist.[13] Not only Pythagoras and Boethius, Augustine and Isidore were known directly or indirectly to the compilers, but so from time to time was the material transmitted in the *artes mechanicae* treatises. While, therefore, Vitruvius is describing an organ many centuries before any Frankish instrument-maker was at work, some examination of that organ is relevant.

In the nature of literate study at this period the liberal arts were more in evidence than the mechanical, and the two fields were seldom integrated even superficially. (They are still not.) The reference to Vitruvius in *Alia musica* does not actually clarify anything about the modes of music beyond implying a theoretical rationale for the number eight. Another treatise, the little pipe-measurement text *Rogatus* associated with Gerbert of Reims refers to major philosophers – Aristoxenos, Boethius, Pythagoras, the Pythagoreans, Macrobius, Censorius, Calcidius and Plato (Sachs 1970: 59–61) – but there is little if any hint of the various technical *ars mechanica* treatises that Gerbert's circle surely knew. Was Gerbert involved in any way with the craft skills and practical theory that must have been behind such achievements as the contemporary organ at Winchester, as might be now assumed (for example Sachs 1980: 255), or were literate and craft activities totally separate in practice? Since the evidence outlined in various ways in the present book suggests the last answer to be 'Yes', the reason could be that what are concerned here are not two distinct areas of study but three: the *ars liberalis* traditions, the *ars mechanica* treatises and the making of organs. As there are fewer sources for the second than the first, so there are fewest of all for the third.

---

12 For convenient word-index, see eds. L. Callebat *et al.*, *Vitruve De Architectura concordance: documentation bibliographique, lexicale et grammatique* (Hildesheim, 1984), 779f. The Greek element in Vitruvius's technical terminology is strong: for the watermill, he knows 'only the Greek name', according to B. Gille, 'Le Moulin à eau', *Techniques et Civilisations* 3 (1954), 1–15, here 1.

13 *Alia musica (Traité de musique du IX siècle). Edition critique commentée avec une introduction sur l'origine de la nomenclature modale pseudo-grecque au Moyen-Age*, ed. J. Chailley (Paris, 1965), 95–6. This section *c.* 875? The reference is to Vitruvius 1.6.4ff, concerning the octagonal Tower of the Winds in Athens.

Both of the major texts concerned partly or wholly with organ-building – *Cuprum purissimum* and Theophilus respectively – are associated in extant copies with older practical treatises such as Vitruvius's *De architectura* and the ninth-century fine-art compendium *Mappae clavicula*: see Chapters 15 and 16.[14] Although a copyist or group of copyists collecting such texts together, as in manuscripts compiled well into the sixteenth century, does not mean that he or they necessarily amalgamated such studies or saw them as mutually illuminating, at least the sources were transmitted together and could have encouraged comparative study. The make-up of *Cuprum purissimum* in particular suggests that as well as transmitting classical treatises on architecture, its compiler selected some information on pipe- and chest-making from an earlier source – or had a practical leaning in this direction himself – and then interpolated it, doing so because those were the areas noticeably absent from the best-known of all *ars mechanica* treatises, Vitruvius's *De architectura*.[15]

Whether their knowledge of Vitruvius depended ultimately on a lost Anglo-Saxon copy of the late eighth century as has been suggested,[16] various influential authors are known to have been familiar with parts or the whole of Book 10 of the *De architectura*. Early authors include those associated with abbeys important in organ-history: Charlemagne's biographer Einhard[17] and adviser Alcuin of Tours (and York), Alcuin's pupil Hraban Maur of Fulda, Hermannus Contractus of Reichenau. Alcuin and Einhard are 'the first two men to show any knowledge of Vitruvius after the Dark Ages', and one fine extant copy (London, British Library, Harley 2767) may have originated in the palace scriptorium of Charlemagne (Reynolds 1986: 441). Later authors familiar with Vitruvius include several with an interest in mechanics: Hugh (and Richard) of St-Victor, Vincent of Beauvais, William of Malmesbury and Theodorich of St-Trond. Those who probably knew some of its contents at least indirectly include the compiler of the *Mappae clavicula* and Bishop Bernward of Hildesheim. Early copies are known to have been in the libraries of Reichenau and Corvey (ninth century), Murbach (the 'Sélestat manuscript', from St Gall?),[18] Salzburg, Bamberg, Regensburg, Fulda (ninth century), Gorze, Toul, Corbie, Rouen, Soissons, Cluny, Montecassino and Bury St Edmunds, at least by the twelfth century, and extant copies made in or before the eleventh century include some originating in northern France (several), Cologne (including St Pantaleon – see pp. 127 and 255) and Hildesheim.[19] This is a very broad sweep, and it seems hardly feasible that Aquitaine, Catalonia or Lombardy had no similar knowledge of the treatise.

[14] Sachs 1980: 34, 252–8 (*Cuprum purissimum*); Dodwell 1961: lvii–lxx (Theophilus); for the *Mappae clavicula*, see below p. 269.

[15] At least one word-formula suggests Vitruvius to have been a point of reference for the author of *Cuprum purissimum*: Sachs 1980: 264.

[16] B. Bischoff, 'Die Überlieferung der technischen Literatur', *Settimane* 18 (Spoleto, 1971), 267–96 and plates 1–3, here 273. On the missing archetype responsible for the two main branches of medieval Vitruvius transmission, see J.-P. Chausserie-Laprée, 'Un nouveau stemma Vitruvien', *Revue des Etudes Latines* 47 (1969), 347–77.

[17] On Einhard, Vitruvius, Theophilus and the Book of Moses, see Chapter 15.

[18] For the treatise 'Bern Anon' containing both *Cuprum purissimum* and the pipe-measurement texts in the 'Sélestat manuscript', see Sachs 1970: 20, 39. Further on the last in K.-A. Wirth, 'Bemerkungen zum Nachleben Vitruvs im 9. und 10. Jahrhundert und zu dem Schlettstädter Vitruv-Codex', *KC* 20 (1967), 281–91.

[19] C. H. Krinsky, 'Seventy-eight Vitruvius manuscripts', *JWCI* 30 (1967), 36–70. On BL Harley 2767 not being a copy made in Cologne, see Reynolds 1986: 441. On the Bury St Edmunds copy, R. M. Thomson, 'The library of Bury St Edmunds in the eleventh and twelfth centuries', *Speculum* 47 (1972), 617–45.

That so many copies of Vitruvius's description of a hydraulis (see below) were therefore made in or passed around the monastic houses of the Carolingian and Ottonian periods is sufficient to explain how any medieval writer or artist got to know of the Roman organ and of the part played by Ctesibius. One might even expect there to be much more reference to it than there is; according to Sachs 1970: 159 (*index nominum*), neither Vitruvius nor Ctesibius is referred to by name in any of the medieval texts concerned with pipe-measurement. But perhaps this is not so surprising since Roman–Greek authors give no detail of pipes themselves. From this fact alone one might conclude that pipe-measurement texts are rather to be seen as one side of the Carolingian attempt to construct a practical theory of music, thus more comparable to music-theory's definitions of mode and scale than to Vitruvius's *ars mechanica* treatise. At the same time, it is possible that since Vitruvius texts had no illustrations,[20] readers were free to conjecture what the water-organ looked like. If this was so, another distinct possibility emerges: it was a reading of Vitruvius that led the artist of the Utrecht Psalter to draw the *pair of cylinders*, the *double tetrachord* and the *altar-like appearance* for the organs of Psalms 150 and '151' (see p. 161).

A question is how far the three areas of study – the *ars liberalis*, the *ars mechanica*, the making of organs – were related. If an arithmetical study of organ-pipe scales (liberal arts) is distinct from the written description of certain crafts (mechanical arts), is the written description of certain crafts any closer to the work of actual craftsmen (organ-builders)? In Vitruvius's ten books, the architect ('leader of builders') is the conceiver, planner and supervisor of temple colonnades and water-organs, both of which would be made by the non-reading or at least non-writing craftsmen who had their own techniques and traditions. Perhaps any such book is marginal to what went on in the workplace:

there are many aspects of Roman civil engineering which we know were skilfully and frequently practised which find no place in *De architectura* at all . . . [Furthermore,] we know of no substantial evidence that Vitruvius's book was valued as a building manual by his contemporaries.[21]

Were organ-archaeology to have produced as much material evidence as, say, aqueduct-archaeology, it is likely that one would want to make similar points about Theophilus's treatise on organ-building. Yet Vitruvius did give information of use to the worker or his supervisor, and medieval treatises referring to organs are sometimes similar in this respect: 'written description of mechanical arts' does overlap 'the work of actual craftsmen' when, for example, it gives concrete measurements. If it is so that concrete measurements were mostly 'self-evident for medieval organ-building' (Sachs 1980: 73) and were the domain of the actual maker, one might wonder why *any* measurements are given, however imprecise or generic. By giving such actual detail, the writer is merging the three areas – literate study, technical description, organ-making – not consistently and never completely but nevertheless discernibly.

---

20 At least, in extant copies: see Krinsky (note 19): 41.
21 N. A. F. Smith, 'Attitudes to Roman engineering and the question of the inverted siphon', *HT* 1 (1976), 45–71, here 50.

Vitruvius's closing remarks on the water-organ distinguish between the reader and the craftsman:

neque	nor is [the theory of this machine]
omnibus expedita ad intellegendum	readily understood by everyone
praeter eos qui in his generibus	beyond those who have experience
habent exercitationem.	in such things.
Quodsi qui parum intellexerit	Anyone who has not well understood
ex scriptis,	it on the basis of what is written,
cum ipsam rem cognoscet,	when he knows the thing itself
profecto inveniet	will certainly find
curiose et subtiliter	that it is curiously and ingeniously
omnia ordinata.	contrived in all respects.

This is a most interesting remark, vital to an understanding of what is written anywhere about organs. It seems that in order to understand, one needs to inspect the object itself, i.e. an object already made by craftsmen with their own traditions. On one hand, then, the reader can go only so far; on the other, the craftsman is independent of what is written. It would have been of little concern to the stonemasons of the eleventh century that the great church of Cluny III (or St-Riquier or Fulda) had an architect who was partly responsible for a plan that followed Vitruvian proportions.[22] Much the same must have been true for the workmen of the Aachen octagon, where there is also some reason for supposing that Vitruvius influenced the layout and the manner in which it was calculated;[23] see also p. 113. Vitruvius belonged to a long, literate tradition that recognized in general terms the validity of simple arithmetical proportion, while stonemasons belonged to a craft with its own tradition, one (like the craft of musicians) that attributed its tools-in-trade to certain great inventors of the past.[24]

A key question about Vitruvius and the water-organ he describes is what either the author or the instrument had to do with organ-builders of his own day. If Roman craftsmen did not read Vitruvius and yet, as we know not least from Vitruvius's own words, organs already existed, had craftsmen learnt from other treatises? In general that must be out of the question. But if there was a continuous, 'subcultural' craft of instrument-makers independent of literature, what then is the literature speaking about – only one of several kinds of instrument, presumably the most complicated? Were there types of Mediterranean hydraules different from those described by Vitruvius or Hero? Have later readers been misled by these treatises to think that the Greeks and Romans knew only the water-organ?

While 'Yes' seems likely to be the answer to all such questions, it does not become any easier to trace the continuous, subcultural craft of organ-making. Whoever was interested in Vitruvius's description of a water-organ, there must still have been a craft of instrument-making during the early medieval centuries. This was independent

---

[22] K. J. Conant, 'The after-life of Vitruvius in the Middle Ages', *JSAH* 27 (1968), 33–8, and C. Heitz, 'Vitruve et l'architecture du Haut Moyen Age', *Settimane* 22 (Spoleto, 1975), 725–52.
[23] See Boeckelmann 1957.
[24] The stonemason's level, square and lathe are attributed to one Theodoros (Pliny, *Natural History* 7.56, 36.19).

of *artes mechanicae* authors (the monks in their libraries) and, even if one sees those monks as occasional supervisors or active craftsmen themselves, the point is that the craft was sustained irrespective of anything that was ever written about it. Perhaps there was no break in tradition between these Roman and medieval subcultural crafts; but that can never be more than conjectural, since one does not know precisely where any organ of 100 BC or AD 1000 was actually made. Perhaps some organs were constructed by general instrument-makers such as a period of settled political conditions would encourage, and the only difficulty for such craftsmen would be casting the bronze pipes. Perhaps other organs were made under the supervision of a literate priest who had learnt the technologies elsewhere (as at Aachen in 826 and Petershausen in *c.* 1130); but presumably he learnt not from reading books but from extant instruments made by craftsmen, so the same questions remain. All such thinking tends to the conclusion that there was indeed a 'continuous, subcultural craft of organ-building' being practised before the fourteenth century contracts name the men, but the *artes mechanicae* authors do not describe it. Like quarks, the existence of an organ-building craft can only be deduced: nobody now has seen it or knows what it was like.

Hero of Alexandria

The *Pneumatika* 1.42 of Hero of Alexandria (mid-first century AD?) describes a water-organ that appears to be less developed, although the underlying information in both Hero and Vitruvius could well derive from the same lost treatise attributed to Ctesibius and described by Philo of Byzantium. As a Greek source on the more restricted subject of pneumatic devices, Hero's description does not compare with Vitruvius's for influence in the medieval West, although it does seem – how, is not known – to have some bearing on certain parts of the organ-treatise text *Cuprum purissimum* (see Chapter 16). Otherwise, circulation of Hero in the West before the late fifteenth century is unlikely to have been widespread, although he was known to Arab translators and, in the twelfth century, to Sicilian.[25]

Hero's writings are on a much bigger scale than Vitruvius's and include, in the *Book on Pneumatics*, extensive accounts of various devices activated by falling or rising water (fire-fighting syphons 1.28, fountains 1.29f, automatic door-opener 1.17–18, a wine-pourer 1.23), by warmed air (1.38–9) or by air-and-water. These are in addition to the regular water-organ (1.42) and a similar device whose wind-raising is activated by a windmill device tripping the lever of a cylinder-pump (1.43 – the last chapter of Book 1). Book 2 includes steam-power and a simple pump (like a bicycle pump, 2.18), in addition to the separate treatise on automata.[26] For the hydraulis only one cylinder is described, not two, and this has generally been taken to mean that Hero's organ was less developed than Vitruvius's. But since no outlet

---

25 M. Boas, 'Hero's *Pneumatica*: a study of its transmission and influence', *Isis* 40 (1949), 38–48.
26 Schmidt 1899A: 193–203 (text in Greek and German, with good figures); English translation in Perrot 1971: 28–34, with plate xxiii.

clack-valve is described by Hero – a vital component – it is possible that the account as we know it does not set out to include everything or describe certain things that would be self-evident. Therefore, directions for a cylinder would apply for two as for one.

The oldest extant source is Venice, Bibliotica Marciana, MS 516 (*c.* 1250), which has a diagram showing eight pipes in what look like pipefeet-sockets, nowhere described in the account but no doubt like those at Aquincum and the 'rings' referred to by Vitruvius. Quite why this of all details is so well documented is not entirely clear – because it is something easy to see for non-expert writers and also conspicuous to later archaeologists? The copy London, British Library, Harley 5589 (sixteenth century) shows only seven pipes.[27] Whether this ambivalence between seven and eight reflects the thinking of much later western scribes or theorists (cf. Theophilus, Chapter 15) cannot be demonstrated in the absence of earlier drawings. But since both numbers had special associations throughout the patristic and medieval period[28] – not least in music- and organ-theory – it is not unlikely that the drawings attached to copies of Hero represent what medieval copyists thought rather than what the ancient Greeks made.[29]

As with Vitruvius and Theophilus, Hero's description is made in such a way as to leave various practical interpretations possible: the reader can extrapolate the principles described to a larger organ, and the general layout can vary widely. It is unlikely that Hero is describing one and only one version of the hydraulis. Nor is this regular water-organ necessarily more 'realistically' described than that whose pump is 'unrealistically' operated by a windmill mechanism, although the drawings in Schmidt 1899A make it appear so to most modern writers (for example Hammerstein 1986: 25). For natural wind-power to be made to operate the reciprocal action of a pump-and-cylinder clearly some gear has to be designed, and one can only guess whether for Hero this was something self-evident, something for an actual maker to devise for himself or something of which he (Hero) has no idea. Such possibilities could explain the many and various *areas of silence* in all the treatises of the *ars mechanica* tradition.

It is generally agreed that for raising the wind of the regular organ, the piston-lever can be operated by foot or body-weight (Schmidt 1899A: 194 and Neuburger 1930: 230), and that for playing the pipes, Hero is describing a spring-loaded key-mechanism. Sliders (πώματα, 'lids') which can be worked either separately or all together (ἤτοι πάντα ἤ τινα αὐτῶν) are pushed to allow the wind up to the pipes and are connected to the keys. These keys take the form of little pivoted 'squares'

[27]   Discussion in Farmer 1931: 159–64.

[28]   Seven, the 'key to the universe' in neoplatonic numerology (Connolly 1980: 16f); eight, the 'number of resurrection' for Sts Augustine, Ambrose, Basil, Jerome and consequently the architects of Carolingian and other octagons (see Heitz 1963: 124f, 137f).
        On the musical relevance of Jewish and Near-Eastern allusions to the 'divine seven' and the 'great eight', see E. Werner, *The Sacred Bridge*, 2 (New York, 1984), 179–80.

[29]   As already suggested in F. W. Galpin, 'Notes on a Roman hydraulis', *The Reliquary*, n.s. 10 (1904), 152–64. It is unrealistic to assume not only that these medieval drawings go back to Hero but that the illustrations in Schmidt 1899A, 'taken from older editions', are such as to 'make an understanding of the text extraordinarily easier' (Hammerstein 1986: 16–17).

(resembling the later organ-square) the top arm of which is pressed down by the finger. The vertical limb of the square pushes in the slider and is tied to a spring of horn, which pulls it back (and therefore the slider out) when the finger is taken off. Although the description and drawing[30] concern a single slider, with single slider-hole and pipe, it is possible that the sliders had several holes, as many as there were pipe-ranks,[31] or alternatively one large hole admitting wind to a latitudinal channel. Perhaps *auloi* for 'the pipes' indicates reeds, as seems to be the case with the pipes of the automata briefly described elsewhere in the treatise (*Pneumatika* 1.17, 1.43, 2.11, 2.35).

From this short summary, it is clear that Hero is not explicit about the number of sliders, the number of pipe-ranks, the type of pipes, any of the dimensions and any of the other design-details down to the material for the keys. In Schmidt's interpretation of the mechanical layout there can be discerned a knowledge of much later organs,[32] in so far as the horn-springs are held in a front longitudinal box-like structure in which only the 'key-tops' are visible, just as they are in a nineteenth-century harmonium. But this only underlines the interpretative rôle necessarily played by the reader of a treatise in the tradition of the *artes mechanicae*: he made his own practical version of what the treatise was outlining, which was so written as to enable him to do this. A more literal interpretation of Hero as in Perrot 1965: 55 may actually be more misleading than Schmidt's since the treatise itself is not to be taken literally.

Muristos and Arabic sources

Two descriptions of organs under the name of one Muristos survive from middle medieval sources,[33] and although neither the pedigree of these sources nor even the date of their 'author' is certain,[34] it is probable that they ultimately derive from the Ctesibius tradition and belong to the Arabic and/or Byzantine body of technical literature that circulated in the eastern Mediterranean, now generally associated with Alexandria.

The first organ has twelve pipes and makes use of a skin for the wind-stabilizer (fed by 'mouths' – probably those of bellows not of men)[35] and of three airtight skins connected by tubes to serve as divisions of a chest. Some kind of valve (a fingerkey?) admits wind to each of the pipes; Farmer 1931: 72 calls them 'stoppers', having 'the form of sliders' like those in some western psalter-drawings. In one copy, they are said to be (and are so drawn) at the middle height of the pipes. Perhaps this means

---

[30]   Also in the Copenhagen manuscript, Copenhagen, Biblioteca Universitatis Hauniensis, Codex Thott. 215. See Drachmann 1963: 193–4.

[31]   But not so understood by Schmidt 1899A: 197, who interprets it as a single hole.

[32]   Schmidt 1899A: 195, reproduced also in later literature such as T. Beck, *Beiträge zur Geschichte des Maschinenbaus* (Berlin, 2/1900), 25.

[33]   An authoritative description and translation are still those of Farmer 1931: 62ff, 127ff.

[34]   One of Farmer's most important (but still unexplored) observations is the similarity of nomenclature between 'Muristos' and 'Aristu' (Muslim version of 'Aristotle', Farmer 1932: 12) and of Arabic orthography between 'Muristos' and 'Ktesibios' (in Arabic script, *ibid.*, 19). The Beirut copy of Muristos is twelfth century, but there are references to his work from the eighth or ninth (*ibid.*, 16, 60, 127, 150).

[35]   The 'mouths' (so called in the text) are those of men, according to Farmer 1931: 70ff (hence Perrot 1965: 244), but are more likely to be those of bellows, according to Hardouin 1966: 47.

that the keys operating the sliders were placed in a row higher than the pipe-mouths, as was probably the case at Aquincum; if so, some kind of 'key-square' as described by Hero must have been used. Although it does not say so, a chest in the form of three skins implies three wooden boxes entirely encasing, or encased by, such skins: if well managed, this construction was both airtight and able to distribute the wind equally, like the horizontal board placed inside the chest of the treatise *Cuprum purissimum* (see p. 280). Linking the skins also means that they shared the same wind-pressure, something not shown in the Utrecht Psalter drawings, where each chest has its own pair of cylinder-pumps. Some genuine 'musical' effect seems to have been intended for the Muristos organ, for although it is uncertain what the notes themselves were (Farmer 1931: 74) or even whether 'twelve pipes' means a nucleus of twelve notes repeated over a longer scale, the description remarks on specific *affetti* produced by various combinations of sustained organ-sound.

The second organ is also described as having three skins, but its wind is compressed by water and feeds a loud siren or military signal-organ of one to four or five pipes. The wind itself is raised by three 'Greek bellows' (*ziqq Rumi* – Farmer 1931: 131, 136), which were interpreted as round, concertina-like ribbed bellows in one of the two drawings found in early copies.[36] But these could be none other than the round metal cylinders as known about from Hero: in the drawing one looks at them from above, and the middle 'rib' could well represent the hoop reinforcing the cylinder-under-pressure of a kind drawn in the Utrecht Psalter (see p. 155). For the possibility that there were western medieval concertina-like bellows, however, see p. 329.

There was another eastern organ, actual or allegorical, known about in the West. The so-called *Letter of St Jerome to Dardanus* (PL 30.213–15)[37] briefly describes an organ in Jerusalem being used as a signal, with a penetrating sound, twelve bronze pipes, a pair of elephant skins and twelve or (depending on the copy) fifteen bellows. It is quoted in the mid-ninth century by Hraban Maur, Bishop of Mainz, as the basis for symbolic exegesis: the twelve pipes, that is to say the twelve apostles, 'give out a huge sound' (*sonum nimium emittit* – PL 111.496–7), the sound of the gospel emanating from Jerusalem itself. Whether or not he meant his report to be entirely symbolic, without actuality, the author of the *Letter* may have been relying on a text-tradition to which the Muristos description of an actual siren also belonged – earlier, later or at much the same time, as the case may be. That both concern technology in Arabic lands makes some such connection plausible.[38] Use of the *Letter* by Hraban does not suggest he knew a siren-organ of twelve pipes, with elephant-hide stabilizer or chest; rather the size of the organ and the travel of its sound (a thousand double spaces) characterize the spreading and the awakening

---

[36] Arabic source, London, British Library, MS Or. 9649, reproduced in Farmer 1931: 134.

[37] A preliminary survey of the *Letter to Dardanus* and its illustrations in various copies, in Hammerstein 1959; further in Seebass 1973: 141–4 and Hammerstein 1986: 65ff. Hammerstein's view that the 'letter' originated not in the fifth but in the ninth century is generally adopted: see earliest copies discussed in D.A. Bullough, *Carolingian Renewal: Sources and Heritage* (Manchester, 1991), 244f. For a well-reasoned interpretation of the *Letter* as allegory, see Richenhagen 1984: 190–3.

[38] Both Farmer 1931: 16f, 60f and Hammerstein 1959: 121–2, note the similarities between the two accounts.

effect of the gospel. The same period saw a description of the singers sent out from Rome to teach chant a century earlier 'as the twelve apostles' (MGH SS 1.734f).

The Muristos sources make no mention of Jerusalem or St Jerome, but they do go on to speak of the author making an organ or siren for the 'King of the Inner Franks' (*Afranjat al-dakhila*) which more than one modern writer has identified as none other than Pippin's organ of 757 (see Chapter 9) and even Roland's horn in the *Chanson de Roland* (see Farmer 1931: 151–2). It would have been one of the models with several pipes and of major dimensions: some 6 m high, with a capacity of 550 litres.[39] If it is so that the Muristos text itself belongs to Pippin's period,[40] the suggestion that the organ of 757 was a siren cannot be easily dismissed. The *Letter to Dardanus* too conveys something of the mystique of Muristos-like sirens to its many readers sitting in Carolingian scriptoria, for it speaks of a *tuba* producing enormous volume from three bronze pipes,[41] presumably – if real – from high pressure provided by a piston-and-cylinder pump of the Alexandrian type. Gospel-allegory or not, this stirred the imagination.

Whatever the connection between these various written sources, one can see that Arabic writings do not offer so very much less than western writings of the same period: copies of Hero's *Mechanics*, reports of Muristos, descriptions of automata and encyclopedia references to *urghan* (ninth to twelfth century)[42] all suggest there to have been in Arab circles at least a theoretical interest in organs. The western legacy of *c.* 1000 differs from this in three particular respects, none of them providing much organological information but nevertheless crucial: western sources include reports of actual organs being placed in monastic churches; there is a developed practical theory of notes and how to produce them with an organ; and there must have been an intermittent or continuous craft of organ-making being practised in many centres removed from royal courts. The last is only hinted at in documentation, and so far one cannot be certain that it was unique to western Christendom. But the great developments in the western organ of the thirteenth and fourteenth centuries may well have been made possible by the fact that it depended on no single, fixed, conventionalized, closed-shop craft of organ-making, as one imagines to have been the case in the eastern Mediterranean.

The Muristos accounts also include elements of technical description that give some idea of organ-makers' procedures. They made various uses of hides (whole skins), such as Theophilus describes; they used brass pipes, the thickness of a stick, as air-ducts between chests, as well as larger tapered ducts from the stabilizer (tapered to increase pressure?); and there were speaking pipes of various diameters, with a 'sound box' for each pipe. While the last evokes the reed-and-boot of a reed-pipe it could also indicate the mouth area of flue-pipes, especially the complex mouths known from the Aquincum organ; another possibility, also hinted at by Aquincum,

---

[39]   For the dimensions etc., Farmer 1931: 128, 151, 153. Also E. Wiedeman & F. Hauser, 'Byzantinische und arabische akustische Instrumente', *Archiv für Geschichte der Naturwissenschaft und der Technik* 8 (1917), 140–66, here 155 ('King of Inner Franks' = *al franga al dâchila*).

[40]   For this possibility, see Hardouin 1966: 23f, 34f.

[41]   Farmer 1931: 120, 128f and plate 2; Hammerstein 1959: 122–4.

[42]   Items in Shiloah 1979: 49, 63, 66 (copy of Hero – ninth century?), 70, 96, 211, 231, 285, 286 (2). The last three are Muristos copies.

is that pipe-sockets or rings fixed on the chest enabled different pipe-resonators to be fitted. The part of Muristos texts concerned with 'varying diameters' is confused and is more likely to refer to pipe-lengths than widths,[43] but as with Hero's directions, leaving such questions open may also be giving the reader useful choice.

There is another detail of importance. Although no information is given on any woodwork, on the bellows or cylinders, or on the pipe-making, all of which were presumably the business of specialized crafts, it is clear that the twelve-pipe organ of Muristos required a framework, a firm structure for the placing of the blowers and their levers (i.e. for the bellows themselves). Some such structure is the element that in the West led to the full timber organ-case; see Chapter 18. Each chest-division has four pipes, the gross lengths of which are x, 2x, 3x and 4x (strikingly like the two sets on the Utrecht Psalter chest for Psalm 150), and it is possible that the chest-division was meant to allow two, three or four pipes to be played all at once. Diatonically tuned or not, the difference in length would give the pipes some kind of blended *quadrillon* or carillon effect such as would be suitable for a penetrating signal-instrument.

A large bell also described by Muristos gave out combined, clanging sounds:[44] it was an egg-shaped, copper-alloy bell of some 8.75 m in circumference, partitioned inside with four chambers (each with an ironstone ball) whose volumes were made proportionately so that they would produce a consonant *quadrillon* effect. Like a huge sleighbell, it was shaken at the end of a rope by men whose ears needed to be stopped. From this it is clear that for signalling purposes, the travel and clangour of bells – and therefore of pipes? – was known to be increased by several pitches sounding at once. Those pumping the siren-organ also needed their ears stopped.

Another detail in the twelve-pipe organ recalls the Utrecht Psalter water-organ: the neck of the round *pnigeus* protrudes through the top of the cistern, 'of a shape consistent with' it (Perrot 1971: 198), which suggests a round cistern for a round *pnigeus* – or could have done so to a psalter-artist reading any such phrase in translation. Furthermore, Muristos, Vitruvius and the Psalter artist all understand the instrument to have a solid base below the cistern and chest. Are the sources for the Utrecht Psalter organs after all written not iconographic, based on some manuscript complex to which Muristos also ultimately belonged?

Aquincum

Despite all their uncertainties, the organ-remains of *c.* 228 found in 1931 on the site of the Roman town of Aquincum do give a certain framework for understanding late Roman organ-technology. The little instrument was found in the cellar of 'what appears to have been the headquarters of a guild of woolweavers' who were associated with fire-fighting duties[45] and is of very modest dimensions: the topboard of the chest is 27 × 8 cm (Kaba 1976: 15).

---

[43] For the 'sound box', Farmer 1931: 66; for variable pipe-lengths rather than pipe-widths, Hardouin 1966: 38–9.
[44] Or was designed to do so: translated in Wiedemann & Hauser (see note 39): 163–6.
[45] W. W. Hyde, 'The recent discovery of an inscribed water-organ at Budapest', *Transactions & Proceedings of the American Philological Association* 69 (1938), 392–410, here 395. (Contains useful bibliography but questionable interpretation of the organ.)

Various details of the general structure, the pipe-making and the keyboard-action emerge from studies of the remains:

wind-raising: although there may well have been a water-cistern with *pnigeus*, there is no evidence now for wind-raising either by bellows or by piston-and-cylinder. Remnants were probably lost in the 1931 dig: so have some others since, such as the rim of what may have been the *pnigeus*, an item listed in the original find.[46] The kind of water-pump found at Silchester and made from a wooden block and some lead piping (see p. 315) suggests what Roman ingenuity could devise with local materials; but it would not easily survive or be recognized for what it was.

bellows: although there is no evidence, a pair is not unlikely for such a tiny organ. The metal ring of 14 cm diameter reported in notes made in the 1930s would have been too large to be the collar of a *conflatorium* of some kind (see Chapter 15), fastening the leather around a rim.[47] A further possibility arises from another remnant found in the dig: a rimmed bronze tube 45 mm long by 30 mm wide probably fitted into the bass of the windchest and held the narrow windtrunk, perhaps from a cistern.

chest and pipes: whether the spruce chest was carved or joined is not clear, but it was lined inside and out with soldered bronze. Key-sliders (with four holes) and their runners are of thick cast bronze, as are the pipe-channel sliders; the latter have one rectangular hole. There were four rows of small, narrow-scaled pipes, three with oak stoppers, one open (Walcker-Mayer: 1970). The open pipes consist of brass plates (79 per cent copper, *c.* 18 per cent zinc – Kaba 1976: 45ff) rolled around a mandrel, with seams soldered on an overlap. The upper lip is soldered on to the curved front edge of the pipe which is cut diagonally (front down to back) at the mouth; the foot was rolled on a conical mandrel, its top pressed in at front and back to make a thin straight windway under the upper lip, then soldered to the upper pipe. There was thus no horizontal languid inside the pipe, but adjustment at the lips was possible. The stopped pipes were, by accident or design, made from a somewhat different alloy (85 per cent copper, *c.* 13 per cent zinc) and were also rolled. According to Walcker-Mayer: 1970 their construction differed, with the high upper lip cut into the front segment of the pipe; the foot is pressed in only at the back, a languid is soldered flat on top of the foot, leaving a semicircular windway at the front, and the upper surface of the languid is soldered to a short cylinder in which the upper pipebody fits. (Was this construction to allow easy adjustment of windway and/or upper lip, or to hold other pipe-resonators when required? Both?) The pipe-feet fitted into a short conical tube soldered on to the topboard, perhaps something like Vitruvius's rings.

---

[46]   The arguments for Aquincum being a water-organ, based on analysis of corrosion patterns in the metal parts, are made in E. L. Szonntagh, 'Is the pipe organ discovered at Aquincum a water organ?', *Scientific Honeyweller* 2.4 (1981), 54–60. On the stopped ranks, see the same author's 'Organ tone-colour and Pipe Dimensions', *Studia Musicologica Academiae Hungaricae* (forthcoming).

[47]   Reported in Hyde (see note 45): 394.

Particularly uncertain are the key-action and the purpose of the four rows of pipes:

> *keyboard*: a metal hook seems to have pulled out the end of the metal slider, presumably producing both a large amount of 'give' in the movement and an unavoidable rattling sound. The hook could have been attached to a 'keyboard': elmwood squares of the kind described by Hero are not impossible to imagine from the remaining fragments. A key would pull the slider with the hook, and the slider was pushed back by a bronze leaf-spring set vertically at the front of the organ. Each key would be some 1.4 cm wide, probably so arranged that its key-surface was the upper not lower arm of the square (Walcker-Mayer: 1970); the pipe-mouths, facing out, would not be covered by the square, and the playing-position could be well above the chest. In another interpretation of the remains, there is no sign of a keyboard, only spring-loaded sliders, and the remnants of wood were part of wooden handles attached to the slider-ends themselves;[48] the hooks then must have been for pulling by hand? Such spring-loaded keyless sliders are not impossible for the earliest medieval Christian organs. Although press-keys would give greater agility, in neither mechanism can it have been easy to repeat a note quickly.
>
> *the rows of pipes*: the poor condition of the pipe-work, with pipe-feet mostly missing, makes interpretation conjectural. Walcker-Mayer 1972: 54–8 proposes a diatonic Pythagorean scale, with four ranks at different pitches:
>
> > open pipes at c'
> > stopped pipes at f, g and a'
> > compass: c' d' e♭' f' g' a♭' a' b' c" d" e♭" f" g"
> > pitch: e♭' = 440Hz

But since neither pitch nor note-names can have corresponded to later convention, it is reasonable to see the compass as the following sequence:

> a h c d e f f♯ g a h c d e

Kaba 1976: 41, however, proposes a diatonic distribution that was 'in all probability' as follows:

> c' d' e' f' g' a' h' c" d" e" f" g" a"

at about modern pitch for the open rank. This crucial question of note-sequence is unlikely ever to be answered, but it is possible that the four ranks provided four different pitches, and/or four different tunings, over one octave or so.

The maker of the metal parts of the organ was evidently well experienced and had 'an excellent knowledge of materials'.[49] Solder was of tin, pipe-material mostly a zinc-copper alloy, other bronze parts purer copper or with greatly variable tin/lead mixtures such as would be normal at the time.

Not the least interesting aspect of the Aquincum organ was an earlier discovery, in 1881, of a contemporary sarcophagus north of Obuda near Aquincum, saluting one Sabina of whom it was said, though she has no known connection with the present organ,

---

[48] S. Szigeti, 'Die ungelösten Probleme der römischen Orgel von Aquincum', *Studia musicologica* 13 (1971), 3–13.
[49] E. Gegus, report in Kaba 1976: 53; on alloys, *ibid.*, 50.

spectata in populo   in the sight of the people,
hydraula grata regebat.   the favourite organist played.   (Kaba 1976: 42)

Regebat might suggest 'holding sway over the people', but it is also the word used by Wulfstan of Winchester for 'ruling the alphabet' or keyboard (see p. 194, line 156). The Aquincum organ itself also has an inscription, a bronze plate that includes the word *hydram*, suggesting *hydra* as an abbreviation for *hydraulis*. Alluding to the organ itself in an organ-inscription is not unknown at a later period (see also the Malmesbury organ, p. 200) and suggests that some of the references to organs in late antiquity also concerned modest organs of the Aquincum type. This was no instrument for theatres and amphitheatres.

Aquincum itself, capital of the province of Pannonia Inferior (western Hungary) and thus on the border of the empire, may have provided the circumstances for such luxury items as domestic musical instruments. It had recently become a *colonia* under Septimius Severus (193–211) and benefited from Caracalla's early third-century reorganization, seeing its major public rebuilding

matched by a growth in the production of luxury goods and even locally made crafts, indicating that for the first time the region was sufficiently prosperous to support local artisans, even if the quality of their work seldom matched the Gallic, Rhaetian, Syrian and Italian products they copied.[50]

Similar remarks could be made about other cities on the borders of the third-century empire, in all points of the compass. However fitfully, such craft-traditions may have survived through to the period of the monastic expansion across the north and west borderlands of the ex-Roman Empire in the tenth century.

[50] P. J. Geary, *Before France & Germany: the Creation and Transformation of the Merovingian World* (New York, 1988), 19. Recent speculation on the organ (J. Minárovics, 'Miert volt az Aquincumi tűzoltóság orgonája víziorgona?', *Budapest Régiségei* 28 (1991), 261–82) strengthens the case for its being a water-organ, though not conclusively.

15

The technologies of Theophilus

The organ parts of the treatise now generally called the *De diversis artibus* and written in the period 1110/40 by the monk Theophilus,[1] have been the subject of various interpretations ever since they were printed in the middle of the nineteenth century in Hopkins & Rimbault's *The Organ* (text plus an English translation). The treatise gives the fullest account of organ-making before the very different work of Henri Arnaut de Zwolle in the fifteenth century (see Chapter 16), and shares with it signs of being both incomplete and something of a compilation. Like Arnaut de Zwolle, Theophilus is describing a type of organ that certainly existed – probably an individual example – but how up-to-date or how widespread its manufacture was can only be guessed, as must be the steps by which organ-making had reached this particular stage. The treatise's relationship to both the general tradition of practical treatises (the *artes mechanicae*) and the brief texts dealing with organ-pipe proportions (the *mensura fistularum*) will be outlined in the present and following chapter.

Point of origin

Identification of Theophilus as Roger of Helmarshausen (a monastery about fifteen miles south of Corvey) was made on the grounds of the phrase *qui et Rugerus* written in a seventeenth-century hand on a twelfth-century copy (Vienna, Österreichische Nationalbibliothek, MS 2527), and though formerly challenged is now generally taken to be plausible.[2] Even so, the question cannot be regarded as settled (see below), and the describing of practical and useful activities can hardly be proof itself that the author was a Benedictine monk, as sometimes proposed (Brepohl 1987: 18). Of the seven most important extant copies of the manuscript, two are from the twelfth century, three from the thirteenth and one each from the fourteenth and fifteenth.[3] Only one of the copies, the thirteenth-century manuscript BL Harley

---

[1]   Title and date according to Dodwell 1961; called *Diversarum artium schedula* in some earlier editions and references. B. Bischoff, in *Mittelalterlichen Studien* (Stuttgart, 1967), 2.175–82 implies a date of *c.* 1100 or so; Van Engen 1980: 158ff finds the third decade of the century the most likely, its area of origin Cologne–Westphalia. In 'Cultural climates and technological advance in the Middle Ages', *Viator* 2 (1971), 171–202, here 194, L. White specifies 1122/3, based on the treatise's putative reaction to writings of St Bernard (see note 36 below).

[2]   Challenged in Hawthorne & Smith 1963: xv–xvi; the question examined in great detail, with information on the personnel of the monasteries concerned, in E. Freise, 'Roger von Helmarshausen in seiner monastischen Umwelt', *FMSt* 15 (1981), 180–293, esp. 193ff.

[3]   Twelfth century: Vienna, Österreichische Nationabibliothek, MS 2527 (Westphalian?) and Wolfenbüttel, Herzog August-Bibliothek, MS 4373 (= cod. Guelph Gudianus lat. 2°69, – from Cologne?). Thirteenth century: London, British Library, Harley 3915; Cambridge, University Library, MS 1131 (= Ee. 9.39); and London, British Library, Egerton 840A. Fourteenth: Leipzig, Universitätsbibliothek, MS 1157. Fifteenth: Paris, Bibliothèque Nationale, lat. 6741. (Dodwell 1961: lvii–lxx and note 43 below.)

3915 (a fair copy probably made in or near Cologne, perhaps from St Pantaleon), contains the complete organ-chapters as known, and it cannot be certain therefore that there never were any more chapters, or further parts of extant chapters, belonging to a treatise which in its present form looks at times like a compilation of different sections. That St Pantaleon probably also had an eleventh-century copy of Vitruvius (Reynolds 1986: 442) may well bear on Theophilus: see below.

Known from a document of 1100 (Dodwell 1961: xli), Roggerus or Rugerus or Rogkerus was a goldsmith with experience of chalice-decoration such as is described in the treatise, a treatise now said to represent

a completely new departure . . . the amount of planning and forethought which should go into the artist's work is admirably understood and explained. Such planning eventually allowed a division of labor, the use of preparatory drawings, and a careful estimate of a project's aesthetic effect.   (Davis-Weyer 1986: 172, 176)

On the other hand, even when the difficulty of understanding some of Theophilus's terms is allowed for, he could not be said to have fully achieved the aims of technological description as they became self-evident to authors of technical books in later periods, including today's. The section on bells, for instance, does not indicate precisely what their several shapes were,[4] and while indeed this may be a detail best left to craftsmen who in Saxony as elsewhere kept to tradition, other basic elements are ambiguous or as good as absent. It is clear that the treatise is no handbook in the modern sense when the preface to Part 1 recommends that the user will read it through frequently (*saepe relegeris*) so as to retain it in the memory (*tenaci memoriae commendaveris*). Although this may not mean memorizing in the way that the psalms were memorized, and was in any case not unusual advice, it suggests that knowledge of the special crafts for those not previously trained in them would have to come from special memorizing. Perhaps it is also inviting the supervisor to establish a system or plan in his mind. Did one memorize in the library, either from reading oneself or having something read aloud, and then go down to the workshop?

The preface to Part 1 also explains why a monk would be describing crafts previously the domain of craftsmen, hinting at why so little technical is written about organs and why anything exists at all. With the treatise the reader will study those things – fine objects for church – that otherwise have to be imported only at great trouble, or learnt about only at great pains, by which Theophilus probably means a long apprenticeship to a master craftsman. Readers should not undervalue the teaching it offers just because it is offered freely and conveniently in a book. With this last remark he may well be countering views held in the twelfth century on the value of making technical descriptions, of putting into writing matters normally transmitted in practice through the crafts themselves, i.e. from one rude mechanic to another. Not all the monastic regions of Europe can have had the same attitudes to these questions, and it is only to be expected that 'practical theory' belonged to some areas rather than others. Where the treatise originated, therefore, is even

---

4   Pointed out by D. V. Thompson, 'Theophilus Presbyter: words and meaning in technical translation', *Speculum* 42 (1967), 313–39. Doubt about who wrote the bell chapters or authorized their inclusion (see Sachs 1973: 93) does not change this point.

more significant than who wrote it. Roger of Helmarshausen has been traced in connection with three particular churches (Stavelot in the Ardennes, Cologne St Pantaleon and finally Helmarshausen)[5] and thus in three different dioceses, Liège, Cologne and Hildesheim. All three monasteries would leave important implications about organ-history.

Stavelot belonged not only to the region of the Meuse in which various technologies were well developed (see pp. 316f) but must have participated, as a major house, in creating that body of music-theory that originated in the area between Prüm and Laon: the *Musica* and *Scolica Enchiriadis*, Hucbald, Regino, possibly Aurelian and others. That area also saw certain characteristic church-plans and church-designs, with complex west ends of various kinds but seldom otherwise with galleries (see Chapter 7). Theophilus's suggestions for making an opening for the organ in the upper wall (in the nave? – see below, Book 3 Chapter 83) may suggest that despite the old-fashioned nature of the organ he was describing, he was thinking in terms of a relatively large instrument, one needing its own location in such churches as Stavelot or St Pantaleon.

St Pantaleon, Cologne, was rebuilt in the years before 1000, with a large three-storeyed westwork, porch/atrium, aisleless nave (like Winchester) and transept-like *porticus* nearer the east end. There was an interim dedication in 980 for work instigated by the same Bruno, Archbishop of Cologne, whose own consecration had seen *organa*:[6] see p. 206. The upper storey of westwork or *porticus* offered an obvious location for any organ the church may have had at this period. Particularly interesting in view of Theophilus's likely connection with St Pantaleon is the recent discovery of the site of a bronze workshop in the monastery, located between the nave and cloister to the north, no longer in use by the later twelfth century but perhaps replaced by a larger shop elsewhere in the monastery. In Cologne as a whole, the technologies necessary for making organs must have been well advanced and the monastery's old connection (*fraternitas*) with St-Saulve, Valenciennes, even raises questions whether all along, from the days of Louis the Pious's organ-builder Georgius onwards (see Chapter 9), there had been a distinct interest in organs pursued by several major monasteries within the region Laon–St-Amand–Cologne–Prüm and including Valenciennes, Lobbes and Aachen. Although nothing certain is known of organs here or in eleventh-century Cologne itself, it would be entirely appropriate for such a treatise as Theophilus's to have originated in the region that also included Hucbald's likely domicile and/or in a monastery that had a copy of Vitruvius.

Helmarshausen was less central but belonged to another interesting circuit of monasteries developing the practical crafts, located between Hildesheim and Fulda and participating in Benedictine reforms (and music-theory?) from Hirsau. In the

---

[5] Documentation in Freise (see note 2): 277ff.

[6] W. Sanderson, 'The sources and significance of the Ottonian Church of Saint Pantaleon at Cologne', *Journal of the Society of Architectural Historians* 30 (1970), 83–96. Plan and history of Cologne St Pantaleon and Helmarshausen in Oswald 1966: 151–3 and 411–12 respectively. Further on Cologne and the Meuse monasteries in Kubach & Verbeek 1976–89.

On the bronze workshop at St Pantaleon, see H. Fussbroich, *Die Ausgrabungen in St. Pantaleon zu Köln*, Kölner Forschungen 2 (Mainz, 1983), 266–7; for a reconstruction of the westwork, *ibid.*, plate 7.

1120s, its church seems to have been a simple three-aisle structure (*c.* 43 × 22 m)[7] with matching east and west apses, plus a west crypt (for the relics?) and at some point a complex west structure. Probably there were no galleries to nave or quire, hence – if the organ chapters of Theophilus's treatise have anything to do with this church – the suggestions for an organ-chamber behind an upper wall? Blank upper walls in nave and quire were also characteristic of a well-known type of church-design in the Meuse valley area; see p. 212.

Whether Theophilus was Roger is a question of more than purely bibliographical interest. Roger was evidently mobile, more so than one would expect of someone called *presbyter professione monachi* (a full monk and priest?), as Theophilus is. At the same time, if he were both mobile and a monk the implication is that someone with knowledge and skill in the arts and crafts moved about a great deal and stimulated interest over large areas. This would have broad implications for the spread of organs and knowledge about them in the period around 1100. So would the very possibility that the treatise was written in response to monastic reform spreading from Hirsau (see below), for many houses were involved in this movement.

   Had Theophilus worked in St Pantaleon, Cologne, before being moved to Helmarshausen, his monastic career would have somewhat resembled that of the *praepositus* Goderannus, a monk called from Cologne to Hildesheim by a bishop known to have been active in the church arts: Bernward (993–1022 – see p. 317). Goderannus may have been involved in the building of the westwork at St Pantaleon, the monastery in which at the end of the tenth century there was the monk Froumund, author of a text on casting metal. In Hildesheim, the *praepositus* evidently worked with a copy of Vitruvius, now the manuscript British Library, Harley 3767.[8] In such ways as these, Cologne, Hildesheim, Helmarshausen and Hirsau are linked together in the practice and study of the crafts.

Chapters on the organ

The easy availability of the Theophilus text[9] makes it convenient to pick out its salient points:

3.81 fistulae graves et acutae et superacutae,
the dimensions of 'deep, high and very high pipes' are given in an outside text (*lectio*), that will be required by the pipe-maker. Whether *lectio* means a formal specification-sheet (pipe-measurement text for makers), as usually assumed, or something more informal (information passed on from a builder) is not certain. For further remarks on *lectio*, see below under 'Theophilus and the *artes mechanicae*'.

---

[7]   The Saxon cathedral of Winchester was 48.6 m long.
[8]   Fussbroich (see note 6): 240 (Goderannus), 267 (Froumund).
[9]   Chapter-numbers here according to Dodwell 1961 and Hawthorne & Smith 1963: xxv–xxvii. Text and translation in Dodwell 1961, Perrot 1971: 232–52, Barry 1989, Brepohl 1987 and (less expert but instructive) Hopkins & Rimbault 1877: 24–31; translation in Hawthorne & Smith 1963/1979.

While the words *graves/acutae/superacutae* are formulaic and need not necessarily imply three octaves, they do allow such a possibility despite Theophilus's note in 3.82 on only 'seven or eight' grooves in the chest. The significance of this 'seven or eight' will also have to be examined at other points in the present chapter.

cuprum purum et sanissimum,

'pure and faultless copper' sheet is 'reduced' (*attenuetur* – beaten or rolled) so that a fingernail makes a through-impression. 'Pure copper' presumably means no lead, but tin would not be regarded as an 'impurity'. Beating produces a work-hardened metal sheet (Barry 1989: 80).

ferrum longum et grossum,

'a long, thick piece of iron' is made as a round mandrel. Various interpretations have been made of the description:

ferrum . . . quod sit	iron . . . which is to be
in circuitu rotundum . . .	round in cross-section;
in una summitate grossius	thicker at one end
et modice attenuatum,	and moderately tapered
	[or flattened?],
ita ut possit imponi in	so that it can be placed into
alterum ferrum curvum	another curved metal piece
per quod circumducatur . . .	through which it is to be revolved . . .
et in altera summitate gracile	and at the other end thin,
secundum mensuram inferioris	according to the size of the lower
capitis fistulae.	head [= end or toe] of the pipe.

Buhle 1903: 89 and Dodwell 1961: 142 understand *in circuitu rotundum* to mean cylindrical, but since the interpretation by Theobald in 1933, Theophilus's pipes have usually been thought to be conical (for example Hawthorne & Smith 1963: 159). The passage could be read to mean that the mandrel is mainly cylindrical but tapered for the foot; cylindrical and thicker at the end where it is fastened to the turning-handle; or conical, in order to enable the pipes to slip off easily. The last seems most likely, assuming that the taper is slight and the pipes therefore less conical than still usually drawn (for example Brepohl 1987: 243).

Alterum ferrum curvum is generally understood as a 'bent iron' or 'crank' for turning the mandrel (Hawthorne & Smith 1963: 58), while Barry speculates that it implies rather a 'burnisher shaped like a half hoop [or bit brace] in which an augur bit is revolved' (Barry 1989: 76–7), something applied to the exterior of the pipe. Either way, the mandrel is turned in its housing.

There is no further information on the toehole except that the pipe-feet are all 'of the same measurement and size' (*unius mensurae et eiusdem grossitudinis*), which may be an approximation, not literally true for a chest larger than one of seven or eight notes as described below.[10] The mandrel gives the length of the longest pipe

[10]   If Theophilus meant that the pipe-feet were *relatively* of the same length and width throughout the rank (relative to the pipe-dimensions), one would expect him to say so more clearly.

and is made 'to a scale that one wishes the pipes to be' (*ad mensuram qua vult esse fistulae*). While at first this may suggest that only one mandrel is used, nothing Theophilus says excludes the possibility that he had in mind mandrels of different sizes – *grave*, *acute* and *superacute*. Another possibility is that on a long (somewhat) conical mandrel, pipes can be cut at different points along the taper, resulting in different diameters both for a rank of pipes and for pipe-feet that could nevertheless have the same length, if so desired. Also, in speaking of a pipe-scale 'as one wishes' (*qua vult*), Theophilus hardly means 'any size whatsoever'. The bottom note of the archetypal hexachordal keyboard, a nominal C, may have varied in pipe-length only between 3' and 4', or any double or half thereof. (In any kind of chorus, multiples and fractions as well as duplications would also be involved, as builders must surely always have known.)

Starting with the larger pipes, the pipe is cut into at the point that the mouth will be, and the edges of the mouth-slot are filed until it is as high (open) as a straw (*festucae*). On the width of the mouth, see below. (Having to file the mouths of bronze pipes means more labour than fine-cutting the mouths of lead-alloy pipes. This may have been a factor in the increasing use of pewter for pipes.)

cuprum circa ferrum,

the copper sheet is rolled 'around the mandrel' and fastened to it with spiralling wire, no doubt because it is springy and inclined to unroll. (This is surely a sign of experience on the writer's part, though not necessarily with organ-pipes.) Mandrel and pipe are placed near the source of heat, and the pipe's long edges are prepared for overlapping (left over right? – Barry 1989: 79) and soldering on the mandrel. Presumably this is also how the Aquincum pipes were made (see Kaba 1976: 21). The mandrel stabilizes the temperature and after the pipe has cooled is turned on a lathe while the pipe is held firm – by the apprentice whose feet work the lathe? – and a curved burnisher is applied, no doubt by the master. This operation equalizes stress in the copper of the pipe and also burnishes its inner surface, making it 'pleasing to the eye, as if turned' on a lathe (*oculis gratiosa appareat, quasi tornata sit*). The thinness of the copper must mean that both inner and outer surfaces are smoothed in the same operation.

percutiatur ipsa fistula cum malleo mediocri,

'let the pipe be beaten with a medium-size hammer' above and below the mouth, until the mouth is pressed in almost to the middle, making a semicircle cross-section. This sounds as if it is pressed in too far, the mouth 'impossibly wide . . . a misconception on Theophilus's part' (Barry 1989: 82). The languid, almost semi-circular and made 'from copper sheet somewhat thicker than the pipe's' (*ex cupro aliquantulum spissiori*) is soldered in. One can test the pipe by blowing it first weakly, then strongly, then very strongly, and 'according to what one hears, one voices the pipe' (*secundum quod auditu discernit, disponat vocem*). Opening the hole (*foramen*) makes a fuller sound (*grossam*), narrowing it makes it less full (*graciliorem*); in this part of §81, *foramen* seems to mean both windway and mouth. When Theophilus says that adjusting either also affects the pitch, he must mean windway or flue[11] since the mouth's cutup cannot be lowered (*fiat strictius*) once it is cut. However, the upper lip and front edge of the languid can be adjusted, and normally are – perhaps Theophilus had not seen this being done?[12]

3.82 de domo organaria,

concerning the chest or 'housing of the organ pipes'. One begins by choosing to make either a wooden or a copper construction; for the copper, see 3.84 below. The wooden chest is made from two thick planks of plane-tree wood (*ligna de platano*).[13] Such timber is thought to have been rare in western Europe in *c.* 1100, and because it has little sap and lasts well when damp,[14] it would be suitable for a glued windchest. The two planks are two and a half *pedes* long, a little more than one *pes* wide, the lower four *digiti* thick, the upper two. Both are hollowed out, joined together only by a casein glue as described by Theophilus in 1.17. Hollowing out of a block, both as a simple box and with its base domed, is the way in which all known early medieval fiddles and lyres were made, the wood itself varying over the centuries or from one region to another.[15] Amongst other near-Eastern peoples, the Turks too knew both hollowed-out wood and cast bronze for instrumental bodies, and in describing both, Theophilus is transmitting an age-old Mediterranean custom, indeed the first and only writer ever to do so in any detail. He does not, however, refer to softening the block of wood first by boiling it in milk, as is found in one Turkish source (Bachmann 1969: 72–3).

In the centre of the lower plank a four-*digiti* hole is made, 'around which let there be left a border of the same wood, of finger thickness' (*circa quod relinquatur de eodem ligno limbus, unius digiti latitudinis et altitudinis*) into which the windtrunk from the collector is fitted. It is not quite clear whether this means that a new moulding is attached or (more likely?) that inside the plank, the hole receiving the trunk is made narrower at the top with a half-inch border preventing it from going higher into the chest. On the upper surface of the lower plank 'channels are hollowed out' (*fiant cavaturae*) for the wind to fill below the pipes belonging to each note. Their number and size are unspecified and are probably meant to agree with those in the upper plank – see next paragraph – but since they are there to send the wind between the windtrunk opening and the slider-key grooves, they could take various forms. (Theobald 1933, Hawthorne & Smith 1979 and Brepohl 1987 make different suggestions.)

---

[11] According to Buhle 1903: 107, adjusting the pitch (tuning) was the point of Theophilus's directions here.

[12] 'Theophilus pipes' as made in recent years by Louis Huivenaar suggest a high pressure (± 10 cm) and strong, breathy sound.

[13] Contemporary Greek writers used the word πλάτανος for the golden tree of the Byzantine throne room: see Brett 1954: 481–2.

[14] Cf. A. R. Emy, *Traité de l'art de la charpenterie* (Liège, 1841), 250. Brepohl 1987: 245 assumes that the wood is imported.

[15] F. Crane, *Extant Medieval Musical Instruments* (U. Iowa Press, 1972) lists fir (for a gusli, p. 8), lime (guslis, 9–10), oak and maple (lyres, 10), boxwood (gittern, 15) and beech (fiddle, 15f), from the sixth to the fourteenth century, with boxwood the most recent. The Sutton Hoo lyre (Anglo-Saxon, early seventh century) had a soundboard nailed on over its hollowed-out soundbox.

septem vel octo cavaturae,

with 'seven or eight grooves' the upper plank is carved out (morticed) right through, and in the bottom of the grooves, slider-keys (*linguae*) are fitted carefully to slide in and out easily, though of course without the wind escaping. How they are made and fitted is not detailed, being a carpentry question, but the cutting and fitting must have been very accurate.

The phrase 'seven or eight' must mean with or without B♭ – either is possible on a chest of these dimensions – but Theophilus does not say so, nor does he as much as hint that a longer chest and greater compass can be extrapolated. But the maker of a keyboard instrument would see scales naturally in terms of repeated sequences, i.e. in octaves. Either he would know this from observation and custom or he would be using some form of outside text (*lectio*) which gave the scaling for seven or eight pipes but pointed out that there can be at least fifteen notes. (For one such text, see Chapter 16). By at least the twelfth century, writers would assume that on instruments the 'seven notes of music' could be at three ranges: the *grave* or lowest octave, the *acute* and the *superacute*. Although a typical writer such as the Cistercian Guido in CS 2.151 may have been speaking of various instruments (*in organis*) when he pointed out that the same seven notes (*septem litterae*) occur at different 'sevenths' (*septenarii* – he does not say 'octaves'), his words could apply to the keyboard. Against this background, it would be strange if Theophilus meant literally 'seven or eight' notes only.

On the top surface of the chest, above each of the grooves which are wider at the top than the bottom, is nailed a sealing strip of wood in which there are as many holes as there are ranks of pipes. The pipes stand in or on these holes. Theophilus then proceeds with two less clear directions:

cavaturae in quibus linguae iunctae sunt, in anteriori parte procedere debent quasi obliquae fenestrae,

'the grooves in which the slider-keys have been fitted should appear in the front part like oblique [horizontal?] windows'. Translations of this passage are 'the front part of the grooves . . . should splay like windows' (Dodwell 1961: 145) and 'the grooves . . . . continue through to the front, like horizontal window-frames' (Hawthorne & Smith 1963: 161–2), while another interpretation sees the oblique windows as a set of extra little blocks glued on at the front of the organ, their front edge bevelled (*obliquae* – Perrot 1965: 317, 318). Horizontal slits in the front seem the easiest interpretation (as Brepohl 1987: 247), but either way the construction was aimed at keeping the slider-key's travel as straight and its housing as airtight as possible when sliding in and out. Yet another interpretation is that *procedere* indicates that the oblique front is not an extra protruding block but on the contrary, a gouged-out indentation in the front face, allowing a key-square to be pushed in fully.[16] Whichever is the truth, the unclear language could suggest that Theophilus is trying to describe something he has seen.

---

[16] The top limb of the key-square is (or continues as) the key-plate, the lower limb pushes in the slider: drawing in Hardouin 1966: 50. But however likely it may be, it cannot be certain that there was a key-square in Theophilus's chest-design.

in posteriori vero parte sub fine ipsarum linguarum fiant foramina aequaliter lata et longa,
'at the rear part of the said part [= the groove], holes are made of equal width and length near to [and within?] the end of the same sliders', two *digiti* square, admitting the wind between lower chest and pipes above. Thus when the slider-key blocking the vertical wind-channel (and therefore somewhat wider than two *digiti*?) is pulled out, either a hole near its end and previously beyond the groove is also pulled out, or as it is pulled out it leaves a gap through which wind already in the channel rises to the pipes. Either way, the key would have to be a tight fit. It does not drop through the groove because it is held by the horizontal slit in front and is wider than the channel below? Important details in the woodworking are omitted here.

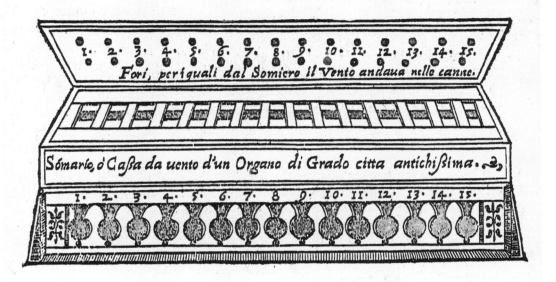

Plate 15 Early organ-chest from Grado, as drawn in G. Zarlino, *Sopplimenti musicali* (Venice, 1588), 291

The very early fifteen-note chest from a church in Grado, described by Zarlino in 1588 (see Plate 15),[17] shows sliders shaped at the player's end with elegant curves and circles, and two rows of pipe-holes piercing a separable topboard. Below this topboard and within the plank-chest are hollowed-out channels fed, it seems, by one square windhole either within the slider (as in Theophilus) or above each slider in the lower part of the upper channels. A pair of bellows was socketed into the back of the chest. According to Zarlino, the length of the chest was one *braccio*, width one quarter; the height looks similar to the width, but the perspective is unclear. This is clearly a small organ, but Zarlino remarks that 'in the church of the saint of

17 Zarlino 1588: 290–1 (e.g. Perrot 1965: plate xxii). So uncertain is Zarlino's perspective (are the 'keys' horizontal?), that one could imagine a pin-action (or a spring-loaded slider) admitting wind not to a 'single hole in the middle of the channel' but to a hole under each pipe. In *Institutioni harmoniche* (Venice, 1588), 290, Zarlino reports on a 'very old organ' found 'many years ago' near Turin that had keys smaller in the treble than in the bass, where a fifth was hard to stretch.

Padua' (S Antonio, Padua? – *nella Chiesa del santo di Padoa*) was 'an old one of suitable enough size' (*un antico di grandezza assai conueniente*).

secundum numerum fistularum,
'according to the number of pipes' per key, the upperboard-strips have carefully made holes in them and are fitted above the sliders (*super linguas sunt iunctae*). Neither Theophilus's text nor Zarlino's drawing suggest that the size of these holes increases for the longer pipes. But since Theophilus's dimensions allow up to three or four ranks, extrapolation could be made for further or larger ranks, even if the text does not say so.

in caudis autem linguarum scribantur litterae,
'furthermore, on the slider-tails are written letters' or the names of the notes, 'by which it can be recognized which is this note and which is that' (*quibus possit cognosci quis ille vel ille tonus sit*). Although this remark recalls the Winchester alphabet and anticipates the Harding Bible's drawing (see Chapter 11), it says more than may appear. Firstly, if the notes were so few as 'seven or eight' and labels were still necessary, then the player was not a regular organist familiar with the keys. Were playing duties – whatever they were – distributed amongst the brothers, who would require no great expertise? Secondly, even if *tonus* meant something as specific as psalm-tone or tonic, which is not out of the question, the important thing for the player was still to know where the semitones lay and whether the *litterae* started at C or at A.[18] Thirdly, if labels were necessary, it would be another reason to suppose that Theophilus's 'seven or eight' notes – like the Harding Bible's eight or the Cambridge Psalter's seven (see p. 177) – were to be understood as indicating not an actual compass but an octave-section of (a 'module' for) a larger compass.

The mechanical movement 'as the slider-keys are pulled out when the organ is played' (*cum linguae cantantibus organis educuntur*)[19] is checked by a copper nail passing through a longitudinal slot in the front end of the slider. The slot is about 1½" long (*dimidii digiti minoris*, 'half a little finger'), the key-travel therefore slightly less. This is an important detail about sliders, unique in the sources. There is no mention of springs, either of the flat-leaf or bent-wire type.

3.84 de domo cuprea,
'concerning the copper chest': directions for making a cast copper chest on the lost wax technique, with dimensions 'according to the number of pipes' (*secundum abundantiam fistularum*). The sliders, which for the copper chest are pierced for each individual pipe, lie on a copper sheet fitted inside the chest. Presumably, the sheet has strip holes for the wind to pass up into the grooves, but Theophilus does not say so. The directions include covering the top of the chest with molten lead, next to the bottom edge of which layer of lead the sliders slide and on the top of which

---

[18]   On (a) clefs indicating the semitones, (b) the note-names, and (c) the question of non-specialist organists, see also Chapter 3.

[19]   It is difficult to suppose that the phrase *cantantibus organis* appears here by chance: see the antiphon for St Cecilia's day, p. 4.

the pipes sit after their holes are drilled through to the sliders' holes. This layer of thick lead 'would probably have worn rapidly in use' (Hawthorne & Smith 1963: 165) and may be evidence that Theophilus was not writing here from experience.

In 3.84 are also included directions on the copper wind-collector and the copper clack-valve for bellows (see below).

3.83 de conflatorio,

'concerning the wind-collector'. According to the number of bellows, the builder is to make holes in the broader (curved) end of a wedge-shaped structure built up from two thick planks of planetree wood glued together after hollowing out with channels inside, one from each bellows and running together into one outlet. The dimensions are: curved end one *pes* and a half wide (*lata* – straight width or the length of the curve?), sides one *pes*, small blunt end one *palmus*. The lower board is one *palmus* thick, the upper three *digiti*.[20] (These measurements sound relative.) The outlet is larger than the inlet holes into which the bellows fit: perhaps in the phrase *fossum deductim usque ad* ('channel led through to . . .'), *deductim* implies that the channel was tapered, becoming narrower, thus increasing the wind-pressure before the collected wind was driven through into the trunk? Strong iron clamps 'tinned on both sides' (*interius et exterius circumstagnatas* – to retard rusting?) are nailed between the inlet holes, binding the two planks together, but only after the whole structure has been wound around with 'strong new linen' (*panno lineo novo et forti* – in one length?) and plastered with the same glue. In view of the modest dimensions of this *conflatorium*, one can assume it matched the one-octave 'chest-module' and was equally open to extrapolation without much increasing the pressure of the wind it was collecting. For a further remark on it, see below.

lignum curvum de quercu,

'a curving log of oak': the windtrunk is made from a well-chosen oak branch, drilled out and (over the curve) burnt through. The curved part is one *pes* long, the straight two: these too look like proportional measurements.

The outer wood of the lower end of the curving trunk is shaped to form a neck one *palmus* square that will fit into the wind-collector's square outlet. The upper end is also cut away (bevelled) for the length of a thumb to be wedged tightly into the bottom of the chest. The whole trunk and its joints at either end are covered with linen[21] and the joints are further sealed with a wide sheet of copper nailed on. A trunk of wood must have been more airtight than one of joined pieces, even if fine joinery was available, and it must have been dressed smooth to take the linen and the copper. Using a curved trunk meant that the bellows could be as large as required, lying horizontally (near the floor, perhaps). Then the chest could lie above, even far above, the bellows, and the feet of the organist could be above the

---

[20] A *palmus* or four-finger unit must have been about 3" or 7.5 cm (Sachs 1980: 258).

[21] Theophilus does not mention the sealing material used later by Arnaut de Zwolle: *corio albo* ('white leather' – kid leather or parchment?), also implied in some late fourteenth-century contracts (see p. 312; for Arnaut, see Le Cerf 1932: 23–4). Is this sealing material another sign of improvements made in the thirteenth century?

wind-collector (see 3.85 below). Although he does not describe the layout in these terms, it seems that in this part of the description Theophilus is assuming extrapolation – that his sizes will in practice be multiplied. It is difficult to see how the feet of the organist would be above the wind-collector if the curved part was only one *pes* long or how the chest could be only two *pedes* or so above the point at which the trunk straightens out.

Some consideration of what Theophilus is implying here is important since he could well be allowing for an interest in making organs of increasing size and placing them in major churches.

3.84 conflatorium quoque formabis in argilla,

'also for the wind-collector a clay mould' can be made and a copper casting produced, instead of the wooden *conflatorium* described above. The windtrunk must be firmly fixed (*firmiter consolidari* – 'soldered fast'?) to the underpart of the copper chest.

Forge-bellows are described by Theophilus elsewhere in Part 3, where they seem to be hand-held (see below) and there is no separate description of bellows in the organ chapters. In 3.84 he remarks only that for the bellows a copper clack-valve should be fitted 'in the head of each and every bellows before the end of the nozzle' (*in capite uniuscuiusque follis ante foramen fistulae suae*). Although none is mentioned, forge-bellows too should have some such valve, otherwise they suck in the hot ashes. Had Theophilus not inspected a pair?

3.85 ut infra monasterium nihil appareat,

'so that nothing be seen below in the *monasterium*' except the 'pipes standing on the chest' (*super quam statuendae sunt fistulae*), the organ can be laid out so that the bellows and keys are on the inner side of the wall, and the organist (*cantor*) is seated with his feet above the wind-collector. The last probably means that the organist, chest and façade could be on the floor above the bellows, not (as understood in Brepohl 1987: 252) literally above the collector. Thus

folles et instrumentum super	the bellows and framework on
quod iaceant secundum	which they lie, according to the
situm loci	nature of the site
ad libitus tuos dispone.	place as you wish.

Instrumentum seems to mean a framework of joists and cross-members supporting the bellows and keeping the trunk rigid, called 'crosses' in non-technical Byzantine descriptions of how organs were set up (p. 149) and used again in 3.85 for the bell-metal furnace bellows (see below).

But where the organ is located is much less clear than first appears, in particular because of the phrase *infra monasterium*. These words appear in earlier Carolingian sources, as at St-Denis in 799 (for a reference to other churches 'within the monastery' enclosure) and Corbie in *c.* 822 (for technical crafts pursued 'within the monastery' confines).[22] If Theophilus uses *monasterium* in its original sense of a

---

[22] St-Denis in B. Bischoff, 'Eine Beschreibung der Basilika von Saint-Denis aus dem Jahre 799', *KC* 34 (1981), 97–103, here 100. Corbie and Abbot Adalhard's statutes, in Schwind 1984: 112.

'secluded chamber',[23] then the phrase would mean 'so that below the chamber in which the organ is secreted, nothing is seen' except the pipes. Or the 'secluded area' could be the monastic quire, down in which the brothers had no desire to see either bellows-blower or organist. Whatever is likeliest, 'down on the floor of the church' as a translation for *infra monasterium* ignores other, well-documented uses of the word.

Neither the general location nor the placement of the organ within that location is quite straightforwardly expressed, although the intended meaning may be simple:

in ipso muro arcus fiat	in the same wall let an arch be made in
in quo cantor sedeat . . .	[= behind?] which the cantor is to sit . . .
est etiam foramen quadrum	furthermore a square opening is [made]
in medio arcus	in the middle of the arch [= arched space]
trans maceriam, per quod	through the masonry, by means of which
domus cum fistulis	the chest with its pipes
exponitur.	is displayed.

Since *arcus* can mean vault, does the phrase mean 'let there be a (new) gallery opening made into the nave' in the otherwise blank wall? The 'square hole' seems to suggest an opening in the wall opening into the nave, presumably with lintel above. What this seems to mean is that in the absence of nave-galleries in German romanesque churches of this area (see p. 115), the upper nave wall has to be specially pierced for the pipe-front, with the organist in a room or passage behind and the bellows-blowers below him. It is also possible to interpret Theophilus's words in the context of a westwork, with its various arches and galleries.

There is no mention of a façade as such, with or without wooden framing. Yet to display the pipes, the front row could be brought forward from the wall and encased in a decorative wooden surround, as is still frequently found with Italian organs well into the nineteenth century: the pipes are in a shallow niche, below an arch within or protruding from the thickness of the wall, and the wooden arch-frame is like the large open side of a shallow six-sided wooden box.[24] In Theophilus's plan, the keyboard placed at the rear makes protruding front-pipes-plus-frame very feasible. Again, Theophilus's whole paragraph implies a much larger organ than the single octave of seven or eight notes and three or four ranks: it is surely not for the sake of eight small *montre* pipes that an arch in the wall has to be opened up.

More information on the layout and location is given in relation to the windtrunk. This is fixed firmly in the masonry, coming up to the chest from below; the bellows themselves are out of sight (and sound?); the chest rests on two iron bars driven into the wall; and the complete organ chamber has a wooden shutter or door (*fenestra lignea*) locked so that 'no unauthorized person passing by knows what is behind it' (*quae dum clausa . . . nemo ignotus superveniens cognoscere valet quid in ea contineatur*).

---

[23] As used by e.g. Eusebius (*c.* 263–*c.* 339): trans. G. A. Williamson, *Eusebius: The History of the Church* (London, 1965), 91. Of eight uses of *monasterium* listed in Blatz's *Novum Glossarium Mediae Latinitatis*, three are for the church building itself (cf. 'minster'). In thirteenth-century processionals, 'the nave of the monastery' can mean the central aisle of the quire (a possible meaning in Theophilus) or the main nave outside the quire (also a possible meaning).

[24] In Italian organs there may be no box, merely a wide, shallow and often square niche in the wall, with a wooden surround on the front side.

This is more likely to be a door into the chamber than a shutter behind or in front of the façade pipes (as in Brepohl 1987: 252), which have their dust-cover. The iron bars not only keep the organ and its windtrunk firmly fixed, but make it unlikely that there was any timber casing for the organ – or if there were, it was not structural. (In turn, this suggests that the eventual timber structuring and casing of organs originated as a practical means for keeping the construction fixed, thus replacing such earlier means as the iron bars.) For someone to be passing behind the chamber-door there must be an inner gallery or at least passageway, as would be found in westworks or in the nave galleries of larger churches in up-to-date monasteries. Perhaps *ignotus* means the people assembling nearby in a gallery, overlooking the liturgy (cf. account of Ramsey Abbey, p. 80); who else would be *ignotus* in a conventual church?

That organs were secreted away is suggested by a contemporary (and highly unusual) reference to St-Donaat, Bruges in 1127, and to Charles Count of Flanders hiding in its organ-chamber:[25]

se in organistro, scilicet	in the *organistrum*, that is
in domicilio quodam organorum	in that kind of little house for the
ecclesiae . . . occultaverat.	church organ . . . he hid himself.

On the shape of this church and parallels it offers to the octagon of Aachen, see Chapter 7. A century and a half later in the old cathedral of Salamanca, the arch of the organ is mentioned (*arca de los órganos*) in or near a north-eastern chapel, along with a door through which one ascends to the instrument (*puerta por donde solían sobir a los órganos*) which is clearly more than a portable (*los órganos grandes* – Llovera 1987: 299–300): from this, it seems that the organ was secreted in a gallery under an arch of some kind, perhaps with a view to the main altar. In all such cases – though so rarely is the organ-location clear – the noise and commotion of an organ in action must have made desirable the removal from sight and hearing of as much of it as possible. But unless the keyboard was at the front of the organ, the organist cannot have been an ordinarily participating member of the choir of monks, and it is difficult to see how he would have a basic part in the liturgy at all.[26]

exterius quoque super organa pannus spissus . . . dependeat,
'also on the outside let there hang over the organ a thick cloth' shaped like a canopy, suspended from a pulley, dropped down over the organ to keep it from dust (*ad arcendum pulverem*) and raised when the organ plays (*dum cantandum est organis*). Mention of the canopy's little wooden ball to which the pulley rope is fastened suggests that Theophilus knew of such a structure. If the canopy did drop over the organ – guaranteed to bring dust with it, one would think – then either the organ protruded from the wall or the canopy was suspended from the lintel/apex of the arch above the

---

[25] J. B. Ross, 'Rise and fall of a twelfth-century clan', *Speculum* 44 (1959), 367–90; and J. Smits van Waesberghe, 'Organistrum, Symphonia, Drehleier', *HmT* (1972), I (1).

[26] By the time of the much later choir organ, such as that on the screen in the Basle Predigerkirche (fifteenth century), the choir, the organist (with his keyboard at the front?) and the bellows-blower were all within sight of each other, no doubt indicating a close cooperation for the *alternatim* chant.

pipe-front. Again there is no mention of an organ-case of wood, and any such canopy suggests that there was not one. If a dropping canopy was bound to raise dust, perhaps the *courtines* at Rouen Cathedral in 1387 or Troyes in 1381 were hanging drapes instead?[27] Hanging curtains of one or other kind, often with conspicuous rings, are a major motif in earlier medieval illustrations such as the Utrecht Psalter, manuscripts made in monasteries of the area and period associated with early organs.

Other Topics in Theophilus

Elsewhere in the treatise, Theophilus describes diverse arts that are involved in or related to the making of organs, although he does not say so.

1.17	how to make the casein glue
	the planing of wood panels [here, ready for gesso artwork]
1.23	gold foil on wood or parchment
1.24	tin foil
1.35	hollowed-out box or chest of oak [no details]
2.17	ruler and compasses (*regula et circino*) employed
2.24–5	casting lead cames for windows
2.27	soldering with a lead–tin alloy
2.31	glass rings [for hanging drapes?]
3.4	bellows for fine work (goldsmith work): a ramskin is used whole (*pellibus arietum*), with an iron pipe at one end [the *fistula*, now often called *tuyère*] taking wind into the forge, and at the rear, two pairs of (small) wooden pieces connected to the skin and worked by the finger and thumb [see below]
3.8	wire-drawing [see Chapter 18]
3.9	the *organarium*, a swage or tool for making gold and silver beads[28]
3.45	the pipe (*fistula*) for communicants to drink from the cup: a thin, conical silver pipe, made by beating a sheet of silver around a tapering iron mandrel; soldered and hammered on the mandrel[29]
3.36 ⎫ 3.39 ⎬ 3.68 ⎭	gilding of silver, copper and bronze
3.67	purifying copper, to remove lead
3.85	for heavy smelting (bell-metal), another kind of wind-raising is described for the furnace:

folles etiam cum instrumentis	also set up bellows with their
suis, in quibus firmiter iaceant,	apparatus, in which they rest steady,
appones, unicuique foramini duos,	two for each wind-outlet,★
et unicuique folli deputabis	and arrange for each bellows
fortes viros duos.	two strong men.
	★each furnace has two or three outlets

3.89	the solder for tinwork: two parts tin to one of lead

[27] For Rouen: N. Dufourcq, *Le Livre de l'orgue français 1589–1789, 1 Les Sources* (Paris, 1971), 24. One hundred and fifty brass rings (*engneaux de laton*) suggest a hanging drape; *pour couvrir la chapelle de dessus* would then mean 'to close off the chapel [vaulted bay?] on the upper floor', or something of this kind. For Troyes: E. Martinot, *Orgues et organistes des églises du Diocèse de Troyes* (Troyes, 1941), 24ff.

[28] Perhaps *organarium* is a scribe's reading for [o]*granarium*, a tool for making round beads or *granae rotundae* (Thompson, see note 4: 320).

[29] Such gold *fistulae*, also soldered, are described in the *Mappae clavicula*: see note 32: 48.

The wholeskin bellows have an intake valve at the rear, a small, 'lozenge-shaped valve which is opened and closed' by finger and thumb (Hawthorne & Smith 1963: 84). Presumably this saves having to pierce the skin elsewhere, but the finger and thumb would soon tire. For heavier smelting or forge work, bellows of boards and leather seem to be meant. The details under 3.85 are not spelled out, presumably because they were familiar (Brepohl 1987: 267): two bellows, each for two strong men, are held firm in their framework. It is likely that the bellows worked in alternation but it is not clear why two men were needed for each; perhaps what is meant is two men per wind-source (i.e. one for each bellows). The general picture is basic to the development of the organ, not only in the type of bellows and the alternating method of blowing them, but in the use of (presumably) a timber structure for the steadying framework. If Theophilus's organ *conflatorium* was rigidly enough fixed for its three (smaller?) bellows to need no such framework, then again he may have been describing an earlier organ-type. The two artefacts organ-with-large-bellows and smelter-with-large-bellows would develop along similar lines.

Two important implications for Theophilus's organ-pipes are contained in the passage dealing with chalice-pipes. In the first place, the (small) mandrel is conical, not cylindrical with an end-cone; in the second it looks as if for Theophilus making organ-pipes was itself an extrapolation of the art of making chalice-pipes, learnt therefore as a monastic craft rather than an instrument-technology as such. While there is no reason to think that either was always the case across Europe, they could well explain the background to organ-making in this particular monastic circle.

The introduction of organs at 3.81 is a marked change of subject after the small-scale gold and silverwork. Bell-founding at 3.85, by far the largest chapter in the whole treatise, follows on the organ chapters with less of an obvious jolt. Throughout the treatise, woodworking is treated only briefly; no joining procedures are described and there is nothing on the preparation of wood comparable to that for the working of metal pipes.[30] The description of bellows looks like a not very expert eye-witness account of a pair of actual bellows rather than a recipe for their manufacture. However, it may be relevant to organs that in 3.4 the use of hands for pumping the bellows is implied, as it is in 3.81 when the bellows-servant (*puer*) sits and pumps gently (*mediocriter flante*) to keep the furnace hot but not too hot. Like chest-making, bellows involve woodwork not the purview of a Theophilus, and the same would be true for key-action and for any other wooden parts of the structure. Thus, in three woodworking areas of an organ – bellows, key-action and casework – sparseness of information cannot be taken to mean that there was nothing to describe.

Writing about crafts and techniques

Rather than truly outlining how to make an organ, Theophilus could well have been describing an actual instrument. But precisely what would spur an early twelfth-century 'monk and priest' to make such a description is a large question,

---

[30] But working with a mandrel can hardly have been new or unfamiliar, at least in ex-Roman provinces.

not least since certain ideas in the treatise anticipate much later craft-description (particularly in Germany?) and can even be said to lead to them,[31] despite the old-fashioned nature of some of its details.

Various attempts have been made to explain why the treatise was written or compiled in the first place. There is the theological background for a German monastic author: 'man's dignity, his creation in the image of God, referred not only to his rationality but also to an inherent ability to devise and develop all good and useful arts', so that the craftsman's labour was 'both a religious duty and a religious exercise' (Van Engen 1980: 151). Some such points needed to be made by Theophilus if it was still generally believed, with John Scottus Eriugena (*Periphyseon* 5.4, *c.* 864), that the mechanical arts were not included amongst those leading to the Source of Knowledge (PL 122.870). In the second place, there was a more practical *raison d'être* for a book on the crafts: as more and more monasteries in north-west Europe were undertaking major building-programmes, guidance on the many necessary technologies may have become desirable, if only for those supervising the work-men. Of any two such reasons the second seems more likely, for however attractive to the modern humanist scholar any 'theological background' might be, it need not have led to a *book* on the crafts, verbalizing them and transmitting them on parchment. Any duty to 'develop all good and useful arts' does not have to take written form, and in vast areas of Christendom never did.

The metallurgical and other heavy crafts discussed in Theophilus's Book 3 are new to the fund of decorative and other light crafts (Books 1 and 2) that belonged to a manuscript tradition for fine-art recipes and techniques, of which the *Mappae clavicula*, probably compiled in the early ninth century, is the best if faulty mani-festation.[32] One tradition of Vitruvius manuscripts often includes excerpts from the *Mappae* (Reynolds 1986: 442), and a German monastery of *c.* 1150 with copies of Vitruvius, Theophilus and the *Mappae* would have a very rich survey of techniques of all kinds. In the case of Theophilus, a big expansion in the number of arts des-cribed in one book – the bringing together of heavy and light arts – must reflect a growing need for scribes in some monasteries to include treatises related to the pro-ductions of metalworkers and builders who were at work in the same community.[33] To whatever extent the brothers themselves were involved in the crafts for the newly built or refurbished abbeys, to that extent written manuals would be useful. That there was less need in the later Middle Ages for manuals to publish 'craft secrets' – even that such secrets became 'owned' by the guilds – is suggested by Theophilus's treatise remaining isolated and not leading to ever fuller handbooks on instrument-making.

---

[31] For example, the opening preface's promise to withhold no secrets of the trade, and the organ chapters' recommendation to the builder to have other information to hand before beginning, anticipate similar points in Andreas Werckmeister's *Erweiterte und vermehrte Orgelprobe* of 1698 (concerning 'secrets', see its Chapter 14; concerning the need for other information, see its Preface). Theophilus's idea of craft-skill as a God-given talent looks like an ancestor of the Lutheran notion of 'the desire for learning'.

[32] C. S. Smith & J. G. Hawthorne, *Mappae clavicula: a Little Key to the World of Medieval Techniques,* Transactions of the American Philosophical Society, n.s. 64.4 (Philadelphia, 1974), 3–6.

[33] Some of the community may have been equally trained as scribes and metalworkers.

Besides, whether or not early technical writings were aiming at the needs of so many new monasteries, their actual usefulness cannot be taken for granted. An author of a treatise or of additions to a treatise can hardly have been trained in how to describe processes or techniques, and he may well have experienced difficulty in writing down his instructions. Literate scribes need not have understood what they were copying or taking down from dictation and thus could easily transmit a garbled version. In any case those instructions need not have described common procedures: it has been remarked of such techniques as gilding described briefly in the *Mappae clavicula* that surviving gilded objects were not made according to the techniques described there.[34] Practising the crafts and writing about them must have been more or less independent arts. Despite these various kinds of problem, however, the large number of new or reformed foundations during Theophilus's period made it useful to have not only some guidelines but also a uniform approach both to the liturgies themselves (chant-books) and to the surroundings for those liturgies (furnishings, equipment).

By the early twelfth century there are several references to the mechanical arts as having a place in the scheme of human knowledge, chiefly in the writings of Hugh of St Victor (1120s).[35] Again, however, it is not clear why such knowledge should take written form, and it is always possible that Theophilus did have some particular reason for assembling his information. One suggestion has been that he was replying to St Bernard's condemnation of florid ecclesiastical art, thus expressing one monk's response to the accusations and reforms of one kind of Cistercian.[36] Furthermore the written form of Theophilus's crafts-description would then correspond to the written form of Bernard's complaints: words could be answered only by other words.

Yet of the three kinds of explanation for Theophilus's treatise – its 'theological background', the energetic monastic building-programme, general reactions to Cistercian 'purity' – the likeliest seems to me the second. It is the simplest and does not need further special pleading as the other explanations do. (The Cistercians themselves copied and preserved technical, practical treatises once their own industrial activities took hold.[37]) Theophilus's justification is that the crafted furnishings are necessary to the Church. The preface to Book 3 quotes the command of Moses to build the tabernacle (Exodus 31.1–11) and David's entrusting 'almost all the needful resources in gold, silver, bronze and iron to his son Solomon' (1 Chronicles 22.14). It then directs the reader:

be inspired henceforth to greater deeds of skill, and with the utmost exertion of your mind prepare to execute what is still lacking in the vessels of the House of God, without which the divine mysteries and service of the Office cannot continue. These are they: chalices, candlesticks,

[34] The treatise is described as 'a collection of workshop recipes badly garbled by several centuries of transmission through monastic scriptoria' in Hall 1979: 48. Remarks on gilding techniques in S. M. Alexander, 'Ancient and medieval gilding on metal – the technical literature', *ibid.*, 65–71, here 71.

[35] Sternagel 1966: 67ff. Hugh of St Victor may have been German-born, likewise 'Richard of St Victor', to whom certain writings are now attributed.

[36] L. White, 'Theophilus redivivus', *TC* 15 (1964), 224–33, where accordingly, with reference to St Bernard's *Apologia*, a date of 1122/3 is proposed for Theophilus.

[37] E.g. the iron-foundries in the Langres area of France (various monasteries) or Coalbrookdale in England (Buildwas Abbey).

censers, cruets, shrines, reliquaries for holy relics, crosses, covers for Gospel Books and the rest of the things which usage necessarily demands for the ecclesiastical rites.[38]

The reference to Exodus 31 is striking since it is there that Bezaleel the craftsman appears, full of wisdom in all manner of workmanship, including bronze and wood: he was also referred to by Eusebius in an address on the new fourth-century basilica at Tyre, a source perhaps known to Theophilus.[39] 'Bezaleel' was also the nickname for Charlemagne's biographer Einhard: the courtier, author, former scribe from Fulda and scholar of Vitruvius who related the story of the relics of SS Marcellinus and Peter translated to the Valenciennes monastery associated with Abbot Georgius, perhaps the organ-builder Georgius (see Chapter 9). Ratger, third Abbot of Fulda (802–17) sent one of his monks to Aachen to be instructed by Einhard in the various arts (*variarum artium* – MGH SS 3.162). From such connections as these it looks as if the idea of a Bezaleel and his rôle in equipping the holy places for the liturgy is well established generations before Theophilus: surely every literate monk knew Exodus 31.

Like other monastic work, the crafts described by Theophilus will drive out sloth and mistaken ideas and will themselves be a pleasurable study (preface to Book 1). He does not quite say that technology is developed *ad gloriam Dei*, but this would be assumed for all the great technological achievements of that period, such as the new vaults of St-Denis (begun *c.* 1140), and is constantly implied in written statements, such as the *Libellus de consecratione S Dionysii* by Suger, Abbot of St-Denis (†1151). Obviously, the making of windows about which Theophilus writes is crucial to the new gothic conception, even if that was not known to Theophilus and took some time to penetrate beyond the Rhine.

One may suspect that it was because of its general expertise in metalwork that 'Germany' played a major part in the fitful documentation of organ-building. Describing crafts seems not to have been important further south and west. Perhaps by the twelfth century the triangle Hildesheim–Goslar–Brunswick[40] had produced a sense of technological competitiveness, inheriting and bequeathing for Saxonia a technical expertise of the kind found earlier in the monasteries of southern Germany.[41] Theophilus himself refers to *Germania*, probably meaning the land south of Saxonia and north of Bavaria, and three places associated with copies of the treatise (including BL Harley 3915) were Cologne, Munster and Altenzella (Altzelle) near Freiberg, Saxony (Dodwell 1961: xxxv). A respect for written *mechanica* may be traceable to a

---

[38] Translated in Dodwell 1961: 64. Theophilus's remark that David entrusted 'almost all' of the materials probably alludes to the phrase in 1 Chronicles 22.14, 'and thou mayest add thereto'. This is the authority to bring to the Temple what seems fitting.

[39] Williamson (see note 23): 384. Bezaleel's gifts in working metal, stone and wood are further described in Exodus 35 and 36, and there are other twelfth-century references to him or to Moses as the ultimate legitimation for man-made crafts (see Whitney 1990: 78–9).

[40] Hildesheim was very active in bronze and stonework by *c.* 1010 (see p. 316). Goslar was the chief German imperial seat by 1050. For the triangle Hildesheim–Goslar–Brunswick, and Roger of Helmarshausen's relation to earlier decorative styles from the Meuse valley, see E. Meyer, 'Der Hildesheimer Rogerwerkstatt', *Pantheon* 32 (1943–4), 1–11, and plate 1 (also in Brepohl 1987).

[41] In his *De carolo magno* of *c.* 883–7 (MGH SS 2.726–63), Notker Balbulus of St Gall refers to a glazier from St Gall at work in Aachen and to a Sangallian bell-founder expert in bronze, copper, tin and silver.

monastic culture centred on Hildesheim already in the ninth century (see Sternagel 1966: 19, 27) and in the eleventh under its bishop Bernward (992–1022). An eye-witness of Bishop Bernward's activites in Hildesheim noted his interest in both liberal and mechanical arts (MGH SS 4.758): handwriting, painting, metal-casting, setting precious stones, architecture, sculpture, goldsmith work, mosaic, brick-making, tile-making, the producing of a Gospel (illuminations? covers?), censers, chalices and crown-candelabra (one of which still exists in Hildesheim Cathedral – see p. 218). The items in such a report are not very different from those in the contemporary poem of Cantor Wulfstan describing the work of bishops of Winchester, showing the period around 1000 to be one in which Benedictine bishops were praised for the technology they developed or stimulated.

Theophilus and the *artes mechanicae*

Although Theophilus's preface does not refer to them, the casting and scaling of bells (3.85–7) and the making of organs (3.81–4) follow the other metalwork described in the treatise. In organological literature, the organ chapters 'escaped the notice of all writers, both foreign and English, who have devoted their time and talents to the consideration of musical antiquities', according to E. F. Rimbault when he re-published the English translation of the British Library copy (Harley 3915).[42] Rimbault was also aware that this copy had three chapters on the organ totally absent from the Vienna, Wolfenbüttel and Cambridge copies.[43] Wolfenbüttel MS 4373 includes 3.81 in the table of contents (*de organis*) but nothing more, while in Vienna MS 2527, 3.81 ends suddenly after sixty-two words. Although the version that does include 3.81–4 appears to do so without breaking continuity or changing style, those chapters are not entirely consistent in detail.

The position of the organ chapters in the treatise, plus their rarity in the copies suggest either that they were additional in some sense or that bells and organs themselves were optional in the list of liturgical requirements. In either case, it is surprising that bells come after organs for they were surely much more common. One distinct possibility is that the treatise is the result of accretion, even straightforward compilation, and that there was no single author 'Theophilus'. Amongst other things, this could explain any old-fashioned details in the description of organs that there might be. Being totally up-to-date may well not have been a priority for the treatise-tradition to which Theophilus belongs: if the 'theological positions' taken in his prologues were a generation or more old – they are now recognized as typical of the period 1060–90[44] – it would be surprising if his organ-technology were any more recent.

---

[42] Hopkins & Rimbault 1877: 23ff. The translation was taken from R. Hendrie, *An Essay upon the Various Arts* (London, 1847).

[43] For manuscripts, see note 3. Further in R. P. Johnson, 'The manuscripts of the Schedula of Theophilus Presbyter', *Speculum* 13 (1938), 86–103.

[44] W. Hanke, *Kunst und Geist: Das philosophische und theologische Gedankengut der Schrift 'De diversis artibus' des Priesters und Mönchs Theophilus Rugerus* (Bonn, 1962), 136.

In style and approach the treatise was intended as a church-orientated contribution to the *artes mechanicae* or written descriptions of the technological arts. In the manuscripts, copies of Theophilus accompany other such treatises from earlier periods: Vitruvius's *De architectura* appears in Wolfenbüttel MS 4373, Vitruvius and others in the copy BL Harley 3915 (see Chapter 14), Palladius's *Opus agriculturae* and others in the Cambridge manuscript (listed in Dodwell 1961: lvii–lxx). Extracts from such treatises, including Theophilus, are often found gathered or compiled with others, but the section on organs is not otherwise known. In an organ treatise of the *artes mechanicae* type, calculations for pipe-measurements will not be included, since they belong to the sphere of theory and the *schola* or *scriptorium* rather than the workshop. It is not clear whether the opening remarks of 3.81:

facturus organa	let him who is to make organs
primum habeat	first have
lectionem mensurae	a treatise on [pipe-]measurement

indicate that Theophilus intended to provide one from elsewhere (as he did for bells), that he had no wish to enter into theory, or that *lectionem* was meant more figuratively (not a physical document but 'an understanding' of the measurements). One further possibility is that since Corvey, and presumably Helmarshausen, had been sharing in the reforms of Hirsau and Abbot William (†1091), Theophilus was writing his Vitruvian treatise in response to them, aiming to meet William's own interests in theoretical pipe-scales, and supplementing them with a practical treatise for the sake of actual builders. It is tempting to think that Theophilus's *lectionem mensurae* was meant to be none other than some text associated with William (as given in Sachs 1970: 86f), and that the authors shared a regional interest in practical matters.

Whatever the case, to make full and complete instructions on building an organ Theophilus would have required much more detail on how to produce sound and pitch from a pipe than appears in any of the known pipe-measurement treatises. It does therefore seem unjustifiably optimistic to describe him as 'exposing in detail the method of calculation for the length of pipes' (Huglo 1981: 109) when his only advice is to look elsewhere for it, to acquire knowledge of it some other way. Perhaps the translation of the passage concerning *lectio* should read 'let him have first chosen a scale of measurement', a sense comparable to that given in Hopkins & Rimbault 1877: 24: he 'should first possess the knowledge of the measure'. During the same period as Theophilus, Hugh of St Victor also used the word in connection with mechanics when he spoke of the treatise *Didascalion* as providing a basis for *lectio et meditatio* in the four branches of knowledge: theoretical, practical, mechanical and logical.[45] *Lectio* here does not mean a list of measurements, for Hugh's discussions are bookish, removed from crafts and undoubtedly remote to the skilled craftsmen themselves. A more fitting question about the practical treatise of Theophilus is whether if the *lectio* he recommended did mean something written it would have

---

[45] Hugh's seven divisions of the mechanical arts are fabric-making, armament, commerce, agriculture, hunting, medicine, theatrics. Such theoretical coverage attracts similar coverage today: cf. Sternagel 1966: 67ff; G. Ovitt, 'The status of the mechanical arts in medieval classification of learning', *Viator* 14(1983), 89–105; R. Baron, *Science et sagesse chez Hugues de Saint-Victor* (Paris, 1957), 73f.

been an old Pythagorean *mensura* text with a starting-length and constant diameter for the pipes (see Chapter 16) or a fuller geometric pipe-table showing all the values. Such values may have been known well before there is written evidence for them. Either way, even if early medieval organ-builders like early harpsichord-makers did not begin with a scaled drawing,[46] they must have set out on the basis of measurements previously followed (as rule-of-thumb?) or thought out (carefully calculated?).

But like other writing in the *artes mechanicae* tradition, it is not at all clear for whom Theophilus's treatise was written. On one hand, like the 'Bern Anon' (see Chapter 16), Theophilus, begins with pipe-making, which is something totally missing from the older *artes mechanicae* books of Vitruvius and Hero, and is of obvious practical use. On the other hand, there is no account of the action other than the sliders, and only from the description of the copper pin checking their pullout (3.82) is there any vivid picture at all of the mechanism. Even then, Theophilus's account is open-ended, for some kind of check would be useful whether or not there was a spring-loaded key attached to the slider. Then there are the questions of how many keys and how many ranks there are. It does not seem logical to assume that the number of notes remained at seven or eight while the ranks increased to five.[47] But one cannot be sure, and it is difficult from such details as this to avoid the impression that Theophilus is assembling his information in such a way as to make it adaptable to many situations. He does not say so, but he is describing specifics for a range of organs.

Conclusion

Since for the casting of the copper organ-chest in 3.84 the reader is referred back to an earlier chapter (3.61), it is clear that the organ chapters are not entirely independent of the rest of the treatise, nor is there any doubt that the treatise is totally distinct from the sixteen chapters of Eraclius's *De coloribus et artibus romanorum* that follow the organ chapters without a break in the manuscript Harley 3915. Therefore, though perhaps never prepared in any complete or final draft, the treatise as we have it can be recognized as an entity with its own style and approach, something for whose organ chapters Theophilus extracted a model from an existing instrument he had examined. Since this could also be true of Vitruvius when he came to describe the water-organ (see Chapter 14), it means that there is still a large gap between what the few writers say and what the many more contemporary makers of organs could do. But a master-craftsman might have been able to read even if he could not write, and Theophilus's three abilities (to observe objects, to order information and to write, prose) would give him or any monastery supervisor a first model on which to build.

46 The question about *lectio* is asked in K.-J. Sachs, 'Die Studien über die Mensura fistularum', in *Orgelwissenschaft und Orgelpraxis*, ed. H. H. Eggebrecht, Veröffentlichungen der Walcker-Stiftung 8 (Murrhardt, 1980), 60–71, here 69. For the suggestion that organ-builders began with a drawing of some kind, see Sachs 1980: 71–3.

47 As in H. Klotz, 'Orgel', *MGG* 10 (1962), 267, 269–70. Also, the tallest pipes would probably be away from the player, on the *monasterium* side of the chest, thus as drawn on *MGG* pp. 269–70 but not 267? In itself, however, Klotz's chorus of 4.2 ⅔.2.1⅓.1 is plausible.

For the pipe-work itself, it could seem to an experienced craftsman today that Theophilus had 'watched pipes being made and voiced, but had probably never done it himself' (Barry 1989: 84). Moreover, it is likely that any instrument on which his account was based, in the Meuse region or in Cologne itself, belonged to a previous period. Like bells, it would have been the work of a specialist in such equipment, someone not necessarily involved in making fine metalwork but able to call on woodworkers or on woodworking skills of his own. If it had had a wind-collector of the type Theophilus describes, it could have been reflecting a general and age-old understanding of such things. Bellows refinements like double tuyères are known in Roman *Anglia*, and the Roman foundry site of Cranbrook in Kent has even yielded a kind of *conflatorium*: a small earthenware 'equalizer' pot, sealed on top with leather and containing two inlet holes (less than 1" diameter) which held the bellows. The bellows pumped in alternation, but the pot was able to send out steady wind through its clay tuyère into the fire. Perhaps organ-builders had developed something of this sort, or perhaps it was from knowing such ancient devices that Theophilus speculated on a *conflatorium* suitable for an organ.

Either way, Theophilus's information was very likely already out of date. But it was also presented in such a way as to make it possible to project a larger instrument and to apply other experience, particularly in woodworking, to an instrument-technology that can never have stood still.

16

Details of 'real organs' in other treatises

The relevance of pipe-measurement treatises

Klaus-Jürgen Sachs's fundamental re-assessment in 1970 and 1980 of a group of medieval writings – the technical treatises on pipe-measurement (*mensura fistularum*) – invalidated a good deal of how writers of the previous hundred years had interpreted these treatises, or what they knew of them. That only a few are the work of a single author and otherwise show signs of being excerpts or compilations was not clear before an authoritative edition was made, and in any case would not have affected the way they were looked at. For it had been usual to regard these treatises, often very brief and formulaic, as prototypes for the practical instruction-manual of the kind that has become familiar only in more recent centuries and for a different readership. Practical conclusions had been inappropriately drawn from writings that were not primarily practical but rather part of a more general corpus of learning, one ultimately founded not on instrument-making as such but on a Pythagorean theory of musical notes.

The most widespread of these conclusions – something that appeared to be supported by the earliest drawings of organs – was the idea that in 'the medieval organ' all pipes of a single rank had the same diameter. It was Sachs who, in a wide-ranging study still strangely undervalued and even neglected by many scholars of medieval music, made clear once and for all that the practicalities of the craft of organ-building were not what the treatises were primarily concerned with. Rather, they were part of a study according to which musical proportion was demonstrated or realized by means of a sequential series of organ-pipes, a divided monochord string or a set of bells: the 'trinitarian ordering by scale, number and weight' (*der trinitarischen Ordnung nach mensura, numerus und pondus*: Sachs 1980: 117).

How far the brief treatises were 'realistic' in the matter of pipe-diameter is implied by the fact that while before the thirteenth century there is no sure indication that the pipe-widths did vary in the treatises' calculations – and then only in the form of quasi-Pythagorean additions to the standard width – nevertheless a constant diameter of between 20 and 30 mm for an octave or even two octaves is small and builders would soon have exceeded it in practice.[1] In other words, craftsmen

---

[1] B. Sudak, 'Genese der mittelalterlichen Theorie des Mensurierens von Orgelpfeifen', *AO* 16 (1982), 217–34.

knew things beyond what theorists describe. (This is not to say that the theorists did not know more – perhaps some did – but that their little treatises had limited intentions.) How realistic early drawings of organs are when they show pipes of more or less unvarying diameter is another and rather different question. For one thing, since drawings could be the result of literate artists knowing the literary sources, they need not be independent evidence. For another, they were not necessarily drawn expertly in any respect (in shape, size, sequence, mouth-design): nor, even if they were, is a constant diameter 'unrealistic' for the short row of pipes in a drawing, whether or not the artist was aiming at a faithful copy. Neither treatises nor representations, therefore, offer straightforward evidence. To a greater extent than used to be imagined – understandably, since evidence is so scarce – both must be marginal to guesses about how organs developed at the hands of their makers.

Yet they cannot be irrelevant because in them are sometimes found practical details of construction, as if the authors/compilers itched to speak of actual organ-building while they were transmitting Boethian note-theory. One example is the treatises' awareness of the end-correction factor for correctly calculating the length of pipes (found in manuscripts from *c.* 1000), for this must have derived from practical experience on somebody's part. This would be so even if the end-correction was itself then expressed in terms of Pythagorean proportion, as it can be. Other elements too probably derive from practical experience – but whose experience, is less certain – as when Aribo (1069/78) remarks that it is 'surer and quicker' to divide anything into three or four than into eight or nine (*certius et velocius* – Sachs 1970: 90), or when Notker Labeo remarks that like the string of a *lira*, an organ-pipe can be too long for its diameter and so have only a 'coarse' tone (*héisa* – Sachs 1970: 98). Notker Labeo also gives a starting-measurement, and texts that were probably derived ultimately from William of Hirsau (see below) include diagrams showing proportional measurements.

For present purposes, these little practical details can help to fill in a few gaps over a period in which so little was documented. The treatise formerly called the 'Bern Anon' is particularly instructive since it belongs to the period of tenth-century reform in the monasteries.

The treatise formerly called 'Bern Anon'

The oldest source for the material known under this name is a compilation of the tenth and eleventh centuries, an 'unhomogeneous and direct joining together of treatments of pipe-measurement and organ-building, furthermore the only one up till then' (Sachs 1980: 34, 253–8). The treatise's organ section comprises seven short texts, four on pipe-scale and three on certain aspects of organ-building (beginning *cuprum purissimum* – see below). In some copies, this material serves as a brief section in a treatise on architecture by M. Cetius Faventinus (third/fourth century, extracted from and citing Vitruvius), which precedes a copy of Vitruvius in the Sélestat manuscript (Reynolds 1986: 445). The organ text seems to have originated for this purpose: something written as a more up-to-date version of the chapter on water-organs in Vitruvius, with practical details not entered into there. The *ars mechanica* tradition to which it belongs probably originated in the monastic scriptoria of north-west France (cf. Hucbald and the *Enchiriadis* treatises) or of southern England, and was copied well into the twelfth century, perhaps even the thirteenth (Sachs 1970: 55–8). This suggests that there was a consistent interest in the contents of such a treatise in libraries, if not in workshops, and no doubt gradually more in libraries and less in workshops.

The treatise juxtaposes theoretical elements with practical, in the process showing many signs that it was compiled from unassimilated fragments of text. The complex makeup could mean that the 'editor' of the architectural treatise compiled the treatise himself, drawing on different kinds of source for different sentences or groups of sentences. The following details are near in time to the Winchester and other organs:

cuprum purissimum tundendo ad summam tenuitatem extenditur,
'the purest copper is worked with hammers to the utmost thinness' and rolled around a cylindrical iron mandrel 'almost four feet long' (*paene quattuor pedibus longo*). The pipe-foot, about one *palmus* long, is conical, its upper diameter – and therefore that of the cylindrical mandrel – the same as a pigeon's egg, its foothole a lark's egg.[2] At the point where the cylindrical part begins, the pipe is cut open, the upper and lower lips pressed in to make it speak ('so that the speech can be formed', *vox possit formari*) when the semicircular languid is soldered in and the joint resoldered. Thus it appears that foot and pipe are made from the same length of copper, and the foot is made conical, apparently on the mandrel. But since nothing is said on the cut and seam of the foot, it is not unlikely that the author was conjecturing from the appearance of a made pipe – perhaps 'he never saw the mandrel, but assumed (wrongly) that it was provided with a tapered foot, as was the finished pipe' (Barry 1989: 87). While the remarks suggest that the pipes in question had the same foot-length, however the foot was made, it is not clear how many pipes there were (see below).

There follow the lengths of pipe calculated for a diatonic sequence of notes 'in which modern melodies mostly lie' (*quo maxime decurrunt modernae cantilenae*). Although this may possibly imply that the organ had something to do with the chant, more likely is that the scale, a Pythagorean pipe-length *mensura* without the additions for practical diameter, is simply that of the notes of post-classical music as learnt from Boethius and others. The author/compiler of a text about organ-pipes would therefore be contributing to the traditional interest of Carolingian monasteries in erecting a theory of notes and making it possible, amongst other things, to classify the Church's chant (see Chapter 2). While the following advice looks practical:

| in septem quoque vocibus | in the seven notes |
| praedictae diapason | of the forementioned octave |

---

[2]   The *ovum columbae* (presumably at its widest circle) has been estimated at between 20 and 37 mm, the *ovum lodicis* between 10 and 16 mm (Sachs 1980: 100, 259; Perrot 1965: 312).

ascendendo et descendendo	both when ascending and descending,
unam quamlibet cantilenam	each and every melody
perficies	you will accomplish (Sachs 1970: 57)

it may be merely saying that the diatonic notes contain all melodies (which is only a theoretical approximation), not that one can now play them all. One version of the text then adds a reference to the B (*b rotundam*) needed 'in certain songs' (*in quibusdam cantibus*). Another version (the earlier?) seems to refer to playing those notes which may be needed but go above present compass, by putting them down an octave; this is possible because any second *ordo* of notes is the same as the first. Whether this implies that the author was aware of compasses beyond an octave,[3] it cannot have been a big step to see that the eighth pipe down from the top doubles the length of the first, the fifteenth that of the eighth.

The fact remains, however, that neither Theophilus nor 'Bern Anon' includes a practical discussion of making and tuning a set of pipes as they would need to have been made and tuned in an actual organ.

ceterum in hydraulis,

'as for the rest, in water-organs' the work involved in making a hydraulis is more difficult but to no greater delectation in the end. This seems to be referring to the engineering challenge of the water-organ, and another brief reference to *hydrauliae* at the end of the text implies the same thing that this does: the author knew Vitruvius's *De architectura*. It does not prove him to have had any first-hand knowledge of the water-organ or even necessarily how it worked, but it may mean that he had seen other parts of the usual organ – the carpentry of the bellows, chests and keys – and recognized them as something less difficult to make than a water-organ.

capsam,

'the chest': materials are not specified, though the sealing of the topboard by molten lead, referred to a little later, must mean the chest was of copper rather than wood. The sentence concerning the chest is confusing:[4]

Capsam, cui superponantur	The chest on which pipes are
fistulae,	to be placed
oportet fieri quadratam aut	must be made square, or
parte altera longiorem, et	longer on the second side, and
per quattuor angulos	at the four corners
	[or: each with four corners?]
singula receptacula	individual receptacles [are made],
reliqua concavitate profundiora,	deeper than the remaining hollow part,
ut ventus divisus aequaliter	so that the equally divided wind
se infundat omnibus foraminibus.	pours into all the [pipe-feet] holes. (Sachs 1970: 57)

---

[3] Not, as Perrot 1965: 339–40 interprets the words, that on a chest with two or more ranks there can be a second rank of pipes an octave higher: such questions arise later in the description.

[4] Theobald 1933: 383ff and W. Nef, 'Der sogenannte Berner Orgeltraktat', *AM* 20 (1948), 10–20, here 11–12, imply that this chest is much the same as Theophilus's.

These could be the words of a non-craftsman describing an actual chest as best he understood it. On one hand, 'receptacles at the corners' is imprecise or simply mistaken; on the other, 'rectangular channels for each note' (below the pipes and above the shallower windbox) would suggest a wooden chest rather than a metal one. It is possible that like Theophilus, the author is setting out to describe both.

The trunk fits into the middle of the base of this chest which is to receive wind 'from the twin bellows on four sides' (*quae per quattuor partes recipiat geminos folles*). Either this means four bellows (one bellows consists of twin boards) or eight (each blower has an alternating pair), and in either case the organ must have much more than an octave or so of pipes. 'On four sides' sounds as if the trunk comes down vertically to a collector around which the bellows are arranged on the four sides of a square, like roots around a tree.

bicorni instrumento perforato recipiuntur,
the pairs of bellows 'are received by a hollow device with two mouths', i.e. each pair is socketed into a wind-collector, probably also of cast copper. A flap-valve of iron or copper is fixed one *palmus* from the windtrunk, i.e. within the wind-collector. (Theophilus, but not the 'Bern Anon' author, makes it clear that each bellows should have its own exhaust-valve, which means that the two-mouthed device here must be small if the valve at the end of each bellows-nozzle is still only one *palmus* away from the trunk?) That the Harding Bible organ (see Plate 10) suggests a hollow device with two mouths precisely of this kind might strengthen the idea that the organ-treatise originated in northern France (Körte 1973: 8), although it could also mean that the Bible artist had read this text.

tabula tenuis, plana, subtilis et recta,
'a thin, flat, well-made and straight table' (i.e. a thin, even sheet) is fixed in place as the upperboard of the windbox part of the chest (*capsae superponenda*), with equidistantly placed holes for the number of pipes required (*secundum numerum fistularum*). Inside the windbox is placed another board, presumably much smaller and facing the entry of the windtrunk − i.e. fixed somehow to lie horizontally not to block but to disperse the wind entering the chest from below by forcing it equally around all of its edges as it rises up to the pipe-holes. Key-sliders or *linguae* (also *tenues, planae, subtiles et rectae*) are fixed above the windbox upperboard − how, it does not say, but presumably they were copper strips separated by battens. The topboard itself of the chest is made from lead, poured on and drilled through from the upperboard, to make holes for the pipe-feet; the sliders are worked free so that they can travel easily. This molten lead anticipates that for Theophilus's copper windchest and would have the same disadvantages in use (see p. 263).

The *ora* or 'mouth' of the slider-grooves is said to run from the front to the back of the chest (*ante et retro*), but this is unlikely to mean that the sliders protruded behind.[5] The grooves may have done so before being plugged at the back, although it is also possible that the author is simply describing something he thought he saw − sliders moving in and out.

[5] Cf. Nef (note 4): 12–13.

a dextra modulantis in sinistram,

'from the right of the one playing, to his left' the pipes on the chest increase in size; thus bass lies to the left. This too sounds like something the author saw, hardly a point for professionals although it does confirm that the row of keys is in sequence. The number of pipes per key can be as many as one pleases, five or ten or 'whatever' (*quotlibet*),[6] but they are to be only *simplae et duplae . . . vox acuta et gravis* ('simple and duple . . . high or low sound'), presumably meaning only unisons and octaves. This is a most important piece of information, though how it was obtained is not known: did the author see a chest of five ranks but was told that it could be ten or more, or had he seen (not made?) such wider chests?

The given pipe-measurements assumed a compass of fifteen sliders, as do the note-names given below.

instrumenta reliqua fiunt,

'the rest of the apparatus is made'. This is the key-action. On pressing a little wooden plate or key (*lamina lignea*), the movement is transferred to an iron pin linking the slider-end with a curved piece of elastic horn. Each slider has such a spring, and the row of springs is fixed in a wooden board in front of the chest. When the key is pressed, the slider-hole lines up with the upperboard hole and wind is admitted to the pipe; when it is let go, the slider blocks the wind. Although there are some uncertainties here in the text and its meaning,[7] the passage does match the compiler's or author's usual descriptive technique, and the general meaning seems clear. The crucial details of how to fix the row of *lamina* or keys are not described, since presumably they belong to woodworking crafts not the concern of this author, but nor is it quite clear why he speaks of the key being depressed from behind (*a tergo depressa lamina*). Is it because although the key is pressed down from above, in relation to the forward movement of the slider to which it is connected by its iron pin, the pushing motion would seem to be 'from behind' the finger end of the slider? Or because the keys are vertical and are pressed from behind towards the player (Riemann 1879: 205–6)? Or because the keys are at the back of the organ, seen from the front? (If the last, it is another detail as observed by a non-expert.) The first is not impossible from the text. But whichever is the case, a visual impression of some kind – how it looks to the observer – is being conveyed.

in laminis,

'on the keys' the *alphabeti litterae* should be written twice, therefore for two octaves. As given in the sources, 'B' means B-natural not B♭ (see remarks below):

      A B C D E F G A B C D E F G H

It may be coincidence that the intervals described in the pipe-scale also correspond to the notes A–a" and that the compiler appears to be consistent, i.e. his 'A' was

---

[6] Sachs 1970: 175 (German translation) as here, but Perrot 1965: 318 (perhaps following Nef (note 4): 14–15) insists that these figures apply to the sliders, not the number of pipes per slider. However, in the clause *simplae et duplae fistulae possunt constitui . . . et ex his quot placuerit* ('simple and duple [unison and octave] pipes can be placed . . . and of these as many as desired'), *his* does not appear to belong to the *linguae* of the next sentence. Nor would only five keys, otherwise unknown in the literature, seem feasible.

[7] See Sachs 1980: 265; Perrot 1965: 318f; Buhle 1903: 86; Körte 1973: 13ff.

meant to be an A (with its third minor) and not a C (with its third major). The last letter of the model scale is uncertain; in one copy of the treatise it appears as

    A B C D E F G a b c d e f g H

and in another

    A B C D E F G a b c d e f g h

so 'H' is not certainly a simple misprint for 'a' (see Sachs 1970: 58 and 1980: 265). If the treatise as compiled is consistent, H need not have been used to mean B-natural since B, the sixth note down from a in the pipe-scale (plus its octave above), is that already. Nor can top A (= a') have been omitted since the total would then be sixteen. Perhaps 'H' is the relic of an earlier convention for using letters beyond A–G; perhaps it is even the scribe's misreading of the doubled $\overset{a}{a}$.

The reason given for labelling the keys – 'so that the player can more quickly know what fingerkey he should play' (*ut citius modulator possit scire, quam linguam debeat tangere*) – is plausible for a compass of two octaves, but says less than it appears to say.

Two particular questions concern the number of pipes and the key-action of *Cuprum purissimum*. Assuming the number of keys and pipes as interpreted above is correct, one of the most important hints in the treatise is that the author knew of organs with more than ten ranks and was quite aware that the number of keys could also vary. With its ten (?) ranks, therefore, Winchester may have been by no means unique, although its forty (?) keys cannot have meant a straight five-octave compass. The treatise does not say whether the choice was open (size varied according to what was required) or depended on age (size varied according to the date of the organ). But it is possible that the ranks and compass as described by a theorist were extrapolated to a larger organ, and that the model organ of both a pipescale-treatise and a psalter-illustration was always smaller than what was known in practice.

The key-action is similar to that of the hydraulis described by Hero (see Chapter 14), and even the two descriptions seem related. Hero's key is a 'square' pivoted in the middle of its lower limb, its upper limb fastened to the end of the slider; not giving such information, 'Bern Anon' leaves the arrangement of the linkwork action much less clear. Perhaps the source was deficient or the compiler did not understand it, or – equally likely – such work was best left to carpenters who devised their own methods on each occasion. Since the Hero texts are not known to have circulated at this time in the Latin monasteries, questions must remain as to whether the source was a now lost section on keyboards in a Vitruvius copy, whether Hero did circulate in a translation now unknown, or whether Hero is the original and only source for the descriptions of the horn-springs. Since all of these are quite unlikely, the last implies what is the most satisfactory solution: the 'Bern Anon' compiler knew another account, not necessarily based on Hero.[8] If organs with horn-springs actually existed in the tenth century, the source of the mechanism could still be literary; if they did not, the reliability of 'Bern Anon' would suffer,

---

[8] Hero himself, or the text-complex named after him, could well have been dependent on earlier sources for at least the wind-raising part of his hydraulic machine.

suggesting his remarks to be a compilation of observation and reading. Whatever is the explanation, the chest and key construction resembles that of Vitruvius or Hero, while more recent if diverse sources served for the remarks on pipe-construction, scale disposition and compass.

Further on 'real details' in pipe-measurement treatises

Even when a concrete measurement is given for the first pipe in a *mensura fistularum* text, as happens in sources associated with William of Hirsau (*c.* 1030–91, see below), the instructions for the scale are not part of a treatise on organ-building as such. Conversely, known treatments of organ-building do not include precise concrete pipe-dimensions despite the parameters implied by certain other dimensions, such as the size of the chest or chest-model in Theophilus. Neither from any treatise (brief) nor from manuscript miniatures (few) would the complete reconstruction now of an early medieval organ be possible, since neither has this aim. At most, they offer 'modules' as a basis on which to plan a full instrument.

Nevertheless, texts do develop towards more recent ideas of practical description and begin to include details formerly within the domain of the craftsman. A progression in the texts may be observed. In the later ninth century, a simple parallel is drawn between the proportions of strings and of pipes (*Scolica enchiriadis*), a branch of theory that gives substance to classical learning, from Plato's *Timaeus* and its later commentators, and from Boethius; then pipes are measured with end-correction and diameter-addition as learnt by experience of pipes themselves; then eventually systematic (geometric) diagrams are made to transmit details of both length and width (Arnaut de Zwolle *c.* 1440, Georgius Anselmi *c.* 1434); finally, fuller details may include the material for the pipes, for the treatment of the mouth, and for the tuning. Some such details as the last, though known about only from thirteenth- to sixteenth-century sources, must have belonged earlier to successive generations of craftsmen. The second stage in such a development must reflect a growing presence of – or awareness of – the organ as a musical instrument, a usable instrument beyond the two-octave row of pipes that gave the old proportion-treatises their 'example' of wind-produced sound to compare with plucked strings and struck bells.[9]

If drawings sometimes transmit practical details 'reliable' as evidence of actual organ-design, so from time to time do the pipe-measurement treatises. One such early text is *Rogatus*, plausibly attributed in a copy of the twelfth century[10] to Gerbert of Aurillac, renowned mathematician, teacher, Archbishop of Reims (991– 8) and subsequently Pope Sylvester II (999–1003). Aurillac was in the vanguard of the Cluniac reform of Benedictine practices, and Gerbert's interests reflect the Order's expansive approach both to traditional learning (his treatise builds on Boethius for theory of proportions) and to the newer technologies (the church itself at Cluny was

---

[9]   Two octaves in a treatise do not imply that a 'real organ' was being described. Although a single octave may appear to be all that is needed to present the basic proportions, in fact the *bisdiapason* appeared in treatments of the monochord and even in the Greek systems (Sachs 1980: 46).

[10]   Madrid, Biblioteca Nacional, MS 9088 f. 125 (Sachs 1970: 27).

developing stone vaults on a new scale). The material on organ-pipes, dated *c.* 980, has been praised for its scope in exceeding all other pipe-measurement texts, its prose-style and its wider mathematical framework.[11] The treatise adds to each pipe-length a comparable proportion from the diameter as a theoretical basis for the phenomenon of end-correction, a phenomenon familiar to observation but one needing 'legitimation' (Sachs 1980: 175). Although the author knows that adjustments can be made at the pipe-mouth, the discussion still barely relates to organs as actual instruments, however. Even the reference to note-names –

litteris quibus organa nostra   letters, with which our organs
notata sunt   have been marked   (Sachs 1970: 65)

– may be part of literary tradition, a way of defining what *litterae* are, whether or not there were many organs with them.

It is significant that the note-letters of *Rogatus* are no longer the Boethian A–LL (a different letter for each note) but octave repetitions returning to A, thus:

A H c d e f g a h c' d' e' f' g' a'

according to the tone–semitone sequence but

F G A B C D E F G A B C D E F in Gerbert's nomenclature.

One B♭ is included in table-calculations, between notes 8 and 9 (see Sachs 1970: 64). Since the F–F–F notation is explained by Gerbert, it may not yet have been customary; later authors in the Cluniac milieu, such as Hermannus Contractus of Reichenau (1013–54), used the terminology A–a–$\frac{a}{a}$ for the two octaves of theory.[12] Presumably the new letter-system was owed to Gerbert's interests, noted in early references to him, in various branches of learning related to music. These branches were not only *musica et astronomia* with which the Gauls (*galliis*) were said to be unfamiliar, but also the kind of learning that led to the making of special apparatus. In Gerbert's case, this included some kind of organ and an astronomical clock, according to William of Malmesbury in the twelfth century, who claimed that they were still there in the church at Reims (see p. 216). Gerbert's *horologia* at Magdeburg and Reims were probably astrolabes, possibly sundials; that at Ravenna, a water-clock.[13]

In epistles, Gerbert referred to *organa* which he appears to have had with him in Italy *c.* 982, perhaps at or in connection with the abbey of Bobbio, in which the abbots of Aurillac evidently had an interest.[14] But it is not clear what *organa* means here, despite usual assumptions (for example Perrot 1965: 290); nor is it certain what

[11] K.-J. Sachs, 'Gerbertus cognomento musicus. Zur musikgeschichtlichen Stellung des Gerbert von Rheims (nachmaligen Papstes Sylvester II.)', *AfMw* 29 (1972), 257–74. On Gerbert possibly being responsible for introducing so-called arabic numerals, see Farmer 1931: 155.

[12] As in H. Oesch, *Berno und Hermann von Reichenau als Musiktheoretiker* (Berne, 1961), 90–3, 207.

[13] S. McCluskey, 'Gregory of Tours, monastic timekeeping and early Christian attitudes to astronomy', *Isis* 81 (1990), 8–22. According to McCluskey, the 'mechanical art' in William of Malmesbury's phrase *horologium arte mechanica* (RBMAS 90.2.196) probably indicates the practical technique of dividing or calculating the divisions on the face of a sundial, and does not imply any kind of moving *mechanism*.

[14] Bobbio is *en route* to one of the Apennine passes used by pilgrims to Rome, a road-system cultivated by the Cluniacs (see A. C. Quintavalle, *Romanico mediopadano: strada città ecclesia* (Parma, 1978), 21, 22, 108 *et passim*).

those things were 'which are made from organs' or 'which arise from instruments' (*quae fiunt ex organis*), listed in a letter of 986/7 and for knowledge of which Gerbert recommended Constantine of Fleury, another Benedictine house under Cluniac reform at the period.[15] Like some contemporary Anglo-Saxon abbeys, the reformed monasteries in the lands of the East and West Franks could well have had an interest both in actual organs and in 'instrumental' teaching-aids for the science of music and its notes. Gerbert, William of Hirsau, Constantine of Fleury and the Abbot of Aurillac represent an interest in various aspects of *organa* held by abbots or bishops in those lands, interests which could then have taken the practical form of having actual organs built. Perhaps one needs to modify the view that the English 'well-documented role' in building monastic organs 'seems to have had no parallel on the continent',[16] since only differences in extant scource-material may be responsible for the Abbot of Winchester's interest in *organa* appearing to take a different form from the Abbot of Hirsau's. This is an uncertain area, and for a different view see pp. 197ff.

Texts associated with William of Hirsau (*c.* 1030–91) were also used by Aribo (1069/78) and contain 'real' detail. *Domnus Willehelmus* had been a Benedictine monk of St Emmeram, Regensburg, became Abbot of Hirsau in 1069 and developed a leadership rôle in the Cluniac reform of German houses. Like Gerbert, some of whose work he seems to have known, William worked on astronomy and had pupils known to write on music. Texts suggest also that his notions of pipe-measurement underwent empirical observation in the course of his studies (Sachs 1980: 205–12). The compass he describes for his 'new art' of pipe-scale in the text *Primae ergo* is two octaves and a third:

C D E F G A B H C D E F G A B H C D E

with both pairs of B♭ and B-natural. Above this the pipes become shrill or ill-voiced (*absonae fiunt*), and those below cannot be blown (*perflari nequeunt*), as 'we will prove' (*provabimus* – Sachs 1970: 85). On the other hand, this remark, plus the scaled diagrams or line-drawings for concrete dimensions of the first or shortest pipe,[17] do not make these pipe-scales any the less useful for scholastic, theoretical study. Nor do the copies of the texts make any apparent effort to preserve an absolute measurement in these lines: the length of the smallest pipe in different copies of *Primae ergo* actually varies from 62 to 140 mm (Sachs 1980: 98).

Similar points about the relation of theory to practice could be made about Aribo, a theorist thought to have worked in another south German house, Freising. Aribo's collection of texts on scaling (pipes, bells, strings) includes practical remarks on making and dealing with pipes. These include advice on soldering the pipe-seam (a strip of tin or some other *lotarium* soldered over the butt-joint, to avoid altering the diameter's size in the process), the mouth (cut across the diameter of

[15] Documentation in Sachs (see note 11): 262–3.

[16] J. McKinnon, 'Musical instruments in medieval psalm commentaries and psalters', *JAMS* 21 (1968), 3–20.

[17] Sachs 1970: plates 14, 15 and 17 (eleventh and twelfth centuries). These diagrams in sources of south German origin anticipate the marginal lines for pipe-lengths, key-lengths and other dimensions in a later treatise produced in the Rhineland: A. Schlick, *Spiegel der Orgelmacher* (Mainz, 1511).

the pipe, so the mouth is pressed in halfway), the windway ('a middle-sized straw' wide – *mediocris festucae*), the diameter (constant, pipes cut from sheets of the same width) and the scaling itself (calculating the notes by alternating fifths and fourths).[18] On one hand, advice may be less practical than appears: the diameter could be constant purely for the purposes of the treatise (for example simply to describe what the relative length of tuned pipes is), and the implication that foot and pipe were cut in one piece from the sheet may be unreliable. On the other hand, there is practical detail in the idea of pipe-sheets being 'thinned along their edges' (*attenuentur praecipue* – filed?) ready for soldering. It is not difficult to imagine that such a writer did want to mix in certain practical details, learnt in various ways, with the pure theory of Pythagorean proportions: to whatever extent this was an attempt to combine theory and practice, so to that extent he was doing something still rather new.

Because of the mixing, however, ambiguities remain. If Aribo's pipe-sheets were filed ready for soldering, then they may have been of copper; but if such metal could be 'bent by the hand of the builder' (*fabrili manu . . . incurvante*) then tin or lead seems more likely (Barry 1989: 86). The oddity is that the question is left open. If copper is taken for granted, then bending by hand is probably not correct; but if tin or lead is the material, then it cannot have been a novelty as one would expect? The organ-chorus is another very uncertain area. In a text apparently including the earlier pipe-scale of William of Hirsau but transmitted by Aribo (*Primam fistulam tantae* – Sachs 1970: 126), there is a reference to multiplying the number of pipes per key. Correct pipe-scaling should be applied to:

quot choros fistularum	as many choruses of pipes as
musici solent ipsi	musicians are themselves accustomed
organico instrumento	to put in the organic instrument
apponere et	and
ad organizandi artem habere.	to have for the art of *organizing*.

Here, both *choros* and *organizandi* have several possible shades of meaning. Despite earlier interpretations that this represents a mixture of unisons and octaves of the kind referred to elsewhere,[19] it is possible that *choros* means simply pipes considered as a set – not a group on the chest sounded by each key but the sum total of pipes considered for purposes of scale-theory. In that case, *choros* would mean a row of pipes, not a mixture-chorus in the later sense. Similarly, while *organizandi* might once have seemed to say that the organ contributed to vocal organum (Perrot 1965: 357), it may mean here simply 'playing music' or 'playing in ensemble music'. Perhaps it does not refer to music at all but to the art of learning how the intervals of music are produced by properly scaled pipes. See also Chapter 19 for some remarks on this important passage.

Another short treatise, the Sélestat manuscript, contains sections that represent pipe-scale treatments of the tenth and eleventh centuries and which are themselves

---

[18]   Sachs 1970: 92. The alternating fifths and fourths anticipate not only the practical scaling of Henri Arnaut de Zwolle in the fifteenth century but the earliest treatments of pipe-tuning in the fourteenth (Sachs 1980: 231).

[19]   E.g. Buhle 1903: 95–96; for such a mixture, see the manuscripts 'Bern Anon' (above) and Sélestat (below).

contained in the treatise-group known formerly as 'Bern Anon' (see above). Their text-section beginning *Mensuram et* (Sachs 1970: 95), also circulating in English copies of the twelfth century, specifies that an octave pipe 'be placed between two larger' (*inter duas maiores fistulas ponatur*) in the sense of 'placed between them on the chest itself'. Per key, the ranks are therefore 8.8.4 (or rather 8.4.8), and the pipe-measurements for one octave can be extrapolated to fifteen or twenty-one notes. It is difficult to see how *ponatur* could, or would be intended to, mean anything other than 'placed on the chest' even if the remark may be merely an indication of what could be done, not what was always done. The details of this organ-type therefore seem to be: a compass of up to three octaves, with three (or even more?) ranks, predominantly unison but with an octave rank (or ranks?) placed between the unisons. This 'placing between' is another sign of practical experience on somebody's part. For it either helps prevent interference across the mouth-eddies or it gives a winding that was more even; probably the former?

The mention in the text *Longissimam* (south German *c.* 1000) of 'instruments which are put into action by water' (*organis . . . quae ad aquam moventur* – Sachs 1970: 97) does not prove that hydraules were still in use or even much understood, for the words are taken from Boethius, as too they had been earlier by Aurelian of Réôme (CSM 21.66). Specification in the text *Mácha dia* (Notker Labeo, *c.* 950–1022?) for the length of the reference-pipe[20] as 'one and a half ells' may have conveyed an absolute measurement in South Germany in *c.* 1000 – something over 3' – but it may also have been given to conform with the pipe's 'casually proposed diameter', as it has been called (Sachs 1980: 101, 315). In short, neither is precise. The text *Longissimam*, one of a family of texts of which *Mácha dia* is a partial translation, begins by speaking of a pipe whose length is as one wishes.

Such translation work was typical of the scriptorium of St Gall at this period (see below) and the material produced there was assured of a wide circulation. Perhaps it is witness to a lively interest in organs, though to conclude this may be no more correct than to assume that an absence of documentation elsewhere means there was no such lively interest. The text *Fac tibi* is partly based on *Mácha dia* and speaks of

octava et quintadecima	octave and fifteenth
in quattuor primis choris . . .	in the first four choruses [= notes]. . .
similiter fac reliquis choris	do similarly with the other choruses [?]
sed quadruplum primis	but the quadruplum [= double octave above]
quattuor convenit,	suits [only] the first four,
reliquis minime	the others very little (Sachs 1970: 115)

which seems to mean that the keys C D E F have ranks of 8.4.2, while G A B H have 8.4 (or 8.4.4 or 8.8.4?). If the author meant this principle to continue on up a longer compass – or if each set of four notes stands for longer stretches of the compass – then this is the first written indication (such as it is) of the accumulated pitches of the Italian *ripieno* or the northern *Blockwerk* of the fifteenth century. This very topic of the Mixture is a paradigm for the organ's evolution: documentation

---

[20] Reference-pipe: the starting point, the pipe from which the others are calculated.

about it is quite incomplete and yet what there is suggests a continuously developing craft at the hands of inventive, alert, practically minded builders.

That a 'builder' (? – *organicus*) might like to go to three octaves or even more (*tria alphabeta vel amplius*) is mentioned in more than one twelfth-century text.[21] Although it is possible that such observations are made purely for the sake of being theoretically complete – *organicus* might mean the *musicus* who is pondering questions of instruments and proportional calculation, not an organ-builder as such – the fact remains that such theory describes a plausible 'actual organ' of the eleventh century. South Germany very likely saw a particular interest in practical matters in its writing and copying of treatises. Whether it did have a culture more at home with mechanical or metallurgical work than was the case in other areas of Europe, St Gall had a history of intense scribal activity in such practical matters as documentation, recording endowments and training monastic scribes in the German vernacular[22] – not unique but able to contribute to 'particular interests in practical matters'.

'Real' detail from some later treatises

Later texts refer to pipe-metal. Beaten tin is specified in the text *Tekhuna hajeschana* (fourteenth-century Hebrew from Toulouse [?], partly with Latin material of the eleventh and twelfth centuries), tin or lead in two fifteenth-century English copies of the text *Circa latitudinem*.[23] These copies give different scalings or ratios of length to circumference for the 'first pipe' (*prima fistularum*) made in the different metals: 7:1 for tin, 5:1 for lead. From the advice that lead is rare and does not suit all parts of the compass, especially the lower pipes (*in inferioribus fistulis*, presumably including the 'first pipe'), it is not clear whether 7:1 is merely the starting ratio for tin, and that higher up it too was 5:1, or something like it. Although there is no further explanation, lead must have been inadvisable for the bigger pipes because of its weight (the sheet was thick?) and the practical difficulties of working it.

Though brief and only imperfectly covering such details as the four-octave compass known in other fifteenth-century sources (Arnaut de Zwolle, Franchino Gaffori), the text *Circa latitudinem* is valuable for including interesting remarks on two further practical matters. First, concerning what seem to be conical pipes:

quaelibet fistula latior erit in	each pipe will be wider in the
parte superiori quam in inferiori	upper part than in the lower
et certa in quantitate,	and to a particular degree [of taper],
quia hoc est pro voluntate	for this is at the choice of the
operantis, dummodo	craftsman, as long as
latitudo sit	the pipe-width [at the mouth?] is
nobilis et apparens.	clearly substantial [?]. (Sachs 1970: 141)

---

21 E.g. Sachs 1970: 124 (here, a copy of an earlier text).
22 Some discussion in Sachs 1980: 200 and further in R. McKitterick, *The Carolingians and the Written Word* (Cambridge, 1989), 120ff.
23 Sachs 1970: 214, 140–1; also Sachs 1980: 335, 362f.

The mouth is a quarter of the diameter, but whether this really does mean a conical pipe and not a cylindrical pipe plus its conical foot, the mouth still seems unrealistic. Is the author's observation imperfect, is *diametri* a mistake for circumference, or is his information very old (see also below)? If one could be sure that their shape was reliably observed,[24] the cylindrical pipes shown in most drawings from the twelfth century onwards would probably mean tin or lead alloy, soldered in the cold and made on wooden mandrels. But there are too many unknowns here: some conicity could have been so slight as to be unrecognized, while elsewhere it could have been exaggerated, both by inexpert artists.

A second point in *Circa latitudinem* concerns the action (*de clavibus*). The little treatise says nothing about it

quia hoc totum in facto consistit	because the whole of this remains in the [sphere of actual] making
et patebit faciliter	and will be easily clear to the
operanti.	craftsman.

A late text, these words summarize centuries of attitude towards such practical matters as action–design and the woodwork of organs: these are practical matters for craftsmen who make their own solutions and need no description in words. However, even in acknowledging the craftsman such writers may be following mere convention, for a well-read theorist would know that Vitruvius had long ago recommended looking at objects already made if one wanted to learn more about them (see Chapter 14).

A second Hebrew text, *Tekhuna chadascha*, has the first known reference to a quint rank. Behind each pipe (as seen by the player) stands one only as large as the fifth above or, failing that, a yet smaller pipe. Behind that stands a pipe half as long as the first, and according to the size of the instrument, each key can have many pipes, 'fourths, fifths and eighths'. Though previously interpreted as a text describing an organ-mixture of fourths, fifths and octaves on each note,[25] this need be no more than an allusion to the theorists' formula *diatesseron, diapente et diapason*. If it contains organological detail at all, it would mean a chorus on Tenor C of c g c', which makes a fifth, a fourth and an octave, the last of which subsumes the other two (*diapason*, 'through all'). Although the treatise apparently offers a chorus of 8.4 as an alternative – 'yet smaller' must mean the octave rather than the fifth? – it could be that the remarks were open to extrapolation, thus leading to the even smaller twelfth and fifteenth ranks. Small ranks of some kind are also hinted at in the treatise *Mensuram et* when it advises replacing the 'missing smaller pipes' (*deficientibus minoribus fistulae* – Sachs 1970: 95), as if the added non-unison ranks vary when the notes ascend. So they would if the compass were long enough. Even if neither treatise

---

[24] One could argue that drawing pipes cylindrically is neither easier nor harder than drawing them conically: in drawings, a gapped row of pipes tends to be conical (e.g. Harding Bible), a close-packed row cylindrical (e.g. Stuttgart Psalter), but cf. the gapped cylindrical pipes of the Utrecht Psalter.

[25] H. Avenary-Loewenstein, 'The mixture principle in the medieval organ: an early evidence', *MD* 4 (1950), 51–7; Perrot 1965: 357. The organum of the *Musica enchiriadis* consisting of four voices (principal/ organal/octave-principal/octave-organal) was an early layout in fourths, fifths and octaves.

yet describes the chorus clearly, nevertheless since a 'minimum module' is what treatises generally seem to offer one can infer the presence of twelfths and fifteenths.

The St Florian Fragment, a source or copy of the thirteenth century, gives other dimensions involved in pipe-making (Sachs 1980: 93–4, 343): foothole diameter a third of the pipe-diameter, pipe-mouth a third of the circumference. The dimensions of pipe-width and foot-taper were to be marked on an iron ruler, thus not occurring by chance in the manufacture.[26] The English text *Incipit mensura* (*c.* 1373) gives a length:circumference ratio of 5:1 for the biggest pipes, with foothole a third for small pipes, a quarter for others; and cutup was probably a quarter.[27]

The impression given by such brief references to pipes is that practice varied widely and that builders were accustomed to a whole range of dimensions for them, as presumably they were for chests and other parts. For instance, if early mouths were always close to a full diameter wide, as in Theophilus, then other or later builders must have consciously reduced them. In the text *Sunt vero* (Georgius Anselmi, 1433/4) several length:diameter ratios are given, each with its own implications for tone. The ratio 7:1 gives a 'tone that penetrates' (*perstrepit*), 15:2 a 'rough and shrill tone' (*sonitum asperum et altum*), 9:1 a 'moderate . . . sweet tone' (*mediocrem . . . suavem sonitum*), and narrower than 9:1, a 'blunt tone' (*obtusum sonum* – Sachs 1970: 142). Though clearly not scientific terms, they nevertheless suggest experience, even experiment, beyond the earlier treatises' statutory ratio of 8:1 for the first pipe.

Finally, two details can be fitfully pursued amongst the treatises: the questions of conical pipes and the emerging tuning-systems. On conical pipes: does the early text known as *Mensuram et* (tenth century) refer to conicity or to cylindrical pipes with tapering feet?

Sic tamen, ut in summitate grossiores, in inferiori parte graciliores semper sint.	But so that at the top they may be always wider, in the lower part narrower.

(Sachs 1970: 93)

(On Theophilus's description, see p. 258.) It seems hardly possible that the writer was simply misled – because the shorter a pipe above its mouth the nearer the whole pipe comes to looking conical, or because feet may have been very long and caused some optical illusion. Similarly, while any description of conicity in the text *Circa latitudinem* (see above) might be both inexpert and archaic, the fifteenth-century text 'Cambrai Anon' (see below) which speaks of conical tin pipes, was neither. Although one must conclude that outward-tapering pipes were an optional pipe-shape – sixteenth-century versions were revivals rather than survivals? – this does not say much about whether the shape was either predominant in the earlier period or particularly associated with copper-working.

By the late fourteenth century some detail on tuning is emerging in that a few theorists now refer to it as something they understand or now find relevant to

---

26 Does the author remark on the measuring rod because it was new to him or because it had become only recently the craftsman's normal tool? The latter seems unlikely.
27 Sachs 1970: 137, discussed in Sachs 1980: 353.

remarks on pipe-measurement. The texts *Incipit mensura* and *Si quis concordiam* (French, fourteenth century) are important for their discussion of tuning methods, setting out on the long road of temperament-coverage that has barely abated to this day.[28] There is no detail in the texts[29] of how the pipes are fine-tuned, but there is awareness of how tempering-problems arise. *Incipit mensura* begins by choosing the best pipe in a given *chorus* of a key (*meliorem fistulam* – the best-toned?); then C G D A E H are tuned by rising fifths, C F B by falling fifths; if there are *falseta* to be tuned, then H F♯ C♯ (the first by a falling fourth – also the second?). The text is not clear enough to confirm Sachs's interpretation that the compass reached as high as h", although references to *omnes b molles* ('all the B♭'s') does suggest that there were more than two such notes. The treatise's remarks are applicable to various compasses. So is the information on F♯ and C♯: the section on B is rounded off with the phrase *et sic est finis* ('and thus ends it') and is then followed by *falsetis vero si concordabis* ('if you really want to tune the sharps'). Arguing back from later history, one could assume that the larger the compass in the treble, the more likely that sharps are included.

The little treatise *Si quis concordiam* advises first voicing the pipes (*intonet calamos*), then placing them above the right keys[30] and tuning by fifths and fourths. Thus C up to G down to D and so on to H, then C up to F and up to B; F♯ up to H. The fourths C–F, D–G being described as *discordia* while the fifths are *concordia* probably means that the fourths are wide, the following fifths (A after D, etc.) somewhat flat, and therefore the thirds of certain chords (triads on C, F and G) more pleasant.

Henri Arnaut de Zwolle

Coming to Arnaut de Zwolle from a study of previous centuries, rather than treating him as a herald of the explosive development of Renaissance organs, gives a particular, perhaps truer focus to his material. The task is to discern what details in his remarks illuminate earlier practices.

The manuscript compilation,[31] begun in about 1440, has both old and new elements: like earlier treatises it gives a string- and pipe-scale (*mensura*), but it also makes clearer than before that there needs to be fine tuning and adjustment of the pipes towards making a temperament.[32] It still likens sound to sweetness, speaking of a certain chair organ with a 'sweetness the likes of which cannot be found under the sun' (*simile dulcedine sub sole irreperibile*); but it is also newly 'technical' about the pipe-work concerned:

[28]   Though outside the scope of the present study, one wonders whether there were any medieval counterparts to 'those gentlemen who tease and torture the strings' in pursuit of minute intervals no-one can hear, according to Plato *Republic* 7.
[29]   Sachs 1970: 139, 140; also Sachs 1980: 354–61, a particularly useful discussion.
[30]   Does this imply that pipes could have been tuned other than on a chest? Perhaps the advice here is for a 'real' organ, no mere theory of proportions?
[31]   Paris, Bibliothèque Nationale, lat. 7295; dating and description in Le Cerf 1932: viif.
[32]   The *mensua* text in Sachs 1970: 145–6; on temperament, Sachs 1980: 367–9.

anteriores principales sunt stannei,	the principals in front are of tin,
omnes vero auxiliantes et posteriores	but all the auxiliaries and
coprincipales sunt plumbei,	co-principals behind are of lead
et sunt calami valde ponderosi,	and are very heavy pipes,
quasi in triplo spissiores	almost three times as thick
calamis stanneis,	as the tin pipes,
tam parvi quam magni.	small pipes as well as large. (Le Cerf 1932: 39)

This is very clear and fits the brief reference to materials in the text *Circa latitudinem* (see above). Also instructive is Arnaut's information that the pipe-mouths on this old organ are irregular in size – wide and narrow, high and low, corresponding to 'no division of the diapason' or regular scale (*nulla est . . . dyapasonis divisi*). Details of the chest, as in Le Cerf 1932: plates II and III, are:

compass from 3' F, with 195 pipes made up as follows:

f–e'   8.4.2.8

f'–e"   8.4.4.2.8

f"–c♯"   8.4.4.2.8.4.8

d"–f"   8.4.4.4.8.4.8

the second complete 8' rank of lead, at the back of the chest.

This was a Blockwerk of early type both in content (only octaves) and in arrangement (the ranks interspersed). For the F–F–F compass, see the remark on Gerbert of Reims above.

Extrapolations from Arnaut's figures for small organs[33] give a Principal Scale somewhat above Normal Scale 8' C, becoming progressively narrower until 1' C is eleven pipes below Normal Scale. Mouth is a quarter of circumference, with quarter cutup and a toehole area the same as or more than the flue. If these dimensions are fully extrapolated, however, the flues would be too wide for large pipes and too narrow for small, and would have been adjusted in practice. (Pipe-scale depends on the size of the organ, according to 'Cambrai Anon': see below.) Tuning appears to be eleven perfect fifths, with H–F♯ a schisma flat, all naturals and B tuned as perfect fifths and all sharps as practically pure thirds.

Some idea of issues of interest in *c*. 1450 are given by brief remarks on *tono cori* (a pitch given by the length of a line in the margin – Le Cerf 1932: plate V), pipe-metal (two weights of tin to one of lead – *ibid*., 49), oxidized lead pipes with small mouths in an old organ of Dijon (*ibid*., 50), 2⅔' ranks in a larger Blockwerk (*ibid*., 54), a tierce-mixture (*ibid*., 56) and perhaps reeds (? *ibid*., 1932: 31–4). But the date of these items is very uncertain.[34] The bellows described by Arnaut (*ibid*., 57–8) were probably new: they had three folds (*costes*) of leathered boards, and outer boards of *c*. 1.585 m × 0.764 m, with a lift of *c*. 0.275 m. In Arnaut's detailed drawings of the smaller keyboard stringed-instruments such as might have interested

---

[33] This and the next two sentences are based on a private communication from Mr Wilson Barry.

[34] Dating Arnaut's 12/24–rank Blockwerk of 8.4.2 2⅔.2 to 1334, as in H. Klotz, *Über die Orgelkunst der Gotik, der Renaissance und des Barock* (Kasel, 1975), 14, is particularly speculative. Nor is Praetorius's observation – that old builders tuned the ranks so that the Blockwerk on each key had perfect untempered fifths (Praetorius 1619: 104) – certainly true of Arnaut's choruses, as suggested by Le Cerf, though this is much more likely.

French makers *c.* 1450, various reliable data are given. The naturals of such instruments were about one medieval inch wide and two long, though there was some variety. Several harpsichord mechanisms, though very likely theoretical constructs only, rely on structural elements that must have been familiar to organ-builders but are described or drawn here for the first time:

> pin action: a 'wooden sticker' (*cavilla lignea*) presses down a spring-loaded jack;
> suspended action: the end-pivoted key hangs below, the jack designed to pluck up the string at one end as the key pulls down its other;
> two kinds of spring: iron or brass wire pallet-spring pushing up the jack in the pin action, a flat brass spring pressing down the jack in the suspended action.

Clearly, fine keyboard-actions were a thing of great interest in the early fifteenth century. The description of a small organ must have been made from an actual sample (*ibid.*, 23–7):

> the chest (*cista*) is made from two 'solid blocks of wood' (*asseres*) glued together, with 'white leather' (*corium album*) between the two;
> leathered grooves (*fissure*) are made in the bottom of the lower block; leading from them and also carved into the upper block are leathered channels (*conductus*) to the toeholes;
> largest pipes to left; or the largest pipes can be in the middle in order to give a pipe-arrangement 'in the form of a bishop's mitre' (*ad modum mitre episcopalis*) if they are fed by channels above the pallets, hollowed out on two levels in the chest blocks;
> the grooves are longer than necessary, and the channels have to turn back to the pipes (thus reducing speech attack?);
> the pin below the frontal end of the key passes through a leather purse (*fossata*);
> the leather-faced pallets (*ventilabia*) are at keyscale (i.e. narrow, directly above the keys) admitting wind to the upper groove via a hole cut in its leather seal below;
> the pallet-tails are glued on with leather and made secure with a wooden batten; 'a little pin or rod of iron wire' (*parvuli claviculi de filo ferreo*) separates the pallets; springs are held in place with another batten; the pallets should not be very wide but 'somewhat high and shaped with a spine' (*aliqualiter alto cum dorso*) to prevent curving;
> bellows can be doubled (*duplex flabellum*) like those of goldsmiths, to 'supply constant wind' (*continue ventum ministrans*); a 'block' between the pair has 'valves' (*asser, ventilabia*) to prevent wind being sucked from one to the other.

Whether some lapses in the descriptions[35] result from the author's method or from the manuscript's unfinished state is unclear. On the other hand, the compass beginning at H agrees with other evidence from the period and is probably to be understood as a means of giving the tetrachord E F G A at two pitches, the one a fourth below the other.

---

[35] E.g. Arnaut gives no hitchpin rail in his harpsichord.

Arnaut's data on large, up-to-date organs give some idea of the various designs of the time that took advantage of inventive mechanisms and a developed technology for making larger pipes. Twelve large 'tenor pipes without mixture ranks' of their own at St-Cyr (at Nevers? – *fistulas tenoris . . . nullas fornituras*) began with a length one and a half times that of the biggest chorus pipe; this must mean that they overlapped the regular chorus, and may therefore have been played by pedal keys? The Cordeliers organ, probably at Dijon, had ten 'larger pipes doubling the tenors at the octave below' (*fistulas grossiores pro subdupla tenoris organorum*). A row of coupling pins or 'stickers could be threaded through' (*caville . . . reducuntur*) to allow the tenors' row of keys[36] to be played by an upper row; from the lower keys (perhaps meaning a pedalboard) iron wires pass through the upper to their own rollerboard connecting with the big subdupla pipes to the side. It is difficult to believe that the stickers, trackers, couplers and rollerboards handled so confidently in such instruments were recent.

In the smaller quire organ at the Cordeliers, there were five *registra*. Although the make-up of the chorus is unclear from Arnaut's words, some conjecture is useful as a guide to what may have been a traditional, small-scaled chorus for liturgical organs:

simplicia principalia in duo divisa,	one-rank principals divided into two,
et quelibet principalis duas quintas	and each principal has two fifths
et unam octavam habet,	and one octave
et sunt ibi 5 registra.	and thus there are five registers. (Le Cerf 1932: 30–1)

Perhaps *registra* specifically means the iron stop-levers. *Simplicia principalia* sounds as if it means a single rank, perhaps divided here into treble and bass and thus distinct from the duplicated principals known from Dutch contracts at this period.[37] 'Two quints' probably included fifths, twelfths or nineteenths. Assuming a small 4' organ, the chorus could have been:

bass 4', treble 4', each with two fifths (or a fifth and a twelfth?) and one octave, thus each half with 4.2⅔.2⅔.2 or 4.2⅔.2.1⅓;

the stop-levers were one for principal bass, one for principal treble, one for the octave, one for both bass fifths, one for both treble fifths (or one for each complete fifth).

Whatever the correct layouts of these instruments, Arnaut describes a transalpine organ-type that by then had achieved extra-large pipes, quint ranks, pallet-chests, more than one keyboard, a rollerboard, a separate coupler and several stop-levers.

---

[36] The account is confusing and does not now make clear if (a) the largest pipes were distinct from the *tenores*, (b) which set it was (if there were two) that had its own keys, and (c) if 'lower keys' means a pedalboard.

[37] E.g. Zwolle 1447, *duppel principalen*: in M. A. Vente, *Vijf Eeuwen Zwolse Orgels 1447–1971* (Amsterdam, 1971), 72, where the contract of 1447 refers to a similar organ in Deventer. On the term 'double', see p. 354.

'Cambrai Anon'

A recent claim that a manuscript from the Cistercian Abbey of Vaucelles[38] goes 'back at least as far as the second half of the fifteenth century' (Barbieri 1989) is based on the information it gives: the organ has a compass of H–g", inverted conical pipes, narrow diameters decreasing rather slowly as the notes rise, presence of large separate pipes (*trompes*) and the choice of two tunings with strong or gentle thirds and sixths (*fortes/douces tierces ou sextes*).[39] The manuscript or its source seems to be the work either of a builder or someone closely observing building-practice.

The length of the longest pipe, which is not given, is also the length of the chest – perhaps an old rule-of-thumb? As in Arnaut (Le Cerf 1932: 29), *Trompes* are recommended to begin a fifth lower than the otherwise lowest note. Perhaps this advice reflected the facts that bass voices are pitched about a fifth lower than tenor voices, not an octave, and/or that held bass notes were likely to be a fourth or fifth lower than the next voice.[40] For *orgues de chapelle* (organs for choir office and mass?), the pipe-length:circumference ratio begins at 6:1, a narrow diapason like that for the front Principale at S Petronio, Bologna (1471–5). For *grandes orgues* it is 7:1, *orgues moyennes* 13:2 and *petites orgues* 5:1. The last is wide because otherwise the pipes 'would have no speech' (*elles n'auroient point de son*). Other fifteenth-century writers record varying length:circumference scales: 7:1, 6:1 and 5:1 in Arnaut de Zwolle (Le Cerf 1932: 15), while Georgius Anselmi of Parma notes that larger churches need pipes of wider scale (Sachs 1970: 142, 221). Such a scale, however, would make the sound less clear if the reverberation were high. Halving of diameter is 'slow', probably with diameters changing 'more rapidly in the low pipes than in the high' and thus 'in favour of the high notes and against the bass' (Barbieri 1989: 9–10). An obscure but probable reference to (old?) pipe-ranks with constant diameter gives an important hint about builders' handling of this factor in practice: mouths became smaller (both width and cutup?) the shorter the pipe for a given diameter.

The pipes are conical. The top:bottom ratio is 7:5, which makes for a tone *plus melodieuse et plus douce*, but some use 6:5 and smaller organs a still smaller taper. The outward tapering is in order that the pipes

puissent mieux vuider	can better transmit	
leurs voix et tons	their voice and tone	(Barbieri 1989: 15)

and for smaller organs the outward taper should be less pronounced, so that this transmission of sound is not achieved *avec trop d'éclat*. It is possible that, all things being equal, conical pipes do produce a more penetrating tone and that no early examples survive only because such tone fell from favour later. Whether the author knew of penetrating tone from experience is only one of the unknowns: others are

---

[38] Cambrai, Médiathèque Municipale, MS 976 (874), ff. 472'–5'.

[39] 'Almost certainly the typical late fifteenth-century contrast between the Pythagorean and syntonic-meantone system' (Barbieri 1989: 5).

[40] In Marin Mersenne's drawing of a *psalterion* (*Harmonie universelle* (Paris, 1636), Part V, Bk. 3, Prop. 26), the bottom string G, which serves as *bourdon*, is a fourth below the next lowest string in a compass of Gc–g'.

whether late medieval representations so seldom show the taper because it was by then (virtually) unknown or because a taper of 6:5 is not easily visible from a distance.

Two other details in 'Cambrai Anon' concern the mouth and the tuning. On mouths: large organs have a mouth of quarter circumference (one third cutup), medium organs two sevenths circumference (two sevenths cutup), small and chapel organs one third circumference (one quarter cutup). The author warns against too large a mouth and recommends a foothole diameter one third the pipe, thus wider and stronger than Arnaut's quarter? (Presumably the circumference measurement of the conical pipe is taken from its largest value, i.e. at the top of the pipe, although this has the effect of reducing the scale even further.) On the tuning: the remark that small organs – meaning treble portatives? – give a good *melodie* when tuned with 'strong' thirds, fifths and sixths may mean conversely that in the case of larger organs, it was their more harmonic function that made it necessary to develop temperaments.

17

Details of 'real organs' in miscellaneous sources

In looking at references to organs over the thousand years between St Augustine and Henri Arnaut de Zwolle, one needs to range particularly freely across the centuries when seeking technical details in sources not primarily concerned with organs. The present chapter gives five further and particularly significant types or species of evidence, starting with the oldest and the one most widely known throughout the period.

Some pre-Carolingian sources

The array of pre-Carolingian references to *organum* occasionally yields a technical-organological detail of importance, whatever the author's source and whatever the requirements of the particular form in which he is writing. Three prime and vastly influential examples are the brief remarks on the organ in psalm-commentaries of St Augustine (†430), St Jerome (†420) and Cassiodorus (†*c*. 585): these alone could be responsible for a large proportion of all the references to organs made over the following centuries.

Augustine's commentary on Psalm 150 discusses the terms used by the psalm:

Organum autem generale	moreover, 'organ' is the general
nomen est omnium	name of all
vasorum musicorum; quamvis	implements of musicians; although
jam obtinuerit consuetudo	now the custom would hold
ut organa proprie	for calling 'organs' specifically
dicantur ea quae	those that
inflantur follibus . . .	are winded by bellows . . .
	[of instruments in general:]
hoc cui folles adhibentur,	that for which bellows are employed
alio Graeci nomine appellant.	the Greeks call by another [or particular] name. (PL 37.1964)

Two particular points stand out here. First, bellows are part of the definition of an organ as given to a wide readership in the fifth century and picked up by later writers (Reckow 1975: 98f). That commentators such as Isidore of Seville use Augustine's definition (*Etymologiae* 2.2) does not imply that actual organs were known at that time and place, however tempted later readers might be to assume it does (for example in Llovera 1987: 81ff). Second, Augustine says that while instruments in general are called *organa*, the Greeks have a more specific name for that with bellows – presumably *hydraulis* or a related term, as used (surmised?) by Hucbald.

Now while Augustine's emphasis on bellows must have influenced at least some of the earlier illustrations, such as that for Psalm 150 in the Stuttgart Psalter (see p. 165), it is not clear how the 'hydraulic instrument' of the classical Alexandrian *artes mechanicae* authors could have become one of the names of an instrument that had no hydraulic element. Perhaps *hydraulis* or *hydra* circulated around the Mediterranean (cf. the Aquincum inscription and the Arabic word-derivatives in Chapter 14) to distinguish the 'hundred-headed' (*hydra*) instrument that had 'pipes' (*auloi*), from all the other 'instruments in general' (*organa*). Although *hydra* does seem to anticipate later musicians' habit of abbreviating instrument-names, the 'hundred heads' is particularly apt. For *hydraulia* to have bellows may not have seemed a contradiction in terms several centuries after Vitruvius, and in any case it is most unlikely that during the centuries from Ctesibius to Augustine organs were made only in the hydraulic form; see p. 243. Besides, the ancient authors themselves, though exhaustively drawn upon by post-medieval scholars, may have given a misleading impression of who used the word for what purpose in common parlance.

Jerome's commentary on Psalm 136/137, which shares some material with Augustine's for the same psalm, includes the following:

Organum autem hominis corpus est.	But the organ is the body of man.
Sicut enim organum ex multis fistulis compositum est,	Thus, as the organ is put together from many pipes,
unum autem modulatione melos mittit,	but one that through musical order brings forth *melos*,
ita et organum nostrum habemus tactum: per ipsum, hoc est per opera, melos et canticum et hymnum referimus Deo.	so we have our organ to hand: through it, that is through works [= *ergon*?], we bring a *melos*, a *canticum*, a hymn before God. (PL 26.1304)

Though conventionally allegorical and apparently less concerned with 'real' organs than Augustine's words, the passage is still useful for the organ-historian because whatever sustained shrieks the hydraulis had formerly contributed to events in the arenas of the Roman Empire, Jerome's words make it difficult to think that organs were capable of nothing more. It must have been known that in the right hands, of player and therefore builder, they could be made to produce *melos* through *modulatione*. And if metaphorically, then actually. Also, even if the point of the passage seems to be to say that actual organs are not necessary – we have the 'organ' of our lives already to hand for pious use – clearly later readers could take the words as some kind of justification for the instrument. Organs placed in a church and producing *well-modulated* sounds would be an allegory for man and man's *opera Dei*, desirable for that reason alone.

In a further commentary on Psalm 150 written a century and a half later, Cassiodorus is more factual:

organum itaque est quasi	thus the organ is like a
turris quaedam	kind of castle (tower)
diversis fistulis fabricata,	made up of diverse pipes,
quibus flatu follium	by which, through the blowing of bellows,
vox copiosissima destinatur;	a very plentiful sound is sent;
et ut eam modulatio	and for this sound
decora componat,	to be properly regulated,
linguis quibusdam ligneis ab	the organ is constructed with certain
interiore parte construitur,	wooden tongues in its interior,
quas disciplinabiliter	which being controlled methodically by
magistrorum digiti reprimentes,	the fingers of masters,
grandisonam efficiunt et	produce a loud-sounding and
suavissimam cantilenam.	very agreeable melody. (PL 70.1052–3)

This is a very useful reference, not only giving important technical details but to some extent clarifying one or two terms met frequently in the early literature, particularly *modulatio* and *suavis*. On *modulatio*: context suggests this to mean specifically the handling of notes to give them musical order (as distinct from signalling noises?), and it would be safe to assume that the words of St Jerome lay behind parts of this reference. On *suavis*: assuming that *grandisonam* is referring to volume-level, the pairing of the words suggests that the sweetness so often invoked in the literature (see Chapter 2) can be matched with loudness – good sound can be sweet *and* loud.

Cassiodorus's words both enlarge on Augustine's definition and may reflect knowledge of previous literature, such as the lines of Claudian (Perrot 1965: 383) in which finger-keys, bronze pipes and (in the interior) agitated water join to produce music. The last is not there in Cassiodorus but a precedent had been set for talking about the interior workings of technical objects. In turn, his use of *turris* may have influenced later writers wishing to convey the idea of any tall piece of complex but self-contained furniture, as when Hraban Maur (†856 – PL 110–31f) uses the word for reporting on the mechanical throne of the Persian king Chosroes (†579). (In this connection, it may be significant that much later Italian contracts frequently refer to groups of pipes in case-fronts as *castelli* – see Donati 1979: 183–4.)

At least four 'realistic' details were conveyed by Cassiodorus to his readers over the centuries that followed:

> pipes are numerous enough to be arranged in a geometric shape of some kind
> and to be likened to a *turris*: perhaps the word implies that there was a tall
> frame (of wood?) around them;
> bellows supply the wind;
> wooden sliders or (more likely?) wooden keys operating sliders (literally
> making use of the individual fingers?) allow individual notes to be played;
> and the resulting sound, both sweet and strong (plentiful? sustained?), is such
> as can play some kind of melodic line.

Although the last is not certain – *cantilenam* might be figurative or as general as Jerome's *canticum* – the organ's appearance, winding, purpose, operation and sound are ably summarized in only a few words, as one might expect of a writer known to have been interested in such *technicalia* as sundials and water-clocks. The information on wooden mechanism, though slight, is unmatched for centuries, and one could wish that many a later medieval reference had built on this precedent.

Cassiodorus's words appear to be less formulaic than those concerning organs in the verse of St Aldhelm (†709), which are still sometimes taken as evidence that the English knew organs in the seventh century. Here the 'wind-filled bellows', 'gilt chests' and 'very large organ' offer some striking images of bellows in action, pipe-chests made of burnished copper (?) and the size of organs compared to other instruments (*ventosis follibus, auratis capsis, maxima organa* – MGH AA 15.2.355–60). But the question is how far previous sources, in words or pictures, could have been responsible for such images in verse concerned with the psalms and their special language, as this was. The largeness of organs is already noted by St Augustine in his commentary on another psalm (Psalm 56 – PL 36.671), and the idea of wind-filled bellows is common. A 'gilt chest' seems to be a newer idea, however; did Aldhelm see such an organ, read about it or even mistakenly use *capsae* to mean pipes? That the last is not out of the question is suggested by the use of the plural (occurring several times in these lines), his likely knowledge of bronze pipes (cf. the Claudian reference above) and the absence otherwise of any term for the pipes of an organ (no *fistulae, calami, voces* etc.). It could still be that Aldhelm had seen an organ with bellows and a gilt chest, but his words are much less like evidence of 'real' organs than those of Augustine or Cassiodorus.

That the lines from Cassiodorus also appear complete in a brief text compiling definitions of musical terms in the psalms and once attributed to Bede (PL 93.1102) suggests that at least some English references to organs before the late tenth century are, as formal texts, totally dependent on earlier literature. This would not prove organs to be unknown, for there are many understandable reasons for using the words of an authoritative predecessor even for a familiar object; nor, however, does it make it any more certain that they were known.

After the psalm commentators

Between Cassiodorus and the thirteenth century, by which later time the larger secular churches were giving new opportunities for organ-building and other skills developed by itinerant craftsmen, such information about organs as did circulate falls under various headings and is summarized elsewhere in this book. First, there was the relevance of Carolingian music-theory in the wake of Charlemagne's *unanimous* chant: in so far as much of this theory was concerned with notes and the relation between them, the organ's note-sequence or compass was important to at least one particular and well-circulating theorist, Hucbald (see Chapter 3). Second, the Boethian tradition for reckoning note-proportions in different materials was realized by theorists most often in terms of organ-pipes, and while the various distinct groups of treatises that result are not exactly about making organs, they do make it inevitable that the organ was, once and for all, a diatonic keyboard instrument (see Chapter 16). Third, another old literary tradition – the *artes mechanicae* – meant not only that one particular engineering book describing an organ-type remained in circulation (Vitruvius, see Chapter 14) but that in some sense it also inspired an organ-treatise unmatched in its practical coverage until at least the fifteenth century (Theophilus, see Chapter 15). Fourth, in the briefer written references to actual organs, found in a whole range of sources but especially in court and church annals there is almost always some technical detail lurking in the words, not always justifying the broader positivistic interpretations given them by most later scholars, but by no means unin-formative (see Chapters 9, 12 and 13). Fifth, although pictorial representation may offer far less technical and 'reliable' information than used to be thought, its mass of non-organological but relevant information is germane and so complex that it cannot yet be regarded as something fully understood (see Chapters 10, 11 and below).

A combination of these various kinds of document may well not result in a history of the organ 750–1250, but each bequeathed approaches that would eventually make it possible for musicians to write histories of the organ. Simple church annals would be succeeded in part by fabric rolls, and these by full book-keeping and minuted accounts from which the history of successive organs could be traced. Music-theory would cover the step-by-step innovations that produced the everyday octave of twelve notes, and while such theory is usually late, often obtuse and seldom with good organological insight, it is nevertheless vital for periods for which there is so little archaeological evidence. Gradually over time the sources of information redefine what is information: old genres such as manuscript illumination work towards modern definitions of 'factual reliability', while new genres such as contracts come into being over much the same period for the expressed purpose of being 'factually reliable'. Four examples of such genres follow, each of them offering some help in the questions asked in Chapter 19.

Technical terms: the example of 'bourdon'

Various kinds of medieval source give clues about developing organ-technology, though usually in a less direct manner than may at first appear to be the case. *Bourdon* is a good example of words that were to become more specialized as technology developed, and while more general uses of the term do not concern us here, its organ-associations do.

In the *De animalibus* of 1256/60, Albertus Magnus remarks on the different pitch-levels of animals' voices, particularly those of the horse family.[1] Producing their voice is

| magnus motor, sicut videmus | a large 'motor', such as we see giving a deep sound |

---

[1] Ed. H. Stadler, *Albertus magnus de animalibus libri xxvi*, Beiträge zur Geschichte der Philosophie des Mittelalters 15, 16 (Münster, 1920), here 16.1269.

in burdonibus,[2] qui sunt	in 'bourdons' [mules?], which are
magnae fistulae organorum	the large pipes of the organs
musicorum,	of musicians.
gravem esse sonum.	

Taken out of context, the phrase *in burdonibus, qui sunt magnae fistulae* appears to be more definitive about organs than was probably intended: while *qui sunt* makes *burdo* look like a word with two senses, Albertus need not have meant anything more than 'mule'. The passage is about mules' voices, which are as deep as 'large pipes' – not extra-large like those of some later Bourdon stops, but the lowest pipes, the bass octave, of a given rank.[3] (The voice of mules is low but not very low.)

However Albertus's words are to be taken, they cannot be evidence for the idea of bourdons being held as drones. Nevertheless, in a period when discriminating vocabulary was being increasingly used – from much the same time comes *cantus firmus* to distinguish one particular use of a given melody – a theorist could soon learn to use 'bourdon' to mean 'held notes', since in the formal music he would be writing about, held notes were most likely to be in this lower part of the compass. Conversely, low notes may have been frequently held. The theorist Anonymous IV (at work in thirteenth-century England, perhaps at Bury St Edmunds) wrote that the tenor note is held in a section of *organum purum* while a voice weaves a 'free' melody above:

tenor totius est G	the whole tenor is G
continuando et G in fine	continuing and G at the close,
modo stabili ut in burdone	in a fixed manner as in the bourdon
organorum.[4]	of organs.

But Anonymous IV was not setting out to say that his monastery's church had an organ with extra-large pipes. Perhaps it did, but such texts are not evidence for them. An astute and musical observer, he meant either 'as in the bourdon register (octave) of instruments/organs' or 'as in the sustained tone found on organs'. The sense of 'mules' does not seem to arise here, although it must have been familiar, especially to an Englishman (see reference to Wulfstan in note 2).

Most references to organs seem to have been made either by inexpert clerks or by writers more learned in literary or non-musical areas, as when Matthew Paris (†1259) told of events in 1235 at St Albans. As the abbot-elect of the abbey was presented, the liturgy proceeded:

incipiatur . . . *Te deum laudamus*	let the *Te Deum* be begun . . .
. . . pulsato classico,	after the [large] bell was rung,

---

2 Albertus Magnus's term for the kind of mule produced by a male horse and female ass is *burdo* (16.1137, cf. 15.38), which has the same voice as a horse (16.1412). In the tenth century, Wulfstan of Winchester had used *burdonibus* for something similar: on English usage, cf. *Dictionary of Medieval Latin from British Sources, fascicle A–B* (Oxford, 1975).

3 Presumably *magnae fistulae organorum musicorum* does indicate organs and not 'large wind-instruments of the musicians'.

4 F. Reckow, *Der Musiktraktat des Anonymus IV*, Beihefte zum Archiv für Musikwissenschaft 4, 5 (Wiesbaden, 1967), here 4.80. This remark of Anonymous IV could well be the 'first regular comparison made between an instrument and a musical phenomenon' (Reckow 1975: 150). On the possibility that 'bourdon' derives from *bord* ('edge, border'), see Walter 1981: 193.

sonantibus chalamis (quos	the pipes (which
'burdones' appellamus)	we call 'mules') sounding
cum horologio.	with the clock.

(RBMAS 28.5.520)

Whether *burdones* here is a veterinary or an organological term, it is used to denote pipes for which the older term *calamis* was more proper or familiar to a well-read scribe.[5] It is not clear whether Matthew Paris means to indicate 'large pipes', something technical-musical (drones) or something derogatory about organs ('mulish in tone'), but presumably it is one or the other. The general picture is clear enough – the bells of the (astronomical) clock were made to sound and the organ-pipes to play as the *Te Deum* was begun and as the new abbot processed to the high altar – but the details are not.

Since held notes in certain organum were held by the tenor voice, and since drone-instruments of the twelfth century had their drone in similar or even higher positions (see p. 32), the word *burdonus* does not always at first carry a sense of deep sound or 'bass'. In fact, the 'buzzing' of *bourdonner* suggests a relatively high pitch, and *burdo* had been used for a buzzing insect several centuries before Albertus Magnus. Nevertheless, by the time of the diagram-layout of a clavichord in Arnaut de Zwolle's treatise (this part of the manuscript *c.* 1460), *barduni* is the name for the lowest of the three octaves (H–h) as distinct from the *naturales* (h–h') and *supernaturales* (h'–f"). These three terms correspond to the *graves–acutae–superacutae* of a much earlier generation (Theophilus 3.81), the *borduni–naturales–falseta* of a fourteenth-century treatise and Albertus Magnus's own terms for animal voices: *gravis, media, acuta.*[6]

From a contract at Rouen in 1382, we learn that the organ there had both extra-large pipes (*plus gros tuiaux*) and *bourdons*: the first needed strengthening, the second revoiced to produce less tone (*amenisier*, 'reduce'). From this it seems that the *bourdons* were *teneurs*, perhaps a separate rank played by its own keys, as distinct from the large (but not larger?) pipes of the chorus. As such, they were probably meant to give a big tone, in certain circumstances a 'booming bass' such as would surely help to establish the idea of a bass line in performances of music. In another French contract of 1421, *bourdons* appear to be simply the lowest pipes, thus in Arnaut de Zwolle's sense.[7] Arnaut too speaks of organs with a set of larger pipes, which he does not call bourdons but *fistulas tenoris grossiores* or *subdupla tenoris organorum* ('larger tenor pipes . . . to double at the lower octave of the organ-tenor' – see below). To the listener and non-technical author, it may not have been clear whether the very large pipes were suboctave (even sub-suboctave) ranks in a chorus, separate bass pipes or simply the low notes of a large compass. Perhaps in the last two cases they were played by their own keys.

---

5   There seems no reason to see *calamis* as meaning 'reeds' in the sense of organ reed-stops, as often suggested (e.g. Marshall 1989: 68), not least since the term 'reed' in neither Latin nor English need have this connotation. If at one point Arnaut (Le Cerf 1932: 41) is referring to an organ reed-stop with the term *calamus* – which is not certain – he must mean some part of the pipe, not reed-stops or reed-pipes in general; elsewhere, he uses it for 'pipe' (see Chapter 17), as do other earlier authors writing 'in the sphere of practical organ-description' (see Sachs 1980: 360).

6   Arnaut de Zwolle in Le Cerf 1932: 13 and plate ix; the earlier treatises in Sachs 1980: 88, 345, 348ff; Albertus Magnus (see note 1): 16.1268.

7   Dufourcq 1971: 25 (Rouen) and 81 (Ste-Marie-de-la-Mer).

From such sources as these – the words of general authors, music-theorists and contract clerks – it is not at all clear how there gradually came about (a) held or drone notes played by the organ and (b) extra-large organ pipes. Presumably the first is earlier than the second, but neither is necessary for the other. It has been supposed that the 32' pipes at Halberstadt (about 9 m, from H)[8] dated from the original organ of 1361, but this seems a century too early, judging by very large pipes known later elsewhere (Chartres, Reims, Rouen, Bologna, Haarlem, Strasbourg). However, if it is so that larger organs are 'extrapolations' of smaller – see remarks on some manuscripts of *c.* 1290 below – there must always have been some organ-builders from at least the twelfth century onwards who stretched their technology to produce the furthest possible extrapolations.

On the other hand, separate bourdon pipes (singles, pairs or fours) on modest or small-size organs become less in evidence in manuscript illuminations of the fifteenth century, just as compass itself was settling to its norm of F–a" at 8' pitch (the longest pipe at 3', 6' or 12'). This is hardly coincidence: perhaps as larger pipes became a normal part of the chorus and compass, they were used less for drones, or, to put it another way, drones become less common the more the lowest pitches assume the character of a 'bass line'.

Technical details in some later representations

A Greek *Book of Kings* (twelfth century) and a Latin psalter (thirteenth) give some technical details for the instrument played by King David.[9] In the first manuscript (Rome, Biblioteca Apostolica Vaticana, graec. 333, f. 45), David bends over a row of organ-pipes: there are two men standing on bellows, a curved windtrunk, David with his fingers in the top of the pipes, and – most strikingly – what looks like a complete wooden structure consisting of frame, rear boards, high arched top, and the usual three-arched stand. Although the book follows ninth-century or earlier archetypes, these features must be up-to-date, whether western or eastern.

In the second manuscript, the Belvoir or Rutland Psalter (see Plate 14), there is technical information concerning pipes, keys and bellows. Here for the first time in a representation (*c.* 1260) appears a keyboard in the form of a row of close-packed keys, suggesting pin-action. Each of the twenty-two (?) large square T-shaped keys, three or four fingers wide, is positioned under its two unequal square conical pipes, but uncertain perspective means one cannot tell whether the keys move vertically or horizontally (hinged at the distal end of the stem). The picture may mean to show that a finger was enough to operate the keys and that they returned automatically. The single bass pipe standing at the treble end looks like a drone, but whether optional (with a key of some kind) or obligatory is unclear. If it were

---

8   As interpreted from Praetorius's compass and specification by Bormann 1966: *passim*, esp. 57.
9   The Book of Kings in C. Eggenberger, *Psalterium aureum Sancti Galli* (Sigmaringen, 1987), plate 107. Belvoir Psalter (London, British Library, Add. 62925, f. 97') in E. G. Millar, *The Rutland Psalter, a Manuscript in the Library of Belvoir Castle*, Roxburghe Club Publications 203 (Oxford, 1937).

not a drone, its key turned a roller or opened a valve under a long hollowed-out channel. The blower has a foot on each of two large bellows, which are attached by rope to a rocking lever above: one is raised as the other is lowered. As the bellows are more realistic than the pipes, so the blower's stance is more realistic than the player's, his job being easy for the non-expert to understand.

However, the picture is riddled with standard conventions of a psalter–illustration showing King David. The organ is joined by a hurdy-gurdy and a row of bells, producing the old trio of pipes–strings–bells, but now in rather more detail than was usual. Both the pipe-shape and the large right-hand pipe recall those in other contemporary psalters, such as the Peterborough Psalter for Psalm 96/97 (Brussels, Bibliothèque Royale Albert Ier, Cod. 9961–2 f.66 – see also below, p. 307) and a French Psalter for Psalm 136/137 (Paris, Bibliothèque Nationale, fr. 13096 f. 46, all three in Jakob 1991: plates 66, 67 and 162). Only Belvoir has square conical pipes, but an artist could interpret common conventions with some individuality, in this case by giving the pipes too wide a scale, showing their tops and attempting some portrayal of the mouths. Even the square T-shaped key in the Belvoir Psalter could be one such individual feature, perhaps being extrapolated from the wide key-strips of the French Psalter; if the latter was younger, both could have derived from an earlier source. Also common (if not universal) was the doubling of the pipe-rank, conveying the idea of a pipe-chorus. From the length of neither could a scale be reliably calculated.

In the Antiphonary of Beaupré, a Flemish Cistercian nunnery (*c.* 1290),[10] three versions of an organ show players' fingers on (a) square portative keys like a checker board, (b) rounded-square keys for the small positive (in the tradition of the Stuttgart Psalter for Psalm 137?) and, (c) for the large positive organ, round discs at the top of a stalk, each 'key' about three fingers wide, presumably a pin-action.[11] As in the Belvoir Psalter, poised fingers may be symbolizing agility rather than showing any actual playing-method. The bellows are like a large leather bag with an upper board shaped to be gripped. There are about twenty-one keys and again an unreal crowd of pipes: a double rank of thirty-two each, with three (six?) extra bourdons. Bourdons are shown for all three organs: for the portative, a pair twice as long as the next longest pipe; for the small positive, the same (?); and for the larger positive, pipes half as long again, as if anticipating Arnaut de Zwolle's length for extra bass pipes (see below). The organ frame and support are also extrapolated: for the portative a shallow stand; for the small positive a bigger support with two gothic arches; for the large positive an arcaded stand, a major piece of timberwork like or standing for the arcading on contemporary choirstalls. The next stage would have been a complete façade-frame and eventually a wooden organ-case enclosing all of the organ.

The resemblance between the three Beaupré organs suggests one of several things. The artist could have conjectured the larger organs from the small, or perhaps

[10] Baltimore, Walters Art Gallery, MS 759 f. 2 (angel playing portative), MS 760 f. 173 (small positive played in a secular setting, r.h. playing while l.h. pumps bellows) and MS 761 f. 270' (larger positive, with tonsured organist playing with both hands, plus bellows-blower); reproduced in *OY* 18 (1987), plates 1–3.

[11] Such as described in Arnaut de Zwolle; Le Cerf 1932: 24, plate xi.

vice versa; and he would do so either because he was familiar with the idea of 'an organ in three versions' or, in the innovative spirit of the times, he could have invented them for his schedule of pictures. It is not unlikely that by the late thirteenth century, and perhaps very much earlier, organ-makers did extrapolate a small unit of design as witnessed elsewhere at the time (see pp. 265, 274) – for example an octave of keys and a set of 2' pipes – into organs of certain sizes, including those very much bigger. More than any other wind instrument, even in the imaginative late Middle Ages, the organ is based on a 'unit of design' that allowed massive extrapolation.

In another contemporary psalter now in Munich,[12] a group of musicians decorating the initial B of Psalm 1 includes three concerned with the organ: one (not tonsured) works a single hand-bellows while two tonsured players in vestments (?) work with their fingers and thumbs three sliders (?) which are tapered, with wider rounded ends. The sliders are on two sides of the rectangular chest, two on one side and four on the other, and all three men appear to be singing, like the other (lay) musicians pictured in this and other miniatures for Psalm 1. Whether the key-levers are sliders or press-keys (short, wide, separately spaced) is unclear,[13] but once again the wind-raising is unambiguous: the bellows are socketed into a deep rectangular reservoir, smaller in top surface than the chest above but comparable in volume. From the top of the reservoir springs a wide trunk that divides into three to enter the chest at top, middle and bottom – a useful detail, doubtless 'reliable' – while on the chest itself stand thirteen inexpertly drawn pipes. They seem to be in pairs and fill the top of the chest in a cluster, probably conveying the visual impression of crowded pipes as received by a non-expert. Such psalter-illustration would not be good evidence for such an organ either in general (is it old, copied from elsewhere? is it an attempt at picturing an ancient organ?) or in detail (sliders may be shown on two sides in order to express *concentus* or the idea of 'two concordant brothers').

Like B-initials in psalters, the C-initial[14] followed certain iconographical conventions that did not make for reliable technical detail in any musical instruments that were included in their decoration. In one thirteenth-century French psalter,[15] David pushes a key-lever with his right hand, but the organ still has the conventional eight pipes of theory. Perhaps the relative rarity of organs in thirteenth-century illustration, compared to the dozens of other conventionalized instruments associated with particular scenes, reflects the fact that new organs were growing in size and complexity: they are no longer simple, easy-to-draw symbols. Other kinds of evidence also suggest this, such as the beginning of documented benefices for maintenance and other costs associated with larger organs, as at Barcelona in 1259[16] and some English cathedrals a century earlier (see Chapter 13).

12 Munich, Universitätsbibliothek, MS 24 quarto f. 2; in Perrot 1965: plate xxvi.
13 The springs and their housing would not be evident in skilful joiner's work.
14 B for *Beatus vir*, C for *Cantate domino*.
15 Paris, Bibliothèque Mazarine, MS 12 (not paginated); in Foster 1977: 32f.
16 F. Baldelló, 'Organos y organeros en Barcelona (siglos XIII–XIX)', *Anuario musical* 1 (1946), 195–237, here 199.

Two other examples of later drawings are typical of the mixture of archaic and 'reliable' or up-to-date details. Psalm 29 of the Luttrell Psalter (East Anglian, *c.* 1340)[17] shows a positive played by the fingers of both hands of a singing lay organist. The manuscript's eight gold-leaf, cylindrical pipes (plus bourdon) may represent burnished copper; the coloured frame, a support of three legs and an oblique pipe-support may represent a timber framework; and the arcaded bench on which the organ stands and the player sits may represent the structure of an organ-gallery. Two bellows, with rounded boards and five (?) folds are being vigorously pumped by hand. No detail can be taken literally – for example the three legs may result from the artist's reading of an older picture in which one leg was a windtrunk[18] – but the design could also stand for a larger organ, 'reduced' for purposes of psalter-illustration. The second example already shows a larger organ: the Peterborough Psalter of *c.* 1315[19] seems to have a width of five or six feet, with gothic wooden (?) end-pieces and a panel under the chest, the whole making a sturdy, joined frame. Other reliable details appear to be the pair of bellows played in alternation (rounded boards, leather folds, studded edges) and the appearance of the performers (tonsured player and blower, the player looking over the top of the pipes). The pipes themselves, two rows with bourdon or bourdons somewhat taller, may not be literally drawn.

Hypotheses from theory and practice: keyboard compass

Some information on two particular keyboard-details can be gleaned from written and pictorial sources: how or why five accidentals (four plus the 'lyric semitone' B) came to be added to the naturals, and how or why the accidentals came to be shorter, narrower keys placed above the naturals. The second question, though less intricate than the first, has its own uncertainties.

In the Norrlanda keyboard (see p. 343), where all the keys protrude singly through the front panel, the sharps are placed above while the B♭ is still one of the naturals.[20] Probably though not certainly, this placing of B had been usual ever since the Winchester organ. The sharps are shorter (less than half length) but as wide as the naturals; both are obviously for single fingers, convex on the upper surface and shallow in section; and the sharps are set only so far above the naturals as is needed for their fall. Hurdy-gurdy keys, with accidentals on an upper level to save space when short strings have to be stopped in close intervals, may have proved how convenient physically were keys placed in this way, but they are unlikely to be earlier than organ-keys so arranged. Besides, there is little choice with hurdy-gurdy

[17] London, British Library, Add. 42130; in E. G. Millar, *The Luttrell Psalter* (London, 1932). Various realistic elements in the Psalter's picture of a watermill (f. 181) are pointed out in Holt 1988: 129f.
[18] Millar points out that 'at least three' organs in the Gorleston Psalter of *c.* 1310 (British Library, Add. 49622) have the same three legs. For examples, see Hickmann 1936: figs. 12, 13.
[19] Brussels, Bibliothèque Royale Albert 1er, Cod. 9961–2 f. 66; also in F. L. Harrison, *Music in Medieval Britain* (Buren, 4/1980), plate xi.
[20] There is also a larger gap between A and B than between B and H, not entirely accounted for by the opened-up joint between the boards of the front panel.

keys, whereas the organ knew some variety: it is little organs that are likely to have had little keys. The convenience of having an octave span of only 18–20 cm when accidentals are put above the naturals is without doubt a late factor: the early organ-player had no obvious reason for wanting a convenient octave span. Earlier still, unless representations of Greek–Roman pipe-rows are totally unreliable, the octave may have had twelve or more notes and yet the key-levers were in one close-spaced row. Thirteenth-century representations do not yet show raised sharps, but the diatonicism of the early keyboard – as of the accompanying hexachord theory – makes it likely that the sharps were always raised, being by definition 'added notes'.

The idea that the keyboard now has twelve notes in each octave because the so-called chromatic scale has twelve can be put vice versa: twelve notes produced a theory of music because that is what keyboards were coming to have.[21] See Chapter 3 for suggestions that the need to transpose gave organs their extra notes quite as much as did the 'requirements of polyphony', which is what certain treatises imply. When Jacques de Liège says that 'virtually throughout' the scale the whole tone is divided (see below), he is speaking of what organ-makers have made or been making for some time: it is a practical as well as a theoretical observation. Accordingly, if larger organ-chests did not always have as many accidentals as smaller,[22] it may be because they focused more on the melody and counterpoint based on the most common chants: it was from practice and experience that makers were working, not pitch-analyses worked out in theory-books. While it may be so that John of Garland's remark concerning accidentals or *falsae . . . necessaria, specialiter in organis* ('necessary things, especially in *organa*' – CS 1.166) does not necessarily mean the organ since *organa* was still a versatile word, organs are still the instruments that most drive home the questions raised. Without a keyboard one did not need to make enharmonically equivalent a tone-division that is in nature different by one comma.

When other theorists refer to F♯ and G♯ (*Summa musice*, Page 1991: 96 and 177), to B and other flats (Jacques de Liège *c.* 1330 – CSM 3.6.146) or a little later to the fourth F♯–C♯ (see Sachs 1970:137), they do so at least partly in reference to the organ keyboard. So does the first known description[23] of a complete chromatic compass G–d″, where the pipe-proportions give C♯:H as 9:8, F♯:H as 3:2, and both D♯:H and G♯:E as 9:7. Such pipe-proportions are a means of quantifying the theoretical relationship, and it is not certain that a builder observed them or, if he did, omitted further practical steps such as making pitch adjustments at the mouth.

In general, documentation before the fourteenth century is meagre, leading to the fair but probably erroneous conclusion that 'organ-making did not know much

---

[21] If it is so that Greek melodic fragments (the Delphic hymns) would have required 'a fully chromatic keyboard with twelve notes in the octave' (C. Stroux in Walcker-Mayer 1972: 74), the twelve would still be a consequence of practical compromise rather than theoretical inevitability.

[22] As late as 1502, the large organ of Freiberg Cathedral seems to have had no keys for C♯ and G♯ (source in U. Dähnert, 'Zur Geschichte der Orgeln in Obersachsen', in *Orgelkunst und Orgelforschung: Gedenkschrift Rudolf Reuter*, ed. W. Schlepphorst (Kassel, 1990), 21–30, here 30).

[23] Sachs 1980: 345–7 = Milan, Biblioteca Ambrosiana, MS D.5 inf. f. 119, appended to copies of Franco and of Marchetto da Padua (1325/50). Sachs points out that in this scheme D♯ and G♯ are further from D and G than C♯ and F♯ are C and F, which supports Handschin's suggestion that D♯ could serve as E♭ and also G♯ as A♭ (see Sachs 1980: 346).

change in the Middle Ages' and that 'there is no reason to believe that other accidentals had been added before the fourteenth century' (Meeùs 1980/1: 71). The scarcity of technical or technological information in this area need not mean that development was static. If theorists generally describe something that is becoming a norm, it is quite possible that at least one accidental (F♯?) had been known on certain organs in the major new churches of the twelfth century. A history of accidentals has to take into account the reasons for them, whatever it is that documents of a period do or do not point out about them.

Of the three obvious reasons for increasing the number of accidentals – for transposition of the *cantus* on an instrument of fixed pitch, for polyphony (voice, organ) using accidentals in order to perfect diminished intervals, for leading notes of the fifth and octave of the main modes in the treble compass – the first is the easiest to underrate. While it may have been an interest in theory *per se* that encouraged in the late fourteenth century various twelve-note octaves including one in which all accidentals were tuned as flats,[24] the earliest accidentals (E♭, F♯) were practical responses to transposition and would have arisen naturally in polyphony.[25] There had been very practical reasons for introducing accidentals. With a keyboard of C D E F G A B H – the basic sequence as described in such treatises as the tenth/eleventh-century group *Màcha dia* (Sachs 1970: 106ff) – the only transcriptions were at the fourth up or fifth down, and it is possible that the B itself was there for that purpose. It certainly is the reason implied in the Vatican Organum Treatise.[26] For whatever purpose he had, an organist could play over a melody at two or three different pitches, for the B enables the hexachordal scales from both G and C to be put down a fifth or up a fourth. The attempt by Berno of Reichenau (†1048) to legitimize in theory the practical usefulness of chromatic notes does so by in effect inviting the reader to see them as transposed versions of the relationship B–H. Thus F♯ is a kind of transposed H.[27]

In addition, Wulfstan's phrase 'lyric semitone' at Winchester suggests, whatever the precise connotation of 'lyric', that the B had its own melodic function, widening the scope for melodic lines as in their way do the fourteenth-century sharps. So far as 'lyric' is a technical term, Wulfstan gave no hint that the B satisfied any need to transpose, although a cantor surely knew such things. Perhaps transposition was a practical professional matter less the concern of writers, for according to Jacques de Liège (*c.* 1330), semitones are found either

in aliquibus artificialibus	in some artificial
instrumentis ut in organis,	instruments such as organs [i.e. with keyboard]
in quibus quasi ubique tonus	where virtually throughout, the tone
in duo semitonia dividitur	is divided into two unequal
inequalia ut plures ibi fieri	semitones, so that more concords
possent concordie	can then be made

(CS 2.271, cf. 294)

[24] See M. Lindley, 'Pythagorean intonation and the rise of the third', *RMA Research Chronicle* 16 (1980), 4–61.
[25] For an early thirteenth-century example, see p. 50.
[26] See I. Godt & B. Rivera, 'The Vatican organum treatise – a color reproduction, transcription and translation', in *Gordon Athol Anderson (1929–1981): in Memoriam* (Henryville, PA, 1984), 264–345.
[27] Further discussion in D. Pesce, *The Affinities and Medieval Transposition* (Bloomington, IN, 1987), 16–18. On Berno's monochord scale, see Sachs 1980: 222, 226–30.

or, to put it more completely,

ut ibi plures cantus	so that then more melodies [?]
possint fieri pluresque	can be made and more
concordiae discantusque	concords and descants
reperiri	can be discovered.

(CSM 3.6.146)

These look like references to chordal harmony and contrapuntal lines on the organ, *reperiri* even suggesting that the musician was able to 'find' certain sounds with the organ keyboard: 'sharpened leading notes' and 'major triads'?

Discovery of such combinations would surely come in part from the array of notes provided in the first instance for transposition on a fixed-note instrument, i.e. for playing over a chant at different points on the keyboard. Organ-makers would have found that the variety of situations in which a row of keys could play a chant depended on the number of major seconds they learnt to divide, and all situations were possible only when all had been divided. Being able to do this would be particularly important when pitch cannot have been standard, whatever alphabet-labels the keys might have. A theorist, however, would emphasize other uses for accidentals. Having notated music in mind, he would know that he could write notes that were logical enough (such as c$\sharp$) but were not found on every fixed-note instrument – and ought to have been.

Perhaps the accidental keys were placed above the others not at first for convenience of the hand but in order to show two things:

what the basic hexachord or heptachord was, i.e. these were the notes left
    physically intact below such 'additions', as if unaffected by them;
where further semitones lay, because a raised key was always preceded and
    followed by a diatonic note a semitone away (so was B, hence eventually
    being raised?).

Showing where the semitones lay was probably a purpose of both alphabet-labels and clefs (see Chapter 3) and would be important whether the scale was a plain heptachord (CDEFGAH), had a B (which created three adjacent semitones) or had one, two, three or four sharps. On such topics as the placing of accidentals, one has to speculate because theorists do not say.

New kinds of source: contracts

The gradual appearance of itemized accounts came about under certain conditions: the clients were large public churches (with priests or canons but not necessarily a convent of monks), the contracted agents were lay craftsmen (who needed payment on account for materials) and the organs were becoming larger and more regularly used (therefore requiring the technological experience of outside experts). Much of the earliest surviving contractual documentation in England – orders for building work of various kinds[28] – comes from royal order-books which, though not itemized contracts themselves, suggest that planning would increasingly require some such specification. Monasteries themselves had hired builders and other craftsmen for centuries before written contracts prove it: Ramsey in the late tenth century and Bury St Edmunds in the late eleventh must be typical examples (further in Salzman 1952: 359, 364).

Terms of agreement concerning organs gradually began to include technical matter, though only from some time after secular contracts had established the convention of itemizing. Thus at Barcelona in 1345, Martín Ferrándiz refers in his contract to three *parts* and to *canons* of the organ,[29] meaning the 'sections' of the keyboard, each with a different number of 'pipes'. These 'sections' may have been the octaves starting at C, and can be understood in two ways. Either there were respectively twelve, sixteen and twenty pipes on each channel (*en cascuna via*) of the upper three 'sections' (c–b, c'–b', c"–f"?) with seven pipes only for the four lowest notes below c (F G A H?), making what looks like a fifteenth-century Blockwerk of 7–12–16–20 ranks; and if *part* means less than an octave, the composition is the same only the compass shorter.[30] Or, since Ferrándiz refers to his instrument having three more notes than the old organ he was replacing (not at the top but in the first of the three *parts*), and since the lowest four notes 'where the bourdons stand' (*hon stan los bordons*) were to have seven ranks, then it could have been a three-octave organ from C, as follows:

> seven ranks C–F ('bourdon' may indicate merely the bottom octave)
> twelve G–H
> sixteen c–b
> twenty c'–a' (c"?).

Although neither the starting-note nor the compass and pipe-total is specified, the terms are clearly moving towards the detail that became conventional in such contracts. Furthermore, the instrument was to have casework of some kind, made of 'good, fine and dry wood' (*caxa . . . de bona e bela e secha fusta*), with other timberwork (*tota la altra obra . . . de fusta*), and 'bellows of good boards and good deerskin' (*manxes ab bones posts . . . de bons cuirs de cervo*). The 'keys' were to be 'of boxwood and holly' (*? . . . claviles . . . de fust de box e de gingoler*) presumably meaning differentiated naturals and sharps; *mols*, which could be either trackers or front guide-pins, must be 'good and stable' (*bones e stables*). Whether the last were trackers or guide-pins, there may be a hint here of the faults frequently found in instruments. The organ, which was to take a year to complete, was to be made within the church, and the chapter was to pay for materials.

At SS Annunziata, Florence, in 1379, many details were entered into the contract, producing a document for understanding the stage reached by the art of organ-

---

[28] Examples from 1237 to 1249 in Salzman 1952: 382–4.
[29] For the following interpretations, cf Baldelló (see note 16): 205–6, and Llovera 1987: 257–68.
[30] I.e., if *part* denotes a shorter sequence of notes with the same ranks before the mixture changes, as well it might, the compass would be shorter; but the Blockwerk would run in the same way.

building that is of almost unrivalled importance.[31] Francesco, presumably Landini, tuned or voiced the organ (*ad temperandum organa*). 'Twelve iron rings' were needed 'for the pedal action' (*duodecim anulis de ferro . . .pro tastando cum pedibus* – pulldowns?) and the chest (*bancatium, capsa*) had paper (*cartarum*) on the underside and was lined with kid-leather (*pelle camusci*) elsewhere. The dimensions of the walnut chest are given as 4 × 1 × 1 ells (*brachia*), and it consisted of several pieces of wood made tight together. This could suggest either joinery work or hollowed-out planks, perhaps by now the former. There were forty-one iron springs for the keys and other iron pieces that could have been used to make tracker-wire for suspended action. Whether such springs and trackers indicated a mechanism with pallet-springs is not totally certain, however: the changeover from key-sliders to pallet-springs is so lacking in documentation (see p. 337) that it is uncertain how the Florence contract is to be understood. Other details are less ambiguous, however: the tin pipes have lead languids, are hammered and re-hammered on wooden mandrels, finally polished and held in place on the chest by a wooden rack; the chest was made of walnut; and the bellows used four calf-skins (*vitellinis*, one for each bellows?). Items in the contract include mandrels, solder-flux, polishing cloths and payment for the pipe-beater. The keys were of refined workmanship: details are not clear but there seems to have been a brass button and leather lining underneath, with copper (brass?) and iron-wire linkwork. The brass button was either decoration or, more likely, a stop to limit keyfall. The case was carved and painted, and there was a cover made of cloth stretched over a frame, which a reference to rope suggests may have been suspended, like Theophilus's (see p. 266). Reference to a board on which a monochord scale was inscribed (*assi ubi signatum est monacordum*) suggests a soundboard fixed in the organ on which a string could be stretched to give the pitches for tuning: a brilliant idea.

Part of the purpose of contracts is to specify materials, presumably because they have to be bought in. A sign of the development can be seen at Wells Cathedral in 1310, when chapter minutes, themselves new sources for such information, provide for felling trees and taking timber for making organs (and their galleries?); by 1338 at York Minster, lead and other materials are at the chapter's charge, and gradually more and more items are specified in contracts.[32] Materials specified for keys at Trier Cathedral in 1386–7 (see p. 347) no doubt reflect the period's refinements in keyboard design and technology. At Notre-Dame, Paris, only because the old organ was sold in 1426 for its 800lbs of pipe-material (Wright 1989: 117) is there any record of its pipes being made of tin. Fourteenth-century Italian contracts often mention tools such as iron mandrel (S Maria, Gemona, 1373), soldering irons (Siena Cathedral, 1372), and casting benches (ditto), as well as musical details such as the

---

[31] R. Taucci, *Fra Andrea dei Servi organista e compositore del Trecento*, Rivista di studi storici sull'Ordine dei Servi di Maria 2 (Rome, 1935), 73–108. Also extracted in Donati 1979. Taken as a group, the contemporary documents from Rouen (see Dufourcq, ñote 33) and Trier (see Bereths 1974) are also as informative.

[32] Wells: ed. W. H. B. Bird, *Calendar of the MSS of the Dean and Chapter of Wells*, Historical MSS Commission, 2 vols (London, 1907), 1.154. York: secondary sources only, in A. Freeman, 'The organs of York Minster', *The Organ* 5 (1926), 193–204, here 193.

XIII semitonis at Treviso in 1347 (Donati 1979: 152, 153, 201, 233). The Treviso contract even specifies that chest and pipes be made to regular scale (*unam bonam cassam, cane ad legalem mensuram* – Donati 1979: 217), but since no further details are given, this must be an example of the contracted item that would previously have been taken for granted.

During the fourteenth century musical aspects of organs are also specified, such as the work on the tenors and chorus pipes itemized in the accounts of Rouen Cathedral in the 1380s (see above). Items in these same accounts include bellows skins (bellows were frequently worked on), metal action-parts (*couplez, resors* – 'trackers, springs?'), curtains, keys (*clefs* – apparently in both senses), revoicing of pipes, tin and a mandrel (? *moules*) for whatever new pipes were necessary, nails, calf-skin and fish-glue.[33] This work was done by craftsmen such as *magister* Godfrey of Furnis *et son valet*, and the ironwork was now contracted for from named blacksmiths. The reference to tin for the new pipes 'to match the others' (*appariller les autres*) makes it clear that the old organ of Rouen being rebuilt at this time also had tin pipes. At Troyes in 1381, it is tinfoil for the pipes that is specified, along with linen and rings for the curtains.[34] By the early fifteenth century many other details often specified include particular materials (oak for the chest, tin for the case-pipes only), and a note on the tone aimed at by the builder ('full and large, well proportioned, clear, well tuned' – *grosses y plenes, ben proporcionades, ben claras et distinctes, ben afinats*); also, comparisons with earlier organs in the neighbourhood are found.[35] This last became common in fifteenth-century contracts for the new big gothic churches of the Netherlands, but the competitive spirit behind it goes back no doubt to the days when individually designed and constructed monastic organs were made in-house and before such novelties as contracts made such things explicit.

---

[33] Dufourcq 1971: 23–6. Both the material (poplar) and the manufacture (by turning) of pipe-mandrels are still charged for in some much later itemized accounts, e.g. in 1605–6 for the organ of King's College, Cambridge (Hopkins & Rimbault 1877: 65).

[34] E. Martinot, *Orgues et organistes des églises du diocèse de Troyes* (Troyes, 1941), 24ff.

[35] All as at Ste-Marie-de-la-Mer in 1421, contract in Dufourcq 1971: 81–2.

18

Wood and metal technologies in early organ-building

The mysteries surrounding the state reached by the organ in 1000 (what was it like?) and its development over the next four centuries (what happened and when?) cannot be solved either by historical documents or by archaeological remains. Not only are both cripplingly scant but what there is may in no way represent any normal activity or what went on in the abbey-workshop undocumented. However, an idea of other crafts practised at the time, closely or distantly related to organs as the case may be, helps to put organ-building into context. Organs were not and are not constructed independently of contemporary techniques in general, even if (as sometimes today) builders may deliberately shun technologies that have been recently developed for other purposes.

Written technology

Despite much attention paid to medieval technology in recent decades, especially its philosophical aspects, there is still something of a dark age about the period 750–1250, particularly who made what, how and where. In so far as literate coverage today is concerned with actual techniques, most attention has been given to the exceptional, to the blossomings of ingenuity in earlier periods (Hero, Vitruvius) or later (Villard, Leonardo), and there is some repetitive emphasis on the few concrete witnesses to a 'Carolingian Renaissance' or a 'Twelfth-century reawakening'. Practical or technical areas are generally covered today just as bookishly as they were in the eleventh century, and it is very difficult to break the literary mould. Well-researched books of today entitled *The Carolingians and the Written Word* or *The Uses of Literacy in Early Mediaeval Europe* could actually be silent on the *artes mechanicae*, on why such technical matters as pipe-measurement should ever be written down, whether 'technical' means 'practical' and whether the Mechanical Arts of literates had anything to do with that of mechanics. One limitation of conventional scholarship is that practical aspects are so often left in the air, though many pages may be written on the philosophy or theology (even etymology) of *mechanica*. Another is that one can easily assume a particular treatise's intention to have been more practical than it actually was.[1] In addition to all this, scholars trained in the humanities will often have a tendency

---

[1] For emphasis on the philosophy of the mechanical arts but little on their practice, see Whitney 1990. For probable misunderstanding of practical intentions: the idea that Gerbert of Aurillac and Reims suggested

to write up the ordinary process of work . . . as if those performing the work were informed by rational, scientific principles

and they will tend to believe in 'technology', the whole idea of which

itself is a fake idea, a construction (as an '-ology') by non-artificers about the artificer's work to make it seem more familiar.[2]

Unfortunately, so little is documented about the organ before 1450 that some such construction seems inevitable.

Because Hero or Villard left notes and diagrams they become a focus for historians, but documents and archaeology give two different pictures. Nothing in the Greek–Roman descriptions of water-pumps suggests that they could be made from a length or two of lead piping held in an ingeniously bored-out wooden block, complete with valves and a receiver, such as was found in the Roman *civitas* capital of Silchester (Usher 1929: 87–8). But written descriptions do not forbid it either, and the Silchester pump is a good reminder that before the period of patents, technical description was likely to be generic, giving accounts of the principles (substance) of construction rather than the specifics (accidents) of any particular example. Specifics concerned with the working of local materials such as wood were not the business of written accounts, even if in theory carpentry was included in the *artes mechanicae* listed by an early ninth-century writer:[3]

mechanica est peritia	'mechanical' is skill
fabricae artis in metallis et	in the art of working in metals,
in lignis et in lapidibus.	woods and stones. (Anon *c.* 800 – PL 101.947)

But for many centuries specifics of woodworking are simply not described anywhere, and even 'workmen' in general are learnt about only obliquely, as in the Venerable Bede's remark of c. 730 concerning one 'unusually gifted in the crafts' but addicted to drink (*fabrili arte singularis* – PL 95.254). Since the organ developed above all as an accumulation of technical specifics and practical solutions, its structual elements have to be traced as best they can from a variety of sources. They will not be found described in the documentation.

Organ-building remained a pragmatical craft. Builders did not need to know any theory of levers from Archimedes or Hero[4] or anyone else to be able to conceive and make pivoted keys; nor did they have to wait for Hero's descriptions of automaton mechanisms to circulate in late medieval monasteries before they could devise the fixed roller. (Bede's gifted craftsman probably could not read, or if he could he was unable to write; he was almost certainly a lay worker, probably freelance, possibly

---

something so specific as 'new finger techniques for playing the organ', in R. McKitterick, *The Frankish Kingdoms under the Carolingians 751–987* (London, 1983), 293, 295, or the assumption that his (?) treatise *mensura fistularum* related to the making of actual organs, in P. Riché, *Gerbert d'Aurillac, le Pape de l'an mil* (Paris, 1987), 51.

[2] M. Fores, '*Technik:* or Mumford reconsidered', HT 6 (1981), 121–37, here 126 and 134.

[3] This on the basis of Isidore of Seville's term *mechanica* (Sternagel 1966: 23). Further on the term in E. Whitney, 'Crafts, philosophy and the Liberal Arts in the early Middle Ages', *Annals of Scholarship* 4.3 (1987), 11–28.

[4] Summarized in M. Clagett, *The Science of Mechanics in the Middle Ages* (Madison, 1959), 15–16, 46–7.

itinerant.) Furthermore, since neither Archimedes nor Hero quite described such simple practical devices as pivoted key-levers or rollers, one has to surmise both that such things were traditionally within the ken of craftsmen and that what natural philosophers were doing instead was taking such well-known devices as these to be the basis for more developed theory, theory that was then written down and transmitted. If this is so, then it is likely that complex mechanical models – particularly the hydraulic organ described by Vitruvius and Hero – were not the only or even the main type of organ known. Perhaps they were described because they were complex and raised matters of scientific principle, while all along craftsmen themselves were making bellows-operated chests of pipes with linkwork to control the wind, and doing so according to no written-down 'technology'.

General on background technologies

At the same time, a period's general level of expertise in technical matters is bound to be relevant. If very complicated bronze water-pumps were known in second-century Spain,[5] so, we can be sure, were organs even if there is no surviving evidence for them. For Charlemagne's craftsmen making the bronze lattice railings of the Aachen octagon (eight sections *c.* 14' × 4'), there would have been no difficulty in making bronze pipes. Similarly, if the monks of Hildesheim had so mastered bronze-casting in the early eleventh century that they could produce for St Michael's the cast-bronze Trajanesque Christian column (3.79 × 0.5 m) and the solid one-piece cast-bronze doors (4.72 × 1.15 m, both column and doors now in the cathedral), they could certainly make bronze organ-chests far bigger than Theophilus's model. Nevertheless, ability in 'background technologies' needs the right circumstances in which organs could develop, hence the importance for the organ-historian of tracing liturgical or musical stimuli. Twelfth-century Cistercian houses could and did develop many crafts,[6] from large-scale mining or heavy forging to fine work with precious metals, but organs were not wanted and were not developed by them at that time.

The splendid metal artefacts at Aachen, Hildesheim and throughout the Meuse valley well before 1100 deserve particular consideration because they are likely to have inspired organ-building directly and because the churches to which they belonged as special furniture were part of active, learned monasteries. At Aachen, all sixteen major works of bronze – eight lattice panels, eight doors (*c.* 795–805) – may have been the work of Byzantine craftsmen who worked elsewhere (St-Denis, Metz, Worms, Regensburg) and took advantage of Meuse-valley ores to set up production in Aachen.[7] Two centuries later, bronze technology had matured to give Hildesheim

---

[5] For the 'Madrid pump' of Roman design, see T. Schiøler, 'Bronze Roman piston pumps', *HT* 5 (1980), 17–38.

[6] E.g. M. T. Hodgen, *Change and History: a Study of the Dated Distributions of Technological Innovations in England*, Viking Fund Publications in Anthropology 18 (New York, 1952), 157ff.

[7] W. Braunfels, *Die Welt der Karolinger und ihre Kunst* (Munich, 1968), 135.

its masterworks – doors, pillar, crown-candelabrum – and a century later still, the large cast bronze font at St-Barthélemy, Liège. The *vita* of Bishop Bernward of Hildesheim (early eleventh century) speaks of him making his own episcopal cross from gold and precious stones and refers to 'his assistant' (*puerum suum*) who actually made the silver crown-candelabrum.[8] Hildesheim under Bishop Otwin (958–84) had already been known for its work in precious metals, and the development of new silver mines near Goslar at the end of the century no doubt helped set the scene for the work of Roger of Helmarshausen (see Chapter 15).

In Italy, some of the various extant eleventh-century bronze doors seem to have come from Constantinople, although Verona was known for its German craftsmen: latter-day Goths and Vandals coming down the valley from Trent and beyond. Such bronze doors were usually built up of separate pieces nailed on wood, thus techno-logically simpler than the Hildesheim casts; similar work could be seen in southern Germany (Augsburg Cathedral doors).

In their different way, the Aachen and Hildesheim masterworks contribute to the question of who the craftsmen were and how far monks were responsible for the work. A confident statement that artists and craftsmen were predominantly laymen[9] does not sufficiently recognize the various categories or degrees of 'monk' and 'lay-brother', or distinguish between heavy and light crafts. Rather, one can imagine various workshop-arrangements in which a man's monastic-degree and ordination-status affected his function, as apprentice, worker, master, supervisor or commissioner. The eastern part of the empire left various references to supervisors or active craftsmen in the monasteries, including the famous monk Tuotilo of St Gall who worked in Metz and Mainz in the late ninth century as painter and musician (MGH SS 2.97–101) and bishops such as Bernward who gathered pupils in writing and painting (MGH SS 4.758). Like the *vitae* of contemporary Anglo-Saxon bishops, such accounts clearly aim to praise certain activities of famous priests, and one cannot be sure that there was anything very unusual in their support for the crafts. From at least the ninth century onwards monasteries across the empire are sometimes recorded as attracting skilled craftsmen to reside in the nearby villages,[10] and pre-sumably certain monasteries specialized in machine-crafts as others did in handwriting or manuscript-illumination.

Although distinctions gradually made in the way crafts are named may not necessarily mean that the crafts were becoming more specialized and specific, nevertheless the reverse could be true: specialized crafts needed specific names. The many distinct job-designations given in sources from German regions – before 1100 there are some eighty known from documents, but between 1100 and 1200 a further hundred[11] – suggests that at least the sources themselves were finding it increasingly

[8] Documentation in K. Algermissen, *Bernward und Godehard von Hildesheim: ihr Leben und Wirken* (Hildesheim, 1960), 45–8, 76, 88ff, 151ff, 191ff.
[9] R. E. Swartwout, *The Monastic Craftsman* (Cambridge, 1932), *passim*, esp. 23ff.
[10] Muri, St-Riquier and Constance, in Swartwout (note 9): 109.
[11] Some details in T. Erb, 'Beobachtungen zum Stand der handwerklichen Arbeitsteilung im 11. Jahrhundert (Regnum Teutonicum)', *Jahrbuch für Wirtschaftsgeschichte* 23.2 (1982), 65–71. Some names of monastic craftsmen are listed and categorized in A. H. Springer, *De artificibus monachis et laicis medii aevi* (Bonn, 1861).

useful to distinguish between, say, one kind of woodworker and another. Pre-Carolingian sources too had regularly distinguished workers in iron from those in copper or in the precious metals.

Woodworking

The wood of northern Europe remained the prime mechanical or structural material throughout the period, although techniques for working it were still 'really based upon a Neolithic tradition' (Singer 1957: 237). Nordic ships of the Viking period were made from planking (including oak) that was lapped over and lashed or nailed to the cross-ribs. The curved ribs were carved from the solid, and the technique of hollowing out – also Neolithic – is still found in wooden boxes of Celtic times. (Perhaps Theophilus does not describe the technique of hollowing out the organ-chest in his Chapter 1.35 because it was so usual.) Drilling, dowelling and pegging are well documented since Roman times. So is turning, at which the Anglo-Saxons became so proficient that their stonework often imitated turned wood (despite its difficulty and pointlessness), as their pilaster strapwork also imitated the lapjoints of wooden beams. Large-scale drilling, presumably by some form of brace and bit, is implied by Theophilus for the making of his windtrunk from a branch of oak, and a 'machine for boring pump barrels from solid tree trunks' must have been known and used.[12] Experienced augur-drilling was also clearly required for the big square dowels running cross-wise through pegged, butt-jointed planks of oak doors in Norman England.[13]

The principles of a main frame jointed with pegs and tenon-and-mortice became very familiar from roof-trussing,[14] but it is still quite uncertain when this method, on a reduced and refined scale, was adopted for the lower or load-bearing part of a wooden organ-structure. The second half of the thirteenth century saw far-reaching developments in woodwork: dowelling to extensive tenon-and-mortice work, with elaborately carved members. Screenwork could be built up in large, repeated sections. The stalls of Salisbury Cathedral (*c.* 1245) and Westminster (*c.* 1255), like those of Winchester Cathedral (*c.* 1308–10, see Plate 16), were themselves a kind of ecclesiastical version of the screens dividing up the great halls of secular castles (Tower of London, 1237), and timber for stalls becomes a familiar item in English abbey-cathedrals from this period (St Paul's 1220, Peterborough 1233–45, Gloucester before 1236). From much the same period one manuscript of the Spanish *cantigas* has a scene in which monks sit facing each other in their stalls.[15] While by 1250 the

---

[12] A. C. Crombie, *Medieval and Early Modern Science*, 2 vols (New York, 2/1959), 1.210. A ninth-century Irish tale concerns a monstrous dog trapped in an alderwood log, along which an arm-length hole has been bored: K. Meyer, *The Death-Tales of Ulster Heroes* (Dublin, 1986), 28.

[13] In C. A. Hewitt, 'The jointing of doors during the Norman period', *AJ* 145 (1988), 374–7.

[14] M. Daumas, *A History of Technology and Invention: Progress through the Ages*, 3 vols (New York, *c.* 1969), 1.520–3.

[15] Tower of London: 'spur of boards, good and becoming', according to Salzman 1952: 260. On the English cathedrals, see C. Tracy, *English Gothic Choir-Stalls 1200–1400* (Woodbridge, 1987), xxiii, 1–2. The *cantigas*: Madrid, Biblioteca del Escorial, j. b. 2, f. 108 (see p. 370).

Engraved by H.Le Keux, from a Drawing by Edw.Blore, for Britton's History &c. of Winchester Cathedral.

WINCHESTER CATHEDRAL CHURCH,

Part of the Stalls of the Choir.

London, Published Dec.r 1.1816. by Longman & C.º Paternoster Row.

Printed by Hayward

Plate 16 Winchester Cathedral, early thirteenth-century wooden choirstalls: J. Britton, *The History and Antiquities of the See and Cathedral of Winchester* (London, 1817), title page

documentation for stalls increases because more of them were being made, it could also be because more were now being contracted for outside the community and records better kept.

Roof-frames made from lap-jointing, tenons and dowels are known in extant English examples from the later twelfth century (Peterborough), with techniques that developed into the complex structures, with scarfing and chase-tenons, of the Salisbury and York chapter-houses *c.* 1275–1300. The Anglo-Saxons had already known efficient joints, including lap-joints with dovetails.[16] Probably, however, the crafts of wooden roof-making had less influence on the wooden parts of organ-building than did the new fashion for wooden stalls, and this not because organs may have been integrated with stalls at an early date but because the gradual replacement of stone benches[17] brought woodworking more often on to the church pavement itself. Timber stalls helped produce wooden organs. The Winchester work shows many of the shapes and decorative details in the Decorated Gothic style that could well have been typical of organ and clock design before the flatter motifs and filigrees of fifteenth-century gothic organ-cases (and late gothic generally) became normal. See Plates 16, 18 and 19. At Xanten, early stalls from the second half of the thirteenth century have much the same kind of gothic detail as Villard de Honnecourt's various drawings (see below).

Simple pine planking with rear battens (cross bars) and tenoned frames remains the method of construction for the extant Swedish (?) organ-cases of the fourteenth (?) century: 'carpenters' work' rather than 'cabinet makers' work' (Kjersgaard 1987: 9). There is not much advance here on, for example, the twelfth-century wardrobe preserved in the Cistercian abbey of Obazine, east of Périgueux. Deal is still the material for the late gothic organ of central Europe, with a weight-bearing frame constructed from deal timbers,[18] but there is nothing certain on when this structure originated for organs and whether its contribution to the sound (deal is more absorbent than the later oak) was a calculated factor. It was probably the late fifteenth century before there were removable tongue-and-groove panels for the side or rear of the case. Dovetail joints, as for cabinet drawers, appear in northern Europe only centuries after they were known in Mediterranean areas,[19] where however they were usually made of hard or rare woods, for small-scaled ivory work or for other fine-scale objects. Framed panels, such as those for bookcase doors – and eventually organ-case doors or wings – are depicted in southern Italy by the sixth century,[20] but such

---

[16] Peterborough, Salisbury and York in C. A. Hewitt, *English Cathedral Carpentry* (London, 1974), 14ff, 76ff. On early techniques, C. A. Hewitt, 'Anglo-Saxon carpentry', *ASE* 7 (1978), 203–29. Denmark: A. Steensberg, 'Byggekonstruktioner i Danmark', *Nordisk Kultur* 14 (1953), 84–90.

[17] Extant examples in the nave of the twelfth-century Cistercian abbey of Le Thoronet. Stone benches other than those around the base of pillars or along sidewalls, have seldom survived.

[18] As too for the gothic organ of Salmanca, *c.* 1500 (see De Graaf 1982).

[19] Singer 1957: 240–1: examples here from the eleventh century.

[20] Singer 1957: 243. One representation of Ezra writing the sacred records, in which a bookcase with panelled doors appears, was copied in Northumbria *c.* 700 (= Florence, Biblioteca Medicea-Laurenziana, Codex Amiatinus). The illustrator may have been merely following convention, for similar bookcase doors are pictured in a fifth-century mosaic in the mausoleum Galla Placidia, Ravenna, with panel-shading as clear as it could be in a mosaic. Bristol City Museum now has a panelled door of the third or fourth century AD, probably from Egypt or at least the Mediterranean.

joinery is known in northern Europe only from the eleventh century at the earliest. That is the period in which the organ may possibly have been moving towards some kind of organ-case, i.e. an upper wooden storey built around the pipes which speak out on one side, all on top of a rigid wood-framed structure holding the chest. But the Swedish organ-remains (see p. 343) suggest that such casework could be constructed without sophisticated 'Italian' joinery. A major unanswered question about the organ is whether it had any fine timber casework before the later thirteenth century.

Although the loose panel in a frame seems not to have (re-)appeared in the North until the thirteenth century, when so many woodworking techniques were being refined, adze-dressed or axe-trimmed planks could take on a planed appearance in skilful hands. Both written accounts and archaeology – panels prepared for gesso-work in Theophilus's treatise §1.17, the little surviving Saxon or Frisian planes from *c.* 700–800[21] – suggest that at least small-scale panelwork may have been very accomplished during these centuries. But panelling is not essential for an organ-case, either above or below impost, and it is likely that organ-timberwork began merely as a structural frame keeping the windtrunk rigidly fixed to the chest. Perhaps lower and even upper parts of organ-cases developed before wood-joinery itself was otherwise widely practised in church. That is quite possible.

Nevertheless, improved wood-planing in the late twelfth and thirteenth centuries no doubt prompted panel-making, perhaps sometimes on a large scale, for organ-cases as for choirstalls. On the choirstalls of St-Denis in the middle of the twelfth century, see Chapter 7.[22] Long benches, probably for the chorus, were developing in the twelfth century from Winchester (an extant example) to Xanten and Kloster Alpirsbach, taking the form of a settle (bench with back and arms).[23] Such benches were probably less simple than the *formulae* shown in the Plan of St Gall over three hundred years earlier.[24] If they had been much the same at first, then the gradual developing of structures with tiered seats and canopies (Winchester, *c.* 1310) could well have come about over much the same period that organs developed their large wooden frames. For example, the stall-enclosed quire of Notre-Dame, Paris, was completed only by the middle of the fourteenth century; by then, the idea of a church-within-a-church was clear to all (like many an extant *coro* in Spain), and either the enclosure would have had an organ incorporated in its upper levels or it would have consciously excluded it, leaving it to be placed in a more public part of the cathedral. Whatever was the case at Notre-Dame itself (see Chapter 20), these alternatives were available in hundreds of major churches across Europe.

[21] W. L. Goodman, *The History of Woodworking Tools* (New York, 1964), 54–6. Extant Roman planes include work from first-century Cologne.

[22] At St-Denis, it is not certain that the new stalls were wood, only that the monks previously sat on marble and bronze (*cupri* – see Panofsky 1977: 52f).

[23] The bench from Alpirsbach did not survive World War II; that at Winchester is made up from massive hewn planks. There also exists at Winchester a curved section of what may have been the settle around the apse of the Norman cathedral, *c.* 1100. (On the later gothic stalls of Winchester, see p. 320.)

[24] It is not certain that the *formulae* in the Plan of St Gall (Chapter 7) were wooden, but some distinctions were drawn in the Plan for bench-seating in different parts of the monastery: *formulae* in the large and smaller churches (movable benches without backs?), *scamnum* (fixed, with backs?) and *sedes, sedile, sedilia* (some separate seats with canopies?) elsewhere.

For the organ-historian the big question about woodworking is: when did organs begin to incorporate woodwork other than for the chest and the framework holding the bellows? What precisely did the 'carpenters' do who joined the coppersmiths in making an Arabic organ, according to one source?[25] Did Byzantine organs have in part a wooden case (see p. 149), and did Cassiodorus's organ-model have wooden keys (see p. 299)? One can make a guess that after bronzework, wooden chests (perhaps lined, as at Aquincum) and wooden keys (like the *linguae* in the treatise 'Bern Anon') came first; then a lap-jointed wooden structure[26] to carry the chest; then butt-jointed sides around and above the pipes to form a case. But there is virtually no direct evidence to support such an interpretation. Theophilus and early illustrators provide only the barest information on the wooden parts, although strangely enough the Utrecht Psalter shows both a rigid wooden (?) base and a decorative wooden (?) framework above the chest-level, thus a kind of façade. For once Theophilus's silence about something (wooden casework) cannot be construed as meaning that it was too obvious to talk about, since his suspended cloth cover must be a kind of casework-substitute.

The later twelfth and thirteenth centuries could well have seen new fundamental approaches to timberwork in organ-building as it did in other large-scale wooden apparatus such as windmills, papermills and fulling mills.[27] The 1230s and 40s were a particularly active time for windmills. By the period of big wooden altarpieces with gothic ornament (for example Oberwesel, *c.* 1330), the complete organ-case in wood was surely known, leading to such refinements as the wooden tester above the organ of Lübeck Cathedral, probably by 1396 (see Jakob 1991: 128). The organ of 1401–3 at the west end of Notre-Dame, Paris, was encased in 1539 (*ligni latus thece* – 'wood to sides and back', Wright 1989: 148) in order to protect it from dust and help project the sound. But surely these were not virtues recognized only recently?

Illustrators may have been slow to reflect the change coming over organs: clear pictorial evidence for surrounding casework is unknown before the mid-fourteenth century (in a Bohemian breviary: Jakob 1991: 126), with the curious exception of a twefth-century Greek manuscript: see above p. 304. Not until the fifteenth century are the three classic components shown, i.e. a case enclosing a mitre-shape display of pipes, a wooden gallery-front, and an organist's stool on a wooden gallery-floor. But far too little is known about the evolution of this total timberwork conception to trace it in detail over the three centuries between Theophilus and Henri Arnaut (*c.* 1130–*c.* 1440).

[25] Said to be ninth century: Shiloah 1979: 376, 380.

[26] Roof-members 'lap-jointed into position, by sidewise pressures', rather than made with mortise-and-tenon joints, are described for English structures *c.* 1200 (including the Benedictine abbey of Peterborough) in C. A. Hewitt, *The Development of Carpentry, 1200: an Essex Study* (New York, 1969), 23–5. The little seven-pipe portative in a painting in the eleventh-century crypt of Bayeux Cathedral seems to be constructed of horizontal wooden strips lap- or butt-jointed.

[27] Cf. E. M. Carus-Wilson, 'An industrial revolution of the thirteenth century', *The Economic History Review* II (1941), 39–60. But the importance of fulling mills and the justification of the phrase 'industrial revolution' have been questioned (e.g. A. R. Hall & N. C. Russell, 'What about the fulling-mill?', *HT* 6 (1981), 113–19), serving again to show the difficulty of correctly assessing technical development. On windmills in eastern England (e.g. Ramsey in the twelfth century), see Holt 1988: 171ff.

One guess would be that as tall wooden stalls became familiar around 1300, so wooden organ-cases were sometimes incorporated, or matched other gothic structures in the quire (such as a bishop's throne, like that at Exeter, *c.* 1320). Something of the kind may be implied by documents describing a quire-screen complete with lectern and organ at Königsberg, East Prussia, in 1333 (*organorum locacione . . . et ambone*). Stalls built up of symmetrical and repeated units would encourage woodworkers to design symmetrical cases for organs, fully possible only when they had also devised roller-boards. Another distinct possibility is that some large instruments were built in the wall as Theophilus suggests, having not a 'tent' suspended over the pipes but panelled doors (or frames over which painted canvas was stretched) closing around the organ, perhaps on to sides of an organ-case built for that purpose. The larger of the two organs in the Lady Chapel at Westminster Abbey in 1304 was probably an example: *in muro cum ij pannis depictis circa eadem extentis* ('on the wall, with two painted cloths stretched around it').[28] From that to the free-standing organ-box of Sion (*c.* 1435) is a small step, as it is to the large swallownest with painted wings of linen at Trier Cathedral (1386 – Bereths 1974: 72f).

Iron wire-drawing

Unless wire is drawn through a perforated iron or steel plate, reducing a strip of metal to a thin rod and then to a thinner wire was done by hammering and filing. Wire-drawing had been known for many centuries before it was described for the first time (by Theophilus, probably for the softer metals). Evidence for the making of iron wire, which is harder to draw and needs to be annealed after each few reductions, has been claimed for Nuremberg by *c.* 1100,[29] and it is possible that both this and Theophilus's remarks are witness to a German technological renaissance in the early twelfth century. The brevity of Theophilus's description may imply that 'it was too well known to need details' (Hawthorne & Smith 1963: 89), though it could also be that the craft belonged to a different trade-occupation than those for which Theophilus was writing: the organ-builder did not make wire but bought it in. The thicker wire or thin rod of iron or steel, such as was forged by Merovingian sword-smiths,[30] could have served for the short sticker of organ pin-actions over the following centuries, were its durability to have made it preferable to wood. The various forms of hammered ironwork made use of in panel or door grills[31] show iron to have been fashioned for purposes of church furnishings long before iron rods and trundles of any kind are documented in organs (for example at Trier Cathedral, 1387).[32]

[28] Königsberg: in W. Renkewitz & J. Janca, *Geschichte der Orgelbaukunst in Ost- und Westpreußen von 1333 bis 1944* (Würzburg, 1984), 1–2. Westminster: without original in A. Freeman, 'The organs of the abbey church at Westminster', *The Organ* 2 (1923), 129–48, here 129.

[29] F. M. Feldhaus, 'Beiträge zur Geschichte des Drahtziehens', *Anzeiger für die Drahtindustrie* (1910), 137, 159, 181.

[30] E. Salin, *La civilisation mérovingienne d'après les sépultures, les textes et le laboratoire*, 4 vols (Paris, 1949–59), 3.94–8.

[31] Some twelfth-century remains in Bobbio and in Parma Cathedral.

[32] *Registra* and expenses for iron are both referred to in the accounts of 1387 at Trier Cathedral: citations in Bereths 1974: 72. H. Klotz, in *Über die Orgelkunst der Gotik, der Renaissance und des Barock* (Kassel, 1975), 13, understands the term to mean stop-registers, but it may rather have had something to do with a carved angel above the organ – meaning the levers that make it work? (Bereths, *ibid.*, thinks this *angelus supra organa* may have been an upper chest, a kind of *Oberwerk*, but a moving statue seems more likely.)

Using waterpower for wire-drawing, as already in fourteenth-century Frankfurt (Feldhaus 1930: 315), increased the flexibility and range of guages. Iron wire suitable for trackers must have been available at least by the mid-fourteenth century when thick guages were used for pulling hammers of clock-bells.[33] This was also the century in which iron wire-drawing is documented in many cities, something so systematically organized by the 1430s in Coventry that the guild of wire-drawers by then recognized categories of workers: smiths for hammering the first strip, brakemen drawing it through the whortle, girdlers annealing it, middlemen removing the scale, wire-drawers operating fine whortles, and crookers cutting and bending the finished wire.[34]

Springs

Fig. 6 Drawing of a Mycenaean *fibula*: see note 36

For the history of the organ, three particular springs are relevant: the flat or leaf spring, the leaf spring bent into a U-shape, and the bent and/or partially coiled round wire-spring.[35] In machinery, the leaf spring gave the earliest reliable movement, and was known as a strip of bronze in the Aquincum organ and in Roman locks and padlocks from at least the first century AD (Neuburger 1930: 338–9). In its shape and functioning the spring *fibula*, a kind of safety pin, is more like the pallet-spring, but in general the springiness must have been too faint and sluggish for the organ (see above). Leaf springs of bronze, of vastly greater dimensions and strength than is necessary for organ-action, were made or proposed by Ctesibius for missile-throwers, according to Philo of Byzantium (Drachmann 1963: 189). These leaf springs contained a small percentage of tin and were hammered after casting and again for a long time when cold, according to Feldhaus 1930: 140. Silence about this basic flectional device in Vitruvius and Hero suggests either that it was little known (Usher 1929: 84–5) or, more likely, that it was too familiar to be described unless it were to have a critical part in some apparatus. Usher also remarks on the springiness of the Roman (and pre-Roman) *fibula*, although the wire part of it was only hammered and filed from the metal strip from which the whole thing was made.

---

[33] H. E. Rose, 'A conjectural reconstruction of the Perpignan clock of 1356', *AH* 15 (1985), 330–54, 491–502, here 345.

[34] M. D. Harris, *Coventry Leet Book 1420–1555*, Early English Text Society (London, 1912), 180–4.

[35] The fully coiled, very thin steel strip-spring now used in clocks appears in the early fifteenth century in locks. Spiral springs were also known to Leonardo: F. M. Feldhaus, *Die Technik der Vorzeit, der geschichtlichen Zeit, und der Naturvölker* (Leipzig, 1914), 289, 445.

In the collections of Greek, Celtic, Roman and Germanic artefacts in European museums are various styles of *fibula* in which thick round bronze wire is wound once or twice exactly like a modern safety pin, except that the wire is less elastic (see Fig. 6).[36] Sometimes the beaten wire is not coiled at the end but somewhere else along its curve.[37] Either way what springiness there was is the *raison d'être* of the object, even if only when wire was drawn would the spring, the reliability and the small amount of effort required be satisfactorily converted for such purposes as the pallet-springs of an organ. Until then, the leaf spring must have remained the one used in organs, either as a strip returning keys to position (as presumably at Aquincum) or in the U-shape for early pallets (as at Norrlanda). The U-shape may have been used very early: extant seventh-century tweezers of Anglo-Saxon origin,[38] bent from a wide strip of bronze, are one type of U-spring though, one imagines, not yet very resilient. On pallets and pallet-springs, see also Chapter 19. Curiously enough, the mechanical principle of late-medieval suspended action – spring-loaded pallet, tracker, key-lever – was paralleled or anticipated by a totally different apparatus, the pole-lathe.

The flexible wooden pole or 'overhead sapling spring' of the pole-lathe is a kind of large, coarse spring. Such a beam above the operator's head holds one end of a rope fastened at the other to a lever below the operator's foot and in-between wound around the axle of a lathe: the foot pulls the rope down, it turns the axle, and the beam pulls it up again. Several drawings from the thirteenth to the fifteenth century show it in use:[39] see Plate 17 for an example. Pole-lathes seem to have remained the 'dominant type of heavy-duty lathe as late as Leonardo da Vinci' (Usher 1929: 322) and are related to the spring beam of the military 'traction trebuchet'.[40] Such a beam was used too for the hydraulic saw of Villard de Honnecourt *c*. 1237,[41] for a vertical saw in the carpenter's window at Chartres and for the heddles of a loom in Boppard-am-Rhein, all before the middle of the thirteenth century (White 1962: 118). The development of the spinning-wheel in the thirteenth century is another instance of the century's experimentation with moving wooden parts. Although in general some of the technical drawings by Villard[42] were probably hypothetical, like some of those by Arnaut de Zwolle or

---

[36] This drawing is based on C. Blinkenberg, *Fibules grecques et orientales*, Historisk-filologiske Meddelser 13.1 (Copenhagen, 1926), 48.

[37] Examples in G. Mansfeld, *Die Fibeln der Heuneburg 1950–1970*, Römisch–Germanisch Forschungen 33 (Berlin, 1973), table 2.

[38] Examples in R. Daniels, 'The Anglo-Saxon monastery at Church Close, Hartlepool, Cleveland'. *AJ* 145 (1988), 156–210, here 182–3.

[39] Paris, Bibliothèque Nationale, lat. 11560 f. 84 is reproduced in Feldhaus 1930: 297, in B. Gille, 'Les développements technologiques en Europe de 1100 à 1400', *Cahiers d'Histoire mondiale* 3 (1956), 3–108, here 75, and elsewhere. Only if the contemporary spinning-wheel is actually earlier can it be described as 'the first known application of a belt-driven transmission' (Mokyr 1990: 51).

[40] A missile-thrower in which ropes pull on the shorter arm of an elastic beam, known from Muslim sources of the seventh or eighth century and Frankish somewhat later. See C. M. Gillmar, 'The introduction of the traction trebuchet into the Latin West', *Viator 12* (1981), 1–8.

[41] H. R. Hahnloser, *The Album of Villard de Honnecourt* (Vienna, 1935). A pair of such poles reconstructed in J. P. Adam & P. Varène, 'La scie hydraulique de Villard de Honnecourt et sa place dans l'histoire des techniques', *BM 143* (1985), 317–32.

[42] Sketchbook drawings (see Sternagel 1966: 112), perhaps 'more likely the album of a guild rather than the work of an individual', according to D. J. de Solla Price, 'Automata and the origins of mechanism and mechanical philosophy', *TC 5* (1964), 9–23, here 18.

Leonardo himself, there is a parallel between the simpler machine drawn in Plate 17 and suspended organ-action. Thus,

beam to rope to foot-lever = pallet-spring to tracker to key-lever

Obviously the miniature scale of the latter would require each element to be much more refined in dimensions and operating weight, with only enough 'give' for easy working. This would require experience of linkwork.

Plate 17 Turner and pole-lathe in a *Bible moralisée* (French, *c.* 1400): Paris, Bibliothèque Nationale, lat. 11560, f. 84

Linkwork

The end-pivoted key of organs, either placed above and pressing down a sticker (pin-action) or hanging from and pulling down a tracker (suspended action), sets in motion a mechanism not in principle more complex than linkwork in Hero's automatic theatre,[43] except that the two organ mechanisms depend on the spring-loaded valve (pallet), something not described by Hero. Hero's own organ key-square – two arms at right angles, the upper depressed by the finger, the lower tied to a horn spring that returns it to rest (see Chapter 14) – is found in other spring-less forms in his automata and theatre-stage equipment.[44] This mechanism offers some parallel to later organ-action since one arm of the square is pulled by a looped wire at its end in exactly the same way that an organ-key pulls its tracker and the tracker its pallet.[45] The square itself must have been familiar enough for much later organ-builders to have used it as a matter of course – without having to re-invent it – for those complex sixteenth-century actions that transferred motion around corners. But stickers-and-backfalls that do not transfer motion around corners (and therefore give better sensitivity to the fingers) remained the principle of such mechanisms as that for Dom Bedos's chair organ in the later eighteenth century.

Trip mechanisms making use of lugs attached to a rotating wheel or axle belong to an unbroken tradition from the Greeks to today, but they are not used in organs even if their principle of return-to-rest – linkwork returning to its original position – is that behind the pallet. The same principle operated in that Arabic automaton, described in a twelfth-century source,[46] in which a single pipe has holes like a flute stopped by a (round?) pallet falling by its own weight plus that of its pivoted lever unless the lever is raised by the pins of a barrel. The various pivoted and angled levers that are crucial to the working of such late-medieval devices as moving statues[47] are smaller, more intricately designed versions of the iron or wood levers of late-medieval stop-mechanisms in an organ, which transfer motion from one plane to another. The organ's roller-with-arms is less complicated than, for example, the roller-with-lugs mechanism for opening doors or releasing drop-curtains in Hero's automatic theatre (Schmidt 1899A: 418–19, 451), but it can only be guessed how and when the former came to be used in organs; see p. 341. Hero's descriptions, like those of the Arabic automata, were not available, necessary or even comprehensible to the twelfth-century carpenter working as he was with moving wooden parts.

---

[43] Text and reconstruction in Schmidt 1899A: 390ff.

[44] E.g. to release balls down a chute in order to imitate thunder: Schmidt 1899A: 406 (see also Bowles 1966: fig. 5).

[45] Examples probably from the late fourteenth century in Kjersgaard 1987.

[46] Text and reconstruction in Farmer 1931: 98–101.

[47] E.g. the wing-flapping cockerel in Strasbourg Cathedral in 1354 (e.g. Bowles 1966: fig. 9).

Clack-valves (flap-valves, check-valves)

The pallet is a spring-loaded clack-valve in the form of a wooden strip, although facing the contact surfaces with soft leather is partly to avoid the 'clack'. It is certain that the principle behind it is ancient. Bellows and pumps needed simpler flap-valves, i.e. without springs. Because such valves, admitting wind or water in one direction only, are what make a pump more than a simple syringe,[48] one can imagine that writers describing an organ-pump (Vitruvius) or bellows (Theophilus) might 'forget' to include them in their descriptions. They are part of the basic definition of such things.

Metal discs, loosely bolted to their seats, are necessary valves for the inflow and outflow in the extant bronze Roman pumps in Madrid (Museo Arqueológico Nacional) and in London (British Museum), and both inlet and outlet flap-valves are described by Vitruvius for his water-pump (*De architectura* 10.7). Vitruvius's organ's inlet-valve seems to have been a shallow bronze cone hanging from a chain held by the teeth of a bronze dolphin-shaped lever, so pivoted that its heavier tail fell, pulling the cone up when the cylinder was not sucking in air. Another sophisticated valve is also known from Roman archaeology: the bronze poppet-valves in a bronze pump found at Bolsena.[49] Important for illustrating the nature of written technology is the fact that nothing faintly resembling the Bolsena valve is described or hinted at in any of the known treatments of the *artes mechanicae*.

Since flap-valves (forced to move by springs, vacuum or exhaust pressure), Vitruvius's dolphin-valves (closing by their lever's gravity) and poppet-valves (closed by their own gravity) were known in bronze a thousand years before Theophilus, one can assume either that spring-loaded wooden keys were also known in his period or that they offered no difficulty in principle. How soon the pallet's triangular cross-section or the action-wire's leather pouches were known will never be certain – pouches only late? – but the ease with which wood and leather are worked makes it unlikely that many generations of organists had to tolerate warped, loose or non-airtight organ pallets.

Bellows

It is strange that the age-old Chinese box-bellows, which allowed one blower to maintain an unbroken stream of wind, remained unknown in the West, not least since one might guess them to be much more easily made than other kinds.[50]

48 T. Ewbank, *A Descriptive and Historical Account of Hydraulic and other Machines for Raising Water, Ancient and Modern* (New York, 16/1879), 262.

49 Singer 1954: 376. These mushroom valves show signs of having been turned on a lathe, according to J. F. Cave, 'A note on Roman metal turning', *HT* 2 (1977), 77–94, here 82. But the lost-wax method of bronze-casting must have made this necessary only at the last stage of production (see also Schiøler (see note 5): 36).

50 J. Needham, *Science and Civilisation in China*, 4.2 *Mechanical Engineering* (Cambridge, 1965), 135–7 and plates clxii–clxiii.

Whole-skin bellows as described by Theophilus (p. 268) are known from early periods and generally keep the three main elements: exhaust pipe (*tuyère*), the skin itself, and the rear intake slit with rims for closing it.[51] Familiar wedge-shaped bellows made from leather and wood, without ribs but with boards rounded at the broader end, are presumably a development of the whole-skin bellows, remaining in use for many centuries and open to such refinement as operation by cam and heavy counterpoise.[52] The steps by which the whole skin became replaced by boards with flexible wedge-shaped leather panels are not clear, but the organ of the Cambridge Psalter (made in Reims, early twelfth century – see Chapter 11) has a pair of what appears to be ribless leather-and-wood bellows, as do an infernal forge in one Catalan manuscript (two rounded wedge-boards, studded at the edges)[53] and bellows in the Belvoir Psalter of *c.* 1290 (see Chapter 17). Ribs cannot have been slow to come in.

An earlier pair of forge-bellows operated by Eve for the smith Adam, in ivory relief-panels of the tenth or eleventh century (Darmstadt, Hessisches Staatsmuseum), have conical, cornucopia-like skins, sewn in parallel sections (with ribs?), each one of the pair, held with a handle across the broader end, pulled out and pushed in to feed a simple *conflatorium*. Such long conical tube-bellows appear for forges in much later centuries, sometimes taking the form of a 'frog's mouth', the round shape preserved with ashen hoops. A variant design is pictured in a fifteenth-century Spanish psalter:[54] apparently, a pair of conical skins, tube-like and ribbed, supply wind to a positive organ. They look a little like concertina bellows. Round-headed nails or studs fixing the leather to the boards are specified in the Trier contract of 1387, with walnut for the boards, iron for the weights and wood for the frame and trunk (*arcus, conductus* – see Bereths 1974: 72f). Such nails are clear in several of the bellows pictured for the Horn of Aristotle in a manuscript of 1326 (Feldhaus 1930: 322) and in the rounded wedge-bellows in the contemporary Gorleston Psalter (Hickmann 1936: figures 12, 13). From such representations as these, it seems that wind-raising for organs – whether pumps for hydraules or bellows for other organs – is particularly well observed, as if organs were an obvious *locus* for the showing of bellows-technology. Perhaps they are: without organ pictures we would have an even vaguer idea today of how bellows in general evolved. It is striking that the Utrecht Psalter's depiction of the cylinders or cylinder-pumps for the three organs is much fuller than it is for the forge-bellows on f. 6' (Psalm 11/12) and f. 74 (Psalm 128/129), which are out of sight behind heat-shields. On f. 74 the blower stands with his right hand gripping the bellows at waist height, and the hearth is at the level of a low organ-chest. But scenes of hearth-bellows operated at waist level behind a protective wall were Roman, with extant representations from the Catacomb of Domatilla and a relief from Aquileia.

---

[51] E.g. R. J. Forbes, *Studies in Ancient Technology*, 9 vols (Leiden, 1955–8), 6.82. For early examples of skin-bellows – the 'first bellows' – in various civilizations, see Frémont 1917: 13ff.

[52] This last in the fifteenth century, for high-draught iron furnaces: Singer 1957: 643.

[53] P. Bonnassie, *La Catalogne du milieu du Xe à la fin du XIe siècle* (Toulouse, 1976), 473f.

[54] Sixteenth-century forge in Frémont 1917: 40. Ash-wood hoops specified at Ely Cathedral in 1396: see D. Gwynn, 'The development of bellows systems in British organs c. 990–1790', *BIOS Journal* 14 (1990), 35–47. Psalter of Alfonso V of Aragon, in Hickmann 1936: fig. 6.

The idea that bellows-organs are older than water-organs though not documented in the same way and rarely discussed, is very reasonable (Usher 1929: 89). The very inclusion of hydraulic pumps in the *artes mechanicae* treatises suggests them to be rare forms of apparatus for a given job of work. Furthermore, if a single pump can give higher and steadier wind than a comparably sized pair of bellows, a question is: Why was this desirable? For gentle melodies played by Roman house-organs modest bellows would have served perfectly well, and the long-held notes or chords of medieval church organs could be fed by many small bellows. It is clear from water-wheels used to drive iron forge-bellows in the early fourteenth century onwards (at Briey by *c.* 1323)[55] that if bellows were large enough or (without waterpower) numerous enough, they could raise whatever blast the job needed.

However, one advantage of pumps for the water-organs used in fulldress ceremonial or the outdoor games of antiquity was their modest size relative to the work done, and it could be that when organs became fixed – as fixed as furnaces needed to be – bellows, which were always easier to make, naturally supplied their wind because there was no need to save space or make the whole thing portable. But the ease with which pumps-and-cylinders could supply constant wind must be evidence of a sort – at least, a very strong hint – that the sound was also meant to be constant, i.e. for playing a siren or high-pitched drone. Little bellows for small organs over the centuries are well enough documented in pairs from the end of the fourteenth century,[56] and suggest either that they were blown in alternation or that one of them served as reservoir or stabilizer, the more necessary if a drone (high or low) was being played. By the early sixteenth century, a set of three rectangular ribbed bellows as illustrated for the regals in Virdung's *Musica getutscht* (Basle, 1511) would mean that two feed-bellows send wind into a stabilizer-bellows, which supplies constant wind to the wind-sensitive regal pipes (Edskes 1980: 82–3). Although the twelve or fifteen bellows feeding an elephant-skin collector/chest as described by Pseudo-Jerome and copied in the ninth century (the *Letter to Dardanus* – see p. 247) passed from memory, builders of any period would recognize the need either for a reservoir or for sheer number of bellows to compensate for windloss.

Many-and-small bellows presumably gave way gradually to fewer-and-larger. This may have been the reason for an item in the books of Orvieto Cathedral in 1388 when the large organ was 'restored' (*? reductum*) so as to require no more than three people to raise enough wind (Donati 1979: 202). The three bellows for the large organ of St-Cyr described by Arnaut de Zwolle (the organ with twelve large bourdon pipes – see Chapter 17) 'are raised with large beams' (*cum magnis baculis levantur* – Le Cerf 1932: 30). Such beams became more necessary the larger the bellows,

---

[55] B. Gille, *Les origines de la grande industrie métallurgique en France* (Paris, 1947), 15. It is suspected that some of the forges in the Domesday Book (1086) had waterpowered bellows: R. F. Tylecote, *The Prehistory of Metallurgy in the British Isles* (London, 1986).
      The notes on and illustrations of various forge-bellows in G. Agricola's *De re metallica* (Basle, 1555) anticipate those of the organ-bellows in Praetorius 1619, and surely influenced or even inspired them.

[56] If bellows in the third century were a whole skin with wooden tuyère, then perhaps they could have the more easily perished or escaped the Aquincum excavators; see Chapter 14. Practical suggestions for pairs of bellows in portative organs, particularly as known from paintings of the late fourteenth century, in G. Bridges, 'Medieval portatives: some technical comments', *GSJ* 44 (1991), 103–16.

but their history is quite unclear: perhaps beams or levers, such as were familiar in various branches of carpentry, were used for bellows-lifting before bellows needed to be large, and actually encouraged them to become larger. In any case such levers remain another of the craftsman's undocumented devices.

At Notre-Dame, Paris, in the fourteenth century there was a further aid to raise wind: a 'wheel engine' (*rota ingenii*) was turned by six or seven servants (*famuli . . . pro vertendo*) hired when the organ was played on special occasions, such as a visit of the king to mass in 1380 (Wright 1989: 146). Several constructions are possible here: a very large pulley or a treadmill, a single or a pair of vertical wheels, or a single or pair of horizontal wheels, in all of which construction a shaft tripped the upper-boards of the bellows sitting in a row.[57] Perhaps there were three men on each of a pair of wheels, with a seventh man keeping time for an even rotation, supplying a large volume of wind for some large pipes and giving a cushion of air as a stabilizer. A firm wooden structure would be necessary for any such system. For the labour involved in making the machine to have been worthwhile, the six men must have been able to produce more wind with it than ordinarily. Although wheels were already familiar for permanent lifting-gear in the roof-space of many a cathedral (several extant examples in England), the Notre-Dame organ-wheel may have been a bigger affair altogether, perhaps occupying one of the spacious nave-galleries below the organ placed on an upper nave wall.

At SS Annunziata, Florence, in 1379 the wood and ropes needed *pro circulis mantacorum* ('for the wheels of the bellows'? – Donati 1979: 209) may have been for simpler wheels, perhaps a set of large pulleys turning on a beam (*una asse . . . supra quam actavit circulos*) with ropes attached to the bellows boards. Both for the Florence and the Paris wheels, however they worked, the bellows must have been weighted, as is recorded at Trier Cathedral in 1387 (Bereths 1974). Though so little is known about all such devices, they do serve as a useful example of the kind of individual solution found in the great cathedrals by ingenious but seldom acknowledged craftsmen.

Clocks

If bells sometimes cast light on how or why organs were used, clocks do on how organs were made, particularly in the timberwork they may both have had in the thirteenth and fourteenth centuries.

While it is not certain how King Hezekiah's water-clock as pictured in late thirteenth- or fourteenth-century manuscripts (see p. 355 and note 42) worked, its conventionalized framing structure, apparently of wood, gives some idea of the kind of thing with which organ-builders were most likely working. See Plate 18. Similar

---

[57] As in the third construction drawn in the late fifteenth-century German *Hausbuch*, which shows three types of leather-and-boards bellows: those operated at waist-height by hand (the *Children of Mercury* scene), two larger pushed/pulled up by an overhead yoke-beam oscillating on an axle turned a few degrees by a hanging beam, and two pressed down by shaped lugs on a horizontal shaft turned by a water-wheel and pulled up by weight-and-pulley. See H. T. Bossert & W. F. Storck, *Das mittelälterliche Hausbuch . . .* (Leipzig, 1912), plates 16, 38, 42; also Hall 1979: plates xvi, xvii.

points could be made about the clock pictured beside Richard of Wallingford, Abbot of St Albans 1327–36, in a manuscript of the fourteenth century[58] where, despite the absence of fine detail, there can be seen a frame and a gothic pediment complete with a typical trefoil, all presumably of wood and matching the design for the Winchester choirstalls. Both the gothic detail and the timber framework of the clock could equally have been made for an organ-builder, particularly if he had also been the clock-maker. Some small extant medieval clocks share gothic details with organs. Like several fifteenth-century organs, a small clock in the British Museum has a castellated top with towers (made from sheet iron)[59] and the rectangular dial-front blocks the view of the inner mechanism precisely as the pipes of an organ-front would. The very ornate, high-gothic metal structure of a clock made for Philip the Good of Burgundy (first half of the fifteenth century) now in the Germanisches Nationalmuseum, Nuremberg, has ornament that includes not only intricate pinnacles and mouldings but a row of gothic roundels such as found on contemporary organs either clustered (left tower at Sion, overall in S Petronio, Bologna) or in a similar row (Van Eyck altarpiece in Ghent).

Presumably the carpentry involved in erecting some of the period's clocks was far greater than that needed for most organs: in the accounts of 1334 for the *hôpital* of the Brotherhood of St-Jacques-aux-Pélerins, Paris, it looks as if it were the clock(s) that required special carpentry:[60]

pour appareillier les ogres	for preparing the organs
et les auloges . . . XXs	and the clocks . . . 20s
pour les charpentiers qui	for the carpenters who
les ostèrent de leur place	lifted them up from their place
et les assirent en une autre	and seated them in another,
et firent un corbiau qui	and made a corbel which
soustient la couverture	supported the roofing
des auloges . . . VJs.	for the clocks . . . 6s.

This is but one document, however: the fourteenth-century organ-corbel or pendentive in Strasbourg Cathedral (1385)[61] now supporting the gallery and organ of 1491 was at least the equal of the clock-corbel at St-Jacques-aux-Pélerins in size and as a feat of timber-engineering. From a flamboyant pendentive-plus-gallery to a flamboyant organ-encasement does not seem a major step: clocks, gallery-fronts and organ-façades give three similar opportunities for deep-carved gothic timber-work. In the end, the organ brought forth some of the tallest and widest examples of such wooden gothic structures, as at Saragossa Cathedral in the mid-fifteenth century.

One extant medieval clock that must be of particular relevance to organs is that in the north-eastern aisle of Beauvais Cathedral, a wooden structure substantially of

---

[58] London, British Library, Cotton Nero D.VII f. 20.
[59] For a note on the *castelli* of fifteenth-century organ-case design in Italy, see above p. 299.
[60] [H. Lengelle] Tardy, *La pendule française des origines à nos jours* (Paris, 1961), 1.2.
[61] H. Reinhardt, 'Petit historique des orgues de la cathédrale, 1260–1714', *Bulletin de la Société des Amis de la Cathédrale de Strasbourg 11* (1974), 57–68.

Plate 18 'King Hezekiah water-clock' in a *Bible moralisée* (French, late thirteenth century): Oxford, Bodleian Library, Bodley 270b, f. 183'

the early fourteenth century though much restored (Plate 19).[62] The clock's seating and housing could well be that of a modest organ: above three free facets of an engaged octagonal stone plinth[63] sit three wooden sides of the clock, one with the

---

[62]   P. Bonnet-Laborderie, *Cathédrale Saint-Pierre histoire et architecture* (Beauvais, 1978), 215. The clock-bell is inscribed *Stephanus Musicus canonicus belvacensis me fecit fieri*. Exterior woodwork restored in the sixteenth century.

[63]   Therefore not unlike a large, gothicized version of the kind of Roman hydraulis-base as seen in the Carthage terracotta (in Perrot 1965: plates xi, xii). It is difficult to see how this could be more than coincidence unless there had been many another unknown water-clock or water-organ built in the intervening centuries on a part-hexagonal plan; perhaps there had.

Plate 19 Early fourteenth-century clock, on octagonal plinth and below a hexagonal gothic canopy (cf. Plate 18) in the north-eastern aisle of Beauvais Cathedral (photo Georges Loëffel).

(later?) dial, two with baluster-panels, the whole crowned with a wooden gothic pavilion (with the familiar trefoil decoration, etc.) housing the bell. In size, location and detail of design, it would not be difficult to imagine an organ here instead: were early organs sometimes placed on a plinth in an aisle, just above the heads of the *plebes* and so out of harm's way though close to eyes and ears? The same motif of three sides of an octagon can be found in the plan of many a later organ or organ-gallery, including both the two organ-cases and the gallery at Strasbourg Cathedral (1491).[64]

There is a further but more elusive factor in common between organs and clocks: they are both more consistently documented when church accounts are kept for work involving outside paid contractors or craftsmen. Cathedral or cathedral-abbey clocks are regularly recorded from the late thirteenth century (Exeter, Norwich, Ely, St Paul's), while fourteenth-century records in France include not only the most conspicuous cathedrals (Reims, Chartres, Beauvais, Strasbourg, Cluny, Lyons, Rouen) but churches known or assumed from Arnaut de Zwolle's manuscript to have had old organs (Dijon, Notre-Dame, Nevers St-Cyr). It was probably in the last few decades before 1300 that organs and clocks came to be regularly encased in timberwork comparable to the new contemporary stalls. How – and how tentatively – either had previously moved in this direction is not known.

---

[64] The 1491 organ has two such shapes (the plan of the front of both the main organ and the chair organ), which 'follow' the plan of the older gallery. Other fifteenth-century applications of this shape include the gallery-front in Dortmund Marienkirche and the pipe-tower in the organ-case at Kiedrich. The Beauvais clock-plinth also anticipates some later pendentives or *trompes* supporting organ-cases or organ-galleries; for a remark on plinths and half-columns, see above p. 129.

19

Further conjectural developments in late medieval organ-building

In instrument-technology the fifteenth century was a hugely inventive period, and it could be that some of the crucial details in the great organs of Bologna or Haarlem, exactly five hundred years after Winchester, were the result of very recent changes of direction, technical or musical. Despite this, some possible stages of development during those five hundred years can be conjectured, if only because later organ-history suggests that there are certain changes that do come about step by step.

Chest and action

The principle behind Theophilus's bronze chest, in which each pipe receives its wind through a boring down into the windbox, supposes a modest width for the chest, as does the material itself. The wooden chest, though equally modest in Theophilus's model, allows more development: a channel under all the pipes of one key means that the key-slider needs to have only one large hole admitting wind to the channel, which may therefore be as long as woodworking skill can devise and the wind can fill evenly. Wood also makes it easier to develop two other crucial elements in chest-design and therefore to increase the potential of organs: chests can become longer (therefore with a bigger compass) and they can be built higher in the organ (to raise the pipes above the key-sliders).

The technique of hollowing out blocks of wood can serve various principles of design:[1]

> two planks carved out and then glued together; with key-sliders, the whole on a small scale but open to extrapolation (Theophilus);
> two planks *ditto* but with a pallet-box below, on a small scale; with keys drawing pallets (Arnaut de Zwolle);
> several planks *ditto* but on a massive scale, individually designed (the Bartenstein organ: see below).

---

[1] Some stringed instruments of modest size, such as citterns, continued to be made from a hollowed-out block well beyond the present period, e.g. a cittern of 1582 in the Victoria & Albert Museum. For the probability that Paul Hofhaimer's regals illustrated in 1519 had a chest made from hollowed-out blocks, see Edskes 1980: 81.

The soundboard of stringed instruments made with the hollowed-out technique is normally glued or nailed on top of the sides,[2] corresponding exactly to Theophilus's perforated strips on which the pipes stand at the top of the chest. These little wooden strips may themselves suggest that Theophilus, or the craftsmen whose work he was describing, were familiar with other kinds of instrument-making.

Wherever pallet-boxes were invented, one can assume that they would help to refine such joinery techniques as were being explored in the course of the fourteenth century for the sake of the casework and other fine furnishings in church. Also, in a way that copper chests clearly could not, the wooden chest became a part of the organ's overall frame construction, being connected with the main framing around it (or vice versa) and giving the structure its stability. The result, such as it can still be seen in the archaic Salamanca organ of *c.* 1500,[3] is a logically coordinated piece of furniture, impossible to imagine in any other material but wood.

Key-mechanism also needed to change in the direction of light wooden construction. With or without spring-loaded levers pulling them, key-sliders would incline to be noisy – rattling in the groove, banging into the end-stop? – and less or more stiff, for if wind-escape and rattling were to be minimized, friction must have increased. The more the pipes and the bigger the size, the worse the key-action for both player and maker. Were the slider with the single hole to be replaced by a wooden clack-valve, loaded with a spring and pushed or pulled open by a lever, either organ-playing would immediately become easier or the makers would soon learn how to make it so by adjusting the various elements of design – the pivotal point of the key, the size of the pallet, the strength of the spring, and so on. It need not be true that spring-loaded pallets working against the wind in the chest were always or at first very heavy even on large organs,[4] though no doubt many were. Furthermore, the keys could be far below the pipes, linked by wire ('suspended action') to the valves and their load light enough for dexterous fingers. In giving a picture of contemporary crafts a drawing of *c.* 1404 could consciously show two organs: one with pin-action and button-keys (a portative) and one with suspended action and longer keys (a positive)[5] (see Jakob 1991: 131). So convenient is the whole arrangement of key, wire and pallet that it seems inevitable, and yet how it all came about is quite unknown.

While one might guess at various possible stages of development,[6] the steps taken by the first builders of pallet-action have passed without record of any kind – one of the most crucial inventions in all instrument technology! Given that some craftsmen,

---

2   Is some such tradition as this the reason why Arnaut de Zwolle's harpsichord soundboard appears to cover completely the side in his plan-drawing of a *clavisimbalum* (Le Cerf 1932: plate VI), though like his clavichords his harpsichord must have had a framed body?
        Brepohl 1987: 247 thinks the strips fitted into rather than on the top of Theophilus's organ-chest, but this would have taken space from the woodblock for no reason.
3   This is the organ frequently dated in the literature to 'about 1380': but see De Graaf 1982 and Edskes 1987.
4   Suggested by Riemann 1879: 210–11, who must be right, however, to assume that the first attempts at long actions were not always successful from the point of view of (later notions of) agility.
5   Tübingen, Universitätsbibliothek, Md 2 f. 171, a medical or astronomical treatise of 1404, illustrating activities of the Children of Mercury: reproduced in Bowles 1982: 27.
6   An interesting attempt in Hardouin 1966: 41, 50–1 does not quite suggest how the steps came to be taken and the pallet to be devised.

in some areas, for some organs, were working in wooden key-action since at least the time of Cassiodorus (see Chapter 17), and that the organ was as open to pragmatic, on-the-spot development as any other instrument if not more, it seems unlikely that the pallet-box was invented from scratch in the fourteenth century, however skilled in so many directions were craftsmen of that period. Nor can a whole range of possibilities have been open to the makers, even if some details varied from region to region and in certain cases persisted into the Baroque organ. It is not unlikely that a simple pin-action, not suspended action, was the place of birth for the pallet, for a hinged lever pressing down the valve seems to be simpler than one pulling it down.

One can imagine early key-slider mechanisms with a spring-loaded square to have taken one such form as the following. The key-square (which could have a key-plate on top and be hidden by a front panel, etc.) was returned to position by the spring (see Fig. 7). If the spring is relocated to return a wind-valve ('pallet') to position rather than the key itself, it needs to be pressed down by a little rod ('pin') from the key (see Fig. 8).

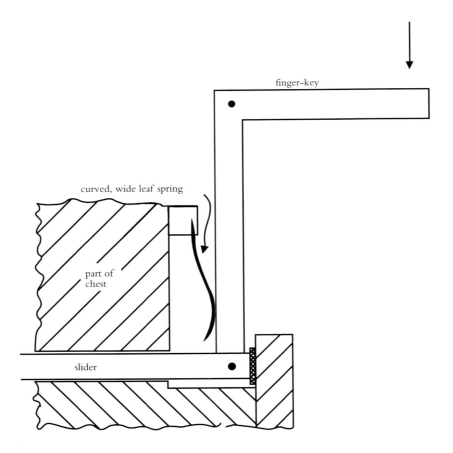

Fig. 7 Action with finger-key square, leaf spring and slider

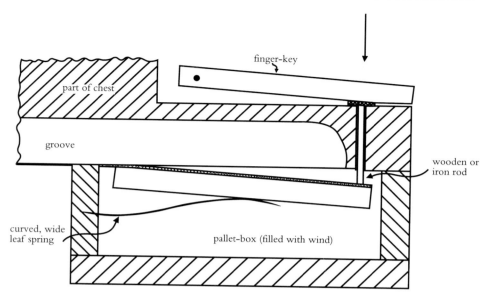

Fig. 8 Action with finger-key, pin, pallet and leaf spring

One can assume that the idea for a wind-valve came first since there would be no point in relocating the spring without it. But why a wind-valve at all? The most obvious answer is that since sliders too easily leaked, something more airtight had to be developed.

The clack-valve, of which the pallet is one particular form, was already well known as a device in one piece of pressurized-air apparatus (bellows) and would be naturally employed in another (organ-chests) when wind had to be controlled. Similarly, the idea of spring-loading the clack-valve need not have been a major step for an organ-maker already familiar with spring-loading the key-squares (as in Fig. 7), although it is also possible that in some cases the valve might have been attached directly to the key without a return-spring. It would thus be both opened and shut by action of the hand, like some old key-sliders and with the same advantages and disadvantages (see p. 52). The valve would need to be slim to the extent that the chest was the same or much the same in length as the row of keys; but since in earlier examples keys need not have been very close together, perhaps the pallets did not at first take one particular form rather than another. The slimmer they were, the longer they had to be if the volume of wind were to be adequate and even. Such details of design required experiment and precision, for the pallet is no ordinary clack-valve.

Although it is impossible to chronicle how organ-size influenced the development of actions, pin-action with pipes above the keys clearly suits a small (not necessarily short-compass) organ, and representations suggest this to have been known by at least the later thirteenth century (carving at León Cathedral – for example, Jakob 1991: 120). But if such action was customary for the gothic portative over the whole period 1250–1450 and beyond, so it could have been for the earlier positive, otherwise for many centuries builders had invented nothing but improved slider-keys, which is hard to believe. It was the increasingly large organ of that period that required other actions: only in much larger organs whose keys need to be (a) of finger-size and (b) without gaps between them, does pin-action become less suitable. Conversely, although the miniature portative keys[7] certainly suit pin-action, so do keys that became common in all manner of keyboard instruments: the short or quite short lever hinged at the distal end.

Any of the elements in the key–pin–pallet–spring linkwork could be old and originally large and 'unrefined'. Any kind of refinement such as the button-keys miniaturized in late portatives could have existed before spring-loaded pallets – Hero's key-square operating a slider could have been contrived to take some such shape. Also, if the keys on a large or somewhat large organ needed to be placed nearer to each other than their ranks of pipes could be, bored channels would have made it possible whether the keys had sliders or pallets. In other words, there need be no inevitable inter-dependence between refined finger-sized keys, pin-action and pallet-springs.

The pallet-spring would be at first a simple leaf spring, as in Figures 7 and 8, and while it may not seem a major step to bend the leaf into a U-shape (as at Norrlanda – see below), the leaf would have to be finely made if it were not to be too strong or lose its elasticity too soon. One must suppose that early springs were not always fine enough for the action of a single finger. Fifteenth-century improvements in wire-drawing, both in iron and brass, meant not only a yet more reliable suspended or pin-action but gave builders a choice of spring for different occasions.[8] The old *fibula* spring (see Fig. 6) would take on new life when made from the wire of late-medieval north-western Europe. As for the stickers of a pin-action: no doubt they could be made of wood, like the short, square hardwood stickers found in some later instruments,[9] but no very early instance of them has survived. Perhaps the stalks of keys shaped like mushrooms really were the stickers.

Keys, trackers and rollerboards

There is a further possibility: that close-spaced finger-sized keys were also the consequence of making small-scale portable organs, not of players desiring finger-dexterity as such. The width of slider-keys, and the width of any space between them depended on what was necessary to grip them (or what hand-weight was necessary for the leaf spring if key-squares operated them) and what physical margins were required for sliders within their grooves. Although close-spaced finger-keys, such as have been universal since the fifteenth century, are musically convenient and desirable, any such desire had to develop.

---

[7] Marshall 1989: 25 and again 86.
[8] A U-shaped spring of wire, less strong than the coiled spring for the larger *Hauptwerk* and *Rückpositiv* pallets, is still used for the little Regal chest in the *Brust* of the Innsbruck Hofkirche organ (1558).
[9] E.g. a seventeenth-century regals in Munich, Deutsches Museum (No. 24139): see R. Menger, *Das Regal* (Tutzing, 1972), plate 11.

However, even if what organists were called upon to play on the large church organs in earlier centuries did not make them think of their keyboards as 'primitive' or 'inconvenient', there is nothing in the 'Bern Anon' theorist or Theophilus or any other documentation to make Arnaut's slim key-dimensions impossible at a much earlier date, at least as one of several options. Refined linkwork of various kinds had long been familiar; see Chapter 18. Aquincum suggests, though it cannot prove, that convenience and dexterity were possible in small organs nine hundred years before Theophilus. But one did not need great agility for the clanging or screeching sound that organs probably provided on some occasions in the early Middle Ages, or for the tenor or bass lines they contributed to later festive music.

Because the organ did not have a single purpose, a single line of historical development is hard to propose, and instruments of different size and therefore mechanism must have co-existed. To imagine all medieval organ-keys as broad, gapped and requiring to be seized (thumped) by the whole hand must be an over-simplification. Very large organs may have had such keys because overall dimensions – including width of channels, size of pallet, length of any linkwork – meant sturdy wooden parts throughout, but such instruments themselves may have been built only from the fourteenth century and then only for musical purposes (making use of large, slow-speaking pipes) for which agility was not needed.

The linkwork required if sliders were to be operated by trackers – square/tracker/square, with a spring for one of the squares – would be so awkward that one can imagine a builder resolving to do away with the horizontally-moving slider and inventing the vertically-moving pallet. This, therefore, is another possible route by which pallets became known. Trackers would become most desirable to transmit key-movement over an intervening vertical distance, removing the chest from the organist's ears. If the compass were not large, as in the fourteen notes of the two top keyboards at Halberstadt (late fourteenth century?) drawn by Praetorius,[10] vertical trackers could have been splayed, drawing down pallets that were placed progressively further from a central vertical the larger the bass pipes were.[11] If the keys were not close-packed but spaced with as much distance between them as on a modern pedalboard, then splaying becomes even more feasible and the keys would to some extent allow for the larger pipes of a larger organ – a further hint that the close-spaced keyboard was a characteristic of the small organ, the open-spaced keyboard of the larger.

Rollerboards were not necessary for every kind of organ known from late fourteenth-century reports any more than trackers themselves were. But without them certain things would follow. If there were no trackers, pin-action became more and more impractical as size increased; if there were no rollers, the biggest and heaviest pipes were all to one side unless a solid chest were bored at some trouble to conduct wind to pipes placed other than in a vertical to the keys. It is very likely

[10]   Praetorius 1619: plate 25: a compass of H–c'.
[11]   Bormann 1966A: 17 assumes a mitre-shape (and therefore a rollerboard?), but it is possible that in the late fourteenth century, such a large organ had short manual keyboards (three in this case?) at least partly for the sake of splaying the trackers for each keyboard.

that rollers originated for a few pipes only, to distribute the weight more evenly (hence the isolated large pipes to the right in some early representations? – see Chapter 17); that rollerboards gradually followed, also at first for a few notes only (see Norrlanda, below); and that the visual advantages of this ingenious device were not only that it allowed the mitre-shape (biggest pipes in the middle) but that it allowed sheer variety of design – with or without side towers, with or without subsidiary mitre-shapes, etc.[12]

How the most extravagant principle of visual design in the fifteenth-century organ – the distantly placed extra-bass pipes or *trompes* – was realized on each occasion is not known, but presumably it was worked out on the basis of one of three techniques by then well established. The pipes sounded all at once and sat on a little chest to which wind could be admitted when a blocking-valve was operated; or a set of small windtrunks originating in the main chest took wind to each pipe, operated either by key-and-pallet or by a separate valve; or (least likely?) long trackers opened a pallet under each pipe. In the case of the late gothic organ of Haarlem (1466), two lead conduits of about 5 cm diameter and 4.5 m long are thought to have taken the wind from the underside of the chest to two pairs of large drum-pipes in a bourdon tower to the right of the organ;[13] presumably, each pair could be sounded separately. On a miniature scale, earlier portatives and positives may well have had some similar system.

However the pallet came about, it is easy to understand how in the late gothic organ large springchests preceded large chests with stop-sliders for each rank of pipes, for the smaller secondary pallet below each pipe in a springchest is no new technology. It merely means that two pallets have to be opened for a pipe to get its wind. Even the spaciousness of the springchest as it developed in northern Italy was traditional. The stop-sliderchest, on the other hand, meant further design-work and experience with airtight joinery or block-gluing,[14] since the slider ran between boards and had to be designed with minimal tolerances. This was surely done for the first time on small organs or on small chests of larger organs: larger organs must always have had some individually designed system, perhaps like that known at Bartenstein, the so-called 'top slider' of the kind still described by Schlick in 1511 (*Oberschleife* – see below). A pair of pallets for the lowest notes, one each from manual and pedal, are known from the Malmö organ of *c.* 1500. They may be as old a means of coupling as the two trackers to one roller and one pallet in the Norrlanda organ.

[12] The Greek–Roman arrangement of diatonic or chromatic note-sequence gave an unvarying long-to-short layout, except in some doubtful drawings described in Chapter 11. For variety in fifteenth-century organ-façades – in mitre or other symmetrical shapes, with bourdon towers, or in chromatic sequence etc. – see note 16 below.

[13] H. van Nieuwkoop, *Haarlemse Orgelkunst van 1400 tot Heden* (The Hague, 1988), 55f.

[14] Bored blocks were still associated with old organs by Andreas Werckmeister, in *Erweiterte und vermehrte Orgelprobe* (Quedlinburg, 1698), 17.

The Swedish organ remnants

As well as the two-rank portative with tallest pipes in the middle, made possible by a conduit bored in the chest-planks at two levels (see Chapter 16), Arnaut de Zwolle gives the design of a larger organ with rollerboard (Le Cerf 1932: plate xiii). Every key in the compass of thirty-one notes (H–f″) is thus transmitted, except c′ and c♯′. The arrangement was for the sake of a mitre-shape plus six larger pipes to left and right (largest on the outside); the organs of Sion (*c.* 1435) and the Innsbruck Hofkirche (1558) have a similar arrangement but on a larger scale. For the Swedish positives at Sundre (inscribed 1370) and Norrlanda (*c.* 1390), the two outer 'towers' were similar to Sion,[15] while at Norrlanda the smaller pipes in the middle flat are in long-to-short sequence, not mitre-shape.

Though small, the Norrlanda organ has several structural characteristics of the major church organ, including a shallow casework (chest 110 cm × 20 cm) that allows some symmetry in the façade design. Double-arm rollers enable keys C♯ D♯ F♯ and G♯ to draw the same roller (and therefore same pipe) as c♯ d♯ f♯ g♯ above, and make an apparent complete compass of C–a. There is no known reference to such octave-transposition via rollers although in music-theory the idea of octave-substitution goes back centuries. There are also eight rollers for eight pedal-keys making double connections: each roller plays two pipes at different pitch per key:

> G+c A+d H+e F+c G+d A+e F+B H+e

or

> H+e F+B A+e G+d F+c H+e A+d G+c

This reconstruction is uncertain and would show something totally unknown from any kind of documentation: the doubled note. Yet the principle of movement being transmitted in one or both lateral directions appears reliable, and the note-doubling (a kind of self-made pedal diaphony) does not contradict other impressions one may have that the early organ contributed to polyphony with diatonic notes producing various diatonic intervals. (Here, the second possibility gives a kind of reversed, diatonic scale with resultant tones of the Bourdon-fifth type.) In any case, of the two dozen or so extant representations of larger fifteenth-century organs, thirteen have some kind of symmetrical pipe-arrangement that would call for rollers if the chest were above a certain size.[16] Most show a deep enough panel between keyboard and pipe-feet for a rollerboard.

Norrlanda's 'keyboard' consists of a row of sturdy keys (three to four fingers long, two wide), almost adjacent and protruding in a row from the front panel; on the B-flat, see below.[17] There were four to six ranks of pipes (including a fifth rank?), thus a small Blockwerk of the kind that makers would have developed from the kind of

---

[15] Remarks on Norrlanda based on P.-G. Andersen, *Orgelbogen* (Copenhagen, 1956), fig. 41 (reconstruction) and Kjersgaard 1987/1988; also W. Adelung, 'On pedal action of [the] Norrlanda organ', *ISO* 28 (1988), 59–60.

[16] One can only conjecture what size this was. For the paintings and drawings, see Bowles 1982, also Jakob 1991: esp. 116–55, which has the most complete collection so far of the extant drawings.

[17] The Norrlanda keyboard is discussed in comparison with that of the Van Eyck altarpiece organ, in E. M. Ripin, 'The Norrlanda organ and the Ghent altarpiece', in *Emsheimer Festschrift*, ed. G. Hillestrom, Musik-historiska Museets Skrifter 5 (Stockholm, 1974), 193–5, 286–8 and G. Corinth, 'A playable reconstruction of the Ghent altarpiece's gothic positive', *ISO Yearbook* (1991), 6–38.

chorus already observed by the theorists of Chapters 15 and 16. Other technical details can be summarized for the late fourteenth century from the extant Swedish remains, organs whose workmanship is of limited sophistication (Kjersgaard: 1987) and therefore, perhaps, very typical:

> *Sundre* had a windtrunk, but five others including Norrlanda had two wedge-bellows socketed into the rear of the chest or pallet-box, as described by Zarlino for the eleventh-century organ (?) of Grado (see Plate 15). Sundre's channels are made up from joined members, but chests otherwise are bored or hollowed out from solid oak. The table at Norrlanda, corresponding to Theophilus's upper plank, measures *c.* 110 × 20 × 2 cm.
>
> *Pallets* are short, broad and thin, pierced with a hole and leathered around and above: the hole admits wind under the surrounding leather of the pallet, which inflates like a little cushion, sealing the gap despite any warp in the pallet-wood but allowing slighter pallet-construction and thus a lighter pallet-spring than otherwise. At Norrlanda, pallet-springs are bent strips of sheet iron, in a U-shape; the pulldown eyes in the pallets are made of iron wire while the pallet guide-pins are of wood.[18]
>
> *The keyboards* begin at C, with B not raised. Sundre appears to have had:
>
> C C♯ D D♯ E F F♯ G A B H c c♯ d e f g g♯ (C♯ plays c♯)
>
> Anga may have had drone-keys on either side of the manual, and perhaps Sundre's pedal played two notes as at Norrlanda. Sundre's finger-keys were about 5 cm wide. An *extant pipe* from Visby is of 30 per cent tin, heavily soldered. It is possible that Norrlanda had stopped pipes for the pedal; its chorus was probably based on 3' F (6' if stopped), with a quint rank.

Sion, Bartenstein, Halberstadt and the organ of *c.* 1400

Recent work at Sion (organ of *c.* 1435)[19] has established a shallow chest (total case-width 29 cm), suspended action and a mitre-arrangement, a compass of H–a" (complete, with a roller for every note, plus a few [?] pedal-pulldowns), and pipes of unusual structure: 99.9 per cent sand-cast lead except for the case-pipes, which have a 97.5 per cent tin front (half of pipe only). Pitch may have been about a tone lower than today's a' = 452.5Hz. Presumably the chorus and physical layout (key-dimensions, position) were like those of Arnaut de Zwolle's organs, and the whole suggests a modest organ-type common to the stretch Dijon–Sion and distinct from the special late gothic designs of the fifteenth century.

Reasons for regarding some organ-remains discovered in *c.* 1928 at Bartenstein, East Prussia, as belonging to an organ built before 1400 were published in 1966 (Bormann 1966B). Although no more than for the Halberstadt organ reported on by Praetorius in 1619 is it clear how much of the Bartenstein organ was original,

---

[18] Arnaut de Zwolle's iron pins (see Chapter 16) may save space?

[19] Jakob 1991: esp. 70–91. For the likelihood that the present location as a swallownest organ on the west wall is original and may reflect the needs of pilgrim processions, *ibid.*, 23. Also M. Wenger, 'L'Orgue de Valère à Sion', CO 42 (1981), 19–20, and Edskes 1987: 21.

both instruments probably illustrate elements of the large organ as seen by German builders towards the end of the fourteenth century.

The large Bartenstein chest of *c.* 4 × 0.6 m was made of five 8 cm planks glued together with casein glue (?) and covered underneath with parchment. A large deal rollerboard of *c.* 4 × 1 m (trapezium-shaped) had rollers some 3 cm thick and octagonal in section; a smaller board of *c.* 1 × 0.7 m (similar shape) was probably a rollerboard for pedal pulldowns. Miscellaneous timber pieces included oak moulding and parts for a 27-note keyboard action.[20] Large folding bellows, of which there seems to have been six, were made from 4 cm deal boards 1.3 × 0.6 cm, with intake valve below; perhaps these were sixteenth-century replacements. The chorus had 420 pipes, conjectured by Bormann to begin at F and end at a' or b', at a pitch about one tone higher than a' =140Hz:

> bass   16.8.4.3.3.2.2.1½.1
> treble 16.8.4.4.3.3.2.2.2.2.1½.1½.1½.1½.1½.1.1.1.1.1.1

The pallet-box was of the familiar type with oak pallets 18 × 4 × 3 cm and iron-wire springs, but the chest was hollowed out of the five-piece solid, with channels and bored ducts to the pipe-feet; the holes for the pipe-feet were made conical (burnt out). Wind to the case-pipes and to the rear mixture pipes passed up through the chest into bored oak beams fitted tightly over the chest-top; these beams[21] slid a short distance along the chest so that the bored holes corresponded either to the lateral channels or not, depending on position. They thus admitted or blocked the wind, as the case may be. The action included two sets of backfalls transmitting movement from the keys at the rear of the organ to the rollerboard in front. Thus the player was behind the organ, as he often was throughout organ-history from Roman mosaics to Theophilus and from him to, for example, the late gothic swallownest organ in the Minoritenkirche, Regensburg.

The position of the organist is another of those elements that play an important part in the history of the organ and yet have left little in the way of evidence. If the player began to sit in front of the organ only when the instrument was too large for him to see over it, one would expect him to be sitting in front, not behind, at Bartenstein; the same applies if he needed to see what was happening below. From this one could surmise that on the contrary, larger organs such as this, even in a gallery of the quire as here, were not used liturgically and therefore needed no fine coordination with music on the church pavement. Fifteenth-century representations (see note 16) regularly show the organist in front, as Arnaut de Zwolle too implied, but this would only confirm that by now he had a liturgical function. The part-hexagonal galleries in late fourteenth-century Strasbourg and elsewhere (see Chapter 18) brought the player very dramatically to the front of the organ. Perhaps it was this up-to-date visibility of the liturgical organist that was the point of showing the organ in fifteenth-century paintings and illuminations – his visible playing meant that the organ was sounding?

[20] In 1361, a 'black monk' of the city of Thorn (Toruń) made an organ with twenty-four case-pipes (Bormann 1966B: 993); no doubt this was the number of notes in the compass.
[21] 'Over-sliders' or *Oberschleifen*; see also Edskes 1987: fig. 3.

The Halberstadt organ is assumed to have had its keyboards (rows of key-levers) at the front, but much about the instrument reported on by Praetorius in the early seventeenth century is unclear, not least its date: supposedly of 1361 but rebuilt in 1495.[22] Ten pairs of bellows[23] and a 15–56 rank chorus from 32' HH seem more characteristic of 1495 than 1361, although if the four differently designed rows of wooden keys (Praetorius 1619: plate XXV) were older than the bellows, one might wonder why they had not been replaced. Was the lowest manual as drawn by Praetorius the original row of press keys pulling down pallets for a compass of

H c c♯ d d♯ e f f♯ g g♯ a h[24]

and connected to foot-levers? It is possible that only later (1495?) was it joined by two other manual rows of fourteen notes; these have shaped keys, while the lowest has plain batten-like levers. It is not clear from Praetorius's drawing whether the rows protruded above each other in one vertical plane or were staggered like modern manuals,[25] but his phrase *über einander liegen* ('lying above each other') suggests the former. While it is difficult to imagine that such rows of levers gave the organist great agility, they did make it possible for him to contribute to festive events by giving a strong-toned sound over all the notes that would be used by hymns and canticles, though at one octave-level only.

Guessing that Bartenstein and Halberstadt still testify to certain very early practices, if not as many as later commentators have sometimes assumed, one may attribute the following to some of the larger northern European organs of *c.* 1400:

size: it looks as if to increase size and sound, builders would devise structures and layouts in order to extrapolate a basic eight, ten or twelve-note design, either by increasing compass or – just as useful for the music an organ might then play – by adding further units ('manuals') of the same.

bellows: a large number of paired wedge-shaped bellows, blown by foot pressure or body weight, made of leather and boards, with folds. Such pairs of bellows would give a 'constant wavering of the wind-pressure . . . more noticeable the more pipes were sounding, above all the full Blockwerk' (Vogel 1983: 38).

chests: several chests or divisions with a compass of not much more than an octave or so; probably with pallets and a pallet-box but sometimes not inconceivably with spring-loaded sliders attached one way or another to press-keys; a keyboard of protruding key-levers, with large gaps between.

pipes: all open metal, of hard impure lead, perhaps tinfoiled; sometimes the largest pipes of an octave or so separated off on to their own chest, or conducted off from the main chest (*trompes*).

---

[22]   Praetorius 1619: 98ff, and Bormann 1966A.

[23]   The blowers hold a horizontal bar, and each foot operates a bellows with three folds, according to Praetorius 1619: plate XXVI.

[24]   Praetorius's letters on the keys. Was the last h in fact an unraised b-flat?

[25]   The woodblock shows the four keyboards recessed individually, as if protruding from the rear wall like inset library shelves; or perhaps the top three keyboards are within one tall recess (*en fenêtre*), the pedal below the bottom 'shelf' as in much later organs?

According to such reasoning, by the late fourteenth century builders had made the following structural elements on a big scale: trackers, rollers, pallet-boxes, pedal-pulldowns and wire-couplers; large folding bellows; a row of short, fairly close-spaced finger-keys with four or five chromatic notes per octave; pipes from *c.* 24' long, perhaps exceptionally including *trompes* or Bourdons (drones?) standing some way from the main case; and multiple ranks (as many as fifty-six per key?), including quints and octave quints.

Keyboards

If any thirteenth-century theorist refers only to two sharps or *ficte musice* (F♯ and G♯ in the *Summa musice* – Page 1991: 96 and 177), one can be sure that builders he did not know about were making more of them. Similarly, when Jacques de Liège remarks that virtually every tone (*quasi unique*) can be divided into two unequal semitones, especially on the organ,[26] this too is a comment after the event, and builders must have known from practice itself that semitones differed in size. Probably F♯ would be the first of the sharps to occur to a builder of a fixed-note instrument because it is needed to perfect the fifth above the only note of the natural scale CDEFGABH that does not otherwise have one, i.e. H.[27] Another reason for F♯ is that the prime transposition of a fourth down for the 'instrumental scale' based on C is impossible without it.

Builders no doubt sometimes produced sharps that were triadic thirds in their own right, as the later E♭ was with G, or A♭ with F (Ramos de Pareja, 1482). But in general, the smaller the semitones E–F, H–C and eventually F♯–G, G♯–A, C♯–D and D♯–E, the more they would create the idea of 'leading notes', especially in the treble. Placed physically above the naturals CDEFGABH, the sharps even look like 'leading notes' to the next natural. For other remarks on sharps and transposition, see Chapter 16. One might also conjecture that as the two-tiered arrangement of the notes allowed players to become more dexterous, melodies would become more flexible and decorative, especially as keys approached finger-size; in turn, the sharps themselves played a part in giving such qualities to melody.

Because woodworking and metalworking traditions differed from place to place, there would have been for centuries many kinds of pipe-work and chest construction. But it is for a rather different reason that keyboards varied widely before the fifteenth century: because all of their details of style and dimension had to be established. These details include length (unfixed for centuries), width, proximity (with or without gaps), arrangement in tiers (shorter sharps) and the materials used (fine woods by the later fourteenth century).[28] No doubt many fifteenth-century key-actions were light and

---

[26] CSM 3.6.146. Such semitones are often said to be for organists 'to accompany choral singing and to play written polyphony' (Page 1987: 117), but see p. 309 for an emphasis on transposition.

[27] An absence of f♯ would mean circumspect handling of H in the diaphony of the *Musica enchiriadis* (see Chapter 2), whether in theory (pedagogy) or practice.

[28] A bone key-plate (♯) from the organ of *c.* 1450 has been found at St Maarten, Groningen, with dimensions 'twice as large' as today's: see B. Wisgerhof, 'Die Orgel der Martinikirche in Groningen', *Ars organi* 30 (1985), 34–9. In the contracted repairs of 1387–8 at Trier Cathedral, boxwood (? *pro ligno palmarum*) is specified for keys: see Bereths 1974: 72.

precise (Edskes 1987: 23), but whether such qualities came from that century's constant experimenting with keyboard instruments or had long been time-honoured aims for organ-builders, is unknown. Changes in Van Eyck's painting suggest that fashion in 1430 was for narrower keys than before, now with sharps raised.

Two particular pieces of evidence bear on keyboard touch and physical appearances in the late Middle Ages, one literary, one archaeological. In the first, a contract at Rouen Cathedral in 1386 already refers to the repair of a keyboard (*clavier*) whose keys are to be 'made uniform and light' (*faire les clenches ounies et douces* – Dufourcq 1971: 25); in 1382 the chest needed work 'in order to weaken those keys which are too strong' (*pour raféblier les clefs qui sont trop fortes* – *ibid.*). While either could refer to the tone of the pipes rather than the particular keys to which they belonged, the first uses a term that seems to be more specific: *clenche*, the key itself, the protruding lever that is like the lift of a 'latch'.[29] 'Uniform and light' must refer to the touch not the tone, and repairs to the pallet-springs during the next century are also carefully specified (Dufourcq 1971: 26). The archaeological evidence is equally suggestive: the untouched keyboard layout at Salamanca (Capilla de S Bartolomé, *c.* 1500) has the row of keys stopped at the front on a crossmember of the lower case-structure. Such a 'keyboard on a shelf' remained a norm for centuries, but its original development – replacing a row of key-levers sticking out from the front plane of the organ (Norrlanda *c.* 1390, Van Eyck painting *c.* 1432, Van der Goes painting *c.* 1476) – must have been the result of deliberation. Neither Arnaut de Zwolle's organ nor his smaller keyboard instruments have this shelf, which probably originated as a structural cross-beam in the interlocking timber construction that constituted a major organ.

Pipe-work

Some pipes, thought to be pre-thirteenth century, were found in Bethlehem in 1906 and have the following characteristics:[30]

> 251 open cylindrical pipes (of which *c.* 220 now in display), made from rolled copper-alloy sheet, each pipe with overlap of 3–5 mm at rear (originally with solder?), pipe and feet in one piece (?), faintly conical. A few white-metal pipes (pewter?); pipe-metal *c.* 0.45–0.9 mm thick, with constant diameter of *c.* 28–9 mm, length from 16.8 cm to *c.* 105 cm; width of rectangular mouth *c.* 23 mm, cutup *c.* 8–11 mm, inside diameter *c.* 25 mm.

The range of pipe-lengths allows nearly three octaves from longest to shortest. Archaeological understanding at the time of recovery being what it was, no other materials were discovered, although early references (note 30) call it a hydraulic

[29] Whatever shape the lift of a latch had (like a cross with a bulbous end?), the word suggests that the finger-keys at Rouen were more than plain batten-like protruding levers.
[30] Private communication from Mr Jeremy Montagu (1983) and the same author's 'The oldest organ in Christendom', *FOMRHI Quarterly* 35 (April 1984), 51–2. Brief references in P. Cheneau, 'L'ancien carillon de Bethléem', *Revue Biblique* 32 (1923), 602–7, and B. Bagatti, *Gli antichi edifici sacri de Betlemme*, Studium Biblicum Franciscanum 9 (1952), 73, 113.

organ. Several features of the pipes – material, shape, diameter – suggest the earliest stages of organ-building.

Except for conical pipes in some early manuscript drawings,[31] representations of pipe-work give little technical data before Arnaut de Zwolle's diagram of a pipe (Le Cerf 1932: plate ix). This conicity cannot be entirely trusted and may be explained in various ways, from the incompetent (the artist was ignorant of musical matters) to the symbolic (the artist was conveying the idea of sound being expelled). See also Chapter 17. Authors or copyists of early pipe-treatises appear not to understand how pipes work or even quite what they look like (see Sachs 1970: plates 17 and 19). Assuming that the open principal type of rank, such as still exists at Sion, Bologna and Rysum, received a variety of voicing according to locally established taste, there still remain very fundamental questions about the development of organ-pipes. Were conical pipes as still described by 'Cambrai Anon' (p. 295) much known in the fifteenth century? Were pipes of tin originally alternatives for pipes of copper and at first found on the same chests, becoming the norm only as compass increased downwards?

As rolled lead pipes with soldered seams had had various purposes since at least the time of the Romans, perhaps copper was preferred for organ-pipes for the sake of durability and looks rather than tone. Was tin when hardened with copper (so-called 'fine pewter')[32] an early option for pure copper or hard bronze? It does not seem unlikely that it was as part of a high-quality alloy that tin originally came to organ-pipes. Since no doubt custom varied from one region to another, some areas – Frisia, Saxonia – may have developed lead more from an early period, using tin in small percentages in the alloy but otherwise developing the organ as essentially a lead-pipe instrument that could enlarge the range of the old Mediterranean hydraulis.

Almost certainly the two other pipe-forms made as regular options – the wooden pipe and the reed – belong not only to the late period around 1400 but particularly to the cult of new, secular, small-scale keyboard instruments: finely worked wooden pipes (open or stopped, flue or regals) were the counterpart of the various types of clavichord and harpsichord built by the professional makers of the mid-fifteenth century. How far wood as an alternative material is related to stopped pipes as an alternative sound can only be guessed. Since it is not unlikely that many a portable organ had pipes of thick paper (which was impervious to some kinds of damage) and that good paper was expensive, wood may actually have been a cheaper substitute, certainly for highly decorated or gilt paper pipes. Stopping wooden pipes must also have been more reliable than stopping paper. On larger organs, as at Arezzo Cathedral in 1454, pipes 'of the most perfect wood' no doubt gave new meaning to the old terms 'sweetness and suavity' (*di legno perfettisimo di dolcezza e soavità* – Donati 1979: 214). The four large wooden pipes in S Petronio, Bologna (1471–5), cannot have been the first such substitutes for metal bass pipes, and as for stopped pipes, it

[31] Including single large bourdons on small fourteenth-century organs (Marshall 1989: 19–21).
[32] See E. S. Hedges, *Tin in Social and Economic History* (New York, 1964), 71. Joining the seams of lead tubes with strips of soft solder is first described in *c*. 100 AD: see trans. C. Bennet *et al.*, *Sextus Julius Frontinus: De aquaeductu urbis Romae* (Cambridge, MA, 1980).

seems unlikely that the Aquincum builder would use stoppers (as it has been assumed he did – see Chapter 14) purely for fine-tuning and not for their tonal qualities and low pitch.

As for reeds, however unfamiliar in general they must have been before Arnaut's time, it is difficult to imagine that reed-tongues and reed-resonators did not supply the sound for the trumpets blown in Hero's automatic devices (statues, temple-doors, etc.) many centuries earlier. Also, against the idea that reed-stops were new at the time of Arnaut de Zwolle's reed-nut measurements (? Le Cerf 1932: plate IV) is the very similarity between such measurements (*mensurae*) and other calculations in the treatise.[33] Although the details are incomplete it looks as if they are there not because reeds are new but because Arnaut or a subsequent author was attempting to fill out the collection of traditional *mensurae* such as a treatise would aim to give.

Of questions concerning pipes, the most crucial historically are those about tin: did its use prompt the greater compass of keyboard and chorus or merely make it possible? The difficulty of voicing very large or very small pipes of copper-alloy could suggest either, but the large pipes of the fourteenth century were surely tin or tin-alloy. Tin's several uses – as filings, as solder (with or without copper) and as thin beaten leaves – were already described in the *Mappae clavicula* (p. 269) and later more fully in Theophilus. Anglo-Saxon objects of pewter in the British Museum suggest that making pipes of pewter (with high or low tin content) would have presented no great difficulty, and it may be the case that at first tin-alloy was a poor substitute for the copper-alloys known at the same period. If this were so, then lead pipes, with lesser or greater amounts of tin, could have been placed behind the front pipes of burnished copper or burnished tin well before fifteenth-century contracts hint at the practice.[34]

Knowledge of tin pipes comes only from a few fourteenth-century contracts (Florence, SS Annunziata, 1332 – Donati 1979: 149) and treatises of much the same period (see Chapter 16). Since tin pipes were evidently polished (Italian contract items in Donati 1979: 149–50), at least part of the point must have been their looks as they were placed in the front of the newly developed casework: silvered cylinders corresponding to the gilt bronze of an earlier period. Lead on the other hand had long been very familiar for water-pipes in monasteries, sometimes on a large scale, as when water had to be brought over some distance.[35] It seems unlikely that only in connection with tin would this ancient lead-technology get applied to organs; Roman organ-pipes of lead or not, later builders must have used it. In any case, it is a major question whether lead or tin pipes had become the norm because they were cheaper and easier to voice and revoice than copper or because they produced a tone increasingly liked by organ-players.

---

[33] E.g. for a clavichord in which the strings are used for a group of different pitches (Le Cerf 1932: 11ff). Such *gebunden* clavichords would have seemed a latter-day exemplum for the old measurement-theory (*mensura*) of monochord strings.

[34] E.g. front pipes of tin (*van finen tinnen ende niet van loe* – 'of fine tin and not of lead') at Louvain in 1445: M. A. Vente, *Bouwstoffen tot de Geschiedenis van het Nederlandse Orgel in de 16de Eeuw* (Amsterdam, 1942), 155; lead pipes at Fano Cathedral in 1424 (Donati 1979: 150, and cf. 159).

[35] Early twelfth-century example in the abbey of Michaelsberg, near Bamberg (MGH SS 15.2.1162).

A guess would be that as pewter alloys became commoner in the twelfth century, organ-compass and the number of chorus ranks increased: and that the softer, flutier tones of the interior ranks made with high-lead pipes (sometimes stopped) became fashionable only as instrumental colours generally were increasingly developed in the fifteenth century. Earlier, and in view of the importance of English tin over the whole period 500–1500,[36] it could be that tin or pewter pipes were first made, or particularly developed, in England. If bronze pipes (copper + tin) had been known there as a consequence of Roman occupation, the copper element could have gradually been reduced – unless special funding were available, as at Ramsey in the late tenth century (see p. 199) – and hardened tin remained, often replaced in turn by cheaper lead.

Like sliders and modern-looking keyboards, stopped pipes suited small organs as they developed in the fifteenth century and perhaps for this reason were seldom found in the Italian church organ, which was in general very spaciously designed. If the only 4' rank in the 8' Salamanca organ of *c.* 1500 was a stopped rank (De Graaf 1982: 23) it must have served as 'colour stop' both in and out of the chorus, and such 'colour' is likely to have become desirable as fifteenth-century builders – members of a secular, guild-like profession – brought into their instruments tokens of contemporary secular taste such as flutes, flageolets, trumpets, crumhorns and the like.[37] They would also find that the chest as it had evolved – with divisions for various sections of the big chorus or Blockwerk – was not suitable for reeds because it sent the wind round too many corners before it reached the reed (Edskes 1987: 17), and that reeds ought therefore to have their own slider or their own chest.

The development of resonators to make reeds imitative belongs to the end of the fifteenth century. One recent suggestion (Edskes 1980: 77) is that early regals or small reeds had been introduced as a separate stop in larger organs because, like the little regals-instrument – another of the period's new keyboard instruments – they were useful for setting one or other of the temperaments then being explored for twelve or more notes to the octave. The whole organ could be tuned from such a rank.

The chorus or Blockwerk

As is clear from fragments of evidence in treatises from the 'Bern Anon' to the 'Cambrai Anon' – thus from 1000 to 1500 – the organ chorus consisted of open pipes of unisons and octaves (and sometimes with quints) grouped for each key. However they developed, quints were undoubtedly less common or obvious to the

---

[36] As shown in the survey by M. Lombard, *Les métaux dans l'ancien monde du Ve au XI siècle*, Etudes d'économie médiévale (Paris, 1974), 187–9. But the history of English tin before the twelfth century is 'problematical' (L. F. Salzman, *English Industries of the Middle Ages* (Oxford, 1923), 70), because again, the mass of documentation begins only in the thirteenth century.

[37] One theme to study when the organ of 1350–1550 is eventually described will be the connection between non-chorus stops and the social function of regional organs. Was the Italian organ slow to develop colours (flutes, mutations, reeds, stopped ranks) because churches seldom had a 'municipal' function in the way of those of the Low Countries and the Rhineland, and thus needed little in the way of colourful variety for popular music?

ear than they became in the chorus of later organs, and in both Arnaut de Zwolle's sample (see p. 292) and in the Italian *ripieno*, the chorus remained centred on the idea of unison and octave reinforcement. In 1471–5, S Martino, Bologna, was still producing relatively few quint ranks at Middle C:

16.16.8.8.8.4.4.2⅔.2.1⅓.1.1.⅔ (*sic*)

The ancestor of this chorus is surely the unisons-and-octave of those early theorists summarized in Chapter 16. The Van Eyck positive probably had 8.4.2.8.

While it may not be correct to see the early theorists' phrase *grave, acute, superacute* as referring to 'three ranks of a mixture' on each key, and while it certainly is jumping to conclusions to suppose an English interest in fifths-music meant that twelfth-century English organs knew quint ranks before German organs did,[38] no doubt there were various kinds of 'tonal reinforcement' contrived by the makers of organs in different church-provinces. Such reinforcement included the superoctave in some cases, eventually the suboctave, all found by organ-makers working in their own inventive traditions, independently of what theorists were writing in their scriptoria. But fifth-sounding ranks are so unlikely to have had much prominence that a question often asked in the past by music-historians – was vocal organum so called because voices singing parallel fifths imitated the fifths of organ-mixtures? – now appears to have come also from a misunderstanding of organs themselves.

One suggestion for quints becoming admitted at all was that 'larger, deeper-sounding pipes produce the fifth rather than the fundamental [8'] when overblown' (Bowles 1961: 17), thus familiarizing ears with the effect of fifths. The idea that narrow-scaled pipes produced rich overtones and that some octaves in a ten-rank chorus could overblow to the second overtone is not new (cf. Riemann 1879: 209), but even if it were plausible it does not suggest when it was that overblown quints were replaced by actual twelfths. It is true that although Theophilus's wide mouths would have worked against overblowing, the high-pressure conical copper pipe with low cutup may have inclined to overblow especially under fluctuating wind-pressure. However, it is difficult to develop this hypothesis further: one could easily conjecture that the overblown second overtone was such as to encourage pipe-makers to do all they could to avoid it, since an overblowing pipe produces a note that is out of tune with its normal speaking neighbours. Furthermore, a present twelfth meant an absent unison, and only when the unisons and octaves were much duplicated would the twelfth have been integrated. Perhaps narrow stopped pipes producing the quintadena tone contributed a twelfth-sounding pitch to the chorus as well as their unison? – but such pipes are not documented or even hinted at before the fifteenth century.

One particular early theorist (South German, eleventh century)[39] alludes to various ranks but not explicitly fifths or twelfths:

---

[38] The three ranks suggested in Meeùs 1980/81: 67; English quint ranks supposed in W. Bachmann, 'Die Verbreitung des Quintieren im europäischen Volksgesang des späten Mittelalters', in *Festschrift Max Schneider zum achtzigsten Geburtstag*, ed. W. Vetter (Leipzig, 1955), 25–9, here 26 (accepted by M. Huglo, in *Corsi* 1989: 360).

[39] Assumed by Gerbert (GS 2) to be Eberhard of Freising, perhaps a pupil of William of Hirsau; further discussion in Sachs 1980: 213–14. See also Chapter 16.

mensura consequenter	'measurement' deals systematically
de tot fistulis loquitur,	with as many pipes
quot choros fistularum musici	as musicians themselves are used to
solent ipsi organico	placing ranks [sets?] of them
instrumento apponere.	in the organ. (Sachs 1970: 126 – see also p. 286)

The only reference to ranks by this theorist seems to be to suboctaves:

suavitatis et ornatus causa	for the sake of sweetness and elegance,
cuique naturali choro	to each natural[40] rank
suum subduplum affigunt.	they add its lower octave.

This could mean either that the notes of the scale are taken down a further octave or that each note on an organ can have its lower octave, even both.[41] The difference between those two need not concern a theorist, and the very ambiguity may mean that builders were working with various octave pitches, the more the bigger the organ. One can only speculate that some such aesthetic (*suavitas*) made musicians desire to add a note's octave, its double octave, an octave below and a twelfth above, perhaps in that order, but the evidence for any kind of quint is slight (see further in Chapter 16). When the *principal* at Rouen Cathedral was reinforced in 1386, starting with one rank and increasing to five over a sixteen-note compass (Dufourcq 1971: 25), it would have included a quint – if it did – only for the top notes. Whether the sixteen-note compass at Rouen was close to Hucbald's scale

     C D E F G A B H c d e f g a b h

or some other such as

     C D E F F♯ G A B H c d e f f♯ a

the number of ranks was gradually increased 'to make the treble a match for the bass' (*affin que le deschant souffise contre la teneur*), which might or might not suggest that it suddenly began to include fifths at the top.

The need for treble reinforcement must often have struck organ-makers in the big gothic churches of the period, and the principle behind it did not contradict what Theophilus (reflecting the practice of some makers *c.* 1100 and earlier) had said about pipe-work. Since Roman times, the part of organ-compass known to builders had been the upper part – 'the treble' as it became – and multiple ranks must have always been necessary in this part of the compass when penetrating sound was required, for processions or in arenas. As western church-organ craftsmen extended the compass downwards there would be more ranks to choose for duplication, since what was 8.8.4 in the treble might be better 8.4.2 in the bass; conversely, as compass extended upwards, a quint rank could add to the spectrum, a concord enabling the builder to avoid adding to the hard-to-tune octave screech at the top. It is hard to believe that the organ-choruses once used for noise in Rome or Constantinople had no fifths in their little treble compasses.

[40] 'Natural', i.e. the eight notes of the basic octave (*ordo*) to which one may add 'as many *ordines* as one likes' (*alios quotlibet ordines quisque adiciat* – ibid.).

[41] Obscurity of this kind does not die out with the eleventh century: in fifteenth-century contracts, it is not always clear whether 'double principal' means 'more than one principal rank' (tin 8' + lead 8'), 'principal doubled by a non-principal' (8' open + a stopped rank) or 'more than unison rank' (16' + 8', 8' + 4').

General on organ-development

It is likely that the period 750–1500 saw spurts of technological advance, not necessarily the same from one area to another and not inevitably in one straight line of development. In the decades around 1000, certain reformed Benedictine abbeys developed various experimental equipment including organs; virtually nothing is certain about them, but what there is conforms to known technologies of the time. One might suppose that each was individually designed, independent of any elsewhere, were it not that despite the sparseness of documentation, we still know of four (perhaps five) Anglo-Saxon organs made in the course of a few years and within two or three days' travel of each other, thus very likely similar in certain respects. After some earlier attempts to describe a few techniques necessary for organ-building, the early decades of the twelfth century saw a fuller attempt made: for one particular area of Benedictine Europe certain church-related crafts were described in a major book, though one that appears not to have circulated widely or inspired successors. Nevertheless, this same period saw fuller records giving a glimpse of other developing technologies such as metallurgy.[42]

The twelfth century also produced a rare comment comparing modern with older achievement. William of Malmesbury, speaking of St Dunstan's gifts to his abbey nearly two hundred years earlier, wrote:

Mirae magnitudinis signa	[he gave] bells of wonderful size,
non quidem, ut nostra	not indeed (as our
fert aetas, dulci	period has it) with a sweet
sed incondito sono	but a jumbled sound,
strepentia,	things making a noise, [and]
organa quae concentu suo	organs which with their blend of sound
in festivitatibus	at festivities
laetitiam populo excitarent.	seem to have aroused gladness in the people.

(RBMAS 63.301–2)

If the comma is misplaced and *strepentia organa* is one phrase, the organs were the 'things making a noise'. In any case, in the two hundred years between Dunstan and William, bells had been made (or played?) so as to produce a great 'sweetness': does this mean that a mere clanging noise had been replaced by tuned bells played in diatonic sequence? The text seems to be an embroidered version of another reference to Dunstan's organs (RBMAS 52.407 – see Chapter 12) and might just be taken to support the idea that screeching organ-sounds of the tenth century had become replaced two hundred years later by a more harmonious organ-sound over a larger compass and with a wider chorus of octave ranks. However, this would be pushing conjecture to the limit.

A third phase is suggested by thirteenth-century documentation: compass was growing downwards, pipe-work of larger dimensions was being mastered, pipe-

---

[42] E.g. steel is mentioned in a text of 1177 in Anjou, but it must have been known earlier: see B. Gille, *Les origines de la grande industrie métallurgique en France* (Paris, 1947), 4, 13.

choruses were expanding, timber structures were surely being developed, and a pallet-action was probably being devised, or at least, the return-action of keys was being improved. During the thirteenth century a 'rebirth of mechanics' gave Europe not only better awareness of Arabic ingenuity but led to such devices as weight-driven clocks in certain gothic cathedrals, perhaps even a mechanical escapement.[43] Organ-chests must have been enlarged at much the same period that weight-driven clocks with moving statuary were developed to new degrees of complexity. At Exeter in 1284, the bell-founder (*campanistario*) is linked in fabric accounts to maintenance duties for the *organa* and *orologium*,[44] something that becomes not uncommon in England in the later Middle Ages. Clustres of important organs in the later thirteenth century, as in the Rhineland, surely reflect an active industry in various church-related technologies in those areas of Europe.

A fourth phase saw the profusion of accomplished crafts during the later fourteenth century, particularly (as they affected organ-building) the techniques of woodworking and tin or pewter casting. Perhaps for the first time this profusion established a pool of organ-knowledge, a widespread fund of techniques available from Durham to the Adriatic, from Castile to the Elbe. But these techniques did not get described on paper any more than the flourishing clock-technology of the fourteenth century did, and similar remarks can now be made about organs as about clocks:[45]

there are no known technical records of early clocks but it is probable that such records were never made; each clock being constructed in accordance with the ideas and experience of the maker. Such records as do exist from the fourteenth century . . . relate to elaborate calendar mechanisms, and the clocks which actuated the mechanisms were regarded as not worthy of mention.

However, more likely than being 'regarded as not worthy of mention' is that technical details of any kind were and had only ever been seldom described: *artes mechanicae* traditions were selective and any such description was exceptional. For whom exactly would any account of either normal or abnormal mechanism appear in written form?

Even in the fifteenth century, an author like Arnaut de Zwolle wrote as one looking in on craft-objects, describing some organs as he found them and making his own suggestions, when he did, not as a traditional instrument-maker but a cultivated Renaissance man. For these purposes he drew 'directly from specific astronomical or horological hardware' for his musical instruments (Bowles 1966: 162), and in the process introduced ideas from outside the old crafts of instrument-making. Organ-makers themselves were probably far less interested in clever gadgets than in

---

[43] E.g. L. Thorndike, 'Invention of the mechanical clock about 1271 AD', *Speculum* 16 (1941), 242–3; L. White 1962: 119–29; C. B. Drover, 'A mechanical monastic water-clock', *AH* 1 (1954), 54–8; A. W. Sleeswyk, 'The 13th century "King Hezekiah" water-clock', *AH* 11 (1979), 484–94. On the employment of magnets in the same century, see G. Hellmann, *Rara magnetica 1269–1599* (Berlin, 1898).

[44] P. Howgrave-Graham, 'Some clocks and jacks, with notes on the history of horology', *Archaeologia* 77 (1928), 257–312, here 268: a tenement granted to the *campanistario* and others for work including the repair of *organa*.

[45] H. E. Rose, 'A conjectural reconstruction of the Perpignan clock of 1356', *AH* 15 (1985), 330–54, 491–502, here 501–2.

applying their ingenuity to developing objects according to traditions of organ-building. The spring-driven clock made by 1430 for the Duke of Burgundy (Bowles 1966: 160) was closer to the work of an Arnaut de Zwolle than of any ordinary organ-builder, for whom the (much?) older spring-loaded pallet must have told him all he needed to know about springs.

Nevertheless, developments as described in a history-book of technology do offer parallels to contemporary organs.[46] Thus Theophilus's treatise belonged to a period of formative development in German mining techniques (Freiberg silver mines, later twelfth century); the early thirteenth century saw both an expansion in iron-producing techniques (almost to the exclusion of other metals) by the industrious Cistercians and the start of a great flowering of gothic timberwork and large-scale wooden furniture; in the same century, weight-driven clocks were made and methods of escapement explored; the fourteenth century now heard clocks striking to mark the secular hours rather than the old monastic *horae*. By that century too, Arnulf of St-Ghislain was speaking of clergy (*clericos*)

qui in organicis instrumentis	who on organic instruments
difficilimos musicales modulos	devise and teach [?] the
quos exprimere vix	most difficult passages of music,
praesumeret vox humana	which the human voice would
adinveniunt atque tradunt.	hardly presume to perform. (GS 3.316)

If this includes organs, and if it is not merely a new complaint about ostentatiously gifted clergy-musicians, it would mean that keyboard-making had made new levels of agility possible. One interesting detail in the remark is that 'difficulty' is coming in as a quality in musical performance. But that instruments were recognized as potentially more agile than voices is already suggested by the theorist Anonymous IV (*c.* 1280).[47]

By the end of the fifteenth century the organ had become rather a uniform type of apparatus. From region to region it allowed a wide-ranging variety in its detail but not in its essentials of wind-apparatus, framing, keyboard and principal chorus-pipes. It approached standardization even if the finished object varied, from the long-compass Italian organ made largely of single ranks to the shorter-compass mixture-organ of northern Europe containing separate divisions. Such standardizations are unlikely before about 1400. The earlier norm, when craftsmen developed their techniques in certain centres that must have been largely independent of each other – and were thus developing at different paces and with different aims in mind – would have given way to something more uniform.

It is an interesting question for the later organ-historian whether such uniformity as there was in key-mechanism came about because it was an 'obvious improvement' on all previous mechanisms or because uniformity is a quality resulting from the manner in which (or the purpose with which) information is transmitted. Several fifteenth-century factors – the secular trades and their craftsmen becoming ever

---

[46]   The examples that follow are from Gimpel 1976: 66–70, 153–5, 168.
[47]   Ed. F. Reckow, *Der Musiktraktat des Anonymus 4*, 2 vols (Wiesbaden, 1967), 1.39 (cf. 45).

more firmly established, the ever-increasing numbers of great churches competing with each other, musical styles and technological knowledge circulating ever more easily – must have contributed to uniformity, although they do not quite explain why the 'unity of this style-epoch was never again reached in the art' of organ-building (Edskes 1987: 11).

How did the organ come to be accepted by the Church?

20

How did the organ come to be accepted by the Church? Some newer hypotheses

A summary of the evidence for the organ, either as an artefact in its own right or as equipment used by the Church, does not lead to an answer to this question. Far too little is documented, and what evidence there is – written, iconographical or archaeological – may be unrepresentative and in some sense arbitrary, as it is surely puzzling and ambiguous.

At the outer time-limits of the question there is a fairly clear situation: one can be reasonably certain what general forms organs might have taken in the year *c.* 250 and again in *c.* 1450 and what part (if any) they played in religious activities at each of those periods. But what happened in between? While this remains very difficult to answer, it would be impossible without knowledge of what the fifteenth century achieved, since even if so much about organs and their music was then quite new, it can suggest what the lines of development had been and what it was in previous centuries that had become totally out of date. Whether the organ's acceptance by the Church originally was thanks to a saint, pope, king, bishop, abbot, individual monastic custom, broad evangelical imperialism or (as I suspect) something much more elusive than any of these – some kind of general technological tradition that would flower periodically when circumstances allowed – there is no doubt that by 1450 the organ had become customary in most representative types of church, in most parts of catholic Europe, and for many of the events that took place in churches.

Since the steps in this development are not known, a series of hypotheses is needed. The nature of the documentation itself – why do we have what evidence we do have, and what is it evidence of? – can be understood only up to a point. It cannot be used to build up a picture of what happened, at least not in the way that evidence is customarily used in scholarship as defined by humanist successors to the same monastic culture. The making and using of organs were not subjects for the kinds of document on which writers of history have come to rely. Hence early sources of information have been both overvalued and undervalued. On one hand, the annalists' remark that the organ was first introduced to Francia in the year 757 has often been accepted, because it seems a positive statement; on the other, an absence of reference to organs in a great gothic cathedral of 1250 has been taken to mean that there was no organ there. Of course, both may be correct. But it is not possible to know, because 'evidence' is not there either in the positive statement or in the absence of statement.

What are the periods and areas in question?

Of all the provinces of the Christian Church, it is the north-west European that is exceptional in promoting the organ as a regular part of its furnishings, and from it alone did the organ spread to be a worldwide instrument. (What that might have meant for the future development of the West's music is touched upon with some trepidation in Chapters 2 to 4.) The churches of Palestine, Syria, Egypt, Numidia, 'Africa', late classical Rome, Byzantium, Asia Minor, Armenia, Georgia and Persia never did come to have organs as regular fixed furniture (except where there was some much later western influence) any more than the synagogue or Temple had them.[1] The occasional association between organ and Church in these provinces – *organa* accompanying the Byzantine emperor as he entered Hagia Sophia or a Numidian bishop as he entered his diocese – only underlines how out of the ordinary it was for the Roman provinces of north-west Europe to adopt and develop it as regular fixed furniture. Like other Mediterranean cities, Christian Rome itself seems barely to have played a part in the story.

Any claim that it was only 'as an automaton' that 'the organ was understood and described in antiquity' (Hammerstein 1986: 88) cannot be sustained, for archaeology (the Carthage terracotta, the organ of Aquincum) and iconography (the Zliten and Nennig mosaics) seem to be all against it. It is possible, for example, that the keys of the first and the organists in the second are not as straightforward as they seem: the keys could be played by automaton barrel stickers, the organists may be artificial automaton figures like those in Hero's treatise. But so many further questions would then arise that this line of enquiry would become more and more attenuated. In any case, it was not on its being known in automaton-form but on its becoming 'fixed furniture' within the main body of churches that the organ's development depended. Its compass gradually extending to give a keyboard-scale made up of successive octaves, the number and size of its pipes gradually increasing, and its structure as a large wooden artefact with precision-linkwork becoming by far the largest musical instrument – all these were consequences of its getting into church. For all depend on the organ becoming more than a portable processional instrument, and to whatever extent the Byzantine court organs of the tenth century also became fixtures in the palace halls – which is not known – one would expect that there too the organ was beginning to grow in the same kinds of way.

It is important to ask, therefore, how *organa* came to be something more than the noisy little devices that were used in classical antiquity and early Christian periods for public jubilation of one kind or another. There are various possible stages through which it could have become something so unexpected as a regular church instrument, and at the outset it must be said that it is not yet clear and perhaps never will be which of them, or what particular combination of them, is the answer.

---

[1] Even if the Temple *magrephah* was a siren-organ of the Muristos type, it may not have been much earlier in date than Muristos (see Chapter 14). Nor did it become a 'church organ'.

First, although writings of early Christian authors, sparse but fairly consistent from Constantine's time to Charlemagne's, referred to organs mostly for figurative purposes, nevertheless it could be that organs never quite went out of favour and did participate here and there in certain church activities, perhaps even in certain services. While an author need not have seen an organ to mention it, or meant by the word *organa* what a previous poet meant by it, nevertheless at least an ideal or poetic acquaintance with organs was sustained, rather like the nineteenth-century poet's knowledge, such as it was, of lyres and dulcimers. If an early psalm-commentary's mention of *organum* does not prove that organs were used in churches of the period, nor does it forbid it. On the contrary, here might lie the simplest explanation of how the organ became a church instrument: northern cantors of the tenth century had organs built in order to take up what it was they interpreted the Mediterranean psalm-commentators of the fifth and sixth centuries as recommending. If St Augustine described an organ in connection with Psalm 150, it must have seemed acceptable – even required – for moments of jubilation and praise.

All that happened to make organs develop, therefore, was that scripture appeared to justify the curiosity always aroused by instruments, leading to more and more of them being made. So too more and more bells were cast.

Second, and on the contrary, Christians associating *organa* with all manner of Roman mischief meant that for as many as eight centuries there was no question of any church having any such object, and it took a particular event in western Europe or an act on someone's part – seventh-century pope of Rome or eight-century king of Francia? – to make it acceptable once more. Memory of the amphitheatre organ had died, and its high-pitched screeching could now join in regal acclamations, taking a role as the signifier of royalty, which itself was a signifier of divine order and could therefore be represented by bishops.[2] In most areas churches larger than oratory chapels were rare for many centuries, but when they did appear they must have been places for occasional public gatherings and as such the natural location for special apparatus, furnishings, vestments, light-effects and sound-effects, not least those apparently authorized by the psalms.

What happened, therefore, was that efforts were suddenly devoted to creating an instrument related to some extent to what was known (even still lying about?) of old Roman *hydraules* but essentially re-designed and rethought in the light of royal patronage and an inevitably changing musical practice.

Third, the organ's acceptance was due to neither of these impulses but to a some--what later revival of organ-building knowledge, without reference to either Roman or early Christian tradition, to the psalm-commentators, kings or popes. Any such revival was typical of the tenth-century spurt of energy taking so many forms in so many monasteries in the lands between East Englia, Catalonia, Campania and

---

[2] It is surely correct to see organs as originally sounding a salute to particular personages: the emperor, then the *vicarius christi*, princes, bishops, counts or other patrons. The passing of time did not remove this idea of an *addressee*, and eventually it became the Church itself, according to D. Schuberth, 'Intellectus organi: Beiträge zur theologischen und kulturellen Einschätzung der Orgel', *MuK* 48 (1978), 187–92, where, however, there are unqualified assumptions that the Aachen organ (a) was kept in church, (b) was for music as such and (c), played in the liturgy.

Thuringia. Since organs involved basic technologies in which there had been no clear break since Roman times (pipes, bellows, woodwork), and since there is no reason to think that the Romans had made only water-organs (though there was no Vitruvius to describe the less intricate bellows-organ), monastery workshops needed only to take up old arts for new purposes.

What happened, therefore, was that from rather primitive conditions in north-western Europe, an evangelical, royally favoured, industrious and clever body of Christians (monks of reformed houses) pressed forward vigorously to master certain techniques – church-building, vault-making, the arts and crafts of metal, stone, glass, wood, linen – and in the process produced a music-making device. This device was not alone but was accompanied by other clever devices (such as clocks measuring hours or seasons)[3] which it outlived. Conditions that seem necessary for technological change (cf. Mokyr 1990) were all present: religious belief reaching out to the people, interest in innovation and diversity, respect for manual labour, and a prevailing competitiveness. To these one might add: distance from early Christian roots.

Fourth, all organs before the later twelfth and even thirteenth centuries were exceptional, each a unique object individually worked, showing neither that there was a consistent tradition for making them nor that the Church had in general accepted them. Although sources make it seem that they were 'clustered' here and there – ninth-century Constantinople, tenth-century England – their use in church was incidental, and they had been made in the first place purely locally, as well as the area's workers in wood, leather and copper knew how. As actual instruments they were only marginally relevant to theorists transmitting Pythagorean proportions or practical music, and organ-makers needed little knowledge beyond what could be learnt from other widely practised crafts like bellows-making or bell-founding.

What happened, therefore, was very little of anything before the huge expansion in church technologies of the late twelfth and thirteenth centuries, when in the wave of prolific and versatile woodworkers of the gothic period, organs found themselves not only in monastic churches but more importantly in the secular cathedrals, from one end of catholic Europe to the other.

A composite explanation?

Now it is not difficult to suppose that all four of these explanations are true in part. All would make it equally possible for the interest in organs to have been stimulated on one hand by psalm-commentaries and on the other by what was known about splendid regal ceremony in which *organa* played a part. A new abbot of 1000 welcomed with the sound of an organ in his church must have felt it to be both psalmic and royal.

---

[3] For some non-mechanical means of measuring hours at the period when reformers required greater regularity in the day – see A. R. Green, 'Anglo-Saxon sundials', *The Antiquaries Journal* 8 (1928), 489–516. For even a simple sundial there had to be both theory (an acknowledged method for calculating the measurements) and practice (masonry skills, metalwork for the gnomon, design for the analogue used): see also p. 284, note 13).

Since the four explanations do not entirely contradict each other a composite statement could be drawn from them, for all known references to *organa* fit in with one or other explanation. Thus:

a few instruments survived from classical times, or the relevant metal and wood crafts did, until the Carolingian Church and its wished-for *unanimitas* of north-western Europe eventually led to organs becoming a fairly normal piece of furniture (and were so authorized by the psalms) in at least the larger episcopal or abbatial church, whose other crafts contributed to the perfection of organ-building by the fifteenth century, at which point organs had become primarily the affair of major non-monastic churches contracting secular craftsmen.

The problem with this statement is that it is too general, and leaves too vague the various steps taken, such as what kind of impetus it was that triggered development in the first place. Nor does it show how the instrument came to have a musical function in the service and what other functions it could have had originally. On the question of impetus: even if Pippin had an interest in organs or the Byzantines thought he did – something for his *cappella*? – there is no evidence that the gift of 757 fathered organs in or out of church. It is true that if *organum* did mean organ – a big 'if' – the gift could have served both the church life and courtly ceremony of Pippin and his son, whether it was a siren- or 'keyboard-organ'; and they could then have given the idea to many an abbot or bishop. But clear evidence for all of this is totally lacking. On the question of function: for the late medieval *alternatim* practice, the organ need have been nothing more than a recent invention, for its mellifluous part in such music required an instrument that probably had little in common with what had once been found in a few tenth-century monasteries.

In other words, the *first* and *fourth* explanations could both be true, in which case the great organs of the fourteenth century were to all intents and appearances a new invention. Of the four explanations, the second is the least convincing, since whatever various historians may have said in the past, the evidence for it is slight as to quantity and suspect as to the political aims of its early transmitters. As some others have also thought (for example Riemann 1879: 195), organs must have been known in north-western Europe before Pippin received the special instrument, whatever it was, from the Emperor of Byzantium. The *first* explanation may be truer in some of its parts than in others: for example, while the organ cannot be shown to have participated in early church activities, it is not out of the question that it had never entirely gone out of favour and that a thin spread of knowledge had survived. Where otherwise did the makers of the Anglo-Saxon organs learn what it was they needed to learn, beyond common skills, for their bells and *organa*? The *fourth* explanation is certainly true for some areas: in pagan northern provinces such as present day Mecklenburg, Christianity had conquered only by the later twelfth century, so that only some decades after this would an organ be recorded. Reference then might be, as it was in England three centuries earlier, to 'a grant for furnishing the organ,' as at Güstrow Cathedral in 1293 (*in subsidium ad organa camparanda*); or the organ might suddenly be specified in a liturgical *ordo*, as in that by the local Bishop of Ratzeburg (1282).[4] The point would be that recently converted Mecklenburg was likely to

---

[4] Cited with source in W. Haacke, *Die Entwicklungsgeschichte des Orgelbaus im Lande Mecklenburg-Schwerin* (Wolfenbüttel/Berlin, 1935), 11. Perhaps the *ordo* here was an ideal, something for optimal conditions?

authorize usage known in the Rhineland or Normandy, and known there for a long time.

Both such references to organs – in records of gifts or in service-orders – mention the instrument *en passant*, as if it were nothing exceptional even in the newer parts of Christian Europe. So does the sudden crop of fourteenth-century references in those areas of Europe that had fewer great churches – around Brunswick, in the Oder region, in West and East Prussia or in most of present day Austria. From the *fourth* explanation, it would also follow that two other important factors were emerging: that by *c.* 1250 a discrete craft of organ-building was arising in each province or even in each diocese (payments were made for outside contractors and their materials) and that organ-sound of a tuneful kind was now desired for regular music in services on certain regular feastdays. Both are suggested by a variety of sources.

The *third* explanation must be true as it concerns the lively activities of monastic houses, but how any tenth-century development of the organ began – what knowledge it was based on – is puzzling. The mystery century is the ninth. Did Anglo-Saxon or East Frankish organs of the tenth or eleventh centuries hang solely on the two *organa* documented at the Carolingian court one and a half centuries or more earlier? That seems impossible. It might be feasible – and then barely – only if there were other instruments made in between and obviously linking them. But since we know of none, except in such uncertain references as Pope John VIII's letter of *c.* 880 (see p. 204), the link is too conjectural to be developed. Yet references to organs in the work of ninth- and tenth-century theorists from Hucbald to Gerbert, whether or not referring to actual and contemporary instruments or conveying real organological understanding, surely reflect some kind of acquaintance with them, somewhere in the writer's knowledge or his source or its source. It must have been that a 'thin spread of knowledge had survived', perhaps even much more than this. But in that case, why is there so little written reference to organs before the thirteenth century and why does so much have to be conjectured?

The answer to this could be more straightforward. Before contracts and endowments were always systematically recorded, the only references at all are incidental. Sometimes, the acts of a generous bishop are recorded, a consecration ceremony is described, the damage in a cathedral fire is itemized, annals make a special note of a job completed: there is no regularity about items recorded under these heads, as is clear when two versions of a consecration exist of which only one mentions *organum* (Cava in the eleventh century – see p. 212). Documents in which reference might be expected – customaries or liturgy-directives – no more refer to the organ than they do to a sundial or the image in a particular window, although the sundial and the image would also in their way contribute to the office or mass. References to secular musical instruments in the ninth and tenth centuries are equally *en passant*,[5] although in the case of these other instruments archaeology has been more successful in providing concrete evidence than it has with organs.

[5] E.g. the reports of an Arab visitor to western Europe, in G. Jacob, *Arabische Berichte von Gesandten an germanischen Fürstenhöfe aus dem 9. und 10. Jahrhundert*, Quellen zur deutschen Volkskunde 1 (Berlin/Leipzig, 1927), 16.

One can only assume that the organ-builders of Winchester, whether English or Frankish, lay or in orders, casual or careful, were *au fait* with current understanding of pipes, scaling, intonation and hexachordal tuning, and that indeed, there was some such current understanding with which to be *au fait*.

What is the evidence for organs in church?

In this form the question is problematic since it implies that its words mean much the same thing then as now.

Evidence in *c.* 1000 is not as it was to become in *c.* 1500, when organ-remnants and written sources provide such a detailed basis for understanding the issues that an instrument of the period could be reproduced today. The types of sources occasionally referring to organs between 750 and 1250 do not include, and may actually have excluded, evidence about organs that is technically reliable in any sense recognized since then. But it is not only technical evidence that is lacking: reference at all to organs is so sparse that they might seem to have been unknown were it not that when one is mentioned, the reference is usually quite incidental. Of all the great abbeys concerned in the making of books and furthering scholarship, only those mentioned *en passant* by Gerbert of Aurillac and Reims (Fleury, Bobbio, perhaps Reims) were directly linked to *organa*, and these were not necessarily 'organs in church'. If Notker Labeo knew about organs directly from an instrument in St Gall, he does not say so. If *organa* were heard when Edward was crowned at Winchester in 1043 and William at Westminster in 1066, the *Anglo-Saxon Chronicle* says nothing about it. Did Malmesbury, secreted in the English Cotswolds, really have some equipment that St Gall did not? Since that is very unlikely, does one put the silence down to indifference, documentation that did not survive, or documentation that had no concern with 'furniture'?

Since the last must be true to at least some extent, it is quite possible that in England too the evidence is incomplete and that there were more organs than those recorded. Perhaps there is some parallel here to other technical objects: watermills and other mills are barely mentioned in England before the later eleventh century when the *Domesday Book* (1086) suddenly lists no fewer than 5,624 of them.[6] Who had made them all and what were they like? As in other woodworking areas, there was an even greater expansion in mill-building during the following century, and it is tempting to guess that there was in organs too.

Organs is a problematic word in the question, yet the portmanteau of meanings of *organa* does provide a kind of evidence, hinting that organs and other instruments were optional parts of certain musical activities, present if available, absent if not. The word was comprehensive enough to include organs and was surely not meant to exclude them. As special objects, organs were no more necessary than gold altar-panels, but they were desirable for much the same reasons, taking part in the

---

[6] C. P. Skilton, *British Windmills and Watermills* (London, 1947), 37. Some 6,082 mills are counted in Holt 1988: 8, a model book for the history of an influential artefact and its context.

ceremonies where possible and being referred to only in occasional documents. While on one hand, therefore, references to *organa* before the period of monastic reform – in poems by Fortunatus (Poitiers, sixth century) or Aldhelm (Malmesbury, seventh) – do not prove that certain early monasteries knew the instrument, on the other hand, the sudden reference to actual organs by *c.* 1000 does not prove that they were previously unknown. If organs had participated optionally in *organa* (ensemble music) in the more splendid abbeys, craftsmen would have learnt enough about the instrument to keep the craft alive.

Against this, however, is not only the allusive nature of poetry, and thus its hard-to-establish value as evidence, but the question whether there really needed to be a discrete and unbroken craft of organ-making. The metalwork, woodwork and leatherwork necessary for making organs offered no special problem to craftsmen provided they understood the arithmetic of hexachordal pipe-making, which was hardly a trade-secret. For the literate monk or a cantor who needed to know, music-treatises from the ninth-century Boethian *Scolica enchiriadis* onwards gave some rules of thumb, even if they were not themselves practical in intent or nature.

In church: the third difficult word in the question is *in* church. Particularly in Mediterranean lands, it is likely that *organa* (instruments, music) belonged out of doors, in atria, porches and processional sites generally; and only practices in north-west Europe brought *organa* into the *templum* itself, which was designed to make possible various activities of the people (*plebes*). *Organa* remained special and were associated with an exceptional abbey-church or with particular events when the *plebes* were witnesses. The distinction between inside and outside the church would not be important were it not that only when the organ became a familiar object within buildings would it have been fixed and able to grow – or would it have grown and therefore needed to be fixed. As furniture it joined other age-old objects made of costly materials – for creating light (lamps, candelabra), fragrance (thuribles, censers) and sound (bells, tabulae) in such monasteries as could afford them. Not for a long time, however: in the eleventh and twelfth centuries, documents of various kinds still show bells being blessed along with communion vessels (for example at Fleury) or mentioned in ordinals (for example at Exeter),[7] but never organs.

What is 'evidence'?

The combination of ambiguous terminology and documentary silence makes evidence difficult to recognize. Without doubt the earliest references to *organum* at Notre-Dame, Paris, between 1189 and 1217 relate not to an organ there, as was understood by some earlier historians, but to the formal vocal polyphony for which the cathedral became famous (Wright 1989: 238, 370). At the same time, sources are silent about an actual organ until fabric accounts and contractual documents from 1332–4 onwards make concrete reference to an instrument (*ibid.*, 144ff). But

---

[7] Fleury: ed. A. Davril, *The Monastic Ritual of Fleury*, Henry Bradshaw Society 105 (London, 1990), 22–3. Exeter: see the index to the *Ordinale Exonensis*, Henry Bradshaw Society 79 (London, 1940).

adding together those two kinds of documentation does not amount to evidence that 'in fact there was no organ in Notre-Dame prior to the fourteenth century' *(ibid.,* 143). Being such a major church with such celebrated music, Notre-Dame is particularly worth looking at from the point of view of examining the 'evidence'.

Depending for hard facts on sources such as fabric rolls or precentor's accounts, which become continuous and reliable only from the end of the thirteenth century in secular cathedrals across Europe, leaves information about earlier furnishings incomplete and no doubt often quite misleading. If there had been any information about such things as organs, it would have been given *en passant* or by chance. Only accounts or contracts needed to be specific, giving information (as eventually at Notre-Dame) on where an organ was placed, who used it when, what its repairs cost, what was required to replace the bellows, etc. For such purposes the documentation will not need to say how old the organ was or how long it had been in use. Of course, were it certain that Notre-Dame had no organ before *c.* 1330, interesting conclusions might be drawn, such as that even the largest secular cathedrals were often slow to adopt the showy monastic organ. But it cannot be certain. Indeed, since the earliest reference at Notre-Dame is to the organ playing on traditional occasions (certain feastdays – Wright 1989: 144), its rôle as a fixed instrument was clearly much the same as that in earlier monasteries. If the instrument was new, it does not seem to have done anything new.[8]

Even when the church was much more modest than Notre-Dame, the sudden mention of an organ at this period (mid-fourteenth century) may raise questions. For example, the small but spectacularly sited Benedictine abbey of Marienberg, South Tirol, had a chronicler at that period who, in referring to a chapel to St Michael in the church, happens to say that the chapel is near the organ (see p. 213, in particular see note 25). But how did an abbey of less than a dozen monks come to have an organ – for teaching purposes, for pilgrims, for events in church, on feastdays with processions? All such reasons are possible, even probable, but in that case there was no reason why this or an earlier organ should not have been there for decades, even centuries, since from the twelfth century on Marienberg had kept much the same character for the whole period – modest, but a conspicuous centre for pilgrims' processions. To the mid-fourteenth century belongs a mass of references to organs in larger churches across the centre of Europe and it is barely credible that they were always or even often the first instrument placed in the church concerned. Trier Cathedral in 1387 is a typical example in that the new organ had the benefit now not only of a contract but of an experienced builder: as at Strasbourg (see p. 332), the organ was of the swallownest type in a gallery on the north wall of the nave, and no doubt it met in all respects the period's requirements for a splendid-looking and splendid-sounding wonder for the *plebes*. It is difficult to believe that this sophisticated structure was the church's first organ and that there had been no previous instrument somewhere on the pavement of aisles or transepts, too antiquated for the tastes of the late fourteenth century.

[8] Conjectures about an earlier organ at Notre-Dame have nothing to do with the old assumption that *Leoninus organista* meant 'Leonin the organist' (example in W. Krüger, 'Aufführungspraktische Fragen mittelalterlicher Mehrstimmigkeit', *Mf* 10 (1957), 279–86, here 284f).

To return to Notre-Dame: contractual, ordinal and similar documents in such large establishments have their own ambiguities. The reference of 1333 to a bell *in choro ad opus organorum* has been understood to mean the bell positioned 'in the quire by the organ' (Wright 1989: 144–5). This is possible but in that case the meaning of words is changing: *organa divinae laudis* in 1269 means one thing (vocal polyphony) and *ad opus organorum* in 1333 another (organ). An early organ at Notre-Dame would certainly have been elsewhere in the church, in an aisle or transept bay (complete by 1180s), as in many a large monastic church. It would not have got into the fabric rolls because such kinds of source barely existed yet.

Any fairly large organ without flexible mechanism, or located some way from the central lectern, would have had a quite different part to play in occasional grand liturgies. Eventually, a small organ could have participated in the organum sung during the many processions at Christmas, Easter and Rogation Day (*ibid.*, 266), as it did on similar occasions in earlier centuries. For while there may well be 'no evidence that an organ . . . was ever used to accompany responsorial chant' at Notre-Dame,[9] nor is there for churches known to have had an organ from the tenth century onwards (on Ramsey Abbey, see p. 80). Even if there were records from *c.* 1175 of an organ in the cathedral, there would be no reason to assume it regularly played in the office's polyphony, such as for the 'interminable tenors' in the vocal organum of Notre-Dame (assumed in Huglo 1981: 111). In other words: if there were a reference to an organ, it would not mean that it regularly participated in vocal organum or psalmody; and if there were no reference, it does not mean that there was no organ.[10]

Not only for organs in church is the evidence problematic. Throughout the centuries there are puzzling gaps in information about them in the various kinds of documentation concerned with the various kinds of music and their performance. The two main sources for the Portuguese–Castilian *Cantigas* repertory of the late thirteenth century show no positive organs in their sumptuous illuminations despite the many wind and stringed instruments in one manuscript (meant to be a comprehensive survey?) and the church interiors with equipment in the other – lamps, candles, crosses, reliquaries, chalices and a bell or two bells hung in a tower.[11] Did the artists not know the church organ or was it too optional and complex for small scenes? Perhaps it was not appropriate either for *cantigas* tales themselves[12] or for the lay personnel composing them: similar paintings of the period on a ceiling in Teruel Cathedral show the same kind of instruments played by professional *juglares*.

---

9   E. Roesner, 'The performance of Parisian organum', *EM* 7 (1979), 174–89, here 174.

10 A similar point could be made about the claim that vocal organum itself was unknown at the comparably grand abbey of St-Denis, in A. W. Robertson, *The Service-Books of the Royal Abbey of Saint-Denis. Images of Ritual and Music in the Middle Ages* (Oxford, 1992), *passim*. Is it correct to argue from an absence of documentation? What kind of counterpoint is plausible in this church?

11 Facs. of Madrid, Biblioteca del Escorial j. b. 2: ed. H. Anglès, *La Música de las cantigas de Santa María de Rey Alfonso el Sabio*, Biblioteca Central Publicaciones de la Sección de Música 19 (Barcelona, 1964). This manuscript includes hurdy-gurdies (f. 154') and portative organ (f. 185'). Facs. of Madrid, Biblioteca del Escorial T. j. I: *Alfonso X el sabio Cantigas de Santa Maria* (Madrid, 1979, Edilán).

12 The illuminations need not be showing actual performance of the *cantigas*: see H. M. Brown, 'Instruments' in *Performance Practice: Music before 1600*, ed. H. M. B & S. Sadie (London, 1989), 15–36, here 17.

When sound contributed to a more regular scene in the *cantigas*, as at a baptism, the miniatures do show the bell(s) being rung or tolled.

But considering in general how many great churches there were across Christian Europe by *c.* 1300, how many dedications, consecrations (of bishops and buildings, abbots and altars), festivals, acclamations, coronations and other splendid public events in church there were each year, it is puzzling how seldom the organ is mentioned in connection with them. Can one suppose not that it was so scarce but that to mention it was exceptional, perhaps something owed to the interests of a particular chronicler? To give one example of a suitable public event: the coronation of Wenceslas II in 1297 in Prague Cathedral, which is known to have had a new organ forty years earlier (see p. 227), is reported by a chronicler who mentions the *Te Deum*, the exulting *plebes*, psalm-singing clerics and the resounding nave (FRB 4.75) but not bells, choral music or organs. Although at least two of these must have played a part in the proceedings, the chronicler's priority seems to have been not to describe the liturgical character of the coronation but to establish its political legitimacy: it was acceptable in the face of God (hence the *Te Deum*), the people (exultant) and the clergy (singing psalms), all of them united (hence the resounding nave). Organs and bells would have added nothing further to this picture of lawfulness and the Lord's anointed.

For the historian today, it is the very *en passant* nature of the first mention of an organ in Notre-Dame in 1332 – like the incidental mention of them elsewhere (expropriated at Lobbes, burnt at Freising, a refuge at Bruges, etc.) – that arouses suspicion and tempts speculation. As far as one can tell from such laconic reference, there is nothing in the presence of these organs that was astonishing to the writers: they are played or repaired or replaced without special comment, as if they were standard items in the church's furnishings. While clearly it is unsatisfactory merely to 'suspect' that there were many more organs than are known about now, the *en passant* mention of them in source after source does encourage one to do so.[13]

Developments in the key periods 950–1000 and 1150–1200?

Since the evidence for such 'key periods' is circumstantial, any explanation is hypothetical; but a case may be made as follows.

In so far as instruments of any kind were made during the ninth and tenth centuries in the wide sector radiating north-west from Rome, they were probably the work of lay craftsmen, although whether such laity were townspeople, employees of a monastery or even novices and other low monastic ranks is unknown. Both lax monasteries and those reformed under the early ninth- and early tenth-century

---

[13] Similarly, minstrels probably played in church for the King of England (on his visits to shrines, etc.) before Wardrobe Books list the payments, as they do only when the late thirteenth century moved towards fuller documentation generally. See R. Rastall, 'Minstrelsy, church & clergy in medieval England', *PRMA* 97 (1970/1), 83–98.

impetus (St Benedict of Aniane and Gorze-Cluny respectively) had lay workers, and the very absence of written material for practical use both before and after the isolated treatise of Theophilus argues for the crafts not being something for ordained monks. Studying *musica* and pipe-proportions may have been monastic in this sense, but making organs was not?

At the same time, the reformed monasteries – re-endowed, re-chartered, rebuilt, re-populated and re-walled – would be exactly the place for collaboration with lay workers, since it was the monastery (or its aristocratic patron) that had the money to employ and to purchase. It did so in such a way as to make its churches the local repository of what was materially valuable and even wonderful, as the Viking invaders or other raiders (such as Hereward the Wake, ravager of Peterborough) knew perfectly well. Æthelwold or St Dunstan did not have to be a friend of music itself to bring organs into their reformed churches (see Chapter 12), rather an energetic priest assembling what they could to make their monasteries technological centres, both for the *plebes* and for the *gloriam majorem Dei*.

Church buildings in which both a monastic community (*fratres*) and a lay community (*plebes*) were accommodated for services had to be newly rebuilt and enlarged in the tenth century. The church at Celles is typical of hundreds in north-western Europe. An eighth-century sanctuary (*cella*), built for a local hermit's relics, small, with no formalized liturgy possible indoors for a large group of people – assuming that in any case Roman liturgical books had penetrated so deeply into the countryside – was replaced in the tenth century by a church in which a westwork of some kind accommodated the *plebes* climbing the spiral staircase up to it, and left a nave for clergy processions, a central space at the crossing for mass and office, and crypts at each end of the church for the pilgrim processions. (Present size and layout of Celles are those of an eleventh-century rebuild.) Such change from relics-sanctuary to 'church' gave craftsmen a good opportunity to develop technologies in stone, metal, wood and glass, and provided a good resonating chamber for music. It would also make it necessary to have an authorized chant-book, and in turn such a book would encourage a more communal liturgy.

Where large communal spaces had long been known, or were associated with forms of liturgy and ceremony that were less intricate and novel – as in the case of the much earlier Mediterranean basilicas – then they saw little if any sudden technological drive in the years around 1000. Offering nothing much new, they also had no need for such new furnishings as stained glass or organs. Nevertheless, organs may still have been far better known in Italy than extant documents suggest. Quite by chance, a modest organ of some Theophilus-like characteristics was described in the sixteenth century by Zarlino (see p. 261) as coming from a conventual church in the city of Grado. The three basilican churches of Grado had the standard plan – spacious nave, aisles, apse, no galleries – and at least one of them (the cathedral) originally had a narthex and atrium.[14] It is reasonable to think of this little organ being moved in and out of the church, with little if any rôle in a liturgy and

---

[14] Plans and sections in G. Bovini, *Grado paleocristiana* (Bologna, 1973), 150–1.

probably no particular location in the building other than what the interests of security would suggest. Again, it seems unlikely that Grado would have an organ when Aquileia and Venice did not; or perhaps it was that when churches in such cities did have organs, they remained only small *organa* for processions and never became anything else.

As for the second period: the later twelfth century gave the organ a somewhat different context. Still a technological wonder for the *plebes*, it was now found more frequently in the major churches – late romanesque or early gothic, abbey or secular cathedral – where there were many convenient locations for it (as there were not in the earlier Roman basilicas of comparable size)[15] and where fuller and fuller furnishing inside the church spaces meant that more and more craftsmen were required.[16] If Theophilus appears to be describing earlier rather than contemporary organs, he would still have been writing for the period of expansion, although it is also possible that there are so few copies of his treatise because it was already out of date. Whatever the case, from a modest construction with conical copper pipes and not much in the way of timber framing, the organ became by the fourteenth century a large piece of wooden furniture with cylindrical pewter pipes, spring-loaded pallets and some deep sounds, probably the deepest man-made sounds that could be heard anywhere on earth.

While a new or reformed abbey of *c.* 1000 may have had both an organ and a notated repertory of chant, the connection between the two is indirect and circumstantial (see Chapter 4). What organs and chant have in common, other than being in part derived from classical and later Roman cultures respectively, is that they belonged to the monasteries of *c.* 1000 which, at least north of Italy, had achieved cultural independence and a tremendous sense of international community. Though existing only by virtue of the apostolic authority claimed by Rome, the monasteries were now creating their own styles and customs in many areas of activity, including all types of equipment. To Mediterranean Christianity many of these styles and customs were quite unknown, and would even have been rather foreign. Once notation developed in the northern monasteries, they no longer needed canonic books from Rome, and on the contrary, it was their new compositions that circulated and developed. Once the same monasteries (including any in Italy)[17] admitted the organ, no reference to Rome or Constantinople or anywhere else was necessary, and it became a part of church life not at all familiar elsewhere.

---

[15] A drawing of Old St Peter's, Rome in 1532/5 shows an organ housed separately in a structure placed in front of the south nave arcade (R. Lunelli, *L'Arte organaria nel Rinascimento in Roma* (Florence 1958), plate 6). However old this organ was, the drawing suggests three things: that basilicas had no upper floors for an organ, that two-storeyed organs as at Winchester (chest above, bellows below) could be wholly contained within one structure, and that a position on the south side of the nave (= geographical north in disorientated churches) was a suitable location for organs.

[16] The crafts that became guilds and corporations in later medieval Europe must have achieved that identity at least partly through the sheer amount of specialized work generated by the great church-building programmes of the twelfth and thirteenth centuries.

[17] The possibility that the classical Italian *ripieno* as known from the late fifteenth century transmits an early conception of the organ more directly than does any northern organ-type, is a further topic to explore in any future evaluation of the late medieval and Renaissance organ.

What did organs do and where did they do it?

One advantage of the organ – its *raison d'être* – is that it sustains a strong and level sound; another is that, like the bagpipes, it can be made with or without a drone. (Possibly the high-pressure water-organ imitated the bagpipes' unbroken sound, i.e. without gaps between the notes of a melody?) Whether in its outdoor appearances the organ played melodies, rhythmic chords, drones, a persistent screeching or various combinations of these, it would follow that when it was placed in the church, it was located near the more public parts: in a west gallery or antechurch, near a south or south-western door, perhaps in a space wide enough for pedestrian spectacle, such as a transept in the large gothic churches. Ailred's twelfth-century picture of the people standing and gaping at the monstrous organ is convincing, whatever his source of information, and one can image them standing in wonder at the astronomical clocks of the next century, or any other mechanism with sounding and moving parts.

In the high gothic churches, however, there are many suitable locations in which an organ can be secreted away and its display-side designed to be visually striking: nave, quire and transept galleries, aisles, screen, triforium levels for a swallownest organ, the upper storey of wooden choirstalls. By 1500, all of these had been made use of. Early evidence suggests a variety of places and heights above the pavement, even if the actual locations are vague. The directions given by Theophilus and the descriptions left at Ramsey and Canterbury place the organ in a gallery; elsewhere, as at Petershausen, it may have been on the floor. If at Malmesbury it had been placed near an altar, perhaps that meant on the pavement nearby. Except for its pipes, an early organ might well have somewhat resembled an altar in shape and size, and even its pipes could look from a distance rather like the retable of a golden altar.

If the Winchester poem is not exaggerating in saying that the noise of the organ went around the town, there is the possibility that its sound was meant to travel, like that of Baroque *Hornwerke* in church-towers of central Europe.[18] Such an effect is clearly related to the siren-organ's held, unwavering sound as it may have been known to Carolingian kings, and its effect on the *plebes* can be imagined. Dunstan's directive at Malmesbury, that his organ should not be removed, does not necessarily mean that it was fixed, only that as with other expensive monastic assets at the time, its legal inalienability had to be claimed, and the instrument's undisturbed presence was not a matter of course.[19] It was meant to play for the people in honour of a particular altar, not be removed to some less public part of the monastery.

---

[18] The Baroque organ of Weingarten Benedictine Abbey has a stop that plays a single C major triad built up of forty-nine pipes (octaves, fifths, thirds, sevenths) and located near the west window, thus near both the entrance and the town below (F. Jakob, *Die grosse Orgel der Basilika zu Weingarten* (Männedorf, 1986), 62).

[19] Two examples at random of the need to claim inalienability: a collection of books brought from Rome by Benedict Biscop (628–89) for Wearmouth–Jarrow was not to be broken up or allowed to perish, according to the terms quoted by Bede (PL 94.722); and at Bages, Catalonia, where there may have been an organ (p. 207), three mills were donated in 1018–19 on condition that no monk or abbot ever gave them away (P. Bonnassie, *La Catalogne du milieu du Xe à la fin du XIe siècle* (Toulouse, 1976), 559).

What were organs like?

Making a compendium of known details by taking the keys and registers of Aquincum, the wooden frame of the Utrecht Psalter organs, Hucbald's compass, the Winchester quantities for pipes and bellows, Theophilus's pipe-forms, bellows and location, all in order to produce a 'typical organ of the early period', would clearly be quite false. And yet, if there were no typical characteristics it is difficult to imagine how makers designed what they did design. If they started from the physical size of a chest, they must have had either an antecedent in mind or set out *de novo* which, if ever the case, became less and less so as time passed. If they started with a special sound in mind — a tonal end-result given by such and such a compass, so many pipes per key, tuned in so many unisons, octaves and twelfths — the carpentry and bellows work must have been more a matter of trial and error.

Most likely is that there was both a 'standard' organ and a range of unique instruments building on but naturally referring back to the standard. For an original standard, the most logical would be the full-sized Roman organ, not with respect to its engineering (in its hydraulic form) but to its physical size, approximate shape, tessitura and, perhaps, tone. The seven or eight notes of music were an obvious starting-point, a basic unit that could be multiplied one way or the other, i.e. in compass or in number of ranks. Although in practice some Roman organs may have had variant scales, the notes C D E F G A B H were sufficient for 'music' as defined by chant in the ninth century, and the organ-keyboard must have played a part in fixing this scale once and for all.

Theophilus's directions for an organ still suggest a 'module' that could be 'extrapolated', although according to what — the maker's experience, the number of pipes required, the size of the church, the function of the instrument etc. — is not clear. Since in 1000 bronze bells of the period looked, sounded and were hung in much the same way from one part of Europe to another — though no doubt with local characteristics in all three respects — it is not out of the question that organs were rather alike and that the building skills circulated as they did for other metallurgical crafts. There being such little reference to organs over this large area could be evidence both for and against the idea that there was a standard organ.

This scarcity in all types of source does raise a whole range of questions about the details. When finger-keys are missing in an early representation, is it because the artist's sources (pictorial, verbal) gave no details? Were there very few organs to be seen by artists or, since good manuscript illumination is likely to have been produced by the very monasteries grand enough to have had an organ, were organs kept from prying eyes? (The Winchester School of illuminators drew no organs because they were too unfamiliar or because they were too mundane?) Since Hucbald's compass (p. 46) may actually be shorter than that of some real instruments, why do psalter organ-pictures almost always show fewer pipes than would have been found on actual organs? Were words and pictures there in order to be liberally interpreted by the knowledgeable? Even if a seemingly unreliable source were ever to turn out to have been accurately portraying a unique organ – the Utrecht Psalter organ a realistic portrayal of an Arabic siren-organ sent to Pippin, for example – one could still extrapolate from it to imagine an organ of a quite different kind, with many pipes, blown by sets of bellows, with finger-activated valves or keys of some kind. Such details as these were indeed pictured in the Stuttgart Psalter which despite its apparent allusion to Roman organs in its tight-packed line of pipes (see Chapter 11), may well convey a realistic size, shape, timber structure, bellows and mode of operation for an organ of the time.

Also supporting the need to extrapolate is the fact that with one or two exceptions, the amount of information does not vary very much over the centuries: the manuscripts Stuttgart and Beaupré (Chapter 17) are comparable, despite the gap of over half a millenium between them. Yet those five centuries must have seen many changes in the way an organ was made even if they did not in the way an illuminator saw his purpose. When, as is usually the case, there is no documentation for a crucial development such as timber framework, the situation in *c.* 1450 can sometimes suggest previous steps of development. For example, the large gothic organ of Haarlem (1463–6) was, like Theophilus's organ, positioned on the wall above the main arcade, but now the pipes did not appear in the front of a specially made opening or have a linen shroud hanging above but were all brought out in front of the wall, held on a long narrow chest and enclosed in a massive but shallow timber case supported on a protruding gallery, in which the organist now sat below the organ façade. Each of these details represents a particular stage of development, and they all depend on the structural principle of the timber framework.

Was the early development consistent?

One could claim that the organ as we know it is essentially an instrument of the fifteenth century, towards which the previous centuries had serendipitously groped and after which its development affects only the various means by which it functions. Or one could assume that technology largely matches need and vice versa, so that earlier instruments were not 'inadequate' however they may appear in the light of later musical demands. Either way, as an example of the questions that arise, one could usefully consider the hypothetical organ-keyboard of *c.* 1000.

If the Winchester organ had sliders pulled out and pushed in by hand, then it offered the organist only a fraction of the facility made possible by the suspended finger-keys of *c.* 1450. And if the little Roman organ of Aquincum already had a spring-loaded mechanism complete with finger-keys, one may well ask why the cantor of Winchester should have been content with a slower key-action than a *pulsator* in Pannonia seven centuries earlier. Because neither he nor the builder knew any better or because he did not need much agility for the sounds he produced in church? The second is much more likely to be the answer, giving some idea of what it was he actually played in the way of drones or clusters or slow *ostinati*. The size of the Winchester organ means that its builder was designing something grander and of course newer than the Roman 'standard organ', something removed from classical tradition and providing a revitalized community[20] with a wonder-machine of great volume though not, perhaps, particularly deep sounds. There is the question, however, whether Winchester did have hand-gripped sliders or whether it so happens that the documentation, in this case a poem, had no reason or language to refer to keys operating them, or did so without enough technical detail for a reader now to be certain. (Rather similar questions could be asked about the treatises of Vitruvius and Theophilus.) Furthermore, even if Winchester had keyless sliders, there must have been a tendency towards a key-action that had easier touch and allowed greater dexterity, not because these are recognized as absolute virtues throughout history but because they are what was achieved in the end, at some cost of time and trouble to the makers of instruments.

If Aquincum did have finger-keys, then, one of several things could follow. Thus Winchester had something similar; or, if it did not, it represented a backward step in the evolution of the keyboard; or if it was typical of larger instruments known here and there over the centuries, then there was a need for big constructions that were quite distinct from the agile little instruments represented by Aquincum on one end of the period and Hans Memling's paintings of portatives at the other. There would be other consequences: if Winchester had little 'Aquincum-like' keys, then the change from spring-loaded keys to spring-loaded pallets could have come about much earlier than otherwise; or if it was backward and did not, then its technology must have been more local, home-produced by general craftsmen rather than by expert instrument-makers. While any of these might be true, it is well to remember that a clamorous, sustained tone-cluster matching the sound of bells is easier to produce with push–pull sliders, and who knows that this is not what organs were built for before the twelfth century and even later?

The art played by organs in the development of music?

No more than the other questions can this be answered with clear evidence and yet it is reasonable to suppose that there is some connection between two particular attributes of western music as it had developed in the later fifteenth century. These were: the concept of a bass line (thus eventually perfect cadences and 'tonality') and the technical perfection of keyboard instruments (thus a compass over several octaves and 'full harmony' supplied by one performer). The connection between a functional bass line and keyboard instruments will always be elusive. Yet it is difficult to think that a three-octave keyboard would not give its player the idea of bass and treble or suggest chords in several parts, irrespective of what theorists of the time might say or fulldress vocal polyphony of the time might imply. The longer the compass, the more one would be drawn to playing long-held drones in

---

[20] From the point of view of their *organa* and the new interest in keeping fuller records, it seems unimportant whether the reform-abbeys of Abingdon, Winchester, Malmesbury and Ramsey represent *bona fide* reformation by the king and abbots or a power-struggle between the king and local barons.

the bass and not the treble, and the more naturally full triads would be played in the upper rather than the lower part of the keyboard.

The usual problems of documentation – pitifully few references to organs, ambiguous terminology, theorists unspecific on technical questions – mean that one has to guess how organs were viewed in *c.* 1000 or so. Assuming that its hexachordal compass was usually short, what an organ would offer was:

> sound produced by means of two mechanical systems (bellows and key-action respectively);
>
> notes fixed in tuning;
>
> notes sustained as long as desirable or technically feasible;
>
> combinations of notes produced by one performer;
>
> the longer the compass, the more the sense of 'up or down' and thus eventually of 'treble and bass';
>
> the longer the compass, the more the ways in which notes could be combined.

Of these, the crucial one is probably the last: the greater the number of notes, the more the organ was an advance on the whole of the Greek–Roman *instrumentarium* and something more specific to the musical world of the Middle Ages. Also, one might guess that the greater the number of an organ's notes, the greater the difference between polyphonic parts in different areas of the compass, i.e. the more that each area developed its own character or characteristics. This cannot be substantiated since it concerns what was naturally improvised, but conjecture is helped by considering the bass, which was and is the area of the compass most dependent on technological development.

In general, the larger the organ the more of a bass tone it would have, since there is a limit to how far small pipes can be multiplied. This may be the single best support for the Winchester organ's having two organists: they duplicated the same pitches and increased volume without needing the large pipes of one long compass? Drones too are likelier to have become a bass effect with organs, probably more so than with other instruments, for the technology developed for the great pipes of Halberstadt and elsewhere gave a new sound-spectrum to listeners. If from the period of Hucbald onwards builders were already seeing that size was a question of extending octave-pitches – the keyboard-compass could have more octaves or its chorus could stretch beyond 8' and 4', eventually (by *c.* 1400?) all the way from 32' to 1' – then it was only a matter of time before the lowest part of any given polyphony became a 'bass line'. Deeper pitches would bring with them particular musical characteristics since bigger pipes speak more slowly than small and need to have a different musical rôle.

Hucbald's repeated remark that instruments begin with a C major hexachord cannot be taken necessarily as a fundamental distinction between sacred and secular music, or instrumental and vocal, since he illustrates the scale he is talking about with an offertory chant – one that circumscribes an octave of C major.[21] Nor in

---

[21]   The terms used in this sentence are of course not Hucbald's: see translation, Babb 1978: 21, 24, 25, 29.

theory does there have to be any significance in what the lowest note of a given compass is.[22] But the remark is still of great interest, for this hexachord in practice helps produce a sense both of 'diatonic major' and of 'bass line', with the lowest note becoming a focal point of return. (In the *Musica enchiriadis*, the repeated C's in certain two-part polyphony may already be moving towards the idea of 'diatonic major' or 'a bass line'.) The very possibility that instrument-makers outside the *monasteria* were all the time making 'C major instruments' while the tonsured literates inside were theorizing on the tones and semitones of Greek tetrachords is clearly important. If in *c.* 1000 the organ was something of a 'noise-making signalling device in C major', it must have lost this when it came to contribute directly to musical practices in the liturgy, eventually playing discreet *alternatim* to the modal chant. Any popular dances it may have played for the public in *c.* 1475, with four-part harmony, two-bar phrases and periodic perfect cadences, would have been a latter-day version of the purer instrumental idioms it had begun with, if it had.

It is to be expected that in the course of several hundred years writers connected the different meanings of the word *organum*. To assume that organs and organum were related would be natural by *c.* 1200 when parallel harmonies were more consistent in some types of polyphony than they had been in the ninth century and when fifth-sounding ranks may have been better known in organs, if less so than usually assumed today. But the organ's acceptance by the Church can have had nothing to do with organum except in its old sense of orderly ensemble music, i.e. a type of music in which *organa* could take part. The name *vox organalis* for the line added to the chant in *Musica enchiriadis* uses the term 'organal' to imply something like 'an integrated voice part made according to the rules for proportional diatonic notes', not that it somehow sounded like an organ. And yet if it were arranged in an orderly fashion and the notes were those of an organic scale, such music could suit such a mechanized instrument like the organ. Were an organ present it could have imitated the effect and even perhaps replaced the organal voice on special occasions, although it may usually have sounded alone or with bells.

The organ was useful for both monastic and lay communities: it had a volume-level higher than other solo instruments, it could sustain its sound, it offered a range of musical effects from solo melody to polyphony or block chords, and for centuries it could do these things so easily that more or less anybody could play it. For good measure, men of great authority – Augustine, Jerome – seemed to authorize it. These combined advantages are impossible with any other instrument and must have made organs desirable whenever or wherever the percussive noise of bells or the mellifluous song of voices was felt to need another source of sound for a festive Church.

---

[22]   However, it is the case that Hucbald's lowest note in the vocal scale (A) has seldom been the lowest note of organs. FF, GG, C, F and c, probably with H in some late medieval instruments, have been normal at different periods.

References

AB The Art Bulletin

Acta SS J. Bollandus, *Acta sanctorum quotquot toto orbe coluntur* . . . [Amsterdam *et al.*, 1643–], ed. J. Carnandet, 69 vols (Paris/Rome, 1863–1940): Jan 21 = vol. 2 (1863), Martii 1 = vol. 7 (1865), Mai 4 = vol. 27 (1866)

AfMf Archiv für Musikforschung

AfMw Archiv für Musikwissenschaft

AH Antiquarian Horology

AJ The Archaeological Journal

AM Acta Musicologica

AO Acta Organologica

Apel 1948 W. Apel, 'The early history of the organ', *Speculum* 23 (1948), 191–216

ASE Anglo-Saxon England

Babb 1978 trans. W. Babb, *Hucbald, Guido and John on Music*, ed. C. V. Palisca (New Haven, CT, 1978)

Bachmann 1969 W. Bachmann, *The Origins of Bowing and the Development of Bowed Instruments up to the Thirteenth Century* (Oxford, 1969)

Baldovin 1987 J. F. Baldovin, *The Urban Character of Christian Worship: the Origins, Development, and Meaning of Stational Liturgy*, Orientalia christiana analecta 228 (Rome, 1987)

Barassi 1983 E. F. Barassi, *Testimonianze organologiche nelle fonti teoriche dei secoli X–XIV* (Cremona, 1983)

Barbieri 1989 P. Barbieri, 'An unknown fifteenth-century French manuscript on organ-building and tuning', *OY* 20 (1989), 5–20

Barry 1989 W. Barry, 'Theophilus on making organ pipes', *JAMIS* 15 (1989), 74–87

Bede *Bede's Ecclesiastical History of the English People*, ed. B. Colgrave & R. A. B. Mynors (Oxford, 1969)

Bereths 1974 G. Bereths, *Beiträge zur Geschichte der Trierer Dommusik*, Beiträge zur mittelrheinischen Musikgeschichte 15 (Mainz, 1974)

BJfhM Basler Jahrbuch für historische Musikpraxis

Blumröder 1983 C. von Blumröder, 'Modulatio/Modulation', *HmT* (1983)

BM Bulletin Monumental

Boeckelmann 1957 W. Boeckelmann, 'Von den Ursprüngen der Aachener Pfalzkapelle', *WRJB* 19 (1957), 9–38

Bormann 1966A K. Bormann, *Die gotische Orgel zu Halberstadt: eine Studie über mittelalterlichen Orgelbau*, 27 Veröffentlichung der Gesellschaft der Orgelfreunde (Berlin, 1966)

Bormann 1966B K. Bormann, 'Die gotische Orgel von Bartenstein vom Jahre 1395', *Ars Organi* 29 (1966), 989–1009

Bowles 1962 E. A. Bowles, 'The organ in the medieval liturgical service', *RBM* 16 (1962), 13–29

Bowles 1966 E. A. Bowles, 'On the origin of the keyboard mechanism in the late Middle Ages', *TC* 7 (1966), 152–62 and figures

Bowles 1982 E. A. Bowles, 'A preliminary checklist of fifteenth-century representations of organs in paintings and manuscript illuminations', *OY* 13 (1942), 5–30

Brepohl 1987 E. Brepohl, *Theophilus Presbyter und die mittelalterliche Goldschmiedekunst* (Vienna, 1987)

Brett 1954 G. Brett, 'The automata in the Byzantine "Throne of Solomon"', *Speculum* 29 (1954), 477–87

Buhle 1903 E. Buhle, *Die musikalischen Instrumente in den Miniaturen des frühen Mittelalters. Ein Beitrag zur Geschichte der Musikinstrumente*, 1: *Die Blasinstrumente* (Leipzig, 1903)

Butler & Morris 1986 L. A. S. Butler & R. K. Morris, *The Anglo-Saxon Church: Papers on History, Architecture and Archaeology in Honour of Dr H. M. Taylor* (London, 1986)

Caldwell 1971 J. Caldwell, 'The organs in the British Isles until 1600', *OY* 2 (1971), 4–12

Callebat 1986 L. Callebat, *Vitruve de l'Architecture Livre X* (Paris, 1986)

Campbell 1950 A. Campbell, *Frithegodi monachi breuiloquium vitae Beati Wilfredi et Wulfstani cantoris Narratio metrica de sancto Swithuno* (Zurich, 1950)

Chailley 1937 J. Chailley, 'Un clavier d'orgue à la fin du XI siècle', *RM* 21 (1937), 5–11

Conant 1959 K. J. Conant, *Carolingian and Romanesque Architecture 800 to 1200* (London, 1959)

CO *Connoissance de l'Orgue*

Connolly 1978, 1980 T. H. Connolly, 'The legend of St. Cecilia: 1, The origins of the cult', *Studi musicali* 7 (1978), 3–37; '2, Music and symbols of virginity', *ibid.* 9 (1980), 3–44

Corsi 1989 *Le polifonie primitive in Friuli e in Europa. Atti del congresso internazionale Cividale del Friuli 1980*, ed. C. Corsi & P. Petrobelli (Rome, 1989)

CS *Scriptorum de musica medii aevi novam seriem*, ed. C. E. H. de Coussemaker, 4 vols (Paris, 1864–76)

CSM *Corpus Scriptorum de Musica*

Davis-Weyer 1986 C. Davis-Weyer, *Early Medieval Art 300–1150: Sources and Documents [1971]*, Mediaeval Academy Reprints for Teaching 17 (Toronto, 1986)

Degering 1905 H. Degering, *Die Orgel, ihre Erfindung und ihre Geschichte bis zur Karolingerzeit* (Münster, 1905)

de Graaf 1982 G. A. C. de Graaf, 'The gothic organ in the Chapel of St. Bartholomew in Salamanca', *ISO Information* 22 (1982), 9–34

Dodwell 1961 C. R. Dodwell, *Theophilus, De diuersis artibus. The Various Arts, Translated from the Latin with Introduction and Notes* (London, 1961)

Donati 1979 P. P. Donati, 'Regesto documentario', in *Arte nell'Aretino seconda mostra di restauri dal 1975 al 1979 . . . Catalogo*, ed. P. P. D. (Florence, [1979]), 148–253

Drachmann 1948 A. G. Drachmann, *Ktesibios, Philon and Heron: a Study in ancient Pneumatics*, Acta historica scientiarum naturalium et medicinalium (Copenhagen, 1948)

Drachmann 1963 A. G. Drachmann, *The Mechanical Technology of Greek and Roman Antiquity* (Copenhagen, 1963)

Du Cange 1678 Charles Du Cange, *Glossarium ad scriptores mediae et infimae latinitatis* (Paris, 1678)

Duchesne 1886–92 L. M. O. Duchesne, *Le liber pontificalis: texte, introduction et commentaire*, 2 vols (Paris, 1886, 1892)

Dufourcq 1971 N. Dufourcq, *Le livre de l'orgue français 1589–1789*: 1, *Les Sources* (Paris, 1971)

Dufrenne 1978 S. Dufrenne, *Les illustrations du Psautier d'Utrecht: sources et apport carolingien* (Paris, 1978)

Dunning 1980 *Visitatio organorum: Feestbundel voor Maarten Albert Vente*, ed. A. Dunning (Buren, 1980)

EHR *The English Historical Review*

Edskes 1980 B. Edskes, 'Das Regal des Orgelmachers Christophorus Pfleger von 1644. Zur Frühgeschichte des Regals', *FM* 2 (1980), 73–106

Edskes 1987 B. Edskes, 'Die Rekonstruction der gotische Schwalbennest-Orgel in der Predigerkirche zu Basel', *BJfhM* 9 (1987), 9–29

EM *Early Music*

EMH *Early Music History*

Engelbregt 1964 J. H. A. Engelbregt, *Het Utrechts Psalterium: een eeuw wetenschappelijke Bestudering* (Utrecht, 1964)

Engelbregt 1973 *Kunst- en Muziekhistorische Bijdragen tot de Bestudering van het Utrechts Psalterium*, ed. J. H. A. E and T. Seebass (Utrecht, 1973)

Eusebius *Historia Ecclesiastica*, PG 20.1–906. Ed. & trans. K. Lake, *Eusebius: the Ecclesiastical History*, 2 vols (London, 1926, 1932)

Farmer 1931 H. G. Farmer, *The Organ of the Ancients from Eastern Sources (Hebrew, Syriac and Arabic)* (London, 1931)

Feldhaus 1930 F. M. Feldhaus, *Die Technik der Antike und des Mittelalters* (Potsdam, 1930)

Fichtenau 1982 H. Fichtenau, *The Carolingian Empire: Sources and Documents [1957]*, Mediaeval Academy Reprints for Teaching 1 (Toronto, 1978, 2/1982)

FM *Forum Musicologicum*

FMSt *Frühmittelalterliche Studien*

FOMRHI *Fellowship of Makers and Researchers of Historical Instruments*

Foster 1977 G. Foster, *The Iconology of Musical Instruments and Musical Performance in Thirteenth-Century French Manuscript Illuminations* (Diss., City University of New York, 1977)

FRB *Fontes Rerum Bohemicarum*, ed. N. Palacky & J. Emler, 5 vols (Prague, 1873–93)

Frémont 1917 C. Frémont, *Origine et évolution de la soufflerie*, Etudes expérimentales de technologie industrielle 50 (Paris, 1917)

Frend 1984 W. H. C. Frend, *The Rise of Christianity* (Philadelphia, PA, 1984)

Fuller 1981 S. Fuller, 'Theoretical foundations of early organum theory', *AM* 53 (1981), 52–84

Gerbert 1774 M. Gerbert, *De cantu et musica sacra*, 2 vols (St Blasien, 1774)

Gimpel 1976 J. Gimpel, *The Medieval Machine: the Industrial Revolution of the Middle Ages* (New York, 1976)

Gregory of Tours *Historia francorum*, MGH SS rer. mer. 1.1, ed. B. Kusch & W. Levison, *Gregorii Turonensis Opera libri historiarum X* (Hanover, 1951)

GS *Scriptores ecclesiastici de musica sacra*, ed. M. Gerbert, 3 vols (St Blasien, 1784)

GSJ *Galpin Society Journal*

Gushee 1973 L. A. Gushee, 'Questions of genre in medieval treatises on music', in *Gattungen der Musik in Einzeldarstellungen. Gedenkschrift Leo Schrade*, ed. W. Arlt *et al.* (Berne/Munich, 1973), 365–433

Hall 1979 B. S. Hall, 'Der Meister sol auch kennen schreiben und lesen: writings about technology *c.* 1400–*c.* 1600 AD and their cultural implications', in *Early Technologies*, ed. D. Schmandt-Besserat (Malibu, CA, 1979), 47–58

Hammerstein 1959 R. Hammerstein, 'Instrumenta Hieronymi', *AfMw* 16 (1959), 117–34

Hammerstein 1986 R. Hammerstein, *Macht und Klang. Tönende Automaten als Realitäten und Fiktion in der alten und mittelalterlichen Welt* (Berne, 1986)

Hardouin 1966 P. Hardouin, 'De l'orgue de Pépin à l'orgue médiéval', *RM* 52 (1966), 21–54

Hawthorne & Smith 1963 J. G. Hawthorne & C. S. Smith, *On Diverse Arts: the Treatise of Theophilus* (Chicago, IL, 1963; corrected reprint New York, 1979)

Heitz 1963 C. Heitz, *Recherches sur les rapports entre architecture et liturgie à l'époque carolingienne* (Paris, 1963)

Heitz 1987 C. Heitz, *La France préromane: Archéologie et architecture religieuse du Haut Moyen Age du IVe siècle à l'an mille* (Paris, 1987)

Hickman 1936 H. Hickmann, *Das Portativ: ein Beitrag zur Geschichte der Kleinorgel* (Kassel, 1936)

HmT Handwörterbuch der musikalischen Terminologie, ed. H. H. Eggebrecht (Wiesbaden, 1982–)

Holschneider 1968 A. Holschneider, *Die Organa von Winchester: Studien zum ältesten Repertoire polyphoner Musik* (Hildesheim, 1968)

Holschneider 1975 A. Holschneider, 'Instrumental titles to the Sequentiae of the Winchester Tropers', in *Essays on Opera and English Music: in Honour of Sir Jack Westrup*, ed. F. W. Sternfeld *et al.* (Oxford, 1975), 8–18

Holschneider 1978 A. Holschneider, 'Die instrumentalen Tonbuchstaben im Winchester Troper', in *Festschrift Georg von Dadelsen zum 60 Geburtstag*, ed. T. Kohlhase & V. Scherliess, (Neuhausen-Stuttgart, 1978), 155–66

Holt 1988 R. Holt, *The Mills of Medieval England* (Oxford, 1988)

Hopkins & Rimbault 1877 E. J. Hopkins & E. F. Rimbault, *The Organ, its History and Construction: a Comprehensive Treatise* . . . (London, 1855, 3/1877)

HT History of Technology

Huglo 1981 M. Huglo, 'Organologie et iconographie médiévales', *Annales d'histoire de l'art et d'archéologie* 3 (1981), 97–113

Huglo 1990 M. Huglo, 'Notes et documents', *RM* 76 (1990), 77–82

Isidore ed. W. M. Lindsay, *Isidori Hispalensis Episcopi Etymologiarum sive Originum libre XX*, Scriptores classicorum Biblioteca Oxoniensis, 2 vols (Oxford, 1911), unpaginated

ISO The International Society of Organ-Builders

Jakob 1991 F. Jakob *et. al.*, *Die Valeria Orgel: ein gotisches Werk in der Burgkirche zu Sitten/Sion*, Ver. des Institus für Denkmalpflege an der E. T. H. Zürich 8 (Zürich, 1991)

JAMIS Journal of the American Musical Instruments Society

Jammers 1962 E. Jammers, *Musik in Byzanz, im papstlichen Rom und im Frankenreich* (Heidelberg, 1962)

JAMS Journal of the American Musicological Society

JSAH Journal of the Society of Architectural Historians

JWCI Journal of the Warburg and Courtauld Institutes

Kaba 1976 M. Kaba, *Die römische Orgel von Aquincum (3. Jahrhundert)*, Musicologia hungarica 6 (Budapest, 1976)

KC Kunstchronik

Kelly 1989 T. F. Kelly, *The Beneventan Chant* (Cambridge, 1989)

Kjersgaard 1987 M. Kjersgaard, 'Technical aspects of Swedish organ-building during the Middle Ages', *ISO Information* 27 (1987), 5–118 and 29 (1988), 29–30

Klukas 1978 A. W. Klukas, *Altaria superioria: the Function and Significance of the Tribune-Chapel in Anglo-Norman Romanesque. A Problem in the Relationship of Liturgical Requirements and Architectural Form* (Diss., U. Pittsburgh, 1978)

Klukas 1985 A. W. Klukas, 'Liturgy and architecture: Deerhurst Priory as an expression of the Regularis concordia', *Viator* 15 (1985), 81–106

KmJb Kirchenmusicalisches Jahrbuch

Körte 1973 K. Körte, 'Die Orgel von Winchester. Rekonstruktionsversuch einzelner Teile', *KmJb* 57 (1973), 1–24

Krautheimer 1937–77 R. Krautheimer, *Corpus basilicarum christianarum*, 5 vols (Vatican City, 1937–77)

Krautheimer 1969 R. Krautheimer, 'The Carolingian revival of early Christian architecture', in *Studies in Early Christian, Medieval, and Renaissance Art* (New York, 1969), 203–56 (= *AB* 24 [1942] 1–38, with postscript)

Kubach & Verbeek 1976–89 H. E. Kubach & A. Verbeek, *Romanische Baukunst an Rhein und Maas*, 3 vols [= catalogue] (Berlin, 1976); vol. 4, *Architekturgeschichte und Kunstlandschaft* (Berlin, 1989)

LaRue 1966 *Aspects of Medieval and Renaissance Music. A Birthday Offering to Gustave Reese*, ed. J. LaRue (New York, 1966)

Le Cerf 1932 *Instruments de Musique du XVe siècle. Les Traités d'Henri-Arnaut de Zwolle et de divers Anonymes (MS BN latin 7295)*, ed. G. Le Cerf & E.-R. Labande (Paris, 1932)

Levy 1984 K. Levy, 'Toledo, Rome and the legacy of Gaul', *EMH* 4 (1984), 49–99

Llovera 1987 J.-M. Garcia Llovera, *De organo vetere hispanico: zur Frühgeschichte der Orgel in Spanien* (St Ottilien, 1987)

McKinnon 1968 J. McKinnon, 'Musical instruments in medieval psalm commentaries & psalters', *JAMS* 21 (1968), 3–20

McKinnon 1974 J. McKinnon, 'The tenth-century organ at Winchester' *OY* 5 (1974), 4–19

McKinnon 1987 J. McKinnon, *Music in Early Christian Literature* (Cambridge, 1987)

McKinnon 1990 *Antiquity and the Middle Ages. From Ancient Greece to the Fifteenth Century*, ed. J. McKinnon, Music & Man 1 (London, 1990)

Mango 1986 C. Mango, *The Art of the Byzantine Empire 312–1453: Sources and Documents [1972]*, Mediaevel Academy Reprints for Teaching 16 (Toronto, 1986)

Marca 1688 Petrus de Marca, *Marca hispanica sive limes hispanicus* (Paris, 1688)

Marshall 1989 K. Marshall, *Iconographical Evidence for the Late-Medieval Organ in French, Flemish and English Manuscripts*, 2 vols (New York, 1989)

MD Musica Disciplina

Meeùs 1980 N. Meeùs, 'Tessitures d'orgues au Moyen Age: une étude préliminaire', *RBM* 34/5 (1980/1), 61–71

MF Die Musikforschung

MGG Musik in Geschichte und Gegenwart

MGH Monumenta Germaniae Historica

AA	*Auctores antiquissimi*, 15 vols (1877–1919)
Cap.	*Capitularia regum francorum*, 2 vols (1883–97)
Conc.	*Concilia, Legum Sectio iii*, 3 vols (1893–1908)
Epist.	*Epistolae merowingici et carolini aevi*, 5 vols (1892–1939)
ius.	*in usum scholarum*, 63 vols (1871–87)
Nec.	*Necrologia germaniae*, 5 vols (1888–1913)
Poet.	*Poetae latinae aevi carolini*, 4 vols (1881–99)
S rer. ger.	*Scriptores rerum germanicarum* (1840–)
S rer. mer.	*SS rerum merovingicarum*, 7 vols (1884–1920)
SS	*Scriptores in folio*, 34 vols (1824–1980)

ML Music & Letters

Mokyr 1990 J. Mokyr, *The Lever of Riches: Technological Creativity and Economic Progress* (New York, 1990)

Morgan 1914 trans. M. H. Morgan, *Vitruvius: the Ten Books on Architecture* (New York, 1914)

MQ Musical Quarterly

MuK Musik und Kirche

Neuburger 1930 A. Neuburger, *The Technical Arts & Sciences of the Ancients* (London, 1930)

NOHM 1954 The New Oxford History of Music II, *The Early Middle Ages to 1300*, ed. A. Hughes (Oxford, 1954)

NOHM 1957 The New Oxford History of Music I, *Ancient and Oriental Music,* ed. E. Wellesz (Oxford, 1957)

NOHM 1990 The New Oxford History of Music II, T*he Early Middle Ages to 1300,* 2nd edition ed. R. Crocker & D. Hiley (Oxford, 1990)

Oswald 1966 F. Oswald, L. Schaefer & H. R. Sennhauser, *Vorromanische Kirchenbauten: Katalog der Denkmäler bis zum Ausgang der Ottonen,* 3 vols (Munich, 1966–71)

OY The Organ Yearbook

Page 1979 C. Page, 'The earliest English keyboard', *EM* 7 (1979), 308–14

Page 1987 C. Page, *Voices & Instruments of the Middle Ages: Instrumental Practice and Songs in France 1100–1300* (London, 1987)

Page 1991 C. Page, *Summa Musice: a Thirteenth-Century manual for Singers* (Cambridge, 1991)

Panofsky 1977 E. Panofsky, *Abbot Suger on the Abbey Church of St-Denis and its Art Treasures* (Princeton, 2/1977)

Parsons 1975 *Tenth-Century Studies: Essays in Commemoration of the Millennium of the Council of Winchester and Regularis concordia,* ed. D. Parsons (London, 1975)

PG *Patrologiae cursus completus, series graeca,* ed. J. P. Migne, 166 vols (Paris, 1857–66)

PL *Patrologiae cursus completus, series latina,* ed. J. P. Migne, 221 vols (Paris, 1844–64)

Perrot 1965 J. Perrot, *L'orgue de ses origines hellénistiques à la fin du XIII siècle: étude historique et archéologique* (Paris, 1965)

Perrot 1971 J. Perrot, *The Organ from its Invention in the Hellenistic Period to the End of the Thirteenth Century,* trans. N. Deane (London, 1971)

Planchart 1977 A. E. Planchart, *The Repertory of Tropes at Winchester,* 2 vols (Princeton, 1977)

Praetorius 1619 M. Praetorius, *Syntagma musicum, 2 De Organographia* (Wolfenbüttel, 1619)

PRMA Proceedings of the Royal Musical Association

RBM Revue Belge de Musicologie

RBMAS Rerum britannicarum medii aevi scriptores [= Rolls Series]

Reckow 1975 F. Reckow, 'Organum-Begriff und frühe Mehrstimmigkeit. Zugleich ein Beitrag zur Bedeutung des "Instrumentalen" in der spätantiken und mittelalterlichen Musiktheorie', *FM* 1 (1975), 31–167

Reynolds 1986 *Texts and Transmission: a Survey of the Latin Classics,* ed. L. D. Reynolds (Oxford, 2/1986)

Richenhagen 1984 A. Richenhagen, 'Zur Orgel als Gegenstand der allegorischen Bibelauslegung in den Schriften der Spätantike und des frühen Mittelalters', in *Orgel und Ideologie,* ed. H. H. Eggebrecht (Murrhardt, 1984), 185–94

Riemann 1879 H. Riemann, 'Orgelbau im frühen Mittelalter (1879)', in *Präludien und Studien: Gesammelte Aufsätze zur Ästhetik, Theorie und Geschichte der Musik,* 3 vols (Frankfurt, 1895), 2.189–211

RM Revue de Musicologie

Ronig 1980 F. Ronig, *Der architektonische Ort der Kirchenmusik vom 4. Jahrhundert bis in die Gegenwart,* Kirchenmusik eine geistig-geistliche Disziplin 4 (Stuttgart, 1980)

Sachs 1970 K.-J. Sachs, *Mensura fistularum: die Mensurierung der Orgelpfeifen im Mittelalter 1, Edition der Texte*, Schriftenreihe der Walcker-Stiftung für orgelwissenschaftliche Forschung 1 (Stuttgart, 1970)

Sachs 1973 K.-J. Sachs, 'Remarks on the relationship between pipe-measurements and organ-building in the Middle Ages', *OY* 4 (1973), 87–100

Sachs 1980 K.-J. Sachs, *Mensura fistularum: die Mensurierung der Orgelpfeifen im Mittelalter 2, Studien zur Tradition und Kommentar der Texte*, SWoF 2 (Murrhardt, 1980)

Salzman 1952 L. F. Salzman, *Building in England down to 1540: a Documentary History* (Oxford, 1952)

Sauer 1964 J. Sauer, *Symbolik des Kirchengebäudes und seiner Ausstattung in der Auffassung des Mittelalters, mit Berücksichtigung von Honorius Augustodunensis, Sicardus und Durandus* (Münster, 2/1964)

Schmidt 1899A W. Schmidt, *Herons von Alexandria Druckwerke und Automatentheater: 1 Pneumatica et Automata* (Leipzig, 1899)

Schmidt 1899B W. Schmidt, *Herons von Alexandria Druckwerke und Automatentheater: Supplementheft* (Leipzig, 1899)

Schuberth 1968 D. Schuberth, *Kaiserliche Liturgie. Die Einbeziehung von Musikinstrumente, insbesondere der Orgel, in den frühchristlichen Gottesdienst*, Veröffentlichungen der evangelischen Gesellschaft für Liturgieforschung 17 (Göttingen, 1968)

Schwind 1984 F. Schwind, 'Zu karolingerzeitlichen Klöstern als Wirtschaftorganismen und Stätten handwerklicher Tätigkeit', in *Institutionen, Kultur und Gesellschaft im Mittelalter: Festschrift für Josef Fleckenstein*, ed. L. Fenske *et al.* (Sigmaringen, 1984), 101–23

Seebass 1973 T. Seebass, *Musikdarstellung und Psalterillustration im frühen Mittelalter. Studien ausgehend von einer Ikonologie der Handschrift Paris Bibliothèque Nationale Fonds Latin 1118*, 2 vols (Berne, 1973)

Settimane Settimane di studio del Centro Italiano di Studi sull'Alto Medioevo (Spoleto)

Shiloah 1979 A. Shiloah, *The Theory of Music in Arabic Writings (c. 900–1900): Descriptive Catalogue of manuscripts in Libraries of Europe and the USA* (Munich, 1979)

Singer 1954 *A History of Technology*, ed. C. Singer *et al.*, 5 Vols (London, 1954–8)

Singer 1957 *ibid. 2 The Mediterranean Civilizations and the Middle Ages c. 700 BC–c. 1500 AD* (Oxford, 1957)

Stäblein 1970 B. Stäblein, *Die Gesänge des altrömischen Graduale Vat. lat. 5319*, Monumenta monodica medii aevi 2 (Kassel, 1970), introduction

Sternagel 1966 P. Sternagel, *Die artes mechanicae im Mittelalter. Begriffs-und Bedeutungsgeschichte bis zum Ende des 13. Jahrhunderts*, Münchener Historische Studien, Abteilung mittelalterliche Geschichte 2 (Kallmünz, 1966)

Strunk 1977 O. Strunk, *Essays on Music in the Byzantine World* (New York, 1977)

Symons 1953 *Regularis Concordia: the Monastic Agreement*, ed. T. Symons (London, 1953)

TC Technology & Culture

Theobald 1933 W. Theobald, *Technik des Kunsthandwerks im 10. Jahrhundert. Des Theophilus Presbyter Diversarum artium schedula* (Berlin, 1933)

Thompson 1902–4 *The Customary of the Benedictine Monasteries of St. Augustine, Canterbury and St. Peter, Westminster*, ed. E. M. Thompson, Henry Bradshaw Society 23 (London, 1902) and 28 (1904)

Usher 1929 A. P. Usher, *A History of Mechanical Inventions* (New York, 1929)

Van Engen 1980 J. Van Engen, 'Theophilus Presbyter and Rupert of Deutz: the manual arts and Benedictine technology in the early twelfth century', *Viator* 11 (1980), 147–63

Vellekoop 1984 K. Vellekoop, 'Die Orgel von Winchester: Wirklichkeit oder Symbol?', *BJfhM* 8 (1984), 183–96

Vogel 1965 M. Vogel, 'Zur Ursprung der Mehrstimmigkeit', *KmJb* 43 (1965), 57–64

Vogel 1983 H. Vogel, 'Das Zusammenwerken von Glocken und Orgelspiel', *Musica sacra* 103 (1983), 33–40

Waeltner 1975 E. L. Waeltner, *Die Lehre von Organum bis zur Mitte des 11. Jahrhunderts* (Tutzing, 1975)

Walcker-Mayer 1970 W. Walcker-Mayer, *Die römische Orgel von Aquincum* (Stuttgart, 1970)

Walcker-Mayer 1972 W. Walcker-Mayer, *The Roman Organ of Aquincum*, trans. J. Godwin (Ludwigsburg, 1972)

Wallace-Hadrill 1983 J. M. Wallace-Hadrill, *The Frankish Church* (Oxford, 1983)

Walter 1981 K. Walter, 'Der Bordun zur Zeit des späten Mittelalters und der frühen Renaissance', in *Der Bordun in der europäischen Volksmusik*, ed. W. Deutsch, Schriften zur Volksmusik 5 (Vienna, 1981), 176–96

White 1962 L. White, *Medieval Technology and Social Change* (London, 1962)

Whitney 1990 E. Whitney, *Paradise Restored: the Mechanical Arts from Antiquity through the Thirteenth Century*, Transactions of the American Philosophical Society 80.1 (Philadelphia, PA, 1990)

Williams 1980 P. Williams, 'How did the organ become a church instrument? Questions towards an understanding of Benedictine and Carolingian cultures', in Dunning 1980: 603–18

Wiora 1955 W. Wiora, 'Zwischen Einstimmigkeit und Mehrstimmigkeit', in *Festschrift Max Schneider*, ed. W. Vetter (Leipzig, 1955), 319–34

Wormald 1953 F. Wormald, 'The Utrecht Psalter', in *Francis Wormald: Collected Writings. Studies in Medieval Art from the Sixth to the Twelfth Centuries,* ed. J. J. G. Alexander *et al.* (London, 1984), 36–46

Wright 1989 C. Wright, *Music & Ceremony at Notre Dame of Paris 500–1500* (Cambridge, 1989)

WRJB Wallraf-Richartz-Jahrbuch

Yorke 1988 *Bishop Æthelwold: his Career and Influence*, ed. B. Yorke (Woodbridge, 1988)

Zarlino 1588 G. Zarlino, *Sopplimenti musicali* (Venice, 1588)

Index of places

Index of names